Programmer's Problem Solver
for the IBM PC, XT & AT

Robert Jourdain

A Brady Book
Published by Prentice Hall Press
New York, NY 10023

Programmer's Problem Solver for the IBM PC, XT & AT

A Brady Book
Published by Prentice Hall Press
A Division of Simon & Schuster, Inc.
Gulf + Western Building
One Gulf + Western Plaza
New York, New York 10023

PRENTICE HALL PRESS is a trademark of Simon & Schuster, Inc.

Manufactured in the United States of America

  5   6   7   8   9   10

Library of Congress Cataloging in Publication Data

Jourdain, Robert L., 1950–
   Programmer's problem solver for the IBM PC, XT, and AT

   Includes index.
   1. IBM Personal Computer—Programming. 2. IBM
Personal Computer XT—Programming. 3. IBM Personal
Computer AT—Programming. I. Title.
QA76.8.12594J67   1986   005.265   85-14926

ISBN 0-89303-787-7

CONTENTS

INTRODUCTION   *ix*

NUMERIC CONVENTIONS USED IN THIS BOOK   *xiii*

1. SYSTEM RESOURCES   1
  1. **Assess the System Resources**   1
    1. Access the 8255 peripheral interface   3
    2. Find out the type of IBM microcomputer   6
    3. Determine the PC-DOS version   7
    4. Find out the number and type of video adaptors   8
    5. Find out the number and type of disk drives   10
    6. Find out the numbers and types of peripherals   12
    7. Assess the amount of RAM   14
  2. **Manage Interrupts**   17
    1. Program the 8259 interrupt controller   19
    2. Allow/disallow particular hardware interrupts   20
    3. Write your own interrupt   21
    4. Make additions to existing interrupts   24
  3. **Manage Programs**   26
    1. Allocate/deallocate memory   28
    2. Run one program from within another   31
    3. Use DOS user-interface commands from within a program   34
    4. Keep a program in memory after it has terminated   35
    5. Load and run program overlays   38
    6. Convert programs from .EXE to .COM type   41

2. TIMERS AND SOUND   45
  1. **Set and Read Timers**   45
    1. Program the 8253/8254 timer chip   46
    2. Set/read the time   50
    3. Set/read the date   52
    4. Set/read the real-time clock   53
    5. Delay program operations   56
    6. Time program operations   58
    7. Control real-time operations   60
    8. Generate random numbers by the timer chip   64
  2. **Create Sound**   66
    1. Program the 76496 sound generator (PCjr only)   67
    2. Make a tone   69
    3. Make a tone simultaneous to other operations   72
    4. Beep the speaker   74
    5. Make a string of tones   76
    6. Make a string of tones simultaneous to other operations   80
    7. Make sliding tones   83
    8. Make sound effects   84
    9. Make simultaneous sounds   87

3. THE KEYBOARD 89
   1. **Monitor the Keyboard** 89
      1. Clear the keyboard buffer 92
      2. Check the buffer for keystrokes 95
      3. Wait for a keystroke and do not echo it on the screen 96
      4. Wait for a keystroke and echo it on the screen 98
      5. Intercept a keystroke without waiting 100
      6. Intercept a string of keystrokes 101
      7. Check/set the status of the toggle and shift keys 104
      8. Write a general-purpose keyboard input routine 106
      9. Reprogram the keyboard interrupt 109
   2. **Access Particular Keys** 114
      1. Use the Backspace, Enter, Escape and Tab keys 115
      2. Use the Shift keys: Shift, Ctrl, and Alt 116
      3. Use the Toggle keys: NumLock, CapsLock, Ins, and ScrollLock .. 118
      4. Use the numeric keypad and cursor keys 119
      5. Use the function keys 121
      6. Reprogram individual keys 122
      7. Assign keyboard macros to individual keys 124
      8. Set up the Ctrl-Break routine 126
      9. Reprogram the PrtSc key 128
   3. **Look up Key Codes and Applications** 129
      1. Assign uses to the keys 130
      2. Look up a scan code 131
      3. Look up an ASCII code 132
      4. Look up a box-graphic code 135
      5. Look up an extended code 136

4. THE VIDEO DISPLAY 137
   1. **Control the Video Display** 137
      1. Program the 6845 CRT controller 140
      2. Set/check the screen display mode 143
      3. Set character attributes/colors 148
      4. Set the screen border color 156
      5. Clear all/part of the screen 158
      6. Switch between two video adaptors 160
   2. **Control the Cursor** 162
      1. Set the cursor to an absolute position 163
      2. Set the cursor to a relative position 166
      3. Turn the cursor on/off 167
      4. Change the cursor shape 169
      5. Read/save/restore the cursor position 171
      6. Create alternative cursor types 173

3. **Write Characters on the Screen** 175
   1. Write a single character on the screen 176
   2. Write a string of characters on the screen 182
   3. Read the character and attribute at a given position 185
   4. Create special characters 187
   5. Look up data for block-graphics characters 191
4. **Draw Dot Graphics** 195
   1. Set the colors for dot graphics 198
   2. Draw a dot on the screen (monochrome card, color card, PCjr) 203
   3. Draw a dot on the screen (EGA) 207
   4. Find the color at a point on the screen 215
   5. Draw lines on the screen 218
   6. Fill areas of the screen 223
   7. Draw graphics using block characters 227
5. **Use Scrolling and Paging** 229
   1. Scroll a text screen vertically 230
   2. Scroll a text screen horizontally 232
   3. Switch between text pages 234
   4. Scroll between text pages 238

5. **THE DISK DRIVES** 241
   1. **Monitor Disk Allocation** 241
      1. Read the file allocation table 243
      2. Determine available disk space 247
      3. Get/set the file size 248
      4. Recover from insufficient disk space errors 250
   2. **Operate on Disk Directories** 252
      1. Read/change the root directory 254
      2. Create/delete a subdirectory 257
      3. Read/change a subdirectory 259
      4. Get/set the current directory 261
      5. Get/set the time and date of a file 262
      6. Write-protect or hide files 263
      7. Read/change the volume label 265
   3. **Prepare for File Operations** 268
      1. Set/check the default drive 270
      2. Create/delete a file 271
      3. Open/close a file 275
      4. Rename a file/move a file's directory location 280
      5. Prepare for file operations 282
      6. Analyze information from the command line 287

　　4.　**Read and Write Files** 289
　　　　1.　Program the 765 Floppy Disk Controller and 8237 DMA chip 291
　　　　2.　Read/write at particular sectors 300
　　　　3.　Write to sequential files 304
　　　　4.　Read from sequential files 310
　　　　5.　Write to random files 315
　　　　6.　Read from random files 320
　　　　7.　Verify data after write operations 323
　　　　8.　Define/recover from disk errors 324

6.　**THE PRINTER** 327
　　1.　**Control Printer Operations** 327
　　　　1.　Initialize the printer port/reinitialize the printer 329
　　　　2.　Test that a printer is on-line 331
　　　　3.　Interpret/recover from printer errors 333
　　　　4.　Switch between two or more printers 335
　　2.　**Set Printing Specifications** 337
　　　　1.　Set text and graphics modes 338
　　　　2.　Control line spacing 340
　　　　3.　Control paper movement 342
　　　　4.　Control the print head position 343
　　　　5.　Set tab positions 344
　　　　6.　Change the print font 345
　　　　7.　Compare IBM printer capabilities 347
　　3.　**Send Data to a Printer** 349
　　　　1.　Output text or graphics data to the printer 350
　　　　2.　Right justify text 354
　　　　3.　Proportionally space text 357
　　　　4.　Print special characters 359
　　　　5.　Perform screen dumps 363

7.　**INPUT-OUTPUT** 367
　　1.　**Access a Serial Port** 367
　　　　1.　Program the 8250 UART chip 369
　　　　2.　Initialize the serial port 370
　　　　3.　Set the current communications port 375
　　　　4.　Monitor the status of the serial port 376
　　　　5.　Initialize and monitor the modem 378
　　　　6.　Transmit data 382
　　　　7.　Receive data 385
　　　　8.　Send/receive data by communications interrupts 389
　　　　9.　Look up a communications control code 393

2. **Create a Device Driver** 395
 1. Set up the device header 397
 2. Set up the device strategy 399
 3. Set up the device interrupt handler 400
 4. Access the device driver 405
 5. Detect/analyze device errors 407
3. **Use Special I/O Devices** 411
 1. Read from/write to a cassette recorder 412
 2. Read the light pen position 414
 3. Take analog input from the game port 417
 4. Take digital input from the game port 420

APPENDICES:
 A. Binary & hexadecimal numbers and memory addressing 423
 B. Bit operations in BASIC 427
 C. Some background on assembly language 431
 D. Integrating assembly routines into BASIC programs 437
 E. Using the ANSI.SYS device driver 439
 F. The 8088 instruction set 440
 G. The 80286 instruction set 446
 H. A glossary for IBM microcomputers 451

INDEX 469

Limits of Liability and Disclaimer of Warranty

The author(s) and publisher of this book have used their best efforts in preparing this book and the programs contained in it. These efforts include the development, research, and testing of the theories and programs to determine their effectiveness. The author(s) and publisher shall not be liable in any event for incidental or consequential damages in connection with, or arising out of, the furnishings, performance, or use of these programs.

INTRODUCTION

Computer programmers are among the great innovators of our times. Unhappily, among their most enduring accomplishments are several new techniques for wasting time. There is no shortage of horror stories about programs that took twenty times as long to debug as they did to "write." And one hears again and again about programs that had to be started over several times because they were not well thought through the first time around. But much less is said of what may be the most successfully mastered time-wasting technique among students of programming: finding information about the machine. Spending hours trying to locate a single, simple fact is a veritable rite of passage for new programmers—as is ripping up reference books in a red-eyed frenzy.

A typical programmer's *morning after* is CRT eye strain, a six foot pile of crumpled printouts, and two dozen reference books all over the floor. Among these books are hardware tech reference manuals, DOS tech reference manuals, language reference manuals, spec sheets on particular chips, hardware manuals for printers and boards, plus a dozen or so computer books, each possessing some prized bit of information required at 3 AM by a particularly intricate bit of code.

Because not many of us have photographic memories (working with computers would make you lose it, anyway), all these books are really needed, since the same old things have to be looked up again and again. The first time through it may require an hour just to zero in on the information. Once found, it still may take untold ages to extract what you need from a lengthy beginner's presentation; or, if your misfortune is to be using a manual written entirely in Swahili, half the afternoon may go into a translation. What is wanted is one big book, with as much as can possibly be packed into it, unencumbered by information not useful for programming, written entirely at intermediate level, covering all IBM micros, and organized in a way that makes the information easy to find. Now where can one find a book like that?

And so I've put together this reference-book-that-is-also-an-instruction-book for all who aspire to write extraordinary programs, but who haven't oodles of time to waste (or $600-800 to spend on all those other manuals and books). The material is organized in two ways. First, the chapters are divided by hardware types, subdivided by features of the hardware, and then set into short entries that each address a particular programming task. For example, one section of the video chapter concerns the cursor, and there the various entries show how to position the cursor, change its shape, turn it on and off, etc.

Second, each discussion is divided into four parts (sometimes fewer). First comes a paragraph or two giving fundamentals. Then the problem at hand is discussed from the viewpoint of programming in a *high-level* language, programming in the *middle-level* BIOS and DOS interrupts, and programming at *low-level* directly upon the auxiliary chips that support the microprocessor. In addition, each of the three or four sections that comprise a chapter begins with a page or two giving the background required to understand the section. These summaries are intended for review, but you could probably use them to fake your way through the first time around.

The discussions of *high-level* programming show the task written in an advanced programming language. While the concepts could as well apply to Pascal or C, the examples are given in BASIC. BASIC was chosen in part because it is the Latin of computerdom, in part because everybody who owns an IBM microcomputer owns BASIC, and in part because Microsoft BASIC makes more extensive use of IBM hardware than any other programming language. Even beginning students of BASIC should be able to use many of these discussions. To extend the capabilities of BASIC, a number of machine language subroutines are provided, and there is an appendix showing how to integrate them into your programs. You can do all sorts of neat things using these routines, such as reprogramming the keyboard or adding paging to the monochrome card.

Middle-level programming shows how a programming task is accomplished using the *interrupts* provided by the operating system. These are powerful little routines that do the drudge work of any computer, like moving the cursor, or reading a disk directory. They are the mainstay of assembly language programming, and the examples given at middle level are written in assembly language. But more and more compilers for high-level languages are allowing access to interrupts, letting the savvy programmer pull off things that the language itself cannot, like reading absolute disk sectors. And so the middle level information is of wider interest than it might at first seem. Only PC-DOS (MS-DOS) is discussed; if you're writing for CPM-86 or the UCSD p-system, you'll need to find documentation elsewhere.

Finally, the *low-level* programming examples show how the particular task is carried out at *chip level*. All of the microcomputers in the IBM family basically share the same architecture, since all are based on the same Intel family of integrated circuits. The chips are accessed through *I/O ports*, which are at your disposal in virtually any language, BASIC included. All of the chips important to programmers are discussed, including the timer chip, the peripheral interface, the interrupt controller, the CRT controller, the floppy disk controller, and the chips that manage serial and parallel ports. While IBM discourages programmers from programming at this level (out of concern that programs won't run on future machines), again and again one discovers capabilities of the machines that can not be reached any other way.

Not all tasks are shown at all three levels. Some are simply impossible in BASIC. Others are not provided for in the operating system. And some are so complicated at low level (many of the disk operations, for example) that they can not be treated here—nor is there much point, since the authors of DOS have already done the work and done it well. In most cases, however, all three levels are shown. By comparing the levels, you can see how a high-level language reaches down to the interrupts and how the interrupts, in turn, operate on the chips that are the heart of the computer.

This book could look awfully intimidating to those who are familiar only with high-level languages like BASIC or Pascal. This is because the middle- and low-level sections are written in assembly language, bestowing upon the pages the aura of the Rosetta Stone. And indeed the book would make an ideal companion for those studying assembler. But don't feel that only a third of the book is at your disposal if you don't know assembly and don't intend to learn it. For one thing, a number of compilers will let you set up and use the operating system functions shown at middle-level, such as Turbo Pascal and Lattice C. And many of the low-level procedures can, in fact, be performed by high-level languages. To enable you to decode what is going on in the assembly language examples, a brief introduction is given in Appendix D. Even if you never use the lower level material, by keeping an inquiring eye on what is going on you will gain a much deeper appreciation of how your high-level language works and of why it sometimes runs into trouble.

Nearly every sub-subsection has its own sample of code. Many are only a few trivial lines. Others are the stripped-down beginnings of an elaborate routine. Very few are stand-alone programs. Rather than fill the book with cutesy examples, I've left just the fragment of code you'd need when you turn to the book for help. By no means is every example intended to be the finest possible rendition. Indeed, in many cases the code has purposely been written inefficiently so that you can better follow it. The idea behind the samples is not so much to provide a source book of program modules as it is to point the way and to start you thinking about the various implications of what you are about to do. But if you like, you can enter a sample *as is* into a program to provide a functioning starting point and then expand it until it is just as baroque as your heart desires. Since all of the examples have been tested, they should also act as a reference to help weed out those *really dumb* mistakes that tend to crop up when long hours of programming have pummeled your mind into a sub-zero IQ.

The prose is this book is dense, to say the least. But I've tried to avoid jargon as much as possible, and there is a glossary of essential Computerese at the end. Except for some highly specialized information, practically every programming-related bit of information available from IBM documentation has been packed in. While it would have been nice to cover absolutely *everything*, the book would have reached 1000 pages, and the forest might have disappeared among the trees. And so for really unusual programming needs—say, to extensively program the floppy disk controller, or to reprogram the AT keyboard—you will have to get hold of the IBM tech reference manuals or the spec sheets from the chip manufacturers. But 99% of programs ought to require no more information about IBM hardware than you will find here. The many different ways of doing the same thing are gone over in the same place, with comparisons of strengths and weaknesses. I've included all of the usual tables of ASCII codes, instruction times, and the like so that this single volume can take care of all of your ordinary reference needs.

There is also a good deal of information here that provides details that the IBM documentation leaves out, such as which control codes are interpreted by which screen-output routines or how various disk functions format files. Some entries give the *how-to* for common programming tasks that are not inherent in the hardware, but that make heavy use of hardware features, such as real-time operations or horizontal scrolling. Space is also given to programmer's tricks that, while not exactly blessed by the Powers Above, can help one get out of a programming tight spot. As things stand now, every programmer has to figure these things out for himself (usually more than once). How ironic it is that the high priests of the Information Age spend so much time re-inventing the wheel, as in the days before papyrus made everything so easy.

The entries also contain information about differences between the various IBM machines. The discussion is based on the standard PC. When the PCjr, XT, or AT differs, individual attention is given to that machine. One line that had to be drawn is that those features of the AT and DOS 3.0 that are directed towards multiuser systems are not covered. This would be a book in itself. With a few noted exceptions, the many examples of code are for a standard PC; but unless stated otherwise, they should run just fine on any of the IBM micros. There is an important limitation, however. Every word of this book assumes the use of PC-DOS version 2.1 or later and the accompanying version of advanced BASIC. Users who won't update to 2.1 don't deserve your innovative programs anyway.

If this book has anything, it has facts—zillions of them—and I do ever so sincerely hope that they are all correct. There also are several hundred program examples, and for these too I have been praying for perfection. But if you think it is easy to keep so much information out of harm's way during multiple edits and revisions, give it a try. If you find something awful, please take a deep breath and think how much worse it could have been using those nasty books written by the competition. Then, sit down and write me a note (care of Brady Co., Simon & Schuster, General Reference Group, 1230 Avenue of the Americas, New York, NY 10020). If you do, the world will be a better place for programmers to live in when this book comes out in a second edition, updated for IBM's latest creations.

Prosperous programming!

Robert Jourdain

Numeric Conventions Used In This Book

Assembly programmers will find nothing unusual in the way numbers and addresses are expressed in these pages. But many high-level programmers are sheltered from addressing systems and non-decimal numbers, and they may be a little confused at first. If you find yourself in that category, don't be put off! This book can serve as a fairly painless way of acquiring a familiarity with this gobbledygook, and your education as a programmer will remain severely constrained without it. Two appendices have been provided to help you along. Appendix A discusses binary and hexadecimal numbers, and how the latter are applied to memory addresses. Appendix B covers more about binary numbers and how they are used in bit-operations. Even if you have no need for this help, do be aware of the following:

1. In deference to less advanced programmers, all numbers are decimal unless followed by an H (for hexadecimal) or a B (for binary). Sometimes the B is omitted after binary numbers when the values obviously refer to bit patterns.

2. Another exception is the eight-digit numbers in the form 0000:0000. These are hexadecimal numbers giving the segment and offset of a memory address. Appendix A explains the meaning of all this.

3. Bits are numbered from 0 to 7 (or 0 to 15), where bit 0 is the least significant bit (that is, when set, bit $0 = 1$ and bit $7 = 128$).

4. An expression such as "ASCII 5" refers to character number 5 of the ASCII set. That is, it refers to a single byte with the value of 5, and not to the ASCII code for the symbol 5, or to a two-byte integer representation of the value 5.

5. Numbers that are placed in brackets and that look something like [2.1.3] are crossreferences to other entries in the book. This one stands for "Chapter 2, Section 1, Entry 3". [2.1.0] refers to the review discussion that begins Section 1 of Chapter 2. You'll find hundreds of these numbers scattered throughout the text. They refer to the place in the book where you can find information of the topic just mentioned. These are only to help the novice. If you understand the discussion, ignore the crossreferences.

6. When working program code is embedded in text, it is always written in bold face.

1
System Resources

Section 1: Assess the System Resources

When a program is loaded, its first job should be to find out where it is: what kind of IBM microcomputer is it running in?...under what DOS version?...how much memory does it have to work with?...are all the required peripherals present? There are three ways to go about finding out this information. Least elegant is simply to prompt the program user for the information (will he or she know the answers?). A far better approach is to take as much information as possible from the dip switch settings on the system board. But these settings are not always adequate. And so the third option is to make direct access to the hardware in question or to try to find the information in the BIOS data area. Since the dip switch settings are the best place to begin looking for information, this section begins with a discussion of the chip where this information is found: the 8255 peripheral interface.

A program can access hardware in only two ways. It can read from and write to any of the port addresses to which hardware happens to be connected (only a small fraction of the 65535 possible port addresses are used). Or the program can read from and write to any of the million-plus addresses in the random-access-memory address space. A comparative summary of port addresses is found at [7.3.0]. Figure 1-1 shows how the operating system and programs are distributed in memory.

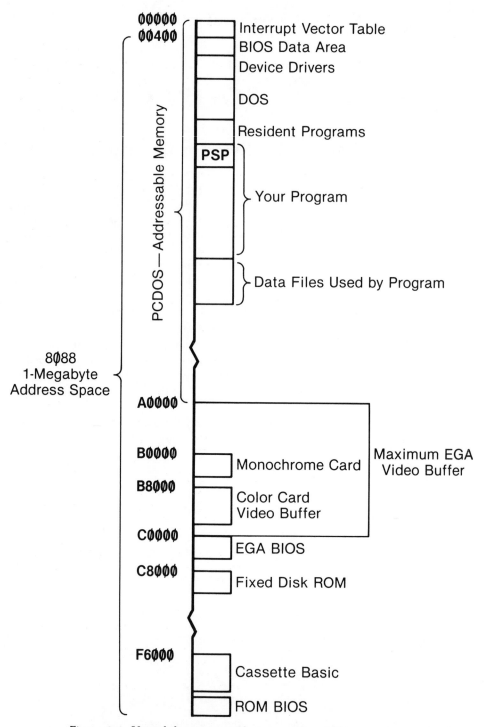

Figure 1-1. Use of the one-megabyte memory address space.

1.1.1 Access the 8255 peripheral interface

The Intel 8255 peripheral interface chip is the best place to begin looking for information about what peripherals are present. The chip is dedicated to a variety of uses. It reports the settings of the dip switches on the system board. It receives the computer's input from the keyboard. And it controls a number of peripherals, including the 8253 timer chip. Among the IBM microcomputers, the AT alone does not use an 8255; instead it stores its configuration information along with a real-time clock on a special battery-powered chip. However, the AT does use the same 8255 port addresses for keyboard operations and to control the timer chip.

The 8255 has three one-byte registers, referred to as Ports A through C. They are located respectively at port address 60H-62H. All three ports may be read, but only Port B may be written to. On a PC, setting bit 7 of Port B to 1 changes the information that Port A holds. Similarly, on a PC, setting bit 2 determines the contents of the low four bits of Port C, and setting bit 3 on an XT does the same. The contents of the registers are as follows:

```
Port A (60H)
            When Port B bit 7=0:
                bits 0-7    PC,XT,PCjr,AT: eight-bit scan codes from keyboard
            When Port B bit 7=1 on PC:
                    bit 0   PC: 0=no diskette drives
                        1   PC: unused
                      2-3   PC: banks of RAM on system board
                      4-5   PC: type of display
                                (11=monochrome, 10=80x25 color,01=40x25 color)
                      6-7   PC: number of diskette drives

Port B (61H)
                    bit 0   PC,XT,PCjr: controls gate of 8253 timer chip channel 2
                        1   PC,XT,PCjr: output to speaker
                        2   PC: select contents of Port C
                            PCjr: 1=alpha modes, 0=graphics modes
                        3   PC,PCjr: 1=cassette motor off
                            XT: select contents of Port C
                        4   PC,XT: 0=enable RAM
                            PCjr: 1=disable beeper and cassette motor
                        5   PC,XT: 0=enable expansion slot error signals
                        6   PC,XT: 1=enable keyboard clock signal
                      5-6   PCjr: select sound source
                                (00=8253 chip, 01=cassette, 10=I/O, 11=76496 chip)
                        7   PC: select contents of Port A, keyboard acknowledge
                            XT: keyboard acknowledge

Port C (62H)
            When Port B bit 2=1 on PC or Port B bit 3=1 on XT:
                bits 0-3    PC: bottom half of configuration switch 2
                                (RAM in expansion slots)
                        0   PCjr: 1=incoming keystroke lost
                        1   XT: 1=maths coprocessor installed
                            PCjr: 0=modem card installed
                        2   PCjr: 0=diskette card installed
                      2-3   XT: banks of RAM on system board
                        3   PCjr: 0=128K RAM
                        4   PC,PCjr: input from cassette
                            XT: unused
```

```
        5    PC,XT,PCjr: output of 8253 channel 2
        6    PC,XT: 1= expansion slot error check
             PCjr: 1=keyboard data
        7    PC,XT: 1= parity error check
             PCjr: 0=keyboard cable connected
When Port B bit 2=0 on PC or Port B bit 3=0 on XT:
    bits 0-3 PC: top half of configuration switch 2 (unused)
        0-1  XT: display type
                 (11=monochrome, 10=80x25 color,01=40x25 color)
        2-3  XT: number diskette drives (00=1, etc.)
        4-7  PC,XT: same as if port B bit 2=1
```

Note that a 0 in one of the register bits corresponds to an "off" setting of a dip switch.

The AT keeps its configuration settings on a Motorola MC146818 chip, along with the real-time clock. The AT has no 8255 chip as such, although the same port addresses are used to control the timer chip and to receive data from the keyboard. The chip has 64 registers, numbered from 00-3FH. To read a register, first send its number to port address 70H and then read it from 71H. The various configuration settings are discussed in the pages that follow. Here is an overview:

Register Number	Use
10H	floppy diskette drive type
12	fixed disk drive type
14	peripherals
15	system board memory (low byte)
16	system board memory (high byte)
17	total expansion memory (low byte)
18	total expansion memory (high byte)
30	expansion memory above 1 megabyte (low byte)
31	expansion memory above 1 megabyte (high byte)

High Level

There are a number of examples in this volume where these ports are accessed. Here a BASIC program finds the number of disk drives installed in a PC. Before reading the two high bits of Port A, bit 7 of Port B must be set to 1. It is essential that you change the bit back to 0 before proceeding or the keyboard will be locked out and the machine will need to be turned off to recover. BASIC does not allow the binary representation of numbers, which makes analyzing bit patterns troublesome. A simple subroutine can change an integer up to 255 (the largest value a port can deliver) into an eight-character binary string. Then a string function like **MID$** plucks out the relevant bits for analysis. See Appendix B for the fundamentals of bit operations in BASIC.

```
100 A=INP(&H61)        'get the value in Port B
110 A=A OR 128         'turn on bit 7
120 OUT &H61,A         'put the byte back in Port B
```

```
130 B=INP(&H60)                    'now get the value in Port A
140 A=A AND 127                    'turn off bit 7
150 OUT &H61,A                     'restore original value to Port B
160 GOSUB 1000                     'convert it to a binary string
170 NUMDISK$=RIGHT$(B$,1)          'get bit 0
180 IF D$="1" THEN NUMDISK=0:GOTO 230 'no disk system
190 C$=LEFT$(B$,2)                 'take the two top bits of the string
200 TALLEY=0                       'keep talley of number of disks
210 IF RIGHT$(C$,1)="1" THEN TALLEY = 2 'figure high bit
220 IF LEFT$(C$,1)="1" THEN TALLEY=TALLEY+1 'add low bit
230 TALLEY=TALLEY+1                'count from 1, not 0
                                   '...and now you have the number of drives

1000 '''Subroutine to convert byte to binary string
1010 B$=""                         'B$ is the string
1020 FOR N=7 TO 0 STEP -1          'keep testing smaller powers of 2
1030 Z=B-2^N                       'subtract from the value of the byte
1040 IF Z>=0 THEN B=Z:B$=B$+"1" ELSE B$=B$+"0" 'assemble string
1050 NEXT                          'repeat for each bit
1060 RETURN                        'all done
```

Low Level

An assembler program finds the number of disk drives in the same way as the example above, but more easily. Again, be sure to restore the original value of Port B.

```
IN    AL,61H          ;get the value in Port B
OR    AL,10000000B    ;force bit 7 to 1
OUT   61H,AL          ;replace the byte
IN    AL,60H          ;get the value in Port A
MOV   CL,6            ;set up to shift AL right
SHR   AL,CL           ;shift top 2 bits six places right
INC   AL             ;count from 1, not from 0
MOV   NUM_DRIVES,AL   ;and now you have the number of drives
IN    AL,61H          ;prepare to restore Port B
AND   AL,01111111B    ;turn off bit 7
OUT   61H,AL          ;replace the byte
```

1.1.2 Find out the type of IBM microcomputer

There are compatibility problems among the various IBM microcomputers. For a program to run on any of the IBM machines and make full use of their capabilities, it must be able to determine the type of machine into which it has been loaded. This information is found in the second from last byte of memory space, at address FFFFE in the BIOS ROM, using the following code numbers:

Computer	Code
PC	FF
XT	FE
PCjr	FD
AT	FC

High Level

In BASIC, simply use PEEK to read the value:

```
100 DEF SEG=&HF000      'point to top 64K of memory
110 X=PEEK(&HFFFE)      'get second from last byte
120 IF X=&HFD THEN...   '...then it's a PCjr
```

Low Level

In assembly language:

```
;---FIND THE COMPUTER TYPE:
            MOV   AX,0F000H        ;point ES to ROMs
            MOV   ES,AX            ;
            MOV   AL,ES:[0FFFEH]   ;get the byte
            CMP   AL,0FDH          ;is it a PCjr?
            JE    INITIALIZE_JR    ;if so, go to initialization code
```

1.1.3 Determine the PC-DOS version

As PC-DOS evolves, it adds new functions, many of which make it far easier to create some kinds of code than did earlier versions. To ensure that software will run with any DOS version, a program would need to be limited to only the functions available in DOS 1.0. DOS provides an interrupt that returns the DOS version number. The number can be used to check the compatibility of your software. Minimally, a program can issue an error message at startup, alerting the user to the need for a different version.

Middle Level ━━━━━━━━━━━━━━━━━━━━━━━━━━━━━━━━━━━

Function 30H of INT 21H returns the DOS function number. The "major version number" (the 2 of 2.10) is returned in AL, and the "minor version number" (the 10 of 2.10) is returned in AH (note that a .1 minor version is reported as AH, not as 1H). AL may contain 0, which indicates a pre-DOS 2.0 version. This interrupt destroys the contents of BX and CX, which return with the value 0.

```
;---FIND DOS VERSION:
            MOV   AH,30H      ;function number to get DOS version
            INT   21H         ;get the function number
            CMP   AL,2        ;check for version 2.x
            JL    WRONG_DOS   ;if less than 2, issue message
```

1.1.4 Find out the number and type of video adaptors

A program may need to find out whether it is running on a monochrome card, a color graphics card, or an EGA, and whether a second adaptor is present. [4.1.6] explains how to switch control from one adaptor to another. The equipment status byte kept in the BIOS data area at 0040:0010 gives the settings on dip switch 1 that tell which card is active. Ideally, bits 5-4 would be 11 if the monochrome card is in control, 10 for 80x25 on the color card, 01 for 40x25 on the color card, and 00 for the EGA. If an EGA is present, however, it may set the bits to a value other than 00, depending on how its own dip switches are set. So you must first use some other means to determine whether an EGA is present, and if not, then the BIOS data will indicate whether the active adaptor is the monochrome card or color card. To check for an EGA, test the byte at 0040:0087. If it equals 0, there is no EGA. If it is nonzero, when bit 3 is 0 the EGA is the active adaptor, and when it is 1, a second adaptor is in control.

When an EGA is present, search for a monochrome or color adaptor by writing a value to the cursor address register on their 6845 chips [4.1.1] and then read the value back to see if it matches. For the monochrome card, send 0FH to port 3B4H in order to index the cursor register, and then read and write the cursor address from port 3B5H. The corresponding ports on the color card are 3D4H and 3D5H. When no card is present, the ports return 0FFH; but since this number could be held by the register, it is not enough just to test for that value.

There are two other questions you may need answered about the EGA: how much memory is present, and what kind of monitor is it connected to? To find the type of display, test bit 1 at 0040:0087; when it is 1 the monochrome display is attached, and when it is 0 a color display is attached. If your program uses the 350-line color mode, it will need to figure out whether the color display is IRGB or R'G'B'RGB, where the latter corresponds to the IBM Enhanced Color Display. This is told by the settings of the four dip switches on the EGA itself. These settings are returned in CL when function 12H of INT 10H is called. The pattern of the low four bits will be 0110 for the Enhanced Color Display. This same function reports the amount of memory on the EGA. On return, BL contains 0 for 64K, 1 for 128, 2 for 192K and 3 for the full 256K of video RAM.

High Level

These code fragments check the current monitor type and mode, and they find out what kinds of video adaptors are present in the machine:

```
100 '''find what adaptor is in control:
110 DEF SEG=&H40              'point to start of BIOS data area
120 X=PEEK(&H87)              'check for EGA
130 IF X=0 THEN 200           'there is no EGA, jump ahead
140 IF X AND 8=0 THEN...       'then the EGA is in control
      .
      .
      .
200 X=PEEK(&H10)              'get equipment status byte
210 Y=X AND 48                'get combined value of bits 4 and 5
220 IF Y=48 THEN...            '...then monochrome (00110000)
```

```
230 IF Y=32 THEN...          '...then 80x25 graphics (00100000)
240 IF Y=16 THEN...          '...then 40x25 graphics (00010000)
```

This example checks for the monochrome card when an EGA or color card is active. The same code will search for the color card if you use port addresses &H3D4 and &H3D5.

```
100 '''find out if monochrome card is present:
110 OUT &H3B4,&HF            'address the cursor register
120 X=INP(&H3B5)             'read it and save value
130 OUT &H3B5,100            'send arbitrary value to register
140 IF INP(&H3B5)<>100 THEN... '...then card present if returns same
150 OUT &H3B5,X              'restore value if card present
```

Low Level

These examples parallel the BASIC examples above.

```
;---FIND WHAT ADAPTOR IS IN CONTROL:
        MOV  AX,40H           ;point ES to BIOS data area
        MOV  ES,AX            ;
        MOV  AL,ES:[87H]      ;see if EGA is present
        CMP  AL,0             ;
        JE   NO_EGA           ;if 0040:0087 is 0, no EGA
        TEST AL,00001000B     ;there is an EGA, now test bit 3
        JNZ  EGA_NOT_ACTIVE   ;if bit 3=1, EGA is not active
             .
             .
EGA_NOT_ACTIVE: MOV  AL,ES:[10H]  ;get the video status byte
        AND  AL,00110000B     ;isolate bits 4 & 5
        CMP  AL,48            ;is it monochrome card?
        JE   MONOCHROME       ;jump if so
                              ;else assume color card
```

Assuming a monochrome card was found, find out if a (non-active) color card is installed:

```
;---IS NON-ACTIVE COLOR CARD INSTALLED?
        MOV  DX,3D4H          ;point to 6845 address register
        MOV  AL,0FH           ;request cursor register
        OUT  DX,AL            ;index the register
        INC  DX              ;point to data register
        IN   AL,DX           ;get current reading
        XCHG AH,AL           ;save the value
        MOV  AL,100          ;use 100 as test value
        OUT  DX,AL           ;send it
        IN   AL,DX           ;read it back
        CMP  AL,100          ;compare
        JNE  NO_CARD         ;jump if no card
        XCHG AH,AL           ;else there is a color card...
        OUT  DX,AL           ;...so restore initial reading
```

1.1.5 Find out the number and type of disk drives

On all machines but the AT (discussed below) the registers of the 8255 peripheral interface chip contain information about how many floppy disk drives a machine has. See the examples at [1.1.1] to get at this information. The information that identifies the *type* of disk is kept in the disk's *file allocation table* (FAT), which keeps track of disk space and usage. The first byte in the FAT holds one of the following codes:

Code	Disk Type
FF	double-sided, 8-sector
FE	single-sided, 8-sector
FD	double-sided, 9-sector
FC	single-sided, 9-sector
F9	double-sided, 15-sector (high density)
F8	fixed disk

A file allocation table is not itself a file. It can be read using the BIOS or DOS functions that directly read particular disk sectors. [5.1.1] contains all of the information you need to find the FAT and read it. Fortunately, the operating system provides a function that returns the identification byte for a disk.

The BIOS data does not indicate how many hard disks are in place, since the dip switches are set only for floppies. However, you can use the operating system function given here to *search* for drives. Instead of one of the above codes, it returns 0CDH when no drive is present. Simply keep testing higher and higher drive numbers until this value occurs.

The AT is unique in that its configuration information tells what kind of disk drives are used. This information is obtained from port address 71H after sending a register number to 70H. For floppy diskettes the register number is 10H. Information for the first diskette is held in bits 7-4 and for the second in bits 3-0. In both cases, the bit pattern is 0000 if no drive is present, 0001 for a double-sided (48 track-per-inch) drive, and 0010 for the high capacity (96 track-per-inch) drive. The fixed disk information is in register 12H. Again, bits 7-4 and 3-0 report for the first and second drives. 0000 indicates that there is no drive. Fifteen other values are possible, reflecting the size and construction of the drive. These codes are complicated; should you need this information for some reason, consult the AT Technical Reference Manual.

Middle Level

Function 1CH of INT 21H reports information about a specific drive. Place the drive number in DL, where 0 = default, 1 = A, etc. On return DX holds the number of clusters in the FAT, AL holds the number of sectors per cluster, and CX holds the number of bytes in a sector. DS:BX points to a byte containing the disk identification code from the FAT, as in the table above. This example finds out the disk type of drive A:

```
;---FIND THE DISK TYPE:
            MOV   AH,1CH      ;function
            MOV   DL,1        ;select drive A
            INT   21H         ;get the information
            MOV   DL,[BX]     ;get the drive type
            CMP   DL,0FDH     ;is it double-sided, 9-sector?
            JE    DBL_9       ;...etc
```

The AT BIOS has a function that reports general drive parameters. This is function 8 of INT 13H. It returns the number of drives in DL, the largest number of sides in a drive in DH, the maximum number of sectors in CL and tracks in CH, and the disk error status code in AH (shown at [5.4.8]).

Another AT BIOS function returns disk type. This is function 15H of INT 13H, which requires the drive number in DL. It returns a code in AH, where 0 = no disk, 1 = diskette without change detection, 2 = diskette with change detection, and 3 = fixed disk. If a fixed disk, CX:DX returns the number of 512-byte sectors.

1.1.6 Find out the numbers and types of peripherals

At startup, BIOS checks what equipment is connected, and it puts together a status register to report its findings. The register is two bytes long, beginning at 0040:0010. The following bit pattern applies to all machines, unless noted otherwise:

```
bit 0           If 1, then diskette drives present
1               XT,AT: 1=math coprocessor present (PC,PCjr: unused)
2-3             11=64K base RAM (AT: unused)
4-5             Active video adaptor (11=80x25 monochrome card,
                    10=80x25 color card, 01=40x25 color card)
6-7             Number of diskette drives (if bit 0=1)
8               PCjr: 0=DMA chip present (PC,XT,AT: unused)
9-11            Number of serial adaptors
12              1=game port attached (AT: unused)
13              PCjr: serial printer attached (PC,XT,AT: unused)
14-15           Number of parallel adaptors
```

Most of the information is straightforward. But note that the information about the disk drives is divided between bits 0 and 6-7. The value 0 in 6-7 indicates that there is one disk drive; to determine that there are none, you must consult bit 0.

The number of serial ports attached can be found by looking into the BIOS data area. BIOS allocates four two-byte fields to hold the *base addresses* of up to four COM ports (DOS uses only two of these). A base address is the lowest number port address of the group of ports that access the COM channel. The four fields begin at 0040:0008. COM1 is at :0008 and COM2 at :000A. The fields contain 0 when there is no corresponding serial port. Thus, if the word at :0008 is non-zero and the word two bytes higher at :000A is zero, there is one serial port.

The AT keeps information about peripherals at register 14H of its configuration chip. First write 14H out to port address 70H, then read the register at 71H. Here is the bit pattern:

```
bits 7-6        00=1 floppy drive, 01=2 floppy drives
5-4             01=displaying in 40 columns on color card
                10=displaying in 80 columns on color card
                11=displaying on monochrome display
3-2             unused
1               1=math coprocessor installed
0               0=no diskette drives, 1=drives installed
```

High Level

In BASIC, simply read the status bytes directly from the BIOS data area. Appendix B explains how bit operations are performed in BASIC. This example checks to see if there are any disk drives by ascertaining whether the low byte of the status register is even or odd (even = no drives).

```
100 DEF SEG=0                   'point to the bottom of memory
110 X=PEEK(&H410)               'get the low byte of the register
120 IF X MOD 2 = 0 THEN 140     'if no remainder after /2, no drives
130 PRINT"Disk drive(s) present 'else, there are drives, give message
140 GOTO 160                    'jump over 2nd message
```

```
150 PRINT"Disk drive(s) absent        'no drives, give message
160 ...                               'continue...
```

To check for COM1:

```
100 DEG SEG=40H                       'point to start of BIOS data area
110 PORT=PEEK(0)+256*PEEK(1)          'get the word at offset 0
120 IF PORT = 0 THEN ...              '...then there is no COM1 adaptor
```

Middle Level

BIOS INT 11H returns the equipment status bytes in AX. There are no input registers. This example checks the number of disk drives.

```
;---GET THE NUMBER OF DISK DRIVES:
          INT   11H                  ;get the status byte
          TEST  AL,0                 ;are there any drives?
          JZ    NO_DRIVES            ;jump ahead if there are none
          AND   AL,1100000B          ;isolate bits 5 and 6
          MOV   CL,5                 ;prepare to shift register right
          SHR   AL,CL                ;shift right five bits
          INC   AL                   ;add 1, so count begins from 1
                                     ;and now the number of drives is in AL
```

Low Level

Assembly programs work just like those shown above for BASIC. Here is an example that reads configuration information on the AT, checking if the math coprocessor chip is installed:

```
MOV   AL,14H              ;register number
OUT   70H,AL             ;send register request
IN    AL,71H             ;read the register
TEST  AL,10B             ;test bit 1
JZ    NO_COPROCESSOR     ;if not set, no coprocessor
```

1.1.7 Assess the amount of RAM

"How much RAM is there?" can mean three things. How much RAM is recorded on the system board dip switchs? How many banks of RAM chips are really resident in the machine? And how much memory is actually unoccupied and available for DOS to assign to your program? A machine might have ten banks of 64K, but the dip switches could be set to 320K to set aside half for some special use. And of the 320K "available," how is your program to know what other software has been loaded and kept resident at either the high or low ends of memory?

Each question is answered in a different way. On the PC and XT the dip switch settings are simply read from Port B of the 8255 peripheral interface chip. See [1.1.1] for how to do this. BIOS keeps a two-byte variable at 0040:0013 that reports the number of K of usable memory. On the PCjr, bit 3 at port address 62H (port C of the 8255 chip) equals 0 when the machine has the 64K expansion option. The AT gives especially good information about memory. On the chip that holds configuration information, registers 15H (low) and 16H (high) tell how much memory is installed on the system board (there are only three valid sizes: 0100H for 256K, 0200H for 512K, and 0280H for 512K plus the 128K memory expansion option). I/O channel memory on the AT is reported by registers 17H and 18H (given in 512K increments). Memory positioned above the one-megabyte range is available from 30H and 31H (again in 512K increments, up to 15 megabytes). If the AT's 128K memory expansion option is installed, bit 7 is set to 1 in register 33. In all cases, first send the register number to port address 70H, then read the register value from 71H.

It is easy to write a routine that directly tests for the presence of RAM at regular intervals in the memory space. Since RAM is installed minimally in 16K units, it is only necessary to check one memory location in each 16K segment to be able to infer that the whole 16K is there. When an address in the memory space is empty, it will read as 233. An arbitrary number other than 233 is written into the location, and the same address is immediately read to see if the number is there. If instead 233 turns up, the particular memory bank is nonexistent. Avoid this technique on the AT, where built-in *exception handling* comes in to action when a write is made to nonexistent RAM. The AT's diagnostics are so good that you can rely on the system's configuration information.

RAM is extensively occupied by parts of the operating system, device drivers, resident interrupt handlers, and DOS memory control blocks. When checking for the memory banks, you must not make any permanent changes in the contents of memory. First *save* the contents of a (presumed) memory location, then check it, and then restore the original contents.

There is one more problem. Should your routine momentarily happen to change the very code that comprises it, a crash could result. Thus it is necessary to choose a location in a 64K block that is away from the offset in which your routine resides. Place the routine early in a program, and use as the offset in a block the same offset as the code segment uses. For example, if the code segment register holds 13E2, then the segment begins at offset 3E2 within the second 64K block of memory. Since your routine is located somewhat beyond this address, it is safe to check the byte at 3E2 in each block. Disable interrupts [1.2.2] lest the code be changed for a hardware interrupt that occurs while the check is made.

Finding out how much memory is actually available to DOS also requires a trick. When a program first receives control, DOS gives it all available memory, including the part of high memory that holds the transient part of DOS (which automatically reloads if it has been overlaid). To run another program from within the current program or to make a program fit for multiuser systems, the allocated memory must be shrunk down to the required size. [1.3.1] explains how this change is made using function 4AH of INT 21H.

The same function can also be used to *expand* allocated memory. Since all memory is allocated when a program is loaded, such expansion is impossible at startup. If you attempt it, the carry flag is set to indicate an error condition, error code 8 appears in AX, and the maximum number of 16-byte paragraphs available is returned in BX. The latter is just the information needed. Simply place a request for an impossibly large block in BX (say, F000H paragraphs), then execute the interrupt. Be sure to execute the function first thing in a program while ES still holds its initial value.

High Level

Interpreted BASIC uses only 64K (although PEEK and POKE can access memory outside of the 64K). The amount of the 64K that is available is returned by the FRE function. The function always takes a dummy argument, which may be either numeric or string. **BYTES = FRE(x)** gives BYTES the number of bytes free. **BYTES = FRE(x$)** does the same. But the string argument forces a "housecleaning" of the data area before the byte count is returned. Note that if the size of the work space is set using CLEAR, the amount reported by FRE will be 2.5 to 4 kbytes smaller, owing to the requirements of the interpreter work area.

The IBM BASIC compiler does not impose the 64K restriction on code and data combined. But the compiler itself is limited in how much memory it can use while it compiles. If space is short, delete all unnecessary line numbers using the /N option at compile time. Also, use shorter words as variable names.

Middle Level

BIOS interrupt 12H checks the dip switch settings and returns in AX the number of kilobytes in the system. This value is calculated from the settings on the 8255 register settings or, in the AT, from the configuration/clock chip. There are no input registers. Keep in mind that the dip switch settings may be incorrect, limiting the reliability of this approach.

To find out how many 16-byte paragraphs are available to DOS, use function 4AH of INT 21H. ES must hold the value it has at startup:

```
;---FIND OUT NUMBER OF PARAGRAPHS AVAILABLE TO DOS:
            MOV   AH,4AH        ;use SETBLOCK function
            MOV   BX,0FFFFH     ;request impossible allocation
            INT   21H          ;now BX holds number of free paragraphs
```

The AT uses function 88H of INT 15H to make an *extended memory check,* which seeks memory that is outside the address range of the CPU when it is in *real address mode.* That is to say, it looks for memory above the one-megabyte mark. The system board must be equipped with 512-640K for this function to operate. The number of 1K blocks of extended memory is returned in AX.

Low Level

The first example checks the number of 64K memory banks in the first ten 64K segments of memory. If you test within the higher six banks of memory space, keep in mind that there are video buffers in the segment starting at B000:0000 (and possibly A000:0000) and ROMs in the segment starting at F000:0000 (and possibly C000:0000).

```
;---TEST EACH MEMORY BANK:
            CLI                     ;disable hardware interrupts
            MOV   AX,CS             ;get the segment value for the code
            AND   AX,0FFFH          ;turn off top 4 bits (set to bottom seg)
            MOV   ES,AX             ;place pointer in ES
            MOV   DI,0              ;let DI count the number of 64K banks
            MOV   CX,10             ;repeat the check for 10 banks
            MOV   BL,'X'            ;use 'X' as the replacement byte
NEXT:       MOV   DL,ES:[0]         ;save the byte at the sample address
            MOV   ES:[0],BL         ;place 'X' at the sample address
            MOV   DH,ES:[0]         ;read the sample address
            MOV   ES:[0],DL         ;replace the original value of the byte
            CMP   DH,'X'            ;does it match what was written?
            JNE   GO_AHEAD         ;if not, don't include in the tally
            INC   DI               ;increment the tally of memory banks
GO_AHEAD:   MOV   AX,ES             ;get ready to increment pointer
            ADD   AX,1000H          ;point to address 64K higher
            MOV   ES,AX             ;set pointer back in ES
            LOOP  NEXT              ;do the next bank
            STI                     ;reenable interrupts
                                    ;and now the tally is in DI
```

Section 2: Manage Interrupts

Interrupts are ready-made routines that the computer calls to perform a common task. There are both *hardware* and *software* interrupts. A hardware interrupt is one that is initiated by hardware, whether on the system board or from a card in an I/O channel. It may be brought about by a pulse of the timer chip, by a signal from a printer, by pressing a key on the keyboard, or by a variety of other routes. Hardware interrupts are not coordinated with the operation of software. When one is called, the CPU stops what it is doing, performs the interrupt, and then picks up where it left off. So as to be able to return to the exact place in the program that it left off, the address of that place (CS:IP) is pushed on to the stack, as is the flag register. Then the address in memory of the interrupt routine is loaded into CS:IP so that the routine is given control. Interrupt routines are often referred to as "interrupt handlers". An interrupt handler always ends with an **IRET** instruction, which undoes the process that started up the interrupt, replacing the original values for CS:IP and the flags, so that the program continues along its way.

Software interrupts, on the other hand, do not really *interrupt* anything. They are essentially no more than procedures that your programs call to perform mundane tasks, like taking a keystroke or writing on the screen. These routines, however, are written within the operating system, not within your programs, and the interrupt mechanism is the means of getting at them. Software interrupts may be nested inside each other. For example, all DOS keyboard-input interrupts use the BIOS keyboard-input interrupt to get a character from the keyboard buffer. Note that a hardware interrupt can take control during a software interrupt. Confusion does not arise from all this activity because each interrupt routine is carefully designed to save all registers that it changes, restoring them at its conclusion so that when it is finished it leaves no trace of its having occupied the CPU.

The addresses of interrupts are called *vectors*. Each vector is four bytes long. The first word holds the value for IP and the second keeps CS. The bottommost 1024 bytes of memory hold interrupt vectors, so there is room for 256 vectors in all. Taken together, they are referred to as the *vector table*. The vector for INT 0 is at **0000:0000**, INT 1 starts at **0000:0004**, INT 2 is at **0000:0008**, etc. If you were to look at the four bytes starting at **0000:0020**, which keeps the vector for INT 8H (the time-of-day interrupt), you would find **A5FE00F0**. Keeping in mind that the low byte of each word comes first in memory, and that the order is IP:CS, the four-byte value translates to F000:FEA5. This is the starting address in ROM for the routine that performs INT 8. Figure 1-2 shows the path a program takes in executing INT 21H.

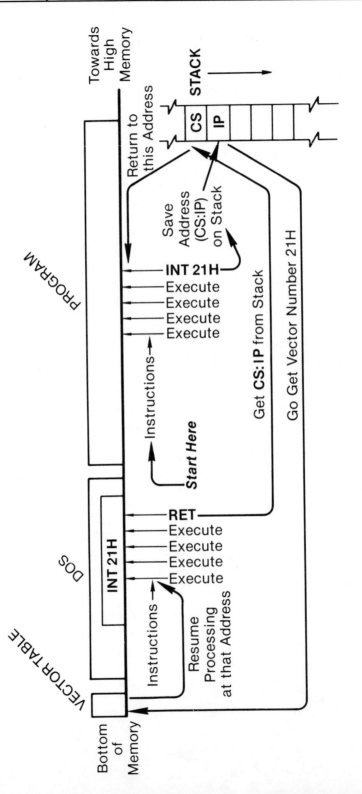

Figure 1-2. The Path of INT 21H

1.2.1 Program the 8259 interrupt controller

The Intel 8259 programmable interrupt controller chip is used in all IBM micro-computers to manage hardware interrupts. Because more than one request for an interrupt can arrive at the same time, the chip has a priority arrangement. There are eight levels of priority, except in the AT, which has 16, and calls to the levels are referred to by the abbreviations IRQ0 to IRQ7 (IRQ0 to IRQ15), which stand for "interrupt request." Highest priority goes to level 0. The extra eight levels on the AT are handled by a second 8259 chip; this second series of levels takes precedence *between* IRQ2 and IRQ3. Interrupt requests 0-7 fit into the vectors for INT 8H-INT FH; on the AT interrupt requests 8-15 are serviced by INT 70H-INT 77H. Here are the interrupt assignments:

Hardware Interrupts By Precedence

IRQ0	timer
1	keyboard
2	I/O channel
8	real-time clock (AT only)
9	software redirected to IRQ2 (AT only)
10	reserved
11	reserved
12	reserved
13	maths coprocessor (AT only)
14	fixed disk controller (AT only)
15	reserved
3	COM1 (COM2 on the AT)
4	COM2 (modem on the PCjr, COM1 on the AT)
5	fixed disk (video vertical retrace on PCjr, LPT2 on AT)
6	diskette controller
7	LPT1

The time-of-day interrupt [2.1.0] is given highest priority because repeatedly missing it would throw off the time-of-day reading. The keyboard interrupt [3.1.0] is invoked when a key is pressed or released; it brings about a chain of events that usually ends in a key code being placed in the keyboard buffer (from there it is retrieved by software interrupts).

The 8259 has three one-byte registers that control and monitor the eight hardware interrupt lines. The *interrupt request register* (IRR) changes a bit to 1 when the corresponding interrupt line signals a request. The chip then automatically checks whether another interrupt is in progress. It consults the *in service register* (ISR) for this information. Additional circuitry assures that the priority scheme is enforced. Finally, before invoking the interrupt, the *interrupt mask register* (IMR) is checked to see whether an interrupt of that level is currently allowed or not. Ordinarily, programmers access only the interrupt mask register at port address 21H [1.2.2] and the interrupt command register at port address 20H [1.2.3].

1.2.2 Allow/disallow particular hardware interrupts

Assembler programs can disable the hardware interrupts listed at [1.2.1]. These are *maskable* interrupts; other hardware interrupts that intercept special errors (such as divide-by-zero) cannot be masked out. There are two reasons to disable hardware interrupts. In one case, *all* interrupts are blocked out so that a critical piece of code can be completely executed before anything else takes place in the machine. For example, interrupts are disabled while a hardware interrupt vector is altered, lest the interrupt occur when the vector is only half changed.

In the second case, only selected hardware interrupts are masked out. This is because those particular interrupts interfere with some time-critical activity. For example, a precisely timed I/O routine could not afford to be waylaid by a lengthy disk interrupt.

Low Level ━━━━━━━━━━━━━━━━━━━━━━━━━━━━━━

Ultimately, the execution of all interrupts relies upon the interrupt flag (bit 9) of the flag register. When it is 0, it honors any interrupt request that the interrupt mask register permits. When it is 1, no hardware interrupt can occur. To set the flag to 1, disabling interrupts, use the **CLI** instruction. To clear the flag to 0, reenabling interrupts, use **STI**. Avoid shutting off interrupts for long periods. The time-of-day interrupt occurs 18.2 times per second, and if more than one request is made for this interrupt while hardware interrupts are disabled, the extra requests are discarded and the time-of-day count falls behind.

Be aware that the machine automatically disables hardware interrupts when a software interrupt is invoked and it automatically reenables them on return. When you write your own software interrupts, you may start the routine with STI if there is reason to keep the hardware interrupts moving. Note also that failing to follow CLI with STI can freeze up the machine, since input from the keyboard is shut out.

To mask out particular hardware interrupts, simply send the appropriate bit pattern to port address 21H, which is the address of the *interrupt mask register* (IMR). The mask register on the second 8259 chip in the AT (IRQ8-15) is at A1H. Set to 1 those bits that correspond to the numbers of the interrupts you wish to mask. The register is write-only. The example below blocks out the disk interrupt. Be sure to clear the register with zeros at the end of a program or the settings will continue after a program is terminated.

```
;---MASK OUT BIT 6 IN THE INTERRUPT MASK REGISTER:
            MOV   AL,01000000B        ;mask out bit 6 (diskette interrupt)
            OUT   21H,AL              ;send to the interrupt mask register
            .
            .
            MOV   AL,0                ;clear IMR at end of program
            OUT   21H,AL
```

1.2.3 Write your own interrupt

There are several reasons for writing your own interrupts. First, most of the ready-made interrupts provided by the operating system are nothing more than common procedures available to all programs, and you may wish to add to this library. For example, many of your programs might use a routine that writes strings on the screen vertically. Rather than link the routine into each program as a procedure, you could set it up as an interrupt that is written as a program that stays resident in memory after termination [1.3.4]. Thus, instead of **CALL WRITE__VERTICALLY** you might have **INT 80H** (keep in mind that calling an interrupt is slightly slower than calling a procedure).

A second reason to write interrupts is to make use of some special hardware interrupts. These interrupts are automatically invoked by some occurence within the computer hardware. In some cases BIOS initializes the vectors for these interrupts to point to a routine that does nothing at all (it contains only an IRET statement). You can write your own routine and change the interrupt vector to point to it. Then, whenever the hardware interrupt occurs your routine is executed. One such routine is the *time-of-day interrupt* [2.1.0], which is invoked automatically 18.2 times a second. Ordinarily this interrupt only updates the time-of-day clock, but you can add any code you like to the interrupt. If your code checks the clock setting and swings into action at designated times, real-time operations are made possible. Other uses include programming a routine for Ctrl-Break [3.2.8], for PrtSc [3.2.9], and for error conditions [7.2.5]. Printer interrupts [6.3.1] and communications interrupts [7.1.8] allow the computer to rapidly switch back and forth between I/O operations and other processing.

Finally, you may wish to write an interrupt that entirely replaces one of the operating system routines, tailoring it to your program's needs. [1.2.4] shows how to write an interrupt within an interrupt that lets you *modify* existing routines.

Middle Level ───────────────────────

Function 25H of INT 21H sets an interrupt vector to a specified address. The addresses are two words long. The high word holds the segment value (for CS), and the low word holds the offset (for IP). To set a vector to point to one of your routines, simply place the segment for the routine in DS and the offset of the routine in DX (follow the order in the example below). Then place the interrupt number in AL and call the function. Any interrupt routine must end with *IRET* rather than the usual *RET* instruction. (IRET pops three words off the stack—the flag register is included—whereas RET pushes only two. If you attempt to test the routine as an ordinary procedure, but as one ending with IRET, the stack will be thrown off kilter.) Note that function 25H automatically disables hardware interrupts when it changes the vector, so there is no danger that midway a hardware interrupt could occur that would make use of the vector.

```
;---TO SET UP THE INTERRUPT:
            PUSH DS                  ;save DS
            MOV  DX,OFFSET ROUTINE   ;offset of the interrupt routine in DX
```

```
              MOV   AX,SEG ROUTINE         ;segment of the interrupt routine
              MOV   DS,AX                  ;place in DS
              MOV   AH,25H                 ;function to set up a vector
              MOV   AL,60H                 ;the vector number (INT 60H)
              INT   21H                    ;change the interrupt
              POP   DS                     ;restore DS

;---THE INTERRUPT ROUTINE:
  ROUTINE     PROC FAR
              PUSH AX                      ;save all changed registers
              .
              .
              .
              POP   AX                     ;restore all changed registers
              MOV   AL,20H                 ;use these two lines for
              OUT   20H,AL                 ;hardware interrupts only
              IRET
  ROUTINE     ENDP
```

Place the following two lines of code at the end of any hardware interrupts you write:

```
              MOV   AL,20H
              OUT   20H,AL
```

It is coincidental that the numbers (20H) are the same in the two lines. If a hardware interrupt does not end with this code, the 8259 chip will not clear its *in service register* so that it reenables interrupts at lower levels than the one just completed. Failure to add the code can easily crash the program; since the keyboard interrupt is likely to be shut out, even Ctrl-Alt-Del will be useless. Note that this code is not required by those interrupt vectors that add extensions to existing interrupts, such as INT 1CH, which adds code to the time-of-day interrupt [2.1.7].

When a program ends, the original interrupt vectors should be restored. Otherwise a subsequent program may call the interrupt and jump to a place in memory where your routine no longer resides. Function 35 of INT 21H returns the current value of a vector, placing the segment value in ES and the offset in BX. Before setting up your own interrupt, get the current value using this function, save the value, and then restore it using function 25H (as above) just before terminating your program. For example:

```
;---IN THE DATA SEGMENT:
  KEEP_CS     DW    0                      ;holds segment for replaced interrupt
  KEEP_IP     DW    0                      ;holds offset for replaced interrupt
;---AT THE BEGINNING OF THE PROGRAM:
              MOV   AH,25H                 ;function number to get INT address
              MOV   AL,1CH                 ;number of the vector (the timer INT)
              INT   21H                    ;now segment is in ES, offset in BX
              MOV   KEEP_IP,BX             ;store offset
              MOV   KEEP_CS,ES             ;store segment

;---AT THE END OF THE PROGRAM:
              CLI
              PUSH DS                      ;DS is destroyed
              MOV   DX,KEEP_IP             ;prepare to restore offset
              MOV   AX,KEEP_CS             ;
              MOV   DS,AX                  ;prepare to restore segment
              MOV   AH,25H                 ;function to set an interrupt vector
```

```
        MOV   AL,1CH              ;number of the vector
        INT   21H                ;now the interrupt is reset
        POP   DS                 ;restore DS
        STI
```

There are a couple of pitfalls to look out for when you write an interrupt. If the new interrupt routine needs to access data variables within, take care that DS is properly set (ordinarily the interrupt can use the stack provided by the calling program). Another consideration is that programs that end via Ctrl-Break will fail to restore interrupt vectors that have been changed unless the Ctrl-Break interrupt itself is programmed to see to it that the job is done [3.2.8].

Low Level

The DOS functions discussed above do nothing more than retrieve or change two words at the low end of memory. The offset of a vector is obtained simply by multiplying the number of the vector by 4. To place the address of INT 16H in ES:BX, for example:

```
;---GET THE ADDRESS OF INT 16H:
        SUB   AX,AX            ;set extra segment to bottom of memory
        MOV   ES,AX            ;
        MOV   DI,16H           ;put INT number (INT 16H) in DI
        SHL   DI,1             ;multiply by 2
        SHL   DI,1             ;multiply by 2 again
        MOV   BX,ES:[DI]       ;put low byte in BX
        MOV   AX,ES:[DI]+2     ;put high byte in ES
        MOV   ES,AX            ;
```

It is inadvisable to go around the DOS functions and set interrupt vectors directly. In particular, in a multitasking environment the operating system may support a number of interrupt vector tables, and the actual physical location of the table may be known only to DOS.

1.2.4 Make additions to existing interrupts

Although unusual, sometimes it is useful to *add* features to an existing interrupt. As an example, consider the software utilities that convert single keystrokes into long user-defined strings of characters (keyboard macros). These utilities may exploit the fact that all standard keyboard input arrives via function Ø of BIOS interrupt 16H [3.1.3]. The basic DOS keyboard-input interrupts call the BIOS interrupt to take a character from the keyboard buffer. Thus one need only modify INT 16H so that it acts as a gateway for the macros, and then any program will receive the macro no matter what keyboard-input interrupt it uses. (Sophisticated keyboard macro programs completely replace the keyboard interrupt, INT 9.)

At this time only BIOS interrupts may be modified. DOS interrupts are *non-reentrant*. A BIOS interrupt, however, can not be *internally* modified because it is on ROM. But you can write a subroutine that precedes and/or follows a BIOS interrupt, and this subroutine will be invoked every time the interrupt is called. In the case of INT 16H, for example, you need only write a routine and point to it the interrupt vector for INT 16H. The original vector for INT 16H meanwhile is transferred to some unused vector, say 60H. The new routine simply calls INT 60H to make use of the original 16H interrupt; that is, when a program calls INT 16H, control is transferred to the special routine, which then calls the original 16H interrupt, which returns to the special routine when it is finished, and the new routine in turn returns to the place in the program that made the call for 16H. Once this is set up, special coding can be placed within the new routine before or after INT 60H is called. Figure 1-3 diagrams this procedure. In summary:

1. Set up the new routine, at some point calling INT 60H.
2. Transfer the interrupt vector for 16H to 60H.
3. Change the 16H vector to point to the new routine.
4. Terminate the program, leaving it resident in memory [1.3.4].

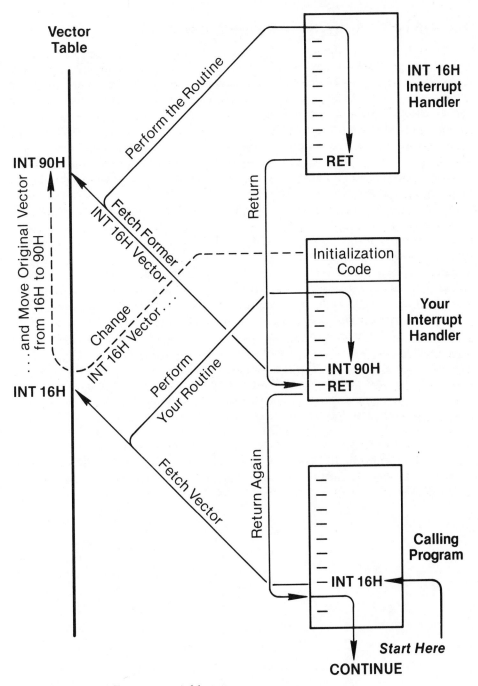

Figure 1-3. Adding on to an existing interrupt.

Section 3: Manage Programs

Most programs are loaded into memory, run, and then abandoned by DOS when the program terminates. High level languages like BASIC ordinarily leave no alternatives. But other options are available to assembly programmers, and this section demonstrates them. Some programs operate as device drivers or interrupt handlers, and their code must be kept in memory ("kept resident") even after other programs have been loaded (interrupt vectors provide the means by which subsequent programs find their way to the resident routines). And sometimes one program may need to run another program from within itself. In fact, DOS allows a program to load a second copy of COMMAND.COM into memory, and the second copy can be used for its usual user-interface facilities, such as the COPY or DIR commands.

Programs may be in two formats, .EXE and .COM. The former allows programs to be larger than 64K, but it requires that DOS do some processing as it loads the program into memory. COM programs, on the other hand, already exist in the image that memory requires. COM programs are especially useful for short utilities. In either case, the code that comprises a program is preceded in memory by a *program segment prefix* (PSP). This is an area 100H bytes large that holds special information DOS requires to operate the program; the PSP provides space for file I/O operations as well [5.3.5]. When an EXE file is loaded, both DS and ES point to the PSP. For COM files, CS also initially points to the PSP. Note that DOS 3.0 has a function that returns the PSP segment number. This is number 62H of INT 21H; there are no input registers, and the paragraph number is returned in BX.

One reason the PSP location is of concern is that its first word contains the number of the DOS interrupt that will terminate the program. When the final RET statement of a program is executed, the values left at the top of the stack direct the instruction pointer (the IP register) to the start of the PSP, so that the termination code is executed as the next instruction of the program. There is more discussion of this feature at [1.3.4] and at [1.3.6].

For reference, here is a map of the PSP fields:

Offset	Field Size	Use
0H	DW	number of DOS function used to terminate program
2	DW	memory size in paragraphs
4	DW	reserved
6	DD	long call to DOS function dispatcher
A	DD	terminate address (IP,CS)
E	DD	ctrl-break exit address (IP,CS)
12	DD	critical error exit address (IP,CX)
16	22 bytes	reserved
2C	DW	paragraph number of the program's environment string
2E	46 bytes	reserved
5C	16 bytes	parameter area 1 (formatted as unopened FCB)
6C	20 bytes	parameter area 2 (formatted as unopened FCB)
80	128 bytes	default disk transfer area/receives command line data

1.3.1 Allocate/deallocate memory

When PC-DOS loads a program, the program is placed at the low end of memory, just above COMMAND.COM and any installed device drivers or other utilities that have been left resident. At this time, all of memory above the program itself is allocated to the program. If the program needs some memory to set up a data area, it can figure out approximately where in memory its own code ends, and then it is free to place the data area anywhere above that. To calculate the end of a program, place a "pseudo segment" at the end of the program, such as:

```
ZSEG    SEGMENT
        ;
ZSEG    ENDS
```

On the IBM assembler, ZSEG will be made the last because segments are arranged in alphabetical order. With other assemblers, actually place it at the end of the source code. In the program itself, simply write **MOV AX,ZSEG**, and AX will then point to the first free segment in memory following the program.

This approach works so long as the program does not assume the existence of memory that is not actually there. Nor does it work in a multiuser environment where several programs may be sharing the same range of memory addresses. As a solution to these problems DOS is able to keep track of 640K of memory in the system, and to allocate *memory blocks* of any size a program demands. A *memory block* is simply a continuous section of memory; it can be as large as there is memory available; in particular, it can be larger than one segment (64K). If too large a block is requested, DOS returns an error message. Any possibility of overlapping blocks is ruled out. In addition, DOS can deallocate, shrink, or expand existing blocks. While a program is not forced to use these means, it is both prudent and convenient to do so. And certain DOS functions *require* that the DOS memory management tools be used, such as when a program is loaded and then left resident [1.3.4] or when one program is run from within another [1.3.2].

Before any memory allocation can be made, the existing block (all of memory from the beginning of the program on up) must be shrunk down to the size of the program. Thereafter, whenever a block is created, DOS sets up a 16-byte *memory control block* that immediately precedes the block in memory. The first five bytes of this field are significant, as follows:

```
byte 0       ASCII 90 if the last block in the chain,
             otherwise ASCII 77
bytes 1-2    0 if the block has been deallocated
bytes 3-4    size of the block in (16-byte) paragraphs
```

DOS references the blocks as a chain. The address of the first block is kept in an internal variable. The variable enables DOS to locate the memory control block of the first allocated block, and from the information contained there it can find the next block, and so on, as shown in Figure 1-4. Once you start using the DOS memory allocation system, you must stick with it. If a program subsequently overwrites areas containing control blocks, the chain will be broken, and DOS will begin returning error messages.

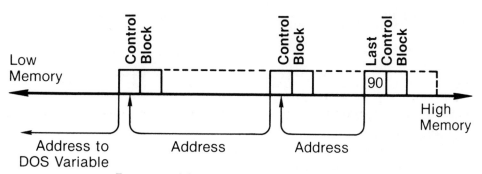

Figure 1-4. Memory Control Block Linkage.

DOS provides three memory allocation functions, numbers 48H-4AH of INT 21H. Function 48H allocates memory, and 49H deallocates memory. The third function ("SETBLOCK") changes the size of memory currently allocated to a program; this is the function that must be executed before the others can be used. Then blocks may be allocated and deallocated freely. A program *must* deallocate all of the blocks it has allocated before terminating. Otherwise memory will be sequestered away from subsequent uses.

Middle Level

All three memory allocation functions of INT 21H use a 16-bit starting address for the memory block they operate upon. This address represents the *segment* in which the block begins (the block always starts at offset 0 in that segment). Thus the actual block starting location is at the memory address represented by this value multiplied by 16. Also, in all three functions, BX contains the number of 16-byte sections of memory ("paragraphs") that are to be allocated or freed. If the function fails, the carry flag is set and AX returns an error code explaining why. The three relevant codes are:

```
7    memory control blocks have been destroyed
8    there is insufficient memory available
9    the memory block address is invalid
```

The allocation function uses codes 7 & 8, the deallocation function uses codes 7 & 9, and the function that changes the allocation uses all three codes. The following code first allocates a 1024-byte block, saving its starting address in the variable BLOCK__SEG. BX holds the number of 16-byte paragraphs requested, and upon return the start address is found as AX:0 (that is, as a 0 offset within the segment value contained in AX). The second part of the code deallocates the same block, as is required when a program terminates. In this case, the value returned in AX is placed in ES. DOS keeps track of the block size and knows how many paragraphs to deallocate.

```
;---ALLOCATE A 1024-BYTE AREA:
          MOV   AH,48H        ;function number
          MOV   BX,64         ;request 64 16-byte paragraphs
          INT   21H           ;attempt the allocation
```

29

```
                     JC    ERROR             ;go to error handling routine if carry
                     MOV   BLOCK_SEG,AX      ;else, AX holds block segment, save it
                       .

;---DEALLOCATE THE SAME AREA:
                     MOV   AX,BLOCK_SEG      ;retrieve start address of the block
                     MOV   ES,AX             ;place it in ES
                     MOV   AH,49H            ;function number to deallocate
                     INT   21H               ;make the deallocation
```

Finally, here is an example of function 4AH. ES holds the segment value of the program segment prefix, that is, of the very first byte in memory at which the program is loaded. ES is initialized to this value at startup. To use SETBLOCK, either call the function at the very beginning of a program (before ES is changed) or else store the initial value of ES for later use.

BX holds the desired block size in 16-byte paragraphs. To calculate the size, place an extra, fake segment in the program that will reside at the end of the source code. On the IBM Macro Assembler, the segments are laid out in alphabetical order, and so this dummy segment can be placed anywhere in the source code so long as it has a name like "ZSEG". On other assemblers, place the dummy segment at the actual end of the source code. The program can read the position of this segment and compare it with its own starting segment, giving the amount of memory required by the program. At the time that the program is loaded, both ES and DS hold the paragraph number for the very beginning of the program at the program segment prefix; in COM files CS also points to this position, but in EXE files it does not.

```
;---REALLOCATE A PROGRAM'S MEMORY (ES HOLDS SAME VALUE AS AT LOAD-TIME):
                     MOV   BX,ZSEG           ;get paragraph # of end of program + 1
                     MOV   AX,ES             ;get paragraph # of start of program
                     SUB   BX,AX             ;calculate program size in paragraphs
                     MOV   AH,4AH            ;function number
                     INT   21H               ;make the reallocation
                     JC    MEMORY_ERROR      ;check for errors, etc...

;---THE DUMMY SEGMENT:
     ZSEG            SEGMENT
     ZSEG            ENDS
```

1.3.2 Run one program from within another

DOS provides the EXEC function (number 4B of INT 21H) to run one program from within another. The first program is called the "parent," and the one that is loaded and run is called the "child."

High Level ───────────────────────────

BASIC 3.0 introduces the SHELL command. With considerable limitations, it lets a BASIC program load and run another program. The format is **SHELL command-string**. The command string may be just the name of a program, or it can be the name plus the parameters that would ordinarily follow the program name on the command line. If no command-string is named, a copy of COMMAND.COM is loaded and the DOS prompt appears. Any DOS commands may be used, and, when finished, typing **EXIT** returns control to the BASIC program.

There are a number of restrictions of the use of SHELL. If the program that is loaded changes the screen mode, for example, the change will *not* be automatically remedied on return. All files must be closed before the program is loaded, and it must not be a program that stays resident after termination. See the BASIC manual for a discussion of several other problems.

Middle Level ───────────────────────────

Function 4BH is more complicated than most, requiring four preparatory steps:

(1) Make space available in memory for the program.
(3) Create a parameter block.
(2) Build a drive, path, and program name string.
(4) Save the SS and SP registers in variables.

Space must be made in memory because DOS assigns the whole of memory to a program when it is loaded. Without freeing some memory there would be no where to load the second program. [1.3.1] explains how it is done using the SETBLOCK function. Once memory is freed, you need merely place in BX the required number of 16-byte paragraphs of memory space, put 4AH in AH, and execute INT 21H to shrink down the memory allocation so that only the number of paragraphs requested is available to the program.

The *parameter block*, to which ES:BX must point, is a 14-byte block of memory in which you must place the following four pieces of information:

```
DW    segment address of environment string
DD    segment/offset of command line
DD    segment/offset of first file control block
DD    segment/offset of second file control block
```

An *environment string* is a string of one or more specifications that DOS follows when it executes a program. The elements of an environment string are the same as those that would be found in a CONFIG.SYS file on disk. For example, **VERIFY = ON** could be placed in the string. Simply begin the string with the first

31

element, end the element with the ASCII Ø character, write the next, and so on. The last element must be followed by two ASCII Ø characters. The string must begin on a paragraph boundary (that is, its address MOD 16 must be Ø). This is because the entry in the parameter block that points to the string holds only a two-byte segment value. All of this may be avoided if the new program can operate with the same environment string as the one that loads it. In that case, simply place ASCII Ø in the first two bytes of the parameter block.

The next four bytes of the parameter block point to a command line for the program being loaded. A "command line" is the string that invokes a program. Loading a program from DOS, it might be something like **EDITOR A:CHAPTER1 \NOTES.MS**. Here, the editor is called and given the name of a file in a subdirectory of drive A to open immediately. When you set up a command line for EXEC, include only the latter information, not the name of the program to be loaded. Precede the command line with one byte that holds the number of characters in the string, and end the string with a carriage return byte, which is ASCII 13.

The last eight bytes of the parameter block point to file control blocks (FCBs). The FCBs hold information for the one or two files named in the command line. If there are no files to be opened, fill the eight bytes with ASCII Ø. [5.3.5] explains how FCBs operate. Since the advent of DOS version 2.0, FCBs have been essentially obsolete, and you may avoid including the FCB information by instead using the DOS 2.0 *file handle* conventions, which access a file by a code number rather than by a control block (also discussed at [5.3.5]).

Finally, you must build a drive, path, and file name string. This is the string that names the program to be loaded. DS:DX points to the string when EXEC is executed. The string is a standard *"ASCII Z string,"* which is nothing more than a drive specifier, a tree directory path, and the file name and extension, ending with an ASCII Ø byte. For example, the string might be **B:\NEWDATA\FILER.EXEØ**, where Ø is ASCII Ø.

Once all of the above information is set up, there remains one final task. All registers are altered by the program that is called. The stack segment and stack pointer must be saved so that they can be restored when control returns to the calling program. Set aside variables to do this. Since DS is also destroyed, these variables can not be retrieved until the statements **MOV AX,DSEG** and **MOV DS,AX** are repeated. Once SS and SP are saved, place Ø in AL to choose the "load and run" option (EXEC is also used for overlays [1.3.5]). Then place 4AH in AH and call INT 21H. At this point essentially two programs are running, and the parent goes on "hold." DOS provides a way for the child program to pass a return code to the parent, so that errors and status may be reported. [7.2.5] explains how this is done. Minimally, on return the carry flag is set if there has been an error, and in this case AX returns 1 for an invalid function number, 2 if the file was not found, 5 for disk problems, 8 if insufficient memory, 10 if the environment string was invalid, and 11 if the format was invalid.

The example given here is the simplest possible, but often the EXEC procedure requires no more. It leaves the entire parameter block as zeros, and does not create an environment string. This means that no command line is passed to the loaded program, and that the environment will be the same as that of the calling program.

You need only change the memory allocation, set up the filename and (empty) parameter block, and save SS and SP.

```
;---IN THE DATA SEGMENT:
    FILENAME      DB    'A:TRIAL.EXE',0       ; load TRIAL.EXE from drive A
    PARAMETERS    DW    7 dup(0)              ;parameter block all zeros
    KEEP_SS       DW    0                     ;variable to keep SS
    KEEP_SP       DW    0                     ;variable to keep SP

;---REALLOCATE MEMORY:
              MOV   BX,ZSEG                   ;get paragraph # of end of program
              MOV   AX,ES                     ;get paragraph # of start of program
              SUB   BX,AX                     ;calculate program size in paragraphs
              MOV   AH,4AH                     ;function number
              INT   21H                       ;make the reallocation
;---POINT TO PARAMETER BLOCK:
              MOV   AX,SEG PARAMETERS          ;ES holds segment
              MOV   ES,AX                      ;
              MOV   BX,OFFSET PARAMETERS       ;BX holds offset
;---STORE COPIES OF SS AND SP:
              MOV   KEEP_SS,SS                 ;save SS
              MOV   KEEP_SP,SP                 ;save SP
;---POINT TO FILE NAME STRING:
              MOV   DX,OFFSET FILENAME          ;offset in DX
              MOV   AX,SEG FILENAME             ;segment in DS
              MOV   DS,AX                       ;
;---LOAD THE PROGRAM:
              MOV   AH,4BH                      ;EXEC function
              MOV   AL,0                        ;choose "load and run" option
              INT   21H                         ;run it
;---AFTERWARDS, RESTORE REGISTERS:
              MOV   AX,DSEG                      ;restore DS
              MOV   DS,AX                        ;
              MOV   SS,KEEP_SS                   ;restore SS
              MOV   SP,KEEP_SP                   ;restore SP

;---AT THE END OF THE PROGRAM CREATE A DUMMY SEGMENT TO MARK END OF CODE:
    ZSEG          SEGMENT                       ;see [1.3.1] for an explanation
    ZSEG          ENDS
```

1.3.3 Use DOS user-interface commands from within a program

Programs can have at their disposal the full range of DOS user-interface commands, such as DIR or CHKDSK. When these services are used from within a program, a second copy of COMMAND.COM is loaded and run. While a good deal of programming can be saved by this approach, it does impose the need for adequate memory for this second copy, and your program could be left at an impasse if not enough is available.

High Level

BASIC 3.0 can load a second copy of COMMAND.COM using its SHELL statement. SHELL is discussed at [1.3.2]. COMMAND.COM is loaded when no file name is specified, so simply writing **SHELL** brings up the DOS prompt. Any of the DOS utilities may be used, including batch files. To return to the calling BASIC program, enter **EXIT**.

Middle Level

The example at [1.3.2] must have a command line added to it in this case. Normally the line begins with a byte giving its length, then the command string itself, and finally ASCII 13. When passing a command to COMMAND.COM, you must place /C before the string (see the DOS manual under *Invoking a Secondary Command Processor*). You also should specify the drive where COMMAND.COM is found, placing the drive prefix at the start of the command string. To have the directory of drive A shown when COMMAND.COM is on drive B, write:

```
COMMAND_LINE   DB  12,'B: /C DIR A:',13
```

The following bit of code sets the command line address into the parameter block used in the example at [1.3.2]:

```
LEA BX,PARAMETERS              ;get offset of parameter block
MOV AX,OFFSET COMMAND_LINE     ;get offset of command line
MOV [BX]+2,AX                  ;place in 1st 2 bytes of block
MOV AX,SEG COMMAND_LINE        ;get segment of command line
MOV [BX]+4,AX                  ;place in 2nd 2 bytes of block
```

1.3.4 Keep a program in memory after it has terminated

Programs left resident in memory may serve as utilities to other programs. Normally such a program is accessed via an unused interrupt vector. DOS treats the program as if it were part of itself, protecting it from being overlaid by programs that are subsequently loaded. Resident programs are usually written in COM form, as discussed at [1.3.6]. They are slightly more difficult to make resident when they are written as EXE files.

Terminating a program with INT 27H causes it to stay resident. At the time that INT 27H is executed, CS must point to the start of the program segment prefix for this function to work properly. In COM programs, CS is initially set to this position, and so you need simply end the program with 27H. In EXE programs, on the other hand, CS initially points to the first byte *following* the PSP (that is, to 100H). In the normal termination of an EXE program, the final RET instruction pops off the stack the first values pushed on to the stack: **PUSH DX/MOV AX,0/PUSH AX**. Since DS initially points to the bottom of the PSP, when these values are popped the instruction pointer is directed to offset 0 in the PSP, which is initialized to contain the code for INT 20H. INT 20H is then executed, and it is the standard function for terminating programs and returning control to DOS. Figure 1-5 diagrams this process. To make INT 27H work in an EXE program, poke 27H into the second byte of the PSP (the first holds the machine code for "INT"), and end the program with the usual RET. For both kinds of file, before INT 27H is executed DX must contain the offset of the end of the program, starting from the beginning of the PSP.

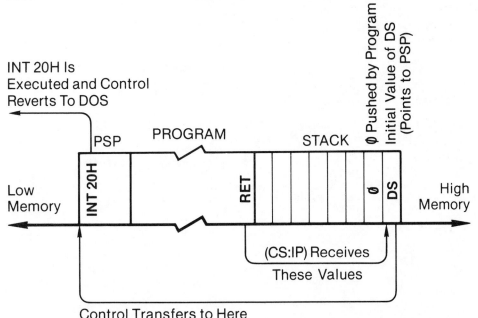

Figure 1-5. Termination of an .EXE program.

Middle Level

The interrupt vector is set up using function 25H of INT 21H, as discussed at [1.2.3] (vector number 70H is used here). Be sure that the routine ends with IRET. Apart from providing the routine, the set-up program does nothing more than initialize the interrupt vector, point DX to the end of the interrupt routine, and terminate. In COM files, simply place the **INT 27H** statement at the end of the program. In EXE files, poke it into the first word of the PSP, and terminate the program using the usual RET statement. Thereafter the routine executes whenever a subsequently loaded program calls INT 70H.

Examples are given here for both COM and EXE files. Both set up the label "FINISH" to mark the end of the interrupt routine (recall that the $ sign gives the instruction pointer value at that point). In the COM file, FINISH gives the offset from the start of the PSP, as required by INT 27H. In the EXE file, the offset is from the first byte following the PSP, and so 100H is added to this value so that this offset too starts from the bottom of the PSP. Note that by placing the routine first in the program, the set-up code can be excluded from the resident portion. Another trick is to use MOVSB to move the code for the routine down into the unused part of the PSP, starting from offset 60H, freeing 160 bytes of memory.

COM file case:

```
;---HERE IS THE INTERRUPT ROUTINE:
     BEGIN:       JMP   SHORT SET_UP      ;jump over the resident routine
ROUTINE           PROC FAR
                  PUSH DS                  ;save altered registers
                    .
                    .
        (the routine)
                    .
                    .
                  POP  DS                  ;restore registers
                  IRET                     ;interrupt return
         FINISH   EQU  $                   ;mark end of routine
ROUTINE           ENDP

;---SET UP THE INTERRUPT VECTOR:
         SET_UP:  MOV  DX,OFFSET ROUTINE   ;put offset of routine in DX
                  MOV  AL,70H              ;interrupt vector number
                  MOV  AH,25H              ;function to set vector
                  INT  21H                 ;set the vector
;---LEAVE THE PROGRAM, STAYING RESIDENT:
                  LEA  DX,FINISH           ;set offset of resident routine
                  INT  27H                 ;quit, and routine stays resident
```

EXE file case:

```
;---HERE IS THE INTERRUPT ROUTINE:
                  JMP  SHORT SET_UP        ;jump over the resident routine
ROUTINE           PROC FAR
                  PUSH DS                  ;save altered registers
                    .
                    .
        (the routine)
```

```
                     .
                     .
                     .
                POP  DS                 ;restore registers
                IRET                    ;interrupt return
        FINISH: EQU  $                  ;mark end point of routine
ROUTINE         ENDP

;---SET UP THE INTERRUPT VECTOR:
     SET_UP:    MOV  DX,OFFSET ROUTINE  ;put offset of routine in DX
                MOV  AX,SEG ROUTINE     ;put segment of routine in DS
                MOV  DS,AX              ;
                MOV  AL,70H             ;interrupt vector number
                MOV  AH,25H             ;function to set vector
                INT  21H               ;set the vector
;---LEAVE THE PROGRAM, STAYING RESIDENT:
                MOV  DX,FINISH+100H     ;set offset of end of resident routine
                MOV  BYTE PTR ES:1,27H  ;poke 27H into PSP
                RET                     ;quit, and routine stays resident
```

Function 31H of INT 21H works in much the same way, except that DX is given the number of 16-byte paragraphs required by the routine (calculate the program size from the start of the program segment prefix—see the example at [1.3.1]).The advantage of this routine is that it can pass an *exit code* to the parent program, providing information on the status of the routine. The parent senses the code via function 4DH of INT 21H. Exit codes are discussed at [7.2.5].

1.3.5 Load and run program overlays

Overlays are parts of programs that remain on disk while the body of the program is resident in memory. When the functions of a particular overlay are required, that overlay is loaded into memory and the program calls it as a procedure. Other overlays may subsequently be loaded at exactly the same place in memory, *overlaying* the prior code. For example, a data base program might load a sort routine and then later overlay it with a report-generation routine. This technique is used to conserve memory. But it works well only for procedures that are not in constant use; otherwise, the frequent disk operations make the program operate much too slowly.

Middle Level ━━━━━━━━━━━━━━━━━━━━━━━━━━━━━━━━━━━━━━

DOS uses the EXEC function to load overlays. This function, number 4BH of INT 21H, is also used to load and run one program from within another when the code number 0 is placed in AL [1.3.2]. When 3 is placed in AL, however, an overlay is loaded instead. In this case, no program segment prefix is built, so the overlay is not set up as an independent program. The function merely loads the overlay, without turning control over to it.

There are two ways to provide memory for the overlays. Either an area inside the body of the main program may be overlaid, or memory outside of the main program must be specially allocated. The EXEC function is given only a *segment* address (a 16-byte boundary) as the location at which the overlay is to be loaded. When the overlay is loaded into a program, the program must calculate a paragraph number that will keep the overlay from encroaching on surrounding code. When memory is separately allocated, on the other hand, DOS provides the program with a paragraph number.

The example below uses the memory allocation method. Since DOS initially allocates all available memory to a program, first function 4AH is used to deallocate excess memory. Then function 48H allocates a block big enough to accommodate the largest overlay that will be set into it. This function returns the segment value of the block in AX, and that paragraph number is the one at which the overlay is loaded and the one at which the overlay is (indirectly) called by the main program. These functions are discussed in more detail at [1.3.1].

Besides the code number 3 in AL, there are two other inputs you must set up for this function. Point DS:DX to a string that gives the path to the overlay file, ending the string with a byte of ASCII 0. Give the entire name of the file, complete with .COM or .EXE ending, since DOS does not read it as if it were searching for a program file.

Finally, point ES:BX to a four-byte parameter block that contains (1) the two-byte paragraph number at which the overlay is to be loaded and (2) a two-byte *relocation factor* that is used for relocating addresses within the overlay (relocation is explained at [1.3.6]). For the paragraph number, use the number returned in AX for the paragraph number of the allocated memory block. The relocation factor gives an offset by which relocatable items in the overlay can be calculated. Use the paragraph number at which the overlay is loaded. Once this is set up, call the function and the overlay will be loaded. Simply by changing the path to the overlay file, the function can be called again and again, loading different overlays each time. On return, if the carry flag is set, there has been an error, and an error code is returned in AX. The code is 1 if the function number was bad, 2 if the file was not found, 5 if there was a disk problem, and 8 if memory was insufficient.

Once the overlay is in memory, it is accessed as a *far* procedure. A double-word pointer must be set up in the data segment to accommodate this call. The segment part of the pointer is simply seg current code segment. The offset of the overlay must be calculated by finding the difference between the code segment and the overlay segment and multiplying the result by 16 (changing the value from paragraphs to bytes). In the example below the two variables OVERLAY__OFFSET and CODE__SEG are placed one after another so that the pointer is set up correctly. The overlay, once loaded, can then be called by CALL DWORD PRT OVERLAY__OFFSET.

The overlay may be a complete program in itself, with its own data and stack segments, although generally the stack segment is omitted so that the calling program's stack is used instead. When the overlay is called, the segment value of its own data segment must be placed in DS.

```
;---END THE PROGRAM WITH DUMMY SEGMENT FOR MEMORY ALLOCATION (see [1.3.1]):
ZSEG            SEGMENT
ZSEG            ENDS

;---IN THE DATA SEGMENT:
OVERLAY_SEG     DW    ?
OVERLAY_OFFSET  DW    ?                ;offset of overlay in code segment
CODE_SEG        DW    ?                ;overlay segment -- must follow OVERLAY_OFFSET
PATH            DB    'A:OVERLAY.EXE'
0BLOCK          DD    0                ;4-byte parameter block for overlay

;---FREE MEMORY:
                MOV   CODE_SEG,CS      ;make a copy of CS
                MOV   AX,ES            ;copy of PSP segment value
                MOV   BX,ZSEG          ;end of program segment address
                SUB   BX,AX            ;calculate the difference
                MOV   AH,4AH           ;SETBLOCK function number
                INT   21H              ;deallocate all other memory
                JC    SETBLK_ERROR     ;carry flag signals error
;---ALLOCATE MEMORY FOR THE OVERLAY:
                MOV   BX,100H           ;allocate 1000H bytes to overlay
                MOV   AH,48H            ;function to allocate memory
                INT   21H              ;now AX:0 points to new block
                JC    ALLOCATION_ERROR ;carry flag signals error
                MOV   OVERLAY_SEG,AX    ;store seg address of overlay block
;---CALCULATE OVERLAY OFFSET IN THE CODE SEGMENT:
                MOV   AX,CODE_SEG       ;subtract overlay segment value
                MOV   BX,OVERLAY_SEG    ;    from the code segment value
                SUB   BX,AX             ;now BX holds number of 16-byte units
                MOV   CL,4              ;shift this number left 4 places
                SHL   BX,CL             ;    to multiply by 16
                MOV   OVERLAY_OFFSET,BX ;save the offset
;---LOAD THE FIRST OVERLAY:
                MOV   AX,SEG BLOCK      ;ES:BX points to parameter block
                MOV   ES,AX             ;
```

```
                MOV   BX,OFFSET BLOCK    ;
                MOV   AX,OVERLAY_SEG     ;put seg address of overlay at first
                MOV   [BX],AX            ;   word of the parameter block
                MOV   [BX]+2,AX          ;use overlay seg as relocation factor
                LEA   DX,PATH            ;DS:DX points to file path
                MOV   AH,4BH             ;EXEC function number
                MOV   AL,3               ;code for overlay
                INT   21H                ;load the overlay
                JC    LOAD_ERROR         ;go to error routine if problem
;---NOW THE PROGRAM GOES ABOUT ITS BUSINESS:
                .
                .
                .
                CALL DWORD PTR OVERLAY_OFFSET     ;call the overlay
                .                                 ; (must use DWORD PTR since
                .                                 ;the overlay is a far procedure)
                .



;---OBSERVE THIS STRUCTURE WHEN WRITING THE OVERLAY:
DSEG            SEGMENT                  ;set up a data segment as usual
                .                        ;skip the stack segment (use the
                .                        ; stack of the calling program)
DSEG            ENDS

CSEG            SEGMENT          PARA PUBLIC 'CODE'
OVERLAY         PROC FAR                 ;far procedure as always
                ASSUME CS:CSEG,DS:DSEG
                PUSH DS                  ;keep copy of calling program's DS
                MOV   AX,DSEG            ;set up overlay's DS
                MOV   DS,AX
                .
                .
                .
                POP   DS                 ;when finished, restore prior DS
                RET
OVERLAY         ENDP
CSEG            ENDS
                END
```

1.3.6 Convert programs from .EXE to .COM type

Assembly language programmers have the option of converting their programs from the usual EXE format to COM format. EXE files have a *header* field that contains information for *relocation*; DOS relocates certain addresses in the program while it loads the program. COM files, on the other hand, are set up in such a way that relocation is not required—they are already in the form in which a loaded program resides in memory. For these reasons, EXE files are at least 768 bytes larger on disk than the COM equivalent (they consume the same amount of RAM once loaded). By avoiding relocation, COM files also load more quickly. There are no other advantages, and many programs are too complex or too large to be converted to COM form.

Relocation is a process that sets addresses that are placed in the segment registers. For example, a program may point to the beginning of a data area by the code:

```
MOV DX,OFFSET DATA_AREA
MOV AX,SEG DATA_AREA
MOV DS,AX
```

The offset in DX is in relation to the setting of the segment register DS. But what value is to be placed in DS itself? The program code requires an *absolute* address, but at what paragraph number DATA__AREA will reside depends on where in memory the program is loaded—and that can vary by the DOS version and by whether other programs have been kept resident in the low end of memory. Only at the time that DOS loads the program is it a certainty where in memory the program begins. For this reason, at the time that the program is linked, all that can be done is to set up any segment values as offsets from the start of the program. Then when DOS performs relocation, the value of the starting location of the program is added to the segment values, giving the absolute location required by a segment register. Figure 1-6 illustrates the relocation process.

COM files have no need of relocation because they are written without any need of these "segment fixups." *Everything* in the program is set up as an offset from the start of the code segment, including all data and the stack as well. For this reason, the whole program cannot exceed 65535 bytes in length, which is the largest offset that addressing can manage (because the high end of this block is used for the stack, the actual space available for code and data is somewhat less than 65535 bytes, although the stack segment can be moved outside the 64K block if necessary). COM files point all of their segment registers to the *bottom* of the program segment prefix; compare this with EXE files, where DS and ES are initialized the same, but CS is set to the first byte *following* the PSP.

Setting up a program in COM form requires adherence to the following rules:

1. Do not set up the program as a procedure. Instead, place a label at the very beginning of the code, such as START, and end the program with the statement END START.

2. Place the statement **ORG 100H** at the start of the code. This sets the point of origination of the code (that is, it sets the instuction pointer). COM pro-

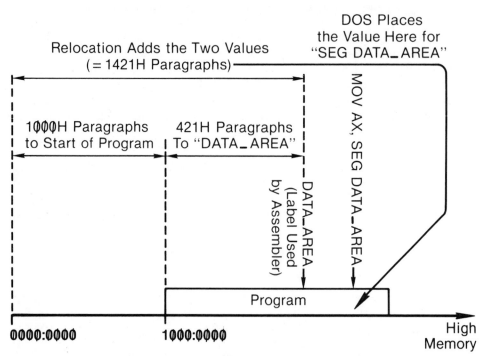

Figure 1-6. Relocation of the memory position of "DATA__AREA".

grams begin from 100H, which is the first byte after the PSP, because CS is set to the start of the PSP, 100H bytes lower. The value 100H is always used. To start the code from elsewhere, place a JMP instruction at 100H.

3. An ASSUME statement sets DS, ES, and SS to match the value of the code segment, as in, for example, **ASSUME CS:CSEG, DS:CSEG, ES:CSEG, SS:CSEG.**

4. The program's data can be placed anywhere in the program so long as it does not interfere with the code. It is best to begin the program with the data, since the macro assembler can create errors during its first pass if references are made to data items not yet encountered. Start the program with a JMP instruction to jump over the data.

5. Segment fix-ups such as **MOV AX,SEG NEW__DATA** are never used. The offset of a label alone suffices. In particular, skip the usual code at the start of a program that sets up the data segment by **MOV AX,DSEG/ MOV DS,AX.**

6. The stack segment is omitted altogether in the initial code. The stack pointer is initialized to the very top of the 64K address space used by the program (recall that the stack grows downwards in memory). In COM programs that must be made smaller than 64K, SS and SP may be changed. Note that when you link the program, the linker gives an error message telling that there is no stack segment. Ignore it.

7. Terminate the program either with a RET instruction or by writing **INT 20H.**

INT 20H is the standard function for terminating programs and returning control to DOS. Even when the program ends with RET, INT 20H is actually used. This is because the first word on the stack is initialized to 0. When the final RET instruction of the program is encountered, the 0 pops off the stack, redirecting the instruction pointer to the start of the program segment prefix. The INT 20H function at that location is executed as the next instruction, causing control to return to DOS. All of this means that you should not push DS and 0 onto the stack at the start of the program (**PUSH DS/MOV AX,0/PUSH AX**) as required by EXE files.

Once a program has been constructed in this way, assemble and link it as always. Then convert it to COM form by using the utility EXE2BIN that is found on the DOS diskette. If the name of the file produced by the linker is MYPROG. EXE, simply type in **EXE2BIN MYPROG**. It will create a program file named MYPROG.BIN. At that point you need only rename the file **MYPROG.COM**. Or write **EXE2BIN MYPROG MYPROG.COM** to make the conversion directly to a file with a .COM extension.

Low Level

This example provides a short, complete program that reads the dip switch setting of how many drives are in the machine and then reports it on the screen. It is an example of the sort of short utility programs for which COM format is ideal.

```
CSEG            SEGMENT
                ORG   100H
                ASSUME CS:CSEG, DS:CSEG, SS:CSEG   ;all segments set to CSEG
;---THE DATA:
  START:        JMP   SHORT BEGIN         ;jump over the data
  MESSAGE1      DB    'The dip switches are set for $'
  MESSAGE2      DB    ' disk drive(s).$'
;---PRINT THE FIRST HALF OF THE MESSAGE:
  BEGIN:        MOV   AH,9                ;function 9 of INT 21H writes strings
                MOV   DX,OFFSET MESSAGE1  ;point DS:DX to the string
                INT   21H                 ;write the string
                PUSH AX                   ;keep the function value to use again
;---GET THE DIP SWITCH SETTING FROM PORT A OF THE 8255 CHIP:
                IN    AL,61H              ;get the byte in Port B
                OR    AL,10000000B        ;force bit 7 on
                OUT   61H,AL              ;replace the byte
                IN    AL,60H              ;get switch settings from Port A
                AND   AL,11000000B        ;isolate the top 2 bits (# drives)
                MOV   CL,6                ;prepare to shift AL right
                SHR   AL,CL               ;move the 2 bits to bottom of register
                ADD   AL,49               ;add 1 to count from 1 to 4, plus
                                         ;    add 48 to convert to ASCII symbol
                MOV   DL,AL               ;put the value in DL
                MOV   AL,61H              ;must restore PB, get the value
                AND   AL,01111111B        ;force bit 7 off
                OUT   61H,AL              ;replace the byte
;---PRINT THE NUMBER OF DRIVES:
                MOV   AH,2                ;use function 2 of INT 21H
                INT   21H                 ;print the number in DL
```

```
;---PRINT THE SECOND HALF OF THE MESSAGE:
                POP  AX                    ;get back the function number
                MOV  DX,OFFSET MESSAGE2    ;get ready to write the second string
                INT  21H                   ;write the string
                INT  20H                   ;end the program
     CSEG       ENDS
                END  START
```

2
Timers And Sound

Section 1: Set and read timers

All IBM microcomputers use the Intel 8253 (or 8254) timer chip to tally pulses from the system clock chip. A number of cycles of the system clock are converted into a single pulse, and chains of these pulses are counted for timing purposes, or they can be sent to the computer's speaker to generate sound of a particular frequency. The 8253 chip has three identical, independent channels, and each can be programmed.

The 8253 chip operates independently of the CPU. The CPU programs the chip and then return to other matters. Thus the 8253 operates like a real-time clock—it keeps its beat no matter what else happens in the computer. However, the longest programmable interval is barely a twentieth of a second. Some other means is required to time minutes and hours. It is for this reason that pulses from channel 0 of the timer chip are tallied in a variable in the BIOS data area. Figure 2-1 diagrams the process. This tally is usually referred to as the "time-of-day count." 18.2 times per second the output from channel 0 invokes a hardware interrupt (the "timer interrupt") which briefly stops the CPU and increases the time-of-day count. A count of 0 signifies 12:00 midnight; when the count reaches the equivalent of 24 hours it is reset to 0. Other times of the day are easily calculated by dividing the count by 18.2 for every second. The time-of-day count is used in most timing operations.

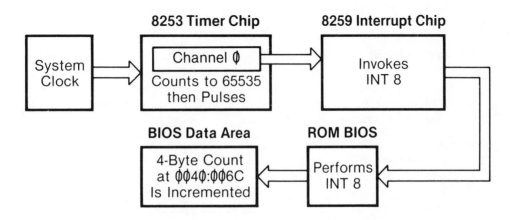

Figure 2-1. Updating the BIOS time-of-day count.

2.1.1 Program the 8253/8254 timer chip

Each of the three channels of the 8253 timer chip (8254 on the AT) consists of three registers. Each group of three registers is accessed through a single port, numbered from 40H to 42H for channels 0 to 2. A port leads to an eight-bit I/O register that sends and receives data for the channel. When a channel is programmed, a two-byte value is sent through the port, low byte first. The number is passed to a 16-bit *latch register*, which keeps the number, and from there a copy is placed in a 16-bit *counter register*. In the counter register, the number decrements by 1 each time a pulse from the system clock is allowed into the channel. When the number reaches zero, the channel issues an output pulse and then a new copy of the number in the latch register is moved into the counter register and the process repeats. The smaller the number in the counter register, the faster the beat. All three channels are always active: the CPU does not turn them on and off. The current value of any counter register may be read at any time without disturbing the count.

Each channel has two lines going into it, and one line coming out. The *out* line conducts the pulse that results from the counting. The destination of these signals varies by the type of IBM microcomputer:

- **Channel 0** is used by the system time-of-day clock. It is set by BIOS at startup so that it issues a pulse roughly 18.2 times a second. A four-byte tally of these pulses is kept in memory at 0040:006C (the least significant byte is lowest). Each pulse invokes the timer interrupt (INT 8), and it is this interrupt that increases the tally. This is a *hardware* interrupt, and so it continues to occur no matter what the CPU is doing, so long as hardware interrupts are enabled (see the discussion at [1.2.2]). The *out* line of channel 0 is also used for timing certain disk operations, and so if you change it you must be sure to restore it to its original reading every time disks are accessed.

- **Channel 1** controls memory refresh on all machines but the PCjr, and it should never be tampered with. The *out* line of the channel is connected to the direct memory access chip [5.4.2], and a pulse causes the DMA chip to refresh all of RAM. On the PCjr, channel 1 paces the conversion of incoming keyboard data from serial to parallel form. The PCjr does not use a direct memory access chip, and when it instead channels data through the CPU, the timer interrupt is shut out. Channel 1 is used to count the intervening pulses of the time-of-day clock so that the count can be updated after disk operations are completed.

- **Channel 2** is connected to the computer's speaker, and it produces simple square-wave signals for making sound. Programmers have more control over channel 2 than the others. Simple sounds may be made to occur simultaneously with other program operations, or more complex sounds may be produced with the full attention of the CPU. Channel 2 may also be disconnected from the speaker and used for timing operations. Finally, the *out* line of channel 2 is connected to the computer's speaker. The speaker will not sound, however, unless a particular setting is made on the 8255 peripheral interface chip.

The two lines going into each channel consist of a *clock* line that feeds the system clock signal from the system clock chip, and a line called the *gate* that turns the clock signal on and off. The gate is always open for the clock signal to channels 0 and 1. But it can be opened and closed on channel 2, and this feature allows special sound techniques. The gate is closed by setting to 1 the lowest bit at port address 61H, which is a register on the 8255 chip; changing the bit back to 0 reopens the gate. [1.1.1] discusses this chip. Note that—like the output of channel 2—bit 1 at 61H is connected to the speaker, and it too may be used to make sound. Figure 2-2 diagrams the 8253 timer chip.

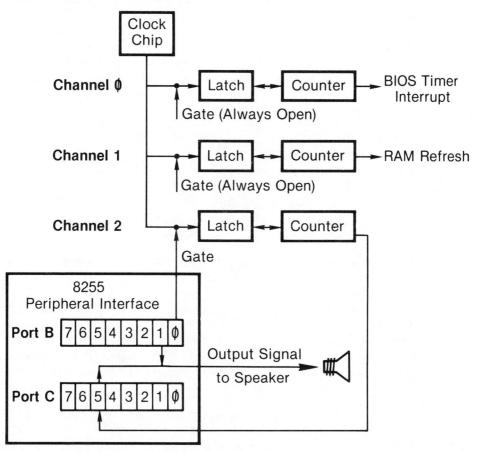

Figure 2-2: The 8253/8254 Timer Chip.

The timer chip can be used directly for timing activities, but this is seldom practical. The input clock rate is 1.19318 million times a second (even on the AT, where the system clock runs faster, the timer chip receives a 1.19 MHz signal). Since the largest number held by 16 bits is 65535, and since that number divides into the clock pulse rate 18.2 times, the longest possible period between pulses is scarcely a twentieth of a second. Most timing operations instead use the BIOS time-of-day count. An interval is timed by reading the time-of-day value and comparing it to some earlier reference value to see how many pulses have passed. Special techniques described at [2.1.7] use the time-of-day count for *real-time* operations.

The 8253 offers hardware designers six modes of operation for each channel. Programmers ordinarily confine themselves to mode 3, both in channel 0 for timing or in channel 2 for either timing or sound. In this mode, once a latch register is given a number, it immediately loads a copy into the counter register. When the number reaches 0, the latch instantly reloads the counter, and so on. During half of the count the *out* line is "on" and during half it is "off." The result is a square wave pattern that is equally useful for making sound and for counting.

An eight-bit *command register* controls how a number is loaded into a channel. This register is located at port address 43H. The command register is given a byte that tells which channel to program, in what mode, and whether one or both of the bytes of the latch will be sent a number. It also shows whether the number will be in binary or BCD (binary coded decimal) form. The bit pattern is as follows:

```
bits    0      if 0, binary data, else BCD
        3-1    mode number, 0-5 (000-101)
        5-4    kind of operation:
                   00 = move counter value into latch
                   01 = read/write high byte only
                   10 = read/write low byte only
                   11 = read/write high byte, then low byte
        7-6    number of channel to program, 0-2 (00-10)
```

In summary, here are the three basic steps for programming the 8253 chip. Once step 3 is completed, the programmed channel immediately begins to function at the new setting.

(1) Send a byte to the command register (43H) that holds the bit pattern that selects the channel, the read/write status, the mode of operation, and the numerical type.

(2) If channel 2, enable the clock signal by setting bit 0 to 1 at port address 61H. (When bit 1 of this register is set to 1, channel 2 drives the speaker. Set it to 0 for timing operations.)

(3) Calculate a counter from 0-65535, place it in AX, and send the low byte and then the high byte to the channel's I/O register (40H-42H).

The three channels of the 8253 are always in operation. For this reason, programs should restore the original settings of the 8253 registers before ending. In particular, if sound is in progress when the program ends, the sound will continue even after DOS takes control and loads another program. Keep this in mind when designing a Ctrl-Break exit routine [3.2.8].

Low Level

In this example channel 0 is programmed to a different value than the setting made by BIOS at start-up. The reason for changing the setting is so that the time-of-day count increments at a rate faster than 18.2 times a second. The rate is changed to, say, 1000 times per second, for the purpose of making precise laboratory measurements. The latch value must be 1193 (1193180 clocks per second/ 10000). To read the current value of the counter register, see the example at [2.1.8]. Prior to disk operations, the original latch value must be replaced, since channel 0 controls their timing. This value is the highest possible—65535 clock inputs between pulses from the channel—and it is made by placing 0 in the latch register (the 0 immediately counts down to 65535).

```
;---SET UP I/O REGISTER:
      COMMAND_REG   EQU   43H            ;set address of command register
      CHANNEL_0     EQU   40H            ;set address of channel 0
                    MOV   AL,00110110B   ;bit pattern for channel 2, 2-byte
                                         ;   counter, mode 3, binary number
                    OUT   COMMAND_REG,AL ;send byte to command register
;---SEND COUNTER TO LATCH:
                    MOV   AX,1193        ;counter for 100 pulses/sec.
                    OUT   CHANNEL_2,AL   ;send LSB
                    MOV   AL,AH          ;shift MSB, since must send from AL
                    OUT   CHANNEL_2,AL   ;send MSB
```

2.1.2 Set/read the time

At start-up, DOS prompts the computer user for the time-of-day. The value entered is placed in the four bytes that hold the time-of-day count (starting at 0040:006C, with the least significant byte lowest). But first it is converted to the form in which the time-of-day is counted, that is, the time is converted to a value that represents the number of (roughly) 18th-seconds that have passed since midnight. This count is continuously updated 18.2 times per second by the timer interrupt. When there is a subsequent request for the time, the current value of the time-of-day count is converted back from its tally of 18ths of a second into the familiar hours-minutes-seconds format. If no value is entered at start-up, the count is set to 0, as if it were midnight. Computers equipped with a clock-calendar chip may automatically set the time-of-day count [2.1.4].

High Level

TIME$ sets or retrieves the time as a string in the format hh:mm:ss, with the hours counted from 0 to 23, starting from midnight. For 5:10 PM:

```
100 TIME$ = "17:10:00"   'set the time
110 PRINT TIME$          'get the time
```

Since TIME$ returns a string, the string functions MID$, LEFT$, and RIGHT$ are required to pick out any particular part of the time reading. For example, to convert the time from 17:10:00 to 5:00, you must cut out the characters from the string that show the hour, convert them to numeric form (using **VAL**), subtract 12, then change the result back to string form:

```
100 T$=TIME$                              'assign the TIME$ string to T$
110 HOURS$=LEFT$(T$,2)                     'get the 2 left characters of T$
120 MINUTES$=MID$(T$,4,2)                   'get the 2 characters showing minutes
130 NEWHOUR=VAL(HOURS$)                     'convert HOUR$ to numeral
140 IF NEWHOUR>12 THEN NEWHOUR=NEWHOUR-12   'subtract 12 if applicable
140 NEWHOUR$=STR$(NEWHOUR)                  'convert new value back to string form
150 NEWTIME$=NEWHOUR$+":"+MINUTES$          'make string of hour, :, and minutes
```

Middle Level

DOS provides interrupts that read and set the time, making the required conversions from the time-of-day count to hours-minutes-seconds. The time is set to an accuracy of 100ths of a second, but since the time-of-day count is updated at only a fifth this rate, the 100ths-second reading is really only an approximation. Function 2CH of INT 21H retrieves the time, and function 2DH sets it. In both cases, CH holds the hour (0-23, where 0 = midnight), CL holds the minutes (0-59), DH holds the seconds (0-59), and DL holds the "hundredth-seconds" (0-99).

In addition, when function 2CH gets the time, AL holds the number of the day of the week (0 = Sunday). The day will be correct only if the date has been set. DOS calculates the day of the week from the date. Note that when function 2DH sets the time, AL flags that the values entered for the time were valid (0 = valid, FF = invalid).

```
;---TO SET THE TIME:
                MOV   CH,HOURS              ;enter the time values
                MOV   CL,MINUTES           ;
                MOV   DH,SECONDS           ;
                MOV   DL,HUNDREDTHS        ;
                MOV   AH,2DH               ;function number for set time
                INT   21H                  ;sets the time
                CMP   AH,0FFH              ;check that time value was correct
                JE    ERROR                ;go to error routine if not

;---TO RETRIEVE THE TIME:
                MOV   AH,2CH               ;function number for get time
                INT   21H                  ;get the time
                MOV   DAY_OF_WEEK,AH        ;take day of week from AH
```

Low Level

If you change the pulse rate of channel 1 of the 8253 chip for a special application, you will need to decode the time-of-day count with your own routines. BIOS turns the count over to 0 after 1.573 million pulses, and this can be changed only by rewriting the timer interrupt. Thus a true *hundredth-seconds* clock can not run for 24 hours without some special programming. Note that the byte at 0040:0070 is set to 0 at start-up, and that it increments to 1 (but not higher) when the clock turns over.

2.1.3 Set/read the date

When the computer is turned on, DOS prompts the user to enter the current date and time. The time is recorded in the BIOS data area. The date, however, is placed in a variable in COMMAND.COM. It is formatted in three successive bytes that hold respectively the day of the month, the number of the month, and the number of the year, counting from 0, where 0 equals 1980. Unlike the time-of-day count, the memory location of the date varies with the DOS version and the position of COMMAND.COM in memory. For this reason the date must always be accessed via the ready-made utilities in BASIC or DOS rather than fetched directly.

Machines equipped with a clock-calendar chip will automatically set the time and date with the aid of special software (usually run at start-up via an AUTOEXEC.BAT file). See [2.1.4] for how to access a clock-calendar chip. Note that when the BIOS time-of-day count rolls over after 24 hours, DOS adjusts the date accordingly.

High Level

DATE$ sets or retrieves the date as a string in the format mm-dd-yyyy. You may use slashes instead of dashes. The first two digits of the year may be omitted. For Halloween of 1984:

```
100 DATE$ = "10/31/84"          'set the date
110 PRINT DATE$                 'show the date

...and the screen displays:   10-31-1984
```

Middle Level

Functions 2AH and 2BH of DOS interrupt 21H get and set the date. To get the date, place 2AH in AH and execute the interrupt. On return, CX contains the year as a number from 0 to 119 that corresponds to 1980-2099 (this is to say that the date is an *offset* from 1980). DH holds the number of the month, and DL holds the day.

```
MOV   AH,2AH       ;function number to retrieve date
INT   21H          ;get the date
MOV   DAY,DL       ;day in DL
MOV   MONTH,DH     ;month in DH
ADD   CX,1980      ;add base value to the date
MOV   YEAR,CX      ;if CX=5, then 5 + 1980 = 1985
```

To set the date, place the day, month, and year in the same registers and execute function 2BH. If the values for the date are invalid, AL returns FF; otherwise it returns 0.

```
MOV   DL,DAY       ;place day in DL
MOV   DH,MONTH     ;place month in DH
MOV   CX,YEAR      ;place year (eg. 1985) in CX
SUB   CX,1980      ;make year an offset from 1980
MOV   AH,2BH       ;function number to set date
INT   21H          ;set the date
CMP   AH,0FFH      ;check if operation successful
JE    ERROR        ;date out of range, go to error routine
```

2.1.4 Set/read the real-time clock

A real-time clock has an independent processor that can count the time without interference from other computer operations. It also has a battery power supply that keeps it running when the computer is turned off. A program can both read and set a real-time clock. Ordinarily, auxiliary software will have set the BIOS time-of-day count and DOS date variables so that they reflect the current setting of the real-time clock. But a program may check to see that these values are current before it uses them, and it can set matters straight if there is a discrepancy.

The various time and date settings on the clock are made through a series of port addresses. Many of the multifunction boards available for IBM microcomputers have a real-time clock, but unfortunately there is no standard chip or range of port addresses. The AT comes equipped with a real-time clock that is based on the Motorola MC146818 chip, and it shares registers on the chip with configuration data for the system. The registers are accessed by first sending a register number to port address 70H and then reading the register value from 71H. The clock-related registers are as follows:

Register Number	Function
00H	Seconds
01	Seconds alarm
02	Minutes
03	Minutes alarm
04	Hours
05	Hours alarm
06	Day of the week
07	Day of the month
08	Month
09	Year
0A	Status register A
0B	Status register B
0C	Status register C
0D	Status register D

Bits in the four status registers perform various functions, of which only the following are of much concern to programmers:

Register A: bit 7	1 =	time update in progress (wait until 0 before reading)
Register B: bit 6	1 =	*periodic* interrupt is enabled
5	1 =	*alarm* interrupt is enabled
4	1 =	*update-ended* interrupt is enabled
1	1 =	hours counted by 24, 0 = counted by 12
0	1 =	daylight savings time enabled

The AT's real-time clock can invoke hardware interrupt IRQ 8. A program may point the vector for this interrupt to any routine it wants performed at a particular time [1.2.3]. Use vector 4AH. Real-time operations created in this way entail less processing overhead than those discussed at [2.1.7] (although at the cost of program portability). The interrupt may be invoked in three ways, all of which are disabled at start-up. The *periodic* interrupt occurs at a regular period. The period is initialized to roughly one millisecond. The *alarm* interrupt occurs when the settings in the three alarm-related registers match their corresponding timing registers. The update-ended interrupt occurs after every update of the register settings on the chip.

INT 1AH is expanded in the AT BIOS to set and read the real-time clock. Since the readings are never more than two decimal digits, the time values are given in binary coded decimal (BCD), where a byte is divided in half, with each digit occupying four bits. This format makes it easy to convert the numbers to ASCII form. A program needs only to shift half of a byte into the low end of a register and add 48 in order to obtain the ASCII symbol that corresponds to the number. On all IBM machines, functions 0 and 1 of INT 1AH read and set the BIOS time-of-day count. There are six new functions to service the AT's real-time clock:

Function 2:   Read the time from the real-time clock
           On return: CH = hours in BCD
                        CL = minutes in BCD
                        DH = seconds in BCD

Function 3:   Set the time on the real-time clock
           On entry: CH = hours in BCD
                       CL = minutes in BCD
                       DH = seconds in BCD
                       DL = if daylight savings, else 1

Function 4:   Read the date from the real-time clock
           On return: CH = century in BCD (19 or 20)
                        CL = year in BCD (offset from 1980)
                        DH = month in BCD
                        DL = day of month in BCD

Function 5:   Set the date on the real-time clock
           On entry: CH = century in BCD (19 or 20)
                       CL = year in BCD (offset from 1980)
                       DH = month in BCD
                       DL = day of month in BCD

Function 6:   Set the alarm on the real-time clock
           On entry: CH = hours in BCD
                       CL = minutes in BCD
                       DH = seconds in BCD

Function 7:   Reset the alarm
           (no input registers)

The alarm setting is made as an offset from the time the setting is made. The maximum period is 23:59:59. As explained above, interrupt vector 4AH must be pointed to the alarm routine. Note that if the clock is not operating (most probably as the result of a dead battery) then functions 2, 4, and 6 set the carry flag.

2.1.5 Delay program operations

When program operations are delayed by empty loops, a good deal of programming time can be wasted testing and retesting the loop for proper duration. Even when the right length is found, it can not be relied upon in all future applications of a program. The loop may vary in speed depending on the compiler used (or, in BASIC, the speed will depend on whether the program is compiled or not). And now that the AT and various IBM "compatibles" have appeared—bringing with them a range of CPU speeds—even assembly language loops may give varying durations. Thus it is always good policy to create precisely *clocked* program delays. The 18.2 times/second pulse rate of the BIOS time-of-day count should be adequate for most needs (see [2.1.1] to increase the pulse rate).

To make a delay of a set duration, a program must calculate how many pulses of the time-of-day count equal that duration. That value is added to a reading of the current value of the count. Then the program keeps reading the count and comparing it to the anticipated value. When the two values are equal, the delay has been achieved and the program moves on. The four bytes that hold the time-of-day count start at 0040:006C (as always, the least significant byte is the lowest in memory). Delays under 14 seconds may be timed by reading the lowest byte alone. The lowest two bytes can time up to an hour (one-half second short of an hour, to be precise).

High Level

In BASIC, use the SOUND statement [2.2.2] with the value 32767 for the frequency. In this case no sound is produced at all. This non-sound lasts for as many time-of-day pulses as you specify. A five-second delay takes 91 pulses (5 x 18.2) Thus:

```
100 SOUND 32767,91          'delays the program for 5 seconds
```

To read the time-of-day count directly:

```
100 DEF SEG=0               'set segment to the bottom of memory
110 LOWBYTE=PEEK(&H46C)     'get lowest byte
120 NEXTBYTE=PEEK(&H46D)    '2nd byte
130 LOWCOUNT=NEXTBYTE*256+LOWBYTE
                           'value of the two low bytes combined
```

Middle Level

Read the BIOS time-of-day count using function 0 of INT 1AH, and add the desired number of 18th-second pulses to that value. Then keep rereading the time-of-day count, each time testing the current value against the desired one. When equal, the delay ends. INT 1AH returns the two low bytes in DX (within which most delays may be counted), and so the two high bytes returned in CX may be disregarded, allowing you to avoid all the fuss of 32-bit operations. In this example, the delay will be 91 pulses, equalling five seconds.

```
;---GET THE BIOS COUNT AND ADD DELAY VALUE:
                MOV   AH,0            ;function number for "read"
                INT   1AH            ;get the time-of-day count
                ADD   DX,91          ;add 5 sec. delay to low word
                MOV   BX,DX          ;store "end of delay" value in BX
;---KEEP CHECKING BIOS TIME-OF-DAY VALUE:
        REPEAT: INT   1AH            ;get the time-of-day reading again
                CMP   DX,BX          ;compare reading to delay value
                JNE   REPEAT         ;go back to REPEAT if not equal
                                     ;else, end of delay, go on...
```

The AT possesses an additional function within INT 15H that performs a measured time delay. Place 86H in AH, and the number of microseconds of delay in CX:DX. Then execute the interrupt.

2.1.6 Time program operations

A program times operations exactly as people do: it takes an initial reading of the system time-of-day count and later compares it to a subsequent reading. The reading can be taken in hours-minutes-second format, but it is messy to calculate the difference between two such readings because the counting system is not decimal. Better to read the BIOS time-of-day count directly, measure the elapsed duration in 18ths of a second, and then convert it to the hh:mm:ss form normally required.

High Level

In BASIC, read the BIOS count directly from memory location 0040:006C. Divide the number by 65520 to figure hours elapsed, 1092 for minutes, and 18.2 for seconds.

```
100 GOSUB 500                      'get the time-of-day count
110 START=TOTAL                    'save the initial count in START
.
(the timed process moves along)
.
300 GOSUB 500                      'get the final time-of-day count
310 TOTAL=TOTAL-START              'figure pulses elapsed
320 HOURS=FIX(TOTAL/65520)         'calculate number of hours
330 TOTAL=TOTAL-HOURS*65520        'subtract hours from TOTAL
340 MINUTES=FIX(TOTAL/1092)        'calculate number of minutes
350 TOTAL=TOTAL-MINUTES*1092       'subtract minutes from TOTAL
360 SECONDS=FIX(TOTAL/18.2)        'calculate number of seconds
370 PRINT HOURS,MINUTES,SECONDS    'the result
380 END
.
500 DEF SEG=0                      'subroutine to read time-of-day
510 A=PEEK(&H46C)                  'get lowest byte
520 B=PEEK(&H46D)                  '2nd lowest
530 C=PEEK(&H46E)                  '3rd lowest
540 TOTAL=A+B*256+C*65535          'tally the count in TOTAL
550 RETURN                         'all done
```

The TIMER function in BASIC returns the number of seconds that have passed since the time-of-day count was last set to 0. Ordinarily this will be the number of seconds since the computer was last booted up. If the time was correctly set at system start-up, TIMER returns the number of seconds that have passed since midnight. Simply write **N = TIMER**.

Middle Level

INT 1AH has two functions to set (AH = 1) and retrieve (AH = 0) the time-of-day count. To read the count, simply execute the interrupt with 0 in AH. On return CX:DX holds the count, with the most significant word in CX. AL contains 0 if the count has not passed the 24-hour value since it was last set. To *set* the count, place the two words in the same registers, and set AH to 1. This example measures an elapsed time under one hour. Only the bottom two bytes of the counter need be consulted. In this case, be sure to allow for a "turnover" condition where the initial reading is higher than the second reading.

```
;---IN THE DATA SEGMENT:
     OLDCOUNT    DW    0                    ;holds the initial time-of-day count
;---TAKE THE INITIAL TIME-OF-DAY READING:
                 MOV   AH,0                 ;set function number
                 INT   1AH                  ;get the count (low word in DX)
                 MOV   OLDCOUNT,DX          ;save the initial count
                  .
                 (the timed process moves along)
                  .
;---LATER, TO CALCULATE TIME ELAPSED:
                 MOV   AH,0                 ;set function number
                 INT   1AH                  ;get the count
                 MOV   BX,OLDCOUNT          ;retrieve the first reading
                 CMP   BX,DX                ;check for "turn over"
                 JG    ADJUST               ;jump to adjust routine if "turn over"
                 SUB   DX,BX                ;else, find difference (=elapsed pulses)
                 JMP   SHORT FIGURE_TIME    ;jmp over adjustment, to time calculation
;---ADJUST FOR TURN OVER:
     ADJUST:     MOV   CX,0FFFFH            ;place largest number (65535) in CX
                 SUB   CX,BX                ;subtract first reading
                 ADD   CX,DX                ;add second reading
                 MOV   DX,CX                ;as above, leave elapsed time in DX
;---BEGIN TIME CALCULATION ROUTINE:
     FIGURE_TIME:                           ;now divide DX by 18.2 for seconds, etc.
```

2.1.7 Control real-time operations

In *real-time* operations, a program issues instructions at specified points in time, rather than issuing them as soon as possible. This technique is usually associated with robotics, but it has many other uses. There is a choice of approaches to real-time operations. In programs that have little or nothing to do between the real-time instructions, the program needs merely to idle along, doing nothing but checking the BIOS time-of-day count to sense when it is time to become active. This technique is little more than a series of delay loops, as described at [2.1.5].

The second approach is more difficult. It is used when a program is constantly busy, but needs to interrupt its operations at specific times in order to carry out some task. An extension is made to the timer interrupt, which is executed 18.2 times per second. Whenever the interrupt occurs, the extension checks the new value of the time-of-day count, and if it matches the count value at which a real-time activity is to begin, the routine initiates the activity. Figure 2-3 illustrates this process. The simple examples given here show how to create within a program a sort of alarm clock that can be set by the user to beep when "time's up." (A more complicated low-level example found at [2.2.6] plays music while the CPU is completely occupied with other matters.)

High Level

BASIC provides primitive control over real-time operations by the *ON TIMER(n) GOSUB* statement. When a program comes upon this statement, it begins to count to the number of seconds given by n. Meanwhile, program operations continue. When n seconds have passed, the program jumps to the subroutine beginning at the specified line number, performs the subroutine, and then returns to where it left off. The counting then starts anew from 0, and the subroutine will be called again after n seconds more.

ON TIMER will not function until it is enabled by a **TIMER ON** statement. It may be disabled by **TIMER OFF**. In cases where the timing should continue but transfer to the subroutine must be delayed, use **TIMER STOP**. In this case it is recorded that n seconds have passed, and the program jumps to the subroutine as soon as another TIMER ON statement is encountered.

Because it repeats, ON TIMER is particularly useful for showing a clock on the screen:

```
100 ON TIMER(60) GOSUB 500           'change the clock every 60 secs
110 TIMER ON                         'enable the timer
  .
  .
500 LOCATE 1,35:PRINT"TIME: ";LEFT$(TIME$,5) 'locate cursor, print the time
510 RETURN
```

Low Level

BIOS contains a special "dummy" interrupt (INT 1CH) which does nothing until you provide a routine for it. At start-up, the vector for the interrupt points to an

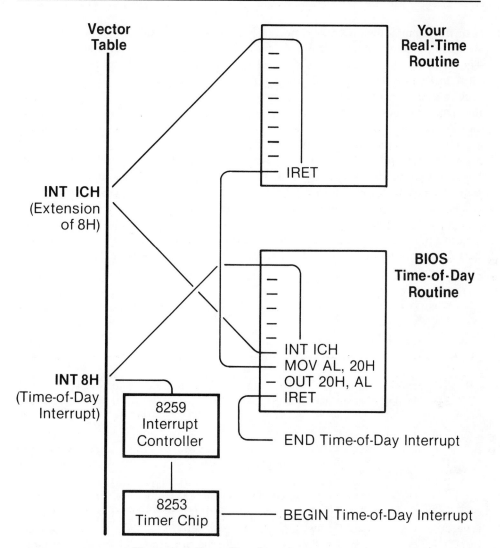

Figure 2-3. Extending the timer interrupt.

IRET (interrupt return) instruction; when the interrupt is called, it simply returns. What is special about INT 1CH is that it is invoked by the BIOS timer interrupt after that interrupt has updated the time-of-day count. That is to say, it is a *hardware* interrupt that automatically occurs 18.2 times per second. You may change the vector for this interrupt to point to a procedure in your program. Then that procedure will be called 18.2 times a second. See Section [1.2.3] about how to write and install your own interrupts.

The procedure you provide should first read the freshly updated time-of-day count, compare it to the count that corresponds to the awaited time, and do whatever is required when the right time arrives at last. Of course, when it is not yet time to perform the real-time operation, the routine merely returns with no further ado. In this way the CPU is kept free for other activity.

In the example below, a routine (unshown) requests from the program user a value up to 60 for the number of minutes that should pass before an alarm goes off. The number, which is stored in MINUTES, is multiplied by 1092, giving the equivalent in time-of-day pulses. A one-hour period fits into 16 bits—longer periods require more complicated 32-bit operations. The number of pulses is added to the low word of the current time-of-day reading, and then it is saved as ALARM-COUNT.

Next, the vector for interrupt 1CH is changed to point to a procedure called ALARM. Remember that once the vector is changed, ALARM will immediately begin to be invoked every 18th of a second. When it is called, it gets the current time-of-day reading via interrupt 1AH, and then it retrieves ALARMCOUNT for comparison. If the two values match, the routine calls a procedure called "BEEP" (also unshown—see [2.2.4]) that beeps the speaker. Otherwise, the routine simply returns. The usual return code for hardware interrupts (**MOV AH,20H/OUT 20H,AL**) is not required, since it is handled by the timer interrupt. Be very careful about saving changed registers.

```
;---IN THE DATA SEGMENT:
    MINUTES       DW   0              ;holds number of minutes until alarm
    ALARMCOUNT    DW   0              ;holds time-of-day for alarm setting

;---SET ALARMCOUNT TO THE AWAITED BIOS TIME-OF-DAY VALUE:
            CALL  REQUEST_MINUTES     ;get from user the minutes until alarm
            MOV   AX,MINUTES          ;move number of minutes to AX
            MOV   BX,1092             ;number of time-of-day pulses/minute
            MUL   BX                  ;multiply—result now in AX
    ;GET CURRENT TIME-OF-DAY VALUE:
            MOV   AH,0                ;function number for time-of-day read
            INT   1AH                 ;get count, low word in DX
    ;ADD THE TWO VALUES:
            ADD   AX,DX               ;add alarm time to current time-of-day
            MOV   ALARMCOUNT,AX       ;set time-of-day value for the alarm
;---CHANGE THE DUMMY INTERRUPT VECTOR:
            PUSH  DS                  ;save the data segment
            MOV   AX,SEG ALARM        ;get segment of the alarm routine
            MOV   DS,AX               ;place segment in DS
            MOV   DX,OFFSET ALARM     ;get offset of the alarm routine
            MOV   AL,1CH              ;number of interrupt vector to change
            MOV   AH,25H              ;DOS function that changes vectors
            INT   21H                 ;change the vector
            POP   DS                  ;restore the data segment

;
;---PROGRAM CONTINUES ALONG...NEW INTERRUPT OCCURS 18.2 TIMES/SEC
;

;---AT END OF PROGRAM REPLACE FORMER INTERRUPT VECTOR:
            MOV   DX,0FF53H           ;original offset for INT 1CH
            MOV   AX,0F000H           ;original segment
            MOV   DS,AX               ;place segment in DS
            MOV   AL,1CH              ;number of interrupt vector to change
            MOV   AH,25H              ;DOS function that changes vectors
            INT   21H                 ;restore the original vector
                                      ;etc...
;---PROCEDURE TO SOUND ALARM:
ALARM           PROC FAR             ;create a far procedure
```

```
                PUSH  AX                  ;save changed registers
                PUSH  CX                  ;
                PUSH  DX                  ;
        ;READ THE TIME-OF-DAY COUNT:
                MOV   AH,0                 ;function number for time-of-day read
                INT   1AH                 ;get count, low word in DX
        ;GET THE COUNT CORRESPONDING TO ALARM TIME:
                MOV   CX,ALARMCOUNT       ;get variable that signals "time's up"
                CMP   DX,CX               ;does the current reading match?
                JNE   NOT_YET            ;if not, leave the routine
        ;SOUND ALARM IF THE TWO COUNTS MATCH:
                CALL  BEEP                ;beep routine is not shown
        ;OTHERWISE, RETURN FROM INTERRUPT:
NOT_YET:        POP   DX                  ;restore changed registers
                POP   CX                  ;
                POP   AX                  ;
                IRET                      ;return from interrupt
ALARM           ENDP                      ;end of the procedure
```

2.1.8   Generate random numbers by the timer chip

Considerable mathematical sophistication is needed to generate a series of random numbers. But sometimes programs require only a single number at a particular instant. In this case the random number can be derived simply by reading the current value from a channel of the timer chip. BASIC uses such a value as the *seed* from which to calculate a random series. Of course, you can not derive a series of random numbers by reading timer settings successively, since the sampling rate will itself be nonrandom.

High Level

BASIC contains a random number generator that can be reseeded using the **TIMER** statement, so that a different series of random numbers is created each time a program is run. Simply write **RANDOMIZE TIMER**, and then use the RND function to call a random number.

```
100 RANDOMIZE TIMER             'automatically reseed the generator
110 PRINT RND,RND,RND           'print three random numbers

...producing:    .7122483    .4695052.   9132487
```

Low Level

Since the counter register of a timer channel is reloaded again and again with a given number (counting down to 0 in the interim), select a counter that equals the desired range of random numbers. Thus, for a random hour of the day, use 23 as the counter.

It is best to use mode 3 in channel 2 (port 42H) of the timer chip [2.1.1]. First set the counter in the desired range (the example below uses 10000, giving a random value from 0000 to 9999). Then, to sample the channel for a random number, instruct the timer chip command register at port 43H to "latch" the current value of the counter register by setting bits 4 and 5 to zero. This transfer to the latch register does not interfere with the ongoing counting. Next, set both bits 4 and 5 of the command register to 1 so that the CPU can read from the latch register. Then two IN instructions will bring first the low byte and then the high byte into the AL register. Finally, reset the latch register to its original value so that the counting continues across the desired range.

```
;---SET THE PORT ADDRESSES:
   COMMAND_REG   EQU   43H            ;set command register address
   CHANNEL_2     EQU   42H            ;set channel 2 address

                 CALL  SET_COUNT      ;set the timer range
                 .
;---THE PROGRAM MOVES ALONG.....AND THEN REQUESTS A RANDOM NUMBER:
                 .
                 CALL  GET_NUMBER     ;get a random number
                 .
                 .
                 .
```

```
;---START CHANNEL 2 COUNTING:
SET_COUNT       PROC
                MOV   AL,10110110B          ;channel 2, both bytes, mode 2, binary
                OUT   COMMAND_REG,AL        ;send instruction byte to command reg
                MOV   AX,10000              ;counter value
                OUT   CHANNEL_2,AL          ;send low byte of counter
                MOV   AL,AH                 ;move high byte to al
                OUT   CHANNEL_2,AL          ;send high byte of counter
                RET
SET_COUNT       ENDP
;---GET A RANDOM NUMBER:
READ_NUMBER     PROC
;---MOVE THE COUNTER VALUE INTO THE LATCH REGISTER:
                MOV   AL,10000110B          ;instructs command register to "latch"
                OUT   COMMAND_REG,AL        ;send the instruction
;---READ THE VALUE OF THE COUNTER:
                MOV   AL,10110110B          ;request for "read/write"
                OUT   COMMAND_REG,AL        ;send the request
                IN    AL,CHANNEL_2          ;get low byte
                MOV   AH,AL                 ;temporarily keep low byte in AH
                IN    AL,CHANNEL_2          ;get high byte
                CALL  SET_COUNT             ;restore value in latch register
                SWAP  AH,AL                 ;reverse high and low bytes
                RET                         ;and now the random number is in AX
READ_NUMBER     ENDP
```

Section 2: Create Sound

BASIC is equipped with elaborate sound facilities, but the operating system makes possible only a single "beep." To make any other sound you must directly program the 8253 timer chip. Channel 2 of the chip is connected to the computer's speaker. When the channel is programmed in mode 3, it produces a square wave of given frequency. Because the speaker is a simple one, it rounds the edges of the square wave, reducing it to a more pleasant sounding sine wave. Unfortunately, the 8253 chip can not alter the amplitude of the wave, so there is no control over the volume of sound from this source.

The speaker receives not one, but two, inputs to make sound. As Figure 2-2 at [2.1.1] shows, in addition to the timer chip, the 8255 peripheral interface [1.1.1] also sends a signal. The pulse rate at either chip can be changed, and combining the actions of the two chips can produce special sound effects.

The PCjr alone possesses a dedicated sound generator chip. It can deliver three simultaneous tones, plus noise for sound effects. The volume of each channel may be set independently. Another unique attribute of the PCjr is that it can manage sound from an external source (such as a cassette player).

2.2.1 Program the 76496 sound generator (PCjr only)

The PCjr is blessed with a four-channel sound generator in which three channels produce tones and the fourth generates "noise" for sound effects. The four channels are independently programmable—with each having its own volume control—and their outputs are combined into a single audio signal. The chip is the TI SN76496N Complex Sound Generator. It has eight registers—two for each channel—all of which are addressed through the single port address C0H. This port address is *write-only*; if an IN (or INP) instruction is used, the entire system will freeze up.

The PCjr has a plug for external audio output. At system start-up the audio channel receives output from the 8253 timer chip. But the channel may be turned over to the sound generator chip, or to either of two external audio inputs. This is done by changing bits 5 and 6 of Port B on the 8255 Peripheral Interface chip (port address 61H—see [1.1.1]). The bit patterns are as follows:

Bits 6 & 5	Function Selected
00	8253 timer chip
01	Cassette audio input
10	I/O channel audio input
11	76496 sound generator

To select the audio source, the PCjr BIOS adds function 80H to INT 1AH. Place in AL a code number from 0 to 3, corresponding to the table above, and call the function. There are no return registers. The 76496 sound generator must use this audio channel, since it cannot drive the PCjr's internal speaker.

Generally speaking, when a byte of data is sent to the sound generator, bits 4-6 hold an identification code telling which of the eight registers the data is directed to. The codes are:

Bits 6-4	Register addressed
000	Tone 1 frequency
001	Tone 1 volume
010	Tone 2 frequency
011	Tone 2 volume
100	Tone 3 frequency
101	Tone 3 volume
110	Noise control
111	Noise volume

In the case of the tone frequency registers, two bytes are required. The bit patterns are:

```
byte 1:    bits 0-3    low 4 bits of frequency data
                  4-6    register identification code
                    7    always set to 1

byte 2:    bits 0-5    high 6 bits of frequency data
                    6    unused
                    7    always set to 0
```

The frequency of a tone is set by sending to the register a ten-bit value that when divided into 111,843 results in the number of cycles per second desired. Thus, frequencies from 110 CPS upward are possible ($111843/2^{10}$). Once the register is initialized (and Port B on the 8255 is properly set), the sound begins immediately and continues until it is shut off. It is not necessary to send another two bytes to change the frequency. If only byte 2 is sent (the high six bits of frequency data), it automatically replaces the corresponding data in the channel that was last addressed. This feature enables tones to smoothly warble and slide.

The noise generator takes only one byte to program. Its bit pattern is:

```
bits 0-1    noise density
        2    noise quality
        3    unused
      4-6    register identification code
        7    always set to 1
```

The noise quality (feed back configuration) is set for white noise (a constant hiss) when bit 2 is 1 and for periodic noise (waves of sound) when bit 2 is 0. The noise density (shift rate) increases with settings for bits 0-1 from 00B to 10B; when set to 11B, the sound varies with the output of tone channel 3.

The volume of each of the four channels is changed by attenuating the basic signal. It is set using only one byte of data. The bit pattern is:

```
bits 0-3    attenuation data
      4-6    register identification code
        7    always set to 1
```

When all four bits of data are 0, the sound is at its maximum volume. When all are 1, the sound is shut off entirely. Any combination of bits can be used to set intermediate volume levels. Bit 0 attenuates the sound by 2 dB (decibels), bit 1 by 4 dB, bit 2 by 8 dB, and bit 3 by 16 dB. Maximum attenuation is 28 dB.

2.2.2 Make a tone

This subsection explains how to make sound while the computer does nothing else; [2.2.3] shows how it is done while other activity is going on. Oddly, for assembly language programmers the latter is simpler. It entails programming the 8253 timer chip, which operates independently of the CPU. In the method shown here, the CPU controls the speaker directly, and so the software must do the work of the timer chip hardware. Although more difficult, this technique allows much more control over the speaker, and most special sound effects [2.2.8] rely on it.

High Level

The BASIC SOUND statement plays a tone over a wide range of frequencies and durations. The frequency is given in cycles per second (37-32767), and the duration is counted in pulses of the BIOS time-of-day reading (0-65535), where there are 18.2 such pulses per second. **SOUND 440,91** plays the tuning note A for five seconds (5 x 18.2). The frequencies of the octave starting at middle C are:

Middle	C	523.3
	D	587.3
	E	659.3
	F	698.5
	G	784.0
	A	880.0
	B	987.7

Frequencies an octave higher are roughly twice these values, and two octaves higher they are twice as great again. Conversely, frequencies an octave lower are about half of these values (a well-tuned piano does not precisely follow the arithmetic intervals).

By virtue of its sound generator chip [2.2.1], the PCjr can use the SOUND statement for three independent channels of sound, and it can control the volume of each. The format is **SOUND frequency, duration, volume, channel.** The volume is from 0 to 15, defaulting to 8. The channel number is from 0 to 2, defaulting to 0. Because the PCjr can use the multivoice and volume control features only over an external speaker, that speaker must first be enabled. Do this by writing **SOUND ON**. **SOUND OFF** restores control to the internal beeper. To play a D minor chord (D-F-A) at low volume, write:

```
100 SOUND ON            ;enable multi-channel sound
110 SOUND 587,50,3,0    ;play D
120 SOUND 699,50,3,1    ;play F
130 SOUND 880,50,3,2    ;play A
```

Low Level

Producing sound from the 8255 peripheral interface adapter entails nothing more than turning on and off at the desired frequency the bit in Port B that is hooked up to the speaker (bit 1). Port B is located at port address 61H (although the AT does not have an 8255 peripheral interface as such, it uses the same port address and bit assignment). If a program changes the bit back and forth as rapidly as possible, the frequency produced is far too high to be useful. Thus delay loops must be inserted between the on-off actions. Remember that bit 0 of Port B controls the gate to channel 2 of the timer chip, which in turn is connected to the speaker. So this bit should be turned off, disconnecting the timer channel. Figure 2-4 shows how this method sets the sound frequency.

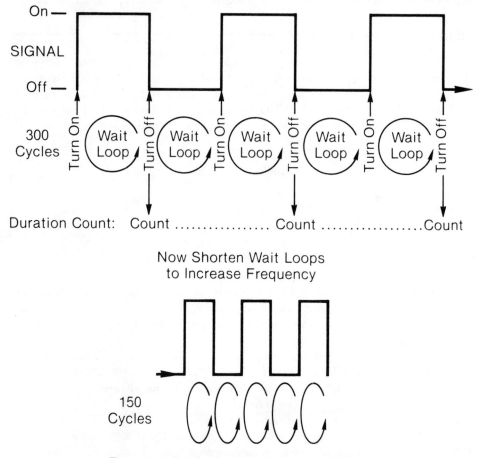

Figure 2-4. Producing sound by the 8255 chip.

In the following example, there are two variables. The one labeled "FRE-QUENCY" is used as the counter in the delay loops between the on-off actions. The smaller the number, the quicker the alternation, and the higher the frequency. The variable "NUMBER__CYCLES", on the other hand, sets the duration of the tone. It tells how many times the whole on-off process should be cycled through. The larger the number, the longer the tone lasts.

Note that hardware interrupts are cleared (deactivated) during this routine. The reason is that the timer interrupt occurs with such frequency and regularity (18.2 times per second) that it audibly modulates the tone. Be cautioned that whenever the interrupts are deactivated, the BIOS time-of-day count falls behind. When a time-of-day reading is subsequently made, it will be thrown off proportionately unless adjustments are made.

```
NUMBER_CYCLES  EQU   1000
FREQUENCY      EQU   300
PORT_B         EQU   61H
               CLI                          ;disable interrupts
               MOV   DX,NUMBER_CYCLES       ;DX counts the length of the tone
               IN    AL,PORT_B              ;get Port B
               AND   AL,11111110B           ;disconnect speaker from timer chip
NEXT_CYCLE:    OR    AL,00000010B           ;turn on speaker
               OUT   PORT_B,AL              ;send the command to Port_B
               MOV   CX,FREQUENCY           ;move the delay for 1/2 cycle to CX
FIRST_HALF:    LOOP  FIRST_HALF             ;make delay while speaker is on
               AND   AL,11111101B           ;turn off speaker
               OUT   PORT_B,AL              ;send the command to Port_B
               MOV   CX,FREQUENCY           ;move the delay for 2nd half of cycle
SECOND_HALF:   LOOP  SECOND_HALF            ;make delay while speaker is off
               DEC   DX                     ;subtract 1 from the number of cycles
               JNZ   NEXT_CYCLE             ;if 0, then duration is exhausted
               STI                          ;reenable interrupts
```

2.2.3 Make a tone simultaneous to other operations

BASIC programmers will find no great distinction made between the techniques for simultaneous and non-simultaneous sound production. But assembly programmers resort to entirely different techniques. Because the 8253 timer chip operates independently of the 8088 CPU, it is trivial to make sounds that continue while other operations are going on. You need merely to program channel 2 of the chip to begin producing a particular frequency, and then later you must reprogram the chip to stop the sound.

High Level

The **SOUND** statement in BASIC can not make simultaneous sound, but the **PLAY** statement *can* if it is especially instructed to do so. **PLAY** is followed by a string that tells what notes (and rests) are to be played, their durations, and other characteristics. The details of PLAY strings are discussed at [2.2.5]. When the string contains the letters **MB** ("music background"), the string is placed in a special buffer and it is performed while other program operations proceed. Conversely, **MF** ("music foreground") stops all other program operations until the string is finished. Here a single tone A is played in the background.

```
100 PLAY "MB A"        'plays A...
110 ...                '...while doing this
```

Note that when in MB mode, the statement **X = PLAY(0)** returns the numbers of notes (up to 32) that remain to be played. When in multichannel mode on the PCjr, this statement returns the number of notes in the buffer of the particular channel (0-2) named within the parentheses.

Low Level

Simply send a counter to channel 2, as explained at [2.1.1]. The chip must first be enabled via Port B of the 8255 peripheral interface (at 61H). Calculate the counter for the latch by dividing 1.19 million by the number of cycles per second desired. The sound will continue until the gate for channel 2 is shut off. So you must reset bit 1 of Port B to 0, or else the sound will continue indefinitely and can be stopped only by rebooting the computer. To precisely time the duration of the tone, use the BIOS time-of-day count, as discussed at [2.1.6]. In this example, the pitch is set to 440 cycles per second. A delay is provided by waiting for a random keystroke.

```
;---ENABLE CHANNEL 2 BY SETTING PORT B OF THE 8255 CHIP:
    PORT_B       EQU   61H           ;set address of PB on the 8255 chip
                 IN    AL,PORT_B     ;get Port B
                 OR    AL,3          ;turn on 2 low bits (3=00000011B)
                 OUT   PORT_B,AL     ;send changed byte to Port B
;---SET UP I/O REGISTER:
    COMMAND_REG  EQU   43H           ;set address of command register
    CHANNEL_2    EQU   42H           ;set address of channel 2
                 MOV   AL,10110110B  ;bit pattern for channel 2, 2 bytes,
```

```
                                            ;mode 3, binary number
                OUT   COMMAND_REG,AL         ;send byte to command register
;---SEND COUNTER TO LATCH:
                MOV   AX,2705               ;the counter: 1190000/440
                OUT   CHANNEL_2,AL          ;send LSB
                MOV   AL,AH                 ;shift MSB, since must send from AL
                OUT   CHANNEL_2,AL          ;send MSB
;---DELAY BY WAITING FOR KEYSTROKE:
                MOV   AH,1                  ;function number of INT 21H
                INT   21H                   ;call interrupt
;---TURN OFF THE SOUND:
                IN    AL,PORT_B             ;get the byte in Port B
                AND   AL,11111100B          ;force the two low bits to 0
                OUT   PORT_B,AL             ;send changed byte to Port B
```

2.2.4 Beep the speaker

Some programs require a variety of warning "beeps." They are easy to create in BASIC, but the operating system provides no "beep" function as such, and it only indirectly allows access to the beeping sound you hear at system start-up. For alternate tones an entire sound-production routine must be programmed at low level. Use a little imagination to tailor the beep to its message. To augur impending doom, create a siren out of sliding tones [2.2.7], or, if the printer is on line, alternate between the computer speaker and printer speaker (output ASCII 7 on the printer data line).

High Level

In BASIC, simply write "BEEP". Here, a likely error is met with a beep and a query:

```
100 INPUT"Enter your age",AGE                          'get age
110 IF AGE>100 THEN BEEP:PRINT"Are you really over 100?"  'error?
                                                       'etc....
```

For beeps of another frequency or duration, use the SOUND statement. The form is **SOUND pitch,duration**, where the pitch is given in cycles per second (3000 is mid-range) and the duration is given in intervals of (roughly) eighteenths of a second. **SOUND 3000,18** makes a mid-range sound for about one second. In this example the speaker rapidly alternates between a high and low sound, scaring the living daylights out of anyone nearby.

```
100 FOR N=1 TO 200          'set the number of alternations
110 SOUND 500,1             'low sound for 1/18th of a sec
120 SOUND 5000,1            'high sound for 1/18th of a sec
130 NEXT                    'repeat
```

Middle Level

The operating system does not offer a function specially made for sound. But you can elicit the familiar "beep" sound simply by "writing" ASCII character 7 "to the standard device" using one of the DOS or BIOS functions—that is, send it to the video monitor. ASCII 7 is interpreted as the "bell" control code, and its symbol is not placed on the screen. Function 2 of DOS interrupt 21H is easiest:

```
MOV   AH,2        ;function to write character on screen
MOV   DL,7        ;send ASCII 7
INT   21H         ;the speaker beeps
```

Note that BIOS function AH of INT 10H does *not* cause a beep when it handles ASCII 7; it displays the character instead.

Low Level

For a simple "beep," the method based on the 8255 peripheral interface chip [1.1.1] is the most concise. The example here roughly replicates the BIOS beep tone heard when the computer is switched on.

```
;---BEEP THE SPEAKER:
                MOV   DX,800        ;counts the number of cycles
                IN    AL,61H        ;read Port B on the 8255 chip
                AND   AL,0FEH       ;turn off the 8253 timer bit
    NEXTCYCLE:  OR    AL,2          ;turn on the speaker bit
                OUT   61H,AL        ;send the byte back to port B
                MOV   CX,150        ;set duration of 1st half of wave
    CYCLEUP:    LOOP  CYCLEUP       ;delay while signal is high
                AND   AL,0FDH       ;turn off the speaker bit
                OUT   61H,AL        ;send the byte to port B
    CYCLEDOWN:  LOOP  CYCLEDOWN     ;delay while signal is low
                DEC   DX            ;dec 1 from the number of cycles
                JNZ   NEXTCYCLE     ;do another cycle if DX not 0
```

2.2.5 Make a string of tones

This subsection shows how to make a timed string of sounds while the computer does nothing else; the next section shows how sound strings are performed while the computer is busy with other operations. When the sound is non-simultaneous, the string may be either a melody or a display of sound effects; when the sound is simultaneous, however, sound effects are not possible.

Sound strings are an advanced feature offered by BASIC. Building the strings from scratch in assembly language requires a good deal of work. Either of the two sound production methods [2.2.2 & 2.2.3] may be used. For both, it is only a matter of starting one tone, timing it, then starting the next, and so on. Every sound string is formed from two data strings, one that holds the frequencies of the successive tones, and another that holds the duration for each (providing different length tones are required). The durations are measured using the BIOS time-of-day count [2.1.6].

High Level

The PLAY statement is one of BASIC's most advanced features. The statement is comprised of a string of notes that is interspersed with information about how the notes are to be played. The notes are written as the letters A - G, and signs for sharps and flats ("accidentals") follow. Sharps are shown by # or +, and flats by -. **PLAY"CC#D"** and **PLAY"CD-D"** are equivalent (but do not use accidentals to show non-black key notes). A second way of naming notes is to calculate a code number from 0 to 84, where 0 equals a rest, and 1 through 84 correspond to the 84 possible notes in the seven octaves, starting from the bottom. Precede the number with the letter **N**: **PLAY"N3N72N44"**.

A seven-octave range is allowed, each reaching from C to B. The octaves are numbered from 0 to 6, and middle C starts octave 3. The current octave may be changed at any point in the string by inserting **O** (the letter "O", not zero) followed by the octave number. All notes that follow are played in that octave until another octave setting is made. When none is initially set, octave 4 is used. **PLAY "O3CO4CO5CO6C"** plays progressively higher Cs. Another way to change the octave is to place the symbols > or < in the string; these respectively switch a tune up or down one octave. **PLAY"O3C>C>C>C"** also plays progressively higher Cs.

Notes may be given different lengths by inserting a code number preceded by the letter L. All notes that follow are given that length until another length code appears. The code is a number from 1 to 64, where 1 is a whole note and 64 is a 64th note. Write L4 to make quarter notes. The tempo at which the notes are played is set by a tempo code, which is the letter T followed by a number from 32 to 255, giving the number of quarter notes per minute. When left unspecified, the note length defaults to L4, and 120 is used for the tempo. To change the length of only a single note and not all that follow, place the value of the length *after* the note, and without the letter L. **PLAY "L4CDE16FG"** plays E as a sixteenth note and all others as quarter notes.

Rests are counted in the same way as note lengths are counted. Place a number from 1 to 64 after the letter P (for "pause"). **P1** gives a whole note pause, and **P64** gives a 64th note pause. Placing a period after a note has the same effect as it does in ordinary music notation: the length of the note is extended by half. A second period extends the length by half as much again.

By default, notes are played for 7/8ths of their specified duration. To play them for their full duration (*legato*), put **ML** in the string. To play them at 3/4ths duration (*staccato*), put **MS** in the string. And to return the texture to normal, write **MN**.

Normally, all other program activity stops until the string has been completed. Use **MB** to cause the string to be played in the background while statements that follow the PLAY statement are executed. To restore the normal situation, write **MF**.

Finally, the PLAY statement allows *substrings* to be played from within a larger string. This means that a part of a string can be set up as an ordinary string variable, and then that variable can be called from within the string that forms the PLAY statement. For example, if S$ = "EEEEE", then in the statement **PLAY"CDXS$;FG"** the note E is repeated five times. Note that the variable name is preceded by the letter X, and it is followed by a semicolon. (For compiled programs another method, using VARPTR$, is required—see the BASIC manual for details.)

This example plays the familiar grandfather clock chimes. The string first sets the melody to play in legato, then sets the tempo and starting octave, and finally lays out the four notes, a pause, and then the same four notes in reverse. The spaces between the codes are entirely for the convenience of the programmer—BASIC ignores them.

```
100 PLAY "ML T40 O3 ECD<G P32 G>DEC"
```

Because of its special sound chip, the PCjr adds two features to the PLAY statement. First, it accepts a V parameter, which sets the volume. The expression **V5** sets (or changes) the volume to level 5. The volume settings range from 0 to 15, with 8 as the default. 0 shuts off sound completely. Second, three strings of sound can be made to sound simultaneously using the PLAY statement. Place all three strings on the same line, separating them with commas. To use these special features, you must first enable the external speaker by writing **SOUND ON**.

```
100 SOUND ON
110 PLAY "..........","..........",".........."
```

Low Level

This example uses the 8253 timer chip to produce sound. It does no more than play a scale of eight notes, but with a little modification it could be made quite versatile. There are three data strings. The first sets the duration of each note as a multiple of an arbitrary delay period (changing the arbitrary period changes the tempo). The second string holds frequencies for each of the eight notes; the values are those that when placed in the latch register of channel 2 of the 8253 chip result in the desired tones. The third string holds the melody in the form of code numbers from 1 to 8 that correspond to the eight frequencies. This string terminates with FF to flag its end. The routine does nothing more than read each note of the melody, look up the corresponding frequency, and place it in channel 2. Then the duration assigned to that note is fed into a delay loop that uses the time-of-day count, and when the delay is finished, the next note is processed. Figure 2-5 diagrams the routine.

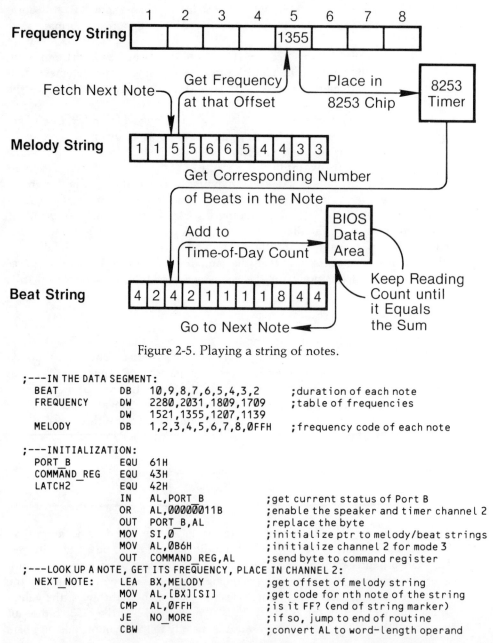

Figure 2-5. Playing a string of notes.

```
;---IN THE DATA SEGMENT:
    BEAT          DB    10,9,8,7,6,5,4,3,2         ;duration of each note
    FREQUENCY     DW    2280,2031,1809,1709        ;table of frequencies
                  DW    1521,1355,1207,1139
    MELODY        DB    1,2,3,4,5,6,7,8,0FFH       ;frequency code of each note

;---INITIALIZATION:
    PORT_B        EQU   61H
    COMMAND_REG   EQU   43H
    LATCH2        EQU   42H
                  IN    AL,PORT_B                  ;get current status of Port B
                  OR    AL,00000011B               ;enable the speaker and timer channel 2
                  OUT   PORT_B,AL                  ;replace the byte
                  MOV   SI,0                       ;initialize ptr to melody/beat strings
                  MOV   AL,0B6H                    ;initialize channel 2 for mode 3
                  OUT   COMMAND_REG,AL             ;send byte to command register
;---LOOK UP A NOTE, GET ITS FREQUENCY, PLACE IN CHANNEL 2:
    NEXT_NOTE:    LEA   BX,MELODY                  ;get offset of melody string
                  MOV   AL,[BX][SI]                ;get code for nth note of the string
                  CMP   AL,0FFH                    ;is it FF? (end of string marker)
                  JE    NO_MORE                    ;if so, jump to end of routine
                  CBW                              ;convert AL to word-length operand
```

```
            ;GET THE FREQUENCY:
                    MOV    BX,OFFSET FREQUENCY ;get offset of the frequency table
                    DEC    AX                  ;AX - 1 so that counting starts from 0
                    SHL    AX,1                ;double AX, since word-length table
                    MOV    DI,AX               ;mov to DI for addressing
                    MOV    DX,[BX][DI]         ;get the frequency from the table
            ;START THE NOTE PLAYING:
                    MOV    AL,DL               ;prepare to send low byte of frequency
                    OUT    LATCH2,AL           ;send to latch register (via I/O reg)
                    MOV    AL,DH               ;prepare high byte
                    OUT    LATCH2,AL           ;send high byte
    ;---CREATE DELAY LOOP:
                    MOV    AH,0                ;function to get BIOS time-of-day count
                    INT    1AH                 ;get the count
                    MOV    BX,OFFSET BEAT      ;get offset of beat string
                    MOV    CL,[BX][SI]         ;get beat value for note number SI
                    MOV    CH,0                ;clear high half of CX to use as word
                    MOV    BX,DX               ;get low word of BIOS count from DX
                    ADD    BX,CX               ;add beat count to current BIOS count
    STILL_SOUND:    INT    1AH                 ;get the count
                    CMP    DX,BX               ;cmp count with end-of-note count
                    JNE    STILL_SOUND         ;if not equal, continue sound
                    INC    SI                  ;else, point to next note
                    JMP    NEXT_NOTE           ;go get the next note
    ;---FINISH UP:
    NO_MORE:        IN     AL,PORT_B           ;get the byte in Port_B
                    AND    AL,0FCH             ;turn off the speaker bits
                    OUT    61H,AL              ;replace the byte in Port_B
```

2.2.6 Make a string of tones simultaneous to other operations

Although BASIC makes it easy, simultaneous music is a tricky bit of *real-time* programming. Only the 8253-based sound production method [2.2.3] may be used, since the 8255-based method [2.2.2] keeps the CPU busy. Accordingly, only strings of pure musical tones—and no sound effects—can be played simultaneously. The basic technique of real-time programming is shown at [2.1.7]. Real-time programs modify the BIOS timer interrupt, which stops the CPU 18.2 times per second to update the BIOS time-of-day count. An extension to the interrupt compares the new time-of-day count to a value representing the desired duration of the sound, and when that value is reached it stops the tone, starts another, and sets up the timing for the new tone.

High Level

A simultaneous tone string is just another option within Advanced BASIC's very elaborate **PLAY** statement, which is discussed at length at [2.2.5]. Simply add **MB** to the beginning of the control string. This stands for "Music Background"; insert **MF** (for "Music Foreground") to cause **PLAY** to revert to stopping all other program operations until the melody is finished. This example plays a scale while drawing and filling a box (it requires graphics capability).

```
100 PLAY "MB T100 O3 L4;CDEFG>ABC"   'play a scale from middle C
110 LINE(10,10)-(80,80),1,BF         'draw a box at the same time
```

Low Level

The routine below is an elaboration of the non-real-time routine shown in the previous subsection. It requires an understanding of how the timer interrupt is reprogrammed, as discussed at [2.1.7]. The routine is pointed to by an interrupt vector, and it is executed 18.2 times a second, at the same time as the BIOS time-of-day count is updated. Normally, only a few lines are actually executed—just enough to determine that no change of sound is required—and the routine returns, freeing the CPU for other tasks.

The BIOS time-of-day count is used to measure the duration of each note. Whenever a change is made from one note to another, the duration of the new note is calculated as a number of pulses of the BIOS time-of-day count, and that value is added to a reading of the current count. The time-of-day value is checked each time the routine is invoked, and when the awaited value finally comes up, a chain of events looks up the next note, programs its frequency into channel 2 of the 8253 chip, and sets up a new duration counter. Extra code is required for the special cases of the first and last notes of the strings.

```
;---IN THE DATA SEGMENT:
  BEAT        DB   10,9,8,7,6,5,4,3,2     ;duration of each note
  FREQUENCY   DW   2280,2031,1809,1709    ;table of frequencies
              DW   1521,1355,1207,1139    ;
```

```
MELODY          DB    1,2,3,4,5,6,7,8,0FFH      ;frequency code of each note
HOLDIP          DW    0                         ;stores original INT 1CH vector
HOLDCS          DW    0                         ;ditto
SOUND_NOW?      DB    1                         ;flags whether sound on or off
FIRST_NOTE?     DB    1                         ;flags special case of 1st note
END_NOTE        DW    0                         ;holds timer count to end note
WHICH_NOTE      DW    0                         ;pts to current note in string
;---INITIALIZE THE INTERRUPT VECTOR:
        ;CHANGE THE VECTOR:
                PUSH  DS                        ;DS is destroyed
                MOV   AX,SEG MELODY2            ;get segment of routine
                MOV   DS,AX                     ;place in DS
                MOV   DX,OFFSET MELODY2         ;get offset of routine
                MOV   AL,1CH                    ;interrupt vector to change
                MOV   AH,25H                    ;function to set vector
                INT   21H                       ;change the vector
                POP   DS                        ;restore DS


;
;---THE PROGRAM MOVES ALONG, CALLS SOUND ROUTINE AT ANY TIME
;


;---AT END OF PROGRAM, REPLACE ORIGINAL VECTOR:
                MOV   DX,0FF53H                 ;put original INT 1C offset in DX
                MOV   AX,0F000H                 ;put original INT 1C segment in DS
                MOV   DS,AX                     ;
                MOV   AL,1CH                    ;number of the interrupt
                MOV   AH,25H                    ;function to change interrupt vector
                INT   21H                       ;replace the original interrupt
                RET


;---HERE IS THE INTERRUPT:
MELODY2         PROC  FAR
                PUSH  AX                        ;save altered registers
                PUSH  BX                        ;
                PUSH  CX                        ;
                PUSH  DX                        ;
                PUSH  DI                        ;
                PUSH  SI                        ;
                PUSH  DS                        ;
                MOV   AX,SS:[114]               ;get original DS from stack
                MOV   DS,AX                     ;restore DS
                CMP   SOUND_NOW?,1              ;is sound required?
                JE    PLAY_IT                   ;if so, move on
                JMP   NOT_NOW                   ;if not, skip the interrupt
   PLAY_IT:     CMP   FIRST_NOTE?,0             ;is this the beginning of a string?
                JE    TIME_CHECK                ;if not, jump to timing loop
                                                ;otherwise, start the melody string
;---INITIALIZATION:
   PORT_B       EQU   61H                       ;set equates for port names
   COMMAND_REG  EQU   43H                       ;
   LATCH2       EQU   42H                       ;
                IN    AL,PORT_B                 ;get current status of Port B
                OR    AL,00000011B              ;enable the speaker and timer channel 2
                OUT   PORT_,AL                  ;replace the byte
                MOV   SI,0                      ;initialize ptr to melody/beat strings
                MOV   AL,0B6H                   ;initialize channel 2 for mode 3
                OUT   COMMAND_REG,AL            ;send byte to command register
                MOV   FIRST_NOTE?,0             ;set flag that melody now in progress
;---LOOK UP A NOTE, GET ITS FREQUENCY, PLACE IN CHANNEL 2:
   NEXT_NOTE:   LEA   BX,MELODY                 ;get offset of melody string
```

```
                       MOV   SI,WHICH_NOTE          ;SI gets pointer to current note
                       MOV   AL,[BX][SI]            ;get code for nth note of the string
                       CMP   AL,0FFH                ;is it FF? (end of string marker)
                       JE    NO_MORE                ;if so, jump to end of routine
                       CBW                          ;convert AL to word-length operand
             ;GET THE FREQUENCY:
                       MOV   BX,OFFSET FREQUENCY    ;get offset of the frequency table
                       DEC   AX                     ;AX - 1 so that counting starts from 0
                       SHL   AX,1                   ;double AX, since word-length table
                       MOV   DI,AX                  ;mov to DI for addressing
                       MOV   DX,[BX][DI]            ;get the frequency from the table
             ;START THE NOTE PLAYING:
                       MOV   AL,DL                  ;prepare to send low byte of frequency
                       OUT   LATCH2,AL              ;send to latch register (via I/O reg)
                       MOV   AL,DH                  ;prepare high byte
                       OUT   LATCH2,AL              ;send high byte
       ;---CREATE A DELAY LOOP:
         TIME_IT:      MOV   AH,0                   ;function to get BIOS time-of-day count
                       INT   1AH                    ;get the count
                       MOV   BX,OFFSET BEAT         ;get offset of beat string
                       MOV   CL,[BX][SI]            ;get beat value for note number SI
                       MOV   CH,0                   ;clear high half of CX to use as word
                       MOV   BX,DX                  ;get low word of BIOS count from DX
                       ADD   BX,CX                  ;add pulse count to current BIOS count
                       MOV   END_NOTE,BX            ;store as value at which to end note
         TIME_CHECK:   MOV   AH,0                   ;function to get BIOS time-of-day count
                       INT   1AH                    ;get the count
                       CMP   DX,END_NOTE            ;cmp count with end-of-note count
                       JNE   NOT_NOW                ;if not equal, quit the interrupt
                       MOV   SI,WHICH_NOTE          ;otherwise, start next note
                       INC   SI                     ;increase the note counter by one
                       MOV   WHICH_NOTE,SI          ;save the note counter
                       JMP   NEXT_NOTE              ;start the next note
       ;---FINISH UP THE ROUTINE:
         NO_MORE:      IN    AL,PORT_B              ;get the byte in Port_B
                       AND   AL,0FCH                ;turn off the speaker bits
                       OUT   61H,AL                 ;replace the byte in Port_B
                       MOV   SOUND_NOW?,0           ;set the play-a-string variable off
                       MOV   FIRST_NOTE?,1          ;set the first-note variable on
         NOT_NOW:      POP   DS                     ;restore altered registers
                       POP   SI                     ;
                       POP   DI                     ;
                       POP   DX                     ;
                       POP   CX                     ;
                       POP   BX                     ;
                       POP   AX                     ;
                       IRET                         ;return from the interrupt
       MELODY2         ENDP
```

2.2.7 Make sliding tones

Sliding tones are made by continuously changing frequency. Both BASIC and low-level programming can achieve them. This sound effect is made more dramatic by slightly shortening the duration of each segment of the tone as it rises, or by slightly lengthening the duration as the tone falls.

High Level ━━━━━━━━━━━━━━━━━━━━━━━━━━━━━━━━━━━━

In BASIC, simply place a SOUND command [2.2.2] in a loop, using very short durations for the tone. Increment the frequency by some multiple of the counter each time through. See [2.2.8] for an example using the PLAY statement, which allows faster transitions.

```
100 FOR N=1 TO 500 STEP 15
110 SOUND 400 + N,1
120 NEXT
```

Low Level ━━━━━━━━━━━━━━━━━━━━━━━━━━━━━━━━━━━━━

It is easiest to use the method of sound production controlled from the 8255 peripheral interface chip. Simply modulate bit 1 of Port B between 1 and 0, using empty timing loops as shown at [2.2.2]. Each time the timing loop is restored by placing a value in CX, slightly increase or decrease that value. Here, the tone rises:

```
;---DISABLE THE TIMER CHIP
     PB          EQU   61H              ;set PB equal to address of 8255 port B
                 IN    AL,PB            ;get the byte at PB
                 OR    AL,1             ;turn off bit 0
                 OUT   PB,AL            ;put the changed byte back in PB
;---SET THE SOUND FREQUENCY AND DURATION
                 MOV   BX,9000          ;initial counter value, decreased below
                 MOV   DX,3000          ;sound will continue for 3000 cycles
     REPEAT:                            ;return here after each cycle
;---TURN THE SPEAKER BIT ON
                 OR    AL,00000010B     ;force bit 1 "on"
                 OUT   PB,AL            ;place "on" byte in PB
                 MOV   CX,BX            ;set counter for 1st half of cycle
     CYCLE1:     LOOP  CYCLE1           ;idle at loop for 1000 repetitions
;---TURN THE SPEAKER BIT OFF
                 AND   AL,11111101B     ;force bit 1 "off"
                 OUT   PB,AL            ;place "off" byte in PB
                 MOV   CX,BX            ;set counter for 2nd half of cycle
     CYCLE2:     LOOP  CYCLE2           ;idle at loop for 1000 repetitions
;---GO ON TO NEXT CYCLE
                 DEC   BX               ;decrement counter, increase frequency
                 DEC   BX               ;and again
                 DEC   DX               ;decrement the remaining duration
                 JNZ   REPEAT           ;do another cycle if DX not 0
                                        ;else, the sound ends...
```

This simple method results in the high range passing considerably more quickly than the low range. Over short intervals this effect is actually desirable; when not, code must be added so that as the tone rises DX is given ever higher values when it is reloaded (6th line of the example).

2.2.8   Make sound effects

Sound effects generally entail a continuous change in the frequency of a tone. Only the PCjr is well equipped for this purpose (see the special discussion at [2.2.1]). On the other machines sound effects cannot readily be produced simultaneously with other program operations.

High Level

Because of the power of the SOUND and PLAY statements, BASIC makes it easy to produce sophisticated sound effects. But all must be constructed out of a pure musical tones, which means that the effect of sound distortion must be created by changing the tones so quickly that the ear blurs them together. For example, a piercing "warble" is created by rapidly switching back and forth between the same tone set several octaves apart:

```
100 FOR N=1 TO 100              'set duration
110 PLAY"l64t255"               'fastest possible tempo
120 PLAY"O1A"                   'play a low A
130 PLAY"O5A"                   'play a high A
140 NEXT                        'repeat
```

When the variation ranges over only a few cycles per second, the result is a sort of vibrato:

```
100 FOR N=1 TO 100              'set duration
110 SOUND 440,1                 'play an A
120 SOUND 445,1                 'play the A slightly sharped
130 NEXT                        'repeat
```

Another technique entails nesting sliding tones within a sequence that itself moves upwards or downwards. Figure 2-6 shows an upward-moving sequence. Many arcade games use this technique:

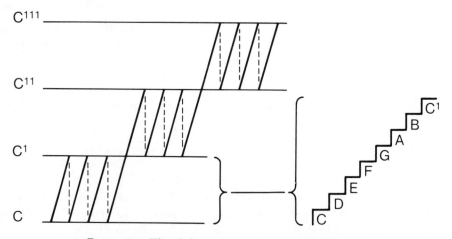

Figure 2-6. The sliding-sliding tone sound effect.

```
100 FOR I=1 TO 10                    'set number of repetitions
110 FOR J=0 TO 6                     'repeat scale 6 times
120 PLAY "mbl64t255o=j;ba#ag#gf#fed#dc#cc#dd#eff#gg#aa#b" 'slide thru a scale
130 NEXT                             'repeat at higher octave (o=j)
140 NEXT                             'repeat the whole sequence
```

The PCjr is much more versatile than the other machines, thanks to its special sound chip. The NOISE statement can generate a variety of sounds, using the format **NOISE source, volume, duration.** The source is a number from 0 to 7 taken from the following table:

0	high pitch periodic noise
1	medium pitch periodic noise
2	low pitch periodic noise
3	periodic noise where pitch varies with channel 3
4	high pitch white noise
5	medium pitch white noise
6	low pitch white noise
7	white noise where pitch varies with channel 3

The volume is given as a number from 0 to 15, where 0 is "off." And the duration is specified as a number of pulses of the BIOS time-of-day count, where there are 18.2 pulses per second.

Low Level

Any of the techniques shown for BASIC are also available through assembly language, although they may take a good deal of programming, as earlier parts of this chapter demonstrate. In addition, assembly programming allows you to create impure tones in which the interval during which the speaker is turned off does not equal the interval during which it is on. This distortion of symmetry makes for a variety of buzzing and clicking sounds. Buzzing results when the difference in the two intervals is, say, 50 to 1. When the difference is 10 to 20 times that, the buzz slows down to individual clicking sounds. In either case, the sound must be produced from the 8255 peripheral interface chip, using the basic technique shown at [2.2.2]. Here is an example of a buzz:

```
NUMBER_CYCLES EQU   300             ;number of times speaker goes on-off
FREQUENCY1    EQU   50              ;time on
FREQUENCY2    EQU   3200            ;time off
PORT_B        EQU   61H             ;address of Port B of 8255 chip
              CLI                   ;disable interrupts
              MOV   DX,NUMBER_CYCLES ;DX counts the length of the tone
              IN    AL,PORT_B       ;get Port B
              AND   AL,11111110B    ;disconnect speaker from timer chip
NEXT_CYCLE:   OR    AL,00000010B    ;turn on speaker
              OUT   PORT_B,AL       ;send the command to Port_B
              MOV   CX,FREQUENCY1   ;move the delay for 1/2 cycle to CX
FIRST_HALF:   LOOP  FIRST_HALF      ;make delay while speaker is on
              AND   AL,11111101B    ;turn off speaker
```

```
              OUT   PORT_B,AL            ; send the command to Port_B
              MOV   CX,FREQUENCY2        ; move the delay for 2nd half of cycle
SECOND_HALF:  LOOP  SECOND_HALF          ; make delay while speaker is off
              DEC   DX                   ; subtract 1 from the number of cycles
              JNZ   NEXT_CYCLE           ; if 0, then duration is exhausted
              STI                        ; reenable interrupts
```

To produce clicking sounds, use the same code, but change the value of FREQUENCY__2 to about 40000.

2.2.9 Make simultaneous sounds

Only the sound generating chip found in the PCjr can produce true simultaneous sound (see the discussion at [2.2.1]). However, in assembly language the two low-level methods of sound production may be combined to simulate the production of two simultaneous sounds. The pulse rates combine to create the effect of a complex wave form. The two sounds are each of diminished intensity, and if they are not widely separated, the result is more like a buzz than like two voices. This trick is really only useful for sound effects.

Low Level

Simply combine the two sound production techniques shown at [2.2.2] and [2.2.3]. Start sound from channel 2 of the timer chip. Then modulate output to the speaker from bit 1 of Port B of the peripheral interface. This second action determines the duration of the sound. Remember to shut off the timer chip when finished.

```
;---START SOUND OUTPUT FROM CHANNEL 2 OF 8253 TIMER CHIP:
                  IN    AL,61H              ;get byte from Port B
                  OR    AL,3                ;turn on bottom 2 bytes
                  OUT   61H,AL              ;send byte back to PB
                  MOV   AL,10110110B        ;bit pattern for 8253 command register
                  OUT   43H,AL              ;send to register
                  MOV   AX,600H             ;counter for channel 2
                  OUT   42H,AL              ;send low byte
                  MOV   AL,AH               ;ready to send high byte
                  OUT   42H,AL              ;send high byte
;---GENERATE A SECOND FREQUENCY FROM THE 8255 CHIP:
   NUMBER_CYCLES  EQU   9000                ;number of times to cycle on-off
   FREQUENCY      EQU   150                 ;delay time for 1/2 cycle
                  CLI                       ;disable interrupts
                  MOV   DX,NUMBER_CYCLES    ;DX counts the length of the tone
                  IN    AL,61H              ;get Port B
                  AND   AL,11111111B        ;disconnect speaker from timer chip
   NEXT_CYCLE:    OR    AL,00000010B        ;turn on speaker
                  OUT   61H,AL              ;send the command to Port_B
                  MOV   CX,FREQUENCY        ;move the delay for 1/2 cycle to CX
   FIRST_HALF:    LOOP  FIRST_HALF          ;make delay while speaker is on
                  AND   AL,11111101B        ;turn off speaker
                  OUT   61H,AL              ;send the command to Port_B
                  MOV   CX,FREQUENCY        ;move the delay for 2nd half of cycle
   SECOND_HALF:   LOOP  SECOND_HALF         ;make delay while speaker is off
                  DEC   DX                  ;subtract 1 from the number of cycles
                  JNZ   NEXT_CYCLE          ;if 0, then duration is exhausted
                  STI                       ;reenable interrupts
;---SHUT OFF CHANNEL 2 OF TIMER CHIP:
                  IN    AL,61H              ;get byte from Port B
                  AND   AL,11111100B        ;turn off bottom 2 bits
                  OUT   61H,AL              ;replace the byte
```

3
The Keyboard

Section 1: Monitor the Keyboard

The keyboard contains an Intel microprocessor which senses each keystroke and deposits a *scan code* in Port A of the 8255 peripheral interface chip [1.1.1], located on the system board. A scan code is a one-byte number in which the low seven bits represent an arbitrary identification number assigned to each key. A table of scan codes is found at [3.3.2]. Except in the AT, the top bit of the code tells whether the key has just been depressed (bit = 1, the "make code") or released (bit = 0, the "break code"). For example, the seven-bit scan code of the <B> key is 48, which is 110000 in binary. When the key goes down, the code sent to Port A is 10110000, and when the key is released, the code is 00110000. Thus every keystroke registers twice in the 8255 chip. Each time, the 8255 issues an "acknowledge" signal back to the microprocessor in the keyboard. The AT works slightly differently, sending the same scan code in either case, but preceding it with the byte **F0H** when the key is released.

When the scan code is deposited in Port A, the keyboard interrupt (INT 9) is invoked. The CPU momentarily sets aside its work and performs a routine that analyzes the scan code. When the code originates from a shift or toggle key, a change in the key's status is recorded in memory. In all other cases the scan code is transformed into a character code, providing it results from a key depression (otherwise the scan code is discarded). Of course, the routine first checks the settings of the shift and toggle keys to get the character code right (is it "a" or "A"?). And then the character code is placed in the *keyboard buffer*, which is a holding area in memory that stores up to fifteen incoming characters while a program is too busy to deal with them. Figure 3-1 shows the path a keystroke takes to travel to your programs.

There are two kinds of character codes, *ASCII codes* and *extended codes*. ASCII codes are one-byte numbers that correspond to the IBM extended ASCII character set, which is listed at [3.3.3]. On the IBM PC, these include the usual typewriter symbols, plus a number of special letters and block-graphics symbols. The ASCII codes also include 32 *control codes* which ordinarily are used to send commands to peripherals, rather than to act as characters on the screen; each, however, has its own symbol which can be displayed by direct memory mapping onto the video display [4.3.1]. (Precisely speaking, only the first 128 characters are true ASCII characters, and it is redundant to speak of "ASCII codes," since "ASCII" stands for "American Standard *Code* for Information Interchange." But programmers commonly speak of "ASCII codes" in order to distinguish them from other numbers.

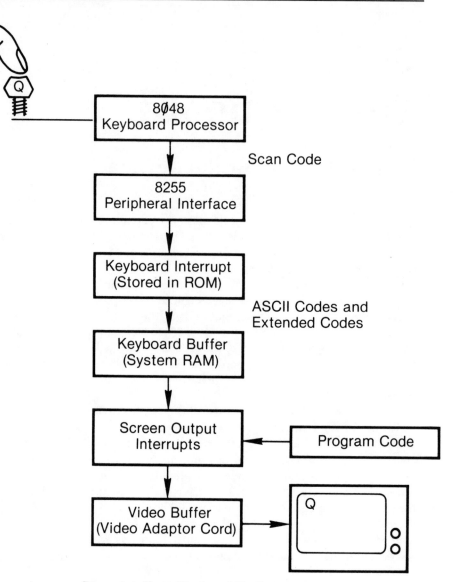

Figure 3-1. From Keyboard To Screen.

For example, "ASCII 8" refers to the backspace character, while "8" is the letter referenced by ASCII 56).

The second kind of codes, the extended codes, are assigned to keys or key-combinations that have no ASCII symbol to represent them, such as the function keys or Alt key combinations. Extended codes are two bytes long, and the first byte is always ASCII 0. The second byte is a code number, as listed at [3.3.5]. The code 0;30, for example, represents Alt-A. The initial zero lets programs tell whether a code number is from the ASCII set or the extended set.

There are a few key combinations that perform special functions and that do not generate scan codes. These combinations include <Ctrl-Break>, <Ctrl-Alt-Del>, and <PrtSc>, plus <Sys Req> on the AT, and <Ctrl-Alt-Cursor left, -Cursor right, -CapsLock, -Ins> on the PC Jr. These exceptions bring about special predefined results [3.2.2]. All other keystrokes must be interpreted by your programs, and if they have a special purpose, such as to move the cursor leftward, your program must provide the code that achieves that effect.

Fortunately, the operating system offers a variety of routines that read codes from the keyboard buffer, including means to receive whole strings at once. Because the routines do just about anything you can ask, it is generally senseless to write your own keyboard procedures, and so there are few low level programming examples in this chapter. However, a discussion of how to reprogram the keyboard interrupt is provided.

3.1.1 Clear the keyboard buffer

Programs should clear the keyboard buffer before prompting for input, eliminating any inadvertent keystrokes that may be waiting in the buffer. The buffer holds up to fifteen keystrokes, whether they be one-byte ASCII codes or two-byte extended codes. Thus the buffer must provide two bytes in memory for each keystroke. For one-byte codes, the first byte holds the ASCII code, and the second, the key's scan code. For the extended codes, the first byte holds ASCII 0 and the second byte holds the code number. This code number is usually the key's scan code, but not always, since some keys combine with shift keys to produce more than one code.

The buffer is designed as a *circular queue*, also known as a *first-in first-out (FIFO) buffer*. Like any buffer, it occupies a range of contiguous memory addresses. But no particular memory location is the "front of the line" in the buffer. Rather, two pointers keep track of the 'head' and 'tail' of the string of characters currently in the buffer. New keystrokes are deposited at the position following the tail (towards higher addresses in memory) and the tail pointer is adjusted accordingly. Once the highest memory location of the buffer space is filled, the insertion of new characters wraps around to the low end of the buffer; thus, the head of the string in the buffer will sometimes be at a higher memory location than the tail. Once the buffer is full, additional incoming characters are discarded; the keyboard interrupt beeps the speaker when this happens. Figure 3-2 diagrams some possible configurations of data in the buffer.

While the head pointer points to the first keystroke, the tail pointer points to the position *after* the last keystroke. When the two pointers are equal, the buffer is empty. To allow for fifteen keystrokes, a sixteenth, dummy position is required, and its two bytes always contain a carriage return (ASCII 13), and the scan code for <enter>, which is 28. This dummy position immediately precedes the head of the keystroke string. The 32 bytes of the buffer begin at memory location **0040:00 1E**. The head and tail pointers begin at **0040:001A** and **0040:001C**, respectively. Although the pointers are two bytes long, only the lower, least significant byte is used. The values of the pointers vary from 30 to 60, corresponding to positions within the BIOS data area. Simply set the value of **0040:001A** equal to the value in **0040:001C** to "clear" the buffer.

Note that it is possible for a program to insert characters into the buffer, ending the string with a carriage return and adjusting the buffer pointers accordingly. If this is done right before exiting a program, when control returns to DOS the characters are read and another program may be loaded automatically.

High Level

In BASIC use PEEK and POKE to fetch and change the values of the buffer pointers:

```
100 DEF SEG=&H40          'set segment to bottom of memory
110 POKE &H1C,PEEK(&H1A)  'equalize the pointers
```

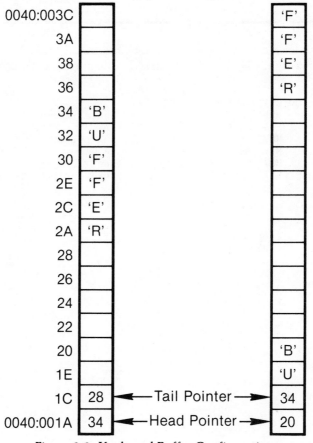

Figure 3-2. Keyboard Buffer Configurations.

This method is not reliable. Some applications may create a buffer elsewhere in memory, and there is also a slight possibility that the keyboard interrupt will break in in the midst of line 110, changing the tail pointer. For these reasons, it is better to leave the buffer pointers alone. Instead, read from the buffer until null is returned, discarding the keystrokes:

```
100 IF INKEY$<>"" THEN 100   'take another keystroke if not null
```

Middle Level

Function C of INT 21H performs any of the DOS keyboard input functions 1, 6, 7, 8, and A (described elsewhere in this section) but clears the keyboard buffer first. Simply place the number of the input function in AL (here it is 1):

```
;---CLEAR BUFFER BEFORE AWAITING KEYSTROKE:
        MOV   AH,ØCH             ;select DOS function ØCH
        MOV   AL,1               ;select key input function
        INT   21H               ;clears buffer, waits for keystroke
```

Low Level

As in the high level example, make the tail pointer equal to the head pointer. To avoid interference by the keyboard interrupt, disable interrupts while the change is made:

```
;---EQUALIZE THE HEAD AND TAIL POINTERS:
            CLI                     ;disable interrupts
            SUB   AX,AX             ;make AX=0
            MOV   ES,AX             ;set ES to bottom of memory
            MOV   AL,ES:[41AH]      ;move head pointer to AL
            MOV   ES:[41CH],AL      ;place in tail pointer
            STI                     ;reenable interrupts
```

3.1.2 Check the buffer for keystrokes

You can check whether or not there has been keyboard input without actually removing a character from the keyboard buffer. The buffer uses two pointers that show the front and end of the queue of characters currently in the buffer. When the two pointers are equal, the buffer is empty. Simply compare memory locations **0040:001A** and **0040:001C** for equality. (One can not merely check for a character at the "front" of the queue, because the buffer is formed as a *circular queue*, and the "front" is constantly changing position [3.1.1]).

High Level

Simply use PEEK to read the two bytes, and compare them:

```
100 DEF SEG=&H40                        'set the memory segment to 0
110 IF PEEK(&H1A)<>PEEK(&H1C) THEN...    '...then a character has arrived...
```

Middle Level

Function B or INT 21H returns FFH in the AL register when the keyboard buffer holds one or more characters, and it returns 00 when the buffer is empty:

```
;---CHECK IF A CHARACTER IS IN THE BUFFER:
            MOV   AH,0BH           ;function number
            INT   21H             ;call interrupt 21
            CMP   AL,0FFH         ;compare to FF
            JE    GET_KEYSTROKE   ;jump to input routine if char present
```

Function 1 of BIOS interrupt 16H provides the same service, but in addition it shows what the character is. The zero flag (ZF) is set to 1 if the buffer is empty, or to 0 if a character is waiting. In the latter case, a copy of the character at the head of the buffer is placed in AX *without* removing it from the buffer. AL returns the character code for one-byte ASCII characters, or it returns ASCII 0 for extended codes, in which case the code number appears in AH.

```
;---FIND OUT IF THERE IS A CHARACTER:
            MOV   AH,1            ;set function number
            INT   16H            ;check if character in buffer
            JZ    NO_CHARACTER   ;jump if zero flag = 1
;---THERE IS A CHARACTER, SO SEE WHAT IT IS:
            CMP   AL,0           ;is it an extended code?
            JE    EXTENDED_CODE  ;if so, go to extended code routine
                                 ;otherwise, take character from AL
```

Low Level

As with the high level example, simply compare the two buffer pointers:

```
;---COMPARE HEAD AND TAIL POINTERS:
            MOV   AX,0           ;use the extra segment
            MOV   ES,AX          ;set the segment to 0
            MOV   AL,ES:[41AH]   ;get one pointer
            MOV   AH,ES:[41CH]   ;get other pointer
            CMP   AH,AL          ;compare the pointers
            JNE   GET_KEYSTROKE  ;jump to input routine if unequal
```

3.1.3 Wait for a keystroke and do not echo it on the screen

Normally, incoming keystrokes are echoed on the screen to show what has been typed. But sometimes automatic echoing is undesirable. One-keystroke menu selections need no echo, for example. And sometimes incoming characters may need error-checking before they are sent to the screen. In particular, any program that accepts extended codes must be cautious of automatic echoing, since the first byte (ASCII Ø) of these codes will be displayed, leaving spaces between the characters.

High Level ━━━━━━━━━━━━━━━━━━━━━━━━━━━━━━━━━

The INKEY$ function of BASIC does not echo. It returns a string that is one byte long for ASCII characters and two bytes long for extended characters. INKEY$ does not wait for a keystroke unless it is placed within a loop that cycles again and again until a character arrives. The loop functions by invoking INKEY$ and then assigning the string it returns to a variable, here C$. When no keystrokes have been received, INKEY$ returns the *null string*, which is a string that is Ø characters long, denoted by two quotation marks with nothing between (""). So long as INKEY$ returns "", the loop repeats: **100 C$ = INKEY$:IF C$ = "" THEN 100**.

The example below assumes that the incoming keystrokes are menu selections and that each selection sends the program to a particular subroutine. The selections are made by striking A,B,C... (resulting in one-byte ASCII codes) or ALT-A, ALT-B, ALT-C... (resulting in two-byte extended codes). To tell the difference, use the LEN function to check whether the string is one or two characters long. If a one-byte ASCII code, a series of IF...THEN statements immediately begin to test the identity of the keystroke, sending the program to the appropriate subroutine. In the case of two-byte codes, control transfers to a separate routine. There the RIGHT$ function eliminates the lefthand character, which, of course, is nothing more than the Ø that identifies extended codes. The ASC function is then used to convert the character from string form to numeric form. Finally, a second series of IF...THEN statements checks the resulting number against those corresponding to ALT-A, ALT-B, etc.

```
100 C$ = INKEY$: IF C$="" THEN 100       'wait for a keystroke
110 IF LEN(C$) = 2 THEN 500              'if extended code, jump
120 IF C$="a" OR C$="A" THEN GOSUB 1100  'is it menu selection a?
130 IF C$="b" OR C$="B" THEN GOSUB 1200  'b?
140 IF C$="c" OR C$="C" THEN GOSUB 1300  'c?
 .
 .
500 C$=RIGHT$(C$,1)                      'get 2nd byte of extended code
510 C=ASC(C$)                            'convert to numeric value
520 IF C=30 THEN GOSUB 2100             'is it menu selection Alt-A?
530 IF C=48 THEN GOSUB 2200             'Alt-B?
540 IF C=46 THEN GOSUB 2300             'Alt-C?
```

Note that line 120 (and those following) could instead have used the numeric values for the ASCII codes for "a" and "A", and so on:

```
120 IF C=97 OR C=65 THEN GOSUB 1100
```

Of course, first C$ would need to be converted to integer form, exactly as in line 510. In programs with a long sequence of these statements, you can save space by changing C so that it always represents either the lower- or upper-case form of a letter. First do some error checking to be sure that the ASCII value of C$ is in the correct range. Then find out if the number is below 91, in which case it is upper case. If so, add 32 to convert it to lower case. Otherwise, do nothing. Then a shorter statement such as **IF C = 97 THEN**... will suffice. Here is the code:

```
500 C=ASC(C$)                        'get ASCII number of the character
510 IF NOT((C>64 AND C<91) OR (C>96 AND C<123)) THEN...
                                     '...then out of range, ignore it
520 IF C<91 THEN C=C+32              'add 32 to value of upper-case letters
530 IF C=97 THEN...                  '... then begin to test the values...
```

Middle Level ━━━━━━━━━━━━━━━━━━━━━━━━━━━━━━━

Functions 7 and 8 of INT 21H wait for a character if none is in the keyboard buffer, and when one arrives, it is not echoed on the screen. Function 8 detects Ctrl-Break (and initiates the Ctrl-Break routine [3.2.8]), while function 7 does not. In both cases, the character is returned in AL. When AL contains ASCII 0, an extended code has been received. Repeat the interrupt and the second byte of the code appears in AL.

```
;---GET A KEYSTROKE:
                MOV   AH,7              ;set function number
                INT   21H              ;wait for character
                CMP   AL,0             ;see if extended code
                JE    EXTENDED_CODE    ;go to extended code routine if so
                  .                    ;otherwise, take character from AL
                  .
;---EXTENDED CODE ROUTINE:
    EXTENDED_CODE: INT  21H            ;now the extended code number is in AL
                CMP   AL,75            ;check if "cursor-left"
                JNE   C_R              ;if not, check next possibility
                JMP   CURSOR_LEFT      ;if so, go to routine
    C_R:        CMP   AL,77            ;...etc...
```

BIOS provides a service that matches the DOS function. Place 0 in AH and call INT 16H. The function waits for a character and returns it in AL. In this case, extended codes require calling the interrupt only once. If 0 appears in AL, an extended code number is found in AH. Ctrl-Break is not detected.

```
;---GET A KEYSTROKE:
                MOV   AH,0             ;function number to intercept keystroke
                INT   16H              ;get the keystroke
                CMP   AL,0             ;is it an extended code?
                JE    EXTENDED_CODE    ;if so, go to special routine
                                       ;otherwise, take ASCII char from AL

;---EXTENDED CODE ROUTINE:
    EXTENDED_CODE: CMP  AH,75          ;take extended code from AH
                                       ;...etc...
```

3.1.4 Wait for a keystroke and echo it on the screen

With text or data entry, keystrokes are normally echoed on the screen. In echoing, characters like the carriage return or backspace are interpreted by moving the cursor accordingly rather than displaying the ASCII symbols for the characters. The echoing begins at whatever point the cursor is currently set, and the text automatically wraps around from the last column to the next line. The wrap requires no special coding because the characters are simply deposited at the next position in the video buffer, and the buffer is essentially one long line containing the 25 lines of the screen.

High Level ───

In BASIC, intercept a keystroke using INKEY$, as shown at [3.1.3]. Then print it before returning to intercept another. Either use the PRINT statement, or else POKE the keystroke directly into the video buffer, using the memory mapping techniques shown at [4.3.1] (the buffer starts at memory segment &HB000 for the monochrome adaptor and at &HB800 for the color adaptor). If you use PRINT, be sure to end the statement with a semicolon, or a carriage return will occur automatically. Below are examples of each method. No attempt is made here to sort out non-character keystrokes. The variable KEYSTROKES$ collects the incoming keystrokes into a data string.

```
100 '''method using PRINT:
110 LOCATE 10,40                        'set the cursor to row 10, col 40
120 KEYSTROKES$=""                      'clear variable that holds incoming string
130 C$=INKEY$:IF C$="" THEN 130         'get a keystroke
140 KEYSTROKES$=KEYSTROKES$+C$          'add the keystroke to a string variable
150 PRINT C$;                           'print the character
160 GOTO 130                            'get next character

100 '''method using POKE (monochrome adaptor):
110 DEF SEG=&HB000                      'set segment offset to start of buffer
120 POINTER=1678                        'position of 10,40 = (2*((10*80)+40))-2
130 KEYSTROKES$=""                      'clear variable holding incoming string
140 C$=INKEY$:IF C$="" THEN 140         'get a keystroke
150 KEYSTROKES$=KEYSTROKES$+C$          'add the keystroke to a string variable
160 POKE POINTER, ASC(C$)               'poke ASCII number of char into buffer
170 POINTER=POINTER+2                   'up pointer by 2 (skip attribute byte)
180 GOTO 140                            'get next character
```

Middle Level ───

Function 1 of INT 21H waits for a character if none is found in the keyboard buffer, then echos it on the screen at the current cursor position. Ctrl-Break is intercepted so that the (programmable) Ctrl-Break routine is executed [3.2.8]. Characters are returned in AL. In the case of extended codes, AL holds ASCII 0. Repeat the interrupt to bring the second byte of the code into AL.

```
;---GET A KEYSTROKE:
            MOV   AH,1            ;set the function number
            INT   21H            ;wait for a character
```

```
                    CMP   AL,Ø              ;extended code?
                    JE    EXTENDED_CODE     ;if so, jump to special routine
                                            ;else, take ASCII character from AL
                       .
;---EXTENDED CODE ROUTINE:
                    INT   21H               ;bring the code number into AL
                    CMP   AL,77             ;check if "cursor-right"
                    JNE   C_R               ;if not, check next possibility
                    JMP   CURSOR_RIGHT      ;if so, go to routine
       C_R:         CMP   AL,75             ;...etc...
```

This function completely ignores the escape key. It interprets a tab keystroke normally. The backspace key causes the cursor to move back one space, but the character in that position is not erased. The enter key causes the cursor to move to the start of the current line (there is no automatic line feed).

3.1.5 Intercept a keystroke without waiting

Some real-time applications cannot stop to wait for incoming keystrokes; they take keystrokes from the keyboard buffer only when it is convenient for the program to do so. For example, idling the CPU while awaiting a keystroke would stop all screen action in a video game. Note that it is easy to test whether or not the keyboard buffer is empty, using the methods shown at [3.1.2].

High Level ───────────────────────

Simply use INKEY$ without nesting it within a loop:

```
100 C$=INKEY$            'check for a character
110 IF C$ <> "" THEN...  'there is a character, so...
120 ...                  'else, there is no character
```

Middle Level ───────────────────────

Function 6 of INT 21H is the only interrupt that receives keystrokes without waiting. The function does not echo characters on the screen, nor does it sense Ctrl-Break. FFH must be placed in DL before calling this interrupt. Otherwise function 6 serves an entirely different purpose—it prints at the current cursor position whatever character is found in DL. The zero flag is set to 1 if there are no characters in the buffer. When a character is intercepted, it is placed in AL. Should the character be ASCII 0, an extended code is indicated, and a second call is needed to bring in the code number.

```
                MOV   AH,6           ;DOS function 6
                MOV   DL,0FFH        ;request function for keyboard input
                INT   21H            ;get character
                JZ    NO_CHAR        ;jump to NO_CHAR if no keystroke
                CMP   AL,0           ;see if character is ASCII 0
                JE    EXTENDED_CODE  ;if so, go to extended code routine
                ...                  ;ASCII character now in AL

EXTENDED_CODE:  INT   21H            ;get 2nd byte of extended code
                ...                  ;code number now in AL
```

3.1.6 Intercept a string of keystrokes

Both BASIC and DOS provide routines to intercept strings of keystrokes. They automatically repeat the single-keystroke input routines described in previous sections, watching for a carriage return to tell that the string is complete. Of course, memory must be allocated to hold each character of the string, and the length of each string must be recorded in order to delimit one string from another. This is done using *string descriptors*, which consist of one or more bytes that hold the address and/or the length of the string. In BASIC the first two bytes of string descriptors hold the address of the string, and the descriptors are kept in an array that is apart from the strings themselves. The string length is held in the third byte of the three-byte descriptors. The DOS function, on the other hand, places the string length at the start of the actual string, and it is up to the program to keep track of the string's location in memory.

High Level ────────────────────────────

BASIC can intercept strings both with and without automatic echoing of the string on the screen. Echoing is easiest, since it is performed by the ready-made string input function, INPUT. INPUT automatically collects the incoming keystrokes, placing each on the screen as it is received. When the enter key is pressed, the input ends and the string is assigned to a specified variable (the ASCII 13 code sent by the enter key is *not* appended to the string). INPUT incorporates the DOS line-editing features, so that typing errors may be corrected before the string is entered. INPUT receives numbers in string form, and it will automatically convert them to numeric form if you specify a numeric variable name for the input. Finally, INPUT can prompt the user for the desired information by automatically writing a string on the screen. The string may be up to 254 characters long. If this length is exceeded, the excess characters are ignored. The basic form is **INPUT"prompt"**, **variable__name**. See the BASIC manual for variations.

```
110 INPUT"Enter your name: ",NAME$     'wait for character string, assign to NAME$
120 INPUT"Enter your age: ",AGE%       'wait for numeric character string, convert
                                       ' it to numeric form, assign it to AGE%
```

The INPUT statement is inadequate when the incoming flow of keystrokes may contain extended codes, as for the cursor movements of a full-screen text processor. Instead, the non-echoing INKEY$ function must intercept each keystroke one by one, then check for extended codes, then check for control codes like the carriage return, and then place only those characters on the screen that belong there. These screen-bound characters are also added, one at a time, to the end of a string variable. Text files are comprised of whole arrays of these string variables. You will find at [3.1.8] an extensive keyboard input routine that shows INKEY$ used this way.

Middle Level ────────────────────────────

Function 0AH of INT 21H inputs strings of up to 254 characters, echoing the input on to the display. This routine continues to add incoming keystrokes to the string until the enter key is struck. DS:DX points to the place in memory where the string will be deposited. On entry, the first byte at this location must contain the number of bytes alloted to the string. After the string is entered, the second byte is given the number of characters actually received. The string itself begins from the third byte.

Allocate just enough memory for the desired string length plus two bytes for the string descriptor and one extra byte for the carriage return. When you set the maximum string length in the first byte, add 1 for the carriage return. The carriage return code—ASCII 13—is entered as the final character of the string, but it is *not* counted in the character tally placed by the function in the second byte of the string descriptor. Thus, to receive a 50-character string, allocate 53 bytes of memory and place ASCII 51 in the first byte. If 50 characters are entered, on return the second byte will contain ASCII 50 and the 53rd byte of allocated memory will contain ASCII 13.

```
;---IN THE DATA SEGMENT:
    STRING      DB    53 DUP(?)          ;space for 50 char string
                                         ;  (2 chars for descriptor, 1 for CR)

;---RECEIVE A STRING FROM THE KEYBOARD:
                LEA   DX,STRING          ;DS:DX points to string space
                MOV   BX,DX              ;make BX also point to string
                MOV   AL,51              ;set string length (+1 for CR)
                MOV   [BX],AL            ;place in first byte of descriptor
                MOV   AH,0AH             ;function number of string routine
                INT   21H               ;receive the string
;---CHECK THE LENGTH OF THE STRING:
                MOV   AH,[BX]+1          ;length now in AH
```

This routine makes use of the DOS line editing functions. Striking the backspace or cursor-left keys deletes the prior character on the screen, and eliminates it from memory as well. The tab key works, extended codes are ignored, and empty strings are permitted (that is, a carriage return without any preceding keystrokes). On the monitor, strings wrap at the end of a line, and the screen scrolls upward when a string reaches the bottom right corner. When keystrokes exceed the alloted length of the string, they are ignored, and the speaker sounds.

DOS provides a second way of receiving a string, and in this case it does not echo it on to the screen. Function 3FH of INT 21H is a general purpose input function that is most commonly used in disk operations. It requires a predefined *handle*, which is a code number used by the operating system to designate an I/O device. The handle for the keyboard is the number 0, and it must be placed in BX. Point DS:DX at the place where the string is to reside, place the maximum string length in CX, and call the function:

```
;---READ STRING WITHOUT ECHOING:
                MOV   AH,3FH             ;function number
                MOV   BX,0               ;handle number
                LEA   DX,STRING_BUFFER   ;DS:DX points to buffer
                MOV   CX,100             ;maximum length of string
                INT   21H               ;wait for input
```

String input terminates when the Enter key is struck, and DOS adds two characters to the end of the string: a carriage return and line feed (ASCII 13 and ASCII 10). Because of these additional characters, when the length of a string is specified as 100 characters, it may occupy up to 102 bytes of memory. The length of the string entered is returned in AX, and this value includes the two terminating characters.

3.1.7 Check/set the status of the toggle and shift keys

The two bytes found at memory locations 0040:0017 and 0040:0018 hold bits showing the status of the shift and toggle keys, as follows:

	Bit	Key	Meaning when bit = 1
0040:0017	7	Insert	Insert mode "on"
	6	CapsLock	CapsLock mode "on"
	5	NumLock	NumLock mode "on"
	4	ScrollLock	ScrollLock mode "on"
	3	Alt shift	key down
	2	Ctrl shift	key down
	1	Lefthand shift	key down
	0	Righthand shift	key down
0040:0018	7	Insert	key down
	6	CapsLock	key down
	5	NumLock	key down
	4	ScrollLock	key down
	3	Ctrl-NumLock	Ctrl-NumLock mode "on"
(others unused)			

The keyboard interrupt immediately updates these status bytes if a toggle or shift keystroke occurs, even if no keystrokes have been read from the keyboard buffer. This is true for the Ins toggle key as well, which is the only one of the eight keys that places a code in the buffer (the Ins status setting is changed even if there is no room for the character in the buffer). Note that bit 3 of 0040:0018 is set to 1 while the Ctrl-Numlock hold state is in effect; since a program is suspended during this state, the bit is of no significance.

The keyboard interrupt checks these status bits before interpreting incoming keystrokes, so when a program changes one of the bits the effect is the same as physically striking the corresponding key. You may wish to set the state of the NumLock and CapsLock keys to assure that input is of the desired kind. Conversely, your programs may need to read the status of the keys, perhaps to echo the current status on the screen. Note that the AT keyboard keeps its toggle indicator lights set correctly even when the status register settings are made by software.

High Level ───

Here, the NumLock key is made to activate the cursor keys by setting bit 5 of 0040:0017 to 0. This is done by ANDing the value at this address with 223 (the bit pattern 11011111B - see Appendix B for the logic behind bit operations). The result is placed in the status byte. The example then sets the bit back to 1 by ORing it with 32 (00100000B).

```
100 DEF SEG = &H40                    'set memory segment to BIOS data area
110 STATUSBYTE=PEEK(&H17)             'get status byte
120 NEWBYTE=STATUSBYTE AND 223        'set bit 5 to 0
130 POKE(&H17,NEWBYTE)                'place new value in the status register
```

Alternatively, to turn the bit ON:

```
120 NEWBYTE=STATUSBYTE OR 32          'set bit 5 to 1
130 POKE(&H17,NEWBYTE)                'place new value in the status register
```

Lines 110-130 may be condensed to the form:

```
110 POKE(&H417,PEEK(&H417) AND 223)
                ...or...
110 POKE(&H417,PEEK(&H417) OR 32)
```

Middle Level

Function 2 of INT 16H gives access to one—but only one—of the status bytes. This is the byte at **0040:017H**, which contains the more useful information. The byte is returned in AL.

```
;---CHECK STATUS OF INSERT MODE
              MOV   AH,2               ;set function number
              INT   16H               ;get the status byte
              TEST  AL,10000000B      ;test bit 7
              JZ    INSERT_OFF        ;if bit is 0 then INSERT is off
```

Low Level

Here the insert mode is forced on by turning on bit 7 of the status byte at **0040:0017** (here addressed as **0000:0417**).

```
              SUB   AX,AX             ;set the extra segment to 0
              MOV   ES,AX             ;
              MOV   AL,10000000B      ;prepare to turn on bit 7
              OR    ES:[417H],AL      ;directly change the status byte
```

3.1.8   Write a general-purpose keyboard input routine

The system of codes used by the keyboard defies simple interpretation. The codes may be one or two bytes long, and there is no simple correspondence between the code length and whether it is for a character or for hardware control. Not all keystroke combinations even produce a unique code, and extra care must be taken to differentiate them. Neither the ASCII codes nor the extended codes are numbered in a fashion that facilitates grouping and error checking. In a word, a general keyboard input routine makes for messy programming.

Examples are given here in BASIC and using INT 16H. They show how to put together much of the information given in this chapter. The general algorithm is shown in Figure 3-3.

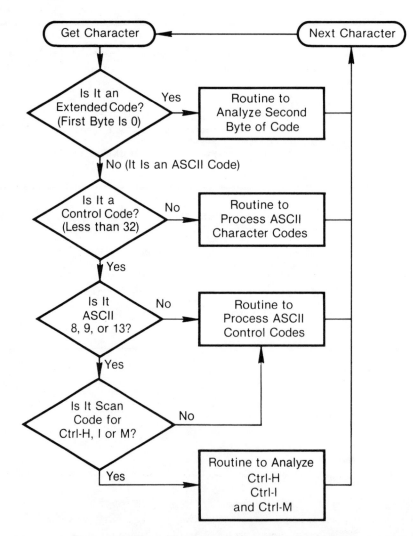

Figure 3-3. Flow Chart For A General Input Routine.

High Level

A keyboard input routine written in BASIC can do all that an assembly language routine can, but with one exception. The INKEY$ function does not have access to scan codes. This means that it is difficult to tell whether ASCII codes 8, 9, 13, and 27 have arisen from the backspace, tab, enter, and escape keys, or from Ctrl-H, I, M and [. The distinction can instead be made by checking the Ctrl key status bit at 0040:0017 at the time the key is pressed. But this ploy fails if the keystroke is stored in the keyboard buffer for any length of time.

```
100 C$=INKEY$:IF C$="" THEN 100              'get a character
110 IF LEN(C$)=2 THEN 700                     'if extended code, go to its routine
120 C=ASC(C$)                                 'else ASCII character, get its number
130 IF C<32 THEN 300                          'if control code, go to its routine
140 IF C<65 OR C>123 THEN 100                 'accept only typewriter keystrokes
150 '''C is a typewriter keystroke -- do with it what you will, for example:
160 S$=S$+C$                                  'make character the next in a string
170 PRINT C$;                                 'echo it on the screen
180 '''...etc...
190 GOTO 100                                  'get next keystroke
 .
 .
 .
300 '''ASCII control code routine
310 DEF SEG=0                                 'point to bottom of memory (BIOS area)
320 REGISTER=PEEK(&H417)                      'get the shift key register
330 X = REGISTER AND 4                        'X=4 if bit 5 is on
340 IF X=0 THEN 500                           'CTRL not down, so go to 4-key routine
350 '''C is a Ctrl-alpha combination -- do with it what you will, for example:
360 IF C=8 then GOSUB 12000                   'Ctrl-H, so create 'HELP screen'
370 '''...etc...
380 GOTO 100                                  'get next keystroke
 .
 .
 .
500 '''4-key routine: decodes ASCII codes 8, 9, 13, and 27 when the Ctrl
510 '      key is up (i.e. as backspace, tab, enter, and escape)
520 IF C=8 THEN GOSUB 5000                    'go to backspace routine
530 IF C=9 THEN GOSUB 6000                    'go to tab routine
540 IF C=13 THEN GOSUB 7000                   'go to carriage return routine
550 IF C=27 THEN GOSUB 8000                   'go to Esc routine
560 GOTO 100                                  'get next keystroke
 .
 .
 .
700 '''extended code routine
710 C$=RIGHT$(C$,1)                           'make C$ = 2nd character only
720 C=ASC(C$)                                 'change to numerical form
730 '''C is an extended code number -- do with it what you will, for example:
740 IF C<71 OR C>81 THEN 100                  'accept only cursor keystrokes
750 IF C=72 THEN GOSUB 3500                   'go to 'cursor up' subroutine
760 '''...etc...
770 GOTO 100                                  'get next keystroke
```

Middle Level

This example differs from the one above in the way that the four special cases for Ctrl-H, I, M and [are treated. Here, when the question arises as to whether the code arises from a single key or a Ctrl key combination, the scan code is checked.

This method is more reliable than checking the Ctrl key status bit, since the scan code is stored in the keyboard buffer, whereas the setting of the Ctrl key status bit is transient.

```
;---GET A KEYSTROKE AND DETERMINE ITS TYPE:
      NEXT:       MOV   AH,0               ;select BIOS keyboard input function
                  INT   16H               ;get a keystroke
                  CMP   AL,0               ;check if extended code
                  JE    EXTENDED_CODE      ;if so, jump to its routine
                  CMP   AL,32              ;check if control code
                  JL    CONTROL_CODE       ;if so, jump to its routine
                  CMP   AL,65              ;see if below range of typewriter chars
                  JL    NEXT               ;if so, get another character
                  CMP   AL,123             ;see if above range of typewriter chars
                  JG    NEXT               ;if so, get another character
;---NOW PROCESS CHARACTER IN AL:
                  STOSB                    ;save character in memory at ES:DI ptr
                  MOV   AH,2               ;choose DOS function to display char
                  MOV   DL,AL              ;put character in DL, as required
                  INT   21H               ;display character (cursor forwards)
                    .                      ;etc.
                    .
                    .
                  JMP   NEXT               ;get next character
;---ANALYZE CONTROL CODES (start with special cases)
      CONTROL_CODE: CMP AL,13              ;is the code ASCII 13?
                  JNE   TAB                ;if not, check next special case
                  CMP   AH,28              ;it's 13 -- was scan code for CR?
                  JNE   C_M                ;if not, go to Ctrl-M case
                  CALL  CARRIAGE_RETURN    ;perform carriage return routine
                  JMP   NEXT               ;go get next keystroke
      C_M:        CALL  CTRL_M             ;perform Ctrl-M routine
                  JMP   NEXT               ;go get next keystroke
      TAB:        CMP   AL,9               ;check whether TAB or Ctrl-I...
                    .
                    .
                  CMP   AL,10              ;after special cases, check others
                    .
                    .
      REJECT:     JMP   NEXT               ;default: go get another keystroke
;---ANALYZE EXTENDED CODES (2nd byte of code is in AH):
      EXTENDED_CODE: CMP AH,71             ;check number against bottom of range
                  JL    REJECT             ;if below, get next char via REJECT
                  CMP   AH,81              ;check number against top of range
                  JG    REJECT             ;if above, get next char via REJECT
;---AH HAS A CURSOR CODE -- ANALYZE IT:
                  CMP   AH,72              ;see if 'cursor up'
                  JE    C_U                ;if so, go to 'cursor up' routine
                  CMP   AH,80              ;see if 'cursor down'
                  JE    C_D                ;if so, go to 'cursor down' routine
                    .
                    .
      C_U:        CALL  CURSOR_UP          ;perform 'cursor up' routine
                  JMP   NEXT               ;get next keystroke
      C_D:        CALL  CURSOR_DOWN        ;perform 'cursor down' routine
                  JMP   NEXT               ;get next keystroke
```

3.1.9 Reprogram the keyboard interrupt

When the keyboard microprocessor deposits a scan code in Port A of the 8255 chip (at port address 60H—see [1.1.1]), it invokes INT 9. The job of this interrupt is to convert the scan code to a character code on the basis of the shift and toggle key settings, and to place the code in the keyboard buffer. (When the scan code is for a shift or toggle key, no character code goes to the buffer (except for <Ins>); instead, the interrupt makes changes in two status bytes located in the BIOS data area [3.1.7]). The BIOS and DOS "keyboard interrupts" are really only "keyboard buffer interrupts." They do not actually "read" keystrokes. Rather, they read the *interpretations* of keystrokes that INT 9 provides. Note that the PCjr uses a special routine (INT 48H) to convert input from its 62 keys into the 83-key protocol used by the other IBM machines. The results of this routine are passed on to INT 9, which performs its work as usual. Via INT 49H, the PCjr also provides for special non-key scan codes that could potentially be set up for peripheral devices that would make use of the infrared (cordless) keyboard link.

It takes a very unusual application to make it worthwhile to reprogram this interrupt, especially considering that DOS allows you to reprogram any key of the keyboard [3.2.6]. Still, if you must reprogram INT 9, this section will give you a start. Read [1.2.3] first to understand in general how interrupts are programmed. There are three basic steps in the keyboard interrupt:

1. Read a scan code and send an *acknowledge* signal to the keyboard.
2. Convert the scan code into a code number or into a setting in the shift/toggle key status register.
3. Place a key code in the keyboard buffer.

At the time the interrupt is invoked, a scan code will be in Port A. So first the code is read and saved on the stack. Then Port B (port 61H) is used to very briefly issue the "acknowledge" signal to the keyboard microprocessor. Simply change bit 7 to 1, then immediately change it back to 0. Note that bit 6 of Port B controls the clock signal of the keyboard. It must always be 1, or the keyboard is effectively turned off. These port addresses apply to the AT as well, even though it does not have an 8255 interface chip.

The scan code is first analyzed to see whether the key was depressed (the "make" code) or released (the "break" code). Except on the AT, a break code is indicated when bit 7 of the scan code is set to 1. On the AT, where bit 7 is always 0, a break code is two bytes: first 0F0H and then the scan code. All break codes are thrown away except those for shift and toggle keys, for which the appropriate changes are made in the shift/toggle status bytes. On the other hand, all make codes are processed. Here again the shift/toggle status may be changed. But in the case of character codes, the status bytes must be consulted to see whether, for example, the scan code 30 indicates an upper or lower case **A**.

Once an incoming character has been identified, the keyboard routine must find its ASCII code or extended code. The example here is much too short to show all cases. In general, the scan code is correlated with an entry in a data table that is accessed by the XLAT instruction. XLAT takes a number from 0-255 in AL and returns in AL a corresponding one-byte value from a 256-byte table that is pointed to by DS:BX. The table may be set up in the data segment. If AL initially contains scan code **30**, then AL receives byte number 30 of the table (the *31st* byte, since we're counting from 0). This byte of the table should have been set to 97, giving the ASCII code for **a**. Of course, a second table would be required for capital **A**, and it would be called instead should the routine find that the shift state is "on". Or, alternatively, some other part of a single table could hold the capital letters, in which case the scan code would need to have an offset added to it.

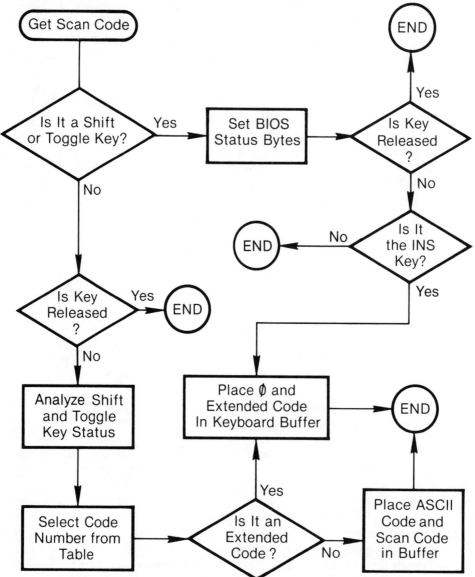

Figure 3-4. The Keyboard Interrupt.

Finally, code numbers must be placed in the keyboard buffer. The routine must first check to see if there is any room in the buffer for another character. [3.1.1] shows how the buffer is constructed as a *circular queue*. Memory location 0040:001A contains the pointer for the head of the buffer, and 0040:001C contains the pointer for the tail. The word-length pointers are offsets within the BIOS data area (which starts at segment 40H), ranging from 30 to 60. New characters are inserted at higher memory positions in the buffer, and when the upper limit is reached, the insertion wraps around to the low end of the buffer. When the buffer is full, the tail pointer is 2 less than the head pointer—except when the head pointer equals 30 (is at the top of the buffer) in which case the buffer is full if the value of the tail pointer is 60.

To insert a character in the buffer, place it at the position pointed to by the tail pointer, then increase the tail pointer by 2; if the tail pointer equals 60, change it instead to 30. That is all there is to it. Figure 3-4 diagrams the keyboard interrupt.

Low Level

An efficient routine requires much thought. This example gives only the rudiments. It intercepts only the lower- and upper-case letters, loading them both into the same table, with the capital letters 100 bytes higher in the table than their siblings. Only the left shift key is attended to, and the current status of the CapsLock is ignored.

```
;---IN THE DATA SEGMENT:
    TABLE          DB 16 DUP(0)              ;skip first 16 bytes of table
                   DB 'quertyuiop',0,0,0,0   ;top row (scan code #16 = q)
                   DB 'asdfghjkl',0,0,0,0,0  ;middle row
                   DB 'zxcvbnm'              ;bottom row
                   DB 16 dup(0)              ;offset upper case to 100 bytes higher
                   DB 'QUERTYUIOP',0,0,0,0   ;caps for top row
                   DB 'ASDFGHJKL',0,0,0,0,0  ;caps for middle row
                   DB 'ZXCVBNM'              ;caps for bottom row

;---AT BEGINNING OF THE PROGRAM, INSTALL THE INTERRUPT:
                   CLI                       ;disable interrupts
                   PUSH DS                   ;save DS
                   MOV  AX,SEG NEW_KEYBOARD  ;make DS:DX point to interrupt routine
                   MOV  DS,AX
                   MOV  DX,OFFSET NEW_KEYBOARD
                   MOV  AL,9                 ;number of interrupt vector to change
                   MOV  AH,25H               ;DOS function to change vector
                   INT  21H                  ;change the vector
                   POP  DS                   ;restore DS
                   STI                       ;reenable interrupts
                   .
                   .
```

(The program continues, perhaps ending and staying resident [1.3.4])

```
;---HERE IS THE KEYBOARD INTERRUPT ITSELF:
NEW_KEYBOARD       PROC FAR                  ;hardware interrupts are far procedures
                   PUSH AX                   ;save all changed registers
                   PUSH BX                   ;
                   PUSH CX                   ;
```

```
                        PUSH  DI                      ;
                        PUSH  ES                      ;
;---GET THE SCAN CODE AND SEND AN ACKNOWLEDGE SIGNAL:
                        IN    AL,60H                  ;get the scan code from Port A
                        MOV   AH,AL                   ;place a copy in AH
                        PUSH  AX                      ;save the scan code
                        IN    AL,61H                  ;get the current reading of Port B
                        OR    AL,10000000B            ;turn bit 7 on
                        OUT   61H,AL                  ;place the changed byte in Port B
                        AND   AL,01111111B            ;turn bit 7 back off
                        OUT   61H,AL                  ;return Port B to its original reading
;---POINT ES TO BIOS DATA AREA:
                        MOV   AX,40H                  ;set ES to bottom of memory
                        MOV   ES,AX                   ;
                        POP   AX                      ;restore scan code to AL
;---CHECK IF SHIFT KEY:
                        CMP   AL,42                   ;left shift down?
                        JNE   KEY_UP                  ;if not, try next possibility
                        MOV   BL,1                    ;if so, prepare to set register bit 1
                        OR    ES:[17H],BL             ;OR the status register directly
                        JMP   QUIT                    ;quit the routine
        KEY_UP:         CMP   AL,170                  ;left shift up?
                        JNE   NEXTKEY                 ;if not, try next possibility
                        MOV   BL,11111110B            ;if so, prepare to set register bit 1
                        AND   ES:[17H],BL             ;AND the status register directly
                        JMP   QUIT                    ;quit the routine
        NEXTKEY:                                      ;continue for all shift/toggle keys

;---IT'S A CHARACTER KEY - INTERPRET THE SCAN CODE:
                        TEST  AL,10000000B            ;code from releasing key?
                        JNZ   QUIT                    ;if so, quit the routine
                        MOV   BL,ES:[17H]             ;otherwise, get shift status byte
                        TEST  BL,00000011B            ;is either shift key down?
                        JZ    CONVERT_CODE            ;if not, jump ahead
                        ADD   AL,100                  ;else capital letter, add TABLE offset
        CONVERT_CODE:   MOV   BX,OFFSET TABLE         ;get ready for table exchange
                        XLAT  TABLE                   ;convert scan code to ASCII code
                        CMP   AL,0                    ;0 returned?
                        JE    QUIT                    ;if so, no entry in table - quit
;---KEY CODE READY - FIND OUT IF KEYBOARD BUFFER FULL:
                        MOV   BX,1AH                  ;offset of head ptr in BIOS data area
                        MOV   CX,ES:[BX]              ;get head pointer
                        MOV   DI,ES:[BX]+2            ;get tail pointer
                        CMP   CX,60                   ;is head pointer at top of buffer?
                        JE    HIGH_END                ;if so, jump to special case
                        INC   CX                      ;increase head pointer by 2
                        INC   CX                      ;
                        CMP   CX,DI                   ;compare it to the tail pointer
                        JE    QUIT                    ;if equal, the buffer is full-quit
                        JMP   GO_AHEAD                ;else, jump over special case
        HIGH_END:       CMP   DI,30                   ;head ptr is 60, is tail ptr 30?
                        JE    QUIT                    ;if so, the buffer is full-quit
;---BUFFER IS NOT FULL -- INSERT THE CHARACTER:
        GO_AHEAD:       MOV   ES:[DI],AL              ;place char in buffer at tail position
                        CMP   DI,60                   ;tail at top of buffer?
                        JNE   NO_WRAP                 ;if not, jump ahead
                        MOV   DI,28                   ;if so, set tail to 28+2=30
        NO_WRAP:        ADD   DI,2                    ;add 2 to get new tail position
                        MOV   ES:[BX]+2,DI            ;place new tail pointer in BIOS data
;---END THE INTERRUPT:
        QUIT:           POP   ES                      ;restore all changed registers
```

```
              POP   DI              ;
              POP   CX              ;
              POP   BX              ;
              POP   AX              ;
              MOV   AL,20H          ;signal end of hardware interrupt
              OUT   20H,AL          ;
              IRET                  ;interrupt return
NEW_KEYBOARD  ENDP
```

Section 2: Access Particular Keys

A keystroke input routine must watch for a variety of keystroke types and conditions, since both one- and two-byte codes may arrive in combination with the shift and toggle keys. Not all keys are logically grouped by the kind of code they issue. The backspace key, for example, generates a one-byte ASCII code, but the delete key makes a two-byte extended code. The Ctrl key produces one-byte codes in combination with the alphabet keys, but two-byte codes otherwise. These irregularities result from the limitations of the ASCII character set: the keyboard interrupt follows the ASCII conventions when possible, but improvises its own codes when not.

This section lists the various key groupings, gives their codes, and explains any anomalies. For the most part, the same information is less conveniently available in the tables of the ASCII codes and extended codes that are found in Section 3 of this chapter. Also discussed here are special features added by BASIC to the keys and special facilities within DOS interrupts that interpret particular keystrokes (such as the backspace).

3.2.1 Use the Backspace, Enter, Escape, and Tab keys

The enter, escape, backspace, and tab keys are the only four non-character keys that generate one-byte ASCII codes. Their codes are among the *control codes* [7.1.9] that comprise the first 32 numbers of the ASCII set. These four codes may also be produced by combinations of letter keys and Ctrl:

```
ASCII   8      backspace    CTRL + H
        9      tab          CTRL + I
       13      enter        CTRL + M
       27      escape       CTRL + [
```

Section [3.2.2] shows how to avoid a mixup between the single keystrokes and the CTRL combinations. Note that the back-tab is produced by a Shift + Tab combination, resulting in the extended code 0;15.

Some of the keyboard input interrupts automatically interpret these four special codes. In BASIC, the INPUT function responds to the backspace, tab, and enter keys. The INKEY$ function does not interpret any of the command codes, since it does not automatically echo on the screen. Your code must do the work. Remember that BASIC provides the TAB function to facilitate cursor movements. Of the BIOS and DOS interrupts, any that echo on the screen also interpret the backspace and tab in their cursor movements. After the code is so interpreted, the ASCII code still appears in AL, to be included in a data string or to be ignored, as the case may be.

3.2.2 Use the Shift Keys: Shift, Ctrl, and Alt

The three kinds of shift key cause only some of the other keys of the keyboard to generate different codes. Shift combinations generally produce *extended codes*. But in two cases they give rise to ASCII codes: (1) when the typewriter-style shift changes the input from the ordinary typewriter keys, and (2) for Ctrl-A to Ctrl-Z, resulting in ASCII codes 1-26. All other combinations result in extended codes, as listed at [3.3.5]. The PCjr has some exceptions which are discussed below.

Inadmissible key combinations produce no code at all. Except in the case of the special Ctrl-Alt combinations, simultaneous depression of the shifts results in only one being effective, with priority given to Alt, then Ctrl, and then Shift. [3.1.7] shows how to check whether a shift key is currently depressed. [3.2.3] explains how to use the Scroll Lock key (a *toggle* key), as a shift key with any key on the keyboard. Other shift key combinations are made possible only by writing a completely new keyboard interrupt that replaces the BIOS routine [3.1.9].

There is a special problem with certain Ctrl key combinations, since Ctrl + H, I, M, and [produce ASCII codes identical to those of the backspace, tab, enter, and escape keys. [3.1.8] shows how an assembly language program can check the scan code of the keystroke to find out whether it was the control key or the letter key that was pressed (the scan code is found in AH when the keystroke is received by INT 16H). Unfortunately, BASIC programs do not have this capability. In this case a program can distinguish between the two by checking the shift status register to see if the Ctrl key is down or not. When bit 2 at address 0040:0017H is set to 1, the Ctrl key is depressed. This method works only at the moment that the keystroke is made, and not if the key code is read out of the keyboard buffer some time later.

The PCjr keyboard has only 62 keys, compared to 83 on a PC or XT, or 84 on an AT. Certain shift key combinations make up for some of the missing keys (combinations using the function keys are shown at [3.2.5]):

PCjr Keystrokes	PC/XT/AT Equivalents
Alt + Fn + 0-9	0-9 (scan codes from numeric keypad)
Alt + /	\
Alt + '	`
Alt + [	!
Alt +]	~
Alt + .	* (scan code when from PrtSc key)
Shift + Del	. (scan code from numeric keypad)

The PCjr keyboard also offers the following unique shift key combinations:

Fn + Shift + Esc	toggles number keys to function keys
Ctrl + Alt + CapsLock	toggles keyboard click feature
Ctrl + Alt + Ins	runs diagnostics
Ctrl + Alt + Cursor left	shifts screen leftwards
Ctrl + Alt + Cursor right	shifts screen rightwards

3.2.3 Use the Toggle Keys: NumLock, CapsLock, Ins, and ScrollLock

With the exception of the Ins key, the toggle keys do not produce a code number that is placed in the keyboard buffer. Rather, they make changes in two status bytes in the BIOS data area at 0040:0017 and 0040:0018. The keyboard interrupt checks these settings before it assigns a code to an incoming keystroke. Your programs can access the status register and change the setting of any toggle key, as explained at [3.1.7].

Other settings in the register show whether a toggle key is currently depressed. This feature allows a program to use toggle keys as shift keys. While no new key codes are created, there are potential applications. For example, <ScrollLock> could be used to add yet another set of shift + function key combinations. A program would receive an ordinary function key code, would check whether or not <ScrollLock> is down, and then would interpret the keystroke accordingly. Note that either of the <Shift> keys reverse the setting of the NumLock key.

The <Ins> key places the code 0;82 in the keyboard buffer, to be read whenever your program chooses. The setting for <Ins> in the status bytes changes immediately, however. Even if there is no room for the <Ins> code in the buffer, the status settings are changed when the key is struck. Both <Ins> and <ScrollLock> have no effect on the other keys of the keyboard (unlike <NumLock> and <CapsLock>). You may define any role you please to them. The IBM Technical Reference Manuals state that <ScrollLock> should be used to toggle in and out of the state where the cursor keys scroll the screen rather than move the cursor.

Of course, you may create all the toggle keys your program needs by simply dedicating keys to that purpose. Although there is no ready-made status register, you can simply assign a variable to each that flags "on" by equalling -1 and "off" by equalling 0. For example, to use F10 to toggle the variable CLOCK on and off:

```
100 '''''Interpret Extended Codes (C = 2nd byte of code):
110 CLOCK=-1                    'start with status on
110 IF X <= 100 THEN NOT CLOCK  'toggles the variable CLOCK
```

3.2.4 Use the numeric keypad and cursor keys

On a PC or XT, the numeric keypad includes the number keys, the Ins and Del keys, and the + and - keys. The AT adds the "System Request" (Sys Req) key, while the PCjr has only the four cursor keys (the others may be emulated by special <shift> and <Fn> combinations, shown at [3.2.2] and [3.2.5]). <NumLock> switches between the cursor and number functions. <Ins> and <Del> operate only when <NumLock> is "on," that is, locked *on* to the numbers. The + and - keys issue the same codes no matter how <NumLock> is set.

The number keys of the numeric keypad issue exactly the same one-byte codes as the number keys at the top row of the keyboard—that is, ASCII codes 48-57 for the numerals 0-9. So do the + and - keys. Assembly language programmers can differentiate between the two key sets by checking the key scan codes, which are found in AH on return from both the INT 16H and INT 21H single-key input routines. Note that either of the typewriter shift keys shifts the keypad keys to the mode opposite that set by the NumLock key. The setting of the CapsLock key has no effect. The "5" key in the center is active only as a number key, and it produces no code number when <NumLock> is set to cursor mode.

Besides the four familiar arrows, the cursor keys include the Home, End, PgUp, and PgDn keys, which often are used to jump the cursor by whole lines or pages. All produce a two-byte extended code. These keys have no direct control over the cursor. They merely issue a code like any other key, and it is the programmer's job to convert the codes to cursor movements on the screen.

Some combinations of the keypad keys and the Ctrl key are available. <NumLock> must be set to cursor-control for these combinations to work. See [3.1.7] for how to make your program set the NumLock key automatically. Here is a summary of the relevant key codes:

ASCII codes:

43	+
45	-
46	.
48 - 57	0 - 9

Extended codes:

72, 75, 77, 80	Cursor Up, Left, Right, & Down
71, 73, 79, 81	Home, PgUp, End, PgDn
82, 83	Ins, Del
115, 116	Ctrl-cursor left, -cursor right
117, 118, 119, 132	Ctrl-end, -PgDn, -Home, -PgUp

The AT has an 84th key, **Sys Req**, which is unique in its function. The key is intended for multiuser systems as a way to enter the main system menu. When the key is pressed down, the code 8500H appears in AX, and INT 15H is executed. Upon release of the key, 8501H shows up in AX, and INT 15H is executed once again. The AT BIOS provides no code for functions 84H and 85H in INT 15H; a simple return is made. But system software can replace the interrupt vector for 15H so that it points to the Sys Req routine. Such a routine must first read AL to see if the Sys Req key has been depressed (AL = 0) or released (AL = 1). Note that INT 15H provides a number of services, some of which might be required of a program using SYS REQ. In this case, the SYS REQ routine must reestablish the interrupt vector it overlays, and if a function number different from 84H or 85H is found in AH, the routine should pass control to the usual INT 15H routine [1.2.4].

3.2.5 Use the function keys

The ten function keys issue different codes in combinations with the Shift, Ctrl and Alt keys, given 40 possible keystrokes. In all cases, the resulting code is a two-byte extended code, where the first byte is always ASCII Ø and the second byte is an arbitrary number as follows:

Code	Keystroke
59-68	F1-F1Ø (alone)
84-93	Shift + F1 - F1Ø
94-1Ø3	Ctrl + F1 - F1Ø
1Ø4-113	Alt + F1 - F1Ø

Too many shift + function key combinations can confuse a program user. But should you need one more group of ten, consider using < ScrollLock > + < Fn > combinations, as explained at [3.2.3].

The PCjr keyboard has only 62 keys, compared to 83 on a PC or XT, or 84 on an AT. Certain function key combinations make up for some of the missing keys, as follows:

PC Jr Keystrokes	PC/XT/AT Equivalents
Fn + 1-Ø	F1-F1Ø
Fn + B	Break
Fn + E	Ctrl + PrtSc
Fn + P	Shift + PrtSc
Fn + Q	Ctrl + NumLock
Fn + S	ScrollLock
Fn + Cursor left	PgUp
Fn + Cursor right	PgDn
Fn + Cursor up	Home
Fn + Cursor down	End
Fn + -	- (numeric keypad scan code)
Fn + =	+ (numeric keypad scan code)

(Combinations using the shift keys are shown at [3.2.2])

3.2.6 Reprogram individual keys

To reprogram a key means to cause it to produce a different code. But by the time programs receive keystroke codes, the keyboard interrupt has already interpreted the incoming scan code and converted it to some predefined ASCII code or extended code. Fortunately, beginning from version 2.0, DOS contains a utility for reprogramming the code assignments. This utility operates only when the keystrokes are intercepted by the DOS keyboard input functions—the INT 16H functions of BIOS continue to interpret the keystrokes normally.

The DOS utility operates by an *escape sequence*. A short string that begins with the *escape* character (ASCII 27) is "output to the standard device," that is, it is treated as if it were being sent to the video display. But owing to the escape code, no characters ever reach the monitor. Rather, the string causes DOS to thereafter reinterpret a particular key that is named in the string. Each key alteration requires its own string, and the same code may be assigned to as many keys as you like.

The general form for the strings is first the escape character (ASCII 27), then [, then the code number for the key that is to be changed, then a semicolon, then the new code number to be assigned to the key, and finally the character **p**. Thus **27,'[65;97p'** changes **A** (ASCII 65) to **a** (ASCII 97). Extended codes are written showing both bytes, with the initial zero byte followed by a semicolon. **27,'[0;68;0;83p'** gives *F10* (0;68) the same code as *Delete* (0;83). You may only assign extended codes found in the extended code table [3.3.5].

There are a number of variants on the basic string. First, character keys may be specified by typing the character itself within quotation marks. Thus **27,'["A";"a"p'** also changes **A** to **a**. Second, whole strings of codes ("macros") can be assigned to a single key by simply writing the characters or their code numbers into the expression. **27,'["A";"A is for Apple" p'** writes *A is for Apple* whenever a capital A is typed. In fact, these escape sequences are really nothing more than a single string in which the first character or code number tells which key is to be redefined, and the remainder of the string shows what is to be assigned. Remember that the code numbers must always be separated by semicolons, and characters must always be surrounded by quotation marks. Codes and characters may be freely mixed. The key-reassignment utility requires that the file **ANSI.SYS** (a device driver) be loaded when DOS is booted. Otherwise the escape sequences are ignored. Appendix E shows how.

Some aspects of keyboard functioning are programmable on a PCjr or AT. The AT procedures are mainly of interest to systems programmers; because these procedures are quite involved and are useful to very few programmers, they are not covered here. See the AT Technical Reference Manual. In the case of the PCjr, BIOS INT 16H has been given two extra functions (AH = 3 and AH = 4), the first of which sets the typematic rate. The "typematic rate" is the frequency at which a key sends its code when it is continuously held down. The second function turns the keyboard click sound on and off. For function 3, place 0 in AL to return to the default typematic rate, 1 to increase the initial delay before typematic action begins, 2 to cut the typematic rate by half, 3 to invoke features 1 and 2, and 4 to turn off the typematic feature. For function 4, place 0 in AL to turn the keyboard click off and 1 to turn it on.

High Level

Unfortunately, the **PRINT** and **WRITE** statements in BASIC do not work with escape sequences. BASIC programs must incorporate a simple assembly language subroutine that makes use of the DOS output interrupt discussed below under "Middle Level." Appendix D shows how to integrate assembly routines into BASIC programs. The example here assumes that the routine will be poked into memory starting at memory address 2000:0000. The DATA statements contain the assembly code. Add a $ sign to the end of the macro code string.

```
100 DATA &H55,&H8B,&HEC,&H8B,&H5E,&H06,&H8B,&H57
110 DATA &H01,&HB4,&H09,&HCD,&H21,&H5D,&HCA,&H02,&H00
120 'poke the routine into memory at 2000:0000
130 DEF SEG=&H2000               'point to 20000
140 FOR N=0 TO 16                'the routine is 17 bytes
150 READ Q                       'read one byte
160 POKE N,Q                     'poke it in
170 NEXT                         '
180 '''change A to a:            '
190 Q$=CHR$(27)+"[65;97p$"       'set up the string
200 ROUTINE=0                    'point to the string
210 CALL ROUTINE(Q$)             'call the routine
```

Middle Level

Use function 9 of DOS interrupt 21H to send the string to the "standard output device." DS:DX must point to the first character of the string in memory, and the string must end with the $ character (24H). Here, **F2** (0;60) is changed so that it functions as **Del** (0;83).

```
;---IN THE DATA SEGMENT:
    CHANGE_KEY    DB    27,'[0;60;0;83p$'

;---TO CHANGE THE KEY ASSIGNMENT:
            LEA    DX,CHANGE_KEY    ;point DS:DX to string
            MOV    AH,9             ;set the function number
            INT    21H              ;and now the key is reassigned
```

3.2.7 Assign keyboard macros to individual keys

A *keyboard macro* is a string of characters that originates from a single keystroke. Macros are programmed into the BASIC interpreter or into the operating system to cut down on typing. Since the string may contain *control codes*, such as the character for a carriage return (ASCII 13), a single macro can perform a chain of commands. To speed program development, for example, one might write a macro that contains all the keystrokes required to compile and link a particular program.

The keyboard macros provided by BASIC work both within BASIC programs and at BASIC's command level. For example, if you program a key to output the word "Orangutan," the INPUT function will receive the whole string when the key is pressed, and an INKEY$ loop will successively read in the nine characters. On the other hand, the DOS macro facility always works at DOS command level, but it works *within* programs only when the programs use the DOS keyboard input functions. Since much commercial software uses BIOS INT 16H, the DOS macros are of limited utility. Of course, macro-like features *within* programs are easily set up in the keystroke input routine. For example, to allow a program user to set a macro for F1, request the string and place it in MACRO1$, and then (in BASIC) write something like:

```
1000 '''Extended Code Input Routine (C = 2nd byte of code)
1010 IF C = 59 THEN LOCATE X,Y:PRINT MACRO1$
```

High Level

BASIC has its own macro facility, but it allows you to program only the 10 function keys, and the strings may be only 15 characters long. The function keys are referred to as "soft keys" in BASIC. The KEY statement assigns the macros to the keys. **KEY 5,"END"** causes function key #5 to send the word **END** to the current cursor position of the screen.

The characters that make up the strings may be written either as strings or as ASCII codes (using CHR$) or as a combination of both. **KEY 5,"A"** and **KEY 5,CHR$(65)** are equivalent. To *enter* a string - as if by the Enter key - add ASCII character 13 to the end. The FILES command, which shows the disk directory, is invoked by F1 once you enter **KEY 1,"FILES" + CHR$(13)**.

BASIC preprograms the ten function keys with common BASIC expressions. You may disable a key by assigning a *null string* to it. **KEY 1,""** causes F1 to do nothing when pressed. The first six characters of each string are automatically shown on the bottom line of the screen by the BASIC interpreter. You can turn this display on and off using **KEY ON** and **KEY OFF**. To fill the screen with the full string assignments, enter **KEY LIST**. Here are some examples:

```
KEY 1,"ERASE"             ;now F1 inputs "ERASE"
KEY 10,"LIST"+CHR$(13)    ;now F10 lists the program
KEY 7,""                  ;disables F7
KEY OFF                   ;turns off the display on line 25
KEY ON                    ;turns line 25 back on
KEY LIST                  ;lists the full strings of all 10 keys
```

To assign macros to other keys in BASIC, you must use the DOS utility described at [3.2.6].

Middle Level ————————————————————————————

Macros are created in DOS using the key-reprogramming facility described at [3.2.6]. The only difference is that the *escape sequence* assigns more than one character to a particular keystroke. The string may be comprised of characters written within quotation marks, or of code numbers, or of both in combination. Here are some examples:

```
27,'["A";"SET"p'              ;assigns SET to capital A
27,'["ASET"p'                 ;variant of above (1st char is key)
27,'[27;"dir";13p'            ;assigns dir <enter> to the escape key
27,'[0;59;copy *.* b:";13p'   ;assigns copy *.* b: <enter> to F1
27,'[0;68;0;72;0;72;0;72p'    ;makes F10 move cursor up three lines
```

3.2.8 Set up the Ctrl-Break routine

When the Ctrl-Break key combination is entered, the keyboard interrupt sets up a flag indicating that there is need for the Ctrl-Break routine to come into action. Control is given to the Ctrl-Break routine only at the time that the program uses a DOS function that is capable of sensing this flag. Normally, only the standard DOS input-output functions can detect Ctrl-Break (numbers 1 - C of INT 21H, but not 6 & 7). But by placing the line **BREAK = ON** in either the AUTOEXEC.BAT or CONFIG.SYS files used by DOS at start up, *all* DOS functions are caused to check for Ctrl-Break whenever they are called. This action slightly slows program execution.

The Ctrl-Break routine exists as a way of exiting a program at any time. When a DOS function senses the Ctrl-Break status, control is directed to the routine pointed to by interrupt vector 23H. DOS sets up the routine to terminate the program in progress. But the routine may be rewritten to any specifications you like. A programmable routine is required so that crucial adjustments can be made before terminating the program. The stack may require adjustment so that SP points to the second word from the top (first word in COM programs) prior to the final RET instruction. Interrupt vectors changed by the program may be restored, and open I/O devices may be closed. If interrupts have been disabled, they can be reenabled. All of this ensures that the computer will be ready to manage another program after the Ctrl-Break termination. Alternatively, the Ctrl-Break routine may simply contain an IRET instruction, which effectively disables the Ctrl-Break feature.

Middle Level

This example exits a program after adjusting the stack. The routine ends with RET rather than IRET, since the effect of the return is to be the same as that of the RET instruction that terminates a program normally. At the time it is used, the stack pointer (SP) must point to the second word on the stack. This assumes that the program is in .EXE form. Remember that the stack places its first word at the highest memory location within the stack segment, the second word below that one, and so on. If the stack size is 400 bytes, point SP to 396. For COM programs, set the stack pointer to the first word on the stack, or simply end the Ctrl-Break routine with INT 20H to terminate.

```
;---HERE IS THE NEW CTRL-BREAK ROUTINE:
     C_B          PROC FAR
                  MOV  AX,396        ;value of 2nd word on the stack
                  MOV  SP,AX         ;adjust stack pointer for return
                  RET                ;return to DOS
     C_B          ENDP
;---CHANGE THE INTERRUPT VECTOR:
                  PUSH DS            ;DS is destroyed
                  MOV  AX,SEG C_B    ;place segment of routine in DS
                  MOV  DS,AX         ;
                  MOV  DX,OFFSET C_B ;place offset of routine in DX
                  MOV  AH,25H        ;function to change interrupt vector
                  MOV  AL,23H        ;number of the vector
```

```
INT   21H                    ;change the vector
POP   DS                     ;restore DS
```

A program can check at any time if a "request" for the Ctrl-Break routine has been made. Place Ø in AL and call function 33 of INT 21H. On return, DL will hold 1 if the status is "on" and Ø if it is not. Placing 1 in AL at entry *sets* the status. In this case, before calling the function, place 1 or Ø in DL to turn the status "on" or "off."

3.2.9 Reprogram the PrtSc key

The PrtSc key produces an asterisk (ASCII 42) when struck alone, and it issues extended code 114 when struck in combination with <Ctrl>. But the <Shift> + <PrtSc> combination has a special status all its own. Other keystrokes cause the keyboard interrupt to deposit their codes in the keyboard buffer (or, for toggle and shift keys, to record their status [3.1.7]). A keystroke can have no impact upon the program in progress until the program gets around to reading it from the buffer. But the <Shift> + <PrtSc> combination causes the keyboard interrupt to immediately turn control over to whatever routine is pointed to by the vector for INT 5. In this way it functions like a *hardware interrupt*.

Interrupt 5 is preprogrammed to dump the contents of the screen onto a printer. But the interrupt vector can be pointed to a procedure dedicated to an entirely different use. For example, an involved simulation program that takes hours to run could be interrupted at any time by Shift + PrtSc to issue a report of preliminary results. You might also want to reprogram PrtSc so that it will send graphics screens to the printer. Another possibility is to use PrtSc as a way to access a program that is loaded and left resident when DOS is booted [1.3.4]. This strategy allows you to write a utility program that can be operated from within other software.

Low Level

Here is the basic form in which to reprogram the routine. Be sure to replace the original interrupt vector (F000:FF54) when you leave the program. Should you fail, all will seem to be well until Shift-PrtSc is pressed, and then the computer will crash (see the more complete example of interrupt programming at [1.2.3]).

```
;---CHANGE THE PRTSC INTERRUPT VECTOR
            CLI                          ;disable interrupts
            MOV   AX,SEG NEW_ROUTINE     ;get the segment of the routine
            MOV   DS,AX                  ;put the segment in DS
            MOV   DX,OFFSET NEW_ROUTINE  ;put the routine offset in DX
            MOV   AL,5                   ;choose the vector to replace
            MOV   AH,25H                 ;DOS function to replace vector
            INT   21H                    ;change the vector
            STI                          ;reenable interrupts
              .
              .
;---SET UP THE PRTSCRN ROUTINE:
    NEW_ROUTINE  PROC FAR
            STI                          ;reenable interrupts
            PUSH AX                      ;save all registers
              .                          ;
              .                          ;
            MOV   CX,100                 ;...your routine
              .                          ;
              .                          ;
            POP   AX                     ;restore all registers
            IRET                         ;perform interrupt return
    NEW_ROUTINE  ENDP
```

Section 3: Look Up Key Codes and Applications

The various key codes and character codes can become confusing. The tables that follow list them all. Watch for the following anomalies:

- The Ins key is the one key that, when struck, both issues a character code to the keyboard buffer *and* makes a change in the shift and toggle key status registers.
- There are four ASCII codes which can be produced in two ways. ASCII 8 is produced by both the backspace key and by Ctrl-H, ASCII 9 by the tab key or Ctrl-I, ASCII 13 by the enter key or Ctrl-M, and ASCII 27 by the Esc key or Ctrl-[.
- The symbols that correspond to the 32 ASCII control codes are not printed on the screen by those key input functions that automatically *echo* characters. They must be displayed by function 10H of INT 10H or by direct memory mapping (both are discussed at [4.3.1]).
- The Ctrl key combinations with the letters of the alphabet all produce one-byte (ASCII) codes. All other Ctrl combinations produce two-byte (extended) codes.
- The <5> key of the keypad is not operational when the NumLock key is set to cursor control.
- The Shift-PrtSc and Ctrl-Alt combinations (and on the AT, the SYS REQ key) are the only cases where key combinations are set up to immediately invoke special routines. Of these, only the former is reprogrammable. The Ctrl-Break interrupt (also reprogrammable) is brought about only when the the Ctrl-Break status is detected by a DOS routine.
- Any ASCII code except 0 can be entered by holding down the Alt key, typing the ASCII number on the keypad, and then letting up the Alt key. Since 0 is excepted, extended codes cannot be entered this way.

Note that there is little you can do to overcome the limitations imposed by inadmissible keystroke combinations. For example, you can not detect <Ctrl-Cursor Up> by intercepting the <Cursor Up> code and then checking the shift status register to see if <Ctrl> is down. Should <Ctrl> be down, no key code would be issued at all.

3.3.1 Assign uses to the keys

There are certain conventions in the use of the keys that should be followed by all programs. These are laid down by the Technical Reference Manual, and if programmers would always observe them, it would be easier for users to move from one program to another. Note, however, the IBM's own software does not rigidly follow these guidelines. The conventions are:

SCROLL LOCK	Toggles the cursor keys in and out of a state where they scroll the screen rather than move the cursor.
CTRL 4/6	Moves the cursor left or right by one word. Alternatively, scrolls the screen horizontally one tab-width to the left or right.
Pg Up	Scrolls backward 25 lines.
Pg Dn	Scrolls forwards 25 lines.
CTRL END	Deletes all text from the cursor to the end of the line.
CTRL PgDn	Deletes all text from the cursor to the bottom of the screen.
HOME	In text, moves cursor to the start of a line, or alternatively, to the start of the document. In menus, switches to the topmost menu.
CTRL HOME	Clears the screen and positions the cursor at top left.
END	Moves cursor to the end of the line, or alternatively, to the end of the document.
BACKSPACE/DELETE	DELETE removes the character under the cursor and moves all that follows one space left. BACKSPACE removes the character to the left of the cursor, moves the cursor to that position, and shifts leftward all that follows.
INS	Toggles in and out of a mode where text is inserted in the midst of other text.
TAB/BACKTAB	Jumps the cursor rightward when Tab alone is struck; jumps the cursor leftward when Shift + Tab.
ESC	Exits from a program or program routine.

3.3.2 Look up a scan code

Every key produces two kinds of scan codes, a *make code* when the key goes down and a *break code* when it is released. Except on the AT, the break codes are 128 higher (bit 7 = 1) than the make codes. Thus, the "T" key creates code number 20 when it is pressed down and number 148 when it is released. The AT uses the same bit pattern for make and break codes, but the break codes are two bytes long, and the first byte is always 0F0H. The PCjr has a special *phantom key scan code*, number 55. This code originates when three or more keys are struck at once, helping to avoid input errors. The keyboard interrupt throws away this code, and it has no associated ASCII code or extended code.

Typewriter Keys

Key	Make Code	Key	Make Code	Key	Make Code
"1" - 2		"T" - 20		"L" - 38	
"2" - 3		"Y" - 21		";" - 39	
"3" - 4		"U" - 22		"'''" - 40	
"4" - 5		"I" - 23		"'''" - 41	
"5" - 6		"O" - 24		"\" - 43	
"6" - 7		"P" - 25		"Z" - 44	
"7" - 8		"[" - 26		"X" - 45	
"8" - 9		"]" - 27		"C" - 46	
"9" - 10		"A" - 30		"V" - 47	
"0" - 11		"S" - 31		"B" - 48	
"-" - 12		"D" - 32		"N" - 49	
"=" - 13		"F" - 33		"M" - 50	
"Q" - 16		"G" - 34		"," - 51	
"W" - 17		"H" - 35		"." - 52	
"E" - 18		"J" - 36		"/" - 53	
"R" - 19		"K" - 37		space bar - 57	

Control Keys

Esc - 1		Ctrl - 29		Alt - 56	
Backspace - 14		left shift - 42		CapsLock - 58	
Tab - 15		right shift - 54		NumLock - 69	
Enter - 28		PrtSc - 55		ScrollLock - 70	

Function Keys

F1 - 59		F5 - 63		F9 - 67	
F2 - 60		F6 - 64		F10 - 68	
F3 - 61		F7 - 65			
F4 - 62		F8 - 66			

Keypad Keys

"7" - 71		"5" - 76		"3" - 81	
"8" - 72		"6" - 77		"0" - 82	
"9" - 73		"+" - 78		"." - 83	
"-" - 74		"1" - 79		Sys Req - 67 (AT only)	
"4" - 75		"2" - 80		Phantom key - 55 (PC Jr only)	

3.3.3 Look up an ASCII code

Code numbers 0 - 31, the *control codes*, are explained in greater detail at [7.1.9]. Note that any ASCII code from 1 to 255 can be entered from the keyboard by holding down the Alt key while typing in the code number on the numeric keypad (with NumLock properly set). When the Alt key is then released, the code is input.

symbol	decimal	hex	binary	symbol	decimal	hex	binary
(null)	0	00	00000000	0	48	30	00110000
☺	1	01	00000001	1	49	31	00110001
☻	2	02	00000010	2	50	32	00110010
♥	3	03	00000011	3	51	33	00110011
♦	4	04	00000100	4	52	34	00110100
♣	5	05	00000101	5	53	35	00110101
♠	6	06	00000110	6	54	36	00110110
•	7	07	00000111	7	55	37	00110111
◘	8	08	00001000	8	56	38	00111000
○	9	09	00001001	9	57	39	00111001
◙	10	0A	00001010	:	58	3A	00111010
♂	11	0B	00001011	;	59	3B	00111011
♀	12	0C	00001100	<	60	3C	00111100
♪	13	0D	00001101	=	61	3D	00111101
♫	14	0E	00001110	>	62	3E	00111110
☼	15	0F	00001111	?	63	3F	00111111
►	16	10	00010000	@	64	40	01000000
◄	17	11	00010001	A	65	41	01000001
↕	18	12	00010010	B	66	42	01000010
‼	19	13	00010011	C	67	43	01000011
¶	20	14	00010100	D	68	44	01000100
§	21	15	00010101	E	69	45	01000101
▬	22	16	00010110	F	70	46	01000110
↨	23	17	00010111	G	71	47	01000111
↑	24	18	00011000	H	72	48	01001000
↓	25	19	00011001	I	73	49	01001001
→	26	1A	00011010	J	74	4A	01001010
←	27	1B	00011011	K	75	4B	01001011
∟	28	1C	00011100	L	76	4C	01001100
↔	29	1D	00011101	M	77	4D	01001101
▲	30	1E	00011110	N	78	4E	01001110
▼	31	1F	00011111	O	79	4F	01001111
(space)	32	20	00100000	P	80	50	01010000
!	33	21	00100001	Q	81	51	01010001
"	34	22	00100010	R	82	52	01010010
#	35	23	00100011	S	83	53	01010011
$	36	24	00100100	T	84	54	01010100
%	37	25	00100101	U	85	55	01010101
&	38	26	00100110	V	86	56	01010110
'	39	27	00100111	W	87	57	01010111
(	40	28	00101000	X	88	58	01011000
)	41	29	00101001	Y	89	59	01011001
*	42	2A	00101010	Z	90	5A	01011010
+	43	2B	00101011	[	91	5B	01011011
,	44	2C	00101100	\	92	5C	01011100
-	45	2D	00101101	]	93	5D	01011101
.	46	2E	00101110	^	94	5E	01011110
/	47	2F	00101111	—	95	5F	01011111

symbol	decimal	hex	binary	symbol	decimal	hex	binary
`	96	60	01100000	Ö	153	99	10011001
a	97	61	01100001	Ü	154	9A	10011010
b	98	62	01100010	¢	155	9B	10011011
c	99	63	01100011	£	156	9C	10011100
d	100	64	01100100	¥	157	9D	10011101
e	101	65	01100101	Pt	158	9E	10011110
f	102	66	01100110	ƒ	159	9F	10011111
g	103	67	01100111	á	160	A0	10100000
h	104	68	01101000	í	161	A1	10100001
i	105	69	01101001	ó	162	A2	10100010
j	106	6A	01101010	ú	163	A3	10100011
k	107	6B	01101011	ñ	164	A4	10100100
l	108	6C	01101100	Ñ	165	A5	10100101
m	109	6D	01101101	ª	166	A6	10100110
n	110	6E	01101110	º	167	A7	10100111
o	111	6F	01101111	¿	168	A8	10101000
p	112	70	01110000	⌐	169	A9	10101001
q	113	71	01110001	¬	170	AA	10101010
r	114	72	01110010	½	171	AB	10101011
s	115	73	01110011	¼	172	AC	10101100
t	116	74	01110100	¡	173	AD	10101101
u	117	75	01110101	«	174	AE	10101110
v	118	76	01110110	»	175	AF	10101111
w	119	77	01110111	░	176	B0	10110000
x	120	78	01111000	▒	177	B1	10110001
y	121	79	01111001	▓	178	B2	10110010
z	122	7A	01111010	│	179	B3	10110011
{	123	7B	01111011	┤	180	B4	10110100
|	124	7C	01111100	╡	181	B5	10110101
}	125	7D	01111101	╢	182	B6	10110110
~	126	7E	01111110	╖	183	B7	10110111
⌂	127	7F	01111111	╕	184	B8	10111000
Ç	128	80	10000000	╣	185	B9	10111001
ü	129	81	10000001	║	186	BA	10111010
é	130	82	10000010	╗	187	BB	10111011
â	131	83	10000011	╝	188	BC	10111100
ä	132	84	10000100	╜	189	BD	10111101
à	133	85	10000101	╛	190	BE	10111110
å	134	86	10000110	┐	191	BF	10111111
ç	135	87	10000111	└	192	C0	11000000
ê	136	88	10001000	┴	193	C1	11000001
ë	137	89	10001001	┬	194	C2	11000010
è	138	8A	10001010	├	195	C3	11000011
ï	139	8B	10001011	─	196	C4	11000100
î	140	8C	10001100	┼	197	C5	11000101
ì	141	8D	10001101	╞	198	C6	11000110
Ä	142	8E	10001110	╟	199	C7	11000111
Å	143	8F	10001111	╚	200	C8	11001000
É	144	90	10010000	╔	201	C9	11001001
æ	145	91	10010001	╩	202	CA	11001010
Æ	146	92	10010010	╦	203	CB	11001011
ô	147	93	10010011	╠	204	CC	11001100
ö	148	94	10010100	═	205	CD	11001101
ò	149	95	10010101	╬	206	CE	11001110
û	150	96	10010110	╧	207	CF	11001111
ù	151	97	10010111	╨	208	D0	11010000
ÿ	152	98	10011000	╤	209	D1	11010001

symbol	decimal	hex	binary	symbol	decimal	hex	binary
⊤⊤	210	D2	11010010	⊖	233	E9	11101001
⊫	211	D3	11010011	Ω	234	EA	11101010
⊨	212	D4	11010100	δ	235	EB	11101011
⊨	213	D5	11010101	∞	236	EC	11101100
⊤	214	D6	11010110	Ø	237	ED	11101101
╫	215	D7	11010111	∈	238	EE	11101110
╪	216	D8	11011000	∩	239	EF	11101111
⌐	217	D9	11011001	≡	240	F0	11110000
Γ	218	DA	11011010	±	241	F1	11110001
■	219	DB	11011011	≥	242	F2	11110010
▬	220	DC	11011100	≤	243	F3	11110011
▮	221	DD	11011101	⌠	244	F4	11110100
▮	222	DE	11011110	⌡	245	F5	11110101
▬	223	DF	11011111	÷	246	F6	11110110
α	224	E0	11100000	≈	247	F7	11110111
β	225	E1	11100001	°	248	F8	11111000
Γ	226	E2	11100010	•	249	F9	11111001
π	227	E3	11100011	·	250	FA	11111010
Σ	228	E4	11100100	√	251	FB	11111011
σ	229	E5	11100101	n	252	FC	11111100
μ	230	E6	11100110	²	253	FD	11111101
τ	231	E7	11100111	■	254	FE	11111110
φ	232	E8	11101000	(blank 'FF')	255	FF	11111111

3.3.4 Look up a box-graphic code

For convenience, these diagrams summarize the ASCII code numbers of the symbols used to construct lines and boxes.

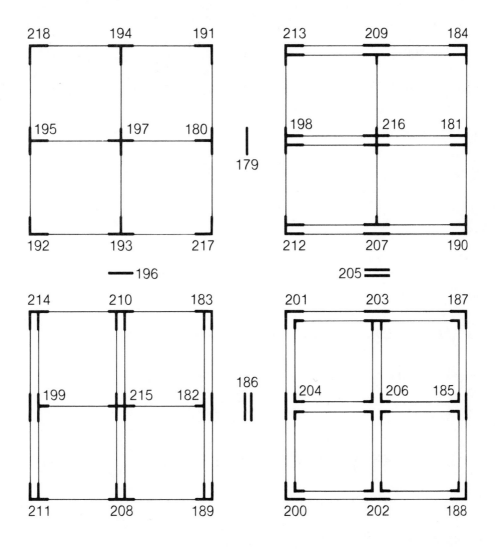

3.3.5 Look up an extended code

VALUE OF 2ND BYTE	CORRESPONDING KEYSTROKE
15	Shift + Tab ("back-tab")
16-25	Alt + Q to Alt + P (the top row of letters)
30-38	Alt + A to Alt + L (the middle row of letters)
44-50	Alt + Z to Alt + M (the bottom row of letters)
59-68	Function keys 1 to 10
71	Home
72	Cursor-up
73	PgUp
75	Cursor-left
77	Cursor-right
79	End
80	Cursor-down
81	PgDn
82	Ins
83	Del
84-93	Function keys 1 to 10 with the Shift key down
94-103	Function keys 1 to 10 with the Ctrl key down
104-113	Function keys 1 to 10 with the Alt key down
114	Ctrl + PrtSc
115	Ctrl + Cursor-left
116	Ctrl + Cursor-right
117	Ctrl + End
118	Ctrl + PgDn
119	Ctrl + Home
120-131	Alt + 1 to Alt + = (the top row of the keyboard)
132	Ctrl + PgUp

4
The Video Display

Section 1: Control the Video Display

This chapter covers the monochrome adaptor, the color graphics adaptor, the PCjr video system, and the enhanced graphics adaptor (EGA). All four video systems are centered upon the Motorola 6845 CRTC (cathode ray tube controller) chip; the EGA in fact uses a custom chip that is based on the 6845 design. The 6845 manages a number of technical tasks that are not ordinarily of concern to programmers. However, it also sets the screen mode, generates and controls the cursor, and (on the color graphics adaptor) assigns colors. The chip is easy to program directly, although operating system routines can handle most of its operations. The PCjr has an auxiliary video chip, the *video gate array*, which is discussed along with 6845 in this section. The EGA uses an architecture that is quite different from the others, and it is discussed separately. There is a general compatibility among the non-EGA systems in their use of port addresses, but there are some important differences. The EGA shares few port addresses with the other systems.

All of the video systems use buffers in which the data for the screen image are mapped. The screen is periodically updated by a scan of this data. The size and memory locations of these buffers varies by the system, by the screen mode, and by the amount of memory dedicated. When multiple screen images are held in the buffer, each image is referred to as a "page." Here is a summary:

Monochrome Adaptor The monochrome adaptor has 4K bytes of on-board memory, starting from memory address B0000H (that is, at B000:0000). This memory provides enough space for only one 80-column page of text.

Color Graphics Adaptor

The color graphics adaptor has 16K of on-board memory, starting from memory address B8000H. This is enough memory for one graphics screen, with no paging, or four to eight text screens, depending on whether they are 40 or 80 columns.

PCjr The PCjr has a video system that is essentially an advanced version of the color graphics adaptor. It is unique in using ordinary system RAM for the video buffer. When BIOS initializes the system, the top 16K of installed memory is assigned to the buffer. Thus the location of the buffer varies depending on whether the system is outfitted for 64K or 128K. Additional blocks of memory can be set aside for more video pages, or the original allocation of 16K may be whittled down to 4K to support only a single text screen.

EGA
The EGA may be equipped with 64K, 128K, or 256K of RAM. Besides serving as the video buffer, this memory also holds the data for the patterns of up to 1024 characters (as explained at [4.3.4]). The starting address of the buffer is itself programmable, so that it begins at A000H for the advanced graphics modes, and at B000H and B800H for compatability with the standard monochrome and color graphics modes. At most, the EGA occupies the two segments from A000H to BFFFH, even when 256K of RAM is present. This is possible because in some modes two or more bytes of video memory are accessed by the same memory address. The number of pages available depends both on the screen mode and on the amount of memory present. Owing to its complexity, the EGA has 16K of ROM that replaces and extends the BIOS video routines. The ROMs start at C000:0000.

In *text* modes the buffers begin with the data for the top row of the screen, starting from the left end. The succession of data wraps around from the right end of one row to the left end of the next, as if the screen were really only one very long row—and from the viewpoint of the buffer, it is nothing more. In *graphics* modes, however, the video buffer may be divided into two or four parts. On the color graphics card and the PCjr the different parts of the buffer hold data for every second or every fourth line of dots on the screen. In the EGA each part of the buffer holds one bit of the two or four bits that define the color of a pixel.

The various video systems all operate in the same way when displaying text. 4000 bytes are allocated so that there are two bytes for each of the 2000 screen positions (25 rows x 80 columns). The first byte holds an ASCII code. Video circuitry converts the ASCII code number to its associated symbol and sends it to the screen. The second byte (the *attribute byte*) holds information about how the character is to appear. On the monochrome monitor, it sets whether the character is shown underlined, intensified, in reverse-image, or as a combination of these attributes. On color systems the attribute byte sets the foreground and background colors of a character. In all cases your programs may write data directly to the buffer, a practice that speeds up screen operations considerably.

All systems but the monochrome card offer a variety of color graphics modes which vary both in resolution and in the number of colors that can be simultaneously displayed. Both the PCjr and the EGA can display up to 16 colors simultaneously, and the EGA can choose the 16 from a palette of 64. When 16 colors are used, every pixel requires four bits of memory, since four bits can hold a number from Ø-15. Similarly, four-color graphics require only two bits per pixel. Two-color graphics can pack the representation of eight pixels into a single byte in the video buffer. The amount of memory required for a particular screen mode is easily calculated by figuring out how many pixels there are and how many bits they require. Text is readily combined with graphics (BIOS *draws* the characters on to the graphics screen), and you can create your own special characters.

4.1.1   Program the 6845 video controller

All of the video systems are built around the Motorola 6845 cathode ray tube controller (the EGA uses a custom chip that is based on the 6845). The chip is used in much the same way in the monochrome card, the color card, and the PCjr; but the EGA is not as compatible, and for this reason it is advised that you avoid programming the chip directly when BIOS can do the job for you. Generally speaking, the 6845 sets up the CRT to operate in one of several alphanumeric or graphics modes. It performs the basic job of interpreting ASCII code numbers and retrieving the data for the corresponding characters from onboard ROM chips (and sometimes from RAM). It decodes the values for attributes or colors and adjusts the screen accordingly. And it creates and controls the cursor. The EGA archtecture divides some of these functions among other chips.

The 6845 has 18 control registers, numbered 0 - 17. The first ten registers fix the horizontal and vertical display parameters. These generally are of no concern to programmers, since the values in the registers are automatically adjusted by BIOS when the screen mode is changed. It is unwise to experiment with these registers since there is a possibility of damage to the monitor. The registers are eight bits long, and some are paired to hold 16-bit values. Numbers 10 & 11 and 14 & 15 set the shape [4.2.4] and location [4.2.1] of the cursor. Numbers 12 & 13 handle paging [4.5.3]. And numbers 16 & 17 report the light pen position [7.3.2]. Most of the registers are write-only; only the cursor address register is read/write, and only the light pen register is read-only. The EGA has six additional registers that are devoted to technical aspects. Number 20 is of most interest; it determines which scan line in a row of characters is used for an underscore.

The 18 registers are accessed by the same port address, which on the monochrome card is 3B5H. It is 3D5H on the color card or PCjr (Note that all port addresses of the monochrome card are the same as for the color systems, except that the middle digit is B rather than D.) The EGA uses either address, depending on whether it is connected to a monochrome or color monitor. To write to a register on the monochrome card, an address register located at port 3B4H (3D4H color) must first be sent the number of the desired register. Then the next byte sent to port address 3B5H will be directed to that particular register. Since the registers that concern programmers are used in pairs, you must first write to the address register, then to one register, then again to the address register, and then to the second register. Because the port numbers are adjacent, it is easiest to address them using INC and DEC, is in the following example:

```
;---WRITE TO 6845 REGISTERS 11 & 12 (DATA IS IN BX):
        ;---SELECT THE LOW-BYTE REGISTER:
                MOV   DX,3B4H          ;port address of the address register
                MOV   AL,11            ;select the register for the low byte
                OUT   DX,AL            ;output to 3B5H goes to #11
        ;---SEND THE BYTE:
                INC   DX               ;increase port address to 3B5H
                MOV   AL,BL            ;put low byte in AL
                OUT   DX,AL            ;put low byte in register #11
        ;---SELECT THE HIGH-BYTE REGISTER:
                DEC   DX               ;reset port address to 3B4H
```

```
        MOV   AL,12              ;select the register for the high byte
        OUT   DX,AL             ;now output to 3B5H goes to #12
;---SEND THE BYTE:
        INC   DX                ;again increase port address to 3B5H
        MOV   AL,BH             ;put high byte in AL
        OUT   DX,AL             ;now second byte is in place
```

On the monochrome and color adaptor there are three other ports that are of importance to programmers. They are numbered 3B8H, 3B9H, and 3BAH on the monochrome adaptor, and 3D8H, 3D9H, and 3DAH on the color adaptor. The first sets the screen mode, the second is primarily concerned with setting screen colors, and the third reports useful information about the display's status.

The PCjr does not use all of these port addresses in the same way. Rather, it keeps some of the information they access in a *video gate array* chip, which was added primarily to give extra control over screen colors. The video gate array is accessed via port address 3DAH. On the color card this port returns a status byte; on the PCjr the port also returns a status byte when IN (or INP) is used, but it accesses the gate array when OUT is used. The registers of the video gate array are as follows:

number	purpose
0	mode control 1
1	palette mask
2	border color
3	mode control 2
4	reset
10H-1FH	palette color assignments

All registers are reached through port 3DAH. First send to the port the number of the register to be accessed, and then send the value for the register. The port toggles back and forth between these address and data functions. *Read* the port to reset it so that it awaits an address. The registers are discussed under the various headings in this chapter.

Of particular interest are the 16 *palette registers* from 10H-1FH. Each register is only four bits long, allowing just enough space to hold the 16 code numbers used by the 16 possible colors. For every character position or dot position on the screen the video buffer contains data that specifies in which color the character is to be displayed. This information is referred to as *attribute data*. Unlike on the color graphics card, the PCjr does not use the attribute data to directly determine the color actually displayed. Rather, the attribute data is regarded as pointing at one of the 16 palette registers, and the number held in that register is the color in which the character is written. Using this technique, a program needs only to change the setting of a palette register, and all characters or dots of corresponding attribute change color. The palette registers work in all screen modes, both for text and for graphics.

The EGA divides these functions between an *attribute controller* chip (located at port 3C0) and two *graphics controller* chips (at 3CC—3CF). The attribute controller holds the EGA's sixteen palette registers, numbered 00-0F. These registers may hold six-bit color codes when the EGA is connected to an Enhanced Color Display, so that any sixteen colors can be used out of a palette of sixty-four. [4.4.1] shows how to program the PCjr and EGA palette registers.

4.1.2 Set/check the screen display mode

The monochrome card supports one screen mode, the color card supports seven, the PCjr supports ten, and the EGA supports twelve. The PCjr system is more versatile than the monochrome or color adaptors, since it offers a wider choice of colors in the two- and four-color modes, and it allows gray-shades in black and white modes. The EGA is far more sophisticated still, supporting a palette of 64 colors, graphics on the monochrome display, and 43-line displays. Here are the various modes:

Number	Mode	Adaptors
Ø	40x25 (320x200) B&W alphanumeric	color, PCjr, EGA
1	40x25 (320x200) color alphanumeric	color, PCjr, EGA
2	80x25 (640x200) B&W alphanumeric	color, PCjr, EGA
3	80x25 (640x200) color alphanumeric	color, PCjr, EGA
4	320x200 4-color graphics	color, PCjr, EGA
5	320x200 B&W graphics (4 gray shades on PCjr)	color, PCjr, EGA
6	640x200 B&W graphics	color, PCjr, EGA
7	80x25 (720x350) B&W alphanumeric	monochrome, EGA
8	160x200 16-color graphics	PCjr
9	320x200 16-color graphics	PCjr
A	640x200 4-color graphics	PCjr
B	reserved by the EGA	---
C	reserved by the EGA	---
D	320x200 16-color graphics (EGA only)	EGA
E	640x200 16-color graphics (EGA only)	EGA
F	640x350 4-color graphics on monochrome display	EGA
10	640x350 4- or 16-color graphics	EGA

The EGA allows eight pages in mode 7, the standard monochrome text mode. Modes 0-6 are fully compatible, using memory in the same way. Providing the configuration switches on the EGA are set for operation with the IBM Enhanced Color Display, the "traditional" text modes are shown in high resolution color, using 8x14 pixel characters, rather than the usual 8x8.

BIOS keeps a one-byte variable at 0040:0049 that holds the current mode number. The byte at 0040:004A gives the number of columns in text modes.

High Level ━━━━━━━━━━━━━━━━━━━━━━━━━━━━

BASIC uses the SCREEN and WIDTH statements to control the screen mode. The PCjr uses these statements somewhat differently from the monochrome and color cards, and it is discussed separately below. SCREEN alone will set the mode for the color adaptor. Follow it first with a code number for the resolution, where:

0	text mode
1	medium resolution graphics mode
2	high resolution graphics mode

SCREEN 1 sets the screen to medium resolution. A second parameter turns color on and off. It is irrelevant for high resolution on the color card, since only B&W is allowed. For text screens, 0 as the second parameter turns color off, and 1 turns it back on. **SCREEN 0,0** makes for a B&W text screen. The opposite applies to graphics screens: 0 turns color on and 1 turns it off. **SCREEN 1,1** creates B&W medium resolution graphics.

All modes are initially shown in black and white. A COLOR statement (see [4.1.3]) must be used to fill the screen in a background color. In graphics modes, the color statement alone suffices to change the whole background to the specified color. But for text screens in color you must follow the COLOR statement with CLS.

Text screens can have 40 or 80 columns. Use the WIDTH statement to set the number of columns. **WIDTH 40** gives 40 columns, and **WIDTH 80** gives 80. No other values are accepted. When the WIDTH statement is used with screens set to graphics modes (**SCREEN 1** or **SCREEN 2**), **WIDTH 40** forces the screen into medium resolution mode, and **WIDTH 80** forces it into high resolution mode. Here are some examples:

```
100 SCREEN 0,1:WIDTH 40      'makes a 40-column color text screen
           ..or..
100 SCREEN 0,0:WIDTH 80      'makes a color display act like monochrome
           ..or..
100 SCREEN 1,0              'setting for medium resolution color graphics
    .
    .
    .
500 WIDTH 80               'changes screen to high resolution graphics
```

The monochrome monitor can be forced into 40-column mode by writing **SCREEN 0:WIDTH 40**. To restore 80-column mode, write **WIDTH 80**. The characters retain their usual width in 40-column mode, so only the left half of the screen is used. Lines wrap around from the 40th column, and the cursor can not be placed on the right half of the screen using LOCATE. CLS clears only the left half of the screen. It is a rare application that would use this feature, but it does allow a program to take input (say, via INPUT statements) while confining the user's typing to the left side of the screen, keeping the right half open for some kind of on-going feedback. Any writing on the right half of the screen would require direct memory mapping, as explained at [4.3.1].

The PCjr uses seven mode numbers in BASIC:

Number	Mode
0	text mode--WIDTH may be 40 or 80 (80 only on 128K machines)
1	4-color medium resolution graphics
2	2-color high resolution graphics
3	16-color low resolution graphics
4	4-color medium resolution
5	16-color medium resolution (only on 128K machines)
6	4-color high resolution (only on 128K machines)

The last four modes require the BASIC cartridge. The page size tells how much memory is required per screen ([4.5.3] discusses paging). A program must allocate adequate memory before it sets a mode. This is done with CLEAR. CLEAR is followed by three numbers that allocate memory, the third of which sets up the video buffer (the first two parameters are discussed at [1.3.1]). For example, the 16K default size for the screen buffer is given by **CLEAR,,16384**. Unfortunately, the size of the video buffer is given in bytes, and the actual size of the buffer is not a round value like 4000 or 32000, but rather 4096 or 32768. Keep in mind that $2K = 2^{11}$, $4K = 2^{12}$, $16K = 2^{14}$, and $32K = 2^{15}$. For three pages of 16K, write **CLEAR,,3*2^14**. This statement should be made at the very beginning of the program, since all variables are cleared when the CLEAR statement is used. Note that when multiple pages are created, page 0 starts at the lowest memory address.

At this writing BASIC does not support the advanced EGA screen modes. [4.4.3] provides a machine language subroutine that lets you set the mode.

Middle Level

Function 0 of INT 10H sets the screen mode. AL holds a mode number from 0 to A. To set the screen for medium resolution color graphics:

```
MOV   AH,0            ;function number
MOV   AL,4            ;mode number for medium resolution color
INT   10H            ;set the mode
```

To *find out* the current graphics mode, use function F of INT 10H. The interrupt returns the mode number in AL. It also gives the current page number in BH, and the number of character columns in AH.

```
MOV   AH,0FH         ;function number
INT   10H            ;get the screen mode information
MOV   MODE_NUMBER,AL ;mode number in AL
MOV   NUMBER_COLS,AH ;number of columns in AH
MOV   CURRENT_PAGE,BH ;current page number in BH
```

DOS also provides *escape sequences* for setting and resetting the screen mode. These require that you load the device driver ANSI.SYS, as explained in Appendix E. The code string is in the form **ESC [= #h**, where # is a mode number given as an ASCII character, and ESC stands for the single ASCII escape character, number 27. For example:

```
;---IN THE DATA SEGMENT:
  MED_RES_COLOR  DB    27,'[=4h$'
  MED_RES_B&W    DB    27,'[=5h$'

;---SET THE SCREEN MODE TO MEDIUM RESOLUTION COLOR GRAPHICS:
                 MOV  AH,9             ;use DOS string-write function
                 LEA  DX,MED_RES_COLOR ;DS:DX points to escape string
                 INT  21H              ;the mode changes
```

Low Level

The color adaptor, monochrome adaptor, and PCjr are discussed separately here, since they vary considerably. The color graphics adaptor has a register that sets the screen mode. It is located at port address 3D8H. Bits 0, 1, 2, and 4 hold the setting. Bit 0 sets the screen to 40 columns when 0, and 80 columns when 1. Bit 1 turns the screen to alphanumeric mode when 0, and to graphics mode when 1. Bit 2 sets the screen to color when 0, and to B&W when 1. And bit 4 sets a graphics screen to medium resolution when 0, and to high resolution when 1 (bit 2 must equal 1). The combinations are:

```
              MODE              bit: 5 4 3 2 1 0
 0. 40x25 B&W Text                   1 0 1 1 0 0
 1. 40x25 Color Text                 1 0 1 0 0 0
 2. 80x25 B&W Text                   1 0 1 1 0 1
 3. 80x25 Color Text                 1 0 1 0 0 1
 4. 320x200 B&W Graphics             0 0 1 1 1 0
 5. 320x200 Color Graphics           0 0 1 0 1 0
 6. 640x200 B&W Graphics             0 1 1 1 1 0
                                     | | | | | |
                                     | | | | | select 80x25 alpha
                                     | | | | select 320x200 graphics
                                     | | | select B&W
                                     | | enable video
                                     | select 640x200 graphics (B&W)
                                     enable blinking
```

Changing these bits does *not* result in a screen mode change. There are many other steps required, including resetting the parameters of the first ten registers at address 3D5H. BIOS efficiently takes care of all this, and there is no sense in doing it from scratch. However, there may be occasion to reinitialize the mode register *in its current mode*, changing bits 3 or 5, which are not really part of the mode setting. When bit 5 is set to 0, it disables the blinking-character attribute; in this case, when the high bit of a character's attribute byte is set to 1, it instead changes the background color to high intensity (see the example at [4.1.3]). Bit 3 of the register controls "video enable." When it is set to 0, the entire screen is forced to border color, but the video buffer is not cleared. The display returns instantly when the bit is changed back to 1. This feature is useful for avoiding screen interference during scrolling [4.5.1]. Some utility programs use it to save wear and tear on the screen phosphors when the computer is turned on but not in use. Note that the two high bits of the register are unused.

The monochrome adaptor has a matching port address at 3B8H. Only three bits are significant. Bit 0 sets the screen to high resolution, which is the only mode the monochrome display is allowed. If this bit is set to 0, the computer crashes. The other two significant bits are numbers 3 and 5, which control "video enable" and blinking, exactly as they do in the color adaptor.

The PCjr divides the information kept at a single port address on the monochrome and color cards. The video gate array has two mode registers, numbers 0 and 3. To access these registers, first send the register number to port address 3DAH, and then write the data to the same address (*reading* this address assures that the first access will be interpreted as an address number). Here are the bit patterns:

```
Register 0:
     bit 0    1=80X25 alpha, and modes 5 and 6, else 0
         1    1=graphics mode, 0=alpha
         2    1=color disabled, 0=color enabled
         3    1=video signal enabled, 0=disabled
         4    1=16-color mode, 0=all other modes

Register 3:
     bit 0    always 0
         1    1=enable blink, 0=16 alpha background colors
         2    always 0
         3    1=2-color graphics, 0=all other modes
```

Like the two adaptor cards, these registers should not be set directly by your programs, since a good deal of other programming is required on the 6845 chip. But each register contains a bit that programs sometimes need to modify, and since the registers are write-only, the entire bit pattern must be understood. These bits are the *video enable* bit in register 0 and the *blink enable* bit in register 3. They function exactly as described above, and their applications are discussed elsewhere in this chapter (at [4.5.1] and [4.1.3]).

The EGA has two registers that control the screen mode. One is at port address 3D5H. This register does not contain bits related to any other purpose, and so there is never reason to access it. The second is at 3C0H, and it contains a bit that chooses whether bit 7 of video text data selects blinking or high intensity. This feature is discussed at [4.1.3].

4.1.3 Set character attributes/colors

When the display is set to alphanumeric mode on any of the video systems, two bytes of memory are given to each row and column position on the screen. The first byte holds the ASCII code number for the character, and the second byte holds the attribute for the character. The color card and PCjr can display in color both a character and the box in which is resides (the background color). The monochrome card is limited to black & white, but it can generate underlined characters, which the color card and PCjr can not. All three video systems can create blinking and reversed image characters. And all three can create high-intensity characters, although on the color card and PCjr the higher intensity characters are regarded as having a different color (the eight basic colors each have high intensity versions, making 16 colors in all). The EGA can do anything that the other systems can, and more. In particular, in enhanced mode it can underline color characters, since the 8x14 character box provides a scan line for this purpose.

Color Attributes:

The same code numbers are used for the screen colors in BASIC and the operating system interrupts. They are:

0.	black	8.	gray
1.	blue	9.	light blue
2.	green	10.	light green
3.	cyan	11.	light cyan
4.	red	12.	light red
5.	magenta	13.	light magenta
6.	brown	14.	yellow
7.	white	15.	bright white

The lowest four bits of an attribute byte set the color of the character itself (bit 3 turns on high intensity). The next three bits set the character's background. And, under normal circumstances, the top bit turns blinking on and off. Thus:

When bit 0 = 1, blue is included in the foreground color
1 = 1, green is included in the foreground color
2 = 1, red is included in the foreground color
3 = 1, the character is displayed in high intensity
4 = 1, blue is included in the background color
5 = 1, green is included in the background color
6 = 1, red is included in the background color
7 = 1, the character blinks

Bits 0-2 and 4-6 hold the same color components for the characters and their backgrounds. These three-bit groups allow eight possible combinations. When the high-intensity bit is on, eight more colors are allowed. The sixteen color codes are derived from these bit patterns, as follows:

Red	Green	Blue	Low Intensity Color	High Intensity Color
0	0	0	black	gray
0	0	1	blue	light blue
0	1	0	green	light green
0	1	1	cyan	light cyan
1	0	0	red	light red
1	0	1	magenta	light magenta
1	1	0	brown	yellow
1	1	1	white	bright white

It is possible to have 16 background colors as well. In this case, bit 7 must act as a high-intensity bit for background, rather than as a blink bit. On the color card, change bit 5 at port address 3D8H to 0, as shown below. Since the port is write-only, all other bits must be reset at the same time. This feature is relevant in only two cases: 80- and 40-column text modes. For 80 column text, send 9 to the port. For 40 column text, send 8. To switch back to blinking, add 32 to either of these values. On the PCjr, set bit 1 to 0 in register 3 of the video gate array. All other bits are 0, except for number 3, which is set to 1 when in a two-color graphics mode. Except in these modes, set the blink bit by first reading port address 3DAH, which readies the video gate array, then send 3 to 3DAH to specify the register, and then 0 to 3DAH to set the bit. Always reenable the blink bit before terminating the program, since other programs may rely upon it.

The EGA also can enable/disable the blink bit, although in this case the port address is 3C0H. First *read* port 3DAH to access the address register at 3C0H. Then send 10H to 3C0H to index the proper register. Finally, write the data to the same address. The register is write-only, so all bits must be set. Blinking is turned on by setting bit 3 and turned off by changing it back to 0. All other bits will be 0 when in a color alphanumeric mode.

On the color card, when characters are written in a color graphics mode they are drawn against the current background color. The statements that write on the screen in BASIC and DOS (INT 21H) both limit themselves to writing characters in the third color of the palette in use (there are two palettes of three colors—see [4.4.1]). In palette 0 the characters are yellow/brown, and in palette 1 they are white. The BIOS character-display routines (INT 10H), however, can specify any of the three colors of a palette. On the PCjr, on the other hand, the color assigned to a particular position in the palette may be changed, and so any colors may be chosen for the characters.

On the PCjr the colors displayed by these code numbers may be changed. Each code number is associated with a palette register in the video gate array [4.1.1]. These registers are numbered from 10H to 1FH, corresponding to codes 0-15. Each four-bit register holds a number from 0-15 that represents the actual color that is displayed when a program statement uses one of the color code numbers. For example, if a line in a program states that a character is to be drawn in code number 0, then whatever color code is held in *palette register 0* determines the actual displayed color. The register is initialized to 0000, so that black will be displayed. But the contents of the register may be changed to, say, 0001, in which case the use of code number 0 results in blue characters. The code numbers used for the palette registers are exactly the same as those used for program statements. Figure 4-1 shows the palette registers as they are initially set, except that the code for green has been changed to display magenta.

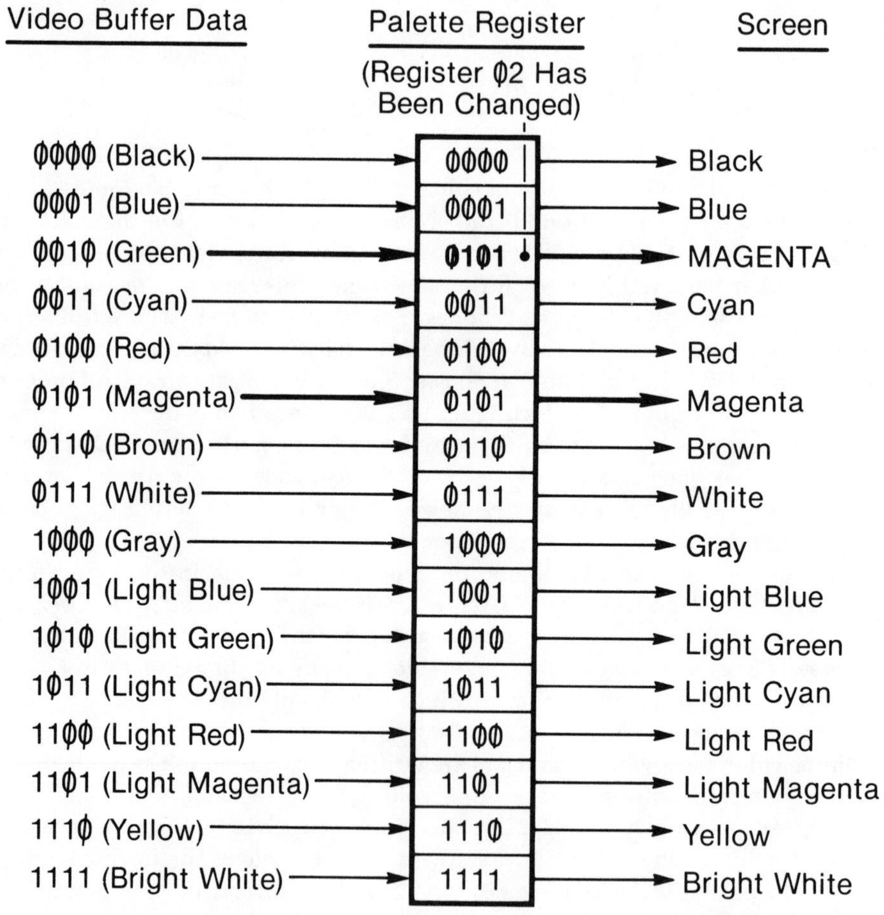

Video Buffer Data	Palette Register (Register 02 Has Been Changed)	Screen
0000 (Black) →	0000	→ Black
0001 (Blue) →	0001	→ Blue
0010 (Green) →	**0101**	→ MAGENTA
0011 (Cyan) →	0011	→ Cyan
0100 (Red) →	0100	→ Red
0101 (Magenta) →	0101	→ Magenta
0110 (Brown) →	0110	→ Brown
0111 (White) →	0111	→ White
1000 (Gray) →	1000	→ Gray
1001 (Light Blue) →	1001	→ Light Blue
1010 (Light Green) →	1010	→ Light Green
1011 (Light Cyan) →	1011	→ Light Cyan
1100 (Light Red) →	1100	→ Light Red
1101 (Light Magenta) →	1101	→ Light Magenta
1110 (Yellow) →	1110	→ Yellow
1111 (Bright White) →	1111	→ Bright White

Figure 4-1. Displaying "green" as magenta.

To program a PCjr palette register, you must first send its number (10H to 1FH) to the video gate array located at port address 3DAH. Then send the data to the same address. To be sure that the array is ready to receive a register number rather than data, first *read* from 3DAH, throwing away the result.

150

The EGA also uses sixteen palette registers. They are located at port address 3C0H, and the palette numbers range from 00-0FH. First *read* port 3DAH to toggle the port to its address register, then send the palette register number to 3C0H, and then the data. When the dip switches on the EGA card are set to enhanced mode (for the IBM Enhanced Color Display), the palette may be selected from 64 colors. In this case, the palette register settings are six bytes long, in the format **R'G'B'RGB**. The RGB bits produce dark colors, and the R'G'B' bits produce brighter ones. When both R and R' are set, for example, a very bright red results. Bits are mixed to produce new hues. Should the palette registers be set up for 64 colors when the EGA is not in enhanced mode, bits 4 & 5 of the registers are ignored, and their contents are treated as an ordinary IRGB pattern. Because the PCjr and EGA use palette registers, the choice of background colors is not limited by using bit 7 of an attribute byte as a blink bit.

Monochrome Characters:

Monochrome characters are slightly more idiosyncratic in their use of the attribute bytes. As with color attributes, bits 0-2 set the foreground color, and bits 4-6 set the background color. These "colors" may only be white or black, of course, and they result from the following bit patterns:

Bit 6 or 2	Bit 5 or 1	Bit 4 or 0	Foreground Attribute	Background Attribute
0	0	0	black	black
0	0	1	underlined white	white
0	1	0	white	white
0	1	1	white	white
1	0	0	white	white
1	0	1	white	white
1	1	0	white	white
1	1	1	white	white

Normal mode is white on black, so bits 0-2 are set to 111 and bits 4-6 are set to 000. Reverse image is created by reversing these assignments. The characters are given high intensity by setting bit 3 to 1; there is no way to give high intensity to the background when a character is displayed in reverse image, nor is underlining allowed in reverse image. In all cases, setting bit 7 to 1 sets the character blinking. All in all there are ten possible combinations that create visible characters. Most of the combinations can be obtained from a variety of bit settings. Here is one setting for each attribute:

Attribute	Bit Pattern	Hex	Decimal
normal	00000111	7	7
intense	00001111	F	15
normal underlined	00000001	1	1
intense underlined	00001001	9	9
reverse image	01110000	70	112
blinking normal	10000111	87	135
blinking intense	10001111	8F	143
blinking normal underlined	10000001	81	129
blinking intense underlined	10001001	89	137
blinking reverse image	11110000	F0	240

Note that there is no underlining in reverse image. This limitation does not apply to the EGA. Use the same bit patterns as for the monochrome card, but program palette registers 0 and 1 to change black to white and white to black.

High Level

BASIC sets the color or attribute of characters by the COLOR statement. All PRINT or WRITE statements that follow a particular COLOR statement are executed with the specifications of that statement. The background color is changed only for the characters subsequently written, not the whole screen. A new COLOR statement has no effect on what has already been written.

Except on the monochrome card, **COLOR 3,4** sets a character's foreground color to #3 (cyan) and its background color to #4 (red). The foreground color codes range from 0-31; numbers 0-15 correspond to the colors listed in the table above, and numbers 16-31 result from adding 16 to any of these values, which results in the same color but causes the character to blink. (In blinking, the foreground alternates between background color and foreground color while the background itself remains unchanged.)

PRINT and WRITE are also able to write characters on *graphics* screens. The color of the characters is always the third color of the current palette, that is, yellow/brown in palette 0, or white in palette 1.

Note that when you start out in color text modes, the screen is in black and white. To set the entire screen to a background color, write a COLOR statement like **COLOR,2** for green background, and then clear the screen using CLS. Whenever you clear the screen during a program, be sure that the most recent COLOR statement has set the current background color to the one with which you want the whole screen filled.

Monochrome attributes are set in much the same way. 0 represents black, and any of the numbers from 1 to 7 represent white. Thus, **COLOR 0,7** makes for black on white ("reverse image"), while **COLOR 7,0** results in white on black (the standard attribute). There is one exception: 1, as a foreground color, gives an underlined character. Adding 8 to any of the foreground values leads to an intensified image.

Adding 16 to any of the values from 0 to 15 causes the character to blink. Thus 7 + 8 + 16 = 31 gives a blinking, intense, white foreground. Background values range only from 0-7.

When you use direct memory mapping [4.3.1], the COLOR statement has no effect. Instead, you must figure out a bit pattern from the tables above, and POKE it directly into each character's attribute byte. Remember that attribute bytes are always at odd-numbered positions in the video buffer. Memory mapping lets you use 16 background colors in BASIC (providing you don't need blinking characters). On the graphics card, write **OUT &H3D8,8** to cause the high bit of each attribute to act as a high-intensity bit for background colors. The following example prints at the center of the screen a dark red '!' over a light red background.

```
100 DEF SEG=&HB800    'point to graphics card buffer
110 OUT &H3D8,8       'use 16 background colors
120 POKE 1000,33      'print '!' at mid-screen
130 POKE 1001,196     'red on light red (11000100)
```

As explained above, the PCjr keeps the blink bit in the video gate array. Here is the same program set up for the PCjr (it is not valid for two-color graphics):

```
100 DEF SEG=&HB800    'point to graphics card buffer
110 X=INP(&H3AH)      'make dummy read to ready gate array
120 OUT &H3AH,3       'request access to register 3
130 OUT &H3AH,0       'turn off all bits in the register
140 POKE 1000,33      'print '!' at mid-screen
150 POKE 1001,196     'red on light red (11000100)
```

Here is an example of changing the color assignment of a palette register. The color code that normally displays blue (0001) is made to be displayed in magenta (0101). The video gate array register number for the register corresponding to color code 1 is 11H.

```
100 X=INP(&H3AH)      'make dummy read to ready gate array
110 OUT &H3AH,&H11    'request register 11H (color code 1)
120 OUT &H3AH,5       'put magenta code in register (0101=5)
```

Middle Level

The BIOS and DOS interrupts are poorly equipped to handle color text. Only function 9 of INT 10H takes an attribute byte when it writes a character. Function A of INT 10H writes single characters without specifying a color or attribute; it simply places the character in the video buffer without touching the adjoining attribute byte, so that the current attribute remains. Function D of INT 10H, the "teletype" routine, also leaves the current attribute bytes alone. All of these functions are discussed at [4.3.1].

The DOS routines of INT 21H that write on the screen *always* write in white on black. Even if the entire screen has been initialized to a particular background color, the DOS routines change the background attribute to black (or "normal") at each character it writes. There is a way around this limitation, however. DOS provides a device driver named ANSI.SYS that can interpret special escape sequences. See Appendix E for background about how to use this feature. The escape sequences are "output" via function 9 of INT 21H, which ordinarily writes strings on the screen. The string in this case consists of the escape character followed by [, and then one or more code numbers from the list that follows. The string ends with the letter **m**, plus the usual terminating **$**. Here are the codes:

0	all attributes OFF (white on black)
1	high intensity ON
4	underscore ON (monochrome display only)
5	blink ON
7	reverse video ON
8	cancelled ON (makes characters invisible)

30	black foreground	40	black background
31	red "	41	red "
32	green "	42	green "
33	yellow "	43	yellow "
34	blue "	44	blue "
35	magenta "	45	magenta "
36	cyan "	46	cyan "
37	white "	47	white "

Note that when DOS routines write characters in graphics modes they ordinarily are confined to code 3 of the current palette. The escape sequences above can set a character's color to any of the palette codes. Use 30 or 31 for background, 32 or 33 for code 1, 34 or 35 for code 2, and 36 or 37 for code 3. In this case, do not specify a background color.

The following example writes two strings on a color display using function 9 of INT 21H. The first is drawn in blue on red, and the second in blinking cyan on red. There is no need to redeclare red as the background color in the second string because the color assignments affect all following write commands (including the BIOS functions of INT 10H) until another assignment is made. Note how easy it is to intersperse the color commands with the strings themselves.

```
;---IN THE DATA SEGMENT:
    STRING_1      DB    'The rain in Spain',0AH,0DH,'$'
    STRING_2      DB    'Falls mainly on the plain$'
    BLUE_RED      DB    27,'[34;41m$'
    BLINK_CYAN    DB    27,'[5;36m$'

;---WRITE THE STRINGS
              MOV   AH,9              ;string-write function
              LEA   DX,BLUE_RED       ;point DX to escape sequence
              INT   21H               ;from now on, all chars blue on red
              LEA   DX,STRING_1       ;point to first string
              INT   21H               ;print the string (+ LF and CR)
              LEA   DX,BLINK_CYAN     ;point to second escape sequence
              INT   21H               ;change foreground to blinking cyan
              LEA   DX,STRING_2       ;point to second string
              INT   21H               ;write the string
```

You should always take care to reset the DOS color attributes to normal at the end of a program, since they can otherwise prevail during programs that follow. Write a final escape sequence that uses code number 0, as listed above.

The PCjr and EGA have a special BIOS function to set the contents of the palette registers. This is subfunction 0 of function 10H of INT 10H. Place the number of the palette register (from 0-15) in BL and the value of the color code (also 0-15) in BH, then execute the interrupt. Subfunction 2 of function 10H sets all palette registers and the border color as well by using a 17-byte array pointed to by ES:DX. Bytes 0-15 of the array are placed in palette registers 0-15, and the 16th byte sets the border color. See [4.1.4] to set the border color alone.

Low Level

As explained above under "High Level", simply memory-map a desired attribute byte after its character. This example is for the color card or PCjr. It sets the screen up as a 25x80 text screen with 16 background colors, then initializes the screen to red on light blue:

```
;---GET SET FOR 16 BACKGROUND COLORS IN 80x25 TEXT MODE:
                MOV   AL,00001001B        ;set blink bit to 0 in color select reg
                MOV   DX,3D8H             ;address of the register
                OUT   DX,AL              ;set the bit
;---INITIALIZE THE ENTIRE SCREEN TO RED ON LIGHT BLUE:
                MOV   AX,0B800H           ;point to graphics video buffer
                MOV   ES,AX              ;
                MOV   CX,2000            ;write attribute at 2000 places
                MOV   BX,1               ;BX points to the attribute bytes
                MOV   AL,10010100B        ;the attribute byte
NEXT_CHAR:      MOV   ES:[BX],AL          ;move the byte to a buffer position
                INC   BX                 ;increment the attribute pointer
                INC   BX                 ;
                LOOP  NEXT_CHAR           ;do the next position
```

4.1.4 Set the screen border color

The border of a character screen may have a different color from the central background color. Any of the 16 colors may be used. Graphics screens, on the other hand, do not technically have a border area. When the background color is set in graphics mode, the whole screen including the border area is set to that color. Operations that write dots on the screen do not access the border area, however; if most addressable pixels are changed to a non-background color, then a border region is effectively created.

High Level

The third parameter of BASIC's COLOR statement sets the border color. The same color code numbers are used that are listed at [4.1.3]. For example, to set the border to light blue, write **COLOR,,8**. The PCjr additionally can change the color by altering the setting in the palette register that corresponds to the color code specified for the border color. See [4.1.3] for a full explanation.

Middle Level

On all video systems, the background color may be set by function BH of INT 10H. This function also sets foreground colors. Place 0 in BH to specify that it is the background color that is to be changed, put the color code in BL, and execute the interrupt. In addition, both the PCjr and the EGA have a dedicated function to set background color. This is subfunction 1 of function 10H of INT 10H. Place 10H in AH, 1 in AL, and the color code in BH. There are no return registers.

Low Level

On the color graphics adaptor, bits 0-3 of port 3D9H (the "Color Select Register") set the border color when the screen is in a text mode. As usual, the ascending order of the bits is *blue, green, red*, and *high intensity*. Because it is a write-only address, the other significant bit in this register must also be set at the same time. This is Bit 4, which when set to 1 causes all background colors to be displayed in high intensity.

```
;---SET THE BORDER COLOR TO LIGHT BLUE:
            MOV   AL,00001001B      ;bit pattern for light blue
            MOV   DX,3D9H           ;address of color select register
            OUT   DX,AL             ;set the border color
```

In the PCjr, the *video gate array* [4.1.1] contains a register that sets the border color. The register is only four-bits wide, where bits 0-3 correspond to blue, green, red, and high intensity when they are set to 1. For light blue, send the bit pattern **1001** to the register. The border color register is number 2 in the video gate array. The register is accessed by first sending 2 to port address 3DAH to request access to the register. Then send the data to the same address. To be sure that the chip is ready to receive a register number rather than data, first *read* port 3DAH. The following example sets the border color to red (bit 2 is turned on).

```
MOV DX,3DAH      ;address of video gate array chip
IN  AL,DX        ;dummy read to ready the chip
MOV AL,2         ;register number
OUT DX,AL        ;send the request
MOV AL,4         ;turn on only bit 2
OUT DX,AL        ;set the border color
```

The border color on the EGA is set by the *overscan register*. This register is number 11H at port address 3C0H. First *read* port 3DAH to toggle the port to its address register, then send 11H to 3C0H as an index, and then send the data. Only the low four bits of the data are significant, unless the EGA is running the IBM Enhanced Color Display, in which case the low six bits set the border color.

4.1.5 Clear all/part of the screen

Clearing the screen can be a matter of merely placing a space character (ASCII 32) at each cursor location of the screen. However, if "non-normal" attributes have been used while writing on the screen, then the attribute bytes of each character must also be reinitialized. The operating system provides an easy way to clear only a part of the screen.

High Level

BASIC provides the **CLS** statement to clear the whole screen. Line 25 will clear only if the function key list at the bottom of the screen has been erased using **KEY OFF**. The attribute bytes are set to ASCII 7. [4.5.1] provides a scrolling routine that can be used by BASIC to clear *windows* on the screen.

Middle Level

The operating system offers several ways to clear the screen. Which you choose may depend on whether the means are already required by the program for some other purpose. The first method is simply to reset the screen mode, using function Ø of INT 10H [4.1.2]. For character screens each box is filled with a space (ASCII 32), and the attribute is "normal" (ASCII 7). Ordinarily this method is a good idea only at the beginning of a program when the screen mode needs setting in any case. On the color graphics adaptor and PCjr, screen mode reinitialization makes the screen flash and bounce. There is no such interference on the monochrome monitor or on the EGA.

```
;---CLEAR SCREEN BY REINITIALIZING MONOCHROME MONITOR:
        MOV  AH,Ø         ;function to set screen mode
        MOV  AL,2         ;code for 25x80 B&W
        INT  10H          ;clear the screen
```

A second method is to use functions 6 or 7 of INT 10H, which scroll the screen. The number of lines to scroll is placed in AL, and when it is Ø, the screen is cleared. The interrupt allows only part of the screen to be scrolled, and hence a window on the screen can be cleared alone. Put the coordinates of the top left corner of the window in CX, and the coordinates of the bottom right corner in DX (row in CH/ DH, column in CL/DL). Set the attribute in which the screen is to be cleared in BH. The coordinates are numbered from Ø.

```
;---CLEAR THE WINDOW BETWEEN 3,4 AND 13,15:
        MOV  AH,6         ;use a scroll routine
        MOV  AL,Ø         ;set number of rows to scroll to Ø
        MOV  BH,7         ;attribute byte for fill
        MOV  CH,3         ;top left row
        MOV  CL,4         ;top right col
        MOV  DH,13        ;bottom right row
        MOV  DL,15        ;bottom right column
        INT  10H          ;clear the window
```

A third method is to use function 9 of INT 10H, which writes a character and attribute as many times as CX specifies. A value of 2000 clears the screen once the cursor is set to 0,0 using the method shown at [4.2.1]. AH holds the space character, AL takes the attribute byte, and BH has the page number.

```
;---SET CURSOR TO TOP LEFT CORNER OF SCREEN:
              MOV   AH,2            ;function to set cursor
              MOV   BH,0            ;page number
              MOV   DX,0            ;coordinates are 0,0
              INT   10H            ;set the cursor
;---WRITE THE SPACE CHARACTER 2000 TIMES:
              MOV   AH,9            ;function number
              MOV   CX,2000         ;number of times to write
              MOV   AL,' '          ;space character in AL
              MOV   BL,7            ;attribute in BL
              INT   10H            ;clear the screen
```

Finally, DOS can perform screen erasures using the special escape sequences that work with the device driver ANSI.SYS. See Appendix E for background. These sequences are strings that begin with the escape character and terminate with a $ sign. The strings are "output" using function 9 of INT 21H, where DS:DX points to the first character of the string. DOS interprets the string without displaying it on the screen. To erase the whole screen, the string is [2J. To erase from the cursor to the end of the line (cursor position included), the string is [K.

```
;---IN THE DATA SEGMENT:
   CLEAR_LINE    DB    27,'[K$'

;---CLEAR FROM CURSOR POSITION TO END OF LINE:
              MOV   AH,9            ;string-writing function
              LEA   DX,CLEAR_LINE   ;point DX to start of string
              INT   21H            ;erase to end of line
```

Low Level

At low level, simply poke the space character and attribute byte directly into the memory buffer using STOSW. Here is an example for the monochrome display:

```
       MOV   AX,0B000H      ;point to monochrome video buffer
       MOV   ES,AX          ;
       MOV   DI,0           ;DI points to start of buffer
       MOV   AL,32          ;space character
       MOV   AH,7           ;normal attribute
       MOV   CX,2000        ;number of times to write
   REP STOSW                ;send AX to ES:DI 2000 times
```

4.1.6 Switch between video adaptors

A machine may be equipped with both monochrome and color cards, or with an EGA and one of the other adaptors. A program may choose which monitor is to be active by changing the value of bits 4 and 5 at memory location 0000:0410. Making both bits 1 chooses the monochrome adaptor. Changing bits 5-4 to 10 selects the graphics adaptor in 80-column mode, and 01 selects 40-column mode. And changing the bits to 00 selects the EGA. In all cases, you must immediately execute a mode-setting command after making the change in the register, since BIOS has many other registers to change before the display will operate correctly.

Note that while the operating system can not drive both adaptor cards at once, programs *can* display on both monitors simultaneously by performing direct memory mapping [4.3.1] upon the video buffer addresses of the "non-active" monitor.

High Level ━━━━━━━━━━━━━━━━━━━━━━━━━━━━━━━━━━━

In BASIC, simply use the following code:

```
100 'Switch to monochrome monitor:
110 KEY OFF:CLS
120 WIDTH 40
130 DEF SEG=0
140 M=PEEK(&H410)
150 POKE &H410,M OR &H30
160 WIDTH 80
170 LOCATE,,1,12,13
180 KEY ON


100 'Switch to color/graphics monitor (80 column mode):
110 KEY OFF:CLS
120 WIDTH 80
130 DEF SEG=0
140 M=PEEK(&H410)
150 POKE &H410,(M AND &HCF) OR &H20
160 WIDTH 80
170 SCREEN 0
180 LOCATE,,1,6,7
190 KEY ON


100 'Switch to EGA (80 column mode):
110 KEY OFF:CLS
120 WIDTH 80
130 DEF SEG=0
140 M=PEEK(&H410)
150 POKE &H410,M AND &HCF
160 WIDTH 80
170 SCREEN 0
180 LOCATE,,1,6,7
190 KEY ON
```

Adjust the WIDTH and SCREEN commands to switch to other initial screen modes.

Low Level

In assembly language, as in BASIC, directly change bits 5 and 4 at 0000:0410.
Reset the screen mode immediately after making the change.

```
;---SWITCH TO MONOCHROME MONITOR:
          SUB  AX,AX              ;make AX 0
          MOV  ES,AX              ;set ES to the bottom of memory
          MOV  DL,ES:[410H]       ;get byte at 0000:0410
          OR   DL,00110000B       ;turn bits 5 and 6 on
          MOV  ES:[410H],DL       ;replace the byte
          MOV  AH,0               ;BIOS function to set screen mode
          MOV  AL,0               ;80 x 25 monochrome mode
          INT  10H               ;set the mode

;---SWITCH TO COLOR MONITOR (40 COLUMNS):
          SUB  AX,AX              ;make AX 0
          MOV  ES,AX              ;set ES to the bottom of memory
          MOV  DL,ES:[410H]       ;get byte at 0000:0410
          AND  DL,11001111B       ;turn bits 5 and 4 off
          OR   DL,00010000B       ;turn bit 4 on
          MOV  ES:[410H],DL       ;replace the byte
          MOV  AH,0               ;BIOS function to set screen mode
          MOV  AL,1               ;40 x 25 color mode
          INT  10H               ;set the mode

;---SWITCH TO EGA:
          SUB  AX,AX              ;make AX 0
          MOV  ES,AX              ;set ES to the bottom of memory
          MOV  DL,ES:[410H]       ;get byte at 0000:0410
          AND  DL,11001111B       ;turn bits 5 and 4 off
          MOV  ES:[410H],DL       ;replace the byte
          MOV  AH,0               ;BIOS function to set screen mode
          MOV  AL,1               ;40 x 25 color mode
          INT  10H               ;set the mode
```

Section 2: Control the Cursor

The cursor serves two functions. First, it acts as a pointer to the place on the screen to which program statements send their characters. Second, it provides a visible reference point on the screen for the program user. Only in the latter case does the cursor actually need to be visible. When the cursor is invisible ("turned off"), it still points to a screen position. This is important because any operating system-supported output to the screen starts at the current cursor position.

The cursor is generated by the 6845 CRT controller chip that is described at [4.1.1]. The chip contains registers that set the cursor's size and position. The 6845 chip makes only a *blinking* cursor, although there are ways for a program to create a non-blinking one [4.2.6]. The rate at which the cursor blinks cannot be changed. In graphics modes no cursor is shown, even though characters are positioned on the screen by means of the same cursor-setting routines as in text modes.

When a video system operates in a mode that allows several display pages, each page has its own cursor, and when you switch between pages, the cursor position shifts to wherever it was when the new page was last operated upon. Some screen modes allow up to eight display pages, and their cursor positions are held in a sequence of eight two-byte variables in the BIOS data area, starting from address 0040:0050H. In each variable, the low byte keeps the column number, counted from 0, and the high byte holds the row, also starting from 0. When fewer than eight pages are used, the variables lowest in memory are used.

4.2.1 Set the cursor to an absolute position

The cursor may be set to absolute coordinates or to coordinates that are relative to its former position [4.2.2]. The absolute coordinates match the 25 rows and 80 (sometimes 40) columns of the screen. High-level languages generally count the screen coordinates starting from 1, so that the top left corner position is 1,1. Assembly language always counts from 0, making this position 0,0.

High Level ────────────────────────────────

BASIC numbers the rows from 1 to 25 and the columns from 1 to 80. The LOCATE statement sets the cursor in the format **LOCATE row,col**. When no cursor settings are made, the cursor jumps to column 1 of the next row whenever a carriage return occurs, and scrolling begins once the 24th line is filled. To write on the 25th line you *must* use LOCATE (first clear the line using KEY OFF). To stop automatic scrolling on lines 24 and 25, follow the PRINT statement with a semicolon (use direct memory mapping [4.3.1] to stop scrolling at 24,80 and 25,80). Here a vertical line is drawn down the center of the screen using one of the block-graphics characters.

```
100 FOR N=1 TO 25        'repeat for each row
110 LOCATE N,40          'set cursor to row n, column 40
120 PRINT CHR$(186);     'print line character (no scroll)
130 NEXT                 'next row
```

When several display pages are in use, the LOCATE statement operates on whatever page of memory is currently "active." If the page shown on the monitor is not the active page, the cursor position on the screen does not change. Note that BASIC has its own variables that keep track of the cursor position. If you hook in an assembly language subroutine that moves the cursor, BASIC will ignore the new cursor position when it resumes control.

Middle Level ────────────────────────────────

The operating system offers two ways to position the cursor at absolute coordinates. Function 2 of INT 10H sets the cursor belonging to a specified page of memory. The pages are numbered from 0, and for the monochrome display the display page (held in BH) must always be 0. DH:DL keeps the row and column, which also are numbered from 0. The cursor changes its position on the screen only if the cursor setting is made for the page in view.

```
;---SET THE CURSOR TO ROW 13, COLUMN 39
        MOV   AH,2         ;function number
        MOV   BH,0         ;display page
        MOV   DH,13        ;row
        MOV   DL,39        ;col
        INT   10H          ;position the cursor
```

The second method for setting the cursor is to use the special device driver **ANSI.SYS**, which may be loaded along with DOS at start-up. Appendix E gives the necessary background. Function 9 of INT 21H is used to output a string that contains the row and column information. The string begins with the escape character (ASCII 27), and it ends with $, which acts as a terminating character. The format of the string is **Esc[row,colH$**, where row and col are numbered from 0, and "Esc" stands for ASCII character 27. For example, **27,'[10;60H$'** sets the cursor to row 10, column 60.

While this method may seem unduly complicated, it is very convenient for writing a series of strings on the screen, since an escape sequence may be treated as just one more string. In this example, a three line message is dispersed across the screen.

```
;---IN THE DATA SEGMENT:
    POSITION_1    DB    27,'[10;30H$'
    STRING_1      DB    'There are two options:$'
    POSITION_2    DB    27,'[13;32H$'
    STRING_2      DB    '(1) Review part I$'
    POSITION_3    DB    27,'[15;32H$'
    STRING_3      DB    '(2) Move on to part II$'
;---PRINT THE STRINGS:
              MOV    AH,9              ;function number to print string
              LEA    DX,POSITION_1     ;offset of 1st cursor string in DS
              INT    21H               ;set the cursor
              LEA    DX,STRING_1       ;offset of 1st text string in DS
              INT    21H               ;print the string
              LEA    DX,POSITION_2     ;etc...
              INT    21H
              LEA    DX,STRING_2
              INT    21H
              LEA    DX,POSITION_3
              INT    21H
              LEA    DX,STRING_3
              INT    21H
```

Low Level

Registers 14 and 15 on the 6845 chip hold the cursor position. You can change the value and the cursor will move to the matching screen position, but the BIOS and DOS interrupts that write on the screen will ignore your setting and resume their prior reading. This happens because each time interrupts are used, they reset the cursor registers using a two-byte value kept in the BIOS data area. There may be up to eight such values, each giving the current cursor position of a video page, starting from 0040:0050. A low-level routine must alter these values in order to completely take over the cursor.

The cursor position is kept in registers 14 and 15 as a number from 0 to 1999, corresponding to the 2000 (25 x 80) character boxes. Take care not to confuse this numbering system with the 0-3999 positions in the video buffer, where each character also has a byte to hold its attribute (shift the buffer pointer right by one bit to obtain the equivalent cursor pointer). Also, watch that you do not reverse the high and low bytes: register 14 is *high*, and register 15 is *low*.

```
;---IN THE PROGRAM:
              MOV    BL,24            ;row in BL (0-24)
              MOV    BH,79            ;column in BH (0-79)
              CALL   SET_CURSOR       ;go set the cursor position
```

```
;---PROCEDURE TO SET THE CURSOR:
  SET_CURSOR     PROC
          ;REQUEST ACCESS TO LOW BYTE REGISTER:
                 MOV   DX,3B4H              ;port number for 6845 address register
                 MOV   AL,15                ;select register 15
                 OUT   DX,AL                ;send the request
          ;CALCULATE THE CURSOR POSITION:
                 MOV   AL,80                ;will multiply number of rows by 80
                 MUL   BL                   ;now rows times 80 is in AX
                 MOV   BL,BH                ;transfer number of columns to BL
                 SUB   BH,BH                ;extend BL through BX
                 ADD   AX,BX                ;add the column count to the row count
          ;SEND THE LOW BYTE OF THE RESULT:
                 INC   DX                   ;next port # is for control register
                 OUT   DX,AL                ;send low byte to register 15
          ;REQUEST ACCESS TO HIGH BYTE REGISTER:
                 MOV   AL,14                ;prepare to send high byte to reg 14
                 DEC   DX                   ;set port number back to address reg
                 OUT   DX,AL                ;send request for register 14
          ;SEND THE HIGH BYTE OF THE RESULT:
                 INC   DX                   ;reset port # to control register
                 MOV   AL,AH                ;put high byte in al
                 OUT   DX,AL                ;send the byte
                 RET
  SET_CURSOR     ENDP
```

4.2.2 Set the cursor to a relative position

Sometimes it is useful to make cursor moves *relative* to the prior position: up one row, left three columns, etc. It is easy enough to adjust ordinary *absolute* cursor positions for this purpose. But for added convenience DOS supplies some commands for relative cursor movements.

Middle Level ━━━━━━━━━━━━━━━━━━━━━━━━━━

The relative cursor move function operates by escape sequences. These are strings that are output to the screen using function 9 of INT 21H. Appendix E provides the necessary background for using them. The strings are especially interpreted by DOS such that the cursor moves, rather than having the characters of the string displayed. A string begins with the escape character, ASCII 27, and the [character, and $ marks its end. The string itself is no more than the number of spaces to move, followed by the code number for the direction. To move three spaces:

```
UP       3A
DOWN     3B
RIGHT    3C
LEFT     3D
```

The numbers are written as ASCII strings. Do not, for example, convert 33C (33 spaces right) to **33,'C'**; it is '33C'. The example below places the numbers 1-8 at regular intervals across the screen, as if to label columns of data. The spacing between the numbers is made by the escape sequence that moves the cursor rightward after each digit is printed.

```
;---IN THE DATA SEGMENT:
   CURSOR_RIGHT   DB    27,'[9C$'

;---SET INITIAL CURSOR POSITION:
                 MOV   BH,0            ;page number
                 MOV   DH,1            ;row
                 MOV   DL,5            ;column
                 MOV   AH,2            ;function to set cursor position
                 INT   10H            ;set the cursor
;---WRITE THE NUMBERS:
                 LEA   BX,CURSOR_RIGHT ;BX will XCHG with DX
                 MOV   CX,8            ;number of numbers to write
                 MOV   DL,'0'          ;start from 0
   NEXT_NUMBER:  MOV   AH,2            ;DOS function to write single char
                 INT   21H            ;write the character
                 INC   DL             ;increment to next ASCII symbol
                 XCHG  DX,BX           ;switch string pointer into DX
                 MOV   AH,9            ;get set to write cursor move string
                 INT   21H            ;move the cursor right 9 spaces
                 XCHG  DX,BX           ;switch the ASCII symbol back into DX
                 LOOP  NEXT_NUMBER     ;do the next number
```

There are also a pair of escape sequences that cause the cursor either to wrap or not to wrap from the end of a line as it is automatically forwarded by the interrupts that write characters on the screen. When set not to wrap, the excess characters are discarded. The sequence is **ESC[= 7h** (or, as data, 27,'[= 7h'). To return to automatic wrapping, use **ESC[= 7l** (27,'[= 7l').

4.2.3 Turn the cursor on/off

The cursor is generated by the 6845 chip. It operates completely apart from video RAM. This means that during direct memory mapping of the display buffer [4.3.1] software must coordinate the cursor movements with the insertion of new characters into the buffer. Note that the 6845 can not create a *non*-blinking cursor, nor can it change the rate at which the cursor blinks. See [4.2.6] for how to construct alternative, "artificial" cursor types.

High Level ――――――――――――――――――――――――――――

The BASIC interpreter automatically turns off the cursor while a program runs. The cursor appears when the INPUT statement is used, but not otherwise. Should your program require the cursor, say for an INKEY$ routine, then it may be turned on by setting the third parameter that follows the LOCATE statement to 1 (0 turns it back off). Recall that the first two parameters following LOCATE set the row and column coordinates for the cursor.

```
        100 LOCATE 15,40,1   ;turn on cursor, set to row 15, column 40
..or..
        100 LOCATE,,1        ;turn on the cursor wherever it is
..and..
        200 LOCATE,,0        ;turn the cursor back off
```

The cursor will remain on through successive LOCATE statements without setting the third parameter each time. But note that the **INPUT** and **INPUT$** statements will turn it off when they are finished.

Middle Level ――――――――――――――――――――――――――――

Assembly programs leave the cursor on unless otherwise instructed. The operating system does not offer specific means to turn off the cursor, but it is easy to do. Simply position the cursor "off the screen," using function 2 of INT 10H to set it at column 1 of "row 26." Remember that the coordinates are counted from 0, so they should be **25,0**.

```
MOV  BH,0    ;page number (always 0 for monochrome)
MOV  DH,25   ;row
MOV  DL,0    ;column
MOV  AH,2    ;function number
INT  10H     ;set the cursor off-screen
```

Low Level ――――――――――――――――――――――――――――

Bit 6 of register 10 of the 6845 chip [4.1.1] turns the cursor off when it is 1 or on when it is 0. This register also holds the value for the "start-line" for the cursor, which along with the "stop-line" found in register 11 determines the thickness of the cursor [4.2.4]. Since the shape of the cursor is no concern when it is turned off, simply place 32 in register 10 to set bit 6 to 1. To turn the cursor back on, you must reset the value of the cursor start-line. For a normal cursor this value is 11. The stop-line for the cursor remains unaffected since it resides in a different register.

```
;---TURN OFF THE CURSOR:
                MOV    DX,3B4H       ;port number for 6845 address register
                MOV    AL,10         ;select register 10
                OUT    DX,AL         ;send the request
                INC    DX            ;next port number accesses registers
                MOV    AL,32         ;32 turns on bit 6, turning off cursor
                OUT    DX,AL         ;turn off the cursor
;---TURN CURSOR BACK ON:                ;(if necessary, readdress register 10)
                MOV    AL,11         ;start-line value (bit 6 will = 0)
                OUT    DX,AL         ;turn on the cursor
```

4.2.4 Change the cursor shape

The cursor can vary in thickness from a thin line to a character-size block. It is built up out of short horizontal line segments, the topmost of which is referred to as the "start line," and the bottommost as the "stop line." On the monochrome display, 14 lines make up the box in which a character is drawn, numbered 0 to 13, starting from the top. Spacing between characters is provided by the top two lines and the bottom three lines. Most characters fit on lines 2-10, although descenders from some characters reach down to lines 11 and 12. An ordinary cursor fills lines 12 and 13, while underlines occupy line 12 alone.

On a 200-line color display, only eight lines make up the box for one character, and the character is drawn on the top seven lines. The eight lines of a box are numbered from 0 to 7, starting from the top, and a normal cursor is formed by line 7 alone. (Note that there is no underlining on a graphics display, since the use of line 7 as an underline would fuse the characters with those below.) A high-resolution color display uses the 14-line monochrome specification in its high-resolution modes and the eight-line mode when it is run in one of the color-graphics compatible modes.

A cursor may be formed from any combination of adjacent line segments. On the monochrome display, a solid block cursor results when the start line is set to 0 and the stop line to 13 (on a graphics display, use 7 as the stop line instead). If the start and stop lines are given the same value, a single-line cursor appears. And when the stop line is a higher number than the start line, the result is a two-part, wrap-around cursor. For example, if the start line is 12 and the stop line is 1, first line 12 is filled, then line 13, then line 0, and lastly, line 1. The cursor takes on the form of two parallel lines that skirt the top and bottom edges of the row it occupies.

BIOS keeps a two-byte variable at 0040:0060 that gives the current values of the start and stop lines. The first byte holds the stop line value and the second holds the start line value.

High Level ─────────────────────────────────

In BASIC, the LOCATE command shapes the cursor, as well as positioning it upon the screen, and turning it on and off. The parameters that set the start and stop lines are the fourth and fifth numbers that follow the word "LOCATE". The other parameters may be omitted so long as the commas that separate them are included. Thus, to create a solid block cursor from lines 2 to 12, write **LOCATE,,,2,12**. Note that BASIC ordinarily turns the cursor off while it is running. See [4.2.3] for how to turn it back on.

Middle Level ─────────────────────────────────

Function 1 of BIOS interrupt 10H sets the cursor start and stop lines. CH takes the start line, and CL takes the stop line.

```
;---SET CURSOR START AND STOP LINES:
                MOV   AH,1        ;function number
                MOV   CH,0        ;start cursor at top line
                MOV   CL,7        ;end cursor at eighth line
                INT   10H         ;
```

Low Level

Registers 10 and 11 of the 6845 CRT controller hold the values for the start and stop lines, respectively. Both registers are accessed via port address 3B5H on the monochrome card or 3D5H on the color card and PCjr. The number of the register must first be sent to the address register at port address 3B4H (see [4.1.1]). The values occupy the low end of each register. The stop line register, number 11, has no other contents. However, the start line register (#10) indicates by bits 5 and 6 whether or not the cursor is showing. Since the cursor appears when both of these bits are set to 0, placing the line number alone in the register will keep these bits set to zero. The other bits of register 10 are unused.

```
;---SET START LINE:
                MOV   DX,3B4H     ;access the 6845 address register
                MOV   AL,10       ;select register 10
                OUT   DX,AL       ;send the request
                MOV   AL,0        ;start line is number 0
                INC   DX          ;next port number accesses control registers
                OUT   DX,AL       ;start line now in register
;---SET STOP LINE:
                MOV   AL,11       ;select register 11
                DEC   DX          ;set port number back to address register
                OUT   DX,AL       ;send the request
                MOV   AL,7        ;stop line is number 7
                INC   DX          ;reset port number to control registers
                OUT   DX,AL       ;stop line now in register
```

4.2.5 Read/save/restore the cursor position

Programs sometimes read and save the cursor position so that the cursor can be temporarily moved to a command line or elsewhere and then returned to its starting point. The current cursor position of any of up to eight pages of memory can be found in the BIOS data area. There are eight two-byte variables, ranging upwards from address 0040:0050. The first position corresponds to page 0, the second to page 1, and so on. The low byte of each variable holds the cursor's column and the high byte holds the row. Both rows and columns are numbered from 0.

High Level

In BASIC, CRSLN retrieves the row and POS the column. POS must be equipped with a dummy argument, so always write it as **POS(0)**. Here, the cursor is moved to the bottom line of the screen, then returned. Note how the cursor is turned back on following the **INPUT** statement [4.2.3].

```
100 ROW=CRSLIN              'get the cursor's row
110 COL=POS(0)              'get the cursor's column
120 LOCATE 25,1            'move cursor to command line
130 INPUT"Enter file name",F$   'get information at the command line
140 LOCATE ROW,COL,1        'restore original position, turn on
```

Middle Level

Function 3 of INT 10H returns the cursor row in DH and column in DL. On entry, place the page number in BH (always 0 for the monochrome card).

```
;---FIND THE CURSOR POSITION
            MOV   AH,3          ;function number
            MOV   BH,0          ;page 0
            INT   10H           ;place row: column in DH:DL
```

DOS provides two escape sequences that save and restore the cursor position. These sequences are special strings that control the monitor when they are "output" to the screen. Background for the use of these sequences is given in Appendix E. The sequence to *save* the position is **Esc[s**, and to *restore* the position, **Esc[u**. There is no need to provide variables to hold the coordinates.

```
;---IN THE DATA SEGMENT:
   SAVE_CURSOR     DB    27,'[s$'   ;Esc sequence to save cursor position
   RESTORE_CURSOR  DB    27,'[u$'   ;Esc sequence to restore cursor position

;---SAVE THE CURSOR:
            LEA   DX,SAVE_CURSOR   ;load offset of string into DX
            MOV   AH,9          ;string output function number
            INT   21H           ;save the cursor position
;---RESTORE THE CURSOR:
            LEA   DX,RESTORE_CURSOR ;load offset of string into DX
            MOV   AH,9          ;string output function number
            INT   21H           ;restore the cursor position
```

Low Level

Registers 14 & 15 of the 6845 chip hold the current cursor position, as explained at [4.1.1]. The high byte is in register 14. The two bytes hold a number from 0 to 1999 in 80-column mode, or from 0-999 in 40-column mode. It is your job to convert the number to row and column coordinates. You could read this value to find the current position of the visible cursor on the screen. But saving the value and restoring it to the register later will not necessarily return the cursor to its former position, especially if your program uses any of the usual screen operations provided by the operating system. This is because BIOS keeps track of the cursor in its own variables so that it can manage paging [4.5.3]. After you reset registers 14 and 15, the cursor will move to the corresponding position, but at the next call to a screen-write interrupt the cursor will jump back to wherever the BIOS variables state that it should be.

4.2.6 Create alternative cursor types

All operating system interrupts that write on the screen use the cursor. You can change the shape of the cursor by the techniques shown at [4.2.4], or the cursor can be made invisible [4.2.3]. Alternative cursor types are possible when the screen is written upon by direct memory mapping techniques [4.3.1]. Here, the "true" cursor is turned off, since it does not direct characters to a particular position in the video buffer. Instead a "false" cursor is created using the attribute byte.

The most effective technique is to set a reverse-image attribute for the character at which the cursor resides. For a white-on-black screen, use ASCII 112 for this attribute. A second possibility is to cause the cursor's character to blink. In this case, simply add 128 to the current attribute to start it blinking and subtract 128 to restore it. Third, try setting the character to non-blinking underline mode (use ASCII 1). Or finally, in single-line applications consider using a special graphics character that *follows* the last character of the line, such as one of the arrow characters displayed by ASCII 17 or 27. Note that when a program receives input in several modes, you can help identify the current mode by showing a particular cursor type.

High Level

This example forms a cursor by setting the character at the cursor position to reverse image. The variable CURSORPOSITION holds the offset in the video buffer of the cursor's character. It is an even number between 0 and 3998. Adding 1 to CURSORPOSITION gives the location of the attribute byte for that character, and placing 112 in it makes the reverse image. The variable FORMERATTRIBUTE keeps the character's usual attribute so that it can be replaced after the cursor moves on.

```
500 '''''routine to analyse incoming extended codes:
.
560 IF EXTENDEDCODE=77 THEN GOSUB 5000          'this line senses <cursor-right> key


5000 '''''subroutine that moves the cursor right one space:
5010 POKE CURSORPOSITION+1,FORMERATTRIBUTE     'restore attribute at old position
5020 CURSORPOSITION=CURSORPOSITION+2           'set the new cursor position
5030 FORMERATTRIBUTE=PEEK(CURSORPOSITION+1)    'store attribute of new position
5040 POKE CURSORPOSITION+1,112                 'turn on cursor at new position
5050 RETURN                                    'all done
```

Low Level

Here is the above example written in assembly code:

```
;---ROUTINE TO MOVE CURSOR RIGHT ONE SPACE (ES POINTS TO BUFFER)
    CURSOR_RIGHT: MOV  BX,CURSORPOSITION   ;get current cursor position in buffer
                  INC  BX                  ;point to that character's attribute
                  MOV  AL,FORMERATTRIBUTE  ;get the former attribute of the char
                  MOV  ES:[BX],AL          ;restore the former attribute
                  INC  BX                  ;point to the char at new position
```

```
        MOV    CURSORPOSITION,BX      ;save the offset of the position
        MOV    AL,ES:[BX]+1           ;get the attribute of the new char
        MOV    FORMERATTRIBUTE,AL     ;save the attribute
        MOV    AL,112                 ;place reverse-image attribute in AL
        MOV    ES:[BX]+1,AL           ;112 goes to next cursor position
```

Section 3: Write Characters On the Screen

There are many means for writing characters on the screen. Some simply place a single white-on-black character at the current cursor position. Other methods are more complicated but give more control over the character's placement and its attribute or color. Special routines write whole strings on the screen. In all cases, at bottom the machine is doing nothing more than placing the character's ASCII code at a specified position in the video buffer; it may or may not place an attribute byte in the following memory address.

Your programs may place these codes into the buffer directly, a technique that is referred to as "memory mapping." Memory mapping tends to require a little more programming than do the functions that the operating system provides for this purpose, but it results in much faster screen operations. The technique is discouraged by IBM because future changes in hardware design could render a program inoperable. But in fact IBM has gone out of the way to make its new hardware conform to the addressing scheme that memory mapping relies upon.

4.3.1 Write a single character on the screen

In BIOS and DOS (and in BASIC as well), all operations that write characters on the screen place the character at the current cursor position and automatically forward the cursor one space. All wrap the cursor from the end of the line, unless special provision is made to throw away any characters beyond the 80th column [4.2.2]. An important difference between the various operations is that some write a character's attribute along with the character, while others do not.

In both high and low-level programming languages, characters can be placed on the screen without using the usual print operations. Rather, direct *memory mapping* is performed, in which the codes for a character and its attribute are directly placed in the memory locations of the video buffer that correspond to a particular cursor position on the screen. The buffer begins at B000:0000 on the monochrome card and at B800:0000 on the color card and on the PCjr. In compatible screen modes, the EGA uses these same buffer addresses. Even numbered positions (starting from 0) hold the ASCII character codes, and odd numbered positions hold the attribute bytes. Figure 4-2 illustrates this layout. The cursor does not follow these operations, and it may be turned off if desired [4.2.3]. In lieu of a cursor, keep variables that act as pointers to the screen.

High Level

BASIC writes both single characters and whole strings with the same statements, either PRINT or WRITE. PRINT is used most; WRITE is a variant with special, seldom used formatting characteristics. PRINT functions with data in three forms. It displays the contents of both string and numeric variables, as in **PRINT S$** or **PRINT X**. It displays characters inserted (within quotes) in the PRINT statement itself, such as **PRINT"These words are printed"**. And it displays the characters that correspond to ASCII codes that appear within the PRINT statement in the form of CHR$ statements, as in **PRINT CHR$(65)**, which writes **A** (ASCII code #65) on the screen.

A single PRINT statement can hold many data items, and any of the three forms of data may be intermixed. The data items are delimited using commas or semicolons. Commas set each subsequent data item at the next tab position on a line. Semicolons cause the items to be printed together on the screen with no intervening spaces (note that PRINT adds a space before any numeric variables it displays; WRITE does not). Normally, a PRINT statement automatically makes a carriage return at its end, so that the next such statement will begin writing on the following line on the screen. To avoid this carriage return, place a semicolon at the end of the PRINT statement, as in **PRINT S$;**.

Use the LOCATE statement to set the cursor position before printing. Without LOCATE statements, PRINT always begins writing at the first column of the line the cursor is on. Successive PRINT statements fill the screen until line 24 is written upon, whereupon the screen scrolls upwards, so that the next PRINT statement also writes on line 24. Only by using LOCATE can PRINT write on line 25; doing so also results in automatic scrolling. To stop the scrolling, end the PRINT state-

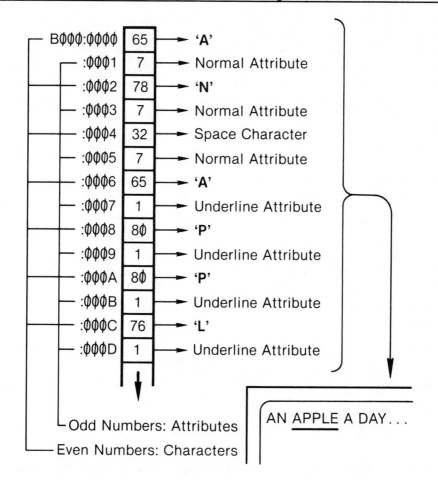

Figure 4-2. Memory mapping on the monochrome adaptor.

ment with a semicolon. This measure, however, will not work at the last columns of lines 24 and 25. To fill these spaces without scrolling, you must use memory mapping, as described below.

You may embed control characters [7.1.9] within a PRINT statement in order to achieve cursor movements "midstring." For example, placing **CHAR$(13)** within a string causes a carriage return at that point. When printed, "One" + **CHRS(13)** + "Two" + **CHRS(13)** + "Three" results in each word starting on a new line. ASCII codes 28-31 respectively move the cursor one space right, left, up, or down. A PRINT statement that contains no data items at all results in a simple carriage return, so that the next PRINT statement begins writing at the line after next.

Memory mapping considerably speeds up screen writing operations in BASIC. It is especially useful for constructing block graphic displays, where boxes may reach down to the lower right corner of the screen. First set the memory segment pointer to &HB000, then use POKE to place each byte in memory. Horizontally adjacent character positions are two bytes apart, with attribute codes in between. On 80-column screens, vertically adjacent positions are 160 bytes apart (two bytes for each character and attribute that make up the 80 columns of a row). The following two examples draw a box around the circumference of the screen using the special double-line graphics characters. The first case mostly uses PRINT statements, and the second case exclusively uses memory mapping. Note how the first case still requires memory mapping at the last columns of rows 24 and 25 to avoid automatic scrolling.

Using PRINT:

```
10 CLS:KEY OFF                    'blank the screen
20 DEF SEG=&HB000                 'access buffer for 24,80 and 25,80
30 LOCATE 1,1:PRINT CHR$(201)     'corner character at 1,1
40 LOCATE 1,80:PRINT CHR$(187)    'corner character at 1,80
50 LOCATE 1,24:PRINT CHR$(186)    'the loop below misses this character
60 LOCATE 1,25:PRINT CHR$(200)    'corner character at 1,25
70 POKE 3838,186                  'column 80 of row 24
80 POKE 3998,188                  'column 80 of row 25
90 FOR N=2 TO 79                  'print the horizontals
100 LOCATE 1,N:PRINT CHR$(205);:LOCATE 25,N:PRINT CHR$(205)
110 NEXT                          '
120 FOR N=2 TO 23                 'print the verticals
130 LOCATE N,1:PRINT CHR$(186):LOCATE N,80:PRINT CHR$(186)
140 NEXT                          '
```

Using Memory Mapping:

```
10 CLS:KEY OFF                    'blank the screen
20 DEF SEG=&HB000                 'point to monochrome buffer
30 POKE 0,201                     'top left character
40 POKE 158,187                   'top right character
50 POKE 3840,200                  'bottom left character
60 POKE 3998,188                  'bottom right character
70 FOR N=2 TO 156 STEP 2          'insert horizontals
80 POKE N,205:POKE N+3840,205     'both top and bottom
90 NEXT                           '
100 FOR N=160 TO 3680 STEP 160    'insert verticals
110 POKE N,186:POKE N+158,186     'both left and right
120 NEXT                          '
```

Middle Level

The operating system offers six routines that write on the screen - three in BIOS and three in DOS. They differ mostly by whether or not they move the cursor after writing a character, whether they cause scrolling, whether they set the character's attribute or color, and which control codes they interpret (some see the backspace character, for example, as just another symbol, which others actually make a backspace on the screen). The six routines are:

```
INT 10H:

function  9      writes character with attribute
          A      writes character without attribute
          E      "teletype" routine (treats screen like a printer)

INT 21H:

function  2      writes character without attribute
          6      writes character without attribute
          9      writes string of characters
```

Functions 9 and A of INT 10H do not interpret any control codes at all. The DOS functions interpret those in the following table. Function E of INT 10H interprets all codes in the table except ASCII 9.

```
ASCII   7   beep
        8   backspace
        9   tab
       10   line feed
       13   carriage return
```

The first two functions of INT 10H do not move the cursor after they write a character. Function 9 of this interrupt writes with an attribute, and function A writes without one, so that the current attribute of a particular position remains. AL holds the character, and BL gets the attribute. The page number is in BH. It must be set even for the monochrome monitor, which, of course, has only one page of memory for the screen to use. In this case, set it to the *first* page, which is numbered as page 0. A special feature of these two BIOS functions is that they print the character as many times as is specified in CX. Ordinarily CX is given 1, but a whole line of characters may be easily printed using a higher count—a useful feature for block graphics. Note that even when multiple characters are written, the initial cursor position remains unchanged. When the line of characters exceeds the space below the cursor, the line wraps around to the top of the screen.

```
;---WRITE A CHARACTER IN REVERSE IMAGE:
        MOV   AH,9                ;function to write with attribute
        MOV   AL,THE_CHARACTER    ;character in AL
        MOV   BL,112              ;attribute in BL
        MOV   BH,0                ;page 1
        MOV   CX,1                ;write the character just once
        INT   10H
```

Rather than constantly restore the count in CX, the BIOS interrupts also offer a "teletype" routine that is more suitable for outputting strings of characters. This is performed by function E. It is set up the same as function A above, but without placing a value in CX. Strings are written simply by changing the character in AL and recalling the interrupt. When used in a graphics mode, the palette color is set in BL; otherwise the current attributes remain.

```
;WRITE A STRING USING THE TELETYPE ROUTINE:
                MOV  AH,0EH            ;teletype function number
                MOV  BH,0             ;page number
                LEA  BX,STRING        ;point BX to the string
NEXT_CHAR:      MOV  AL,[BX]          ;mov a character to AL
                CMP  AL,'$'           ;is it '$' (end of string)?
                JE   ALL_DONE         ;if so, quit
                INT  10H              ;write the string, cursor forwards
                INC  BX               ;point to next char
                JMP  SHORT NEXT_CHAR  ;go get next character
ALL_DONE:
```

INT 21H of DOS offers generally more useful routines, since they all forward the cursor and cause the screen to scroll after the bottom line is accessed, as well as interpreting some of the common control codes. The DOS functions write to whatever page has been set by function 5 of INT 10H [4.5.3]. There are two functions designed to write a single character, numbers 2 and 6. The former senses Ctrl-Break [3.2.8]; the latter does not. (When Ctrl-Break is entered from the keyboard, the Ctrl-Break routine does not execute until a function that can detect it is used.)

Both functions write characters in white on black unless special provision is made for color via the ANSI.SYS device driver [4.1.3]. In general, you need only place the character in DL, place the function number in AH, and invoke INT 21H. However, function 6 is special in that it has a second life as a keyboard input function. It acts in this role only when it is given the character FF in DL [3.1.5]. In all other cases, it writes on the screen whatever is in DL. In the next example, function 6 alternates between receiving and printing a character ([3.1.4] discusses routines that combine both of these features).

```
          MOV AH,6          ;function number
NEXT:     MOV DL,0FFH       ;if FF in DL, gets keystroke
          INT 21H           ;execute the interrupt
          JZ  NEXT          ;if no character, keep trying
          CMP AL,13         ;got a character, is it CR?
          JE  END_INPUT     ;if so, quit
          MOV DL,AL         ;otherwise, move the character to DL
          INT 21H           ;now function 6 prints the character
          JMP SHORT NEXT    ;go get the next
```

Low Level

At bottom, all output to the monitor is memory mapped. The technique is discouraged so as to sustain compatibility through generations of machines, but IBM has gone to lengths to see to it that the video buffers of its microcomputers are structured the same and positioned in memory at the same range of addresses. Because the buffers are structured so that attributes are interleaved with character bytes, character data cannot be moved from memory to the buffer using a simple MOVSB instruction, since the pointer to the buffer must increment by 2 after each one-byte transfer. Still, screen operations are *much* faster using this technique. Note that memory mapping does not work when writing characters in graphics modes. In this case the video buffer size is 16K or 32K, and BIOS *draws* each character, pixel by pixel. Note also that memory mapping does not make use of the cursor to position characters. If desired, the cursor can be moved along with the input [4.2.1], or it may be turned off and a *pseudo*cursor can be created [4.2.6].

```
;---IN THE DATA SEGMENT:
   SAMPLE_STRINGDB  'PRINT THIS STRING$';data string ends with {3$} terminator

;---WRITE OUT THE STRING:
              MOV  AX,0B000H          ;monochrome monitor
              MOV  ES,AX              ;point to video buffer
              LEA  BX,SAMPLE_STRING   ;BX points to the string
              MOV  DI,CURSOR_START    ;starting point in buffer for string
   NEXT:      MOV  AL,[BX]            ;get a character
              CMP  AL,'$'            ;is it end of string?
              JE   ALL_DONE           ;if so, quit
              MOV  ES:[DI],AL         ;else put the character in the buffer
              INC  DI                 ;increase buffer pointer by 2
              INC  DI                 ;
              INC  BX                 ;increase string pointer by 1
              JMP  SHORT NEXT         ;go get next character
   ALL_DONE:                          ;move on
```

The color card and PCjr (but not the EGA) present special problems in memory mapping. When the buffer memory is written to at the same time as it is read for output to the screen, interference occurs on the screen. The problem is avoided by waiting for an "all clear" signal before beginning to write. Continuously read the value of port address 3DAH. When bit 0 equals 1 it is safe to begin writing. (3DAH is the port by which the PCjr sends data to its video gate array; when read, it returns a status register just like the color card.)

```
;---WAIT UNTIL ALL CLEAR:
              MOV  DX,3DAH            ;port address for status register
   CHECK_AGAIN: IN  AL,DX            ;get the value
              TEST AL,1              ;is bit 0 set?
              JZ   CHECK_AGAIN       ;if not, keep trying
;---NOW WRITE THE MESSAGE:
              LEA  BX,MESSAGE        ;message in data segment, ends with $
              MOV  DI,2000           ;start writing at center screen
              MOV  AH,01000001B      ;set the attribute to blue on red
   NEXT_CHAR: MOV  AL,[BX]           ;get one character of the message
              CMP  AL,'$'           ;is it the end of the string?
              JE   ALL_DONE          ;if so, move on
              MOV  ES:[DI],AX        ;otherwise, write the character
              INC  BX                ;increase pointer to the string by 1
              INC  DI                ;increase pointer to the buffer by 2
              INC  DI                ;
              JMP  SHORT NEXT_CHAR   ;do the next character
   ALL_DONE:                         ;move on
```

You must experiment to find out how many characters your routine can write, without interference, in a single cycle. Keep in mind that when the loop is first entered, the test bit may equal 1, but there may not be enough time left in the cycle to complete a write operation.

The PCjr is specially wired so that output to the addresses used by the video buffer of the color graphics card are *redirected* to the place in the PCjr's memory where the buffer actually resides. This feature helps make software compatible for the two systems.

4.3.2 Write a string of characters on the screen

Routines that display whole strings of characters are very useful, but they can impose restrictions on the content of the string. Pay attention to which *control codes* (tab, space, etc.) are interpreted and which are not. Until the advent of the AT, the BIOS did not have a function to display strings, although PC-DOS always has had one. The BIOS function offers more control over character attributes. Of course, use of the new BIOS function presents compatibility problems with all of the earlier machines. Note that the EGA has ROMs on board that extend the BIOS, and that the string-display function is one of these extensions. Thus any PC or XT may have access to the BIOS routine.

High Level ━━━━━━━━━━━━━━━━━━━━━━━━━━━━━━━━━━━━━━━

BASIC writes strings the same way that it writes individual characters. Simply use **PRINT S$**, where S$ is any string up to 255 characters that the program has constructed or transported into memory. Ten of the *control codes* are interpreted. They include:

ASCII	7	beep
	9	tab
	10	line feed
	11	cursor home
	12	form feed (erases screen, cursor home)
	13	carriage return
	28	cursor right
	29	cursor left
	30	cursor up
	31	cursor down

All other codes appears as symbols on the screen.

Middle Level ━━━━━━━━━━━━━━━━━━━━━━━━━━━━━━━━━━━━━

Function 9 of INT 21H displays a string. DS:DX points to the first character of the string. The string must end with the $ character, which means that $ itself cannot be part of the string. The string may be any length. The function does not automatically send the cursor to the start of the next line after the string is printed; to cause this, append 0AH (line feed) and 0DH (carriage return).

```
;---IN THE DATA SEGMENT:
    FIRST_STRING  DB    'This is the first string in memory',0AH,0DH,'$'
    SECOND_STRING DB    'And this is the second string$'

;---PRINT THE STRING:
                  MOV   AH,9                ;function number to print string
                  LEA   DX,FIRST_STRING     ;load the offset of FIRST_STRING in DX
                  INT   21H                 ;prints string at cursor position
                  LEA   DX,SECOND_STRING    ;load pointer to SECOND_STRING
                  INT   21H                 ;write 2nd string at start of new line
```

The following control codes are interpreted:

	ASCII	7	beep
		8	backspace
		9	tab
		10	line feed
		13	carriage return

DOS function 40H of INT 21H is also useful for writing strings on the screen. It requires that you know the length of the string, since the string requires no terminating character; it is especially handy for dumping text files on the screen. This function was designed primarily for output to files. It requires a *handle*, which is an ID number assigned to a particular file or peripheral. The video display has a ready-made handle, number 1. Place the handle in BX and the number of bytes in the string in CX. Then point DS:DX at the string. The function writes text with a normal (white-on-black) attribute. Note that there is no need to "open" the video display the way you must open a file in order to use this function. Here is an example:

```
;---OUTPUT 1000 BYTES OF TEXT:
            MOV   AH,40H       ;function number
            MOV   BX,1         ;handle for video display
            LEA   DX,STRING    ;point DS:DX at the string
            MOV   CX,1000      ;number of bytes to display
            INT   21H
```

DOS provides a number of *escape sequences*, which are special strings that control hardware. When they are output by function 9 of INT 21H, these strings control the cursor, the video mode, the character color, and some aspects of the keyboard. Appendix E discusses how they are used. When programs write many strings on the display, escape sequences are often the easiest way to position the cursor and set the string color. This is because an escape sequence itself is treated as just another string in the series of strings that are displayed.

On the AT, or in machines equipped with the EGA, function 13H of BIOS INT 10H displays a string. Point ES:BP to the string, and place the length of the string in CX. DX is given the cursor position at which the string starts (calculate it as an offset from the start of the page the string is written on, not counting attribute bytes). BH takes the page number. Finally, place a code number from 0-3 in AL to specify how the string is to be displayed:

AL = 0	string is all characters, cursor is not moved
AL = 1	string is all characters, cursor is moved
AL = 2	string alternates characters and attributes, and cursor is not moved
AL = 3	string alternates characters and attributes, and cursor is moved

When AL = 0 or 1, place the attribute in BL. All characters will be written in this attribute. The backspace, carriage return, line feed, and bell (ASCII 7) codes are interpreted as commands by this function, rather than as printable characters.

Low Level

The restriction on the use of $ makes function 9 useless for many applications. Yet this is the only interrupt available on all machines that displays strings of unspecified length. Consider writing your own interrupt ([1.2.3] shows how) that uses the memory mapping techniques shown at [4.3.1]. Instead of '$', use a special character as the string terminator, such as ASCII 0. Add routines to interpret only those control codes you need. The resulting code will be much faster than that provided by DOS.

4.3.3 Read the character and attribute at a given position

Ordinarily, a program takes data from its variables in memory and places it in the video buffer for projection onto the screen. The program in a sense "knows" what is on the screen. But there are situations in which the video buffer is itself used as a work area (as in cut-and-paste graphics programs) so that the current contents of the screen are unrecorded in program memory. In these cases it may be necessary to read from the screen rather than write to it. A BIOS function reads the character and attribute at a particular screen position; otherwise it can be found by memory mapping [4.3.1] in reverse. To find the character and attribute at row 0, column 39 (1,40 in BASIC) in 80-column mode, add (0 x 160) plus (39 x 2) and take the two bytes at that offset in the video buffer. See [4.5.3] if offsets for paging are required. Note that reverse memory mapping will not work with characters written in graphics mode.

High Level

BASIC uses the SCREEN function to find a character or attribute (this statement is entirely separate from the SCREEN statement that sets the video mode). **SCREEN 5,10** retrieves the ASCII code (0-255) of the character at row 5, column 10 (rows and columns are numbered starting from 1). To retrieve the attribute/color of the character instead, add 1 as a third parameter, as in **SCREEN 5,10,1**. When used in a graphics mode, 0 is returned if the indicated screen position does not contain an (unmodified) character.

The attribute is also returned as a code number up to 255. Because BASIC does not permit the use of numbers in binary form, it is a little tricky to sort out the bit pattern of the attribute. The foreground color is equal to **ATTRIBUTE MOD 16**. Once you have the foreground color, the background color is calculated as (((**ATTRIBUTE - FOREGROUND**)/16) **MOD 128**). When the attribute is greater than 127 the character is blinking (or, if you have set it up as such, it has an intensified background [4.1.3]). Appendix B discusses bit operations in BASIC.

Middle Level

Function 8 of INT 10H returns the character and attribute at the current cursor position. Place in BH the value of the current display page (numbered from 0, and always 0 for the monochrome adaptor). The character code is returned in AL, and its attribute byte in AH. This function is so versatile as to be able to read characters in graphics modes, reporting the palette color in AH. It works even for user-defined character [4.3.4]. This example checks the character and attribute at 0,39 on page 2 of the graphics adaptor:

```
;---SET THE CURSOR POSITION:
            MOV   AH,2         ;function to set cursor
            MOV   DH,0         ;set cursor row
            MOV   DL,39        ;set cursor column
            MOV   BH,0         ;set the page number
            INT   10H          ;position the cursor
```

4.3.3   Read the character and attribute at a given position

```
;---FIND THE CHARACTER AND ATTRIBUTE:
          MOV  AH,8              ;function to find character/attribute
          MOV  BH,2              ;page 2 (always 0 on monochrome card)
          INT  10H               ;now AH:AL holds attribute:character
```

Low Level

Calculate the offset and perform memory mapping in reverse. Add a page offset
if required. This example gets the character and attribute at 7,39 on page 2 of the
graphics card:

```
;---FIND THE CHARACTER AND ATTRIBUTE AT 7,39 IN PAGE 2:
          MOV  AX,0B800H         ;address of graphics buffer
          MOV  ES,AX             ;ES points to first byte of buffer
          MOV  DI,1000H          ;page offset
          MOV  AL,80             ;multiply number of rows by 160
          MOV  BL,7              ;place row number in BL
          MUL  BL                ;now AX has (rows-1) times 160
          MOV  AX,39             ;place column number in AX
          ADD  BX,AX             ;add rows and columns
          SHL  BX,1              ;double number for attribute bytes
          MOV  AX,ES:[BX][DI]    ;now AH:AL holds attribute:character
```

4.3.4 Create special characters

Only the monochrome adaptor cannot display characters of the programmer's own design. The color card allows 128 user-defined characters, the PCjr allows 256, and the EGA allows 1024, of which 512 may be on line at once. On the color adaptor the ROM BIOS contains data for drawing only the first 128 characters of the ASCII set (numbers 0-127). The second 128 characters are not available for your use unless you re-create them using the technique explained here. Note that DOS 3.0 provides the GRAFTABL command to supply the required data for the second 128 characters. The PCjr has on board the data for the second 128 characters. The EGA has complete character sets for both 200- and 350-line screens.

Characters on the graphics card and PCjr are designed within a box that is 8x8 pixels. Eight bytes hold the data for each character. Each byte holds the settings for a row of pixels, starting with the top row, and the high bit (number 7) corresponds to the leftmost pixel of the row. When the bit equals 1, the pixel shows. To design a character, you must determine the bit patterns for the eight bytes and place them in sequence in memory. Figure 4-3 shows how eight bytes can form a diamond.

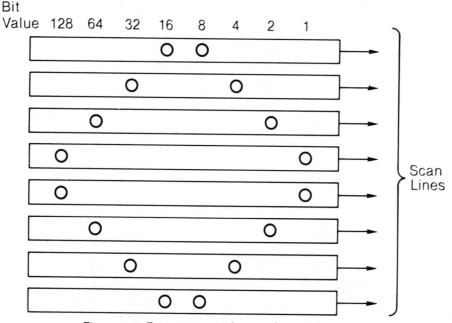

Figure 4-3. Bit patterns to form a diamond.

One hundred twenty-eight characters together require 1024 bytes, although there is no requirement that all characters be set up in memory. A special interrupt vector (a permanent pointer in low memory, see [1.2.0]) is set to point to what would be the first byte for the first character of the extended set, that is, to character number 128. When the code 128 is sent to a character position in the video buffer, these first eight bytes are looked up and displayed. If the character is 129, the ninth through sixteenth bytes are displayed, and so on.

The interrupt vector is number 1FH, which is located at address 0000:007C. Place the address of the offset in the low word (low byte first), and the address of the segment in the high word (again, low byte first). Note that you can create higher code numbers without setting aside memory for lower ones; simply adjust the vector to some lower address that is actually outside of the block that contains the character data. The eight-byte sequences that draw ASCII characters 128-255 are given at [4.3.5]. On the PCjr, vector 1FH points to the second 128 ASCII characters, and vector 44H points to the first 128. Either vector can be redirected, allowing a full 256 user-defined characters.

The EGA is much more complicated, and much more versatile. When a text mode is initialized, one of the two character sets (8x8 or 8x14) is copied from the EGA ROMs on to bit map 2 of the video buffer. This part of the buffer is treated as if it were broken into blocks, and the standard character set is placed in block 0. Providing the EGA is equipped with adequate memory, three more blocks of character data may be set up. The size of a block depends on the number of scan lines used in the character. Characters that are 8x8 need 8 times 256, or 2048 bytes. When more than one block of characters is enabled, bit 3 of the attribute byte of a character determines which block the character data will be taken from.

Which block is used depends on the settings of bits 3-0 in the *character map select register*, which is located at port address 3C5H. First send 3 to 3C4H to index the register. Bits 1-0 give the number of the character block that is enabled when bit 3 of an attribute byte is 0, and bits 3-2 do the same for when bit 3 is 1. When the pattern is the same in both pairs of bits, the dual character set feature is disabled, and bit 3 of attribute bytes reverts to setting character intensity. In this case, only block 0 is enabled. Nothing stops you from placing your own characters at whatever positions you choose within this block, however. And if you overwrite the standard character set, you can replace it at any time from the ROM data.

High Level

In BASIC you must take care to place the character data outside of the memory area used by the program. If lots of memory is available, place the data at the high end; if there is a danger of conflict, use the CLEAR command to limit how much memory BASIC can use. Then poke the address of the starting byte of the data into the interrupt vector. The following example sets up a square box as character 128. A DATA statement holds the values that make up the character. They are either 255 or 129; in the first case all bits are 1, and in the second case only the end bits are 1. See Appendix B about calculating the decimal values of bit patterns.

```
100 '''''Place the data beginning at memory segment &H3000:
110 DATA 255,129,129,129,129,129,129,255 'data for 1 character
120 DEF SEG=&H3000                        'poke at &H30000
130 FOR N=0 TO 7                          'there are 8 bytes
140 READ Q                                'read 1 byte
150 POKE N,Q                              'poke it
160 NEXT                                  'etc.
170 '''''Set the interrupt vector:
180 DEF SEG=0                             'point to bottom of memory
190 POKE 124,0                            'poke offset
```

```
200 POKE 125,0              '
210 POKE 126,0              'poke segment
220 POKE 127,&H30           '
230 '''''Print the character:
240 LOCATE 12,12:PRINT CHR$(128) 'and now char 128 exists
```

Middle Level

On the color card or PCjr, use function 25H of INT 21H to set the interrupt vector, which is number 1FH. On entry, DS:DX points to the first byte of the data block. See [1.2.3] for more information. The example creates two characters, numbers 128 and 129. They are mirror images of each other, and written in sequence they form a small rectangle.

```
;---IN THE DATA SEGMENT:
  CHARACTER_DATA DB 11111111B,10000000B,10000000B,10000000B
                 DB 10000000B,10000000B,10000000B,11111111B
                 DB 11111111B,00000001B,00000001B,00000001B
                 DB 00000001B,00000001B,00000001B,11111111B

;---SET UP THE INTERRUPT VECTOR:
            PUSH DS                 ;save DS
            LEA  DX,CHAR_DATA        ;offset of character data in DX
            MOV  AX,SEG CHAR_DATA    ;segment of character data in DS
            MOV  DS,AX               ;
            MOV  AH,25H              ;interrupt to set vector
            MOV  AL,1FH              ;number of the vector to change
            INT  21H                 ;set the vector
            POP  DS                  ;restore DS

;---PRINT THE CHARACTER:
            MOV  AH,2                ;DOS function to write single char
            MOV  DL,128              ;first character
            INT  21H                 ;write it
            MOV  DL,129              ;second character
            INT  21H                 ;write it
```

On the EGA, function 11H of INT 10H manipulates the character sets. This function can be quite complex when it is used to create special screen modes, but its basic application is straightforward. There are four subfunctions. When AL is 0, user-defined data is transferred from elsewhere in memory into a special character block. When AL is 1 or 2, the 8x14 and 8x8 ROM data sets are respectively copied into a block. And when AL is 3, the function sets the block assignments in the character map select register, as described above. In the latter case, simply place the relevant data in BL and call the function. To load the ROM data, place the block number in BL and execute the function. To load your own data, point ES:BP to it and place the number of characters to transfer in CX, the offset (character number) in the block at which to begin the transfer in DX, the number of bytes per character in BH, and the number of the block in BL. Then call INT 10H. Here is an example:

```
;---INSTALL 128 USER DEFINED CHARACTERS AT TOP END OF BLOCK 0:
            MOV  AX,SEG CHARACTER_DATA   ;point ES:BP to the data
            MOV  ES,AX                   ;
            MOV  BP,OFFSET CHARACTER_DATA ;
            MOV  CX,128                  ;number of characters
```

189

```
MOV   DX,128                    ;starting offset
MOV   BL,0                      ;block number
MOV   BH,8                      ;8x8 character box
MOV   AL,1                      ;subfunction number
MOV   AH,11H                    ;function number
INT   10H                       ;transfer the data
```

You can retrieve status information about the character sets using subfunction 30H of function 11H of INT 10H. Without setting any input registers, CX returns the number of bytes per character in use, and DL tells how many rows fit on the screen (which depends on both the character size and the vertical screen resolution).

4.3.5 Look up data for block-graphics characters

Here are the eight-byte sequences required to draw block characters with the color graphics card. Their use is explained at [4.3.4].

ASCII number	Symbol	Sequence (in hexadecimal)							
128	Ç	78	CC	C0	CC	78	18	0C	78
129	ü	00	CC	00	CC	CC	CC	7E	00
130	é	1C	00	78	CC	FC	C0	78	00
131	â	7E	C3	3C	06	3E	66	3F	00
132	ä	CC	00	78	0C	7C	CC	7E	00
133	à	E0	00	78	0C	7C	CC	7E	00
134	å	30	30	78	0C	7C	CC	7E	00
135	ç	00	00	78	C0	C0	78	0C	38
136	ê	7E	C3	3C	66	7E	60	3C	00
137	ë	CC	00	78	CC	FC	C0	78	00
138	è	E0	00	78	CC	FC	C0	78	00
139	ï	CC	00	70	30	30	30	78	00
140	î	7C	C6	38	18	18	18	3C	00
141	ì	E0	00	70	30	30	30	78	00
142	Ä	C6	38	6C	C6	FE	C6	C6	00
143	Å	30	30	00	78	CC	FC	CC	00
144	É	1C	00	FC	60	78	60	FC	00
145	æ	00	00	7F	0C	7F	CC	7F	00
146	Æ	3E	6C	CC	FE	CC	CC	CE	00
147	ô	78	CC	00	78	CC	CC	78	00
148	ö	00	CC	00	78	CC	CC	78	00
149	ò	00	E0	00	78	CC	CC	78	00
150	û	78	CC	00	CC	CC	CC	7E	00
151	ù	00	E0	00	CC	CC	CC	7E	00
152	ÿ	00	CC	00	CC	CC	7C	0C	F8
153	Ö	C3	18	3C	66	66	3C	18	00
154	Ü	CC	00	CC	CC	CC	CC	78	00
155	¢	18	18	7E	C0	C0	7E	18	18
156	£	38	6C	64	F0	60	E6	FC	00
157	¥	CC	CC	78	FC	30	FC	30	30
158	Pt	F8	CC	CC	FA	C6	CF	C6	C7
159	ƒ	0E	1B	18	3C	18	18	D8	70
160	á	1C	00	78	00	7C	CC	7E	00
161	í	38	00	70	30	30	30	78	00
162	ó	00	1C	00	78	CC	CC	78	00
163	ú	00	1C	00	CC	CC	CC	7E	00

ASCII number	Symbol	Sequence (in hexadecimal)							
164	ñ	00	F8	00	F8	CC	CC	CC	00
165	Ñ	FC	00	CC	EC	FC	DC	CC	00
166	ª	3C	6C	6C	3E	00	7E	00	00
167	º	38	6C	6C	38	00	7C	00	00
168	¿	30	00	30	60	C0	CC	78	00
169	⌐	00	00	00	FC	C0	C0	00	00
170	¬	00	00	00	FC	0C	0C	00	00
171	½	C3	C6	CC	DE	33	66	CC	0F
172	¼	C3	C6	CC	DB	37	6F	CF	03
173	¡	18	18	00	18	18	18	18	00
174	«	00	33	66	CC	66	33	00	00
175	»	00	CC	66	33	66	CC	00	00
176	░	22	88	22	88	22	88	22	88
177	▒	55	AA	55	AA	55	AA	55	AA
178	▓	DB	77	DB	EE	DB	77	DB	EE
179	│	18	18	18	18	18	18	18	18
180	┤	18	18	18	18	F8	18	18	18
181	╡	18	18	F8	18	F8	18	18	18
182	╢	36	36	36	36	F6	36	36	36
183	╖	00	00	00	00	FE	36	36	36
184	╕	00	00	F8	18	F8	18	18	18
185	╣	36	36	F6	06	F6	36	36	36
186	║	36	36	36	36	36	36	36	36
187	╗	00	00	FE	06	F6	36	36	36
188	╝	36	36	F6	06	FE	00	00	00
189	╜	36	36	36	36	FE	00	00	00
190	╛	18	18	F8	18	F8	00	00	00
191	┐	00	00	00	00	F7	18	18	18
192	└	18	18	18	18	1F	00	00	00
193	┴	18	18	18	18	FF	00	00	00
194	┬	00	00	00	00	FF	18	18	18
195	├	18	18	18	18	1F	18	18	18
196	─	00	00	00	00	FF	00	00	00
197	┼	18	18	18	18	FF	18	18	18
198	╞	18	18	1F	18	1F	18	18	18
199	╟	36	36	36	36	37	36	36	36
200	╚	36	36	37	30	3F	00	00	00
201	╔	00	00	3F	30	37	36	36	36
202	╩	36	36	F7	00	FF	00	00	00
203	╦	00	00	FF	00	F7	36	36	36
204	╠	36	36	37	30	37	36	36	36

ASCII number	Symbol	Sequence (in hexadecimal)							
205	=	00	00	FF	00	FF	00	00	00
206	╪	36	36	F7	00	F7	36	36	36
207	╧	18	18	FF	00	FF	00	00	00
208	╨	36	36	36	36	FF	00	00	00
209	╤	00	00	FF	00	FF	18	18	18
210	╥	00	00	00	00	FF	36	36	36
211	╙	36	36	36	36	3F	00	00	00
212	╘	18	18	1F	18	1F	00	00	00
213	╒	00	00	1F	18	1F	18	18	18
214	╓	00	00	00	00	3F	36	36	36
215	╫	36	36	36	36	FF	36	36	36
216	╪	18	18	FF	18	FF	18	18	18
217	╛	18	18	18	18	F8	00	00	00
218	╔	00	00	00	00	1F	18	18	18
219	■	FF	FF	FF	FF	FF	FF	FF	FF
220	▬	00	00	00	00	FF	FF	FF	FF
221	▌	F0	F0	F0	F0	F0	F0	F0	F0
222	▐	0F	0F	0F	0F	0F	0F	0F	OF
223	▀	FF	FF	FF	FF	00	00	00	00
224	α	00	00	76	DC	CB	DC	76	00
225	β	00	78	CC	F8	CC	F8	C0	C0
226	Γ	00	CC	C0	C0	C0	C0	00	00
227	π	00	FE	6C	6C	6C	6C	6C	00
228	Σ	FC	CC	60	30	60	CC	FC	00
229	σ	00	00	7E	D8	D8	D8	70	00
230	μ	00	66	66	66	66	7C	60	C0
231	τ	00	76	DC	18	18	18	18	00
232	φ	FC	30	78	CC	CC	78	30	FC
233	Θ	38	6C	C6	FE	C6	6C	38	00
234	Ω	38	6C	C6	C6	6C	6C	EE	00
235	δ	1C	30	18	7C	CC	CC	78	00
236	∞	00	00	7E	DB	DB	7E	00	00
237	ø	06	0C	7E	DB	DB	7E	60	C0
238	ε	38	60	C0	F8	C0	60	38	00
239	∩	78	CC	CC	CC	CC	CC	CC	00
240	≡	00	FC	00	FC	00	FC	00	00
241	±	30	30	FC	30	30	00	FC	00
242	≥	60	30	18	30	60	00	FC	00
243	≤	18	30	60	30	18	00	FC	00
244	⌠	0E	1B	1B	18	18	18	18	18
245	⌡	18	18	18	18	18	D8	D8	70

ASCII number	Symbol	Sequence (in hexadecimal)							
246	÷	30	30	00	FC	00	30	30	00
247	≈	00	76	DC	00	76	DC	00	00
248	°	38	6C	6C	38	00	00	00	00
249	•	00	00	00	18	18	00	00	00
250	·	00	00	00	00	18	00	00	00
251	√	0F	0C	0C	0C	EC	6C	3C	1C
252	ⁿ	78	6C	6C	6C	6C	00	00	00
253	²	70	18	30	60	78	00	00	00
254	■	00	00	3C	3C	3C	3C	00	00
255	(blank 'FF')	00	00	00	00	00	00	00	00

Section 4: Draw Dot Graphics

The color graphics adaptor uses three graphics modes, the PCjr uses six, and the EGA uses seven. How to set these modes is shown at [4.1.2]. The video memory requirements of these modes vary considerably, depending on the screen resolution and the number of colors used. In its advanced graphics modes, the EGA uses memory in a very different way from the other video systems, but it emulates their memory use exactly in the three graphics modes it shares.

First consider the color card and PCjr systems. Two colors (including black and white) require but one bit of memory for every dot on the screen. Four colors take two bits, and sixteen colors take four (eight-color modes are avoided because the three bits that would be required do not divide evenly into the eight bits of a byte). In all screen resolutions there are 200 dots vertically. Low resolution (available only on the PCjr) uses 160 dots horizontally, medium resolution uses twice that (320 dots), and high resolution doubles the number again (to 640 dots). The number of Kbytes of memory required for each mode is shown at [4.5.3].

When in two- or four-color modes, the PCjr has the choice of any of the 16 colors available. The color adaptor is more limited. In two colors it is always restricted to black and white, and in four colors it can choose only the background color from the 16, while the three foreground colors must be taken from either of two ready-made palettes. Palette 0 holds the colors brown, green, and red; palette 1 holds cyan, magenta, and white.

Unlike text data, in modes 4-6 and 8-A graphics data is laid out over a video page in parts. In most modes, the data is split in two, and the first half of the buffer holds data for the even-numbered lines of the screen, and the second half keeps data for the odd-numbered lines (the lines are numbered downwards from the top of the display). In the PCjr's 16-color modes, however, the 32K buffer that is used is divided into four parts, with each part holding data for every fourth line.

In four-color modes, the first byte in the buffer gives the leftmost horizontal dots on line 0, with the highest bits holding the information for the leftmost pixel. The next byte holds data for the next segment of the line, and so on. 80 bytes are required per line. The 81st byte keeps the information for the left end of *line 2*. Sixteen-color modes use roughly the same arrangement, but 160 bytes are required for a line, and each part of the buffer holds data for only half as many lines. On the color graphics adaptor, even lines stretch from offset 0000 to 1F3FH and the odd lines from 2000H to 3F3FH. The gap between 1F3FH and 2000H is ignored. On the PCjr, the corresponding locations vary considerably, depending on the mode and the number of pages used. The PCjr is specially wired so that output to the 16K starting at segment B800H is redirected to the actual memory addresses in which the data resides. This feature facilitates writing programs that run on both the color card and the PCjr.

For screen modes DH through 10H on the EGA, memory is organized quite differently. It is split up into one, two, or four *bit planes*, in which a single plane is organized as in the high-resolution blank and white mode discussed above: when a byte of data is sent to an address in the video buffer, each bit corresponds to a pixel on the screen, laid out as a horizontal segment with bit 7 leftmost. Picture four such bit planes, residing side-by-side at the same address in the video buffer. This leaves four bits for each pixel, which provides for sixteen colors. Figure 4-4 shows the various memory schemes.

Characters may be written while in graphics mode. They are not created in the usual way; rather, BIOS draws them dot by dot without changing the background color. For this reason, there is no such thing as reverse-image or blinking characters in graphics modes. Nor is there a cursor. BIOS is also capable of reading and comparing the dots at a cursor position to see what character is present. The characters are positioned at one of the usual row and column positions, which means that they always begin at an eight-pixel boundary.

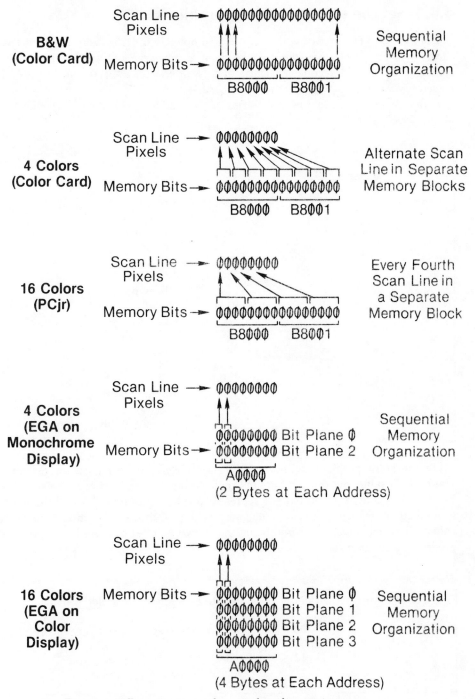

Figure 4-4. Four strategies for graphics layout in memory.

4.4.1 Set the colors for dot graphics

The PCjr and EGA work with color in a completely different way from the color card. They use *palette registers* that let them at any time change the color that is displayed by the color codes. Because of this difference, the two systems are discussed separately, starting with the color card.

Both systems use the same basic series of color codes, which is exactly the same as that used for character colors:

Code Number	Bit Pattern	Color
0	0000	Black
1	0001	Blue
2	0010	Green
3	0011	Cyan
4	0100	Red
5	0101	Magenta
6	0110	Brown
7	0111	White
8	1000	Gray
9	1001	Light Blue
10	1010	Light Green
11	1011	Light Cyan
12	1100	Pink
13	1101	Light Magenta
14	1110	Yellow
15	1111	Bright White

On the color graphics adaptor, color is allowed only in medium resolution graphics. Two bits out of each byte in the video buffer are given over to each pixel. The four possible bit combinations represent one background color and three foreground colors. The background color may be any of the 16. The three foreground colors, however, must be chosen from one of two palettes that are limited to three predetermined colors each. They are:

Code number	Bit pattern	Palette 0	Palette 1
0	00	background color	background color
1	01	green	cyan
2	10	red	magenta
3	11	yellow/brown	white

While you can change between palettes at any time, all colors already written on the screen will change accordingly. The only way to use colors from outside of the two palettes is by artificially treating one of the palette colors as the background color, which requires filling the whole screen in that color whenever the screen is cleared (use memory mapping for this). Then the true background color can "show through" as a foreground color. This technique results in a screen border like that of text screens. Graphics screens do not otherwise set a special border color because the whole screen is set to the background color, even though the border-area pixels are not addressable. Note that BIOS keeps a 1-byte variable in its data area that holds the current palette number. It is located at 0040:0066H. Changing this number does not change the palette setting; conversely, if you change the palette color through means other than an operating system function, you should update this setting.

Characters may be interspersed with dot graphics. The color in which characters appear depends on which routine is used to write the characters. The simpler routines default to the third color of the current palette. But there are ways to use any palette color and to intermix characters written in different palette colors. See the discussion at [4.1.3].

The EGA and PCjr have extra flexibility in their use of color attributes, no matter which video mode they operate in. In 16-color graphics, the four bits laid down in memory for a particular dot on the screen give a bit pattern that is not directly translated into the corresponding color in the above table. Rather, the number refers to one of 16 *palette registers*. Each of these registers holds the bit pattern for the color that will actually be displayed. If all 16 registers are given the pattern 0100, then no matter what attribute is used in memory for a pixel, it is displayed in red. The value in register 0 is used as the background color. Figure 4-1 at [4.1.3] diagrams this mechanism. In two- and four-color modes, only the first two or four palette registers are relevant.

The palette registers enable a program to change everything displayed in one color to another without making any other changes in the video buffer. What's more, objects can be made to magically disappear and reappear. This is done by changing to background color the value found in the palette register that corresponds to the attribute in which the objects are drawn. For example, say that the background color is black (0000) and that an object is drawn using the attribute 1110, so that it appears in whatever color is given in palette register 15 (yellow is the default value for this register). By changing register 15 to 0000 (the black background color) the object disappears from view. But the object is still defined in memory by virtue of being written with the attribute 1110, rather than the attribute 0000, as would be used by all background dots. The object can be made visible again by changing palette register 15 back to 1110. Not all yellow objects would need to disappear, since some could be drawn using a different attribute that also corresponds to a palette register containing the code for yellow.

The EGA can use six bits of a palette register, rather than four, when it is connected to an IBM Enhanced Color Display. Sixty-four colors are made possible, using the pattern R'G'B'RGB. R, G, and B produce dark colors, and R', G', and B' produce lighter ones. The various combinations create the 64 hues. As always, 111111 is white and 000000 is black. Note that the 64 colors are available through the palette registers no matter what screen mode the EGA is running in. When working in four color graphics (as on the color card), only the four lowest palette registers will be active, but they may contain any color.

High Level ───────────────────────────

When the color card is in a graphics mode, BASIC treats the COLOR statement differently than for a text mode. First comes the background color as a number from 0 to 15, and then the palette number is given, either 0 or 1. For example, **COLOR 2,1** sets the whole screen to the background color green (#2) and activates palette 1. Thereafter the three foreground colors are specified by their palette numbers: 1 for cyan, 2 for magenta, and 3 for white (e.g. in PAINT statements). To *turn off* color in medium-resolution mode, write **SCREEN,1**. Note that no memory is saved by using black and white in medium-resolution. The PCjr uses the COLOR statement this way only for SCREEN 1. For SCREEN 3 to SCREEN 6 the format for the statement is **COLOR foreground, background.** The foreground is a number from 1-15 in a 16-color mode or from 1-3 in a four-color mode. It must not be 0, which is always the background color.

There are special statements to set the contents of palette registers: PALETTE and PALETTE USING. PALETTE sets the color corresponding to any attribute. **PALETTE 9,11**, for example, causes dots drawn with palette color 9 (normally light blue) to be shown in color 11 (light cyan). To change all palette registers back to their initial settings, so that register 0 contains 0, register 12 contains 12, etc., simply write **PALETTE**. Note that in the modes SCREEN 4 and SCREEN 6 the palette registers are initialized so that the attributes of colors 1-3 are the same as those of palette 1 on the color graphics card. This is done for the sake of compatibility.

All 16 palette registers may be set by a single statement, PALETTE USING. PALETTE USING dumps the contents of a 16-element integer array into the palette registers. By keeping several such arrays, a program can quickly switch back and forth between various color schemes. Each element of the array must be a number from 0 to 15, or else -1, in which case no change is made in the contents of the corresponding register. For example, to reverse the usual color scheme, create an array where ARRAYNAME(0) = 15, ARRAYNAME(1) = 14, etc. Then write **PALETTE USING ARRAYNAME(0),** and the contents of ARRAYNAME are dumped into the palette registers. The 0 indicates the starting position in the array from which the data for the registers is taken. Longer arrays may be used, with the data taken from any starting point so long as there are 16 elements between it and the end of the array. **PALETTE USING ARRAYNAME(12)** would take data starting from the 12th byte of the array. Note that PALETTE USING operates for both text and graphics modes. Here is an example:

```
100 DEF INT A-Z          'all variables integers
110 DIM SCHEME1(16)      'array for color scheme #1
120 DIM SCHEME2(16)      'array for color scheme #2
130 DATA 3,5,9,2,4,12,15,1,6,7,14,13,8,11,10,0
140 DATA 0,11,13,7,1,12,2,5,10,8,14,6,15,4,9,3
150 FOR N=0 TO 15         'for each palette register
160 READ Q                'read color code
170 SCHEME1(N)=Q          'place in the array
```

```
180 NEXT                        'go get next
190 FOR N=0 TO 15               'repeat for second array...
200 READ Q                      '
210 SCHEME2(N)=Q                '
220 NEXT                        '
230 PALETTE USING SCHEME1(0)        'set the registers
    .
    .
500 PALETTE USING SCHEME2(0)        'change them mid-program
```

Middle Level

Function BH of INT 10H sets both background and palette colors—but not at the same time. To set the background, place 0 in BH, and then put a color code from 0-15 in BL. To set the palette, place 1 in BH, and put either 0 or 1 in BL. This example sets the background to cyan and chooses palette 0:

```
;---SET BACKGROUND AND PALETTE COLORS:
                MOV     AH,0BH          ;function to set graphics colors
                MOV     BH,0            ;first, choose background color
                MOV     BL,3            ;code for cyan background
                INT     10H             ;set the color
                MOV     BH,1            ;now set the palette
                MOV     BL,1            ;choose palette 1
                INT     10H             ;set the palette
```

On the PCjr this function works in exactly the same way in four-color modes, setting up registers 1-3 in either of the same color schemes that are used by the color card. In a two-color mode, a 0 in BL makes for white as color 1, and a 1 makes for black. This function has no effect on the 0-15 arrangement used by the 16-color modes. In all cases, however, the background color may be set by placing 0 in BH and a code in BL.

Low Level

On the color card, port address 3D9H accesses the "Color Select Register." The register operates in graphics modes differently than for text modes (described at [4.1.3]). Bits 0-3 hold the background color information in the usual format (respectively, the blue, green, and red components, and intensity). Bit 5 selects the palette; when the bit is 0, the palette is number 0. In graphics modes no other bits are significant. The register is write-only, so you must include both the background and palette bits when making a change in either.

```
                MOV     DX,3D9H         ;color select register address
                MOV     AL,00100110B    ;bit pattern for cyan, palette 1
                OUT     DX,AL           ;send it
```

Since they use palette registers, the above example does not apply to either the PCjr or the EGA. Instead, simply load the desired values into these registers. On the PCjr the registers are numbered from 10H to 1FH. All registers are accessed through the same port address, 3DAH. Every other value received by the port is taken as a register address. So first send the register number and then the color code for that register. To be sure that the port is awaiting a register number, *read* from it and throw away the result. For example, to place the color light blue (1001) in palette register 2H:

```
;---PLACE CODE FOR LIGHT BLUE IN PALETTE REGISTER 2:
            MOV DX,3DAH                 ;video gate array address
            IN  AL,DX                   ;read the port to clear it
            MOV AL,12H                  ;register number
            OUT DX,AL                   ;send the register number
            MOV AL,00001001             ;code for light blue
            OUT DX,AL                   ;send the color
```

On the EGA the palette registers are at 3C0H, and they are numbered from 00 to 0FH. Read port 3DAH (not 3C0H) to be sure an index is awaited. When the IBM Enhanced Color Display is connected and the dip switches are set accordingly, six-bit values are placed in the registers.

4.4.2 Draw a dot on the screen (monochrome card, color card, PCjr)

Because of the organization of graphics information in the video buffer, drawing a dot entails changing individual bits within memory. The two-, four-, and sixteen-color modes require that one, two, and four bits respectively be changed to set a single dot. These operations can consume a tremendous amount of processor time, as evidenced by how slowly much graphics software operates. Careful forethought often leads to ways of setting all of the bits of a particular byte at once, rather than accessing the same byte four or eight times. Keep this in mind before blindly opting to use the simple dot-by-dot techniques shown here.

High Level

BASIC provides the PSET and PRESET statements to change the color of individual dots. The names stand for PointSET and PointRESET. They are nearly the same. Both are followed by the column and row coordinates of the dot, placed in parentheses. Note that coordinates are given in the order x,y—that is, first the column and then the row; this is the reverse of the row-column order by which the LOCATE statement positions text on the screen. **PSET(50,80)** or **PRESET(50,80)** set the dot color at column 50, row 80. PSET may be followed with a color code that is in the range permitted by the current screen mode. When no color is given, the highest number code that the screen mode allows is used. PRESET, on the other hand, names no color. It always returns the dot to background color (code 0). For example:

```
100 PSET (100,180),3      'set dot at 100,180 to palette color 3
110 PRESET (100,180)      'change the dot back to background color
```

PSET and PRESET ordinarily use a coordinate system where the top left corner of the screen is numbered 0,0. The WINDOW statement lets you redefine the coordinate system so that, for example, the top left corner is -100,100, center-screen is 0,0, and the bottom right corner is 100,-100. In this instance, the statement would be written as **WINDOW(-100,100)-(100,-100)**. (The new coordinates have no effect upon the 25x80 (or 25x40) system by which the LOCATE statement positions characters on graphics screens [4.2.1]).

As in a LINE statement [4.4.5], the first number in each of the pairs of parentheses gives horizontal, x-axis coordinates. They could both be positive or negative, so long as they are not identical. The left edge of the screen is always assigned the smallest number (which may be the largest *negative* number). Thus, even by reversing the coordinates of the example to **WINDOW(100,-100)-(-100,100)** the value -100 is given to the left end of the x-axis.

The second number of each coordinate pair gives the vertical boundaries of the screen. Again, whichever value is smallest is given to the bottom edge of the screen, no matter which coordinate pair it is matched with. The largest positive value (or smallest of two negative values) is assigned as the value of the y-axis at the top line of the screen. The direction of increasing value can be reversed so that the largest value is at the bottom of the screen and vice-versa. Simply add the word SCREEN to the statement, as in **WINDOW SCREEN** (-100,100)-(100,-100).

A program may direct points to be set at areas outside of the screen coordinate system. For example, a circle could be centered off-screen, so that only an arc of it is in view. Note also that the coordinates given by WINDOW statements may be continuously changed to "zoom" or "pan" an image. The image must be redrawn, and sometimes erased, each time the WINDOW coordinates are changed.

The PMAP statement converts coordinates between the usual *physical* system and a *world* system set up by a WINDOW statement. PMAP uses four code numbers:

0	convert x from world to physical
1	convert y from world to physical
2	convert x from physical to world
3	convert y from physical to world

The statement takes the form **PMAP(position,code)**. For example, say that you have set up a system of world coordinates using WINDOW. The top left corner of the screen is given (-100,100), and the bottom right is given (100,-100). What is the pixel position of the center point of the screen (0,0) using the usual 320 x 200 physical system, where the top left is 0,0? To find X, write **X = PMAP(0,0)**, and to find Y, write **Y = PMAP(0,1)**. X will be given the value 160, and Y will be 100.

Middle Level

Function CH of INT 10H sets a dot. DX holds the row, and CX the column, both counted from 0. The color code is placed in AL. Note that the contents of AX are destroyed during the interrupt. When the interrupt is used repeatedly from within a loop, be sure to PUSH AX before, and POP it afterwards.

```
;---PRINT A DOT AT 100,180:
                MOV   AH,0CH          ;function to set dot
                MOV   AL,3            ;choose palette color 3
                MOV   CX,100          ;row
                MOV   DX,180          ;column
                INT   10H             ;draw the dot
;---"ERASE" THE DOT:
                MOV   AH,0CH          ;replace function (AX destroyed)
                MOV   AL,0            ;use background color to "erase"
                MOV   DX,100          ;row
                MOV   CX,180          ;column
                INT   10H             ;erase the dot
```

While the palette color is placed in the low bits of AL, the top bit is also significant. When it is equal to 1, the color is exclusive-ORed (XORed) with the color currently in place. Recall that in the XOR operation a bit equals 1 solely in the case where, of two bits compared, only one is presently turned on. If both of the bits compared are 1, or if neither is 1, then the bit is set to 0. In two-color modes this means that XORing a bit reverses its setting. The whole screen can be reversed by XORing every pixel. In four- or sixteen-color modes, on the other hand, areas of the screen can be made to change their colors. For example, say that in four-color medium resolution an area is entirely covered by pixels of either palette code 1 (bit pattern 01B) or palette code 2 (10B). What happens if every pixel in the area is XORed with 11B? 01B becomes 10B, and 10B becomes 01B—the colors are reversed.

Low Level

At low level one accesses the video buffer directly ("memory mapping"). First you must calculate the offset of the dot (a) within the buffer and (b) within the byte that contains the bits that set the dot. Then bit operations make the proper setting. Note that if you choose to use this technique on the PCjr when in one of the 16-color modes that use a 32K page, output to the addresses starting at paragraph B800H will not be redirected properly. Instead direct the operations to their actual locations below segment 2000H.

To find the dot, first calculate whether it is on an even or odd numbered row. In this example, the row is placed in CX, and the column in DX. If bit 0 of DX is 0, the row is an even number. Even rows begin at offset 0 in the buffer. On the other hand, if the row is odd numbered, add 2000H to point to the beginning of the second half of the buffer.

Next, divide the number of rows by 2, since the count is for only even or odd rows, and multiply the number by 80 for the 80 bytes that make up a row. By using the **SHL** instruction to make the division, the result will give the number of bytes in all rows *preceding* the row that the dot resides on.

Rather than next calculate the number of columns in the current row, it is best to first figure the position of the two bits within the byte that holds them. This is done by reversing all bits in the column count (after storing a copy), and then taking the bottom two bits. These show whether the two bits of the pixel are in the first, second, third, or fourth position within the byte. Multiplying the position by 2 gives the bit number of the first of the two bits of the pixel.

Next, it is time to calculate the number of bytes in the row leading up to the byte holding the pixel. In medium-resolution, divide the number of columns by 4; in high-resolution, divide by 8. Add together the three offsets: the row byte-count, the column byte-count, and the even/odd line offset within the buffer. Then get the byte out of the buffer.

Finally, perform the operations on the relevant bits of the byte. Rotate the byte until the two pixel bits are at the bottom. The rotation is counted using the bit-position value calculated above. Then turn off both bits and OR them with the desired palette code. Re-rotate the bits to their former position, and send the byte back to the video buffer.

```
;---IN THE DATA SEGMENT:
PALETTE_COLOR    DB    2

;---CALL THE ROUTINE:
                 MOV   AX,0B800H          ;point to graphics buffer
```

```
                       MOV   ES,AX                ;
                       MOV   CX,100               ;row in CX
                       MOV   DX,180               ;column in DX
                       CALL  SET_DOT
                         .
                         .
;---FIGURE NUMBER OF BYTES IN ROWS PRIOR TO PIXEL'S ROW:
   SET_DOT             PROC
                       TEST  CL,1                 ;is it an odd numbered row?
                       JZ    EVEN_ROW             ;if not, then jump ahead
                       MOV   BX,2000H             ;put offset for odd rows in BX
                       JMP   SHORT CONTINUE       ;jump ahead
   EVEN_ROW:           MOV   BX,0                 ;put offset for even rows in BX
   CONTINUE:           SHR   CX,1                 ;half the number of rows
                       MOV   AL,80                ;multiply by 80 bytes per row
                       MUL   CL                   ;now AX holds bytes up to prior row
;---FIGURE POSITION OF 2 BITS WITHIN THE BYTE:
                       MOV   CX,DX                ;copy the column count
                       NOT   CL                   ;reverse bits
                       AND   CL,00000011B         ;now CL has bit position 3-0
                       SHL   CL,1                 ;CL x 2 gives bit position of 1st bit
;---TALLY NUMBER OF BYTES IN COLUMN OFFSET:
                       SHR   DX,1                 ;divide number of columns by 4
                       SHR   DX,1                 ; (keep bottom 2 bits)
;---FIGURE OFFSET OF THE BYTE THAT NEEDS CHANGING:
                       ADD   AX,DX                ;add column offset to row offset
                       ADD   BX,AX                ;add above to buffer offset
;---CHANGE THE BITS:
                       MOV   AH,ES:[BX]           ;get the byte at that position
                       ROR   AH,CL                ;move relevant bits to bottom of byte
                       AND   AH,11111100B         ;blank out the bottom 2 bits
                       MOV   AL,PALETTE_COLOR     ;palette color in AH
                       OR    AH,AL                ;change the bits to the palette color
                       ROL   AH,CL                ;rotate bits back to correct position
                       MOV   ES:[BX],AH           ;replace the byte
                       RET
   SET_DOT             ENDP
```

4.4.3 Draw a dot on the screen (EGA)

Graphics on the EGA are complicated. From the CPU's point of view, screen modes 0 through 7 operate exactly as on the color card or PCjr, but modes DH through 10H are completely different. The memory organization of these memory modes varies, depending on how many colors are used, and how much RAM is installed on the card. See Figure 4-4 at [4.4.0].

In modes D, E, and 10H, memory is organized in four *bit planes*. A single plane is organized as in the color card's high-resolution black and white mode discussed at [4.4.2]: when a byte of data is sent to an address in the video buffer, each bit corresponds to a pixel on the screen, laid out as a horizontal segment with bit 7 leftmost. Picture four such bit planes, residing side-by-side at the same address in the video buffer. This leaves four bits for each pixel (giving 16 colors), where each bit is in a separate byte on a separate bit plane.

But how can you write four different bytes of data when they are at the same memory address? The answer to this question is *not* that four bytes are sent in sequence to the address. Rather, one of three *write modes* can alter all four bytes on the basis of a single byte of data received from the CPU. The effect of the CPU data depends on the settings of several registers, including two mask registers that determine which bits and which bit planes are to be affected.

To understand these registers, you must first know about the four *latch registers*. These hold the data from each of the bit planes at whatever memory position was last accessed. (Note that the term *bit plane* is used to refer to both the entire extent of the video buffer, and to the one-byte swatches of the buffer temporarily held in these latch registers). When the CPU sends data to a particular address, that data may change or entirely replace the latch register data, and then it is the latch register data itself that is written into the video buffer. *How* the latch registers are influenced by the CPU data depends on which write mode is used and how certain other registers are set up. Whenever a video memory address is *read*, the latch registers are filled by the four bytes from the four bit planes at that location. The latch registers are easily manipulated so that their contents may be ORed, ANDed, XORed, or rotated, greatly facilitating fancy graphics and scrolling.

The bit mask register and map mask register act on the latch registers, protecting particular bits or bit planes from being changed by the CPU data. The *Bit Mask Register* is a write-only register at port address 3CFH. First send 8H to 3CEH to index the register. Setting a bit to 1 in this register masks out a bit across all four bit planes, so that the corresponding pixel on the screen is immune to change. The hardware still operates in byte-size units, however, so the "unchanged" bits are in fact *rewritten* into the four bit planes. The data for these masked-out bits is whatever resides in the latch registers, and so the program must be sure that the current contents of the latch registers are those of the relevant memory address. For this reason, the memory address is read before being written to.

The *Map Mask Register* is at port address 3C5H. The register is write-only. Before sending data, send 2 to this address as an index. Bits 0-3 of this register correspond to bit planes 0-3; the high four bits of the register are not used. When bits

0-3are 0, the corresponding plane is unaffected by write operations. This feature is used in different ways by the various write modes, as you will see below.

The three write modes are set by the *mode register*, a write-only register at 3CF that is indexed by first sending 5H to the port. The write mode is set in bits 0 and 1 as a number from 0 to 2. Bit 2 should be 0, as should bits 4 through 7. Bit 3 sets up one of two modes for reading from the video buffer. The bit may be set to either 1 or 0. The EGA BIOS initializes the write mode to 00.

Write Mode 0:

In the simplest case, write mode 0 copies the byte of CPU data into each of the four bit planes. For example, say that 11111111B is sent to a video memory address when all bits and all bit planes are enabled (that is, none are masked out using the registers discussed above). Every bit in all four planes is set to 1, so that the bit pattern for each of the corresponding pixels is 1111B. This means that the eight pixels are shown in color code 15, which is initialized to bright white, although the palette registers allow it to be any other color, of course.

Now, consider the same case, but sending the value 00001000B. The bit pattern for pixel 3 is 1111, and for the others it is 0000, which corresponds to black (at start-up). And so in this case only pixel 3 would appear on the screen (again as bright white), and the other seven pixels would be "off." Even if the other seven pixels were already set to display a color, they would all be switched to 0000.

Next, consider using a color other than 1111B. If you send the palette code of the desired color to the map mask register, the register will mask out certain bit planes in a way that creates that color. For example, if you want the color code to be 0100, send 0100 to the map mask register. Bit planes 0, 1, and 3 will then be immune from changes. When you send 11111111B to the address, that value will be placed only in bit plane 2, and the bit patterns for each pixel will be 0100. If you send 00001000B to the address, pixel 3 will have the pattern 0100B, and all other pixels will be 0000B.

There is a complication, however. The map mask register *disables* bit planes, but it does not zero them. Say that bit plane 0 is filled with 1's, and that bit planes 1 and 3 are filled with 0's. If you disable these three planes and then write 11111111B to the video address, bit plane 2 will be filled by 11111111B, and bit plane 0 will keep its 1s, so that the resulting color code for each pixel will be 0101B. There are cases where you may wish to use this feature as a means of adjusting screen colors. But generally it is necessary to *clear* all four bit planes (that is, all four latch registers) before writing in any color other than 1111B or 0000B. This is done simply by sending 0 to the address. Be sure that all four bit planes are enabled when doing this.

The discussion up to now has concerned writing eight pixels at once. What about writing fewer pixels? In this case, existing pixel data must be preserved, of course, and this is done by seeing to it that the current contents of the video address are stored in the latch registers. Then the *bit map register* is used to mask out those pixels that are not to be changed. When a bit is set to 0 in this register, the data sent from the CPU for that bit is ignored, and instead the data for the bit that is found in the latch registers is used. Whether the bit in the CPU data is a 1 or a 0 makes no difference; if you are changing only bit 2 and all others are masked out, the data you send to the CPU could be ØFFH, or 4H, or any other value in which bit 2 is turned on. If bit 2 is off, Ø is placed in that position in all enabled bit planes.

Generally, a program must first *read* any memory position to which it is about to write fewer than eight pixels. There are two read modes (discussed at [4.4.4]), and it does not matter which is selected. The read operation "primes" the latch registers with the four bytes of data from that memory address. The data returned to the CPU by the read operation may be discarded.

Now, all of this comprises only the most *basic* functioning of write mode Ø. You can make matters much more complicated if you like. One option is to modify the latch contents before writing, using logical operations. The *data rotate register* uses the following bit pattern to provide these services:

```
bits 2-0      rotate count
     4-3      00      data unmodified
             01      data ANDed with latch contents
             10      data ORed with latch contents
             11      data XORed with latch contents
     7-5      unused
```

The data rotate count, from Ø to 7, sets how many bits the data is rotated before it is placed in the latch. Normally the value is Ø. Similarly, bits 4-3 are ØØ except when the data is to be ANDed, ORed, or XORed. By clever manipulation of these features, the same data can result in different colors and images, all without any additional CPU processing. The data rotate register is indexed by sending 3 to port address 3CEH; then send the data to 3CFH.

Finally, write mode Ø can be made to operate completely differently by enabling the *set/reset* feature. Here, a particular color is kept stored in the low four bits of the *set/reset register* (also located at 3CFH, and indexed by sending Ø to 3CEH). There is a corresponding register, the *enable set/reset register* which enables any or all of these four bits by setting its own low bits to 1. When all four bits in the set/reset register are enabled, they are placed in all eight locations of the bit plane when data is received from the CPU, and the CPU data is completely discarded. When fewer than all four of the set/reset bits are enabled, the CPU data is placed in the unenabled bit maps. Note that the bit mask register will prevent the set/reset data from being written to certain pixels, but that the map mask register setting is ignored by the set/reset feature. BIOS initializes the enable set/reset register to zeros so that it is inactive. It is located at 3CFH and is indexed by sending 1 to 3CEH.

Write Mode 1:

Write mode 1 is for special applications. In this mode, the current contents of the latch register are written to the specified address. Recall that the latch registers are filled by a read operation. This mode is extremely useful for rapidly transferring data during scroll operations. The bit mask register and map mask register have no effect on this operation. Nor does it matter what value it is that the CPU sends to the particular memory address—the latch contents are dumped without alteration.

Write Mode 2:

Write mode 2 provides an alternate way of setting individual pixels. The CPU sends a value in which only the four low bits are significant, and these four bits are taken as a *color* (palette register index). This is to say that the bit pattern is inserted *across* the four bit planes. The pattern is replicated across all eight positions at that memory address unless the bit mask register has been set up to protect certain pixels from being changed. The map mask register is active, as in write mode 0. Of course, the CPU must send a whole byte to the memory address, but only the low four bits are significant.

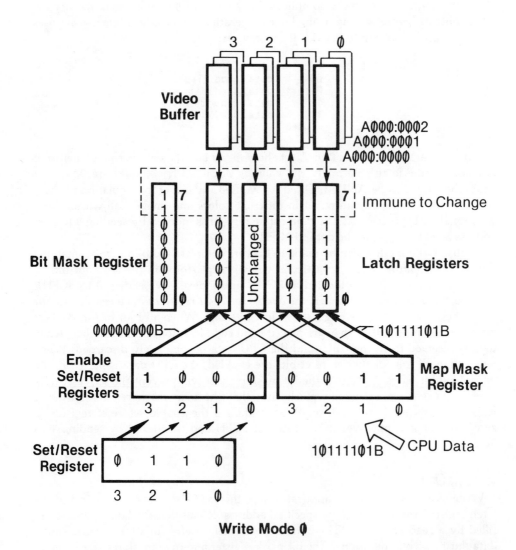

Figure 4-5. The EGA graphics write modes.

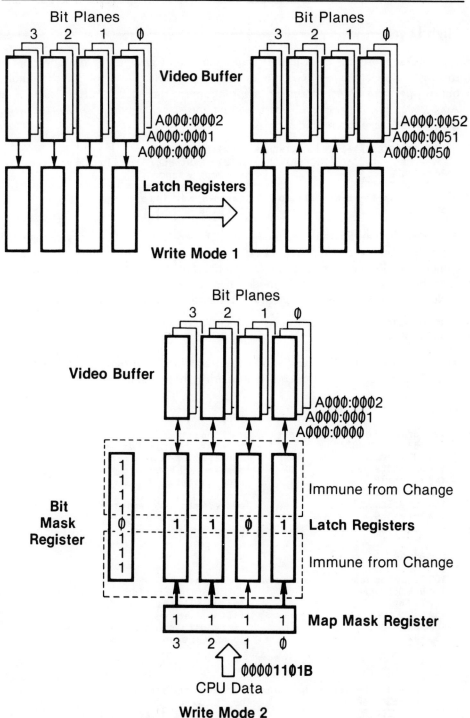

Figure 4-5 (cont.). The EGA graphics write modes.

High Level

BASIC supports the EGA in the "traditional" color graphics card modes. But at this writing the advanced EGA modes are not available. Thus you have no choice but to perform direct memory mapping onto the video buffer starting at A000:0000. The biggest problem is setting the screen mode. Use the following machine language subroutine:

```
10 S$=CHR$(&H2A)+CHR$(&HE4)+CHR$(&HB0)+CHR$(&H0D)
                +CHR$(&HCD)+CHR$(&H10)+CHR$(&HCB) 'the machine routine
20 DEF SEG                       'set memory segment
30 Y=VARPTR(S$)                  'point to string descriptor
40 Z=PEEK(Y+1)+PEEK(Y+2)*256     'calculate string address
50 CALL Z                        'call the subroutine
```

The fourth byte of S$ holds the mode number, here mode D. You may change it to any value you please. Appendix D explains how this routine fits into BASIC. It is completely self-contained; there is no need to set aside memory to hold the machine code. Be sure to restore the prior mode when finished.

Next, set the proper write mode. Here is the sequence to set write mode 2:

```
50 OUT &H3CE,5          'index the mode register
60 OUT &H3CF,2          'select mode 2
```

The original write mode should also be restored when the program is finished.

Finally, here are samples of code that perform the actual memory mapping:

Write Mode 0:

```
100 'draw red pixel at top left corner of the screen:
110 DEF SEG=&HA000              'point to the video buffer
120 OUT &H3CE,8                 'address the bit mask register
130 OUT &H3CF,128               'mask out all bits but 7
140 X=PEEK(0)                   'read current contents into latches
150 POKE 0,0                    'clear
160 OUT &H3C4,2                 'address map mask register
170 OUT &H3C5,4                 'set red as the color
180 POKE 0,&HFF                 'draw the pixel
```

Write Mode 1:

```
100 'copy top scan line to the scan line below:
110 DEF SEG=&HA000              'point to video buffer
120 FOR N=0 TO 79              'for all 80 bytes in the line
130 X=PEEK(N)                   'fill the latches
140 POKE N+80,Y                 'empty latches at scan segment below
150 NEXT                        'go do next scan line segment
```

Write Mode 2:

```
100 'draw a red pixel at the top left corner of the screen:
110 DEF SEG=&HA000              'point to the video buffer
120 OUT &H3CE,8                 'address the bit mask register
130 OUT &H3CF,128              'mask out all but bit 7
140 X=PEEK(0)                   'fill the latch registers
150 POKE 0,4                    'send red as the color
```

Middle Level

The EGA supports the standard BIOS graphics functions. Draw pixels using function CH of INT 10H, just as for the color card and PCjr. On entry, DX holds the row, and CX the column, both counted from 0. The color code is placed in AL. The contents of AX are destroyed during the interrupt.

```
;---DRAW A PIXEL AT 50,100:
                MOV   AH,0CH         ;function to set dot
                MOV   AL,12          ;choose palette register 12
                MOV   CX,100         ;column
                MOV   DX,50          ;row
                INT   10H            ;draw the dot
```

Low Level

Examples of the three write modes are given below. Before using them you must set a screen mode that uses the video buffer at A000:0000. Use the ordinary BIOS function; for example, to set mode D:

```
                MOV   AH,0           ;function to change mode
                MOV   AL,0DH         ;choose mode D
                INT   10H            ;change the mode
```

Be sure to restore the prior mode when finished. You will also need to set the write mode. Here is an example that sets write mode 2:

```
                MOV   DX,3CEH        ;point to address register
                MOV   AL,5           ;index register 5
                OUT   DX,AL          ;send the index
                INC   DX             ;point to mode register
                MOV   AL,2           ;choose write mode 2
                OUT   DX,AL          ;set the mode
```

Finally, here are examples of the three write modes:

Write Mode 0:

```
;---DRAW RED PIXEL AT TOP LEFT CORNER OF SCREEN:
                MOV   AX,0A000H      ;point ES to buffer
                MOV   ES,AX          ;
                MOV   BX,0           ;point to first byte of the buffer
;---MASK ALL BITS BUT BIT 7:
                MOV   DX,3CEH        ;point to address register
                MOV   AL,8           ;register number
                OUT   DX,AL          ;send it
                INC   DX             ;now point to data register
                MOV   AL,10000000B   ;the mask
                OUT   DX,AL          ;send the data
;---CLEAR CURRENT LATCH CONTENTS:
                MOV   AL,ES:[BX]     ;read contents in
                MOV   AL,0           ;get ready to clear
                MOV   ES:[BX],AL     ;clear it
;---SET UP MAP MASK REGISTER FOR RED:
                MOV   DX,3C4H        ;point to address register
                MOV   AL,2           ;map mask register index
                OUT   DX,AL          ;set the address
                INC   DX             ;point to data register
```

```
                    MOV   AL,4                  ;color code
                    OUT   DX,AL                 ;set the color
      ;---DRAW THE PIXEL:
                    MOV   AL,0FFH               ;send any value with bit 7 on
                    MOV   ES:[BX],AL            ;pixel written
```

Write Mode 1:

```
      ;---COPY A SCAN LINE TO THE SCAN LINE BELOW:
                    MOV   CX,80                 ;eighty bytes in a scan line
                    MOV   BX,0                  ;start from first byte of buffer
                    MOV   AX,0A000H             ;buffer address
                    MOV   ES,AX                 ;point ES to it
      NEXT_BYTE:    MOV   AL,ES:[BX]            ;fill latch registers with data
                    MOV   ES:[BX]+80,AL         ;empty latch at scan segment below
                    INC   BX                    ;point to next byte
                    LOOP  NEXT_BYTE             ;go do next
```

Write Mode 2:

```
      ;---DRAW RED PIXEL AT TOP LEFT CORNER OF SCREEN:
                    MOV   AX,0A000H             ;point ES to buffer
                    MOV   ES,AX                 ;
                    MOV   BX,0                  ;point to first byte of the buffer
      ;---SET UP BIT MASK REGISTER:
                    MOV   DX,3CEH               ;point to address register
                    MOV   AL,8                  ;bit mask register
                    OUT   DX,AL                 ;address the register
                    INC   DX                    ;point to data register
                    MOV   AL,10000000B          ;mask out all bits but bit 7
                    OUT   DX,AL                 ;send the data
      ;---DRAW A RED PIXEL:
                    MOV   AL,ES:[BX]            ;fill the latch registers
                    MOV   AL,4                  ;red
                    MOV   ES:[BX],AL            ;draw the pixel
```

4.4.4 Find the color at a point on the screen

For the graphics modes of the color card and PCjr, finding the color of a pixel at low-level entails no more than reversing the procedures that write one: a program reads from video memory and isolates the relevant bits. The EGA, however, can not be accessed this way in modes DH - 10H, since there are two or four bytes of memory at any particular address. The card has two *read modes* to deal with this difficulty. Keep in mind that on the PCjr and EGA, once you find the color code for a pixel, you still must check the current palette register setting for that code in order to find the color it is associated with.

Any programming language can access the two EGA read modes. Mode 0 returns the byte found at any one of the bit planes at the particular address. Mode 1 seeks a specified color code and returns a byte in which a bit is set to 1 when the corresponding pixel has that color. Bit 3 of the *mode register* determines which read mode is in effect (0 = mode 0). This register is at port address 3CFH, and you must first send 5 to 3CEH to select the register. Ordinarily, all other bits in this write-only register are set to 0, except for bits 0 & 1, which set the write mode. Since BIOS sets these two bits for write mode 0 (so that they are both 0), normally you need only send 0 to the register to bring about read mode 0, or send 8 to invoke read mode 1.

Read mode 0 requires that you first set the *map select register*. The sole purpose of this register is to set which bit map is to be read. So send a number from 0 - 3 to it. The register is at port address 3CFH, and 4 must first be sent to 3CEH to index the register.

Read mode 1 is more complicated. First the *color compare* register must be given the bit pattern of the color code you are seeking. The code is placed in the bottom four bits of the register; the high four bits are not significant. The register is at port address 3CFH, and it is indexed by first sending 2 to 3CEH. When the memory position is read, a byte is returned with 1's for every pixel that matches that color. However, by using the *color don't care* register, one or more bits of the color code can be ignored when the comparison is made. Normally the four low bits of this register are set to 1; zeroing one of these bits causes the contents of the corresponding bit plane to be ignored. For example, ordinarily if the bit pattern for pixel #3 (bit 3) at a particular address is 0110, and the color compare register contains the value 0010, it will return a byte in which bit 3 = 0 when the color don't care register is all 1's. But if the color don't care register contained 1011, bit 3 would be set to 1 in the byte returned to the CPU.

The color don't care register is at 3CFH, and it is indexed by sending 7 to 3CEH. The high four bits are not significant. Note that IBM documentation (August 2, 1984) states that the register operates in the opposite way, so that a 1 in the register makes the comparison operation ignore a bit plane. Experimentation shows otherwise.

Neither of the two read modes can quickly tell the color of a particular pixel. In read mode 0, four separate reads are required, one for each bit plane, and then the relevant bits must be masked out of each byte. In read mode 1, on the other hand, it could take up to sixteen reads before a 1 is returned for a particular pixel, showing that it is the specified color. While the EGA is relatively slow in this particular operation, it moves quickly for other needs.

High Level

BASIC provides the POINT function to return the color of a pixel. The palette color of the pixel at column 200, row 100 is found by **Q = POINT(200,100)**. The value given to Q is an ordinary color code number. If a point off-screen is named, POINT returns -1. When the coordinate system of the screen has been changed by a WINDOW statement [4.4.2], the POINT statement observes the new system.

POINT can also report the position of the last pixel drawn. Using the ordinary coordinate system where 0,0 is the top left corner or the screen, **Q = POINT(1)** gives to Q the x coordinate of the pixel, and **Q = POINT(2)** gives the y coordinate. If a WINDOW statement is in effect, **Q = POINT(3)** and **Q = POINT(4)** provide the respective x and y coordinates in the specified coordinate system. When no WINDOW statement is operational, the second two statements operate like the first two.

At this writing, BASIC does not support the EGA in its advanced modes (D-10H). In these modes a program must directly read the contents of the video buffer. Here is an example using read mode 1 that searches for color code 0001 or 1001:

```
100 OUT &H3CE,5        'address the mode register
110 OUT &H3CF,8        'set read mode 1
120 OUT &H3CE,2        'address color compare register
130 OUT &H3CF,1        'search for 0001
140 OUT &H3CE,7        'address color don't care register
150 OUT &H3CF,7        '7=0111B, so will seek 0001 or 1001
160 DEF SEG=&HA000     'point to EGA buffer in modes DH-10H
170 X=PEEK(0)          'read first byte
180 IF X<>0 THEN...    '...then 0001 or 1001 was found
```

Middle Level

Function D of INT 10H returns the color code of a specified pixel. The BIOS on board the EGA assures that this function works with any screen mode. Place the row number (counting from 0) in DX, and the column number (also from 0) in CX. The result is returned in AL.

```
;---FIND THE PALETTE CODE OF 100,200:
        MOV   AH,0DH         ;function number to read dot
        MOV   DX,100         ;row number
        MOV   CX,200         ;column number
        INT   10H            ;and now the palette code is in AL
```

Low Level

In the color card and PCjr graphics modes, simply reverse the memory mapping process by which a pixel is set, as shown at [4.4.2]. Use the same example found there, but end it this way:

```
;---CHANGE THE BITS (starting point for the change):
              MOV   AH,ES:[BX]        ;get byte from correct position
              ROR   AH,CL             ;move 2 relevant bits to bottom of AH
              AND   AH,00000011B      ;make out other bits
              RET                     ;and now AH holds the palette code
```

For EGA modes DH-10H, manipulate the registers discussed above. The following example uses read mode 0 to read bit plane 2 at memory address A000:0012.

```
;---SET THE READ MODE:
              MOV   DX,3CEH           ;index register
              MOV   AL,5              ;address the mode register first
              OUT   DX,AL             ;send the index
              INC   DX                ;point to the register itself
              MOV   AL,0              ;all bits off for read mode 0
              OUT   DX,AL             ;set the mode
;---SET WHICH BIT PLANE TO READ:
              DEC   DX                ;point back to index register
              MOV   AL,4              ;address the map select register
              OUT   DX,AL             ;send the index
              INC   DX                ;point to the register itself
              MOV   AL,2              ;request bit map 2
              OUT   DX,AL             ;send the value
;---READ THE BIT MAP:
              MOV   AX,0A000H         ;buffer starts at A000:0000
              MOV   ES,AX             ;point ES to the buffer
              MOV   BX,12             ;offset in buffer
              MOV   AL,ES:[BX]        ;read bit plane 2
```

Finally, here is an example that seeks color code 0010 or 1010 using read mode 1:

```
;---SET THE READ MODE:
              MOV   DX,3CEH           ;index register
              MOV   AL,5              ;address the mode register first
              OUT   DX,AL             ;send the index
              INC   DX                ;point to the register itself
              MOV   AL,8              ;set bit 3 for read mode 1
              OUT   DX,AL             ;set the mode
;---SET THE COLOR COMPARE REGISTER:
              DEC   DX                ;return to index register
              MOV   AL,2              ;address of color compare register
              OUT   DX,AL             ;send the index
              INC   DX                ;point to the register itself
              MOV   AL,0010B          ;the color code
              OUT   DX,AL             ;send the code
;---SET THE COLOR DON'T CARE REGISTER:
              DEC   DX                ;back to the index register
              MOV   AL,7              ;address of color don't care register
              OUT   DX,AL             ;send the index
              INC   DX                ;point to the register itself
              MOV   AL,0111B          ;accept either 1010 or 0010
              OUT   DX,AL             ;send the value
;---SEEK THE COLOR:
              MOV   AX,0A000H         ;buffer starts at A000:0000
              MOV   ES,AX             ;point ES to the buffer
              MOV   BX,12             ;offset in buffer
              MOV   AL,ES:[BX]        ;read the buffer position
              CMP   AL,0              ;any bits set?
              JNZ   FOUND_IT          ;if so, go find out which ones
```

4.4.5 Draw lines on the screen

The simplest way to draw lines on the screen is to calculate at which point the next dot of a line resides and then change the bits of the byte that hold that point. Such operations are slow, although they are often unavoidable. It is better, when possible, to calculate the range of screen positions that hold a particular color. Then the required bit operations need be done on only one byte, and that byte can be placed in a range of corresponding position in the video buffer.

High Level ————————————————————————

BASIC draws straight lines with the LINE statement. **LINE (20,10)-(40,30)** draws a line from column 20, row 10 to column 40, row 30. Both rows and columns are numbered from 0. You may omit the first coordinate, in which case drawing originates from the last point drawn in the previous graphics statement. The second coordinate may also be specified *relative* to the prior point by writing **LINE -STEP(xoffset,yoffset)**.

The LINE statement also holds specifications for the color and pattern of the line. The color code immediately follows the listing of the coordinates; **LINE (50,50)-(60,60),2** draws the line in color 2. When no color is given, it defaults to number 3. The *style* feature lets lines be dotted in any way you please. A binary pattern is written in decimal or hexadecimal form. For example, the pattern **1010101010101010**, which is equal to &HAAAA, results in a line where the dots alternate between the given color and the background color. Write the pattern specification as the third parameter following the coordinates. For example, **LINE (30,30)-(40-40),3,,&HAAAA** produces the above pattern in color code 3.

BASIC also provides routines to draw rectangles and circles. Rectangles are drawn using the LINE statement. In this case the coordinates describe the top left and bottom right corners of the box. Simply write **B** (for "box") as the third parameter following the coordinates. **LINE (50,50)-(100,100),1,B,&HAAAA** draws a square 50 dots on a side in palette color 1, using the style pattern explained above. Write **BF** instead to draw a rectangle filled in the designated color (do not set a style pattern in this case).

Circles are drawn by the CIRCLE statement. It is based on the formula, **CIRCLE (x,y),r,color,start-angle,stop-angle,aspect.** The x-y coordinates give the screen address of the center of the circle, and r gives the radius in pixels; all other information is optional. The color is a color code that defaults to 3. The start- and stop-angles can be set to draw only an arc of a circle (when omitted, a whole circle is drawn). The angle is measured as a positive or negative quantity starting from the rightwards horizontal. Measure it in *radians* (there are 2*PI radians in 360 degrees (6.292 radians), and 1 degree = .0174532 radians). The aspect is a ratio that adjusts horizontal to vertical dimensions. A round circle results when it is 5/6 in medium resolution or 5/12 in high resolution. Smaller numbers make for horizontally extended ellipses; larger ones create the opposite. In summary, **PI = 3.14159:CIRCLE (200,50),30,2,PI/2,PI,10/6** results in an arc centered at row

50, column 200, with a 30-pixel radius, drawn in color 2, encompassing only the top-left quadrant of a vertically extended ellipse.

More complex lines may be drawn with the DRAW statement, which is extremely versatile. DRAW is followed by a string (set in parentheses) in which code numbers give the sequence of orientations and lengths of the segments that make up the line. For example, **DRAW"E12F12G12H12"** draws a diamond. Set the initial point with PSET (discussed at [4.4.2]); otherwise it defaults to center-screen. The basic codes consist of a letter followed by the number of pixels of segment length. The codes are as follows:

```
Ux          Move up (x pixels)
Dx          Move down
Rx          Move right
Lx          Move left
Ex          Move diagonally up and right
Fx          Move diagonally down and right
Gx          Move diagonally down and left
Hx          Move diagonally up and left
```

In medium resolution, 100 pixels horizontally and 100 pixels vertically result in line segments of approximately equal length (the y to x *aspect ratio* is actually 5/6). In high resolution, the horizontal line would be roughly half the length of the vertical one. Because of the greater distance between the pixels, diagonals that form a hypoteneuse across a box have the same number of pixels as the longest side of the box, even though the segment itself is longer.

To draw diagonals at angles other than 45 degrees, use the code letter M. This code will draw the next line segment to either an absolute or relative position on the screen. For an absolute position, list its x and y coordinates. **DRAW"M50,60"** extends the line to column 50, row 60. Add plus and minus signs before the letters. If the current point on the x axis is 100, +50 will extend the line to column 150, and -50 will extend it to column 50. To move from 100,100 to 120,70, write **DRAW"M+20,-30"**.

The line need not be continuous. When the letter **B** is placed before a code, the code moves "the point of the pen" as specified, but without actually drawing the segment. For example, **DRAW"L10BU5R10"** draws two parallel horizontal lines. To draw more than one segment outward from a single point, precede a code with the letter N. In this case, "the point of the pen" returns to its starting point after drawing the segment.

There are a number of special codes which can be placed anywhere in a string, and which affect all codes that follow (until another such code makes a different specification). Set the color of line segments by the letter C followed by a color code. **DRAW"C2D5"** draws a line downwards in color 2. Change the scale in which a figure, or part of a figure, is drawn by setting the scale factor. Add to the string the letter S followed by the factor. The factor is a number that is divided by 4. The factor is normally set to 4, which makes the scale equal to '1'. Changing the factor to 8 doubles the size of the figure drawn. In this case, write **DRAW "S8U12D12"**...etc.

You may tilt the axes of the entire coordinate system using either of two codes. The code letter A turns the axes counterclockwise by 90-degree increments. A0 turns it not at all, A1 turns it by 90 degrees, A2 by 180 degrees, and A3 by 270 degrees. Similarly, the **TA** turns the axes by a specified number of degrees, numbered from 0 to 360 (counterclockwise), or from 0 to -360 (clockwise). **DRAW"A1L10"** and **DRAW"TA90L10"** both result in a leftward-drawn line being directed 90 degrees downward instead.

A DRAW statement may contain string variables that themselves contain valid codes. This feature enables a program to reuse *parts* of figures in different drawings. Within a DRAW statement, place the name of the string after the letter X and follow the string name with a semicolon. For example:

```
100 S$="U12R15U45L32"
110 DRAW"XS$;"
```

A number of strings may be combined in a single DRAW statement, interspersed with any of the other codes. Note that any of the numbers used with codes in DRAW statements may themselves be variables. In this way a single DRAW routine can easily be made to vary in its configuration, color, scale, and orientation. Place an equals sign between the code letter and the variable name, and follow the name with a semicolon. For example, to set the color by a variable, write **DRAW"C = PCOLOR;"**. The BASIC compiler requires that these variables be referenced by means of a VARPTR$ function. In this case, write the statement as **DRAW"X" + VARPTR$(S$)** or **DRAW"C = " + VARPTR(PCOLOR)**. Complex drawings may be stored in an array and returned to the screen at any time. See [4.4.6] for a discussion.

Low Level

The routine below uses Bresenham's algorithm to draw a straight line between any two points. It uses the BIOS function that sets pixels, and it could be made even faster by replacing the function with a direct memory mapping routine *in line.* Like all fast algorithms, it avoids multiplication and division operations. A line is treated as a series of two kinds of segments: those that move diagonally, and those that move either horizontally or vertically. In lines with a slope greater than 1, the straight segments are vertical, and otherwise they are horizontal; the first task of the algorithm is to figure out the slope. Then an adjustment factor is calculated that sees to it that a certain number of straight segments are longer than the rest. Finally, a complicated loop switches back and forth between plotting the diagonal and straight segments. BX alternates between positive and negative values, flagging which kind of segment to draw. Here, the data is set up for a diagonal from one corner of the screen to the opposite:

```
;---IN THE DATA SEGMENT:
        START_X                 DW 0
        END_X                   DW 319
        START_Y                 DW 0
        END_Y                   DW 199
        COLOR                   DB 2
        DIAGONAL_Y_INCREMENT    DW ?
        DIAGONAL_X_INCREMENT    DW ?
        SHORT_DISTANCE          DW ?
```

```
                STRAIGHT_X_INCREMENT              DW ?
                STRAIGHT_Y_INCREMENT              DW ?
                STRAIGHT_COUNT                   DW ?
                DIAGONAL_COUNT                   DW ?
;---SET SCREEN MODE:
                MOV  AH,0                     ;function to set mode
                MOV  AL,4                     ;320x200 color
                INT  10H                      ;set the mode
;---SET INITIAL INCREMENTS FOR EACH PIXEL POSITION:
                MOV  CX,1                     ;holds increment for x axis
                MOV  DX,1                     ;holds increment for y axis
;---CALCULATE THE VERTICAL DISTANCE:          ;keep it in CX
                MOV  DI,END_Y                 ;subtract starting point
                SUB  DI,START_Y               ;  from ending point
                JGE  KEEP_Y                   ;jmp ahead if negative slope
                NEG  DX                       ;otherwise, y increment is -1
                NEG  DI                       ;make the distance a positive value
KEEP_Y:         MOV  DIAGONAL_Y_INCREMENT,DX    ;y increment is 1
;---CALCULATE THE HORIZONTAL DISTANCE:        ;keep it in DX
                MOV  SI,END_X                 ;subtract starting point
                SUB  SI,START_X               ;  from ending point
                JGE  KEEP_X                   ;jmp ahead if negative slope
                NEG  CX                       ;otherwise, x increment is -1
                NEG  SI                       ;make the distance a positive value
KEEP_X:         MOV  DIAGONAL_X_INCREMENT,CX    ;x increment is 1
;---FIGURE WHETHER STRAIGHT SEGMENTS ARE HORIZONTAL OR VERTICAL:
                CMP  SI,DI                    ;is horizontal longer than vertical?
                JGE  HORZ_SEG                 ;if so, jump ahead
                MOV  CX,0                     ;else, no x-axis change when straight
                XCHG SI,DI                    ;place long distance in CX (DX short)
                JMP  SAVE_VALUES              ;save these values
HORZ_SEG:       MOV  DX,0                     ;no y-axis change when straight
SAVE_VALUES:    MOV  SHORT_DISTANCE,DI        ;save value of short distance
                MOV  STRAIGHT_X_INCREMENT,CX   ;one value is 1, one is 0, so
                MOV  STRAIGHT_Y_INCREMENT,DX   ;straight line is vert or horz
;---CALCULATE ADJUSTMENT FACTOR:
                MOV  AX,SHORT_DISTANCE        ;short distance into AX
                SHL  AX,1                     ;double short distance
                MOV  STRAIGHT_COUNT,AX        ;save it for straight loop
                SUB  AX,SI                    ;2*short distance - long distance
                MOV  BX,AX                    ;save it as loop counter
                SUB  AX,SI                    ;2*short distance-2*long distance
                MOV  DIAGONAL_COUNT,AX        ;save it for loop
;---PREPARE TO DRAW THE LINE:
                MOV  CX,START_X               ;set starting x coordinate
                MOV  DX,START_Y               ;set starting y coordinate
                INC  SI                       ;increase long axis by 1 for end point
                MOV  AL,COLOR                 ;place color code in dx
;---NOW DRAW THE LINE:                        ;SI & DI set coordinates for x & y
MAINLOOP:       DEC  SI                       ;decrement counter for long distance
                JZ   LINE_FINISHED            ;quit after last pixel
                MOV  AH,12                    ;function to draw pixel
                INT  10H                      ;draw it
                CMP  BX,0                     ;draw straight segment when BX < 0
                JGE  DIAGONAL_LINE            ; else, draw diagonal segment
;---DRAW STRAIGHT LINE SEGMENTS:
                ADD  CX,STRAIGHT_X_INCREMENT  ;set up x and y increments
                ADD  DX,STRAIGHT_Y_INCREMENT  ; for straight segment
                ADD  BX,STRAIGHT_COUNT        ;add to adjustment factor
                JMP  SHORT MAINLOOP           ;go do next pixel
```

```
;---DRAW DIAGONAL LINE SEGMENTS:
DIAGONAL_LINE:   ADD   CX,DIAGONAL_X_INCREMENT    ;set up x and y increments
                 ADD   DX,DIAGONAL_Y_INCREMENT    ; for diagonal segment
                 ADD   BX,DIAGONAL_COUNT          ;subtract from adjustment factor
                 JMP   SHORT MAINLOOP             ;go do next pixel
LINE_FINISHED:
```

4.4.6 Fill areas of the screen

Careful forethought can eliminate much of the painful slowness at which many programs fill areas of graphics screens. When the fill is based on simple calculations that operate dot-by-dot, then time-consuming bit operations are required. Smarter code can sometimes figure out whether all bit-positions of a particular byte in the video buffer will be given the same color; when so, the byte is given a predefined value that sets all bits to the correct color. In this way, the byte does not need to be repeatedly operated upon, each time setting bits for only one of the pixels that the byte holds information for.

[4.3.4] explains how to create special 8x8 dot characters in whatever pattern you choose. Although they are restricted to normal character positions, such characters can greatly facilitate graphics fills. A solid 8x8 pattern may be written over all positions within several rows and columns, filling the area several times faster than pixel-by-pixel drawing would. This kind of character graphics can be freely intermixed with dot-addressed graphics. Block graphics are also a good technique for fills that are tiled or dithered.

High Level

BASIC provides the PAINT statement to fill a closed figure of any shape. You need only specify a single, arbitrary point within the area and the routine takes care of the rest. A palette color may be set for the fill, so that, for example, **PAINT (100,110),2** paints in palette color 2. The painting works outward from the point until non-background-color pixels are encountered. Alternatively, you may specify a boundary color, and the painting continues outward in all directions until pixels of that color are located. In this way, lines of other colors *within* the boundary can be occluded by the paint operation. The boundary color follows the palette color for the fill; thus, **PAINT (100,180),2,3** paints in color 2 up to lines in color 3. Note, however, that this routine does not fill "around corners"; that is, once a limiting color is encounter along a particular vertical or horizontal trajectory, no further pixels along that trajectory are filled, even if the shape is an irregular one that reaches around. The following example draws two overlapping boxes in cyan and magenta and then fills the latter in white. The segments of the cyan box that overlap are painted over.

```
100 LINE (50,70)-(270,130),1,B      'draw box in cyan
110 LINE (100,30)-(220,170),2,B     'draw overlapping box in magenta
120 PAINT (101,31),3,2              'fill the second box in white
```

Be aware that the LINE command can itself fill in a box, using 'BF' (for "box fill") instead of 'B'. See [4.4.5].

The PAINT statement has a "tiling" feature that lets you fill areas in a specified pattern. A "tile" which in medium resolution is four dots wide and up to eight dots deep (8 x 8 in high resolution) is repeated over the designated area. The pattern is described as a series of bytes that hold the bit pattern of successive rows of the tile. In medium resolution, the bit pattern 10000011 gives four horizontal dots, the first in color 2, the next two in background color, and the last in color 3. The pattern equals 131, or &H83 (see Appendix B for a discussion of bit operations in BASIC). Reversing the pattern to 11000001 would give 193 (&HC1). These might be combined in the string **CHR$(&H83) + CHR$(&HC1)**, forming a tile that is four pixels wide and two pixels deep. Up to eight bytes may be included in such a string, making for a depth of up to eight pixels. Such a string is used in a PAINT statement in place of the palette color. Here a square is filled in the above pattern:

```
100 LINE (100,100)-(150,150),1,B      'draw the box
110 PAINT (125,125),CHR$(&H83)+CHR$(&HC1),1    'tile it in
```

Note that peculiarities of the tiling pattern can sometimes cause the PAINT routine to stop before it has completed the fill. BASIC provides a solution in the *background* parameter for the PAINT statement. If you have trouble, consult the BASIC manual for details.

The DRAW statement, which draws complex lines, also can fill an area. It is discussed at [4.4.5]. The "current point" (from which the next line segment is drawn) must be led into any area bound by a border of a particular palette color. Place within the DRAW string the code letter P, followed by the palette color in which to paint, and then the palette color of the boundary. To draw a box in palette color 1 and then fill it in color 3, write **DRAW"U10R10D10L10BH1P3,1"**. Here, the first four codes draw the walls of the box, then the code 'BH' moves the point into the box without drawing a segment, and then the P code causes the box to fill. Much more complex shapes can be filled this way. Note that it is not necessary to jump to a point within the figure without drawing a line segment along the way. However, the final segment must be of a different color than the boundary that is filled.

BASIC also has a way of filling areas of the screen with a predefined image. The image, which may be of any dimensions, is stored in an array, and it may be projected on the screen at any position. Ordinarily, one creates the image on the screen using the many tools available and then stores it in the array using the GET statement. The array may then be placed in a sequential file [5.4.3] so that a program can load it and project the image. The GET statement lists the top left and bottom right coordinates of the box that contains the image, giving first the column and then the row of each coordinate pair. Then the array name is given, without placing it in quotes. For example, **GET(80,40)-(120,60),ARRAY3** places all of the pixels in the defined box in the array named ARRAY3.

The one-dimensional array, like any other, must be defined beforehand using a DIM statement. The array may consist of elements of any precision. To calculate the required size of the array, first figure how many bytes are needed to hold the image. The formula for this is **4 + INT((x*bitsperpixel + 7)/8)*y**. Here, 'bitsperpixel' equals 1 in high resolution and 2 in medium resolution. The letters x and y refer to the number of pixels along the horizontal and vertical sides of the image block. 'INT' indicates that you should round downwards if the division by 8 results in a remainder. Finally, figure how many elements the array requires to hold that number of bytes. Each element is two bytes in an integer array, but four for single-precision and eight for double-precision.

To call the image from the array and display it on the screen, use the PUT statement. This statement requires only the coordinates of the top left corner of the area on the screen where the image is to be placed. Follow the coordinates with the array name. For example, **PUT (40,30),ARRAY1** places the image with the top left corner at column 40, row 30. The PUT statement optionally takes a final parameter that determines the colors in which the image is drawn. When omitted, the image appears exactly as it was recorded by GET. This is equivalent to writing **PUT (40,30),ARRAY1,PSET.** Otherwise, there are several other options. If instead of PSET you write PRESET, palette color 0 in the original image is printed in color 3, or vice-versa, and color 1 is replaced with color 2, or vice-versa.

There are three other cases which involve using the logical operators AND, OR, and XOR. Like PRESET, these words replace PSET in the example above. See Appendix B for a discussion of the three operations. Each operation entails comparing the bits of the existing pixel on the screen with the bits of the pixel in the image that will overlay it. In high resolution, where there is only one bit per pixel, the operations are straightforward. But in medium resolution, various color transformations occur because of the combinations made possible by two bits per pixel.

AND turns a bit on only if the bit is on for both the screen pixel and the image pixel (from the array). In high resolution, this means that a pixel in the image appears only when the matching pixel on the screen is already turned on. All other pixels in the area are turned off. In medium resolution, the two bits of each pixel are ANDed together. If a pixel on the screen is 01 and the corresponding pixel of the image is 10, then neither bit is turned on (since neither bit is 1 in both cases), and the pixel on the screen changes to 00, which is background color.

OR turns on a bit if the bit is on in either the screen pixel *or* the image pixel. In black and white, OR superimposes the image on to the existing image. But in color, again you must calculate the effects. Palette codes 1 (01) and 2 (10) combine into 3 (11), but so do codes 0 (00) and 3 (11).

Finally, XOR turns on a bit only if the bit is on in one, and only one, of the two bits compared. XORing an entire area of a black and white screen with 1 causes the image to reverse (1 and 1 result in 0, and 1 and 0 result in 1). In medium resolution, all colors change when XORed. The result is to superimpose the XORed image. But more importantly, when the image is XORed a second time, the screen reverts to being exactly as it was before. The image is effectively erased. This technique is useful for animation, in which case the image is XORed twice at one position, then XORed twice at an adjacent point, and so on.

Low Level

There are a number of approaches to graphics fill routines. None is ideal, since there is necessarily a tradeoff between the speed of the routine and the complexity of the figure that it can handle. Any routine that fills areas pixel-by-pixel is bound to be slow, no matter how elegantly it is conceived. Keep in mind that nearly every pixel affected will reside in a byte in which all pixels are changed to the same color. Making several accesses to the same byte through a complicated routine takes much more time than setting the whole byte by a single access to the video buffer. For example, clearing the screen pixel-by-pixel takes several seconds on a PC when the BIOS function is used, but memory mapping is instantaneous:

```
        MOV   AX,0B800H          ;point ES to screen buffer
        MOV   ES,AX              ;
        MOV   CX,8192            ;fill all bytes, even between 2 parts
        MOV   AX,0               ;put 0 in each byte
        MOV   DI,0               ;DI points to each byte in turn
REP STOSW                        ;write AX 8192 times
```

Many routines fill one horizontal line at a time, seeking the boundary color to the left and right and filling as they go. Since the lines are comprised of contiguous bytes of data, take each byte from the video buffer and quickly examine whether the boundary color is present anywhere in it. If not, replace the byte with an entire byte of fill color. Otherwise, resort to the usual pixel-by-pixel approach for that byte.

There is an extremely fast way of figuring out whether the boundary color appears within a byte of video data. Say that in four-color medium resolution the routine is seeking palette color 1 as the boundary color. The bit pattern for this color is 01, so first make an entire byte of those patterns: 01010101. Then use NOT to reverse each bit, so that the value becomes 10101010. XOR this value with a byte of data taken from the video buffer; the result will be a byte in which *both* bits in a field are 1 only in those fields that hold the bit pattern for the boundary color. After XORing the data, use NOT to reverse the digits so that boundary color fields are 00. Then use TEST to seek fields of 0 value. If such a field is found, the boundary color has been located, and the routine jumps to code that operates on pixels one-by-one, in the traditional fashion. Using word-length data makes this procedure even faster.

```
        MOV   AL,ES:[BX]         ;get a byte from the video buffer
        XOR   AL,10101010B       ;both bits on if boundary pattern
        NOT   AL                 ;both bits off if boundary pattern
        TEST  AL,11000000B       ;test bits 7-6
        JZ    FOUND_BOUNDARY     ;jump if boundary color found
        TEST  AL,00110000B       ;test bits 5-4
        JZ    FOUND_BOUNDARY     ;jump if boundary color found
        TEST  AL,00001100B       ;test bits 3-2
        JZ    FOUND_BOUNDARY     ;jump if boundary color found
        TEST  AL,00000011B       ;test bits 0-1
        JZ    FOUND_BOUNDARY     ;jump if boundary color found
        MOV   AL,FILL_COLOR      ;no boundary color, so fill
        MOV   ES:[BX],AL         ;replace byte in video buffer
        .                        ;...go get next byte
        .
FOUND_BOUNDARY:                  ;...instead, use BIOS to read and
                                 ;   set pixels in this boundary byte
```

Where feasible, consider designing your graphics so that the edges of rectangular shapes reside on two-, four-, or eight-pixel boundaries so that direct memory accesses can completely fill them. Although not as fast, another option is to create user-defined block characters [4.3.4], printing them over the edges of the fill area. There is much room for ingenuity here, and there often is no good reason for sluggish graphics.

4.4.7 Draw graphics using block characters

When graphics displays are drawn dot by dot, they can take up too much computing time, particularly when the graphics are animated. One way to increase speed is to reduce some or all of the graphics shapes to figures that can be constructed out of 8-by-8 dot patterns. These patterns are created as user-defined characters, as shown at [4.3.4]. Once the patterns are set up, they are written on the screen very quickly and with little code. The patterns may be mixed with dot-addressed graphics, just like ordinary characters. One way to quickly fill a shape is to repeat a *solid* block character within the shape. Note that these characters are always positioned at the usual cursor positions.

Middle Level ─────────────────────────────

This example draws a human figure that is two characters wide and two characters high. As explained at [4.3.4], interrupt vector number 1FH is pointed to the beginning of the character data. The four characters can be printed with ordinary BIOS and DOS routines. It would be easy to create a second set of characters showing the figure with legs and arms in a different position. The two character sets could then be alternated at adjacent cursor positions—making erasures between—to give the illusion of a man walking across the screen.

```
;---IN THE DATA SEGMENT:
  CHARACTER_DATA DB 00110000B          ;top-left quadrant of figure
                 DB 01100111B
                 DB 01100111B
                 DB 00110011B
                 DB 00011111B
                 DB 00001111B
                 DB 00001111B
                 DB 00000111B

                 DB 00000011B          ;top-right quadrant of figure
                 DB 10001100B
                 DB 10011000B
                 DB 00110000B
                 DB 11100000B
                 DB 11000000B
                 DB 11000000B
                 DB 10000000B

                 DB 00001111B          ;bottom-left quadrant of figure
                 DB 00011111B
                 DB 00011100B
                 DB 00011000B
                 DB 00011000B
                 DB 00110000B
                 DB 01100000B
                 DB 00010000B

                 DB 11000000B          ;bottom-right quadrant of figure
                 DB 11000000B
                 DB 11000000B
                 DB 11000000B
```

```
                DB 01100000B
                DB 00010000B
                DB 00011110B
                DB 00000000B

;---SET UP THE INTERRUPT VECTOR:
                PUSH DS                         ;interrupt destroys DS
                MOV  DX,OFFSET CHAR_DATA ;offset of character data in DX
                MOV  AX,SEG CHAR_DATA    ;segment of character data in DS
                MOV  DS,AX                      ;
                MOV  AH,25H                     ;function to set interrupt vector
                MOV  AL,1FH                     ;number of the vector
                INT  21H                        ;set the vector
                POP  DS                         ;restore DS

;---DRAW THE FIGURE:
;---POSITION CURSOR FOR TOP ROW:
                MOV  AH,2                       ;function to set cursor
                MOV  DH,13                      ;row 13
                MOV  DL,20                      ;column 20
                MOV  BH,0                       ;page 0
                INT  10H                        ;set the cursor
;---DRAW TOP TWO CHARACTERS:
                MOV  DL,128                     ;get character 128
                MOV  AH,2                       ;function to write/forward cursor
                INT  21H                        ;write it
                MOV  DL,129                     ;get character 129
                INT  21H                        ;write it
;---POSITION CURSOR FOR BOTTOM ROW:
                MOV  DH,14                       ;row 14
                MOV  DL,20                       ;column 20
                MOV  AH,2                        ;function to set cursor
                INT  10H                         ;set the cursor
;---DRAW BOTTOM TWO CHARACTERS:
                MOV  DL,130                      ;get character 130
                MOV  AH,2                        ;function to write/forward cursor
                INT  21H                         ;write it
                MOV  DL,131                      ;get character 131
                INT  21H                         ;write it
```

Section 5: Use Scrolling and Paging

Scrolling and paging are two ways of transferring blocks of information from memory to screen. In *scrolling*, one edge of the screen is shifted inward, erasing the information on the opposite side. Then the area that has been opened up is filled from memory. Repeating this action line after line creates the illusion of a scroll.

On the other hand, *paging* is based on keeping several screens of information in the video buffer at the same time, switching the video display from one or another. Paging is not possible on the monochrome adaptor since it contains only enough memory for one character screen. The other video systems can manage multiple pages in most screen modes. Paging is particularly useful for constructing time-consuming screens out of view; once finished, the screen may be displayed instantly. A pseudo-paging routine for the monochrome adaptor is given at [4.5.3]. It is particularly useful for dealing with slow screen output in BASIC.

4.5.1 Scroll a text screen vertically

When a text screen is scrolled upwards, lines 2 through 25 are rewritten upon lines 1 through 24, and the next line of a data is taken from memory and written on line 25. By being written over, the top line of data is "lost," although it continues to exist in memory. Downward scrolling works in like fashion.

High Level ─────────────────────────────

BASIC is notoriously slow in its screen operations. For rapid scrolling you will want to use the following machine language subroutine, which does nothing more than make use of INT 10H, as described under *middle level* below. The routine scrolls the whole screen or any window within it. Appendix D shows how to integrate machine subroutines into your programs. Your BASIC program must specify the coordinates of the top left and bottom right corners of the window, counting 0-24 and 0-79. Also required is a parameter telling whether the scroll moves upwards or downwards (6 or 7, respectively), the number of lines to scroll (if 0, the window clears), and the value of the attribute byte for the lines that are blanked out (7 for "normal"). Use integer variables. The example below makes the whole screen scroll downwards one line, and then fills the vacated line.

```
100 '''data for the subroutine:
110 DATA &H55,&H8B,&HEC,&H8B,&H76,&H12,&H8A
120 DATA &H24,&H8B,&H76,&H10,&H8A,&H04,&H8B
130 DATA &H76,&H0E,&H8A,&H2C,&H8B,&H76,&H0C
140 DATA &H8A,&H0C,&H8B,&H76,&H0A,&H8A,&H34
150 DATA &H8B,&H76,&H08,&H8A,&H14,&H8B,&H76
160 DATA &H06,&H8A,&H3C,&HCD,&H10,&H5D,&HCA
170 DATA &H0E,&H00
180 '''place the data at segment value &H2000:
190 DEF SEG=&H2000                         'place data at &H20000
200 FOR N=0 TO 43                          '44 bytes
210 READ Q                                 'read one byte
220 POKE N,Q                               'place it in memory
230 NEXT                                   'next

300 '''in the program:
310 GOSUB 270                              'scroll down one line
320 LOCATE 1,1:PRINT TEXT$(LINEPTR);       'write line of text at 1,1

500 '''scroll subroutine:
510 DEFINT A-Z                             'use integer variables
520 TLR=0                                  'top left row
530 TLC=0                                  'top left column
540 BRR=24                                 'bottom right row
550 BRC=79                                 'bottom right column
560 NUMROWS=1                              'scroll one row
570 DIR=7                                  'scroll downwards
580 FILL=7                                 'fill in normal attribute
590 DEF SEG=&H2000                         'point to machine routine
600 SCROLL=0                               'start at first byte
610 CALL SCROLL(DIR,NUMROWS,TLR,TLC,BRR,BRC,FILL)   'make the scroll
620 RETURN                                 'all done
```

Middle Level

Function 6 of INT 10H scrolls any part of the screen upwards, and function 7 scrolls it downwards. In both cases AL holds the number of lines to scroll, and when AL = 0, the entire screen is cleared instead of scrolled. CH:CL holds the row and column for the top left corner, and DH:DL holds the coordinates for the bottom right. The row(s) that are scrolled away from are cleared, and they are given the attribute code placed in BH.

```
;---SCROLL UPWARDS ONE LINE:
        MOV   AH,6          ;function number to scroll upwards
        MOV   AL,1          ;number of rows to scroll upwards
        MOV   CH,0          ;coordinate of top left row
        MOV   CL,0          ;coordinate of top left column
        MOV   DH,24         ;coordinate of bottom right row
        MOV   DL,79         ;coordinate of bottom right column
        MOV   BH,7          ;attribute of cleared line
        INT   10H           ;make the scroll
                            ;now fill bottom line with text...
```

Low Level

Scrolling the whole screen vertically is a trivial task, since in memory the right end of one line continues at the left end of the next. Moving everything in the video buffer 160 bytes upwards in memory (80 columns x 2 bytes per character) results in scrolling the screen downwards by one line. If you write your own scroll routine using direct memory mapping, be careful of the screen interference that occurs on the color card and in the PCjr. This problem is discussed at [4.3.1]. The usual solution is to keep checking a status byte until it gives the go-ahead to write data into the video buffer. You will need to experiment to see how much data can be written in a cycle.

An alternate solution is to turn off the screen entirely during the scroll operation and then instantly restore it. To "turn the screen off" means that the projection of data from the video buffer is disabled, but the buffer itself is untouched. This process is used by the BIOS scroll routine above; although it is unpleasant to the eyes, it is not as bad as the interference it averts.

To turn the screen off on the color graphics adaptor, set bit 3 at port address 3D8H to 0. Changing the bit to 1 instantly turns the screen back on. The port address is for the Mode Select Register on the color graphics card. This one-byte register is write-only, so a program cannot just read it, change bit 3, and then replace the byte. Rather, you must determine the settings for the other bits of the register as well (listed at [4.1.2]). On the PCjr this bit is located in Mode Control Register 1 in the video gate array. [4.1.1] explains how to access and program this register.

4.5.2 Scroll a text screen horizontally

Horizontal scrolling is sometimes required for special text processing, such as in program editors. The operating system has no special facilities for it. For this reason it is more complicated than vertical scrolling—but not by much. Consider the case in which you want the screen to scroll leftwards by five columns. The five columns on the left are to be overlaid, the other text is shifted left, and the rightmost five columns must be blanked out. Since the video buffer is one long string, if every character in it is moved downwards in the buffer by ten bytes, the net effect is that the leftmost five characters of every line wrap around to the right edge of the line above. Thus the screen is shifted leftwards by five columns, moving the five discarded columns to the right edge of the screen. All that remains is to blank out the right edge. This is easily done with the *vertical* scrolling routine [4.5.1], which can be set up to operate on only part of the screen, and which blanks out that area when it is told to scroll by zero lines. Figure 4-6 illustrates this method.

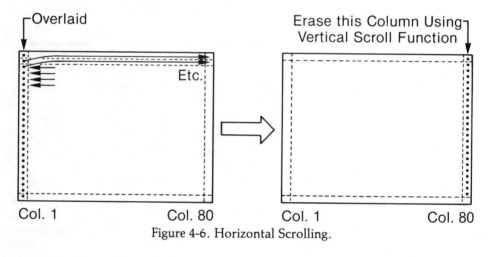

Figure 4-6. Horizontal Scrolling.

Low Level ━━

This example scrolls leftwards by five columns. It is easy to modify it to scroll rightwards as well and to move by a specified number of columns. By using direct memory mapping to shift the characters, this technique results in a practically instantaneous scroll.

```
;---SHIFT EVERYTHING DOWNWARDS BY 10 BYTES:
            MOV   AX,0B000H        ;point DS and ES to monochrome buffer
            MOV   ES,AX            ;
            MOV   DS,AX            ;
            MOV   SI,10            ;shift from SI...
            MOV   DI,0             ;...to DI
            MOV   CX,1995          ;move all but 5 of 2000 characters
      REP   MOVSW                  ;make the shift
;---BLANK OUT THE RIGHT EDGE:
            MOV   AH,6             ;vertical scroll function of INT 10H
            MOV   AL,0             ;0 lines to scroll blanks out window
```

```
        MOV   CH,0              ;top left row
        MOV   CL,75             :top left column
        MOV   DH,24             ;bottom right row
        MOV   DL,79             ;bottom right column
        MOV   BH,7              ;attribute to use for blank
        INT   10H               ;clear the window
```

4.5.3 Switch between text pages

Because all video systems except the monochrome card have enough memory for several video buffers, several screens may be constructed at once, and whichever is required at the moment may be displayed. Rather than move data around in video memory, the monitor is sent data from different parts of video memory. The number of pages possible varies by video system and screen mode. Here is a comparison:

Mode	Type	Number pages	Buffer start
0	alpha	8	B800
1	alpha	8	B800
2	alpha	4/8	B800
3	alpha	4/8	B800
4	graphic	1	B800
5	graphic	1	B800
6	graphic	1	B800
7	alpha	1/8	B000
8	graphic	variable	B800
9	graphic	variable	B800
A	graphic	variable	B800
D	graphic	2/4/8	A000
E	graphic	1/2/4	A000
F	graphic	1/2	A000
10	graphic	1/2	A000

Modes 8-A are PCjr graphics modes; the number of pages varies depending on how much read/write memory has been allocated for the video buffer. The page size is 2K or 4K for alpha modes, 32K for four colors in high resolution or 16 colors in medium resolution, and 16K for all other modes. Modes D-10 are confined to the EGA. The number of pages varies by how much RAM is mounted. Modes F and 10 minimally require 128K. Mode 7 allows one page for the monochrome card, and eight with the EGA.

The monochrome adaptor does not have memory aboard for extra pages. There is no reason why a section of main memory cannot be set aside as a screen buffer. In this case, paging is achieved by quickly exchanging the entire contents of the memory buffer and the video buffer (which is located at B000:0000). Think of the buffer in main memory as a "pseudopage." While not true paging, the result is much the same so long as the data is shifted by an assembly language routine.

When paging is used, care must be taken that operations that write on the screen are directed to the proper page. A program is not required to write on the page currently displayed. In fact, it is often desirable to construct screens "off stage" and then bring them to view instantaneously. This technique is particularly useful when making complicated screens in BASIC that take long to write. BIOS keeps a one-byte variable in its data area that reports which page is currently displayed. The variable ranges from 0 to 7. It is located at 0040:0062.

High Level

BASIC uses the SCREEN command to set which page is written upon (the *active* page), and which is displayed (the *visual* page). The pages are numbered from 0 to 3 for 80-column text, or from 0 to 7 for 40-column text. The third parameter following **SCREEN** sets the active page. **SCREEN,,2** causes all PRINT statements to write upon page 2. The fourth parameter sets the visual page. **SCREEN,,,1** causes page 1 to be the one currently shown. Taken together, **SCREEN,,2,1** writes on screen 2 while displaying screen 1. When the display page is left unspecified, it automatically becomes the same as the active page.

To set aside memory for paging on the PCjr, use the CLEAR statement. This statement sets the total amount of memory devoted to the screen buffer, which at start-up is 16384 bytes. To add a second 16K page, write **CLEAR,,,32768.** Additional text pages require 4096 bytes each. Providing memory is set aside in this way, the paging commands of the SCREEN statement operate as described above. The PCjr alone has an extra parameter for this SCREEN statement that erases pages (that is, returns them to background color). See the BASIC manual for details. Also unique to the PCjr is the PCOPY statement, which copies an image from one page to another. **PCOPY 2,1**, for example, copies the whole of page 2 onto page 1.

Although the monochrome adaptor hasn't enough memory for paging, there is a way to provide a sort of "pseudopaging." The machine language subroutine below treats a block of memory as a display page. When the subroutine is called, it *exchanges* the contents of the video buffer with the contents of this memory area. Thus the effect is as if there were two display pages. (Appendix D explains how to use machine subroutines in BASIC programs.)

You must set aside a 4000-byte memory block for the pseudopage in addition to the memory that will hold the machine subroutine. In the example below, the block starts at segment value &H2000 and the machine routine is placed at &H2200. The segment value of the block is contained within the 9th and 10th bytes of machine code, and you can easily change it. You will find that the address &H2000 is expressed as &H00,&H20 in the DATA statement. This is because the least significant digits are always placed in the lowest memory locations. If you want to position the block at, say, 1234:0000, then change bytes 9 and 10 to &H34,&H12.

You may need to clear the pseudopage of any garbage left by other programs. Lines 230-260 accomplish this by poking ASCII 32, the space character, into every byte (32 acts as a "normal" attribute byte). A program can write to the screen normally and then transfer the contents to the pseudopage. But if you want to write directly to the pseudopage you must use direct memory mapping.

```
100 '''''the machine code:
110 DATA &H1E,&H06,&HB8,&H00,&HB0,&H8E,&HC0
120 DATA &HB8,&H00,&H20,&H8E,&HD8,&HBF,&H00
130 DATA &H00,&HBE,&H00,&H00,&HFC,&HB9,&HD0
140 DATA &H07,&H26,&H8B,&H1D,&HAD,&HAB,&H89
150 DATA &H5D,&HFE,&HE2,&HF6,&H07,&H1F,&HCB
```

```
160 '''''poke the code into memory
170 DEF SEG=&H2200                  'point to location for routine
180 FOR N=0 TO 34                   'start from first byte
190 READ Q                          'read a byte of the routine
200 POKE N,Q                        'poke it
210 NEXT                            '
220 '''''clear the pseudopage of garbage:
230 DEF SEG=&H2000                  'point to start of pseudopage
240 FOR N=0 TO 3999                 'for each char and attribute...
250 POKE N,32                       'poke in 32
260 NEXT                            'until whole buffer cleared

500 '''''write directly to pseudopage:
510 DEF SEG=&H2000                  'point to pseudopage
520 S$="PSEUDOPAGE"                 'write "pseudopage" mid-page
530 M=LEN(S$)                       'get length of string
540 FOR N=1 TO M                    'for each character of the string...
550 POKE N*2+2000,ASC(MID$(S$,N,1))   'poke at memory position after next
560 NEXT                            '...leaving it in video buffer format

600 '''''now use the routine:
610 PRINT"SCREEN 1"                 'print message on screen as usual
620 DEF SEG=&H2200                  'point to the machine subroutine
630 PSEUDOPAGE=0                    'start at the beginning
640 CALL PSEUDOPAGE                 'exchange screen and pseudopage
650 CALL PSEUDOPAGE                 'switch them back
660 ...
```

Middle Level

Function 5 of INT 10H chooses which page is currently displayed. Simply place the page number in AL:

```
;---SET THE VISUAL PAGE:
            MOV   AH,5              ;function number
            MOV   AL,2              ;page number (numbered from 0)
            INT   10H               ;set the page
```

This function does *not*, however, specify the page that is written upon. Any of the BIOS interrupts that write on the screen (functions of INT 10H) require that the number of the page to be written upon be given as one of the input registers. But the DOS screen interrupts all write upon the page currently in view. Thus, for "off-stage" operations you must use INT 10H.

To *find* the current page, execute function F of INT 10H, which gives the video status. The page number is returned in BH.

Low Level

Display pages are chosen by changing the point in video memory from which the monitor receives its data. This point in memory is set by registers 12 (high byte) and 13 (low byte) on the 6845 chip, which are together referred to as the *start address.* The values for the page boundaries in the B800 buffer are as follows:

	40 COLUMNS	80 COLUMNS
page 0	0000H	0000H
1	0400H	0800H
2	0800H	1000H
3	0C00H	1800H
4	1000H	
5	1400H	
6	1800H	
7	1C00H	

[4.1.1] explains how the 6845 registers are programmed, and [4.5.4] contains an example in which the start address is programmed. In the latter example, simply give BX one of the values in the table above. All of this only sets the page that is displayed, of course. To *write* to a particular page from low level, use one of the values from the table as an offset into the video buffer during direct memory mapping operations.

Because direct memory mapping is so rapid, the illusion of paging is easily created on the monochrome monitor. Set aside a 4000-byte block of RAM to hold the page. Although the monochrome adaptor cannot be made to read directly from user memory, the contents of the memory block and of video memory can be switched so quickly that no one would know the difference. The following routine toggles the contents of the two.

```
;---IN THE DATA SEGMENT:
  PSEUDO_PAGE   DW    2000 DUP(720H)      ;initialize buffer to spaces

;---TOGGLE BETWEEN THE PSEUDO_PAGE AND VIDEO BUFFER:
              MOV   AX,0B000H            ;point ES to the video buffer
              MOV   ES,AX                ;
              MOV   AX,SEG PSEUDO_PAGE   ;point DS to the pseudo-page
              MOV   DS,AX
              ;
REPEAT:       MOV   DI,0                 ;point DI to start of video buffer
              MOV   SI,OFFSET PPAGE      ;point SI to start of pseudo-page
              CLD                        ;set direction flag for "forward"
              MOV   CX,2000              ;get set to move 2000 words
NEXT_WORD:    MOV   BX,ES:[DI]           ;put byte from video buffer in BX
              LODSW                      ;word from pseudo-page in AX (SI+2)
              STOSW                      ;word from AX to video buffer (DI+2)
              MOV   DS:[DI]-2,BX         ;put byte from BX into pseudo-page
              LOOP  NEXT_WORD            ;do the next
```

The PCjr keeps a Page Register at port address 3DFH. The bit pattern is as follows:

```
    bits 2-0     sets which page (of up to 8) is displayed
         5-3     sets which page (of up to 8) is written
                     upon when output is address to B800H
         7-6     =00 for all alpha modes
                 =01 for 16K graphics modes
                 =11 for 32K graphics modes
```

4.5.4 Scroll between text pages

Because text pages are adjacent to each other in the video buffer, a short array of text can be laid out entirely within that memory. Then the text can be scrolled up and down across the screen without actually moving it around in the buffer. Instead, the screen is caused to start showing the contents of the buffer beginning from different points, creating the illusion of scrolling. This technique is known as *hardware scrolling.*

Hardware scrolling is achieved by changing the display's "start address," which is a number that points to the character in video memory that is to be displayed at the top left corner of the screen. Adding 80 to the number "scrolls" the whole screen upward one line, and subtracting 80 scrolls the screen downwards. In 40-column mode, add or subtract 40 instead. Figure 4-7 diagrams hardware scrolling.

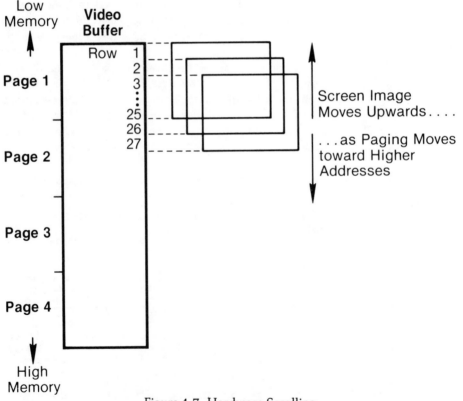

Figure 4-7. Hardware Scrolling.

Note that the Start-Address Register does not count attribute bytes; you must calculate memory positions differently than for direct memory mapping. Also be aware that, although there is blank memory along the boundaries between pages (96 bytes between 80-column pages, 48 bytes between 40-column ones), the 6845 chip sees to it that these areas are skipped over, so that the scroll appears to be continuous from one page to another. Hardware scrolling occurs so quickly that you may wish to incorporate a delay routine so that the program user has time to control how far the screen shifts.

BIOS keeps the current value of the start address register in a variable in its data area. The two-byte variable is located at 0040:004EH.

Low Level

The start address is contained in registers 12 (high byte) and 13 (low byte) on the 6845 chip. [4.1.1] explains how the chip operates. Before each byte of the address is sent to port address 3D5H, the number of the register it is destined for must be sent to port address 3D4H. In this example the screen is scrolled upwards by one line. The variable START_ADDRESS holds the address of the first character of the current top line of the screen.

```
        MOV   BX,START_ADDRESS    ;start at beginning of buffer
        ADD   BX,80               ;move one line (80-column Mode)
        ;
        MOV   DX,3D4H             ;output to the address register
        MOV   AL,12              ;address register 12
        OUT   DX,AL              ;send the request
        ;
        INC   DX                ;now output to the command registers
        MOV   AL,BH             ;high word of start address in AL
        OUT   DX,AL             ;send it to register 12
        ;
        DEC   DX               ;back to the address register
        MOV   AL,13            ;address register 13
        OUT   DX,AL            ;send the request
        ;
        INC   DX              ;back to the command registers
        MOV   AL,BL           ;low word of start address in AL
        OUT   DX,AL           ;send it to register 13
```

5
The Disk Drives

Section 1: Monitor Disk Allocation

All disks, whether floppy or fixed, are organized in the same fashion. The surface of the disk is laid out as a series of concentric rings, called *tracks*, and the tracks are divided radially into *sectors*. For example, standard 5-1/4-inch floppy disks have 40 tracks, and under DOS 2.0, each track is broken into nine sectors (15 sectors on the 1.2M floppy, and 17 on the fixed disks). The sector size is 512 bytes, and 512 bytes x 9 sectors x 40 tracks x 2 sides adds up to the 360K capacity of the diskette. All types of disk use the 512-byte sector size in PC-DOS.

A file is divided among as many sectors as are required to hold it. Only a few sectors on the outside rim of the diskette are reserved for special purposes. The others are available on a "first-come, first-served" basis. This means that as the disk is filled with data the sectors are gradually filled up, moving inwards to the center of the disk. When files are deleted, sectors are freed, and with time the available space comes to be scattered around the diskette, dispersing new files and making them slow to read and write.

Fixed disks have some special characteristics. Often they are comprised of two or more parallel disks, each with a pair of heads to read from the two sides. Taken together, all tracks a given distance from the center are referred to as a *cylinder*. Because the heads for all of the disks move in tandem, economy of motion is achieved by filling all tracks in one cylinder before moving inward to the next. Groups of cylinders may be devoted to different operating systems. The DOS FDISK program can, in fact, *partition* a fixed disk into up to four sections of varying size. For this reason, the specifications of a fixed disk can vary greatly.

Disk sectors are defined by magnetic information written by the utility that formats the disk. The information includes an ID number for each sector. BIOS numbers the sectors from 1-8, 1-9, or 1-15, depending on the disk capacity. Tracks are not marked magnetically; rather, they are mechanically defined as an offset of the read/write head from the outer edge of the disk. Tracks are numbered from 0-39 on 5-1/4-inch floppies, or higher on disks of greater capacity. The BIOS disk functions reference a particular sector using both track and sector numbers. The DOS functions, however, regard all sectors of a disk as a single chain numbered upwards from 0, so that every sector has its own *logical sector number*.

For floppy disks, the first sector (track 0, sector 1) is given the *boot record*, which is a small program that enables the computer to operate the disk drives well enough to read other parts of DOS. Next comes two copies of the *file allocation table*, which keeps track of the allocation of disk space (the second copy is for safety's sake). And then comes one copy of the *root directory*, which lists files and references to subdirectories and tells where on the disk they begin. Finally, there are two small DOS programs, IBMBIOS.COM and IBMDOS.COM, which are read at startup, and which give the computer the capability needed to find and load COMMAND.COM, which, of course, is the body of the disk operating system.

Fixed disks have a *master boot record* which contains a *partition table* that enables the disk to be partitioned between several operating systems. The partition table contains information about where the DOS partition begins on the disk, and the first sector at that partition contains the DOS boot record. The partition is otherwise organized like a floppy.

5.1.1 Read the file allocation table

Disks use a *file allocation table* (FAT) to allot disk space to files and to keep track of free sectors. For reasons of reliability, two copies of the FAT are kept on all disks. They are located in sequence at the lowest possible logical sectors numbers, beginning from side 0, track 0, sector 2 (sector 1 is always taken by the *boot record*). The number of sectors used by a FAT varies by the size and type of disk. Note that under DOS 3.0 the size of the FAT entries may be 16 bits for fixed disks. The discussion here assumes 12-bit entries; see the DOS Technical Reference manual for information about 16-bit entries.

The file allocation table works by keeping track of every *cluster* of sectors on the diskette. A cluster is a group of standard, 512-byte sectors (no matter the disk type, DOS always works in 512-byte sectors). Groups of sectors are used to keep the FAT size small. However, the large clusters used by fixed disks waste disk space when small files are recorded (a 500-byte utility still takes up 4K of disk space). Here are the various cluster sizes and FAT sizes used by the IBM microcomputers:

Disk Type	Sectors/Cluster	FAT Size (sectors)
160K floppy	1	1
180K floppy	1	1
320K floppy	2	2
360K floppy	2	2
1.2M floppy	1	7
10M fixed	8	8
20M fixed	4	40

Large cluster size tends to waste disk space, but when large disks have a small cluster size, the FAT becomes large. During disk operations, DOS loads a copy of the FAT into memory, keeping it there if possible, and so a large FAT can take up a good deal of RAM. Because most ATs have plenty of RAM, a much larger FAT is deemed acceptable. Hence the 20M fixed disk has smaller clusters than the 10M disk, promoting efficient utilization of disk space. The 1.2M floppies use a single-sector cluster size because they are primarily intended as a backup medium for the fixed disk, and so compactness is most important.

Every position in a file allocation table corresponds to a particular cluster position on the disk. Files usually range across a number of clusters, and a file's directory entry contains the *starting cluster* at which the first part of the file is stored. By looking up the position in the FAT that corresponds to the starting cluster, DOS finds the number of the cluster in which the next bit of the file is found. This cluster also has its own corresponding entry in the FAT, which in turn contains the number of the next cluster in the chain. For the last cluster occupied by a file, the FAT contains a value from FF8H to FFFH. Unused clusters (or freed clusters) are given the value 000, and bad sectors are given FF7H. Finally, values from FF0 to FF7 are used to indicate reserved clusters.

A cluster number uses three hexadecimal digits, which is a value contained by 1-1/2 bytes. In order to keep file allocation tables small, the numbers for two adjacent clusters are kept in three consecutive bytes of the table. DOS automatically takes care of the necessary arithmetic.

The first three bytes of a FAT are not used for cluster numbers. The first byte gives a code about the disk type (see [1.1.5]), and the next two bytes are both FFH. Since these table positions are occupied, the clusters are counted starting from 2, with 2 and 3 taking up the second triplet of bytes in the table.

DOS 3.0 can generate FATs that have 16-bit entries. These are required for fixed disks over 10M, which have more than 4086 clusters. Figure 5-1 shows the relationship between the FAT and disk clusters.

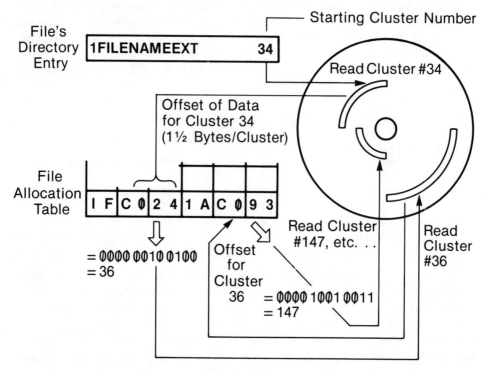

Figure 5-1. The File Allocation Table.

There is seldom good reason to make direct changes in the file allocation table. DOS takes care of all file operations, and it provides services that analyze the table for data about space availability on the disk. But for certain special needs, such as unerasing files or creating block device drivers, direct access to the FAT is unavoidable. Use the following rules to read the FAT directly.

To find the next cluster:

1. Multiply the cluster number by 1.5.
2. Get the two bytes at the resulting offset (rounded down).

3. If the cluster number is even, take the low 12 bits; otherwise take the high 12 bits.

To convert the cluster number to a logical sector number:

1. Subtract 2 from the cluster number.
2. Multiply the result by the number of sectors in a cluster.

High Level

This example reads the FAT and looks up the value under cluster number 6. [5.4.2] explains the initial code that reads the FAT sectors. The result is a 12-bit value expressed as three hexadecimal digits (four bits each), returned in string form. In the example two 2-digit hexadecimal numbers are combined, and either the right or left three digits are taken as the result. When BASIC converts a character to hex form, it returns only one digit if the first is 0, and so the deleted 0 must be restored for this method to work properly.

```
100 '''read FAT sectors
110 DEFINT A-Z 120 DATA &H55,&H8B,&HEC,&H1E,&H8B,&H76,&H0C,&H8B
130 DATA &H04,&H8B,&H76,&H0A,&H8B,&H14,&H8B,&H76
140 DATA &H08,&H8B,&H0C,&H8B,&H76,&H06,&H8A,&H1C
150 DATA &H8E,&HD8,&H8B,&HC3,&H8B,&H00,&H00,&HCD
160 DATA &H25,&H59,&H1F,&H5D,&HCA,&H08,&H00
170 DEF SEG=&H1000                'place machine code at 1000:0000
180 FOR N=0 TO 38                 'read 39 bytes of data
190 READ Q:POKE N,Q               'move to memory
200 NEXT                          'next byte
210 READSECTOR=0                  'start subroutine from first byte
220 BUFFER=&H2000                 'transfer data to buffer at 2000:0000
230 LOGICALNUMBER=1               'starting sector for FAT on 360K disk
240 NUMBERSECTORS=2               'two sectors in FAT
250 DRIVE=0                       'read drive A
260 CALL READSECTOR(BUFFER,LOGICALNUMBER,NUMBERSECTORS,DRIVE) 'get sectors
270 '''find the cluster number in the data
280 DEF SEG=&H2000                'point to the FAT data
290 CLUSTERNUMBER!=6              'get cluster number 6
300 C!=CLUSTERNUMBER!             'make copy
310 C!=INT(C!*1.5)               'multiply by 1.5 and round down
320 X=PEEK(C!)                    'read two bytes at that position
330 Y=PEEK(C!+1)                  '
340 X$=HEX$(X):Y$=HEX$(Y)         'convert to hexadecimal strings
350 IF LEN(X$)=1 THEN X$="0"+X$   'make strings two bytes if truncated
360 IF LEN(Y$)=1 THEN Y$="0"+Y$   '
370 H$=Y$+X$                      'combine the numbers into one string
380 '''see if even or odd numbered cluster, and patch together numbers:
390 IF CLUSTERNUMBER! MOD 2 <> 0 THEN 420 'jump for ODD case
400 NEXTCLUSTER$=RIGHT$(H$,3)     'even number: take left three digits
410 GOTO 430                      'jump ahead
420 NEXTCLUSTER$=LEFT$(H$,3)      'odd number: take right three digits
430 PRINT NEXTCLUSTER$            'print the result
```

Middle Level

DOS function 1CH provides information about the file allocation table, but it does not return the FAT itself. Place the drive number in DL, where 0 = default,

1 = A, etc. On return DX has the number of clusters in the FAT, AL has the number of sectors per cluster, and CX has the number of bytes in a sector. DS:BX will point to a byte that contains the initial FAT byte that is a code describing the disk type; these codes are listed at [1.1.5].

Low Level

It is far easier to access a FAT in assembly language. Note how the cluster number is multiplied by 1.5 by making a copy of the number and shifting it rightward one bit to divide it by two, then adding the copy to the original. This method automatically rounds the result down. The code that reads the FAT sectors into memory is discussed at [5.4.2].

```
;---IN THE DATA SEGMENT:
            BUFFER   DB 1024 DUP(0)     ;set up space for 2 sectors

;---READ THE FAT INTO MEMORY:
            LEA   BX,BUFFER             ;point to data buffer
            MOV   DX,1                  ;logical sector number
            MOV   CX,2                  ;2 sectors
            MOV   AL,0                  ;drive A
            INT   25H                   ;read sectors
            POP   CX                    ;balance stack (see [5.4.2])
;---GET THE CLUSTER NUMBER:
            MOV   AX,3                  ;put cluster number in AX
            MOV   CX,AX                 ;make copy
            MOV   DX,AX                 ;make second copy
            SHR   DX,1                  ;divide second copy by 2
            ADD   CX,DX                 ;add the 2 copies (= x1.5)
            ADD   BX,CX                 ;add as offset to buffer pointer
            MOV   DX,[BX]               ;get the 2 bytes at that offset
            TEST  AX,1                  ;is the cluster number odd?
            JNZ   ODD_CLUSTER           ;jump if so, else it's even:
            AND   DX,0000111111111111B  ;get number by clearing high 4 bits
            JMP   SHORT CONTINUE        ;jump over "odd" case
ODD_CLUSTER:    MOV   CL,4              ;prepare to shift right
            SHR   DX,CL                 ;shift down top 12 bits
CONTINUE:                              ;and now the next cluster is in DX
```

5.1.2 Determine available disk space

Although the next subsection explains how to recover from full-disk errors, there is no medicine like prevention. Programs should monitor the available disk space and inform users of an impending shortage. If space is short, the user can leave the program and correct the problem without loss of data.

High Level ━━━━━━━━━━━━━━━━━━━━━━━━━━━━━━━━━━━━

The following assembly routine returns in the variable CLUSTERS the number of clusters available on a specified disk. Place the drive number in DRIVENUM, where $1 = A$, $2 = B$, etc. Appendix D explains how assembly language subroutines are integrated into BASIC programs.

```
10  DEFINT A-Z               'must use integer variables
20  DRIVENUM=1               'put drive number here
30  CLUSTERS=0               'initialize clusters with any value
40  DATA &H55,&H8B,&HEC,&H8B,&H76,&H06,&H8B
50  DATA &H14,&HB4,&H36,&HCD,&H21,&H8B,&H7E
60  DATA &H08,&H89,&H1D,&H5D,&HCA,&H04,&H00
70  DEF SEG=&H1000           'place routine at 10000H
80  FOR N=0 TO 20            'for each byte of the routine...
90  READ Q:POKE N,Q          'read it and poke into memory
100 NEXT                     '
110 FREESPACE=0              'pointer to start of routine
120 CALL FREESPACE(CLUSTERS,DRIVENUM) 'call the routine
130 PRINT"CLUSTERS: ";CLUSTERS  'print the number of clusters
```

Middle Level ━━━━━━━━━━━━━━━━━━━━━━━━━━━━━━━━━━

Function 36H of INT 21H tells how much disk space is free. The only input register is DL, which contains the drive number. The default drive is noted by 0, drive A by 1, etc. On return, BX contains the number of clusters available, AX tells how many sectors there are in a cluster, and CX tells how many bytes are in a sector. A little multiplication produces the desired result. The following example checks that there is at least 2K of disk space remaining on a double-sided floppy:

```
MOV  AH,36H       ;function number
MOV  DL,1         ;drive A
INT  21H          ;go get the disk space
CMP  BX,2         ;at least 2 clusters (2K) free?
JL   RUNNING_OUT  ;if not, alert the program user
```

5.1.3 Get/set the file size

A program may need to check file size for a variety of reasons. One is to calculate the number of records a file contains. Another is to determine the end-of-file position where the file pointer may be set in order to *append* new data to a file without changing the existing data.

File size, of course, is automatically set by the DOS functions. Sometimes a program may need to reserve disk space for future use. In this case, simply open the file in random access mode and write a record at as high a position as you would like the file to be long. The records between the high "dummy" record and the file proper will be filled with whatever data happens to be in the disk sectors allocated to the file by this action.

High Level

In BASIC, the LOF ("length of file") function returns the exact number of bytes allocated to a file (be cautioned, however, that old, 1.x versions of BASIC return the number of 128-byte blocks used by a file). The file must be opened, and it is referred to by the file buffer number under which it is opened. The format is $X = LOF(1)$, etc. The following example finds out how many 64-byte records are contained in a file opened as #3:

```
100 OPEN"FILENAME" AS #3              'open the file
110 RECORDLEN=64                      'define record size
120 NUMBERRECORDS=LOF(3)/RECORDLEN    'calculate number of records
```

Middle Level

FCB function 23H of INT 21H reports the number of records in a file. By giving the file a one-byte record length, its size is returned in bytes. Point DS:DX to an opened file control block. Then call the function. If the file is not found, AL returns with FF. Otherwise AL returns 0, and the number of records is placed in the random record field of the FCB (bytes 33-36). To work properly, the FCB's record length field must be set after the FCB is opened but before the function is called; the two-byte field is located at offset 14 in the FCB. If the file is not evenly divided by the given record length, the number of records reported is rounded upwards. Here is an example in which a record length of 1 is used:

```
;---FIND THE SIZE OF A FILE:
            LEA   DX,FCB        ;point DS:DX to FCB
            MOV   BX,DX         ;copy the pointer into BX
            MOV   CX,1          ;record size in CX
            MOV   [BX]+14,CX    ;move into FCB record size field
            MOV   AH,23H        ;function that reports file size
            INT   21H           ;call the function
            MOV   AX,[BX]+33    ;get low part of file size count
            MOV   CX,[BX]+35    ;get high part of file size count
                               ;now CX:AX has file size
```

It is also possible to *set* file length using file control blocks. Use the *random block write* function, which is discussed at [5.4.5]. This function has a special case where if the number of records to be written is set to 0, then the file length is set to the number of records specified in the random record field.

The file handle method has no function that directly reports file size, but it is possible to calculate the size by moving the file pointer from the beginning to the end of the file. When the file is opened the pointer is automatically set to its first byte. The pointer is moved by function 42H of INT 21H. Place the code number 2 in AL, directing the pointer to the end of the file. BX takes the file handle. CX:DX holds the offset from the end of the file to the position at which the pointer is set, so place 0 in both of these registers. Then call the function. On return DX:AX contains the new position of the pointer as an offset from its prior position—that is, it contains the file length (DX holds the most significant part). If an error occurs, the carry flag is set and AX returns 1 if the function number was invalid, or 6 if the handle was invalid. Don't forget to reset the pointer to the start of the file, if this is desired. Place 0 in AL, CX, and DX, and call the function again. Here is an example:

```
;---OPEN THE FILE:
            LEA   DX,FILE_PATH          ;point DS:DX to path string
            MOV   AL,0                  ;open for reading
            MOV   AH,3DH                ;function to open file
            INT   21H                   ;open it
            JC    OPEN_ERROR            ;check for errors
            MOV   HANDLE,AX             ;save the file handle
;---FIND THE FILE LENGTH:
            MOV   AH,42H                ;function to move pointer
            MOV   AL,2                  ;code to set to end-of-file
            MOV   BX,HANDLE             ;file handle in BX
            MOV   CX,0                  ;0 in CX and DX
            MOV   DX,0                  ;
            INT   21H                   ;move the pointer
            JC    POINTER_ERROR         ;error?
            MOV   FILESIZE_HIGH,DX      ;store the file size
            MOV   FILESIZE_LOW,AX       ;
```

5.1.4 Recover from insufficient disk space errors

Programs can crash when they attempt to write to a full disk. It is often easy to avoid this condition, even in BASIC, by checking available disk space beforehand [5.1.2]. Once the error occurs, try to give the program user options about how to deal with it. Let him edit out part of the data. Or let him erase some other file on disk and then try the write operation again. Most radically, let the user insert a different diskette to receive the data. This last approach must be undertaken with great care. First close all open files. Then prompt the disk change. Once the user indicates that a new disk is in place, *create* a new file and then write out the data.

High Level ─────────────────────────────────

In BASIC, set up an error trapping routine, as shown at [7.2.5]. If a BASIC statement attempts to write to a file on a filled disk, error condition #61 occurs. Control may be transferred to an error-correction routine that informs the user of the problem and allows him to correct it without loss of data.

```
100 ON ERROR GOTO 5000          'enable error trapping
     .
     .
200 OPEN FILENAME$ FOR OUTPUT AS #1'open file
210 FOR N=1 TO ARRAYLEN          'start to write an array to disk
220 PRINT#1,ARRAY$(N)            'write one element
230 NEXT                         'next
     .
     .
5000 IF ERR=61 THEN 5100         'an error has occurred: disk full?
5010 IF ERR=.....                'other errors...
     .
     .
5100 '''full-disk error recovery:
5110 BEEP:PRINT"Disk full -- choose an option:"
5120 PRINT"(A)   Re-edit the file"
5130 PRINT"(B)   Delete some other file from disk"
5140 PRINT"(C)   Use different diskette"
     .
     .
        (recovery routines here)
     .
     .
5500 RESUME
```

Middle Level ───────────────────────────────

All DOS functions that write to disk are capable of some kind of error code that indicates a full disk. Here is a summary of these codes:

Access Method	Function	Name	Return Error Code
File Control Block	15H	Sequential Write	AL = 1
	22H	Random Write	AL = 1
	27H	Random Block Write	AL = 1
File Handle	40H	Write to File/Device	CX < > BX

Monitor these error conditions after *every* operation that writes to disk. No critical error condition occurs, so it is easy to recover. Just test for the error code each time one of the functions is invoked, and create as elaborate a recovery routine as you like.

Section 2: Operate On Disk Directories

Every disk has one *root directory* from which all directory searches begin. The root directory may hold entries that refer to *subdirectories*, which in turn may hold references to other subdirectories, resulting in a *tree structured* directory system. The root directory is always found on particular disk sectors; subdirectories are kept as ordinary disk files, so they may be located anywhere on disk. Note that a hard disk may have up to four root directories if it has been partitioned into four parts, although DOS will only "see" its own root directory. Directories vary in size depending on the size of a disk and how it is partitioned. The following table shows the size and locations of the root directories of the various disk types:

Disk Type	Directory Size	Directory Entries	Logical Starting Sector
160K floppy	4 sectors	64	9
180K floppy	4	64	9
320K floppy	7	112	15
360K floppy	7	112	15
1.2M floppy	14	224	29
10M fixed	————variable————		
20M fixed	————variable————		

Depending on how they are partitioned, fixed disks vary in the size of their directories and their logical starting sectors. When the entire disk is given over to PCDOS, both the XT and AT fixed disks allot 32 sectors to the root directory, giving 512 entries.

Both root directories and subdirectories use 32 bytes to hold the information for a single file, no matter the type of disk. Thus each sector contained in a directory holds 16 entries. Each 32-byte field is broken down as follows:

bytes	0- 7	File name
	8-10	File name extension
	11	File attribute
	12-21	(reserved)
	22-23	Time file last accessed
	24-25	Date file last accessed
	26-27	Starting cluster
	28-31	File size

No period is written between the file name and its three-byte extension. Both are left-justified in their fields, and empty bytes are padded with spaces (ASCII 32). The file attribute tells whether a file is hidden, read-only, etc. [5.2.6]. It also defines special directory entries, such as subdirectories or volume labels. The time and date information is compressed, and reading the values requires bit operations [5.2.5].

The starting cluster refers to a position in the *file allocation table* (FAT), which is discussed at [5.1.1]. The FAT keeps track of free space on the disk, and it assigns the sectors in which a file is written. The FAT may allocate space in groupings larger than one sector, and these groupings are referred to as *clusters*. A file is laid out along a chain of clusters, and the FAT contains a corresponding chain of entries that indicate where the clusters are located on the disk. The directory needs to point to the start of a file's chain of entries in the FAT, and that is what the *starting cluster* value does. Since files usually do not evenly divide into clusters, the *file size* field is required to give the file's exact size in bytes.

5.2.1 Read/change the root directory

A disk directory is divided between the root directory (discussed here) and subdirectories (discussed at [5.2.3]). When the program user enters the name of a particular file to work on, it can be useful to check whether the file is indeed present. Ordinarily, changes in the root directory are made in the course of normal file operations or through special DOS functions. However, the directory may be *directly* accessed. There is greater need of this approach in high-level languages, where the DOS utilities are largely unavailable.

The root directory is read and changed by placing the whole of it into memory using the techniques shown at [5.4.2] that read absolute disk sectors. These operations leave no space between the sectors when they deposit them in memory. The buffer containing the sector data may be thought of as a series of 32-byte fields, and a pair of pointers may be used to move about the directory. One pointer is always a multiple of 32, and it points to the start of a directory entry. The second pointer is added to the first to locate one of the fields within a 32-byte entry. The data in memory may be changed as required, and then the entire buffer is written back to the disk.

There are two methods of reading absolute disk sectors, and in both instances only one number in the code differs between the read- and write-cases. Since an error in writing to disk can easily disable the disk and all its contents, take special care. First be sure that the sector-read operation has performed correctly in all respects. Only then should you test the sector-write code, making it an exact duplicate of the code used for reading, except for the function number change.

High Level

BASIC displays the directory using the FILES command. Only the file names are listed. **FILES** gives the directory on the default drive; to specify the drive, write **FILES"A:"**, etc. Alternatively, information for a particular file can be displayed by writing **FILES"A:MYFILE.DAT"**. The filename may include * and ?, as in DOS. The FILES statement supplies file information to the computer user, but sometimes it is the program that needs to check for the presence of the file. In this case the file is opened for sequential input, and if it does not exist an error condition is intercepted. See the discussion and example at [5.2.3].

To retrieve *any* information from the root directory, use the machine language subroutines shown at [5.4.2]. Once the directory data is in memory, set up pointers as described above and search the memory buffer at 32-byte intervals. The example below searches for the directory entry of an erased file. When files are erased the first byte of the file name is changed to E5H, but the remainder of the entry is left intact. Of course, the disk space for the file is deallocated in the file allocation table. A routine that unerases a file needs to know the starting cluster in the FAT. The example locates this two-byte cluster number at offset 26 in the directory entry.

```
100 '''read the directory sectors into memory at segment &H2000:
110 INPUT"Enter erased filename ",FILENAME$          'prompt user for filename
120 IF LEN(FILENAME$)>12 THEN BEEP:GOTO 110          'error
130 IF INSTR(FILENAME$,".")>9 THEN BEEP:GOTO 110     'error (etc...)
140 '''pad filename and extension with spaces
150 Y=INSTR(FILENAME$,".")                      'check position of extension period
160 IF Y=0 THEN FIRSTPART$=FILENAME$:GOTO 230   'no extension, jump ahead
170 EXTENSION$=LEFT$(FILENAME$,LEN(FILENAME$)-Y) 'isolate extension
180 EXTENSION$=EXTENSION$+STRING$(3-LEN(EXTENSION$),"") 'add trailing spaces
190 FIRSTPART$=RIGHT$(FILENAME$,Y-1)            'isolate first part of file name
200 FIRSTPART$=FIRSTPART$+STRING$(8-LEN(FIRSTPART$),"") 'add trailing spaces
210 FILENAME$=FIRSTPART$+EXTENSION$             'assemble the complete name, no period
220 '''now go find the erased file:
230 MID$(FILENAME$,1,1)=CHR$(&HE5)              'make first character &HE5
240 DIRPTR=0                                    'pointer to 32-byte entries
250 FIELDPTR=26                                 'set field pointer to cluster number
260 FOR N=1 to 112                              '112 dir entries on dbl sided diskette
270 X$=""                                       'clear X$
280 FOR M=0 to 10                               'put together the filename string
290 X$=X$+PEEK(DIRPTR+M)                        'get each character in turn
300 NEXT                                        'next
310 IF X$=FILENAME$ THEN 340                    'matches the modified input string?
320 NEXT                                        'if not, go check next entry
330 PRINT"Too Late -- file entry obliterated":END  'not found
340 X=PEEK(DIRPTR+FIELDPTR)                     'found it! Get 1st byte of cluster no.
350 Y=PEEK(DIRPTR+FIELDPTR+1)                   'get 2nd byte of cluster number
360 Z=X+256*Y                                   'Z now has the complete cluster number
```

Middle Level

DOS provides two pairs of file-searching functions, one for files opened under the *file control block* method, and one for files opened under the *file handle* method. One function of each pair searches for the first occurrence of a file name in a directory, and the second searches for subsequent occurrences when global characters are given in the file name. Only the file handle method can search subdirectories.

FCB Method:

Function 11H of INT 21H searches for the first occurrence of a file. Point DS:DX to an *unopened* FCB and execute the function. Upon return, AL will hold 0 if the file has been found, and FF if it has not. The DTA is filled with information from the directory. For normal FCBs, the first byte in the DTA is the drive number (1 = A, etc.), and the next 32 bytes receive the directory entry. For extended FCBs, the first seven bytes of the file match the first seven of the extended FCB, the eighth byte is the drive specifier, and the next 32 are the directory entry.

```
;---IN THE DATA SEGMENT:
    FCB         DB    1,'NEWDATABAK',25 dup(0)

;---SEARCH FOR THE FILE:
              MOV   AH,11H          ;function to search directory
              LEA   DX,FCB          ;point to the FCB
              INT   21H             ;make the search
              CMP   AL,0            ;successful?
              JNE   NO_FILE         ;if not, go to recovery routine
              LEA   BX,DTA          ;now DS:BX points to directory entry
```

After function 11H has been used, function 12H can search for all subsequent entries when the file name contains global characters. Only the ? symbol may be used in the file name (and not *). This function works exactly as the first, and if a second match is found, the information in the DTA for the first is overlaid.

File Handle Method:

Function 4EH of INT 21H finds the first match to a file name. Point DS:DX to a string giving the path to the file. For example, **B:EUROPE \ FRANCE \ PARIS** points to the file PARIS. The string may have up to 63 characters, and it is followed by one byte of ASCII 0. The file name may contain global characters, including both ? and *. Place the attribute(s) of the file in CX; if normal, the value is 0, otherwise consult [5.2.6] for attribute values.

Upon return, the carry flag is set if the file was not found. If found, the function fills the DTA with information about the file. Note this special use of the DTA by the *file handle* method of access—the DTA is generally used by the DOS FCB functions. The first 21 bytes of the DTA are reserved by DOS for searches for more matches. The twenty-second byte gives the file's attribute, followed by two bytes holding the time, and two more holding the date. The next four bytes keep the file size, low word first. And finally the file name is given in a variable length string that ends with ASCII 0. A period (ASCII 46) separates the file name and its extension, and neither are padded with spaces.

```
;---IN THE DATA SEGMENT:
    PATH          DB    'B:FRANCE\PARIS\4EME',0

;---SEARCH FOR THE FILE:
              MOV   AH,4EH              ;function number
              LEA   DX,PATH             ;point DS:DX to path string
              MOV   CX,0                ;normal file attribute
              INT   21H                 ;search for the file
              JC    NO_FILE             ;jump if not found
              LEA   BX,DTA              ;point DS:BX to DTA
              MOV   AL,[BX]+21          ;now file's attribute is in AL
```

The next occurrence of the file name (when global characters are used) is found by function 4FH of INT 21H. It is set up the same as 4EH, and it can only be used *after* 4EH, with the DTA pointer unchanged. When there are no more matches, the carry flag is set and 18 appears in AX.

5.2.2 Create/delete a subdirectory

A program can create and delete subdirectories, so long as certain preconditions are met. To create a subdirectory, there must be at least one empty slot in the root directory. To delete a subdirectory, it must be empty of all files and all references to other subdirectories. Further, you can not delete a subdirectory that is the *current* directory (the one to which all directory operations are by default directed). Note that it is impossible to delete the root directory.

High Level

BASIC provides the MKDIR ("make directory") and RMDIR ("remove directory") commands. Both are followed by a standard directory path of up to 63 characters, including the drive specifier. The path is placed in quotes. To add a directory called *STORKS* to the subdirectory *BIRDS*, simply write **MKDIR"B:MAMMALS\BIRDS\STORKS"**. Once this statement is executed, a file named STORKS is created for use as a subdirectory, and its existence is recorded as an entry in the subdirectory file named BIRDS. To delete the same subdirectory, first remove all files from it [5.3.2]. Then use the statement **RMDIR"B:MAMMALS\BIRDS\STORKS"**.

The above example assumes that the root directory is the current directory. But the entire path need not be listed if the current directory is somewhere along the way to the subdirectory operated upon. Hence, if BIRDS were the current directory, the STORKS subdirectory could be created or deleted using **MKDIR "\STORKS"** or **RMDIR"\STORKS"**.

Middle Level

Since file control blocks serve only the root directory, the methods that create and delete subdirectories must use file handles.

Create a Subdirectory:
Point DS:DX to a string giving the drive and path to the directory in which to place the subdirectory entry. The string must end with an ASCII 0 byte. To open a subdirectory called "PRIMATES" in the root directory of drive A:, simply write the string as **A:\PRIMATES"**. To open the subdirectory within another subdirectory called MAMMALS, write **A:\MAMMALS\PRIMATES**. The drive specifier **A:** may be omitted if the disk is in the default drive, and the path need originate only from the current directory. Place 39H in AH and execute INT 21H; a new directory will be created if the path is valid. Otherwise the carry flag is set to 1 and AX contains the error code 3 ("path not valid") or 5 ("access denied"). This example sets up the PRIMATES subdirectory:

```
;---IN THE DATA SEGMENT:
    PATH        DB    'A:MAMMALS\PRIMATES',0

;CREATE A SUBDIRECTORY NAMED "PRIMATES":
            LEA   DX,PATH            ;point DS:DX to path string
```

```
        MOV  AH,39H              ;function number
        INT  21H                 ;create the subdirectory
        JC   ERROR_ROUTINE       ;intercept errors
```

Remove a Subdirectory:

To remove a subdirectory, set up a string exactly as shown in the above example that creates a subdirectory. Then place 3AH in AH and call INT 21H. Again, error codes 3 or 5 are returned in AX if the function fails (code 5 may indicate that the directory is not empty).

5.2.3 Read/change a subdirectory

Subdirectories are much like root directories, except that they are kept in ordinary files rather than at an invariable sector location. Subdirectories are never confused with ordinary files because a directory entry that represents a subdirectory uses a special attribute byte (bit 5 is set to 1—see [5.2.6]). Subdirectories begin with two special 32-byte entries, the first named by a single period, and the second by two periods. These orient the subdirectory to other directories around it. References to lower subdirectories appear just like file entries.

Supposedly a subdirectory can be read like any other file, so it would seem an easy matter to load one into memory. But unfortunately the designers of DOS elected to place 0 in the file-length field in directory entries that refer to subdirectories. As a result, DOS assumes the file to be of 0-length, and it refuses to read it. There is no simple way to overcome this problem.

High Level ────────────────

In BASIC, the FILES command can use standard path names to show a subdirectory; for example, **FILES"B:MAMMALS \ BIRDS"** displays all of the files in the subdirectory "BIRDS". FILES may also be used to find out if a particular file is present in a directory. For example, **FILES"LEVEL1 \ NEWDATA"** checks for the file NEWDATA and displays the filename if it is found. While this may be useful to the user, often it is the program itself that needs to be alerted to whether or not a file exists. To accomplish this, try to open the file for sequential input. If it is not found then error condition 63 occurs. Set up an error recovery routine, as explained at [5.4.8]. Then use a variable to flag whether or not the file has been found ("EXISTS" in the example below). If the program does not need the file opened, be sure to close it before moving on.

```
100 ON ERROR GOTO 1000          'initialize error recovery
110 EXISTS=1                     'set flag to "file exists"
120 INPUT"Enter file name: ",S$  'request file name from user
130 OPEN S$ FOR INPUT AS #3      'open file for sequential input
140 IF EXISTS=0 THEN BEEP:PRINT"File does not exist"
                                 ' inform user that no file, etc.
  .
  .
  .
1000 IF ERR=53 THEN 1500         'is it error for non-existent file?
1010 IF ERR=64 THEN ...          'capture bad files names, etc...
  .
  .
1500 EXISTS=0                    'set flag showing file not found
1510 RESUME 140                  'resume line following error
```

Middle Level ────────────────

The file handle functions that access the root directory [5.2.1] can just as easily reference any subdirectory. To dump the entire contents of a subdirectory, simply use function 4EH to search for *.*, and then repeat the search operation using function 4FH. When there are no more files, the carry flag will be set and AL will contain 18. Each time an entry is found, the DTA receives data about the file, including its entire path string (note the use of the DTA with a file handle function). The following example displays the path strings of all normal files in a subdirectory.

```
;---IN THE DATA SEGMENT:
    PATH        DB      'A:MAMMALS\*.*',0
    DTA         DB      256 DUP(?

;---SET DTA:
                LEA     DX,DTA              ;point DS:DX at DTA
                MOV     AH,1AH              ;function to set DTA
                INT     21H                ;set the DTA
;---SEEK FIRST FILE:
                MOV     AH,4EH              ;function to seek 1st filename match
                LEA     DX,PATH             ;point to path string
                MOV     CX,0                ;read files of normal attribute only
                INT     21H                ;go search for *.*
                JC      ERROR              ;if an error, go to recovery routine
;---DISPLAY THE FILE NAME:
    NEXT_LINE:  LEA     BX,DTA              ;point BX to the DTA
                ADD     BX,30               ;add offset of filename
    NEXT_CHAR:  MOV     DL,[BX]             ;get a character of the filename
                CMP     DL,0                ;is it the last in the string?
                JE      END_STRING          ;if so, jump ahead
                MOV     AH,2                ;otherwise, function to display char
                INT     21H                 ;display character and forward cursor
                INC     BX                  ;increment pointer to DTA
                JMP     SHORT NEXT_CHAR     ;go get the next character
;---OUTPUT CARRIAGE RETURN/LINE FEED AT END OF EACH LINE:
    END_STRING: MOV     AH,2                ;function to display character
                MOV     DL,13               ;carriage return
                INT     21H                 ;write it
                MOV     DL,10               ;line feed
                INT     21H                 ;write it
;---LOOK FOR NEXT FILE:
                LEA     DX,PATH             ;point to path string
                MOV     AH,4FH              ;function to search next match
                INT     21H                 ;call the function
                JC      FINISHED            ;quit if no more matches
                JMP     SHORT NEXT_LINE     ;go write out name of next match
    FINISHED:
```

5.2.4 Get/set the current directory

The *current directory* is the directory in which DOS searches for a file that is specified without a path name. If not set otherwise, the current directory is the root directory.

High Level ———————————————————————————————

BASIC sets the current directory using CHDIR. The command is followed with a string giving the path to the directory to which to move. The string may have up to 63 characters, including a drive specifier, and it is placed within quotation marks. **CHDIR"C:MAMMALS \ PRIMATES \ GIBBONS"** makes GIBBONS the default subdirectory. To move to the root directory, write **CHDIR" \ "** or **CHDIR"B: \ "**.

BASIC 3.0 can report the path to the current directory, exactly as the DOS **PATH** command does. Simply enter **PRINT ENVIRON$("PATH")**.

Middle Level ———————————————————————————————

Function 3BH of INT 21H sets the current directory. Point DS:DX to a string in standard directory-path form, and end the string with one byte of ASCII 0. For example, **B:BIRDS \ PARROTS \ POLLY** would make POLLY the current directory. The **B:** could be omitted if B: is set as the default drive [5.3.1]. To make the root directory of drive A the current one, write **B: ** . This example sets POLLY as the current drive:

```
;---IN THE DATA SEGMENT:
      PATH       DB    'B:BIRDS\PARROTS\POLLY',0

;---MAKE POLLY THE CURRENT DIRECTORY:
               MOV  AH,3BH          ;function number
               LEA  DX,PATH         ;point DS:DX to path
               INT  21H             ;set the current Directory
```

To find out which directory is current, use function 47H of INT 21H. DS:SI points to a 64-byte data area in which the path will be written. DL is given the drive number, where 0 = "default", 1 = A, 2 = B, etc. On return, the function returns the string without a drive specifier. If a non-existent drive was called, AL returns with error code 15. The string begins with the name of the first subdirectory in the chain, not with a backslash. An ASCII 0 byte signals the end of the string. This example assigns the name of the current directory to the variable "CURRENT_DIR":

```
;---IN THE DATA SEGMENT:
   CURRENT_DIR  DB    64 DUP(?)

;---GET THE CURRENT DIRECTORY:
               MOV  AH,47H          ;function number
               LEA  SI,CURRENT_DIR  ;point to data area
               MOV  DL,1            ;drive A
               INT  21H             ;place the string at DS:SI
```

5.2.5 Get/set the time and date of a file

Counting from 0, bytes 22-23 of a 32-byte directory entry hold the time at which a file was last accessed. Bytes 24-25 hold the date. The bit patterns are:

```
TIME:   bits 11-15      hours (0-23)
              5-10      minutes (0-59)
               0-4      seconds (0-29 in two-second intervals)

DATE:   bits  9-15      year (0-119, as an offset from 1980)
               5-8      month (1-12)
               0-4      day (1-31)
```

The day of the week is not recorded; DOS calculates it from the other information. Also note that, as always, the low byte of these two-byte values precedes the high byte in memory.

Middle Level

The *file control block* method of file access can get at a file's date, but not its time. When the FCB is opened by function FH of INT 21H, the two-byte date field is filled in the format shown above. This field is located at offset 14H in the FCB [5.3.5].

The *file handle* method, on the other hand, can both fetch and set a file's time and date. Function 57H of INT 21H performs all operations. To **set** the time and date, place the file handle in BX and 1 in AL. To **retrieve** the time and date, place 0 in AL instead. In both cases the date goes in DX, and the time in CX. The bit pattern is exactly as shown in the table above. The DOS technical reference manuals state that an exception is made, and that the low bytes of information are in CH and DH, and vice-versa. This in fact is not the case. The carry flag is set to 1 if an error occurs, in which case AX returns 1 if the number in AL was invalid or 6 if the file handle was no good. The following example finds the hour of the day in a file's time setting:

```
;---IN THE DATA SEGMENT:
        PATH    DB 'B:NEWDATA.BAK',0
;---OPEN THE FILE:
                LEA   DX,PATH           ;point to path string
                MOV   AH,3DH            ;function to open file
                MOV   AL,0              ;open to read
                INT   21H               ;open it
                JC    OPEN_ERROR        ;jump to error routine if problem
;---GET THE TIME AND DATA SETTINGS:
                MOV   BX,AX             ;move file handle to BX
                MOV   AL,0              ;code to fetch time
                MOV   AH,57H            ;function number
                INT   21H               ;go get the file's time
                JC    TIME_ERROR        ;jump to error routine if problem
;---SHIFT 'HOUR' BITS TO BOTTOM OF CH:
                MOV   CL,3              ;shift down bits 11-15
                SHR   CH,CL             ;hour value is now in CH
```

5.2.6 Write protect or hide files

DOS uses six different file "attributes," which give a file name a special status. A file may have several of these attributes concurrently (but not all). The attribute is set by the 12th byte of a 32-byte directory entry. The low six bits are significant, and the others are set to 0. The bits are:

```
if bit  5 = 1,   then the file has been written to since the last backup
        4 = 1,   then the file is a subdirectory
        3 = 1,   then the file is not a file at all, but the volume label
        2 = 1,   then the file is classified as a "system" file
        1 = 1,   then the file is hidden from directory searches
        0 = 1,   then the file is made "read-only"
```

Bit 5 is the "Archive Bit" used by the BACKUP and RESTORE commands of DOS. The bit is set to 0 after a backup and changed to 1 when the file is worked on again. The next time backups are made, unchanged files can be identified and ignored.

High Level

BASIC does not allow you to set a file attribute directly. Consult [5.2.1] for how to read the directory into memory, find a file, make changes, and then rewrite it to disk. Once the directory is laid out in memory, the attribute bytes are found at offsets 11, 43, 75, etc. If you must, read the current attribute byte and change only one bit, using the bit operations techniques shown in Appendix B. It is easier just to write all attributes anew. Take care—mistakes can be disastrous. This example finds the attribute of a file named "NEWDATA.AAA".

```
100 'load the directory sectors at &H2000 and then...
110 DEF SEG=&H2000                  'point to start of directory data
120 FILENAME$="NEWDATAAAAA"         'search for filename without "."
130 DIRPTR=0                        'pointer to directory
140 FOR N=1 to 112                  'check each entry (dbl sided floppy)
150 X$=""                           'temporary string to hold file name
160 FOR M=0 to 10                   'for each character of file name...
170 X$=X$+PEEK(DIRPTR+M)            'add it to the temporary string
180 NEXT                            'get next character of file name
190 IF X$=FILENAME$ THEN 220        'compare filenames, jump if match
200 NEXT                            'otherwise, go check next entry
210 PRINT"File not found":END       'no match found, give error message
220 X=PEEK(DIRPTR+11)               'match found, get attribute byte
230 IF X AND 32 <> 0 THEN PRINT"File not backed up"   'analyze attribute
240 IF X AND 16 <> 0 THEN PRINT"File is a subdirectory"
250 IF X AND 8 <> 0 THEN PRINT"Volume Label name -- not a file"
260 IF X AND 4 <> 0 THEN PRINT"File is a system file"
270 IF X AND 2 <> 0 THEN PRINT"File is a hidden file"
280 IF X AND 1 <> 0 THEN PRINT"File is read-only"
```

Middle Level

Function 43H of INT 21H can both change and find a file's attribute, but only if the file has been opened using the *file handle* method rather than the *file control block* method. There is no complementary function for FCBs. The attribute byte may be set when the file is created [5.3.2] by using an *extended* file control block. But if you subsequently open the FCB, change the attribute byte setting, and then close the file, the original attribute will remain. While you could change the attribute by some roundabout method, it is far easier to simply use the file handle function.

To use function 43H, place 1 in AL to give the file the attribute byte placed in CX (that is, in CL, but with CH equal to Ø). Alternatively, place Ø in AL to have the function return the file's current attribute byte in CX. In both cases, DS:DX points to a string giving the file's path. As always, it may have 63 characters, including the drive specifier. The end of the string is marked with an ASCII Ø byte (not counted as one of the 63 characters). This example gives the "hidden" status to the file OVERDUE:

```
;---IN THE DATA SEGMENT:
        PATH    DB    'A:ACCOUNTS',0

;---TURN ON THE "HIDDEN" ATTRIBUTE BYTE:
        MOV   AH,43H              ;function number
        MOV   AL,0                ;get the attribute byte
        LEA   DX,PATH             ;point DS:DX to the file's path
        INT   21H                 ;place attribute byte in CX
        JC    ERROR_ROUTINE       ;jump to recovery routine
        OR    CL,10B              ;turn on bit 1
        MOV   AH,43H              ;function number
        MOV   AL,1                ;replace the byte
        INT   21H                 ;and now the file has hidden status
```

The carry flag is set to 1 if an error occurs. In this case, AX returns with 2 if the file was not found, 3 if the path was not found, and 5 if there were other problems ("access denied").

5.2.7 Read/change the volume label

The volume label of a floppy disk is nothing more than a directory entry with a special attribute byte. The label fills the first 11 bytes of the entry, as would a file name and its extension. The attribute byte at offset 11 holds the value 8 (bit 3 = 1). The date and time fields are also filled in. One property of this attribute is that it prevents the entry from being displayed when the DIR command is used.

The label can occupy any position in the directory. It is found simply by testing all attribute bytes in sequence until the value 8 appears. Erase the label by placing E5 in the first byte of the entry—the attribute byte itself does not need to be changed. To change the label, write over the first 11 characters (use spaces, if required, to write over *all* 11). And to add a volume label to a disk that does not have one, search out an empty directory field and write in the label and the attribute; nothing more is required.

High Level ━━━━━━━━━━━━━━━━━━━━━━━━━━━━━━

The discussion at [5.4.2] explains how to read and write absolute disk sectors from BASIC. For a standard double-sided diskette, use 0 for the side number, 0 for the track number, 6 for the sector number, and 7 for the number of sectors to read or write. Once the data is loaded at the designated buffer, the examples given here can be used to change or add a volume label. Then the sectors are rewritten to disk. Be careful: mistakes could mean loss of all information on the disk. This example searches for the volume label and changes it:

```
100 'load the sectors at, say, &H1000, and then...
110 DEF SEG=&H1000
120 DIRPTR=11                        'pointer to first attribute byte
130 FOR N=1 TO 112                   'test all 112 directory entries
140 IF PEEK(DIRPTR)=8 THEN 180       'jump below if it is volume label
150 DIRPTR=DIRPTR+32                  'increase pointer to next entry
160 NEXT                             'go check attribute byte of next entry
170 PRINT"NO VOLUME LABEL FOUND":END         'no label
180 INPUT"Enter the new volumn lable ",V$    'prompt user for new label
190 IF LEN(V$)>11 THEN BEEP:PRINT"11 characters only":GOTO 180  'error
200 V$=V$+STRING$(11-LEN(V$),32)     'pad the string with spaces to 11 chars
210 DIRPTR=DIRPTR-11                  'point to start of the entry
220 FOR N=1 TO LEN(V$)               'for each character of the label
230 POKE N,MID$(V$,N,1)              'poke into the volume label position
240 NEXT                             'next character
250 'and now rewrite the sectors to disk...
```

Low Level ━━━━━━━━━━━━━━━━━━━━━━━━━━━━━━

The example below assumes that you have set up a 3584-byte data buffer to hold all seven sectors of the directory of a 360K floppy. The buffer is called DIR_AREA. The first example finds the label and displays it, or, failing to find a label, it displays a message telling that there is no label. For convenience, the code sets up the area to hold the sectors in the data segment; it is better to allocate memory for the task and then deallocate it afterwards [1.3.1].

```
;---IN THE DATA SEGMENT:
  VOL_STRING    DB      'The volume label is $'
  NO_LABEL      DB      'There is no volume label $'
  DIR_AREA      DB      3584 dup(?)            ;holds 7 sectors
;---READ IN THE 7 DIRECTORY SECTORS:
                MOV     AX,SEG DIR_AREA     ;get segment of buffer
                MOV     ES,AX               ;ES:BX points to the buffer
                MOV     BX,OFFSET DIR_AREA  ;get offset of buffer
                MOV     DL,0        ;drive number
                MOV     DH,0        ;head number
                MOV     CH,0        ;track number
                MOV     CL,6        ;directory starts at sector 6
                MOV     AL,7        ;7 sectors on double-sided diskette
                MOV     AH,2        ;function number to read sectors
                INT     13H         ;read the directory into memory
;---CHECK ATTRIBUTE BYTES UNTIL FIND ONE EQUALLING 8:
                MOV     CX,112              ;number of directory entries
                ADD     BX,11               ;point to first entry
  TRY_AGAIN:    MOV     AL,[BX]             ;get the first entry
                CMP     AL,8                ;does it have the volume attribute?
                JE      GOT_IT              ;if so, jump below
                ADD     BX,32               ;otherwise, increase pointer to next
                LOOP    TRY_AGAIN           ;go check next entry
;---DISPLAY MESSAGE TELLING THAT THERE IS NO VOLUME LABEL:
                MOV     AH,9                ;DOS function to print string
                LEA     DX,NO_LABEL         ;point to string
                INT     21H                 ;print it
                JMP     SHORT CONTINUE      ;skip below
;---DISPLAY MESSAGE GIVING VOLUME LABEL:
  GOT_IT:       MOV     AH,9                ;DOS function to print string
                LEA     DX,VOL_STRING       ;point to string
                INT     21H                 ;print it
                SUB     BX,11               ;move pointer from attri to label
                MOV     CX,11               ;will write all 11 chars
                MOV     AH,2                ;DOS function to write character
  NEXT_CHAR:    MOV     DL,[BX]             ;place character in DL
                INT     21H                 ;write it, forward cursor
                INC     BX                  ;point to next character
                LOOP    NEXT_CHAR           ;go get it
  CONTINUE:
```

To erase the label, place the following code at GOT_IT:

```
  GOT_IT:       MOV     AL,0E5H             ;code to mark empty dir field
                SUB     BX,11               ;point BX to start of field
                MOV     [BX],AL             ;change 1st byte of field
```

To change the volume label, instead use this code at GOT_IT. It assumes that you have set up elsewhere the 11-byte string NEW_LABEL.

```
  GOT_IT:       LEA     SI,NEW_LABEL        ;point SI to new label
                SUB     BX,11               ;point BX to start of label
                MOV     DI,BX               ;place pointer in DI
                MOV     CX,11               ;11 chars to move
        REP     MOVSB                       ;move the string
```

To *add* a label, write it in as above, but also set the attribute byte to 8 (you can simply append ASCII 8 to the string holding the new label, since the attribute byte immediately follows the label itself).

Finally, in all cases that change the directory, write the directory back to disk. Mistakes in this code tend to be unforgiving.

```
;---WRITE CHANGED SECTORS BACK TO DISK:
            MOV   AX,SEG DIR_AREA      ;same input registers as above
            MOV   ES,AX
            MOV   BX,OFFSET DIR_AREA
            MOV   DL,0
            MOV   DH,0
            MOV   CH,0
            MOV   CL,6
            MOV   AL,7
            MOV   AH,3                 ;function number to write sectors
            INT   13H
```

Section 3: Prepare for file operations

Programs written in high level languages need only *open* a file and all of the required preparatory work for file operations is automatically performed. Assembly language programmers, however, must set up special data areas that are used by file I/O. PC-DOS uses two methods of file access, the *file control block (FCB) method* and the *file handle method.* The FCB method descends from the days before PC-DOS made use of tree-structured directories; it can only access files in the current directory. The file handle method can reach files anywhere in a tree directory no matter which is set as the current directory.

Because tree directories are now widely used, the FCB method has become essentially obsolete; DOS continues to support this method in order to maintain compatibility with older software, and for this reason it is covered here. But your programs should always use the file handle method. The file handle method offers the additional advantage that it is easier to set up. In some applications, however, the read/write operations themselves may be somewhat more complicated than in the FCB method. For example, random file operations using the file handle functions require that a program calculate each record's offset within the file, whereas the corresponding FCB function accepts a record number and performs the calculations itself.

Files must be "opened" before data can be read or written. To open a file means to set up and initialize a special data area that DOS can use to keep crucial information about the file, such as its name and drive specifier, the size of the file's records, etc. High level languages like BASIC automatically set up these areas. A file control block is such a data area, and when the FCB method is used, the program sets up the block and DOS reads and manipulates its contents. The FCB is initially given only the name and drive of a file; once it is opened, information is entered into the block about the size of the records the file is organized in and about the location in the file from which access should begin.

In the file handle method, on the other hand, DOS automatically sets up a data area for the file at an unspecified location. DOS then creates a unique 16-bit code number for the file, and thereafter that "handle" is used by DOS functions to identify which opened file to operate upon. All that must be provided to find the file is a standard DOS path string with an optional drive specifier and with backslashes separating subdirectory names. These strings differ from those used with the DOS A> prompt only in that they terminate with a byte of ASCII Ø so that the program can tell where the string ends (the IBM manuals dub them "ASCIIZ strings").

The operations that move data to and from files require that you specify an area in RAM in which the data is to be deposited or from which it is to be taken. This buffer is defined by allocating an area of memory and setting a pointer to its first byte (that is, to the buffer's lowest position in memory). If too much data is transferred, the buffer overflows, possibly destroying data at higher addresses. The buffer can be used as a *transfer* buffer, handling only a small amount of data for a read or write operation. Or the buffer can be placed at the area in memory where the program actually keeps and manipulates the data that is transferred.

The file control block functions define the transfer buffer by a pointer kept by DOS at all times. The buffer is referred to as the *disk transfer area*, or *DTA*. Unfortunately, the IBM technical literature also refers to *the pointer* that defines the buffer as the "DTA", although it is better to think of it as the "disk transfer area pointer." Once the DTA pointer is defined by a special function, all file operations use that pointer until it is changed. The file handle functions, on the other hand, require you to define the starting address of the transfer buffer each time a function is called, and they ignore the DTA pointer used by the file control block functions. Figure 5-2 shows the two file access methods.

Identify File	Drive, Name and Extension Fields in FCB	Handle Placed in BX (Obtained by Opening File Using ASCIIZ String)
Set Starting Point for Read/Write	((Current Block × 128) + (Current Record)) × Record Size →─ Calculated from Random Record Number	Set File Pointer
Set Number of Bytes to Read/Write	Record Size (May Read/Write Multiple Records)	Set Number of Bytes in CX

Figure 5-2. The two file access methods.

5.3.1 Set/check the default drive

Programs can save themselves some work by setting a default drive to which all data file activity is directed. If early in a program the user is invited to choose the default drive, there will be no confusion as to what goes where.

High Level

The following lines of BASIC code switch the current drive using a machine language subroutine. The subroutine is only seven characters long. It is placed in the string X$, and the variable Z is made to point to the first byte of the routine. Appendix D explains how assembly routines are integrated into BASIC programs. Set the number of the drive in line 110, where $0 = A$, $1 = B$, etc. No error condition occurs if a non-existent drive is set as the default, so be careful. Do not attempt to combine lines 120 and 130 of this routine, since the BASIC interpreter will not process them correctly.

```
100 DEF SEG                                      'set segment to bottom of BASIC data area
110 NUMBER=0                                     'choose drive A
120 X$=CHR$(180)+CHR$(14)+CHR$(178)+CHR$(NUMBER)+CHR$(205)+CHR$(33)+CHR$ (203)
130 Y=VARPTR(X$)                                 'get string descriptor (string address at Y+1)
140 Z=PEEK(Y+1)+PEEK(Y+2)*256                    'calculate address of string
150 CALL Z                                       'perform the machine subroutine
```

Middle Level

Function EH of INT 21H sets the default drive. Simply place the drive number ($0 = A$, $1 = B$, etc.) in DL and execute the interrupt. This function returns in AL the number of drives in the machine. Note that 2 is returned when the machine has only one drive. A better way to determine the number of drives is shown at [1.1.5].

```
MOV   AH,0EH      ;function number
MOV   DL,1        ;code for drive B
INT   21H         ;set B: as the default drive
```

Function 19H of INT 21H reports which disk drive is currently the default drive. There are no input registers. AL returns with a code number, where $0 = A$, $1 = B$, etc.

5.3.2 Create/delete a file

A file may be created without placing any information into it. A directory entry is set up, and the file length field in the directory is set to 0. When the file is deleted, this directory entry is not actually removed, it is merely made non-operational by changing the first byte of the entry (the first character of the file name) to E5H. Thereafter the entry can be overwritten by that of a newly created file. At the time of file deletion, changes are also made in the file allocation table so that the sectors used by the file are freed for use by others. The contents of the sectors are not themselves erased. Hence it is possible to recover a deleted file—but be warned that the operations on the file allocation table are intricate.

High Level ───────────────────────────────

BASIC has no special command that creates a file. Instead, when OPEN is used, it searches the directory for the file name it is given and creates a new file if the name is not found. If a new file is opened and closed without any write operations between, it remains in the directory with a one-byte length, and a cluster of disk space is allocated to it (the single byte is the Ctrl-Z character—ASCII 26—that is used to terminate a standard ASCII file). See [5.3.3] for details of the OPEN statement.

The CLOSE statement does not conversely *delete* a file. Rather, the KILL command performs this task. The file must not be open while deleted. Simply place the file name in quotes, as in **KILL "A:ACCOUNTS.DAT"**. Or, if the file is in a subdirectory, use a standard path string, such as **KILL "A:\FINANCES\ACCOUNTS.DAT"**. In either case, the drive specifier is required only if the file is not on the default drive. Note that you can not use this method to delete a subdirectory (which is a kind of file)—use RMDIR instead [5.2.2].

Middle Level ──────────────────────────────

A file may be created or deleted using either the *file control block* or *file handle* methods. Creating the file by one method in no way restricts future access to the file by that method alone. But because a file is opened at the same time that it is created, it should be created using the same method of access as you wish to use at that time. When files are created and then closed with nothing placed in them, the file keeps a slot in the directory with 0 in the file size field, but no disk space is allocated to the file. It is important to understand that when a sequential file is opened for writing data (but not appending data), it is these file-creation functions that are used, since the file is reduced to zero-length and then entirely rewritten.

FCB method:

Function 16H of INT 21H creates and opens a file. Set up an FCB with the file's name and drive, and point DS:DX to it. Then call the function. The directory is searched and, if a match is found, the existing directory entry is reused so that the created file overwrites the file by that name. To avoid inadvertently destroying an

271

existing file, first check for a match to the file name using function 11H of INT 21H [5.2.1]. When there is no matching name, a new directory entry is created and AL returns 0; if the directory is full, AL returns FF. Use an extended file control block [5.3.5] to give the file a special attribute (e.g., read-only status) [5.2.6]. Once opened, the new file is initialized to 0 length, and it is allocated a cluster of disk space. Here is an example:

```
;---IN THE DATA SEGMENT:
        FCB     DB    1,'MYFILE    DAT',25 DUP(0)

;---CHECK FOR EXISTING FILE:
                MOV   AH,11H               ;function to search for file name
                LEA   DX,FCB               ;point DS:DX to the FCB
                INT   21H                  ;make the search
                CMP   AL,0                 ;if file already exists, AL=0
                JE    WARN_USER            ;jump to error routine if so
;---CREATE THE FILE:
                MOV   AH,16H               ;else, function number to create file
                INT   21H                  ;create the file (DS:DX already set)
```

Use an extended file control block to create a file with a special attribute, such as read-only status. The attribute bytes are discussed at [5.2.6]. Add a seven-byte header to the usual FCB, starting with FFH, then five bytes of ASCII 0, and then the desired attribute byte. A hidden file requires that bit 1 of the attribute byte be set to 1. To hide the file opened in the above example, write:

```
FCB     DB    0FFH,5 DUP(0),2,1,'MYFILE    DAT',25 DUP(0)
```

Function 13H of INT 21H deletes a file. Point DS:DX to an *unopened* FCB and execute the function. If no match is found for the file name, AL returns with FF; otherwise AL is given 0. Global characters (question marks, but not asterisks) may be used in the file name, in which case more than one file may be deleted by a single call to the function. Here is an example:

```
;---IN THE DATA SEGMENT:
        FCB     DB    1,'MYFILE DAT',25 DUP(0)

;---DELETE 'MYFILE':
                MOV   AH,13H               ;function number
                LEA   DX,FCB               ;point DS:DX to FCB
                INT   21H                  ;delete the file
                CMP   AL,0FFH              ;check for failure
                JE    DELETE_ERROR         ;jmp to routine if failed
```

File Handle Method:

Function 3CH of INT 21H creates and opens a new file by the file handle method. Point DS:DX to a string giving the file's path and name in standard DOS format, including an initial drive specifier if the file is not on the default drive. The string must end with an ASCII 0 byte. Place an attribute byte [5.2.6] for the file in CX (0 for a normal file). Then execute the function. If successful, on return the carry flag is set to 0 and AX contains a handle for the new file. An error has occurred if the carry flag is set to 1, and in that case AX contains 3 if the path was not found, 4 if all file buffers are already open, or 5 if the directory is full or if the file already exists but is marked read-only. Note that if the directory already contains a file by that name, the existing file is truncated to Ø length, effectively destroying it. To avoid mistakes, use function 4EH of INT 21H to check for a match beforehand.

```
;---IN THE DATA SEGMENT:
        PATH    DB      'B:LEVEL1\LEVEL2\FILENAME.EXT',0

;---CHECK FOR A MATCH TO THE FILENAME:
                MOV     AH,4EH          ;function to check for match
                LEA     DX,PATH         ;point DS:DX to the path
                INT     21H             ;see if there is a match
                JNC     WARN_USER       ;don't go on if match found
;---CREATE THE FILE:
                MOV     AH,3CH          ;else use function to create file
                MOV     CX,0            ;normal attribute
                INT     21H             ;create the file (DS:DX,CX still set)
                JC      OPEN_ERROR      ;go to error routine if carry flag set
                MOV     HANDLE,AX       ;store a copy of the file handle
```

DOS 3.0 adds a new function to create files by the file handle method. This is number 5BH of INT 21H. It operates exactly as function 3CH above, except that it produces *extended error codes* for better error checking. These are explained at [7.2.5].

To *delete* a file by the file handle method, use function 41H of INT 21H. Again, point DS:DX to a string giving the file's path and name. Global file name characters are not allowed. Then call the function. If the carry flag is 1, the function has failed; AX will hold 2 if the file was not found and 5 if there was a disk drive problem. Note that you cannot delete read-only files with this function; change the file's attribute [5.2.6] before deleting it. Here is an example:

```
;---IN THE DATA SEGMENT:
        PATH    DB      'B:LEVEL1\LEVEL2\FILENAME.EXT',0

;---DELETE THE FILE:
                MOV     AH,41H          ;function number
                LEA     DX,PATH         ;DS:DX points to the directory path
                INT     21H             ;delete the file
                JC      DELETE_ERROR    ;go to error routine if carry flag set
```

DOS version 3.0 has a special function (5AH of INT 21H) that creates a temporary "nameless" file. DOS generates a name of its own for the file and checks to see that it does not already exist in the directory. This feature averts any possibility that a program's temporary files might match the name of an existing disk file, destroying it. On entry, DS:DX must point to a string that traces the path up to the directory in which the temporary file will be created. End the string with a backslash. Place the file's attribute in CX (normally Ø). On return AX holds the file handle, unless the carry flag is set to 1, in which case AX holds error information. The arbitrary file name is appended to the end of the path string. This function can return *extended error codes*, which exist only in DOS 3.0; they are explained at [7.2.5]. The file is *not* automatically deleted by this function—the program must use function 41H (above). This example causes DOS to create a temporary file and later deletes it:

```
;---IN THE DATA SEGMENT:
    PATH        DB      'B:LEVEL1\LEVEL2\',12 DUP(0)

;---CREATE THE TEMPORARY FILE:
                MOV     AH,5AH              ;function number
                LEA     DX,PATH             ;point DS:DX to the path
                INT     21H                 ;make the temporary file
                JC      CREATION_ERROR      ;error routine is carry flag=1
                                            ;...handle now in AX
                  .
                  .
                                            ;...later, to delete file:
                MOV     AH,41H              ;function number
                LEA     DX,PATH             ;repoint DS:DX to path string
                INT     21H                 ;delete the temporary file
                JC      DELETION_ERROR      ;error routine is carry flag=1
```

5.3.3 Open/close a file

To "open" a file means to set aside small blocks of memory to hold information about the file and to act as a way station (a buffer) through which data moves between the file and memory. High level languages automatically set up these blocks for you; assembly language does not. When a file is opened, the directory is searched for its presence. When found, DOS takes information from the directory about the file, such as its size and date. Later, when the file is closed, DOS updates this directory information. Closing a file also "flushes" out the DOS data transfer buffer, sending to disk the last information directed to the file. Failing to close files before ending a program can result in loss of data.

If a program operates on many files, be sure to keep an eye on how many are open at any one time. DOS 2.1 allows up to 99 files to be open at once, with the default being 8 (change the number with the DOS *FILES* command); BASIC allows no more than 15. Each file takes up memory for the parameter block and buffer. And the memory for each file is put aside *before* any files are opened, so that the memory is unavailable to the program even when the specified number of files are not open. For this reason, you can conserve memory by setting the largest admissible number of files to no more than required, using the methods shown below.

High Level ━━━━━━━━━━━━━━━━━━━━━━━━━━━━━━━━━━━━

When BASIC opens a file, it searches the directory for it, and if it is not found, a new file by the given name is created. There are two ways of writing a statement that opens a file, and in most instances one does as well as the other. The only difference is that one form is rather cryptic, while the second comes closer to natural language in its expression. In either statement you must supply at least three pieces of information. First, the name is required; since it is a string, it is placed within quotes. Second, a number from 1 upwards is assigned to the file as the ID number by which other statements read or write to the file. And third, you must specify for what purpose the file is being opened, that is, whether it is for random access, for a sequential read, or whatever. To open the file MYFILE.TXT to write to a sequential file ("OUTPUT" or "O"), where the file accessed is the one opened as #2, write either:

```
OPEN "O",#2,"MYFILE.TXT"
```

...or...

```
OPEN "MYFILE.TXT" FOR OUTPUT AS #2
```

Note that in either case the number #2 refers to file buffer 2. The number may be any value that does not exceed the number of file buffers allowed. If six files are supported simultaneously, the number must be from 1 to 6. However, file buffer #1 does not need to be used before a file can be opened under number #2. BASIC sets the number of files buffers to 8 by default, and you can change the number to from 1 to 15. Of these, four are used by BASIC for its own purposes, so that in the default condition only four are available for I/O. Use the F: parameter when

BASIC is loaded in order to set the number of buffers. For example, if you type **BASICA/F:10** when starting up BASIC, ten buffers are created, and six are available for file operations.

A second parameter, **S:**, sets the size of the file buffers. All buffers are the same size. The default is 128 bytes, and the value may be as large as 32767. For sequential files it may be set to 0, saving a little memory. For random files it must be as large as the largest record size. Note that if records are 512 bytes long and the buffer size is set to 512, faster disk operations result. **BASICA/S:512/F:10** opens 10 buffers with a 512-byte record size. Each file takes 188 bytes plus the buffer size, so 7K of memory is consumed by this configuration. The number of file buffers opened must not be more than allowed by DOS.

Cryptic Form:

The first form of the OPEN statement shown above uses single letters to designate the kind of file operation desired. There are three options:

```
"O"    output data to a sequential file
"I"    input data from a sequential file
"R"    both read and write data to and from a random file
```

Sequential files can not be written to while they are opened for reading, and vice-versa. Typically, a sequential file is opened, read in its entirety into memory, and then the file buffer is closed. After changes have been made, the file is reopened (via any file buffer) for output, and the file is written back to disk, overlaying the sectors that hold the file and possibly taking up some more.

There are a few things to note about this form of the OPEN statement. The file name should contain a drive specifier if the file is not found on the default drive (the drive from which BASIC was loaded). Also, the file name may be given as a string showing the path to a file located in a subdirectory, as in **OPEN "I",#1,"A:\LEVEL1\LEVEL2\MYFILE.TXT"**. In addition, note that you can tack on a *record length* specification to the end of the statement, as in **OPEN "R",#3,"B:MYFILE.TXT",52**. In this case, every record will take up 52 bytes of disk space. If a FIELD statement does not make use of all 52 bytes, the remainder is wasted. This parameter is essential in random file operations. Most sequential file operations do not require a record length setting, but you can speed up file operations by setting the record size to 512. The record length may be from 1 to 32767 bytes, and it defaults to 128.

Natural Language Form:

The second form of the OPEN statement does exactly the same as the first, except that it uses complete words. Rather than write "O" or "I", write **OUTPUT** and **INPUT** (without quotes), as in **OPEN "FILENAME" FOR INPUT AS #1**. For random files, give no such specification at all, as in **OPEN "MYFILE.TXT" AS #2**. In addition, you can specify **APPEND** to write data starting from *the end* of a sequential file, without overwriting any of the existing data, as in **OPEN "B:MYFILE.TXT" FOR APPEND AS #3**. As with the first form discussed above, the statement also takes an optional specification of record length. Just append

LEN = **number** to the end of the statement. For example, **OPEN "C:MYFILE.TXT"
AS #1 LEN = 52** opens a random file with 52-byte records.

Often a program will take the name of a file from the program user. To use this
file name, in the OPEN statement simply substitute for the name of the file the
name of the string that holds the file name. Error checking is required to be sure the
name is acceptable.

```
100 INPUT"Enter file name: ",F$          'get file name from user
110 IF INSTR(F$,".")<>0 THEN 130         'jump if it has an extension
120 IF LEN(F$) > 8 THEN 500 ELSE 150     'if longer than 8 chars, error
130 IF LEN(F$) > 12 THEN 500             'if longer than 12 chars, error
140 IF LEN(F$)-INSTR(F$,".")>3 THEN 500  'if extension over 3 chars, error
150 OPEN F$ FOR INPUT AS #1              'open the file
        .
        .
500 INPUT"Improper file name -- enter another: ",F$   'get another name
510 GOTO 110                             'analyze new name
```

Closing Files:

Closing files is trivial. To close all that are open, simply write **CLOSE.** To close a
particular buffer, or several buffers, write **CLOSE #1** or **CLOSE #1,#3,** etc. It is
important to close *all* files before a program terminates. Data may remain in the
buffer that has not yet been output to disk. Note that the END, NEW, RESET,
SYSTEM, and RUN commands close all file buffers, but they do not flush the buffers. Once closed, the file can be reopened using any available buffer number.

Middle Level

DOS provides different functions for opening and closing files depending on
whether a program uses the *file control block* method or the *file handle* method of
access. In either case, only pre-existing files may be opened. A separate function
[5.3.2] creates new files.

FCB Method:

Function FH of INT 21H opens an existing file. You must first set up a file control
block, as shown as [5.3.5]. Before opening the FCB, fill in only the file name and
drive specifier (Ø = default, 1 = A:, etc.). Point DS:DX to it and call the function.
On return AL will hold Ø if the file was successfully opened, and FF if the file was
not found. If Ø was used as the drive specifier, the number will be changed to that
of the default drive.

Only after the file has been opened should you set the record size (defaults to 128
bytes), or the random record or current record fields (these are discussed in the sections concerning sequential and random operations). When opened, the current
block field is set to Ø, and the date and time fields are filled in from directory information.

To close a file using the FCB method, point DS:DX to the opened FCB and call
function 10H of INT 21H. If successful, information about the file's size, time, and
date will be set in the directory, and AL will return Ø. But if the file name is not
found in the directory, or if it is found in a different position, a disk change will be
indicated by AL returning FF.

```
;---IN THE DATA SEGMENT:
        FCB     DB      1,'FILENAMEEXT',25 DUP(0)
;---OPEN THE FILE:
                MOV     AH,0FH          ;function number
                LEA     DX,FCB          ;point DS:DX to the FCB
                INT     21H             ;opens the file
                CMP     AL,0            ;check for errors
                JNE     OPEN_ERROR      ;jump to routine if error
                  .
                  .
;---CLOSE THE FILE:
                MOV     AH,10H          ;function number
                LEA     DX,FCB          ;point DS:DX to the FCB
                INT     21H             ;close the file
                CMP     AL,0            ;check for error
                JNE     CLOSE_ERROR     ;jump to recovery routine
```

File Handle Method:

Use function 3DH of INT 21H to open files. Point DS:DX to a string giving the path and file name, with drive specifier if required. The entire string should be no more than 63 bytes long, and it must be followed by an ASCII 0 byte. Place an "access code" in AL, where 0 opens the file for reading, 1 opens it for writing, and 2 opens it for both. Upon return, AX will hold the 16-bit handle by which the file is thereafter identified. The file pointer is set to the beginning of the file. The record size is set at one byte—this is because random file operations under the handle method are not specially buffered: in essence, random files are treated like sequential ones, and the same functions deal with both. This function opens both normal and hidden files. On return the carry flag will be set to 0 if the file opened successfully. If not, the flag will be set to 1, and AX will hold 2 if the file was not found, 4 if the program has attempted to open too many files, 5 if there was a disk access problem, and 12 if the access code placed in AL was invalid. Here is an example:

```
;---IN THE DATA SEGMENT:
    PATH            DB      'A:LEVEL1\FILENAME.EXT',0

;---OPEN THE FILE FOR BOTH READING AND WRITING:
                MOV     AH,3DH          ;function number
                MOV     AL,2            ;open for reading or writing
                LEA     DX,PATH         ;point DS:DX to path string
                INT     21H             ;open the file
                JC      OPEN_ERROR      ;jump to error routine if problem
                MOV     HANDLE,AX       ;save a copy of the handle
```

Function 3EH of INT 21H closes files opened under the file handle method. Simply put the handle in BX and execute the function. On return, the carry flag will be set to 0 if successful, and to 1, with AL = 6, if the file handle was invalid.

```
;---CLOSE THE FILE:
                MOV     AH,3EH          ;function number
                MOV     BX,HANDLE       ;place file handle in BX
                INT     21H             ;close the file
                JC      CLOSE_ERROR     ;go to error routine if carry flag set
```

Function 45H of INT 21H creates a second file handle from an existing, opened handle. BX is given the existing handle, and AX returns the new one. Function 46H of INT 21H, on the other hand, links a second handle (placed in CX) to an opened handle (in BX) so that the former refers to the same file or device as the latter.

5.3.4 Rename a file/move a file's directory location

Renaming a file can entail nothing more than changing the first 11 characters of the file's directory entry. In a tree structured directory, however, the entire directory entry may be moved to another subdirectory, redefining the path to the file. A single command can both rename a file and move it to another directory.

High Level

The NAME command in BASIC renames a file. It can also move the file to a different directory. List first the existing name and then the new name for the file, placing them separately in quotes, as in **NAME "OLDFILE.EXT" AS "NEWFILE.-EXT"**. In this case, a file in the root directory is renamed. File paths may be used to change the names of files located in subdirectories. For example, **NAME "B:LEVEL1 \ OLDFILE.EXT" AS "B:LEVEL1 \ NEWFILE.EXT"** changes "OLD-FILE.EXT" to "NEWFILE.EXT".

Note that the complete path must be given for the new file name. If you were instead to write **NAME "B:LEVEL1 \ OLDFILE.EXT" AS "NEWFILE.EXT"**, then the file would not only be renamed, but it also would be transferred to the root directory. To move a file from one subdirectory to another without changing its name, write **NAME "A:SUBDIR1 \ OLDFILE.EXT" AS "A:SUBDIR2 \ OLDFILE.-EXT"**. Files may *not* be moved between disks using this method. Because files of the same name may be kept in different directories, another possible error is to attempt to move like-named files together. In this case, error code 58 is returned [5.4.8].

Middle Level

DOS can rename files using both the *file control block* method and the *file handle* method. The former may operate only upon files in the current directory.

FCB Method:

Use function 17H of INT 21H. Point DS:DX to an opened file control block. Place the new name for the file in the FCB starting at offset 11H (this is a "reserved area" of the block). The second name may use the global character ?, in which case the characters at those positions in which it appears are not changed. Upon return, if the new name has already been used elsewhere in the directory then AL = FF, otherwise AL = 0. This example changes the file **ACCOUNTS.DAT** to **DEBTS.DAT**.

```
;---IN THE DATA SEGMENT:
    FCB         DB   1,'FILENAMEEXT',25 DUP(0)
    NEWNAME     DB   'NEWNAME EXT'          ;11 characters to replace old name

;---PLACE NEW FILENAME IN VARIABLE CALLED ''NEWNAME'', THEN...
                MOV  SI,OFFSET NEWNAME      ;point DS:SI to the new filename
                MOV  AX,SEG FCB             ;ES:DI points to FCB
                MOV  ES,AX                  ;
                MOV  DI,OFFSET FCB          ;
                ADD  DI,11H                 ;start at offset 11
```

```
            MOV   CX,11              ;11 bytes in a filename
      REP   MOVSB                    ;transfer the 11 bytes
            LEA   DX,FCB             ;point DS:DX to the FCB
            MOV   AH,17H             ;function to change name
            INT   21H               ;change the name
            CMP   AL,ØFFH            ;test for error
            JE    RENAME_ERROR       ;go to error routine if problem
```

File Handle Method:

Function 56H of INT 21H renames and moves files. DS:DX points to the usual DOS path string (to 63 characters) that gives the name of the file to be renamed, and that terminates with an ASCII 0 byte. ES:DI points to a second string that gives the new name and path. The drive specifiers (if any) must match. If the paths are different, the file is moved to a different subdirectory, as well as being renamed. To move a file without renaming it, simply give the same name but a different path in the second path string. On return, if an error has occurred, the carry flag is set and AX contains 3 if one of the paths was not found, 5 if there was a disk error, and 17 if different drives were specified. This example moves ACCOUNTS.-DAT from the subdirectory "GAINS" to the subdirectory "LOSSES".

```
;---IN THE DATA SEGMENT:
      OLDPATH     DB    'A:GAINS\ACCOUNTS.DAT',Ø
      NEWPATH     DB    'A:LOSSES\ACCOUNTS.DAT',Ø

;---CHANGE THE FILE'S PATH:
            LEA   DX,OLDPATH         ;point DS:DX to old path
            MOV   AX,SEG NEWPATH     ;point ES:DI to new path
            MOV   ES,AX              ;
            MOV   DI,OFFSET NEWPATH  ;
            MOV   AH,56H             ;function number
            INT   21H               ;move the file
            JC    ERROR_ROUTINE      ;go to error routine if carry flag set
```

5.3.5 Prepare for file operations

High-level languages like BASIC automatically perform the preparatory work for file operations. But assembly language programs have work to do before they can create or open a file. The requirements differ depending on whether the program uses the *file control block* or the *file handle* method of file access. In general, for either method you must set up a string or parameter block that names the file, and also a buffer for the data transfers. DOS provides separate sets of read/write functions for the two methods.

Middle Level ━━━━━━━━━━━━━━━━━━━━━━━━━━━━━━━━━━━━━━

File Control Block Method:

The file control block method of file access requires that you construct a parameter block that initially contains just enough information about the file so that it can be found in the directory. Although an FCB has many fields, generally only a few need to be filled; once the file is opened, DOS fills in much of the remainder of the information. Note that a special field is tacked on to the front of the block to make an *extended FCB*, which is explained below. Here is the FCB structure:

Drive (DB)
: A number telling which drive the file is found on. 1 = drive A, 2 = drive B, etc. If set to 0, DOS uses the default drive, and it replaces the 0 with the number of the default drive.

Name & Extension (11 bytes)
: Left-justify the eight-byte file name, and fill the remaining spaces with blanks (ASCII 32). The same applies to the three-byte extension. No period symbol is placed between the two.

Current block (DW)
: DOS organizes files in blocks of 128 records, numbered 0-127. For example, it treats random record #129 as record #0 of block #1 (counting for both records and blocks starts from 0). There are no special markings in the file that delimit blocks and records. Rather, the offsets of blocks and records are calculated on the basis of the record size, which is set in the next field of the FCB.

Record size (DW)
: All DOS functions that read and write to files work in units of *records*. For random files it is essential that the record size be set to match that of the random records placed in the file. For sequential files the record size is not critical, but a small record size can slow down file operations. Because the sector size is 512 bytes, a 512-byte record size is optimal. DOS automatically places the default value 80H (128) in the record size field when the file is opened. So be sure to set the field *after* opening the FCB.

File size (DD)   The size is given to the nearest byte. It is filled in by DOS when the file is opened.

File date (DW)   The date is written in by DOS when the FCB is opened. The format is given at [5.2.5].

Current record (DB)   The current record is the counterpart of the current block field. The records are numbered 0-127. Random record #200, which is located in block 1, would have current record number 71 ((200-128)-1).

Random record number (DD)
                        Rather than require that the program calculate the block and record positions of random records, DOS does the work itself. In random file operations, simply place the record number in this four-byte field. When the random file operation is performed, DOS places the proper values in the current block and current record fields. Remember that the most significant byte is the highest in memory.

The relationship of the current record field, current block field, and random record field is shown in Figure 5-3.

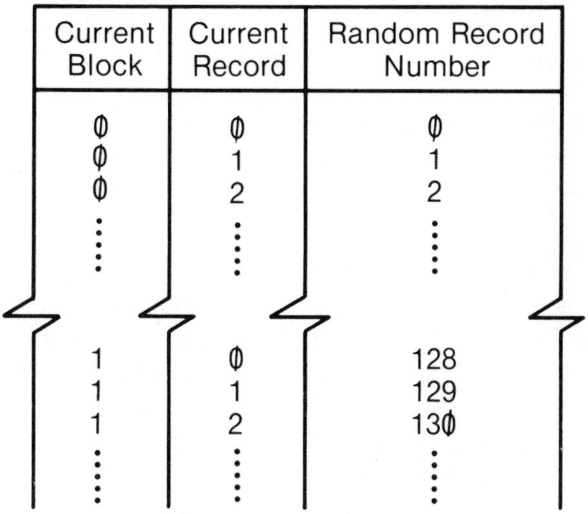

Current Block	Current Record	Random Record Number
0	0	0
0	1	1
0	2	2
⋮	⋮	⋮
1	0	128
1	1	129
1	2	130
⋮	⋮	⋮

Figure 5-3. The organization of random records in an FCB.

It is easiest to set up an FCB as a variable in a program's data segment. If the name of the file to be opened is invariable, the name can be written directly into its field. Initialize the remainder of the block with ASCII 0. Only after the FCB has been opened (using function FH of INT 21H, as shown at [5.3.3]) should you write the remaining information into the block. Note that the FCB for a simple sequential operation using a 128-byte record size requires no further preparation. Once the

FCB is set up, subsequent file operations access it by pointing DS:DX to it. The simplest form is:

```
FCB     DB    1,'FILENAMEEXT',25 DUP(0)
```

Alternatively, set the FCB up as a structure:

```
FCB             STRUC
DRIVE_NUM       DB   0
FILE_NAME       DB   8   DUP(?)
FILE_EXT        DB   3   DUP(?)
BLOCK_NUM       DW   0
RECORD_SIZE     DW   0
FILE_SIZE       DD   0
FILE_DATE       DW   0
RESERVED        DB   10  DUP(0)
CURRENT_REC     DB   0
RANDOM_REC      DD   0
FCB             ENDS
```

This approach makes it easy for a program to place data into the FCB, since labels exist for every field. Depending on the type of file operation, the fields pose the following requirements:

1. To access random files you must set the record size and the record number in the random record field.
2. To access sequential files from the beginning you need only set the record size, providing that you initialize the current block and current record fields to 0 (simply initialize the entire FCB to 0's except the drive specifier and file name). When opened, the record size field is set to 128; if that suffices, no further initialization is required.
3. To access sequential files midway, or at the end, you must set the current block and current record fields (here your program must do the calculating itself).

The program segment prefix [1.3.0] has a field large enough to hold a file control block. This space is provided for every program, and so it is economical to make use of it, especially in COM programs. The FCB field is located at offset 5CH in the PSP. In COM programs, use ORG to set up the FCB, as follows (here, the default DTA—which is discussed below—is also labeled):

```
;---AT THE BEGINNING OF THE CODE SEGMENT:
                    ORG   5CH
FCB                 LABEL    BYTE
DRIVE_NUM           DB   0
FILE_NAME           DB   8 DUP(?)
FILE_EXT            DB   3 DUP(?)
BLOCK_NUM           DW   0
RECORD_SIZE         DW   0
FILE_SIZE           DD   0
FILE_DATE           DW   0
RESERVED            DB   10 DUP(0)
CURRENT_REC         DB   0
RANDOM_REC          DD   0
                    ORG   80H
```

```
DTA            LABEL   BYTE
               ORG   100H
               ASSUME CS:CSEG,DS:CSEG,SS:CSEG
                .
                .
```

An *extended FCB* is used to create or access files that have special attributes, such as hidden files and read-only files. The various attributes are explained at [5.2.6]. Extended FCBs are seven bytes longer, with the additional seven bytes *preceding* the usual block. The first byte is FF, which indicates the special status. It is followed by five bytes of ASCII 0, and then by the attribute byte itself. When opening a file using an extended FCB, DS:DX points to the first of the additional seven bytes (FF), rather than to the drive specifier as for normal FCBs. Here is the general form, in which 2 is the value of the attribute byte and 1 is the drive specifier:

```
FCB    DB    0FFH,5 DUP(0),2,1,'FILENAMEEXT',25 DUP(0)
```

File Handle Method:

The file handle method is easier to set up than the FCB method. For this method, you need only set up a string giving the file's path, just as in standard DOS commands. For example, **B:COMPILE \ UTILITY \ PASCAL** names the file PASCAL in the subdirectory UTILITY. The strings are limited to 63 characters, including the drive specifier. When the file is opened (using function 3DH of INT 21H—see [5.3.3]), DS:DX is pointed to the first byte of this string. DOS does all the work of parsing the string and finding the file, and once the file is opened DOS returns a 16-bit ID number for the file in AX. The ID is called the file handle, and it is used in all subsequent operations that operate on the file.

The Data Buffers:

A program must specify a location in memory where incoming data is deposited or outgoing data is removed. This space in memory can be a transfer buffer that acts as a way station for the data. Or the memory space can be the actual location at which the data resides when it is processed. A transfer buffer typically is set to the size of one record, and it may conveniently be set up as a string variable in the data segment, as in the example below. Large data work areas, on the other hand, should be allocated by DOS using the memory allocation methods given at [1.3.1]. Setting up, say, a 10000-byte data area in the data segment itself makes the program 10000 bytes larger on disk, which is wasteful.

The buffer used by the FCB method of file access is called the "disk transfer area," or DTA. This buffer is pointed to by a word-length pointer that is kept by DOS and that can be changed by your programs. IBM documentation often refers to this DTA pointer simply as "the DTA." Since only the start of the buffer is specified, nothing stops data from being deposited beyond the end of the DTA, so you must see to it that this never happens. The DTA pointer is set by a special DOS function, and once it is set, all read/write functions automatically access it. This means that the functions themselves do not have to contain the transfer buffer address.

When the DTA is made synonymous with the memory area in which the data is processed, it may be necessary to constantly change the DTA so that file operations can access particular fragments of the data. In a single sequential read operation or in a single random block read operation, DOS automatically places one record after another in the DTA. Be sure to allot enough space to hold the number of records the program has requested. The DTA cannot be more than one segment (64K) long.

Use function 1AH of INT 21H to set the DTA pointer. Point DS:DX to the first byte of the DTA and execute the function. That is all there is to it. Here is an example:

```
;---IN THE DATA SEGMENT:
        DTA     256  DUP(?)

;---SET UP THE DTA:
              LEA   DX,DTA              'point DS:DX to DTA
              MOV   AH,1AH              'function to set DTA
              INT   21H                 'set the DTA
```

Function 2FH of INT 21H reports the current DTA pointer setting. There are no input registers. On return, ES:BX holds the segment and offset of the DTA.

The program segment prefix [1.3.0] provides every program with a 128-byte ready-made DTA from offset 80H to 9FH. You may wish to use it if memory is scarce. The DTA pointer is initially set to point to this buffer, so there is no need to set the pointer at all if it is used. This default buffer is especially easy to use in COM files, where DS points to the bottom of the PSP. EXE files may require a little extra coding to access the default DTA. Note that to *find* the current setting of the DTA pointer you must use function 2FH of INT 21H. There are no input registers. On return ES:BX points to the DTA.

The DTA pointer is not used in the file handle method of file access. The functions that read and write data always contain the address at which the data buffer is located. It is entirely up to you whether the data is moved to an intermediary buffer or to its final location in memory.

5.3.6 Analyze information from the command line

When loaded, many programs allow the user to place additional information on the DOS command line, usually to indicate the name of the file that the program will first work on. This information is dumped into the 128-byte region beginning at offset 80H in the program segment prefix [1.3.0]. (This same area is also used as the default DTA, as discussed at [5.3.5]). The first byte at 80H tells how many characters there are in the string, and then the string itself follows.

For programs that use the file handle methods to work on files, the form in which a file name is entered from the command line should be adequate for file operations. Just require that the program user adhere to the standard DOS protocol for path strings. File control blocks, on the other hand, require that a string like 'A:ACCT.BAK' be converted to the form 1,'ACCT   BAK'. DOS has a special function that makes this conversion from the first information following the program name on the command line. This procedure is referred to as "parsing."

Middle Level ─────────────────────────────

The filename should be the first information to follow the name of the program being loaded. The name may be separated from the program name by : . ; , = + **TAB SPACE.** And the end of the filename may be delimited by : . ; , = + **TAB SPACE** \ < > | / " [ ] and any of the control characters (ASCII 1-31).

Function 29H of INT 21H parses the filename. Point DS:SI to offset 81H in the PSP. Remember that when the program is loaded both DS and ES point to the bottom of the PSP. ES:DI must point to a memory area that is to serve as the file control block for the new file. The bit settings in AL determine how the parsing is to be performed. Only bits 0-3 are significant:

---

bit 0   1 = Leading separators are ignored.

   1   1 = The drive ID byte is set in the FCB only if specified in the command line.

   2   1 = FCB filename changed only if the command line contains a filename.

   3   1 = FCB filename extension changed only if the command line contains filename extension.

Once this information is set, the program can call the function. If no drive specifier is found in the command line, the default drive is assumed. And if no filename extension is present, it is assumed to be blanks (ASCII 32). Should an asterisk appear in the file name, it is converted to the appropriate number or question marks in the filename entry of the FCB. AL returns 1 if the filename contains ? or *, and it returns FF if an invalid drive was specified.

On return, DS:SI points to the first character after the filename at offset 81H. Additional command line information must be deciphered by your own code.

ES:DI points to the first byte of the newly formatted FCB. If no valid filename has been created at the FCB, ES:[DI] + 1 is a blank. Here is an example that places the code in the FCB area of the PSP, starting at offset 5CH:

```
;---PARSE THE COMMAND LINE, SETTING UP A FCB AT 5CH IN THE PSP:
                MOV   AH,29H              ;function number
                MOV   SI,81H              ;DS:SI points to filename
                MOV   DI,5CH              ;ES:DI points to FCB area
                MOV   AL,1111B            ;set code byte
                INT   21H                 ;set up the FCB
                MOV   AL,ES:[DI]+1        ;get status information
                CMP   AL,32               ;no file set up?
                JE    ERROR_ROUTINE       ;if not, jump to error routine
```

Section 4: Read and Write Files

There are two basic ways to access files, sequentially and randomly. Although computer literature commonly refers to "sequential files" and "random files," the files themselves reside on disk in exactly the same way: as a continuous sequence of bytes. There is no indication in the directory or anywhere else that a particular file is "sequential" or "random." What differentiates the two kinds of files is the *layout of data* and the corresponding *method of access*. Any random file can be accessed sequentially, and any sequential file can be accessed randomly, although there is seldom reason to do so, especially in the latter case.

Sequential files place data items one after the other—no matter their length—separating the items with a pair of characters, first the carriage return (ASCII 13) and then the line feed (ASCII 10). High-level languages like BASIC insert these delimiting characters automatically, while assembly language programs must take the trouble of inserting them after each variable is written to the file. Both numbers and strings may be saved in sequential files. Strings take up one byte for every character in the string. Numbers are conventionally written in string form, although they could as well be written in numeric form. Thus BASIC automatically writes out the value "128" as a three-digit string, although an assembly language program could write it as a two-byte integer, or even as a one-byte code—anything goes so long as the file will be reread by software that understands the format. For the sake of compatibility, writing numbers as strings is advised.

There is no requirement that each number or string be separated by a carriage return/line feed pair, but when the pair is omitted the program must provide a way of separating the data. Ten integers could be stored as a 20-byte data element, for example. On the other hand, very large data elements, such as a paragraph of text, may be divided into several data elements (a standard text file is nothing more than a document broken down into strings of manageable size, saved in sequential form). Because the data items are of varying length, it is impossible to know just where in the file a particular item is located. And so a program must read the file from its beginning to find a particular item, counting the number of carriage return/line feed pairs until it encounters the desired item. It is for this reason that files of this format are called "sequential." Generally, the entire file is transferred from disk to memory.

Random files pre-allocate a fixed amount of space to each data item. When a particular data item does not fill the entire space allotted, the excess is filled with spaces. If every item occupies ten bytes, then it is easy to look up the 50th item, since one can calculate that it starts at the 491st byte of the file (that is, byte #490, since counting begins from 0). Generally, a related set of items is grouped together into a *record*. Each record holds several *fields*, which provide a set number of bytes into which to place each data item. For example, a record may have fields for age, weight, and height. The respective fields for each might be two bytes, three bytes, and five bytes. Taken together, they would form a record ten bytes long. A random file could consist of thousands of such records. Each record follows immediately upon the prior, with no delimiters like the carriage return/line feed pairs used in sequential files. However, the records may be written in any order, so that record 74 may be written even though record 73 has not been (disk space would still be allocated for record 73, and the record would contain whatever data happens to be in the sector to which the record is assigned). Unlike sequential files, random files remain on disk. Only the particular records that are operated on at any particular moment are present in memory.

When file control blocks are used to access random files, DOS is told the size of each record in the file (all must be the same for any one file). This allows a program to ask for any record by number, and DOS then calculates exactly where that record is located on disk. When the file handle method of access is used for random files, the program must itself calculate the position of particular records.

DOS keeps a *file pointer* for every file buffer. It points to the nth byte of the file, defining the place in the file at which the next read or write operation begins. In a sequential over-write operation, the file pointer is initially set to the beginning of the file, and the pointer constantly increments as more and more data are written out to the file. When data is appended to a sequential file, the file pointer is initially set to the end of the file. When a single record is accessed in a random file, the location of the record is calculated as an offset from the start of the file, and the pointer is set to that value; then a record's worth of data is read or written to the file. DOS ordinarily looks after the file pointer, but programs can take control and manipulate the pointer for special ends.

The only low-level example in this section is of single-sector read/write operations. Reading or writing whole files is nothing more than a sequence of these single-sector reads or writes, programming the floppy disk controller chip anew for each sector. Full-scale file operations are enormously complex at this level, as the hefty size of COMMAND.COM suggests. Still, by studying the discussion of low-level operations along with those about the file allocation table [5.1.1] and disk directories [5.2.1], you will come to appreciate how disk operating systems work.

5.4.1 Program the 765 Floppy Disk Controller and 8237 DMA Chip

The NEC 765 floppy disk controller chip controls floppy disk drive motors and heads, and it manages the flow of data to and from disk sectors. A single controller, mounted on the disk drive adaptor, runs up to four drives. Except in the arcane field of copy protection, programmers almost never need to program the FDC chip directly. The disk management routines of BIOS and PC-DOS are both efficient and reliable, and it can be quite risky to write one's own routines, since bugs could damage a disk's directory or file allocation table, rendering the disk useless.

The discussion that follows is intended only to get you started. The BIOS listing at the end of any IBM Technical Reference Manual contains the code for an elaborate routine that formats diskettes, reads and writes sectors, and resets and reports the status of the diskette system. Once you absorb the material here, study the BIOS routine to continue your education in low-level disk operations. You will also need the Intel documentation for the 8272A FDC chip, which is the same as the NEC chip. This documentation lists the interrupts generated by the FDC, which the IBM documentation does not. The 8272A information is found in the "Microsystem Components Handbook, Volume II".

The FDC performs fifteen operations in all, of which only three are discussed here: seek operations and single-sector reads and writes. Understanding how these operations work will enable you to perform any of the twelve others, providing you have the information mentioned above. Reading a file basically entails looking it up in a directory [5.2.1], tracking its disk locations through the file allocation table [5.1.1], and performing a series of single-sector read operations. The example listed below reads a single disk sector. There are six steps in this procedure:

1. Turn on the motor and wait briefly for it to come to speed.
2. Perform the seek operation, and wait for an interrupt that announces its completion.
3. Initialize the DMA chip to move the data to memory.
4. Send the read instructions to the FDC and then wait for an interrupt indicating that the data transfer is complete.
5. Take status information about the FDC.
6. Turn off the motor.

The FDC is operated through only three I/O ports. There are in fact more than three registers on the chip, but most are loaded through a single port address. The three ports are:

```
3F2H                    digital output register
3F4H                    status register
3F5H                    data register
```

The first step is to access the digital output register. It has the following bit pattern:

bits 1-0	selects a drive, where	00 = A	
		01 = B	
		10 = C	
		11 = D	
2	0=reset the floppy disk controller		
3	1=enable FDC interrupt and DMA access		
7-4	1=turn on drive motors D – A (bit 4 = A)		

This register is write-only, and so all bits must be set at once. The example below uses drive A, and the bit pattern required is 00011100. This pattern selects drive A, keeps bit 2 set to 1, enables the FDC system, and turns on drive A. *Do not* set bit 2 to 0 at any time, or you will have to recalibrate the drive, an action that is seldom necessary.

To "recalibrate" a drive means to retract its head to track 0. The operation is made by sending a simple command sequence to the FDC chip. The FDC monitors the current head position by keeping track of all changes it makes in the head position from its initial setting at track 0. When the FDC is reset by briefly changing bit 2 of the digital output register to 0, the reading for the current head position is set to 0 no matter at which track the head actually resides, making the recalibration necessary. Ordinarily, an FDC reset is required only after a disk error has occurred which is so serious that the current state of the disk controller and drive is unknown.

Note that selecting a drive and turning on its motor are separate actions. The FDC can access only one drive at a time, but more than one motor can turn simultaneously. Motors may be left running for a few seconds after data transfer is complete in anticipation of further disk accesses. This strategy avoids the loss of time that would result from repeatedly waiting for the motor to come up to speed. Conversely, the motor should not be left on all the time because diskettes would wear out prematurely.

The FDC chip operates in three phases: the command phase, the execution phase, and the result phase. In the command phase, one or more bytes is sent to the *data register*. The sequence of bytes is strictly fixed, and it varies by the command. The FDC then undertakes the command, and during that time the FDC is in the execution phase. Finally, during the result phase, a number of status bytes are read from the data register. It is imperative that there be no error in the number of bytes sent to, and read from, the data register during the command and result phases.

The number of command and result bytes varies among the disk operations that the FDC performs. Any IBM Technical Reference Manual supplies the data for all fifteen operations. The first byte of a command is a code that names the desired operation. The code number is held in the low five bits of the byte, and in some cases additional information is encoded in the high three bits. In most cases, the second command byte gives the drive number (0-3) in its two lowest bits and the head number (0 or 1) in bit 2; all other bits are ignored by the FDC. In a seek operation only one more byte is required, and this is the number of the new track. Reading or writing a sector requires seven more command bytes, and they are identical in either case. The third through fifth bytes give the current track number, the head number, and the sector number. And then there follows four bytes of technical data required by the FDC.

The first of these technical data is the number of bytes in a sector, which is coded as 0 for 128, 1 for 256, 2 for 512, and 3 for 1024. Diskettes created by PC-DOS have 512-byte sectors, of course. Next is the *end-of-track* (EOT) data, which gives the final sector number of a cylinder; this value is 9 for 360K floppies. Finally, there is a byte that gives the *gap length* (GPL, set to 2AH), and the *data length* (DTL, set to FFH). The Technical Reference Manuals contain a table that explains other input parameters, such as those used for disk formatting. DOS keeps the four technical parameters in memory in a parameter table called the *disk base*. The disk base is pointed to by interrupt vector 1EH. The four values are arranged in the order that the FDC requires them, starting from offset 3. The following table shows the command sequence for the three operations shown in the example below. In the bit patterns, X's indicate that the setting of a bit is irrelevant, H stands for the head number, and DD stands for the drive number.

Operation	Byte#	Function	Setting for Head 0, Track 15, Sector 1
Seek:	1	code number: 00001111	1FH
	2	head and drive: XXXXXHDD	00H
Read a Sector:	1	code number: 01100110	66H
	2	head and drive :XXXXXHDD	00H
	3	track number	0FH
	4	head number	00H
	5	sector number	01H
	6	bytes in a sector	02H
	7	end-of-track	09H
	8	gap length	1AH
	9	data length	FFH
Write a Sector:	1	code number: 01000101	45H
	2-9	same as for reading a sector	

You must be sure that the FDC is ready before you send or read a byte from the data register. Bits 7 and 6 of the *status register* provide this information. Here is the bit pattern of the entire register:

```
bits 3-0      1 = disk drive D-A in seek mode
     4        1 = FDC read or write command in progress
     5        1 = FDC in non-DMA mode
     6        1 = FDC data register ready to send data
              0 = ready to receive data
     7        1 = FDC ready to send or receive data
```

Before starting disk operations it is a good idea to check that bit 6 is set to 0, indicating that the FDC is waiting for a command. If it is waiting to send data then an error has occurred. When a byte of data is sent to the data register, bit 7 of the status register goes to 0; keep reading the register until the bit changes back to 1, and then send the next command byte. Similarly, consult this status bit before reading a status byte from the data register during the result phase. The example below ends with two procedures that perform these functions.

When the seek operation is complete, the FDC invokes INT 6, the diskette interrupt. While one could as easily sense the end of the seek operation by polling the status register, the interrupt is monitored in the example given here. When the interrupt occurs, the BIOS interrupt handler sets bit 7 of the *seek status* byte in the BIOS data area, located at 0040:003E. This is the sole result of the interrupt. Keep polling this byte until bit 7 is set, then reset the bit to 0 and continue on to the next step of the sector-read operation.

The next step is the initialization of the 8237 direct memory access chip. This chip transfers data between peripheral devices and memory, a job that could instead be handled by the CPU. In fact, in the PCjr, where there is no DMA chip, the FDC sends data directly to the CPU, which in turn moves it to memory. The clock speed of the CPU is barely adequate to this task, however, and all interrupts are shut out while the data transfer is made so that no data will be lost. This means that in the PCjr input from the keyboard or a modem is shut out. The timer interrupt is also ignored, but the time-of-day count is updated afterwards by a special routine that uses channel 1 of the 8253 timer chip to count the pulses made during disk operations. All other IBM machines have DMA chips, and the CPU is free during data transfers.

The PC and XT use the four-channel 8237 DMA chip. Channel 0 is dedicated to *memory refresh*; it constantly restores the charge in the RAM memory cells. If you operate on this channel, the machine is likely to crash. Channel 2 is dedicated to disk operations, and the other two channels, numbers 1 and 3, are available (via the system board slots) to add-on hardware. Unfortunately, memory-to-memory transfers require two channels, and channel 0 must be one of them, so these transfers are not possible on the PC and XT. The AT, however, has seven channels of direct memory access, and DMA is automatically used by the MOVS instructions, greatly improving performance.

Before initializing a channel, a program must send a code to the chip telling it whether it is reading from or writing to the floppy disk controller. This one-byte code is 46H for reading, and 4AH for writing. The code must be sent to each of two separate port addresses, numbers 0BH, and 0CH.

Each channel of the 8237 chip uses three registers. One 16-bit register, the *count register*, is given the number of bytes of data to transfer. This value should be set to 1 less than the number of bytes desired. For channel 2, this register is accessed through I/O port 05H; send the two bytes of the count in succession, with the least significant byte first.

The other two registers hold the address of the buffer in memory to or from which data is transferred. This address is set up as a 20-bit value, so that, for example, 3000:ABCD is expressed as 3ABCD. The low 16 bits are sent to the *address register*, which for channel 2 is at port address 04H. Send the least significant byte first. The high four bits go to a *page register*, which is at 81H for channel 2. When a byte is sent to this register, only the low four bits are significant. If the buffer is set up in the data segment, you will need to add the values of DS and the buffer offset to derive the 20-bit value. The addition may result in a carry to the page register value. For example, if DS is 1F00H and the buffer offset is 2000H, then the resulting address will be 1F000 + 2000 = 21000H.

Once the three registers are set up, send 2 to port address 0AH to enable channel 2. This leaves the DMA chip waiting for disk data, and the program should immediately start sending the command codes to the FDC. Here is a summary of the steps in programming the 8237 chip:

1. Send a read or write code.
2. Calculate the 20-bit memory address of the buffer to which the data is to be sent, and place it in the channel 2 address and page registers.
3. Place the value of the number of bytes to transfer (minus 1) in the channel 2 count register.
4. Enable the channel.

After sending the command bytes, again wait for an interrupt, and monitor it in the same way as for a seek operation. Then read the status bytes. These are as follows:

Operation	Byte #	Function
Seek:	none	-
Read:	1	status byte 0
	2	status byte 1
	3	status byte 2
	4	track number
	5	head number
	6	sector number
	7	bytes/sector code (0-3)
Write:	1-7	same as read

Here are the bit patterns of the three status bytes:

```
Status byte 1:  bits  7-6      00=normal termination
                               01=execution begun, could not complete
                               10=invalid command
                               11=failed because disk drive went off line
                      5        1=seek operation in progress
                      4        1=disk drive fault
                      3        1=disk drive not ready
                      2        number of selected head
                      1-0      number of selected drive

Status byte 2:  bit   7        1=requested sector beyond last sector number
                      6        unused (always 0)
                      5        1=data transfer error
                      4        1=data overrun
                      3        unused (always 0)
```

```
              2        1=cannot find or read sector
              1        1=cannot write because of write-protection
              0        1=missing address mark in disk formatting

Status byte 3:   bit  7        unused (always 0)
              6        1=encountered deleted-data address mark
              5        1=cyclic redundancy check error in data
              4        1=track indentification problem
              3        1=scan command condition satisfied
              2        1=scan command condition not satisfied
              1        1=bad track
              0        1=missing address mark
```

As you can see, much of the status information is devoted to disk formatting, which does not concern us here. There is a fourth status byte, however, that produces useful information:

```
Status byte 4:   bit  7        1=disk drive fault
              6        1=disk is write-protected
              5        1=disk drive is ready
              4        1=current head position is known
              3        1=disk is double-sided
              2        number of selected head
              1-0      number of selected drive
```

You can retrieve this fourth status byte by sending the "Sense Drive Status" command to the FDC. The first byte of this two-byte command is the number 4, and the second is a byte in which bits 1 & 0 hold the drive number and bit 2 holds the head number. Status byte 3 is the only result value. Note that after every disk operation where you use the BIOS or DOS services, the resulting status bytes are placed in the BIOS data area, starting at 0040:0042. The operating system also keeps a diskette status byte at 0040:0041, where the bit pattern is as follows:

bit pattern	error
80H	attachment failed to respond
40H	seek operation failed
20H	FDC failed
10H	data error (bad CRC) on data read
09H	attempt to DMA across 64K boundary
08H	DMA overrun
04H	requested sector not found
03H	tried to write on write-protected disk
02H	address mark not found
01H	bad command sent to FDC

In conclusion, here is a complete disk-read routine, which transfers one sector of data from track 12, sector 1, head 0 of drive A to a 512-byte buffer in the data segment. The seven status bytes are also delivered to a holding buffer. This routine is designed for a PC or XT. You will need the PCjr or AT technical reference manuals to work on those machines. On the AT, change the delay loops to account for the greater processor speed, and remember to add a **JMP SHORT $ + 2** statement between successive OUT commands that are directed to the same port address. Fixed disks operate in a similar manner, and you should be able to transfer the concepts you have learned here to other situations.

```
;---IN THE DATA SEGMENT:
  BUFFER          DB 512 DUP(?)
  STATUS_BUFFER   DB 7 DUP(?)


SECTOR_READ      PROC                        ;begin the single-sector read procedure
;---TURN ON MOTOR:
                 STI                         ;be sure interrupts are enabled
                 MOV  DX,3F2H                 ;address of digital output register
                 MOV  AL,28                   ;set bits 2, 3, and 4
                 OUT  DX,AL                   ;send the command
;---WAIT FOR MOTOR TO COME TO SPEED (1/2 second delay):
                 CALL MOTOR_DELAY             ;count 9 turns of BIOS clock
;---PERFORM SEEK OPERATION:
                 MOV  AH,15                   ;code number
                 CALL OUT_FDC                 ;send to FDC
                 MOV  AH,0                    ;drive number
                 CALL OUT_FDC                 ;send to FDC
                 MOV  AH,12                   ;track number
                 CALL OUT_FDC                 ;send to FDC
                 CALL WAIT_INTERRUPT          ;wait for INT 6
;---WAIT FOR HEAD TO SETTLE (25 MSEC):
                 MOV  CX,1750                 ;count for empty loop (PC or XT)
    WAIT_SETTLE: LOOP WAIT_SETTLE             ;idle for 25 milliseconds
;---BEGIN INITIALIZATION OF DMA CHIP:
                 MOV  AL,46H                  ;code to read data from FDC
                 OUT  12,AL                   ;send the code to 2 addresses
                 OUT  11,AL                   ;
;---CALCULATE ADDRESS OF TRANSFER BUFFER:
                 MOV  AX,OFFSET BUFFER        ;get buffer offset in DS
                 MOV  BX,DS                   ;put DS in BX
                 MOV  CL,4                    ;ready to rotate high nibble of DS
                 ROL  BX,CL                   ;rotate to bottom four bits of BX
                 MOV  DL,BL                   ;copy BL to DL
                 AND  DL,0FH                  ;blank top nibble of DL
                 AND  BL,0F0H                 ;blank bottom nibble of BX
                 ADD  AX,BX                   ;add BX into AX (DS into offset)
                 JNC  NO_CARRY                ;if no carry, DL is page value
                 INC  DL                      ;but if carry, first increment DL
    NO_CARRY:    OUT  4,AL                    ;send low byte of address
                 MOV  AL,AH                   ;shift high byte
                 OUT  4,AL                    ;send high byte of address
                 MOV  AL,DL                   ;fetch page value
                 OUT  81h,AL                  ;send page number
;---FINISH INITIALIZATION:
                 MOV  AX,511                  ;count value
                 OUT  5,AL                    ;send low byte
                 MOV  AL,AH                   ;ready high byte
                 OUT  5,AL                    ;send high byte
                 MOV  AL,2                    ;get set to enable channel 2
                 OUT  10,AL                   ;all done, DMA waits for data...
;---GET POINTER TO DISK BASE:
                 MOV  AL,1EH                  ;number of vector that points to table
                 MOV  AH,35H                  ;function that fetches vector
                 INT  21H                     ;now ES:BX points to disk base
```

```
;---SEND READ PARAMETERS:
                MOV   AH,66H              ;code for single-sector read
                CALL  OUT_FDC            ;send it
                MOV   AH,0̅               ;head and drive number
                CALL  OUT_FDC            ;send it
                MOV   AH,1̅2              ;track number
                CALL  OUT_FDC            ;send it
                MOV   AH,0̅               ;head number
                CALL  OUT_FDC            ;send it
                MOV   AH,1̅               ;record number
                CALL  OUT_FDC            ;send it
                MOV   AH,E̅S̅:[BX]+3        ;sector size code (from disk base)
                CALL  OUT_FDC            ;send it
                MOV   AH,E̅S̅:[BX]+4        ;end-of-track number (from disk base)
                CALL  OUT_FDC            ;send it
                MOV   AH,E̅S̅:[BX]+5        ;gap length (from disk base)
                CALL  OUT_FDC            ;send it
                MOV   AH,E̅S̅:[BX]+6        ;data length (from disk base)
                CALL  OUT_FDC            ;send it
                CALL  WAIT̅_INTERRUPT     ;wait till INT 6 marks end of transfer
;---READ THE RESULT BYTES:
                MOV   CX,7               ;7 result bytes from reading a sector
                LEA   BX,STATUS_BUFFER   ;place them in a buffer
      NEXT:     CALL  IN_FDC            ;get a byte
                MOV   [B̅X̅],AL            ;place in buffer
                INC   BX                ;point to next byte of buffer
                LOOP  NEXT              ;go get next byte
;---TURN OFF MOTOR
                MOV   DX,3F2H            ;address of digital output register
                MOV   AL,12             ;leave bits 3 and 4 on
                OUT   DX,AL             ;send the new setting
                RET                     ;end of sector-read procedure
SECTOR_READ     ENDP


WAIT_INTERRUPT  PROC                    ;waits for INT 6, resets status byte
;---M̅ONITOR INT 6 STATUS IN BIOS STATUS BYTE:
                MOV   AX,40H             ;segment of BIOS data area
                MOV   ES,AX             ;place in ES
                MOV   BX,3EH             ;offset of status byte
     AGAIN:     MOV   DL,ES:[BX]        ;get the byte
                TEST  DL,80H            ;test bit 7
                JZ    AGAIN             ;keep looping if not yet set
                AND   DL,01111111B      ;reset bit 7
                MOV   ES:[BX],DL        ;replace status byte
                RET                     ;continue...
WAIT_INTERRUPT  ENDP


OUT_FDC         PROC                    ;sends byte in AH to FDC
                MOV   DX,3F4H            ;status register port address
   KEEP_TRYING: IN    AL,DX             ;fetch value
                TEST  AL,128            ;is bit 7 on?
                JZ    KEEP_TRYING        ;if not, keep looping
                INC   DX                ;ready, so point to data register
                MOV   AL,AH             ;value was passed in AH
                OUT   DX,AL             ;send the value
                RET                     ;all done
OUT_FDC         ENDP

IN_FDC          PROC                    ;returns byte (in AL) from FDC
                MOV   DX,3F4H            ;status register port address
```

```
        ONCE_AGAIN:   IN    AL,DX            ;fetch value
                      TEST  AL,128           ;is bit 7 on?
                      JZ    KEEP_TRYING      ;if not, keep looping
                      INC   DX               ;ready, so point to data register
                      IN    AL,DX            ;read a byte from the data register
                      RET                    ;all done
IN_FDC                ENDP
```

5.4.2 Read/write at particular sectors

Reading and writing particular disk sectors is a technique used mostly to access a disk's directory or file allocation table, where the sectors are always positioned at the same location. While reading the sectors is harmless enough, *writing* absolute sectors requires that the code be completely accurate the first time it is used. A mistake could make the directory or FAT unreadable, effectively destroying all data on the disk.

Both BIOS and DOS offer functions for reading and writing to particular sectors. They specify the sectors differently. On the PC, XT, and PCjr, the BIOS routine requires information about the side number (0 or 1), track number (0-39), and sector number (1-8). Because of the eight-sector limitation, this method is essentially obsolete on these machines. On the AT, however, the sector number may be 8, 9, or 15, and the track numbers may range to either 39 or 79. The DOS functions specify the sector by a single number, referred to as the *logical sector number*. Starting from the outside rim of the disk and moving inward, the sectors are assigned consecutive higher numbers. This method may be used with a disk of any size and kind.

The logical sector count begins from side 0, track 0, sector 1, and it continues to side 1, track 0, then goes on to side 0, track 1, etc. (On large fixed disks, the entire outside *cylinder* is counted first.) Depending on how the disk is formatted, the logical sector number increases by a certain amount with every track. For a 360K floppy, each track (taking both sides) adds 18 to the number. But the calculation is slightly complicated by the fact that the numbering begins from 0. Thus the first sector of track 3 on side 1 might at first seem to be 3*18 for tracks 0 - 2, plus 9 for side 0 of track 3, plus 1 to point to the first sector of track three on side 1. This equals 64. The logical sector number is 1 less than this number. Figure 5-4 compares the BIOS and DOS methods of naming disk sectors.

High Level

BASIC does not provide direct access to disk sectors. Use the following machine language subroutine. Appendix D explains the logic behind how such routines are set up. The example reads the nine sectors of track 3 on side 1 of a 360K floppy. The routine itself is positioned in memory at segment address &H1000, and the contents of the sectors is deposited starting from segment address &H2000 (recall that an absolute address equals a segment address multiplied by 16). To instead *write* from this address to the sectors, change the seventh from last byte of program data, &H25, to &H26. Everything else remains the same.

```
100 DEFINT A-Z                              'all variables are integers
110 DATA &H55,&H8B,&HEC,&H1E,&H8B,&H76,&H0C,&H8B   'the assembly routine
120 DATA &H04,&H8B,&H76,&H0A,&H8B,&H14,&H8B,&H76
130 DATA &H08,&H8B,&H8B,&H0C,&H8B,&H76,&H06,&H8A,&H1C
140 DATA &H8E,&HD8,&H8B,&HC3,&HBB,&H00,&H00,&HCD
150 DATA &H25,&H59,&H1F,&H5D,&HCA,&H08,&H00
160 DEF SEG=&H1000                          'place the routine at &H10000
170 FOR N=0 TO 38                           'for each byte of the routine...
180 READ Q:POKE N,Q                         'read each byte and poke into memory
```

```
190 NEXT                                    'next byte
200 READSECTOR=0                            'execute the code from first byte
210 BUFFER=&H2000                           'place sector data at &H20000
220 LOGICALNUMBER=62                        'logical sector 62
230 NUMBERSECTORS=9                         'read 9 sectors worth
240 DRIVE=0                                 'drive 0=A, 1=B, etc.
250 CALL READSECTOR(BUFFER,LOGICALNUMBER,NUMBERSECTORS,DRIVE)
260 '''and now the sectors are in memory, starting from 2000:0000
```

Middle Level

BIOS uses function 2 of INT 13H to read sectors, and function 3 of INT 13H to write sectors. In both cases, DL holds a drive number from 0 - 3, where 0 = A, etc. DH has the head (side) number, 0 - 1. CH holds the track number, from 0 - 39, and CL keeps the sector number, from 0 - 8. AL is given the number of sectors to be read. Only eight are allowed, which is more than enough for most purposes. ES:BX points to the starting point in memory at which the transfer is to be deposited, or from which it is taken. On return, AL holds the number of sectors read or written. The carry flag is set to 0 if the operation was successful. If it is 1, then AH holds the disk operation status bytes that are described at [5.4.8].

```
;---IN THE DATA SEGMENT:
    BUFFER          DB      4000 DUP(?)          ;create a buffer (or allocate memory)

;---READ SECTORS:
                    MOV     AX,SEG BUFFER        ;point ES:BX to the buffer
                    MOV     ES,AX                ;
                    MOV     BX,OFFSET BUFFER     ;
                    MOV     DL,0                 ;drive number
                    MOV     DH,0                 ;head number
                    MOV     CH,0                 ;track number
                    MOV     CL,1                 ;sector number
                    MOV     AL,1                 ;number of sectors to read
                    MOV     AH,2                 ;function number for "read"
                    INT     13H
```

DOS interrupts 25h and 26h respectively read and write absolute sectors. Place the beginning logical sector number in DX, and point DS:BX to the transfer buffer. CX is given the number of sectors to read or write, and AL takes the drive number, where 0 = A, 1 = B, etc. All registers are destroyed except the segment registers. On return the flag register remains on the stack, leaving the stack off balance. Be sure to POP this value off the stack immediately upon return (in the example, it is arbitrarily POPed into CX).

```
;---IN THE DATA SEGMENT:
    BUFFER          DB      5000 dup(?)          ;set up a buffer (or allocate memory)

;---READ SECTORS:
                    PUSH    DS                   ;save all required registers
                    MOV     AX,SEG BUFFER        ;point DS:BX to the buffer
                    MOV     DS,AX                ;
                    MOV     BX,OFFSET BUFFER     ;
                    MOV     DX,63                ;logical sector number
                    MOV     CX,9                 ;read whole track
                    MOV     AL,0                 ;drive A
```

```
        INT   25H                    ;DOS function to read sectors
        POP   CX                     ;pop flags from stack to any register
        POP   DS                     ;restore registers
        JNC   NO_ERROR               ;jump below if carry flag 0
        CMP   AH,3                   ;test for write-protected disk
          .                          ;etc.....
          .
          .
NO_ERROR:                            ;continue...
```

On return the carry flag will be set to 1 if there has been an error, in which case AH and AL contain separate error status bytes that are largely redundant. If AH is 4, then the requested sector was not found, and if it is 2, the disk formatting is faulty. If AH is 3, an attempt was made to write on a write-protected disk. All other values in AH indicate a hardware failure.

Low Level

Disk operations at low level require you to directly program the disk controller chip and the direct memory access chip. Because these operations are particularly involved, they are discussed separately at [5.4.1].

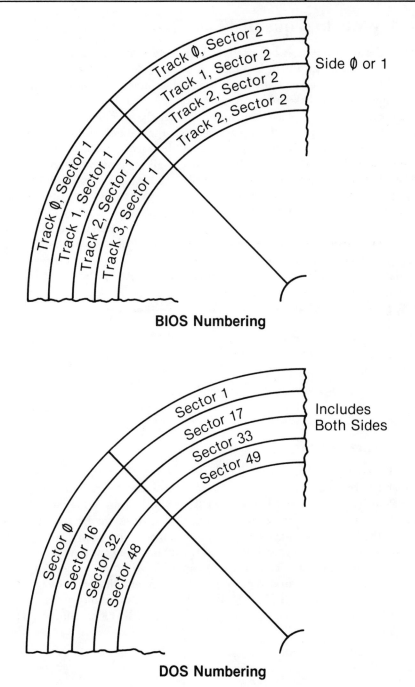

BIOS Numbering

DOS Numbering

Figure 5-4. BIOS & DOS organization of disk sectors.

5.4.3 Write to sequential files

From the programmer's perspective, high-level languages appear to operate on sequential files one data item at a time. A single statement "writes" the contents of a variable into the sequential file, delimiting variables by interspersing a carriage return/line feed pair. Assembly programs, on the other hand, deal with the data in one-record units. They place the data in a buffer that is one or more records large, adding carriage return/line feed pairs between the data elements, but not between the records. Particular data items may span two records. Then a DOS function is used to write one or more records to disk. At all programming levels, DOS may not actually physically write data on the disk each time a data output command is used. Rather, in the interest of economy, DOS waits for its output buffer to fill before sending it to disk.

Note that BASIC automatically appends an ASCII 26 character (Ctrl-Z) to the end of the sequential files it writes. This is required of standard ASCII text files. The DOS functions do not add this character; your program must write it in as a final data item. Random files are not terminated with ASCII 26.

High Level

BASIC prepares to write to a sequential file by opening the file in sequential mode, using the OPEN statement. The statement has two forms, and which to choose is a matter of preference. The formats are:

```
100 OPEN "MYFILE" FOR OUTPUT AS #1
```

...or...

```
100 OPEN "O",#1,"MYFILE"
```

The "O" in the second statement stands for "output". The symbol #1 designates the number 1 as the code number by which to refer to the file in statements that access the file, such as in **WRITE #1** or **INPUT #1**. In both cases, a file named MYFILE is opened and made ready to receive sequential data. If no file by that name is found on disk, the OPEN statement creates one. And if the file already exists, its contents are overwritten, so that when it is closed it contains only the new data written into it. To *append* data to the end of a sequential file without changing its prior contents, open it using the first type of OPEN statement shown above, in the form **OPEN "MYFILE" FOR APPEND AS 1**. See [5.3.3] for more information.

Data is written to the file using the PRINT# or WRITE# statements. They share the form:

```
100 PRINT#1,S$
```

...or...

```
100 WRITE#1,X
```

#1 refers to the file ID number (the "file descriptor") assigned by the OPEN statement. The first example writes a string variable to the file, and the second writes a numeric value, but each can write either. Numeric values are written into sequential files in string form, even though they are taken from non-string variables. For example, 232 is a two-byte integer in numeric form, but if X = 232, then PRINT#1,X places three bytes in the file, using the ASCII codes for the symbols 2, 3, and 2.

The PRINT# and WRITE# statements differ in how they separate one data item from the next in a file. Which is best depends on the characteristics of the data. The chief difference between the two statements is that WRITE# places extra delimiters around the data items. Consider the case where a statement outputs several variables, in the form **100 PRINT#1,A$,Z,B$** or **100 WRITE#1,A$,Z,B$**. In this case, the carriage return/line feed pair is placed in the file only after the last of the three variables (note that string and numeric variables may be mixed). How can the three variables then be distinguished? If PRINT# is used, they cannot. The three items are joined into a continuous string. But when WRITE# is used, each data item is enclosed in quotes, and commas are placed between the items. Later, when the items are read back from the file, BASIC automatically strips away the quotes and commas that were added by the WRITE# statement.

There are a number of minor points to consider. One is that the whole problem of delimitation can be solved by simply writing only one variable in each PRINT# or WRITE# statement. In this case, PRINT# separates all items with the carriage return/line feed pair, and WRITE# does the same, but also surrounds the item with quotes (which wastes file space). Further, WRITE# should not be used with strings that contain quotes themselves, since the first internal quote will erroneously signal the end of the variable when the string is read back. Finally, note that when several variables are printed with the same statement, both PRINT# and WRITE# format the data exactly as if it were to be printed on the screen. Thus, **PRINT#1,A$,B$** spaces B$ apart from A$, while **PRINT#1,A$;B$ does not;** the file will be padded with spaces accordingly.The PRINT# statement can be used in the form **PRINT#1 USING…**, where all of the usual screen PRINT USING formats are available to format output to the file.

In general it is most economical to use the PRINT# statement, writing only one data item at a time. This method gives over the least amount of file space to delimiters, and it allows a string of any composition to be read back without error. The more complicated delimitation schemes required by writing multiple variables with a single PRINT# or WRITE# statement can lead to trouble, especially when one variable is read as two, so that the correct position in the data sequence is lost.

After all data has been written, simply close the file to secure the data. Write **CLOSE** to close all files that are open, or **CLOSE#1** to close file #1, **CLOSE#1,#3** to close files #1 and #3, etc. Although BASIC is sometimes forgiving of unclosed files, this is not the case here. PRINT# and WRITE# statements output data to the file buffer; the information is written on disk only when the buffer is filled. The last data entered is flushed out to disk by the CLOSE statement. Omitting the statement can result in lost data. Here is an example:

```
100 OPEN"A:NEWSEQ" FOR OUTPUT AS 1     'open for sequential output
110 A$="aaaaa"                         'three strings to write
120 B$="bbbbb"                         '
```

```
130 C$="ccccc"                          '
140 WRITE#1,A$,B$,C$                     'write the strings
150 CLOSE                                'flush buffer
```

Middle Level

DOS can write sequential files both by the file control block method and the file handle method. The FCB method provides a function that is specifically tailored for writing sequential files. The file handle method, on the other hand, has only a general-purpose function to write to files, but it is just as easy to use for this purpose. In either case, the way in which a file is opened is important in sequential operations. If data is to be *appended* to a sequential file, an ordinary "open" function is used. However, when the file is to be overwritten, the function that "creates" a file is required. Such a function truncates the file to 0 length so that its subsequent length will be no greater than the amount of data written into it.

FCB Method:

Function 15H of INT 21H writes sequential files. Prepare the file control block and disk transfer area as shown at [5.3.5]. If the entire file will be overwritten, open it with function 16H, which "creates" the file, truncating its length to 0. If you merely "open" the file using function 0FH, then remnants of the old file will remain at the end of file should the new file length be less than the old one. On the other hand, if you wish to *append* data to the file, use the "open" function.

Once the file is opened, point DS:DX to the start of the FCB and call function 15H to write one record's worth of data. The amount of data in a record depends on the value placed in the *record size* field at offset 14 in a normal FCB; this value defaults to 128 bytes. If the record size is less than the 512-byte disk sector size, the data may be buffered until enough has accumulated to warrant an actual disk-write operation; thus a sequential record may have been successfully written even if the disk drives do not turn. When the file is closed, any data remaining in the buffer is flushed on to the disk. Upon return from function 15H, AL holds 0 if the operation was successful, 1 if the disk has become full, and 2 if the data transfer segment is too small.

In the following example, five 256-byte records are written to disk. The records might be a mass of text data. This data is laid out in a memory area labeled **WORKAREA.** The DTA pointer is initially set to the beginning of this area, and after each record is written the DTA setting is changed so that it points 256 bytes higher. Note that ordinarily memory is specially allocated for such a work area [1.3.1], but for simplicity this example uses a buffer set up in the data segment.

```
;---IN THE DATA SEGMENT:
    WORKAREA    DB    2000 DUP(?)        ;data buffer
    FCB         DB    1,'FILENAMEEXT',25 DUP(0)

;---POINT DTA TO THE WORKAREA:
                LEA   DX,WORKAREA        ;DS:DX points to DTA
                MOV   DI,DX              ;keep copy
                MOV   AH,1AH             ;function to set DTA
                INT   21H               ;set the DTA
```

```
;---OPEN THE FILE:
               MOV    AH,16H              ;function to open file for overwrite
               LEA    DX,FCB              ;DS:DX points to the FCB
               INT    21H                 ;open the file
;---SET RECORD SIZE:
               LEA    BX,FCB              ;point BX to FCB
               MOV    AX,256              ;256 byte record size
               MOV    [BX]+14,AX          ;set record size
;---SEND THE DATA:
               MOV    CX,5                ;number of record to write
  NEXT_RECORD: MOV    AH,15H              ;function for sequential write
               LEA    DX,FCB              ;point to FCB
               INT    21H                 ;write the data
               CMP    AL,2                ;write error?
               JE     CONTINUE            ;if so, go to recovery routine
               CMP    AL,1                ;disk full
               JE     DISK_FULL           ;go to full disk routine
;---TRANSFER OK, RESET DTA:
               ADD    DI,256              ;add 1 record to DTA position
               MOV    DX,DI               ;point DS:DX to new DTA
               MOV    AH,1AH              ;function to set DTA
               INT    21H                 ;set DTA to new position in data area
               LOOP   NEXT_RECORD         ;go write the next record


;---LATER, CLOSE THE FILE:
               LEA    DX,FCB              ;point DS:DX to FCB
               MOV    AH,10H              ;function to close file
               INT    21H                 ;close it
```

The file control block method is unwieldly for appending data to the end of
sequential files. Unlike the file handle method, in which you can point to the end of
the file, here you must manipulate the current record and current block fields. Read
the last data-bearing record into the DTA and fill its empty space with the first of
the data you want appended. Then rewrite that record to its former position in the
file, following it with as many additional new records as are required. Open the file
using function 0FH.

File Handle Method:

Be careful about how you open a file for sequential output by the file handle
method. Because the same function is used to write to random files, when the file is
closed its length is not set to the ending position of the file pointer. For example,
say that a 2000-byte text file is taken from disk and pared down to 1000 bytes in
memory. If a simple "open" command (function 3DH) has opened the file, then
after the new, shorter version of the text is written to disk and the file is closed, the
length of the file remains 2000 bytes, with the new text having overlaid the first
1000 bytes. For this reason, to open a file for sequential over-write, use function
3CH of INT 21H [5.3.2]. This function normally *creates* a new file, but if the file
already exists, it truncates it to 0 length. To *append* data to a sequential file, however, use the ordinary "open" function, 3DH of INT 21H [5.3.3].

Consider first the case of completely overwriting the file. After the file is opened
by function 3CH, the file pointer is set to 0, so there is no need to set its position.
Place the file handle in BX and the number of bytes to be written in CX. Then point
DS:DX to the first byte of the output data and execute function 40H of INT 21H.

On return, if the carry flag has been set, there has been an error, and AX holds 5 if there was a disk drive problem, or 6 if the file handle was bad. Otherwise AX holds the number of bytes actually written; if there is a disparity, it is most probably attributable to a full disk. Do not fail to provide error recovery for this situation, since, if the program crashes, the original contents of the disk file are lost (owing to the truncation to 0 length). To check disk space, see [5.1.2]. Here is an example:

```
;---IN THE DATA SEGMENT:
        PATH        DB      'B:FILENAME.EXT',0  ;directory path
    DATA_BUFFER     DB      2000 DUP(?)         ;or allocate memory for buffer [1.3.1]
;---OPEN THE FILE USING THE "CREATE" FUNCTION:
                    LEA     DX,PATH             ;point DS:DX to directory path
                    MOV     CX,0                ;file attribute (here, normal)
                    MOV     AH,3CH              ;function number
                    INT     21H                 ;truncate file to 0 length
                    JC      OPEN_ERROR          ;catch errors
                    MOV     HANDLE,AX           ;keep copy of handle
;---WRITE 1000 BYTES OUT TO THE FILE:
                    MOV     AH,40H              ;function number
                    MOV     BX,HANDLE           ;handle in BX
                    MOV     CX,1000             ;number of bytes to write
                    LEA     DX,DATA_BUFFER      ;DS:DX points to data buffer
                    INT     21H                 ;write the data
                    JC      OUTPUT_ERROR        ;go to error routine if carry
                    CMP     CX,2000             ;1000 bytes successfully written?
                    JNE     FULL_DISK           ;go to error routine if problem
```

To *append* data to a sequential file, open it with function 3DH of int 21H, placing 1 in AL if the program will only write data, or 2 in AL if both reading and writing are to take place. The file length is left unchanged, although it will increase as data is appended. The file pointer must be set to the end of the file or else existing data will be overwritten. This is accomplished by function 42H of INT 21H. Place the subfunction number 2 in AL to set the pointer to the end of the file, and put the file handle in BX. CX:DX points to the offset from the end of the file at which writing is to start, so place 0 in each. Then execute the function to set the pointer. On return, a set carry flag indicates an error, and AX holds 1 if the function number in AL was invalid, and 6 if the file handle was invalid. Once the pointer is set, the write operation proceeds exactly as above:

```
;---IN THE DATA SEGMENT:
    PATH        DB      'B:FILENAME.EXT,0  ;directory path
    DATA_BUFFER DB      1000 DUP(?)        ;or allocate memory for buffer [1.3.1]

;---OPEN THE FILE:
                LEA     DX,PATH             ;point DS:DX to directory path
                MOV     AL,1                ;code to open for writing only
                MOV     AH,3DH              ;function number
                INT     21H                 ;open the file
                JC      OPEN_ERROR          ;go to error routine if carry
                MOV     HANDLE,AX           ;keep copy of handle
;---SET FILE POINTER TO END OF FILE:
                MOV     BX,AX               ;file handle in BX
                MOV     CX,0                ;CX:DX gives 0 offset from end of file
                MOV     DX,0                ;
                MOV     AL,2                ;code number for end-of-file
                MOV     AH,42H              ;function to set file pointer
```

```
                INT   21H                     ;set the pointer
                JC    POINTER_ERROR           ;go to error routine if carry
;---APPEND 300 BYTES TO THE FILE:
                MOV   AH,40H                   ;function number
                MOV   BX,HANDLE                ;handle in BX
                MOV   CX,300                   ;number of bytes to write
                LEA   DX,DATA_BUFFER           ;DS:DX points to data buffer
                INT   21H                      ;append the data
                JC    OUTPUT_ERROR             ;go to error routine if carry
                CMP   CX,300                   ;300 bytes successfully written?
                JNE   FULL_DISK                ;go to error routine if problem
```

5.4.4 Read from sequential files

Reading sequential files is much the same as writing them, except that the process is reversed. In BASIC, data is taken from the file and put into individual variables or into a data array. In assembly language, the data is placed in a buffer in memory. In the later case, the data is transferred record by record, and it is the responsibility of the program to separate the data items contained in the records. A "record" here refers to the size of the units in which the file is read.

High Level

Reading sequential files in BASIC is less complicated than writing them, since there are only two choices about how to go about it, depending on what characters in the file are to be recognized as marking the end of a data item. The INPUT# statement recognizes commas and quotation marks as data separators, as well as carriage return/line feed pairs. The LINE INPUT# statement recognizes only the CR/LF combination, and thus it can read whole lines of text that contain the other delimiters. This capability is essential for text processing.

To read three items with the INPUT# statement, first open the file, as discussed at [5.3.3] (for example: **OPEN"A:NEWSEQ" FOR INPUT AS 1**). If the file has been opened as #1, then **INPUT #1,X\$,Y\$,Z\$** assigns the first three elements in sequence to the three string variables. When using numeric variables, as in **INPUT #1,X,Y,Z**, be sure that the numeric type of the variable matches the variable found in the file. A double-precision number must be read into a variable that is itself double-precision so that it will be large enough to hold eight bytes. An alternative way of reading three data items is to place them in an array:

```
100 DIM ITEM$(40)      'create 40-element string array
100 FOR N=0 to 39      'for each element...
110 INPUT #1,ITEM$(N)  'read it, and place it in the array
120 NEXT
```

To read the nth item in a sequential file, a program must still read all items that precede it. Simply set up a loop that keeps reading data items, but do not save the data as it arrives.

The LINE INPUT# statement operates in much the same way as INPUT#, except that it can take only one variable at a time, and the variable is always a string. The variable may be up to 254 characters long, which is the longest that a data item can be if it was created by BASIC. A carriage return/line feed pair contained in the original data is included in the string that LINE INPUT# returns. This feature enables text files to keep track of paragraph endings.

The EOF ("end of file") function may be used to figure out when all data items in a file have been read. The function returns -1 if the file has been exhausted and 0 otherwise. The buffer number under which the file was opened is required by the function; for example, if the file was opened as #2, then **X = EOF(2)**. The following example reads an entire text file into an array:

```
100 OPEN "TEXT.AAA" FOR INPUT AS #2   'open for sequential input
110 DIM TEXT$(500)                    'allow 500 lines
```

```
120 LINECOUNTER=0                    'counts array lines
130 LINE INPUT #1,TEXT$(LINECOUNTER)  'get 1 line
140 IF EOF(2) THEN 170               'if end of file, quit
150 LINECOUNTER=LINECOUNTER+1        'increment line counter
160 GOTO 130                         'read next line
170 ...                              'continue...
```

The INPUT$ statement reads a specified number of characters from a sequential file. It is the responsibility of the program to figure out where the various data elements begin and end. The format for a file opened as #1, in which 30 bytes are to be read, is S$ = INPUT$(30,#1). Although you can specify the number of bytes to be read, be aware that this number cannot exceed 254 since this is the maximum size of the string variable into which the data is placed. INPUT$ is useful for transferring a body of data into a contiguous memory area. For example, the following code dumps the first 200 bytes of a sequential file into the monochrome display buffer so that it is displayed on the screen, control characters and all:

```
100 OPEN"A:NEWFILE" FOR INPUT AS #1   'open file
100 CLS:DEF SEG=&HB000                'clear screen, point to video buffer
110 FOR N=0 TO 9                      'get 10 groups of 200 bytes
120 S$=INPUT$(20,#1)                  'get 1 group
130 FOR M=1 TO 20                     'take each byte and place it at...
140 POKE N*160 + M*2,ASC(MID$(S$,M,1))  '... even-numbered positions
150 NEXT M                            'go get next byte
160 NEXT N                            'go get next group of 200
```

Middle Level

As for all file operations, DOS can read sequential files using either the *file control block method* or the *file handle method*. Only the first has a function specially designed to write sequential files. The file handle method uses a more general function, manipulating it in the particular way required for sequential access.

FCB Method:

Function 14H of INT 21H reads sequential files. Set up a file control block and disk transfer area, as explained at [5.3.5]. Open the file using function F of INT 21H [5.3.3]. With DS:DX pointing to the first byte of the FCB, function 14H reads one record of the file each time it is called. You may set the record size at offset 14 in the FCB. Do this *after* the FCB is opened since DOS inserts a default value of 128 when it opens the file.

Each time the function is called the data is loaded into memory starting at the first byte of the DTA. If the DTA is designed as a small transfer buffer, then before reading the next record the DTA contents must be transferred to the file's data area in memory. Alternatively, the DTA pointer may initially be set to the starting memory address at which the file is to reside, and after each record is read the pointer is incremented by the record size so that it points to the place at which the next record is to be deposited.

By setting the *current record field* (DB, offset 1FH) and the *current block field* (DW, offset CH) to values other than 0, a sequential file can begin reading from any point (make the settings *after* the FCB is opened). After each read, the current record field is automatically incremented by 1, and after 128 records the current block field is also incremented. On return, AL holds 0 if a whole record was successfully read. Upon encountering the end of the file, AL holds 1 if function 14H returned no data at all, and AL holds 3 if part of a record was encountered.

This example reads two records from a file, placing them in sequence in the data area where they are required. The record length is set to 256 bytes. The two records are read within a loop, and after the first is read, the DTA position is changed so that the DTA begins at the next empty byte in the data area.

```
;---PLACE FCB IN THE DATA SEGMENT:
        FCB       DB    0,'OLDDATA DAT',25 DUP(0)
        DATA_AREA DB    512 DUP(?)              ;will use as the DTA
;---SET DTA TO START OF THE DATA AREA:
                  LEA   DX,DATA_AREA            ;point DS:DX to DTA
                  MOV   DI,DX                   ;keep a copy in DI
                  MOV   AH,1AH                  ;function to set DTA
                  INT   21H                     ;set the DTA
;---OPEN THE FILE:
                  LEA   DX,FCB                  ;DS:DX points to the FCB
                  MOV   AH,0FH                  ;function to open file
                  INT   21H                     ;open the file
                  CMP   AL,0                    ;error?
                  JNE   OPEN_ERROR              ;go to routine if so
;---SET RECORD SIZE TO 256 BYTES:
                  LEA   BX,FCB                  ;point DS:DX to FCB
                  MOV   AX,256                  ;record size
                  MOV   DS:[BX]+14,AX           ;place value in FCB record size field
;---READ THE DATA:
                  MOV   CX,2                    ;number of records to read
    NEXT_RECORD:  MOV   AH,14H                  ;function for sequential read
                  LEA   DX,FCB                  ;point DS:DX to FCB
                  INT   21H                     ;read 1 record
                  CMP   AL,0                    ;transfer OK?
                  JE    CONTINUE                ;jump to error routine if problem
                  CMP   AL,2                    ;error?
                  JE    READ_ERROR              ;go to routine if so
                  .                             ;else, end of file condition...
                  .
    CONTINUE:     ADD   DI,256                  ;add record size to DTA counter
                  MOV   DX,DI                   ;point DX to new DTA position
                  MOV   AH,1AH                  ;function to set DTA position
                  INT   21H                     ;change the DTA
                  LOOP  NEXT_RECORD             ;go get the next record
;---LATER, CLOSE THE FILE:
                  LEA   DX,FCB                  ;point DS:DX to the FCB
                  MOV   AH,10H                  ;function to close a file
                  INT   21H                     ;close it
                  CMP   AL,0FFH                 ;error?
                  JE    CLOSE_ERROR             ;if so, go recover
```

File Handle Method:

Function 3FH of INT 21H can read data from a file sequentially. This function is used for all file reading done via file handles, including random files. The file is opened by function 3DH of INT 21H, with the code number 0 placed in AL for reading only, or 2 for reading and writing. When opened, the file pointer is automatically set to the first byte of the file. The function that reads from the file specifies how many bytes to read, and once that is done the file pointer points to the byte following the last byte read, ready for the next call to the function. Note that the file pointer is unique to the file—operations on other files do not affect its position.

A program may set up a small data transfer buffer, say of 512 bytes, and repeatedly call the read function without attending to the position of the file pointer. Alternatively, a program may in one stroke transfer the entire file directly to the place in memory where it is to reside. In the latter case you can simply request that the function read more bytes than there are in the file, since reading stops after the last byte of the file. However you still must calculate the exact file length so that you know where the data stops in the buffer into which it is read.

Find the file size by moving the file pointer to the end of the file. This is done right after the file is opened, when the file pointer is set to the beginning of the file. Place the code number 2 in AL and call function 42H to move the pointer to the end of the file. And put 0 in both CX and DX, which otherwise would offset the pointer from the end-of-file position by whatever value they hold. On return from this function, DX:AX contains the new position of the pointer as an offset from the start of the file—that is, it contains the file length. Be sure to reset the pointer to the beginning of the file before starting to read; this is done in exactly the same way, except that AL is given 0. If an error occurs in function 42H, the carry flag is set and AX returns 1 if the function number was invalid and 6 if the handle was invalid.

Now the program is ready to read from the file. Put the file handle in BX and the number of bytes to read in CX, then execute the interrupt. On return, AX holds the number of bytes actually read. If AX is 0, then the end of the file has been overrun. For other errors, the carry flag is set to 1 and AX holds 5 if there was a hardware error and 6 if the handle was invalid. The following example reads an entire short file into a memory buffer. For convenience, the buffer is set up in the data segment, which significantly increases the size of the program on disk. It is better for your programs to create the buffer using the memory allocation techniques shown at [1.3.1].

```
;---IN THE DATA SEGMENT:
     PATH          DB     'A:FILENAME.EXT,0    ;directory path string
     DATA_BUFFER   DB     1000 DUP(?)          ;buffer
     HANDLE        DW     ?                    ;stores file handle
     FILESIZE      DW     ?                    ;stores file size


;---OPEN THE FILE:
               LEA    DX,PATH                  ;point DS:DX to directory path
               MOV    AL,0                     ;code to open file for reading
               MOV    AH,3DH                   ;function to open file
               INT    21H                      ;open the file
               JC     OPEN_ERROR               ;go to error routine if carry
               MOV    HANDLE,AX                ;make copy of the handle
;---SET FILE POINTER TO END OF FILE:
               MOV    AH,42H                   ;function to set pointer
               MOV    AL,2                     ;code for end of file
               MOV    BX,HANDLE                ;file handle in BX
               MOV    CX,0                     ;offset in CX:DX is 0
               MOV    DX,0                     ;
               INT    21H                      ;set pointer, DX:AX returns position
```

```
                    JC      POINTER_ERROR1          ;go to error routine if problem
                    MOV     FILESIZE,AX             ;store file size (assume < 64K)
;---RESET FILE POINTER TO START OF FILE:
                    MOV     AH,42H                  ;restore function number
                    MOV     AL,Ø                    ;code for start of file
                    MOV     CX,Ø                    ;restore CX and DX to Ø
                    MOV     DX,Ø                    ;
                    INT     21H                     ;set the pointer
                    JC      POINTER_ERROR2          ;go to error routine if problem
;---READ THE ENTIRE FILE:
                    MOV     AH,3FH                  ;function number to read from a file
                    MOV     BX,HANDLE               ;put file handle in BX
                    MOV     CX,FILESIZE             ;number of bytes to read
                    LEA     DX,DATA_BUFFER          ;DS:DX points to buffer
                    INT     21H                     ;read the file
                    JC      READ_ERROR              ;go to error routine if problem


;---LATER, CLOSE THE HANDLE:
                    MOV     BX,HANDLE               ;handle in BX
                    MOV     AH,3EH                  ;function to close handle
                    INT     21H                     ;close it
                    JC      CLOSE_ERROR             ;check for error
```

5.4.5 Write to random files

Random files are not physically different from sequential files, they differ only in their mode of access. Random files assume that all data is organized in records of a fixed size, so that the position of any record of data can be calculated (sequential files must find the nth data element by counting the delimiters between the elements, starting from the beginning of the file). DOS automatically performs this calculation. Any program can perform this work itself, however, by setting the file pointer to the desired position and reading sequentially however many bytes there are in a record.

High Level ━━━━━━━━━━━━━━━━━━━━━━━━━━━━━━━━━

[5.3.3] explains the format for opening a random file in BASIC. Unlike sequential files, a single random file may be read and written to at the same time, without closing and reopening the file in between. The OPEN statement ends with a number giving the size of one record of the file. For example, **OPEN "R",1, "NEWDATA", 20** sets the record size to 20 bytes in the file NEWDATA (opened in file buffer #1).

Once the file is opened, the records can be partitioned into their component variables using a FIELD statement. A FIELD statement tells how many bytes of the record are given to each variable. For example, a 20-byte record might be divided up as **FIELD 1,14 AS LASTNAME$,2 AS DEPOSIT$,4 AS ACCTNUM$**. In this statement, the initial number 1 indicates that the FIELD statement is defining the layout for the records of the file opened as number #1. The data is placed in the record in exactly the same order as the FIELD statement records it. The RSET and LSET statements move data into the fields, fitting each item against either the right (RSET) or left (LSET) end of the field, and padding unused room (if any) with space characters. For example, in the 14-byte field that is tagged LASTNAME$, the name "SMITH" is inserted by **RSET LASTNAME$ = "SMITH"**, or, if N$ is given the value "SMITH", then **RSET LASTNAME$ = N$**. LSET could as easily be used as RSET. When the data is later read from the field into a variable, the variable is given all 14 characters. If RSET has been used, the program would have to delete the extra spaces from the left of the string variable, but if LSET had been used the excess spaces would be on the right.

Note that all of the variable names in a FIELD statement are for strings. In random files BASIC treats all variables—numbers included—as strings. A numeric variable must be "converted" to a special form before it is set into its field, and it must be "reconverted" when it is later read back. The word "converted" is written in quotes because BASIC does not actually change the number from the way that it is represented in memory; it just treats the number in a special way. Numeric fields in a FIELD statement require two bytes for integers, four for single-precision numbers, and eight for double-precision numbers—the same number of bytes that these values require in memory. To convert them to "string form," use the MKI$, MKS$, and MKD$ functions, which make the numeric-to-string conversion for variables of integer-, single- and double-precision type respectively. Normally, these functions are combined with an RSET or LSET statement, as in **RSET ACCTNUM$ =**

MKI(X), where X is an integer variable if ACCTNUM$ has been allotted only two bytes in a field statement.

Once all fields have been filled by RSET and LSET statements, the record is written to disk using PUT#. **PUT#1,245** places the data in record number 245 of the file that has been opened as #1. The record number may be omitted, in which case the data is written to the record number that is 1 greater than the last record written to (beginning with record 1). The entire record is written over, even if all fields have not been filled with data. Note that the fields in the buffer are not cleared after a PUT operation, so a data item such as the current date needs to be RSET into the buffer only once, and thereafter it will be written to all records that are accessed in that session. THE LOC function returns the number of the last record written to. If the file is opened under buffer #3, write **X = LOC(3)**.

The LOF (length of file) function returns the length of a file in bytes. Divide this number by the record size in order to determine the number of records contained in the file. Adding 1 to this value gives the record number to use in order to *append* new records to a file. If the file is opened through buffer #2 with a 32-byte record size, write **RECORDNUM = LOF(2)/32 + 1**.

The following example opens a random file with a 24-byte record size, and partitions the record into three variables. The program user is prompted for the data for each field, and when it is complete, the record is appended to the file. Line 120 calculates the initial record number. Note that the data may not be physically written to the disk each time a record is PUT. Several records may accumulate in the output buffer before this is done.

```
100 OPEN "R",1,"A:NEWDATA.DAT",24        'open #1 with 24-byte records
110 FIELD 1,18 AS LASTNAME$,2 AS AGE$,4 AS WEIGHT$   'partition the records
120 R=LOF(1)/24+1                         'number of last record + 1
130 CLS                                   'clear screen for messages
140 INPUT"Enter name: ",N$               'get the name (string variable)
150 INPUT"Enter age: ",A%                'get the age (integer)
160 INPUT"Enter weight: ",W!             'get the weight (single-precision)
170 RSET LASTNAME$=N$                     'place name in field
180 RSET AGE$=MKI$(A%)                     'place age in field
190 RSET WEIGHT$=MKS$(W!)                  'place weight in field
200 PUT #1,R                              'write the record
210 R=R+1                                 'point to next record for next time
220 PRINT:PRINT"Do another y/n?"         'query user
230 C$=INKEY$:IF C$="" THEN 220          'wait for response
240 IF C$="y" or C$="Y" THEN CLS:130     'if yes, go do another
250 CLOSE                                 'otherwise close the file
```

Middle Level

As with other DOS file operations, there are two methods of writing random files, one using file control blocks and one using file handles. For both you must set up a data transfer buffer that is at least the size of the random records to be written.

File Control Block Method:

Open the file control block using function 0FH, and point DS:DX to it. Once the file is opened, place the random record number in the random record field of the

FCB. Then call function 22H of INT 21H, which will transfer the data from the DTA to the file buffer set up when the FCB was created. The data may not be immediately written to disk if the record size is smaller than the file buffer size. Rather, the disk write will occur only when subsequent calls to function 22H have filled the buffer.

Upon return from function 22H, AL holds 00 if the transfer was completed successfully. Otherwise it holds 1 if the disk has inadequate space or 2 if the disk transfer segment had not enough space to write one record (that is, if the buffer size set for DOS was smaller than that specified in the FCB).

```
;---IN THE DATA SEGMENT:
        FCB     DB    1,'NEWDATA     ',25 DUP(0)
        DTA     DB    256 DUP(?)


;---OPEN THE FILE AND SET FCB FIELDS:
                MOV   AH,0FH              ;function number
                LEA   DX,FCB             ;point DS:DX to FCB
                MOV   BX,DX              ;copy FCB offset into BX
                INT   21H               ;open the file
                MOV   AX,256             ;256 byte record size
                MOV   [BX]+14,AX         ;place in record size field
                MOV   AX,233             ;record number
                MOV   [BX]+33,AX         ;put in random record field (low)
                MOV   AX,0               ;0 for high word of field
                MOV   [BX]+35,AX         ;put in random record field (high)
;---TRANSFER DATA FROM DTA TO FILE:
                MOV   AH,22H             ;random write function number
                LEA   DX,FCB             ;point DS:DX to FCB
                INT   21H               ;write the data
                CMP   AL,0              ;error?
                JNE   WRITE_ERROR       ;if so, go to recovery routine


;---LATER, CLOSE THE FILE:
                LEA   DX,FCB             ;point DS:DX to the FCB
                MOV   AH,10H             ;function to close a file
                INT   21H               ;close it
                CMP   AL,0FFH           ;error?
                JE    CLOSE_ERROR       ;if so, go recover
```

Often programs work on a sequence of random records at once, moving them to and from memory as a single unit. DOS provides a special function for FCB access called a *random block write*. It is function 28H of INT 21H. On entry, DS:DX points to an opened FCB in which the random record field has been set to the number of the first of the series of records that are to be written upon. This function is almost exactly like that in the above example. The only difference (besides the different function number) is that CX is given the number of records in the block (do not confuse the concept of "block" with the blocks of 128 records by which DOS keeps track of records—a program may read any number of records, beginning at any point).

CX returns with the number of records actually written. AL holds 0 if all records were written successfully and 1 if disk space was insufficient, in which case no records are written at all. Unlike function 22H, this function automatically increments the current record, current block, and random record fields in the FCB so that they point to the record following the last one read. Note that if CX is set to 0 on entry, the file length is set to the number of records specified by the random record field. In this way, disk space can be reserved for future use by the file.

File Handle Method

DOS makes no distinction between sequential and random files when using the file handle method of access. Your program must calculate the location in the file at which any particular record begins and set the file pointer to it. The file pointer is positioned using function 42H of INT 21H. Place the file handle in BX and the offset in the file into CX:DX (CX contains the high part of the value). Then put a code number from 0 - 2 in AL. When 0, the pointer is moved to an offset that is CX:DX bytes from the beginning of the file; if 1, the offset is to the point CX:DX bytes higher than the current offset; and if 2, the pointer is moved to the end of the file *plus* the offset (that is, it extends the file). Negative numbers are not allowed for relative offsets. On return DX:AX contains the new pointer location (with DX as the high part of the value). If the carry flag is set to 1, an error has occurred. AX will contain 1 if the code number in AL was invalid, or 6 if the handle was invalid.

Once the file pointer is positioned, a random record is written using the same function used for sequential files, 40H of INT 21H. On entry, BX contains the file handle and CX tells how many bytes to write. DS:DX points to the first byte of the data to be written. Upon return, AX holds the number of bytes actually written. If it differs from the number placed in CX, the disk is probably full (see [5.1.4]). As usual, the carry flag is set to 1 if there has been an error. In that case, AX contains 5 if there has been a disk drive problem, and 6 if the file handle was invalid.

The file pointer is to a file's image on disk what a DTA is to a data set's image in memory. It can be moved around to access particular parts of the data. By carefully manipulating the file pointer in random file operations, the contents of a particular field of a particular record can singly be taken from the disk and deposited precisely where required in memory.

```
;---IN THE DATA SEGMENT:
    HANDLE       DW    ?                ;stores file handle
    FILEPATH     DB    'A:NEWDATA',0    ;directory path string
    RECORD_BUFFER DB   30 DUP (?)       ;holds record ready for output
;---OPEN THE FILE:
                 MOV   AH,3DH            ;function number
                 MOV   AL,1              ;code to open file for writing
                 LEA   DX,FILEPATH       ;point DS:DX to path string
                 INT   21H              ;open the file
                 JC    OPEN_ERROR        ;go to error routine if carry flag set
                 MOV   HANDLE,AX         ;keep copy of file handle
;---CALCULATE THE RECORD POSITION AND SET FILE POINTER:
                 MOV   AX,30             ;record size is 30 bytes
                 MOV   CX,54             ;write record #54 (55th record)
                 MUL   CX               ;now DX:AX has record offset
                 MOV   CX,DX             ;move high word of offset to DX
                 MOV   DX,AX             ;move low word of offset to CX
                 MOV   AL,0              ;sets pointer to start of file
                 MOV   AH,42H            ;function to set file pointer
                 MOV   BX,HANDLE         ;handle in BX
                 INT   21H              ;set the pointer
                 JC    POINTER_ERROR     ;go to error routine if carry flag set
```

```
;---WRITE THE RANDOM RECORD:
          MOV   AH,40H              ;function number
          MOV   BX,HANDLE           ;file handle in BX
          MOV   CX,30               ;record size
          LEA   DX,RECORD_BUFFER    ;DS:DX points to record buffer
          INT   21H                 ;write the record
          JC    WRITE_ERROR         ;go to error routine if carry flag set
```

Unlike the FCB method, the file handle method makes no special provision for writing *blocks* of random file records. But your program needs only to calculate how many bytes comprise the block of records that is to be written.

5.4.6   Read from random files

Reading random files reverses the process of writing them. DOS calculates the position of a record within a file on disk, then reads the record and deposits it in memory. A program must then divide the record into fields of the exact same dimensions as the fields used when the record was constructed. Don't forget to remove any space characters that were used to pad the fields. The discussion of *writing* data to random files [5.4.5] contains information that will help you better understand the information here.

High Level

To read a random file, open it and define the record fields just as was explained for writing random files. Then use GET# to read a particular record from disk. **GET#1,23** reads record number 23 from the file opened under buffer #1. When the record is read, the variables named in the FIELD statement are automatically given the corresponding values in the record. For example, if the FIELD statement is **FIELD 1,20 AS X\$,2 AS Y\$**, then after the statement **GET#1,23** is executed, X\$ will hold the string in the first 20 bytes of record 23 and Y\$ will hold the second ten bytes. There are no statements corresponding to RSET and LSET that must be used to remove the data from their fields.

In the case of numeric data, recall that they had to be converted to string form using MKI\$, MKI\$, or MKD\$. To reassign these values to proper numeric variables so that they may be manipulated or printed, reconvert them using the corresponding functions CVI, CVS, CVD. If Y\$ holds an integer, then write $Y\% = CVI(Y\$)$ and the reconversion is made, with Y% holding the original value of the variable before it was specially processed for random files. If you were to display the string value of the variable, you would find a number between 0 and 65535 encoded as two ASCII characters.

This example opens the file created by the example at [5.4.5] and displays the data found in any record requested:

```
100 OPEN "A:NEWDATA" AS 1 LEN=24          'open the file
110 FIELD 1,18 AS LASTNAME$,2 AS AGE$,4 AS WEIGHT$   'partition the records
120 CLS:INPUT"What is the record number";R       'request a record number
130 IF R*24 > LOF(1) THEN BEEP:PRINT"No such record":GOTO 120'past end of file?
140 GET #1,R                              'get the record
150 PRINT LASTNAME$,CVI(AGE$),CVS(WEIGHT$)    'print the data
160 PRINT:PRINT"Do another y/n?"          'request another?
170 C$=INKEY$:IF C$="" THEN 170           'loop until keystroke
180 IF C$="y" OR C$="Y" THEN 120          'go get another if requested
190 CLOSE                                 'else close the file
```

Middle Level

The FCB method of file access has two functions that read random records. The file handle method, on the other hand, uses the same function that it uses to read sequential files. The two access methods are treated separately.

FCB Method:

Function 21H of INT 21H reads single random records. A second DOS function, 27H, reads *blocks* of consecutive random records; it is discussed below. Set up a file control block as discussed at [5.3.5] and open it [5.3.3]. After the FCB is opened, enter into the FCB the record size of the random files (DW at offset 14) and the number of the record that is to be read (DD at offset 33). Once DS:DX is pointed to the first byte of the FCB, call function 21H to read the record, and it will be deposited in memory starting at the first byte of the DTA.

When a record is successfully read, AL returns with 0. This outcome does not necessarily indicate that there has been no error, however, since an improper record size could cause parts of adjacent records to be returned as if they were a single record. If a request is made for a record number larger than the number of records contained by the file, AL returns 1 or 3. When 3, the very end of the file has been read, and *part* of a record of data has been read. When 1, no data was read at all.

This example reads one record and deposits it in the DTA:

```
;---IN THE DATA SEGMENT:
      FCB         DB   1,'OLDDATA    ',25 DUP(0)


;---OPEN THE FILE AND SET FCB FIELDS:
                  MOV  AH,0FH              ;function number
                  LEA  DX,FCB              ;point DS:DX to FCB
                  MOV  BX,DX               ;copy FCB offset into BX
                  INT  21H                 ;open the file
                  MOV  AX,55               ;55 byte record size
                  MOV  [BX]+14,AX          ;place in record size field
                  MOV  AX,22               ;record number to read
                  MOV  [BX]+33,AX          ;put in random record field (low)
                  MOV  AX,0                ;0 for high word of field
                  MOV  [BX]+35,AX          ;put in random record field (high)
;---TRANSFER DATA FROM DTA TO FILE:
                  MOV  AH,21H              ;random read function number
                  LEA  DX,FCB              ;point DS:DX to FCB
                  INT  21H                 ;read the data, place at DTA
                  CMP  AL,0                ;error?
                  JNE  READ_ERROR          ;if so, go to recovery routine
;---LATER, CLOSE FILE:
                  MOV  AH,10H              ;function to close file
                  LEA  DX,FCB              ;point DS:DX to FCB
                  INT  21H                 ;close it
```

To read blocks of consecutive records into memory at once, use function 27H of INT 21H. It is set up exactly like function 21H, above, except that in addition CX is given the number of records to be read, and upon return CX holds the number of records actually read. The values returned in AL are also the same as those for function 21H. Unlike in function 21H, the FCB fields that keep track of records (the random record, current block, and current record fields) are automatically incremented to point to the next unread record when this function is used.

Note that in both single and multiple random record readings, the *current block* and *current record* fields of the FCB are set from the initial value of the random record field. If you know the value of the current block and record, but not the corresponding random record number, use function 24H of INT 21H to do the calculation for you. There are no input registers other than to point DS:DX to the opened FCB. Upon return the random record field is filled with whatever value matches the settings of the other two fields.

File Handle Method:

The previous section shows how to write random records using the file handle method. Set up a random-read routine in exactly the same way, calculating the offset in the file to which to direct the file pointer. Point DS:DX to a buffer into which the record is to be deposited, then execute function 3FH of INT 21H. On entry, CX contains the record size, and BX holds the file handle.

```
;---IN THE DATA SEGMENT:
    HANDLE        DB    ?                    ;stores file handle
    FILEPATH      DB    'A:OLDDATA',0        ;directory path string
    RECORD_BUFFER DB    30 DUP (?)           ;buffer for 1 record
;---OPEN THE FILE:
              MOV   AH,3DH                   ;function number
              MOV   AL,0                     ;code to open file for reading
              LEA   DX,FILEPATH              ;point DS:DX to path string
              INT   21H                      ;open the file
              JC    OPEN_ERROR               ;go to error routine if carry flag set
              MOV   HANDLE,AX                ;keep copy of file handle
;---CALCULATE THE RECORD POSITION AND SET THE FILE POINTER:
              MOV   AX,30                     ;record size is 30 bytes
              MOV   CX,54                     ;write record #54 (55th record)
              MUL   CX                        ;now DX:AX has record offset
              MOV   CX,DX                      ;move high word of offset to DX
              MOV   DX,AX                      ;move low word of offset to CX
              MOV   AL,0                       ;sets pointer to start of file
              MOV   AH,42H                     ;function to set file pointer
              MOV   BX,HANDLE                  ;handle in BX
              INT   21H                        ;set the pointer
              JC    POINTER_ERROR              ;go to error routine if carry flag set
;---READ A RANDOM RECORD:
              MOV   AH,3FH                     ;function number
              MOV   BX,HANDLE                  ;handle in BX
              MOV   CX,30                       ;record size
              LEA   DX,DATA_BUFFER             ;DS:DX points to record buffer
              INT   21H                        ;write the record
              JC    READ_ERROR                 ;go to error routine if carry flag set

;---LATER, CLOSE THE HANDLE:
              MOV   BX,HANDLE                   ;handle in BX
              MOV   AH,3EH                       ;function to close handle
              INT   21H                          ;close it
              JC    CLOSE_ERROR                  ;check for error
```

5.4.7 Verify data after write operations

DOS can verify the accuracy of disk data transfers at the time they occur. Errors occur so seldom that the verification measures ought ordinarily to be avoided, since they slow down disk I/O. But when they are required there are two ways to make the verification. One is to place the command **VERIFY = ON** in a CONFIG.SYS file, which is automatically read when DOS boots up. Thereafter, *all* disk operations are verified. This is the only verification measure available to BASIC. A second method is to leave the VERIFY parameters "off," and to use a special DOS function to verify only those disk operations that are critical. When the verification procedure finds an error, it brings about a critical error condition, as described at [7.2.5].

Middle Level ━━━━━━━━━━━━━━━━━━━━━━━━━━━━━━━━━━

Function 2EH of INT 21H switches verification on and off. Place 1 in AL for "on" and 0 in AL for "off." Also put 0 in DL. Then execute the interrupt. There are no result registers.

```
;---TURN ON VERIFICATION:
          MOV   AL,1              ;code number
          MOV   DL,0              ;required input register
          MOV   AH,2EH            ;function number
          INT   21H              ;complete
```

To find out what the current verification setting is, call function 54H of INT 21H. There are no input registers. On return, AL = 1 if "on," and AL = 0 if "off."

5.4.8 Define/recover from disk errors

Disk operations are so complicated that there are a large number of possible errors. Most disk errors are discussed along with the operations in which they may occur. Here they are brought together in one place to help you create a general purpose procedure for recovery from disk errors.

Disk errors are of two kinds, which you may think of as "soft" or "hard." Soft errors result from inappropriate requests for file access: the file requested may not exist, or disk space may run out before all of a file can be written. Hard errors, on the other hand, result from the faulty sequencing or timing of disk operations, as might occur from bad alignment or from flaws in the disks themselves. In the latter case it is a good idea to "reset" the disk before proceeding.

High Level

[7.2.5] explains how to set up an error recovery routine. An ON ERROR GOSUB statement shifts the program to an error recovery subroutine when any critical error occurs. The subroutine first finds out the BASIC error code number, and for disk errors the following are provided:

52   Bad file number. No file has been opened under the buffer number designated (#1, #2, etc.).

53   File not found. Used with LOAD, KILL, NAME, FILES, and OPEN.

54   Bad file mode. Attempted to access a file differently than the way it was opened, e.g., by trying to input from a sequential file that was opened for output.

55   File already open. Tried to open a file that is already open, or to KILL a file that is still open.

58   File already exists. Tried to rename a file (using NAME) with a name found elsewhere in the directory.

61   Disk full. See [5.1.4] for a special discussion of this error.

62   Input past end. Tried to read more variables from a sequential file than it contains. Use EOF to avoid this error, as explained at [5.4.4].

63   Bad record number. Tried to read or write to a record numbered higher than the number of records the file contains.

64   Bad file name. Used with KILL, NAME, and FILES.

67   Too many files. The directory has no room for more entries. Alternatively, an attempt was made to open one more file when the maximum number of simultaneously opened files had already been reached.

70   Disk is write-protected.

71   Disk is not ready. Most likely, the disk drive door is open.

72   Disk media error. There may be damage to the disk. This error also sometimes occurs with hardware faults.

74   Specified wrong disk in RENAME operation.

75   Path/file access error. Tried to open a subdirectory or
          volume label as if it were a file. Or tried to open a read-
          only file for writing. This error also occurs if you attempt
          to remove the current directory. Used with OPEN, NAME,
          MKDIR, CHDIR, and RMDIR.

76   Path not found. The path was incorrectly specified, or it
          does not exist. Used with OPEN, MKDIR, CHDIR, and RMDIR.

Once the routine has decoded the error, the user may be informed of the problem. When the user indicates that the problem has been corrected, a RESUME statement sends the program back to the line where the error occurred. The RESUME statement may end with a line number so that the program returns to the *beginning* of an entire sequence of disk operations, no matter where the error occurred (note that files do *not* close when an error occurs). The following example recovers from full-disk errors and write-protection errors:

```
100 ON ERROR GOSUB 5000                    'start up error trapping
  .
  .
600 '''disk operations begin here
  .
  .
5000 '''error recover subroutine
5010 IF ERR=61 PRINT"Disk Full":GOTO 5100
5020 IF ERR=70 PRINT"Disk Is Write Protected":GOTO 5100
  .
  .
5100 PRINT"Correct the problem, then strike any key"
5110 C$=INKEY$:IF C$="" THEN 5110
5120 RESUME 600
```

Middle Level

Function 1 of INT 13H returns a byte in AL that gives the status of the disk drives. The bit pattern is as follows:

bit 0-1   01=invalid command, or, if bit 3=1,
              tried to transfer data over 64k boundary
          10=address mark not found
          11=write attempt to write-protected disk
    2   1=specified sector not found
    3   1=DMA overrun operation (data lost during transfer)
              or, if bit 0=1, attempted transfer across a
              64k boundary
    4   1=data was read incorrectly, must try again
    5   1=controller failure
    6   1=seek operation failure
    7   1=drive failed to respond (time-out error)

Each DOS disk function uses only a few of the available disk error codes, or sometimes none at all. In all cases, the carry flag is set to 1 when an error occurs. If there is an error, its code number is placed in AX. Here are the codes relevant to disk operations:

1   Invalid function number
2   File not found

3	Path not found
4	Maximum number of files already open
5	Access denied (hardware error)
6	Invalid file handle
15	Invalid drive was specified
16	Tried to remove the current directory
17	Not same device
18	No more files (when searching directory using
	global filename characters)

Recovery from these soft errors is a simple matter. Some alert you to *programming* errors. Others are attributable to the program user. When the drive itself does not respond correctly a *critical error* occurs. [7.2.5] shows how to write a routine to deal with critical errors.

DOS 3.0 introduces *extended error codes*. These may be retrieved by function 59H of INT 21H when the carry flag indicates an error has occurred. See [7.2.5] for a discussion.

6
The Printer

Section 1: Control Printer Operations

DOS can handle three parallel devices (LPT1-3), and this chapter shows how to control them. Serial printers are controlled exactly as parallel printers, except for the way in which the data is sent to the printer; for this information, see Section 1 of Chapter 7. Each parallel device has its own adaptor. An adaptor is manipulated through three I/O registers, and the port addresses of these registers are different for each adaptor. The BIOS data area contains the base address of each adaptor. A base address gives the lowest address of the group of three port addresses. The base address for LPT1 is at 0040:0008, for LPT 2 it is as 0040:000A, and so on. Which adaptor is assigned to which LPT number is not certain, as the table below shows. For this reason a program that accesses the parallel port directly should *look up* the addresses it uses. Note that a base address is initialized to 0 when no corresponding adaptor is installed.

Adaptor	Data Output	Status	Control
Monochrome card (PC/XT/AT)	3BCH	3BDH	3BEH
PC/XT Printer adaptor PC Jr Printer adaptor AT serial/parallel card (set as LPT1)	378H	379H	37AH
AT serial/parallel card (set as LPT2)	278H	279H	27AH

The *data output register* is the port address to which each byte of data is sent on its way to the printer. The *status register* reports a variety of information about the printer; the CPU may continuously monitor it in order to sense when it is all right to send data. The status register also reports that a printer error has occurred. The *control register* initializes the adaptor and controls the output of data. It also can set up the parallel port for interrupt operations, so that the printer will interrupt the CPU when it is ready for another character, leaving the CPU free for other matters. Here are the bit patterns in the status and control register:

Output Register:

	bit	0	0=normal setting, 1=causes output of byte of data
		1	0=normal setting, 1=automatic line feed after CR
		2	0=initialize printer port, 1=normal setting
		3	0=deselect printer, 1=normal setting
		4	0=printer interrupt disabled, 1=interrupts enabled
	5-7		unused

Status Register:

	bit	0-2	unused
		3	0=printer error, 1=no error
		4	0=printer not on line, 1=printer on line
		5	0=printer has paper, 1=printer out of paper
		6	0=printer acknowledges receipt of character, 1=normal
		7	0=printer busy, 1=printer not busy

There is no good reason for any program to lack the error recovery routines needed to deal with printer problems. A well written program should begin by checking that a printer is on line. If more than one printer is connected, the program should let the user choose the one he prefers. And the print routine should be able to recover from printer errors of any kind, preferably without requiring that the entire document be redone.

6.1.1 Initialize the printer port/reinitialize the printer

Programs should initialize each printer port (LPT1-LPT3) prior to its first use. Printer ports should also be reinitialized after a printer error condition is corrected. Do not confuse printer port initialization with the initialization of the printer itself. Printer initialization is essentially a matter internal to the printer. It occurs automatically when the printer is turned on, and in most cases a printer cannot truly be reinitialized without switching it off and then back on. But a program *can* reinitialize a printer in the sense that it can restore the initial parameters it uses for printing, cancelling all of the special fonts, tab settings, etc. It is considered good etiquette to reset the printer this way when a program is finished with it.

High-level languages automatically initialize the printer port, but assembly language programs require a short routine for this purpose. Restoration of initial print parameters, on the other hand, is a problem for all programs. Some printers, such as the newer Epson printers, have a "Master Reset Code" by which the printer is entirely reset. But since all printers do not have such a code, a program must make provision in its exit code to reset any parameters it may have changed. For example, it might output the codes for "italics off," "compressed mode off," etc. Remember to include a call to this procedure in a Ctrl-Break exit routine.

Keep in mind that on many printers, characters are not printed until an end-of-line carriage return is received (or until a line's worth of data is input). Characters can wait in the printer buffer indefinitely, even after the program that originated them has terminated. When a fresh data transmission begins, these lingering characters are printed. To avoid this problem always clear the buffer before starting to print; and, as good etiquette, clear the buffer when your programs are finished. This is done by sending ASCII 24 to the printer (no print parameters are altered).

Middle Level ───────────────────────────────

Function 1 of BIOS INT 17H initializes a printer port and returns a byte giving the port's status. Place in DX the port number, from 0-2 for LPT1 to LPT3, then call the interrupt. A printer status byte (identical to that discussed at [6.1.2]) is returned in AH.

```
;---INITIALIZE LPT1:
            MOV   AH,1          ;function to initialize printer
            MOV   DX,0          ;LPT1
            INT   17H           ;make the initialization
```

Low Level ───────────────────────────────

The output control register of each printer adaptor has a bit that causes the adaptor to initialize. This register is located at the port address that is 2 higher than the base address of the adaptor. Recall that the base address for LPT1 is kept at 0040:0008, for LPT2 it is at 0040:000A, etc. Only the low five bits of the output control register are significant. Bit 2 is the printer initialization bit, and ordinarily it is set to 1. To initialize the adaptor, set this bit to 0 for a thousand turns through an empty loop (3000 on the AT, or time 1/20th second using the BIOS time-of-day count [2.1.5]). Only bit 3 ("printer selected") needs to be set to 1 at this time. So send 12 to the port, make the delay, and then send the usual (non-interrupt) initialization value to the register, which is 8.

This example initializes LPT1:

```
;---INITIALIZE LPT1:
                MOV   DX,ES:[8]     ;move base address to DX
                INC   DX            ;add 2 to the base address
                INC   DX            ;
                MOV   AL,12         ;initialization value
                OUT   DX,AL         ;start the initialization
        DELAY:  MOV   AX,1000       ;begin delay loop
                DEC   AX            ;decrement the counter
                JNZ   DELAY         ;loop 1000 times
                MOV   AL,8          ;normal value for the control register
                OUT   DX,AL         ;time's up -- end initialization
```

6.1.2 Test that a printer is on-line

A program should always test that a printer is on line before starting to send output. It is easy to ascertain that a printer is not ready, since bit 3 of the printer status register is set to 1 in this case. But it is more difficult to find out exactly *why* the printer is not ready: whether it is turned off, deselected, or out of paper. This is because printers of different manufacture bring about different bit patterns in the status register even when they are in an identical state. Although the status register has bits that should show the three printer states, the bit patterns that actually occur with these conditions may not be in accord (bit 3 should show that the printer is turned off, bit 4 that it is deselected, and bit 5 that paper has run out). The values below are returned in the status register by the Epson "standard" that is generally followed by IBM:

Value	Bit Pattern	Interpretation
223	11011111	printer ready
87	01010111	printer not ready
119	01110111	printer out of paper
247	11110111	printer turned off

The input status register is located at the port address that is one greater than the *base address* of the printer. The base address for LPT1 is kept at 0040:0008, for LPT2 it is at 0040:000A, etc. Keep in mind that if the printer was turned off, it will take a while to self-initialize once it is switched on. Do not begin printing until the input status register indicates that the printer is on line and ready to receive data.

High Level

This routine tests whether the printer is on line and tells the program user what to do if it is not. It uses the values in the table above. As mentioned above, this approach is not useful for general print routines that access many different printers, but it is appropriate when you write printer-specific device drivers. Note that line 120 derives the value of a two-byte number by multiplying the high byte by 256 and adding it to the low byte. 1 is added to the result as the offset of the input status register address from the base address.

```
100 '''Get the LPT1 address and see if a printer is ready:
110 DEF SEG=&H40                         'point to the BIOS data area
120 PRTRBASE=PEEK(9)*256+PEEK(8)+1       'get the input status register address
130 IF INP(PRTRBASE)=223 THEN 180        'if printer is ready, jump
140 BEEP                                 'else beep, analyze, print messages:
150 IF INP(PRTRBASE)=87 THEN LOCATE 1,1:PRINT"Strike the SELECT key":GOTO 150
160 IF INP(PRTRBASE)=247 THEN LOCATE 1,1:PRINT"Turn the printer on":GOTO 160
170 IF INP(PRTRBASE)<>223 THEN 170       'wait until initialization finished
180 '''Printer is now on line -- begin print operations:   'etc...
190 LPRINT Z$
```

Middle Level

Use function 2 of INT 17H to fetch the printer port status byte. On entry, DX contains the LPT number (0-2 for LPT1-LPT3). This function turns off the three unused bits of the byte, and it XORs two others, so the bit patterns differ from those listed above:

Value	Bit Pattern	Interpretation
144	10010000	printer ready
24	00011000	printer not ready
184	10111000	printer turned off

Again, be aware that these numbers differ from printer to printer. The more general "off or not ready" status is indicated when bit 3 of the register is set to 0.

Low Level

This example takes a simpler route and merely checks the "on line" bit of the status register. Use the base address of LPT1 to get the status byte.

```
;---IN THE DATA SEGMENT:
    MESSAGE        DB 'Printer not ready -- strike any key when OK$'

;---CHECK TO SEE IF ON LINE:
                MOV   AX,40H       ;point ES to BIOS data area
                MOV   ES,AX        ;
                MOV   DX,ES:[8]     ;get the base address
                INC   DX           ;offset to status register
                IN    AL,DX        ;put status byte in AL
                TEST  AL,1000B     ;test bit 3
                JNZ   GO_AHEAD     ;jump ahead if printer on-line
;---PRINT ERROR MESSAGE AND WAIT FOR KEYSTROKE:
                MOV   AH,9         ;function to display string
                LEA   DX,MESSAGE   ;DS:DX points to message
                INT   21H          ;print the error message
                MOV   AH,7         ;function to wait for keystroke
                INT   21H          ;wait for keystroke (no echo)
    GO_AHEAD:                      ;program continues...
```

6.1.3 Interpret/recover from printer errors

Error checking must not stop once a program ascertains that a printer is on line. Printer errors can occur at any time while the printing is going on, and a program must be ready to recover. While a printer is capable of many sorts of errors, only three are reported back to the computer. These are the "out of paper" error, the "not on line" error, and a general purpose "error has occurred" message. As [6.1.2] explains, not all printers report these error conditions in the same way, but *theoretically* the input status register uses the following bit pattern:

```
bit 3  =  0 when a printer error has occurred
    4  =  0 when the printer has gone off line
    5  =  1 when the printer has run out of paper
```

Bit 4, in particular, may not operate as it is supposed to. The input status register is located at the port address that is one greater than the *base address* of the printer. The base address for LPT1 is kept at 0040:0008, for LPT2 it is at 0040:000A, etc.

At low level, when a program sends data to a printer, it constantly monitors bit 7 of this register to see if the printer is ready to accept another character. It is an easy matter to check bit 3 at the same time to see if an error has occurred. If the errors that *should* be indicated by bits 4 and 5 have occurred, at least bit 3 will have become 0. The program can then do its best to analyze the error, and then it can prompt the user to correct the situation. Note that the DOS function that outputs characters to the printer (number 5 of INT 21H—see [6.3.1]) can be made to continuously monitor for time-out errors by means of the MODE command. Before loading a program that uses function 5, enter **MODE LPT1:,,P** (or better still, place the command in an AUTOEXEC batch file).

All of these errors require that printing stop and that action be taken before it can begin again. It is frustrating to the program user when much of a long document must be reprinted because of a printer error. Careful design of a recovery routine should allow a program to resume printing from the top of the page on which the error occurred. Always store a copy of the pointer to the output data whenever a new page is begun. When an error recovery procedure comes into action, it can order the user to reset the page to top-of-form, and then printing can recommence at the start of the page where printing left off.

High Level

BASIC provides two error conditions for printers. Error code 24 occurs when the printer is de-selected, and code 27 occurs when the printer is turned off, or if it runs out of paper. These codes are detected using the error-trapping technique explained at [7.2.5]. Unfortunately, only code 27 is trapped efficiently. Code 24 takes approximately half a minute to register, during which time the program freezes. It is not very useful to read the status register directly before each print operation. This works before printing begins, but not if the printer is deselected while printing is in progress. For what it is worth, here is the error-trapping routine:

```
100 ON ERROR GOTO 1000                              'enable error trapping
    .
    .
1000 '''begin error recovery routines:
1010 IF ERR=24 OR IF ERR=27 THEN GOSUB 2000:RESUME  'is it a printer error?
    .
    .
2000 BEEP:LOCATE 1,1:PRINT"Printer Not Ready"        'inform user of problem
2010 PRINT"Strike any key when ready"
2020 IF INKEY$="" THEN 2020                          'loop until key struck
2030 RETURN                                          'go back to program
```

Middle Level

Whenever function 0 of INT 17H outputs a character to the printer, it returns the printer status byte in AH. Check the value of this byte after every character is sent. BIOS slightly modifies the status byte. Normally, bit 0 is not significant, but in this case it is set to 1 when a "time-out" (printer off line) error occurs. The following example detects two kinds of errors: a general "printer not ready" condition and the "out of paper" condition. The example assumes that at the beginning of each page (that is, after every form feed) the program saves a pointer to the start of the output data, placing it in the variable STARTING_PTR. This enables the program to recommence from the top of the page rather than from the beginning of the document. Of course, the printer must be fully reinitialized before recommencing, so that all formatting parameters are restored. (This example merely illustrates error checking—it is not a working print routine).

```
;---IN THE DATA SEGMENT:
    MESSAGE1      DB    'Printer off-line -- strike any key when ready$'
    MESSAGE2      DB    'Printer out of paper -- strike any key when ready$'

;---SEND A CHARACTER AND CHECK FOR ERRORS:
    NEXT_CHAR:    MOV   AH,0              ;function number
                  MOV   DX,0              ;choose LPT1
                  MOV   AL,[BX]           ;BX points to data
                  INC   BX                ;increment data ptr for next time
                  INT   17H               ;send the character to the printer
                  TEST  AH,00001000B      ;isolate bit 3 (error flag)
                  JZ    NEXT_CHAR         ;go do next character if no error
                  TEST  AH,00100000B      ;isolate bit 5 (no paper)
                  JZ    OFF_LINE          ;if not out of paper, jump ahead
                  MOV   AH,9              ;prepare to print no paper message
                  LEA   DX,MESSAGE2       ;point DS:DX to string
                  INT   21H               ;print the string
                  JMP   SHORT RECOVER     ;jump ahead
    OFF_LINE:     MOV   AH,9              ;prepare to print time-out message
                  LEA   DX,MESSAGE1       ;point DS:DX to string
                  INT   21H               ;print the string
    RECOVER:      MOV   BX,STARTING_PTR   ;restore top-of-page pointer
                  MOV   AH,0              ;function to wait for keystroke
                  INT   16H               ;wait
                  CALL  PRTR_INITIALIZA   ;reinitialize printer parameters
                  JMP   NEXT_CHAR         ;start over from top of page
```

6.1.4 Switch between two or more printers

Computers equipped with multiple parallel ports may have two or more printers attached. Output may be switched between the printers in two ways. One way is by using only those printer output statements that specify which printer is used. You may wish to design the code so that the specification can be changed.

The second way of switching printers is to allow LPT1 to be used by default, but to change the printer that is addressed by LPT1. This is done by switching the base address used by LPT1. This base address is kept in the BIOS data area at 0040:0008. Exchange it with the base address for LPT2 or 3 (at 0040:000A or :000C) and a different adaptor will be accessed as LPT1.

High Level

In BASIC, if the printer has been opened by the statement **OPEN "LPT1" AS #1**, then to change printers first CLOSE #1 and then open the second printer using the statement **OPEN "LPT2" AS #1**. Thereafter all **PRINT #1** statements will direct their output to the second printer. This change is not so easily made in programs that use the LPRINT statement, since LPRINT sends all output to LPT1 by default. In this case you must exchange the printer base addresses. The following BASIC code does just that, switching LPT1 and LPT2. Used a second time, it switches the addresses back to their initial configuration.

```
100 DEF SEG=&H40          'point to bottom of BIOS data area
110 X=PEEK(8)             'get low byte of LPT1 address
120 Y=PEEK(9)             'high byte of same
130 POKE 8,PEEK(10)       'transfer low byte of LPT2 address
140 POKE 9,PEEK(11)       'transfer high byte
150 POKE 10,X             'switch low byte of LPT1 to LPT2
160 POKE 11,Y             'high byte of same
170 SYSTEM               'leave BASIC
```

This is a handy program to invoke when ready-made software does not address the desired printer. It can be compiled and kept on disk, say by the name OTHERPRN, and then one need merely type that name (from the DOS prompt) to toggle between printers. If you have no compiler, make a batch file named OTHERPRN.BAT, and place in the file the line **BASIC OTHERPRN**. When you type **OTHERPRN**, the batch file loads BASIC, which automatically runs OTHERPRN.BAS, and then BASIC is exited. Be sure BASIC.COM resides on the disk. Keep in mind that you must resist the temptation to test this program before it has been saved on disk, since it erases itself when it is run.

Low Level

One way an assembly language program can change the printer to which it sends data is by always using function 0 of INT 17H for output [6.3.1]. This function requires that the printer number be placed in DX. Supply this number from a variable, so that it can be changed at any time. The second possibility is to exchange the base address of LPT1 with that of LPT2 or LPT3. The following program does just that. Like any short utility, it should be written in .COM form, as explained at [1.3.6].

```
;---EXCHANGE BASE ADDRESSES OF LPT1 AND LPT2:
                MOV   AX,40H              ;segment of BIOS data area
                MOV   ES,AX               ;point ES to data
                MOV   BX,8                ;offset of LPT1 base address
                MOV   DX,ES:[BX]          ;save LPT1 base address
                MOV   AX,ES:[BX]+2        ;save LPT2 base address
                MOV   ES:[BX],AX          ;switch LPT2 base address
                MOV   ES:[BX]+2,DX        ;switch LPT1 base address
```

Section 2: Set Printing Specifications

Special codes are sent to a printer to set the many specifications for page format, type style, etc. These codes are sent to the printer like any other data. Some are no more than one-byte codes from the first 32 bytes of the ASCII character set. These are *control codes* (listed at [7.1.9]), and they initiate such common printer operations as line feeds and form feeds. Most print specifications, however, are sent as *escape sequences*, where one or more code bytes follow the escape character, which is ASCII 27. The initial escape character informs the printer that the character(s) that follow are to be interpreted as commands, rather than as data. Such escape sequences generally have no terminating character, since the printer "knows" the length of each sequence. Only in the few cases where the escape sequence is of variable length is a terminating character required, and that character is always ASCII 0.

In almost all cases, the specifications made by these codes stay in effect until they are explicitly undone. Once the code for underlining is received, for example, underlining continues indefinitely until the code that stops underlining is sent. The printer's buffer may be cleared without affecting the specifications. But if there is a printer error and the printer is reset (turned off and back on), then all specifications must be restored.

Most codes that set print specifications are interspersed throughout the data they affect. For example, data for a word that is to be boldfaced is preceded by an escape sequence that turns boldfacing on and followed by an escape sequence that turns it off. Since there is no universal standard for the various codes, sophisticated printing requires that printer drivers be written for every printer that is to be supported. Each driver converts instructions generated by the print routine into the protocol used by the particular printer.

Sending the codes is straightforward in assembly language, but in BASIC you must remember to follow the statements that send the codes (like LPRINT or PRINT#) with a semicolon. Otherwise the statements will automatically follow the codes with a carriage return/line feed pair.

The discussions and examples in the following pages are largely based on the *IBM Graphics Printer*. The codes used by this printer are as "standard" as any printer protocol can be. This is largely because they are based on the protocol used by Epson printers (the first IBM printers were Epsons) which make up about a third of all printer sales. The control codes used by the IBM printers are compared at [6.2.7]. While the information given in this section may not specifically apply to the printers you write for, most of the principles will.

6.2.1 Set text and graphics modes

A printer is always in text mode unless it is specially placed in a graphics mode. The command that invokes a graphics mode must state how many bytes of graphics data follow (never more than one line) and once that number of bytes has been interpreted as a graphics image, the printer returns to text mode. For this reason, there is no code that *turns on* text mode.

The number of graphics modes varies from printer to printer. In all cases the escape code that invokes the graphics mode is followed by two bytes that specify how many bytes of graphics data follow (low byte first). To calculate the value of the two bytes, divide the number of data bytes by 256 and place the result in the second byte and the remainder in the first byte. These two bytes are immediately followed by the data bytes themselves.

Each byte defines a bit pattern that corresponds to the eight vertical dots of one position along the line. The low bit (1) corresponds to the bottom of the column formed, and the high bit (128) corresponds to the top. For example, to print a pyramid, first send a byte in which only the bottom bit is turned on, then a byte with the bottom two bits turned on, etc. After the eighth byte, reverse the series. The value of the first byte is 1, then 3 (1 + 2), then 7 (1 + 2 + 4), then 15 (1 + 2 + 4 + 8), etc. Figure 6-1 diagrams this pattern.

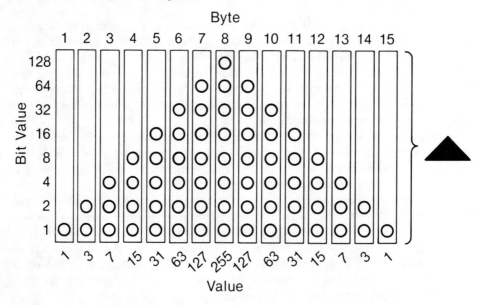

Figure 6-1. Bit patterns that print a pyramid.

To print the pyramid in BASIC on an IBM Graphics Printer, write the following code:

```
100 LPRINT CHR$(27);CHR$(75);CHR$(15);CHR$(0);CHR$(1);CHR$(3);
        CHR$(7);CHR$(15);CHR$(31);CHR$(63);CHR$(127);CHR$(255);
        CHR$(127);CHR$(63);CHR$(31);CHR$(15);CHR$(7);CHR$(3);CHR$(1);
```

The first two CHR$ bytes start up the 480-dot graphics mode, the next two tell that fifteen bytes of graphics data follow, and then the sequence of data bytes is listed. Of course, this could be programmed much more cleverly so that the fifteen bytes of data are generated by a loop. Note that all kinds of problems can occur when the number of bytes specified does not accord with the number of bytes given. To add space between graphics figures, output a number of 0-value bytes. In BASIC, when more than 80 bytes of graphics data are output to a single line, be sure to set the printer to "infinite width." Write **WIDTH "LPT1:",255**.

The IBM Graphics Printer has four graphics modes which are more or less "standard." They are:

27,75 480-dots per line. The "normal" mode. Maximum 480 bytes of data per statement.

27,76 960-dots per line. Twice the horizontal resolution, but printed at half the speed ("double density"). Maximum 960 bytes of data per statement.

27,89 960-dots per line, printed at normal speed ("high speed double density"). Two horizontally adjacent dots may not both be printed, since the pins in the print head do not have enough time to refire. If an attempt is made to do so, the second dot is ignored. Maximum 960 bytes of data per statement.

27,90 1920-dots per line, printed at half speed ("quadruple density"). Horizontally adjacent dots must be at least 3 dots apart (that is, print 1, skip 2). Maximum 1920 bytes of data per statement.

The denser modes generally can not print one dot after another when they are horizontally adjacent. To fill in between the dots, take the carriage back to the left margin, move the print head slightly to the right, and make a second pass using the same data. Here is a comparison of the dot densities that are elicited by the same control codes on different printers:

Code	Graphics Printer	Color Printer	Compact Printer	Proprinter
27,75	480 dots	1108 dots	560 dots	480
27,76	960 dots	2216 dots	--	960
27,89	960 dots	2216 dots	--	960
27,90	1920 dots	4432 dots	--	1920

The color printer is unique among the IBM printers in that it can set the *aspect ratio* of graphics images. This ratio reflects the difference between the horizontal and vertical distances between dots. Ordinarily a 1:1 ratio is desirable, since graphics calculations become difficult otherwise. But when dumping a graphics image from the video display, an aspect ratio is required that is the same as the screen's ratio. In a medium resolution screen mode, five dots vertically equal the same physical distance as six dots horizontally. This makes the aspect ratio 5:6, and it is the default value assumed by the color printer. Only 1:1 and 5:6 ratios are allowed.

6.2.2 Control line spacing

Except on printers with special plotting capabilities, all printing is done in lines. Even graphics images are comprised of lines, although in this case no space is left between them. ASCII 10 is the standard line feed control code. Sending it to the printer (without a preceding escape character) causes the paper to move forward by whatever spacing has been specified. Ordinarily, if no line feed is sent along with a carriage return (ASCII 13), the print head returns to the left edge of the paper so that it may rewrite over the same line. However, the line feed can be made to occur automatically after every carriage return. The printer's dip switch settings may activate this feature. Or it can be done by turning on bit 1 of the *output control register* (see [6.1.0]). Many printers can toggle the auto-line feed feature on and off using the code **27,53**, and some can make *reverse* line feeds (**27,93**).

The graphics printer defaults to 1/6 inch line spacing (that is, it writes six lines per inch), and it can be returned to this mode by sending **27,50** (this code is also used in combination with a variable line-spacing code that is discussed below). There are two other ready-made spacings for this printer, 1/8 inch and 7/72nd inch. Their respective control codes are **27,48** and **27,49**.

Fine gradations of line spacing are also possible. The graphics printer uses three codes that can shift the platen in very small gradations. All three use a two-byte escape sequence followed by the number of 72nds or 216ths of an inch to space by. The vertical distance between the centers of two dots is 1/72nd inch. Spacing 8/72nds inch leaves no space between lines (= 9 lines/inch). Standard 6 lines/inch spacing is given by 12/72nds inch. Finally, 1/216th is 1/3rd of 1/72nd. Movements of this size enable the print head to be slightly offset from dot centers so that on a second pass dots are joined to achieve better print quality. Here are the escape sequences:

Movement	Escape Sequence
72nds inch	27,65,n (where n = 1 to 85)
216ths inch	27,51,n (where n = 1 to 255)
216ths inch	27,74,n (where n = 1 to 255)

The command for 72nds inch spacing does not become active until a second control code is used: **27,50**. As explained above, this second code may also be used alone to restore the printer to 1/6th inch line spacing. If **27,65,n** has been used at any time, however, you will need to restore 1/6 inch spacing by sending **27,65,12,27,50**. The two codes for 216ths inch spacing are not identical. The first causes all subsequent line feeds to follow its specifications; the second operates for only a single line feed, and thereafter the line spacing reverts to its former setting.

This table compares the line spacings made by the same control codes on several IBM printers:

Code	Matrix Printer	Graphics Printer	Color Printer	Compact Printer	Jet Printer	Wheel Printer	Pro Printer
27,48	1/8	1/8	1/8	1/9	1/8	1/8	1/8
27,49	7/72	7/72	6/72	1/9		9/96	7/72
27,50	1/6	1/6	1/6	1/6	1/6	1/6	1/6
27,51		n/216	n/144				n/216
27,65	n/72	n/72	n/72			n/72	n/72
27,74		n/216	n/144				n/216

No matter how line spacing is changed, the printer keeps track of the forward and backward motions of the platen so that the skip-over-perforation is always made at the correct place.

6.2.3 Control paper movement

The paper in a printer is moved by line feeds, vertical tabbing, and form feeds. A dip switch setting in the printer determines whether the printer automatically skips to a new page when it encounters the perforation between pages. If the perforation is not skipped over, print may end up right on top of it. The skip leaves three lines of space at the top and bottom of each page. The printer does not actually sense the perforation; rather, it assumes at start-up that the top of the page is properly aligned, and then it keeps track of the number of line feeds it has made. A program can override the dip switch setting by sending control codes to the printer. **27,56** stops the printer from skipping over the perforation, and **27,57** causes it to skip.

The Graphics Printer uses a code that sets the number of lines skipped at page breaks. The code is **27,78,n**, where n is the number of lines from 1 to 127. For example, **27,78,10** causes the printer to skip 10 lines. If the line spacing is set to 1/6th inch, so that an 11 inch page holds 66 lines, then after printing 56 lines the printer makes a 10-line skip. It is up to your program to initially forward the paper by five (blank) lines so that the 55 lines of text are centered on each page.

If forms are used that have a different length from the usual eleven inches, the page length must be changed so that the skips occur at the correct place and so that form feeds move the paper to the proper position. The page length can be set either by the number of lines or by a length given in inches. To set the number of lines per page, send the code **27,67,n**, where n is the line count. The same escape sequence is used for setting the form length in inches, except that the page length is written as **0,n**, where n may be from 1 to 22 inches. For the standard page, send **27,67,0,11**.

6.2.4 Control the print head position

Print is positioned on the page in part by moving the paper [6.2.3] and in part by moving the print head. The head can be positioned anywhere, but not simply by specifying a lateral coordinate. Rather, the print head is positioned as an offset from the left extreme of its reach. There are no sensors in a printer that report the current position of the print head. Your program must keep track of the position if it must be known. It is a good idea to start printer output with the control code **27,60**, which moves the head to the left extreme without making a line feed (a carriage return can accomplish the same).

In printing text, there are several ways to move the print head to a particular position. It is moved rightward by sending to the printer one or more *space* characters or *tab* characters, and it is moved leftward by sending one or more *backspace* characters, or by the carriage return charcter. The movements are made essentially continuously—do not think of them as you would similar operations on a manual typewriter. So long as your program knows the initial position of the print head it can combine line feeds with spacing, tabs, and backspacing to format print exactly as you like. Printers that can make *reverse* line feeds can easily function as a plotter.

Graphics modes can move the print head by small fractions of an inch. When printing text, a graphics mode can be entered to achieve variable spacing between words. Unfortunately, this process slows the printer considerably. See the example at [6.3.2].

There is a special code that causes the print head always to return to the left margin before printing a line, canceling bidirectional printing. While this feature slows down printer operation considerably, it helps position the print head more accurately. It is especially useful in graphics work. To turn unidirectional printing on, send **27,85,1**, and to turn bidirectional printing back on, send **27,85,0**.

6.2.5 Set tab positions

Depending on the printer, both horizontal and vertical tab positions may be set (the IBM graphics printer has no vertical tabs). Horizontal tabs are defined as offsets from the left margin, given in spaces. In some cases up to 112 horizontal tab positions are allowed. Similarly, vertical tabs are defined as offsets from the top of the page, and here the measurement is made in line spacings. For most IBM printers, the maximum is 64 vertical settings.

The first two bytes of the code for setting horizontal tabs is **27,68**, and for vertical tabs it is **27,66**. For both kinds of tabs, the two initial code bytes are followed by a string of bytes giving the tab positions in ascending order. Place an ASCII 0 byte at the end of the string to mark its end. To set horizontal tabs at columns 15, 30, and 60, send **27,68,15,30,60,0** to the printer. And to set vertical tabs at lines 8 and 12, send **27,66,8,12,0**. Note that if the page length differs from 11 inches, it must be set before the vertical tab positions. Vertical tabs are canceled by **27,67**.

Note that most printers do not have *margin settings* as such. Left margins may be set up by tabbing, or by outputting the appropriate number of space characters at the start of each line. For precise margin settings, switch into a graphics mode and output a number of ASCII 0 bytes. Right margins are created simply by limiting the line length.

6.2.6 Change the print font

An 8-1/2-inch wide page holds up to 80 normal characters per line when each character is given the same width. Proportional spacing [6.3.3] may fit a few more characters per line. Compressed print, on the other hand, fits 132 characters on a line, double-width print fits 40, and compressed double-width fits 64. Be cautioned that intermixing the varying widths on a single line can make formatting difficult.

Most dot matrix printers offer a variety of special font modes. Here are the standard options as used on the IBM Graphics Printer:

Compressed Print:

To turn on the compressed print mode, send the one-byte control code **15**. To turn the mode off, send **18**. An 8-1/2 inch wide page can have 132 characters per line in this mode.

Double-Width Print:

To start the printer writing in double-width characters, send the one-byte control code **14**. Double-width character mode is unusual in that the printer automatically turns it off when it receives a line feed or carriage return. Since these characters are ordinarily confined to single-line titles, this feature is convenient. To turn off the mode mid-line, send **20**.

Emphasized Print:

In emphasized print, each character is printed twice at exactly the same position. This makes the dots darker, giving a *boldface* appearance. Printer speed is halved. To turn the mode on, send the control code **27,69**. To turn the mode off, send **27,70**.

Double-Strike Print:

In double strike mode the paper is shifted 1/216th of an inch before a second pass of the print head. Better formed characters result, and there is a slight boldfacing of the print. The printer speed is cut in half. Turn the mode on by sending the control code **27,71**, and turn it off by **27,72**.

Underlined Print:

Underlining may be performed in two ways. Graphics printers have an underline mode that causes an underline to be placed under all characters, spaces included. For the IBM Graphics Printer, the mode is turned on by sending **27,45,1**, and it is turned off by sending **27,45,0**. Printers that do not have an underline mode can create underlining by making a second pass over the line of print, printing the understore character (ASCII 95) where underlining is required, and spaces (ASCII 32) at all other positions. A second pass is performed simply by making a carriage return (ASCII 13) without a line feed (ASCII 10). Making second passes does not interfere with the printer's calculation of page length.

Subscripted/Superscripted Print:

On graphics printers, subscripted or superscripted text is compressed vertically. To begin superscripting, send the control code **27,83,0**, and to begin subscripting, send **27,83,1**. It is possible to shift directly from one to the other. To turn this feature off so that printing resumes on the current line, send **27,84**.

Some modes can not be used in combination with others. If you want to use four modes at once, consult the following table. Each of the six columns gives an allowed combination.

Combination	1	2	3	4	5	6
Normal	X	X				
Compressed			X	X		
Emphasized					X	X
Double Strike	X		X		X	
Sub/Superscript		X		X		X
Double Width	X	X	X	X	X	
Underline	X	X	X	X	X	

6.2.7 Compare IBM printer capabilities

The following table compares the control codes of the IBM printers. The information is not adequate to program many of the codes (you will need the IBM documentation) and in some cases unique codes have been omitted. The table is intended to show the range of printer capabilities, and to point out which codes are "standard". Note that the codes for the first four printers are available through the *Options and Adapters* series of Technical Reference Manuals, and that the codes for the others are found in their accompanying *Guide to Operations* manuals.

Code	Function	Matrix Printer	Graphics Printer	Color Printer	Compact Printer	Jet Printer	Wheel Printer	Pro Printer
Paper Movements:								
10	Line feed	X	X	X	X	X	X	X
11	Tab vertically	X		X	X	X	X	X
12	Form feed	X	X	X	X	X	X	X
13	Carriage return	X	X	X	X	X	X	X
27,52	Set top of page			X			X	X
27,56	Ignore paper end	X	X					
27,57	Cancel ignor paper end	X	X					
27,66	Set vertical tabs	X		X	X	X		X
27,66	Clear vertical tabs							X
27,78	Set skip perforation		X	X	X	X		X
27,79	Cancel skip perforation		X	X	X	X		X
Print Head Movements:								
8	Backspace			X		X	X	X
9	Tab horizontally	X	X	X	X	X	X	X
27,60	Move print head to left	X	X	X				
27,62	Set horizontal motion index					X		
27,68	Set horizontal tabs	X	X	X	X	X	X	X
27,68	Clear horizontal tabs							X
27,77	Automatic justification			X				
27,80	Proportional spacing ON/OFF		X			X		
27,82	Reset tabs to defaults			X	X		X	X
27,85	Unidirectional print ON/OFF		X	X			X	
27,88	Set left/right margins			X			X	
27,100	Variable forward space			X				
27,101	Variable backspace			X				
Line/Character Spacing:								
27,48	1/8 inch line spacing	X	X	X		X	X	X
27,48	1/9 inch line spacing				X			
27,48	7/72 inch line spacing	X	X					
27,49	7/72 inch line spacing							X
27,49	9/96 inch line spacing						X	
27,49	6/72 inch line spacing			X				
27,49	1/9 inch line spacing				X			
27,50	Start 27,65 variable feed	X	X	X				
27,50	1/6 inch line spacing	X	X	X	X	X	X	X
27,51	Variable line feed (n/216)		X					X
27,51	Variable line feed (n/144)			X				
27,53	Automatic line feed ON/OFF			X	X	X	X	X
27,65	Variable line feed (n/72)	X	X	X			X	X
27,67	Set page length	X	X	X	X	X	X	X
27,74	Variable line feed (n/216)		X					X
27,74	Variable line feed (n/144)			X				
27,93	Reverse line feed			X			X	
27,104	Half line feed forward						X	
27,105	Half line feed reverse						X	

Code	Function	Matrix Printer	Graphics Printer	Color Printer	Compact Printer	Jet Printer	Wheel Printer	Pro Printer
Fonts:								
11	15 characters per inch ON						X	
14	Double width print ON	X	X	X	X	X		X
15	Compressed print ON	X	X	X	X	X		X
18	Compressed print OFF	X	X		X	X		X
1810	characters per inch ON			X		X	X	
20	Double-width print OFF	X	X	X	X	X		X
27,45	Underline ON/OFF		X	X	X	X	X	X
27,58	12 characters per inch ON			X			X	X
27,69	Emphasized print ON	X	X	X				X
27,70	Emphasized print OFF	X	X	X				X
27,71	Double-strike print ON	X	X	X		X		X
27,72	Double-strike print OFF	X	X	X		X		X
27,83	Subscript/superscript ON		X	X		X	X	X
27,84	Subscript/superscript OFF		X	X		X	X	X
27,87	Double-width print ON/OFF		X	X	X	X		X
27,91	Color underline ON					X		
27,95	Overscore ON/OFF							X
Special character sets/colors:								
27,54	Select character set 2		X	X		X	X	X
27,55	Select character set 1		X	X		X	X	X
27,61	Download fonts						X	X
27,73	Change print quality			X		X		X
27,92	Print control codes			X			X	X
27,94	Print any character			X			X	X
27,97	Shift ribbon at page end			X				
27,98	Select ribbon band 4			X				
27,99	Select ribbon band 3			X				
27,109	Select ribbon band 2			X				
27,121	Select ribbon band 1			X				
Graphics Modes:								
27,75	480-dot bit-image graphics		X					X
27,75	560-dot bit-image graphics				X			
27,75	1108 dot bit-image graphics			X				
27,76	960-dot bit-image graphics		X					X
27,76	2216-dot bit-image graphics			X				
27,89	960-dot normal speed		X					X
27,89	2216-dot bit-image graphics			X				
27,90	1920-dot bit-image graphics		X					X
27,90	4432-dot bit-image graphics			X				
27,91	Set image resolution/color					X		
27,110	Set aspect ratio			X				
Miscellaneous:								
7	Bell	X	X	X			X	X
17	Select printer	X		X		X	X	X
19	Deselect printer	X		X		X	X	
24	Clear buffer	X	X	X	X	X	X	X
27,81	Deselect specific printer			X				X

Section 3: Send Data to the Printer

Sending data to the printer is trivial in high-level languages, and there are several operating system functions that make it easy for assembly language programs as well. Low-level programming requires more work, but it allows more options. Generally, a low-level print routine sends a character to the printer and then constantly monitors the input status register of the serial port to which the printer is attached. The next character is sent only when the printer signals that it is ready (the printer may not actually print the character at once—it may save it in the printer's own buffer until a line's worth of characters has been received).

In addition, low-level routines may use the *printer interrupt*, or they may simulate the action of this interrupt. Through special programming the printer can be made to interrupt the CPU when it is ready for another character. The interrupt routine quickly sends the next character along its way, and then the CPU returns to its other chores. This method is used for *background printing* (also known as spooling). Because the physical motions of the printer are so slow compared to the speed of the computer's electronics, the output of characters to the printer takes up only a few percent of the CPU's time. The interrupt lets the remaining time be used productively.

While sending data to a printer is a fairly simple bit of programming, setting up the output data can be terribly complex. Most of the extraordinary feats we are accustomed to seeing printers perform are accomplished by combining text and graphics data with the various printer codes discussed earlier in this chapter. By combining text and graphics modes on the same line, right justification and proportional spacing are made possible. In addition, any graphics printer can create special characters of any design, and by careful manipulation of line spacing and overstriking, any of the IBM block characters may be printed.

6.3.1 Output text or graphics data to the printer

The CPU may devote its full attention to sending data to the printer, or it may print "in the background" by using the printer interrupt. A third alternative is to have the program send characters to the printer at regular intervals, as a sort of "pseudo-interrupt." This method is not as closely coordinated with the printer's operations as true interrupts; but printer operations, after all, are not time-dependent.

No matter how the data is output, just one character is sent to the printer at a time. High-level languages provide functions that appear to send whole strings of data at once, but these functions break the strings down into individually transmitted characters. Usually high-level languages send a carriage return/line feed pair after each string. Assembly language programs, on the other hand, must set up all of this. The cost is that there is more coding to do, but the benefit is that there is more flexibility, particularly with error checking.

High Level ────────────────────────────────

BASIC provides the LPRINT and PRINT# statements for sending data to a printer. LPRINT requires no special preparation, but PRINT# requires that the printer be opened just like a file, using the statement **OPEN "LPT1" AS #1**, or **OPEN "LPT3" AS #2**, or whatever. The LPRINT statement always addresses LPT1, whereas PRINT# can address any printer number.

A carriage return/line feed pair is automatically inserted after every LPRINT and PRINT# statement, unless the statement is followed by a semicolon. To avoid inadvertent line feeds, make it a habit to follow all control sequences with a semicolon. Do the same for any strings of text you want printed adjacent to one another. Be aware, however, that many printers do not begin printing until they have received data for a whole line. This is signaled either by a carriage return or by 80 characters (or whatever) having been received. Be sure to send a final carriage return to "flush" the last characters from the printer's buffer.

The printer automatically wraps around from the end of the line. The default width of a printer line is 80 columns, but full-width printers may use more. Lines written with compressed or expanded characters may also require a change of the printer width. To change the number of columns printed before the print head wraps around, write **WIDTH "LPT1:",n**, where n is the desired number of columns. When a string is printed that is as long as the line length, or longer, the print head wraps around, effectively performing a carriage return/line feed. This means that when the string length exactly matches the line length, a second line feed is make if the string is followed by a carriage return/line feed pair.

In graphics printing the printer is ordinarily set to "infinite width." To bring this about, set the width to 255 by writing **WIDTH "LPT1:",255**. If you fail to include this statement, when a long stream of graphics data is output, after every 80 bit patterns are printed BASIC will insert the patterns for the line feed and carriage return characters. These extra characters will be counted in the tally of data bytes for the graphics statement so that subsequent printer statements will be thrown off.

A single LPRINT statement may contain several data items in a variety of forms. The information may be written into the statement itself, as in **LPRINT"The Rain In Spain"**, or it may be referred to by variable names, as in (X$ = "The Rain In Spain":LPRINT X$). Special characters may be included by using CHR$. Control sequences are normally sent this way; for example, **LPRINT CHR$(10)** sends a line feed control code to the printer. CHR$ is most often used for ASCII codes that are not represented by a common (keyboard) symbol. All kinds of data can be combined in the same statement. Place semicolons between the items to have the items printed adjacent to one another, or use commas to have each item begin at the next tab position. This is to say that an LPRINT statement is printed exactly as a similarly formatted PRINT statement would be displayed on the screen. Here are some examples:

```
100 LPRINT S$;" and ";Y$              'combines three strings
110 LPRINT X,Y,Z                      '3 numbers spaced as on screen
120 LPRINT "The total is ";X          'combines string and numeric values
130 LPRINT "The ";CHR$(27);CHR$(45);CHR$(1);"real";
                  CHR$(27);CHR$(45);CHR$(0);" thing."
                                      'underlines the middle word
```

The PRINT# statement can use the same data types as LPRINT, and it also can include many data items in one statement and can mix data of different types. Semicolons and commas operate in the same fashion. Here are some examples that parallel those above:

```
100 OPEN "LPT1:" AS #2
110 PRINT#2,S$;" and ";Y$
120 PRINT#2,X,Y,Z
130 PRINT#2,"The total is ";X
140 PRINT#2,"The ";CHR$(27);CHR$(45);CHR$(1);"real";
                  CHR$(27);CHR$(45);CHR$(0);" thing."
```

Middle Level

Function 0 of INT 17H sends one character to the printer. Place the character in AL and the printer number in DX. On return AH holds a status register that should constantly be monitored to detect printer errors. [6.1.3] explains how to do this. To output a stream of data, set a pointer to the buffer holding the data, and write a routine like this:

```
;---OUTPUT DATA TO LPT1:
                MOV   CX,NUMBER_CHARS     ;CX counts number bytes output
                MOV   DX,0                ;choose LPT1
    NEXT_CHAR:  MOV   AH,0                ;function to send 1 byte to printer
                MOV   AL,[BX]             ;BX points to data buffer
                INT   17H                 ;send the character
                TEST  AH,8                ;test error bit
                JNZ   PRNTR_ERROR         ;if problem, jump to recovery routine
                INC   BX                  ;increment data pointer
                LOOP  NEXT_CHAR           ;go get next byte
```

The standard DOS interrupt for printer output is function 5 of INT 21H. Simply place the character in DL and call the function. It always accesses LPT1, and there are no return registers.

```
;---OUTPUT DATA TO LPT1:
            MOV   AH,5                ;DOS function number
            MOV   DL,CHAR             ;move output character to DL
            INT   21H                 ;send it
```

Another way to output data to the printer is by function 40H of INT 21H. This function is the standard output function used by the *file handle* method of access to a file or device [5.3.0]. In this case, the function uses a special, ready-made handle (identification number) for the printer. This number is 0004, and it is placed in BX. The function only accesses LPT1, so to use a different printer you will need to switch the base addresses [6.1.4]. DS:DX points to the output data, and CX holds the number of bytes to send. For example:

```
;---OUTPUT 120 BYTES OF DATA TO LPT1:
            MOV   AH,40H               ;function number
            MOV   BX,4                 ;predefined handle for printer
            MOV   CX,120               ;number of bytes to send
            LEA   DX,PTR_DATA          ;point DS:DX to the data
            INT   21H                  ;send the data
            JC    PRTR_ERROR           ;jump to recovery routine if error
```

On return the carry flag is set if there has been an error, in which case AX holds 5 if the printer was off line, or 6 if you used the wrong handle number. Note that there is no need to *open* a device when a pre-defined handle is used.

Low Level

A byte of data is sent to the printer by placing it in the *output data register*, the port address of which is the same as the base address for the printer. Remember that the base addresses for LPT1-3 are the port addresses found at offsets 8, 10, and 12 in the BIOS data area (beginning at 0040:0000). Once the data is sent to the register, briefly turn on the *strobe* bit of the output control register, which is located at the port address that is 2 higher than the data register. The strobe bit is number 0, and it need be set to 1 only very briefly to initiate transmission of the data in the data register. The print routine may *immediately* change the strobe bit back to 0.

Once the byte of data is sent, the program must wait for the printer to signal that it is ready for another. This is done in two ways. When ready, the printer briefly pulses the *acknowledge bit* of the input status register. This register is located at the port address that is 1 greater than the base address of the printer. The acknowledge bit is number 6, and it normally is set to 1. The acknowledge pulse sets the bit to 0 long enough that an assembly language program is sure to catch it if it constantly monitors the register.

An alternative way of knowing that the printer is ready for another byte of data is to constantly monitor bit 7 of the status register, which is set to 0 when the printer is busy and to 1 when it is free to receive data. If you write a low-level print routine in interpreted BASIC or some other very slow language, use this method.

The following example checks the BIOS data area for the base address of LPT1, and then it writes data from a buffer pointed to by BX. The program monitors the status register for its busy signal, and at the same time it checks bit 3 to see if there has been a printer error.

```
;---GET READY:
                MOV   AX,40H              ;point ES to bottom of BIOS data area
                MOV   ES,AX               ;
                MOV   DX,ES:[8]           ;put base address of LPT1 in DX
                MOV   BX,DATA_START       ;BX points to data buffer
;---SEND A CHARACTER:
     NEXTCHAR:  MOV   AL,[BX]             ;place character in AL
                OUT   DX,AL               ;send the character
                INC   DX                  ;point DX to output control register
                INC   DX                  ;
                MOV   AL,13               ;bit pattern to pulse strobe line
                OUT   DX,AL               ;send the strobe signal
                DEC   AL                  ;normal bit pattern for control reg
                OUT   DX,AL               ;turn off strobe signal
;---CHECK FOR ERRORS, WAIT TILL PRINTER READY:
                DEC   DX                  ;point DX to status register
     NOT_YET:   IN    AL,DX               ;get status byte
                TEST  AL,8                ;error?
                JZ    PRTR_ERROR          ;jump to error routine if a problem
                TEST  AL,80H              ;printer busy?
                JZ    NOT_YET             ;if so, loop
                INC   BX                  ;printer ready, increment data pointer
                DEC   DX                  ;point DX to data register
                JMP   NEXTCHAR            ;go print next character
```

When bit 4 of the printer control register is set to 1, the printer interrupt is enabled. When interrupts are used, a program does not have to wait for a "not busy" signal from the printer by continuously monitoring the printer status register. Instead, a program may send a character to the printer and then go about some other business; when the printer is ready for the next character, it sends an acknowledge signal (bit 6 of the status register is briefly set to 1), and the printer interrupt is automatically invoked. The interrupt routine sends the next character to the printer and returns, whereupon the main program continues along its way until it is again interrupted for a character. When the output data is exhausted, the interrupt must shut itself off. The printer interrupt is set up much like the communications interrupt, which is discussed at [7.1.8].

Unfortunately, a design flaw makes the interrupt feature of the first printer adaptors unreliable. On some cards it works and on others it does not. Only in the case of the AT's serial/parallel card can you always trust it. Instead, use the timer interrupt, as explained at [2.1.7]. Set the 8253 timer chip so that the interrupt occurs at a rate somewhat slower than the rate at which the printer can handle data. Then write an interrupt handler that sends a character to the printer each time the time-of-day interrupt occurs. In order to ensure proper synchronization, have the routine check the "printer busy" bit of the status register (bit 7), and if indeed the printer is still busy, have the routine return without sending a new character.

6.3.2 Right justify text

True right justification entails dividing the extra space at the end of a line so that it is distributed equally between all words. Some printers have a special mode that automatically performs justification. The IBM Color Printer has this capability; sending **27,77,0** causes on-board circuitry to interpret the incoming data and format it perfectly. Otherwise, a printer must vary the width of the spaces between words by switching into a graphics mode when it prints a space character. In graphics modes the space widths can be adjusted by one-sixth or less of a character width. Unfortunately, many printers very briefly stall while changing between text and graphics modes, so this method can be very slow. An alternate approach is to make spaces using the usual ASCII 32 character, dispersing the extra spaces as evenly as possible across the line. The more difficult graphics approach is shown here.

The steps to formatting a right justified line of text are as follows. First, the number of columns in the line must be calculated from the page format settings. Then the number of characters required by each successive word is entered into a tally that includes the spaces between the words. A separate count is kept of the number of spaces. When the talley comes to exceed **80** (or whatever width the printer is using), then the last incomplete word is eliminated from the talley, along with its preceding space. The number of excess columns in the line is multiplied by 6, which is the number of horizontal dots in a character, and the resulting number is divided by the number of spaces between the words.

After each word is printed, the printer is set to 480 dots-per-line graphics mode, and it sends a number of bytes of ASCII 0. Each byte moves the print head one dot rightwards. The number sent should be 6 for the ordinary space, plus the result of the division of the extra space. Finally, if the remainder of the division is not 0, send one extra byte of 0 to each space until the remainder is exhausted.

In summary, consider a case in which a particular line contains twelve words, totaling 61 letters, plus eleven spaces between the words. This leaves eight columns unused in an 80-character line. The eight columns are multiplied by six to give 48 dots worth of horizontal space. Since there are eleven spaces in the line, each space may be given four extra dots of space, and there still remain four surplus dots, one of which is added to each of the first four spaces. The first four spaces have six dots for the normal spacing, plus five extra, equalling eleven. The other spaces are ten dots wide. To send this data to the printer, set up code that sends a single ASCII 0 byte and place it in a loop that repeats as many times as there are bytes of 0 required. Figure 6-2 illustrates this process.

The example below shows the basics of right justification. Take care to provide code for special cases, such as single "words" that are longer than one line (e.g., a long string of dashes). The routines also need modification to deal with the situation in which there are only a few words on a line, as at a paragraph ending. Don't allow these words to be spread across the full width of the page.

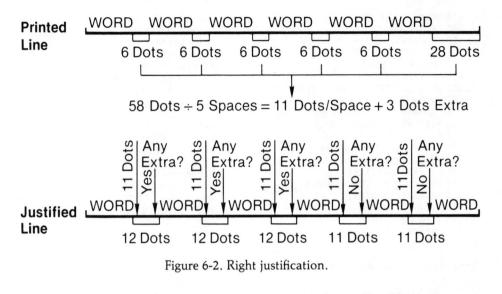

Figure 6-2. Right justification.

High Level

In this example, BUFFERPTR points to the point in a data buffer from which the next line of output begins.

```
100 S$="This text will be printed with right justification using the printer
    alternately in text modes and graphics modes."
110 STRINGPTR=1                      'points to the data string S$
120 COLUMNS=1                        'counts column positions 1-80
130 SPACES=0                         'counts number of spaces in the line
140 '''figure out how many words will fit on a line
150 C$=MID$(S$,STRINGPTR,1)          'get a character
160 IF C$<>' ' THEN 190              'if not a space, jump ahead
170 LASTSPACE=COLUMNS                'if a space, keep track of position
180 SPACES=SPACES+1                  'add 1 to tally of spaces
190 COLUMNS=COLUMNS+1                'increment column pointer
200 STRINGPTR=STRINGPTR+1            'increment data pointer
210 IF COLUMNS=81 THEN 230          'jump ahead if end of line
220 GOTO 150                        'otherwise, go get next character
230 IF C$<>' ' THEN 270             'if last char not a space, jump ahead
240 COLUMNS=79                      'else, line length is 79 chars
250 SPACES=SPACES-1                 'don't count the last space
260 GOTO 340                        'go figure spacing
270 C$=MID$(S$,STRINGPTR+1,1)       'test if col 80 is last char of word
280 IF C$<>' ' THEN 300             'next char will be spc if so, else jump
290 GOTO 340                        'if so, go figure spacing
300 COLUMNS=COLUMNS-LASTSPACE       'col 80 is mid-word, backtrack
310 STRINGPTR=STRINGPTR-COLUMNS+1   'set back data pointer for next line
320 COLUMNS=LASTSPACE-1             'number columns is 1 less than last spc
330 SPACES=SPACES-1                 'decrement tally of spaces
340 '''figure out number of dots per space
350 EXTRASPACES=80-COLUMNS          'figure extra spaces at line end
360 TOTALSPACES=EXTRASPACES+SPACES  'add in spaces between words
370 TOTALDOTS=6*TOTALSPACES         'multiply by 6 dots per space
380 DOTSPERSPC=TOTALDOTS\SPACES     'divide by spaces and get quotient
390 EXTRADOTS=TOTALDOTS MOD SPACES  'divide by spaces and get remainder
400 '''now print out the first line of the string
```

```
410 OPEN "LPT1:" AS #1                          'open printer
420 PRINTPTR=1                                  'points from start of data buffer
430 C$=MID$(S$,PRINTPTR,1)                       'get a character
440 PRINTPTR=PRINTPTR+1                          'increment pointer
450 IF C$=" " THEN 500                           'if a space, jump to spacing routine
460 PRINT#1,C$;                                  'otherwise, print the character
470 IF PRINTPTR=COLUMNS+1 THEN 590               'if end of line, quit
480 GOTO 430                                     'otherwise, go get next character
490 '''here is the spacing routine
500 PRINT#1,CHR$(27)+"K";                        'switch to 480-dot graphics mode
510 NUMBERDOTS=DOTSPERSPC                        'NUMBERDOTS sets number 0's sent
520 IF EXTRADOTS=0 THEN 550                      'if no extra dots, jump ahead
530 NUMBERDOTS=DOTSPERSPC+1                      'else add an extra dot
540 EXTRADOTS=EXTRADOTS-1                        'decrement tally of extra dots
550 PRINT#1,CHR$(NUMBERDOTS);                    'send number of graphics chars (low)
560 PRINT#1,CHR$(0);                             'send number of graphics chars (high)
570 FOR N=1 TO NUMBERDOTS:PRINT#1,CHR$(0);:NEXT   'send graphics 0's
580 GOTO 430                                     'space finished, go get next char
590 PRINT#1,CHR$(13)                             'at very end, send carriage return
```

Low Level

The corresponding assembly language routine is too long to include here. It would work much as the BASIC example above, except that there is no need to set up a separate string variable to hold the line. Just set pointers within the data buffer to the beginning and end of the line that will be printed.

6.3.3 Proportionally space text

Generally speaking, proportional spacing requires a special printer that contains information in its ROM about the width of each character. The IBM Color Printer has a proportional spacing mode which is turned on by the sequence **27,78,1**, and turned off by **27,78,0**. A program that formats output to the printer in this mode must know the width of each character (found in the documentation). With this data it can calculate how many unbroken words can be fit onto a line.

Be cautioned that some dot matrix printers automatically double-strike proportional text. If the words in a line are separated by extra graphics-mode spacing, the printer may go back for the second pass after each word, rather than doing the whole line at once. Since printers are relatively slow when changing the direction in which the head travels, in this case right justified proportional text can take a very long time to print out, and it can place undue wear on the printer. This problem does not apply to single-strike proportional spacing. Note that the IBM color printer can automatically combine proportional spacing with its automatic justification feature so that no special coding is required.

Ambitious programmers can cause *any* graphics printer to perform proportional spacing. The program must store in memory the bit patterns of each character (see [6.3.4]). Rather than send ASCII codes to the printer, which call on the character data held in the printer's ROMs, the bit patterns are used to construct a graphics image of a line of text. Then the entire string of data is output in a graphics mode. This approach requires a good deal of memory to hold the character data, but it allows precise control of the printed image.

High Level ────────────────────────────

This example turns on proportional mode and prints the first line of a program's output data. The widths of the proportional font are read into the array FONTWIDTH from a sequential file.

```
100 '''''read in the array of font widths
110 DIM FONTWIDTH(127)                            'array to hold font widths
120 OPEN "FONTS" FOR INPUT AS #1                  'open file holding widths
130 FOR N=32 to 127                               'file has codes for ASCII 32-127
140 INPUT #1,FONTWIDTH(N)                         'read a width into the array
150 NEXT                                          'next width
160 '''''figure out how many characters can fit on the line:
170 CHARPTR=0                                     'CHARPTR points to buffer
180 LINE$=''''                                    'holds data for 1 line
190 LINELENGTH=0                                  'counts length up to 480 dots
200 WHILE LINELENGTH<480                          'keep adding chars until line full
210 C$=PEEK(BUFFERPTR+CHARPTR)                    'get character from data buffer
220 LINELENGTH=LINELENGTH+FONTWIDTH(ASC(C$))      'add char width to tally
230 LINE$=LINE$+C$                                'add character to LINE$
240 CHARPTR=CHARPTR+1                             'increment the character pointer
250 WEND                                          'go get next character from buffer
260 '''''end of line, search LINE$ backwards until end of last word found
270 IF C$='' '' THEN 310                          'last char a space? if so, jump
280 FOR N=LEN(LINE$) TO 1 STEP -1                 'search backwards from end of line
290 IF MID$(LINE$,N,1)='' '' THEN 310             'is character a space?
300 NEXT                                          'if not, go get next
```

```
310 LINELENGTH=N-1                          'if so, prior char is the end of line
320 '''''initialize proportional spacing and send data
330 LPRINT CHR$(27);CHR$(78);CHR$(1);       'code to start proportional spacing
340 FOR N=1 TO LINELENGTH                   'for each character
350 LPRINT PEEK(BUFFERPTR+N-1);             'print it
360 NEXT                                    'go get the next character
```

Low Level

An assembly language program would work in much the same way as the BASIC example above. One advantage in assembly is that the XLAT instruction is available to facilitate the look-up of the character widths. Place the character in AL, point DS:BX to the table, and invoke XLAT. The character width will be returned in AL:

```
;---LOOK UP THE CHARACTER WIDTH:
                LEA   SI,DATA_BUFFER        ;point to printer data
                LEA   BX,WIDTH_TABLE        ;point to character width table
                MOV   AL,[SI]               ;get a byte of data
                XLAT  WIDTH_TABLE           ;place its proportional width in AL
                                            ;etc...
```

6.3.4 Print special characters

Most printers do not support the full IBM character set, yet most programs use the special block graphics characters. It can be very useful to be able to print these characters, and it is not terribly difficult to do so on any dot matrix printer that has graphics capability. Rather than rely on the printer's ROM for the data with which to create the character, the print program itself must contain this information, and it must manipulate the printer in special ways to get it on to the page.

Printing special characters in itself is trivial. Simply break down the character into six bytes in which the bit patterns correspond to the dot patterns of the six columns of dots that make up a character. For example, to print the horizontal double-line character, ASCII 205, a program must output the bit pattern **00100100** six times in 480-dots-per-line mode. This amounts to exactly one character width, since 6/480 equals 1/80th of a line. To invoke this particular graphics mode, send **27,75**. Then send the number of bytes of graphics data coming, using two bytes with the low byte first: **6,0**. Finally, send six bytes of the pattern itself, which in this case is the sum of the values of bits 2 and 5 (4 + 32 = 36). The entire sequence is **27,75,6,0,36,36,36,36,36,36**. More precise graphics modes may be used for finer resolution; generally the extra overhead in computing time is negligible relative to the speed of printer operations.

There is a special problem when block graphics characters must connect vertically one to another. Printers normally print a line of eight-dot columns, then skip downwards by twelve dots, so that a four-dot margin is left between the lines of characters. Block characters must print across the margin, and in some cases a single character is twelve dots high. Because most print heads have only eight pins, the only solution to this problem is to make two passes to form the character, moving the paper forward before the second pass. In this case, the line feed character (ASCII 10) is not used at all. Rather, the printer alternates between making special four-dot spacings and then eight-dot spacings. During the second pass half of the pins will overlap where dots have already been printed, and each of these pins must always be sent 0 so that they do not fire.

To forward the paper by four dots, send the sequence **27,65,4,27,50**, and to forward it by eight dots, send **27,65,8,27,50**. An automatic carriage return results. While the first pass occurs, create a temporary line of text that is to be printed during the second pass. If a character is an ordinary one, place a space character (ASCII 32) in the corresponding position of the temporary second line. But where the character is a special graphics character that prints across the four-dot margin, place its ASCII code in the matching second-line position. For example:

Character position:	1	2	3	4	5	6	7	8	9	10
ASCII code:	205	32	98	111	114	105	110	103	32	205
2nd line code:	205	32	32	32	32	32	32	32	32	205

A separate table must be kept of the dot patterns for the second pass. For a doubled descending line, the table contents for the first pass would be 0,255,0,255,0,0, and for the second pass it would be 0,15,0,15,0,0. Note that in the second and fourth bytes of the second-pass code, the top four bits are left 0 to avoid overstriking.

In summary, when printing begins, the first character is checked to see if it is a special graphics character, and, if not, it is simply sent to the printer as an ASCII code. A space character is entered in the temporary string used for the second pass. Then the next character is processed. When a graphics character appears, the six bytes that encode it are looked up in a table, and the printer enters 480-dot graphics mode, initializes for six bytes, and then sends the data. The printer then automatically reverts to character mode. The corresponding position in the second-pass string is given the ASCII code of the graphics character. This process continues until the end of the line, then a four-dot line feed is ordered. In the second pass, each character is again considered in turn. If it is a space, then print the space character (that is, print nothing at all, but forward the print head). And if it is a graphics character, look up the second-pass code in a separate table and print it using the same graphics technique used for the first pass. Reuse the second-pass string for each line of print. Figure 6-3 diagrams this procedure.

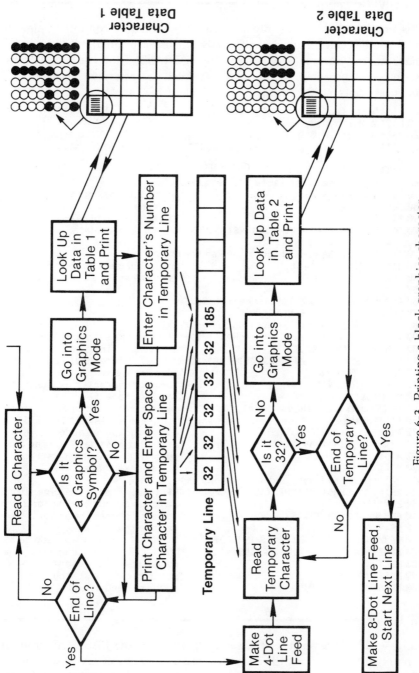

Figure 6-3. Printing a block-graphics character.

High Level

This example divides text into two columns so that a continuous line divides them down the center. For simplicity, only one line is printed, but the example can be made to print a whole page by creating a FOR/NEXT loop at lines 325 and 505. To show two approaches, the first pass is printed character by character, while the second pass prints out the entire line as a single string.

```
100 '''''data table for first pass (ASCII chars 179 and 180 only)
110 DATA 0,0,255,0,0,0
120 DATA 4,4,255,0,0,0
130 '''''data table for second pass (ASCII chars 179 and 180 only)
140 DATA 0,0,15,0,0,0
150 DATA 0,0,15,0,0,0
160 '''''place the first table into an array
170 DIM FIRSTPASS$(45)                  'holds 1st-pass data for special chars
180 FOR N=1 TO 2                        'fill the array
190 Y$=''''                             'Y$ takes all 6 bytes per character
200 FOR M=1 TO 6:READ X:Y$=Y$+CHR$(X):NEXT        'read data
210 FIRSTPASS$(N)=Y$:NEXT                         'place in array
220 '''''place the second table into an array
230 DIM SECONDPASS$(45)                 'holds 2nd-pass data for special chars
240 FOR N=1 TO 2                        'fill the array as above
250 Y$=""
260 FOR M=1 TO 6:READ X:Y$=Y$+CHR$(X):NEXT
270 SECONDPASS$(N)=Y$:NEXT
280 '''''print the text in the following string
290 TEXT$="Here is one column "+CHR$(179)+" Here is the second column"
300 TEMP$=STRING$(80,32)                'create a string of spaces for pass 2
310 GRAPHICS$=CHR$(27)+CHR$(75)+CHR$(6)+CHR$(0)   'graphics mode control string
320 OPEN "LPT1:" AS #1                  'open printer
330 FOR N=1 TO LEN(TEXT$)               'for each character of the text...
340 C$=MID$(TEXT$,N,1)                  'get the character
350 IF C$<CHR$(128) THEN PRINT#1,C$;:GOTO 400   'if not special, print, get next
360 '''''assume any other characters are block graphics (ASCII 179-223)
370 PRINT #1,GRAPHICS$;                 'go into graphics mode
380 PRINT #1,FIRSTPASS$(ASC(C$)-178);   'print 1st pass data for the character
390 MID$(TEMP$,N)=C$                    'put marker in 2nd pass string
400 NEXT                                'go get next character
410 '''''space by 8 dots and make second pass
420 PRINT #1,CHR$(27)+CHR$(65)+CHR$(4)+CHR$(141);  'make the line spacing
430 Z$=''''                             'Z$ holds output string for 2nd pass
440 FOR N=1 TO LEN(TEXT$)               'for each character of text...
450 C$=MID$(TEMP$,N,1)                  'get the character
460 IF C$=CHR$(32) THEN Z$=Z$+" ":GOTO 480        'if a space, add to string
470 Z$=Z$+GRAPHICS$+SECONDPASS$(ASC(C$)-178)      'else add special char sequence
480 NEXT                                'go get next character
490 PRINT #1,Z$                         'print the whole string
500 PRINT #1,CHR$(10);                  'add line feed at end
```

Low Level

An assembly program uses the same algorithm as the BASIC program above. When only a few of the ASCII characters are used, you can save space by creating a table that compresses them together, so that their positions in the table are not proportional to their positions in the ASCII set. Then set up a small table using the XLAT instruction and have it provide the index used to find character data in the data table.

6.3.5 Perform screen dumps

A text screen dump is simple enough if all of the characters used are contained in the printer's ROM and if none are shown on the screen in special attributes, such as with an underline or in reverse image. In this simplest case a program needs only to set the printer width to 80 characters and then read the characters from the video buffer one-by-one, sending them as an unbroken data stream to the printer. If the printer ROMs lack special characters, such as the IBM block graphics characters, then a program must set up its own data table for the characters and output them to the printer in graphics mode. Because these characters may connect across line spacings, special programming is required [6.3.4].

Special character attributes each have their own problems. Check the attribute of each character as it is read from the video buffer ([4.1.3] discusses the bit patterns for the various attributes). When a character is underlined or intensified, turn on and off the printer's underline or boldface modes. If the character is reverse-image, however, the same problem arises as with many of the block graphics characters: the reverse-image area should descend to the top edge of the line below. Follow the prescriptions given at [6.3.4], and fill in solid dots on the second pass. Depending on the printer, you may need to create special character data tables for reverse image characters, since when they are printed, the surrounding dots may be too close to each other, obscuring the dark area that forms the character. Double-striking is out of the question in this case. A simple solution to the reverse-image problem is to use a graphics mode to display a text screen, then use one of the printer's graphics modes to dump the screen.

Graphics dumps present another sort of difficulty. A byte of printer data represents eight vertical dots. But a byte of video graphics data represents eight horizontal dots. A conversion routine is required, as shown in Figure 6-4. Fetch eight bytes at a time from the screen, taking those that correspond to an 8-by-8 dot area. Then use logical operators to move the bits, as shown in the examples below.

Be aware that most dot matrix printers distort the screen image. This is because they tend to use a 1:1 aspect ratio, while the screen uses 5:6 (the aspect ratio compares the number of horizontal dots per inch to the number of vertical dots per inch). Correctly speaking, it is actually the screen's aspect ratio that creates the image distortion, since programs must alter the data for the image so that it will appear as it should (a circle on the screen, for example, is created by the mathematical image of an ellipse). When the video data is dumped onto a printer, these adjustments must be reversed. Some printers have special graphics modes that can print out the screen image without distortion, and the IBM color printer can alter the aspect ratio of *any* of its graphics modes.

High Level

This BASIC routine prints a simple copy of a text screen, ignoring special attributes:

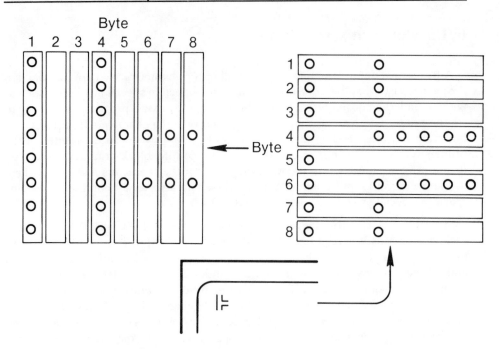

Figure 6-4. A graphics screen dump of one character cell.

```
10 OPEN "LPT1:" AS #1              'open the printer
20 DEF SEG=&HB000                  'point to the monochrome video buffer
30 PRINT #1, CHR$(13)              'reset print head to left
40 FOR G=0 TO 3998 STEP 2          'for every other byte of buffer...
50 PRINT #1,CHR$(PEEK(G));         'read it and print it
60 NEXT                            'next byte
```

Rearranging the bit patterns for a graphics dump is time consuming in BASIC. Place in an array (here, BYTE$) the eight bytes from an 8-by-8 dot block of screen area. Create a second array (VERTICAL$) and initialize its elements to 0, then change the bits of its elements 1-by-1, as follows:

```
500 FOR M=0 to 7                   'for every bit...
510 FOR N=0 TO 7                   'of every byte...
520 X=ASC(BYTE$(N))                'get the value of the byte
530 Y=2(7-M)                       'make a mask with 1 bit turned on
540 Z=X AND Y                      'see if that bit is on in the byte
550 IF Z<>0 THEN VERTICAL$(M)=CHR$(ASC(VERTICAL$(M)) OR 2 N)
                                   'if so, turn on the same bit in
                                   '  the corresponding position in the
                                   '  second array
560 NEXT N                         'next bit
570 NEXT M                         'next byte
```

Low Level

Assembly language can make the bit conversions much more quickly. Here is a routine that is terribly fast because it keeps everything on the chip (it also is a little large—you might want to write up the BASIC algorithm shown above instead). The routine works by keeping the eight *result* bytes in the CX, DX, BP, and DI registers. A byte of screen data is placed in AL, and then CL, CH, DL, and DH are moved in sequence into AH. A single bit is shifted from AL into AH each time, and when four shifts have been made, CX and DX are exchanged with DX and BP, and then it is all done again. This process is repeated for each of the eight screen bytes, and when it is complete, the converted image is held on the chip registers, with the leftmost byte of printer data in CL. These are dumped on to the printer and reinitialized to 0, and then the process starts all over again with another eight bytes from the screen. To begin with, fetch the eight bytes from the screen and place them in a buffer called BUFFER. Place 0 in AX, CX, DX, BP, and DI. Then:

```
                    LEA    BX,BUFFER          ;point to video data buffer
                    MOV    SI,0               ;points to offset in buffer
GET_BYTE:           MOV    AL,[BX][SI]        ;fetch a byte
DO_HALF:            XCHG   AH,CL              ;get CL, CH, DL, and DH,
                    SHL    AX,1               ; shifting a bit from AL
                    XCHG   AH,CL              ;
                    XCHG   AH,CH              ;
                    SHL    AX,1               ;
                    XCHG   AH,CH              ;
                    XCHG   AH,DL              ;
                    SHL    AX,1               ;
                    XCHG   AH,DH              ;
                    XCHG   AH,DH              ;
                    SHL    AX,1               ;
                    XCHG   AH,DH              ;
;---BEGIN SECOND HALF OF THE BIT MOVES:
                    XCHG   CX,BP              ;switch CX and DX contents
                    XCHG   DX,DI              ;
                    CMP    SI,7               ;if all bytes converted, print
                    JE     PRINT_BYTES        ;
                    INC    SI                 ;otherwise point to next byte
                    JMP    SHORT GET_BYTE     ;go get it
;---PRINT THE BYTES:
PRINT_BYTES:        PUSH   DX                 ;save DX
                    MOV    AH,5               ;DOS printer output function
                    MOV    DL,27              ;escape code
                    INT    21H                ;send it
                    MOV    DL,75              ;graphics mode code
                    INT    21H                ;send it
                    MOV    DL,6               ;will send 6 bytes
                    INT    21H                ;
                    MOV    DL,0               ;
                    INT    21H                ;
                    CALL   PRINT_2_BYTES      ;send contents of CX
                    POP    CX                 ;
                    CALL   PRINT_2_BYTES      ;send former contents of DX
                    MOV    CX,BP              ;
                    CALL   PRINT_2_BYTES      ;send BP contents
                    MOV    DX,DI              ;
                    CALL   PRINT_2_BYTES      ;send DI contents
                    .
                    .
        (go do next group of eight bytes)
                    .
                    .
```

```
PRINT_2_BYTES  PROC NEAR
               MOV  AH,5              ;DOS print function
               MOV  DL,CL             ;CL first
               INT  21H               ;print it
               MOV  DL,CH             ;CH next
               INT  21H               ;print it
               RET
PRINT_2_BYTES  ENDP
```

7
Input/Output

Section 1: Access a Serial Port

In asynchronous communications, the machine sends or receives bytes of information one bit at a time. The timing *between* the bytes of data is not important, but the timing of the sequence of bits that make up a byte is critical. The signal on the line goes high and low, corresponding to logical 1s and Øs, and the line is said to be *marking* when the level is high (= 1) and to be *spacing* when the level is low (= Ø).

The line is held in the marking condition whenever it is not transferring data. At the onset of the transmission of a byte of data, the signal drops to Ø during the *start bit.* Then the eight bits of data (sometimes fewer) follow as a pattern of highs and lows. The last data bit is optionally followed by a *parity bit* used in error detection, and then the sequence concludes with 1 or more stop bits, which are comprised of a high signal. These stop bit(s) begin the marking state that continues until the transmission of the next byte of data begins; the number of stop bits used is significant because they set the *minimum* amount of time that must pass before the next start bit. Figure 7-1 diagrams this sequence.

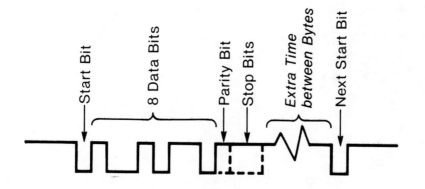

Figure 7-1. The transmission of one byte of serial data.

Of course, both the transmitting and receiving stations must use the same protocol for these bit patterns, and they must operate at the same transmission speed (measured in bits per second (bps), also referred to as *baud*). Errors can easily occur, and the serial hardware offers a variety of status information, both for the port itself, and for the modem that the port is connected to. The modem's job is to convert the signal generated by the serial port into an acoustic signal that can be transmitted across phone lines. Most modems also provide a number of advanced communications features, such as automatic dialing and answering, most of which are not supported by the serial port itself.

7.1.1 Program the 8250 UART chip

Serial communications is so complicated that special chips have been designed to do the work of forming and timing the strings of bits that comprise serial data. Such a chip is called a *universal asynchronous receiver transmitter*, or UART. Without UARTs, communications programming would be extremely complicated. The IBM microcomputers user the Intel 8250 UART.

DOS supports two communications ports, and hence two UARTS. Their base addresses are kept at 0040:0000 for COM1 and 0040:0002 for COM2. (A base address is the lowest two-byte port address of the group of port addresses by which the UART is accessed). On all machines but the PCjr, COM1 starts at 3F8H and COM2 at 2F8H; the PCjr keeps its internal modem at 3F8H and COM1 at 2F8H. For convenience, the discussion here refers to the registers numbered 3FxH, but the same specifications apply to the registers at 2FxH.

The 8250 has ten programmable one-byte registers by which to control and monitor the serial port. Most are devoted to initializing the port, a process that can be rather complicated. The ten registers are accessed through seven port addresses, numbers 3F8H - 3FEH (or 2F8H - 2FEH). In five cases, the register accessed at a particular port address depends on how bit 7 is set in the *line control register*, which is the only register at port 3FBH. Here are the registers:

```
3F8H (OUT, bit 7=0 at 3FBH)     Transmitter Holding Register
3F8H (IN, bit 7=0 at 3FBH)      Receiver Data Register
3F8H (OUT, bit 7=1 at 3FBH)     Baud-Rate Divisor (low byte)
3F9H (IN, bit 7=1 at 3FBH)      Baud-Rate Divisor (high byte)
3F9H (OUT, bit 7=0 at 3FBH)     Interrupt Enable Register
3FAH (IN)                       Interrupt Identification Register
3FBH (OUT)                      Line Control Register
3FCH (OUT)                      Modem Control Register
3FDH (IN)                       Line Status Register
3FEH (IN)                       Modem Status Register
```

Of the ten registers, only six are necessary for simple serial communications. The *transmitter holding* register holds the byte of data about to be sent [7.1.6], and the *receiver data* register keeps the most recently received byte of data [7.1.7]. The *line control* and *line status* registers initialize and monitor the serial line, using the baud rate placed in the two baud-rate divisor registers [7.1.2]. Of the remaining four registers, the *modem control* and *modem status* registers are used only for modem communications [7.1.5], and the two interrupt-related registers are used only in interrupt-driven routines [7.1.8].

Interrupts are used in communications for reasons of efficiency. Simple communications routines constantly monitor the line status register, waiting for an incoming character, or waiting until the register indicates that it is all right to transmit another byte of data. Because the CPU operates very quickly relative to the 300 or 1200 bit-per-second rate at which serial data typically moves, this method can be wasteful of CPU time that might otherwise be devoted to processing the incoming/outgoing data. For this reason the 8250 may be set up to bring about an interrupt whenever a character arrives, an error occurs, etc. The interrupt momentarily brings into action a procedure in your program that would, say, output the next character from a communications buffer.

7.1.2 Initialize the serial port

When a communications port is initialized ("opened"), all of the parameters by which it operates are set. These parameters include the word length, the number of stop bits, the parity setting, and the baud rate. The *word length* is the number of bits that form the basic data unit. While we are accustomed to working in eight bits, seven bits is adequate for standard ASCII files (where all characters are below ASCII 128), and as few as four bits may be suitable for the transmission of numeric data.

High Level

BASIC opens the communications channel as a file, and as such it must be given a file identification number:

```
OPEN"COM1: ............" AS #1
```

Placed within the quotation marks is all the information required to initialize the serial port, each entry separated from the prior by a comma. The initialization data is always entered in the following order:

Baud rate	given as an integer: 75, 100, 150, 300, 600, 1200, 1800, 2400, 4800/, or 9600 bits per second. Defaults to 300 baud.
Parity	given as a one-character code: O for ODD parity; E for EVEN parity (the default); N for NONE (no parity); S for SPACE, where the parity bit is always 0; and M for MARK, where the parity bit is always 1. If eight data bits are used, specify N; if four bits are used, do *not* use N.
Data bits	given as the integer 4, 5, 6, 7, or 8, with 7 as the default value.
Stop bits	given as the integer 1 or 2, with 2 as the default for 75 and 110 bps, and 1 for all others. When the number of data bits is 4 or 5, 2 stands for 1 1/2 stop bits. "1 1/2" bits is possible because in communications a bit is a *unit of time*, and hence it is divisible.

The statement **OPEN "COM1:" AS #1** opens COM1 for 300 bps communications with even parity, using seven data bits and one stop bit. **OPEN "COM1:1200,O,8,1"** sets up the port for 1200 bps communications with odd parity, eight-bit characters, and one stop bit. Note that you can end one of the OPEN statements with the expression **LEN = number,** where the number sets the maximum block size by which GET and PUT instructions may handle data (128 bytes is the default). There are a number of modem-control commands that optionally may be included with these specifications ([7.1.5] explains the special terminology found here):

RS	Suppresses the "Request To Send" signal. If this command is omitted, OPEN"COM... turns on RTS.

CS   Causes the "Clear To Send" line to be checked. This command may optionally be followed by a value (from 0-65535) that gives the number of milliseconds to wait for the signal before a "Device Time-out" error occurs—for example, **CS500**. The default value is 1000, unless RS is specified, in which case it is 0.

DS   Causes the "Data Set Ready" line to be checked. An optional parameter is allowed, as for CS above. The default value is 1000.

CD   Causes the "Carrier Detect" line to be checked. An optional timing parameter is allowed, as for CS above. The default value is 0.

LF   Causes a line feed (ASCII 10) to automatically follow every carriage return (ASCII 13). Used for serial output to a printer.

PE   Enables parity checking, causing a "Device Time-out" error if a parity error occurs.

These special commands may be placed anywhere in the OPEN"COM... statement and in any order. Note that normally the CTS and DSR signals must be turned on or the OPEN statement will fail and a "Device Time-out" error will occur. In summary, here is an OPEN"COM... statement that includes all parameters except RS and LF:

```
OPEN"COM1:1200,O,7,1,CS2000,DS2000,CD,PE" AS #1 LEN=256
```

Middle Level ━━━━━━━━━━━━━━━━━━━━━━━━━

BIOS function 0 of INT 14H initializes the serial port. DX is given the number of the communications channel (COM1 = 0, COM2 = 1). AL takes a byte that gives the initialization data, as follows:

```
bits 1-0        Word length.   10=7 bits & 11=8 bits.
     2          Number of stop bits.   0=1 & 1=2.
    4-3         Parity.   00 or 10=none.   01=odd & 11=even.
    5-7         Baud rate.      000=110 bps
                                001=150
                                010=300
                                011=600
                                100=1200
                                101=2400
                                110=4800
                                111=9600
```

This example initializes the port to an eight-bit word length with one stop bit and even parity. The baud rate is 1200 bps.

```
;---ASSIGN VALUES TO THE PARAMETER VARIABLES:
            MOV   WORDLENGTH,00000011B      ;8-bit word length
            MOV   STOPBITS,00000000B        ;1 stop bit
            MOV   PARITY,00011000B          ;even parity
            MOV   BAUDRATE,10000000B        ;1200 baud
;---INITIALIZE COM1:
            MOV   AL,0                       ;clear AL
            OR    AL,WORDLENGTH              ;initialize the bits from 4 variables
            OR    AL,STOPBITS                ;
```

```
OR    AL,PARITY           ;
OR    AL,BAUDRATE         ;
MOV   AH,0                ;function to initialize serial port
MOV   DX,0                ;select COM1
INT   14H                 ;initialize the port
```

Low Level

Whether for input or output, minimally four registers of the 8250 chip must be initialized for serial operations. These are the two baud-rate divisor registers, the line control register, and the interrupt enable register.

Baud-rate initialization:

The *baud-rate divisor* is a number that divides the rate of the system clock (1190000 cycles/second) to give a result that equals the desired baud rate. For example, for 1200 bps the baud-rate divisor would be 96, since 119000/96 equals roughly 1200. The larger the divisor, the slower the baud-rate. Baud rates of 300 and under require a two-byte number for the divisor, and for this reason the 8250 chip needs two registers to hold the divisor. The high byte is sent to 3F9H (or 2F9H), and the low byte to 3F8H (2F8H). In both cases, bit 7 of the line control register at 3FBH (2FBH) must be set to 1 before sending values; otherwise these two addresses direct the values to other registers (see [7.1.0]). Here are some values required by common baud rates:

Baud Rate	3F9H	3F8H
110	04H	17H
300	01H	80H
600	00H	C0H
1200	00H	60H
1800	00H	40H
2400	00H	30H
3600	00H	20H
4800	00H	18H
9600	00H	0CH

Always set the baud rate registers first since they are the only ones that require that bit 7 equal 1 in the line control register. Then set the contents of the line control register, making bit 7 equal 0 so that all subsequent register accesses are correct. Since the line control register is write-only, there is no way to set bit 7 back to 1 without redoing all of the bits in the register. Note that the PCjr uses different divisors—see the technical reference manual if you need them.

Line Control Register Initialization:

The bit settings for the line control register at 3FBH (or 2FBH) are as follows:

bits 1-0	Character length. 00=5 bits, 01=6 bits 10=7 bits, 11=8 bits.
2	Number of stop bits. 0=1. 1=1.5 if the character length is 5, else =2.
3	Parity. 1=parity bit is generated, 0=not.
4	Parity Type. 0=odd, 1=even.
5	Stick Parity. Causes parity to *always* be 1 or 0. 0=disabled. 1=always 1 if bit 3=1 & bit 4=0, or 1=always 0 if bit 3=1 & bit 4=1 or 1=no parity if bit 3=0.
6	Set Break. Causes output of string of 0s as signal to remote station. 0=disabled, 1=break.
7	Toggles port addresses of other registers on chip.

Ordinarily bits 5 - 7 are set to 0. The others are given the values of the desired communications protocol.

The interrupt-enable register:

Even when interrupts are not used, you should access the interrupt-enable register to be sure that interrupts are disabled. Simply place 0 in the register. The interrupt identification register may be ignored.

The remaining initialization registers are concerned with modems. Modems, of course, are required only for distant communications and not for the control of nearby devices such as a serial printer. [7.1.5] explains how to initialize the modem control register.

In this example the base address of COM1 is found in the BIOS data area and the various registers are initialized for 1200 baud, seven-bit data, even parity, and one stop bit.

```
;---GET BASE ADDRESS OF COM1:
               MOV   AX,40H              ;point ES to BIOS data area
               MOV   ES,AX               ;
               MOV   DX,ES:[0]           ;get base address for COM1
;---INITIALIZE THE BAUD RATE DIVISOR REGISTERS FOR 1200 BPS:
               ADD   DX,3                ;point to line control register
               MOV   AL,10000000B        ;turn on bit 7
               OUT   DX,AL               ;send the byte
               DEC   DX                  ;point to MSB of baud rate divisor
               DEC   DX                  ;
               MOV   AL,0                ;MSB for 1200 bps
               OUT   DX,AL               ;send the byte
               DEC   DX                  ;point to LSB of baud rate divisor
               MOV   AL,60H              ;LSB for 1200 bps
               OUT   DX,AL               ;
;---INITIALIZE THE LINE CONTROL REGISTER:
               MOV   AL,0                ;initialize AL to 0
               OR    AL,10B              ;7-bit data length
               OR    AL,000B             ;1 stop bit
               OR    AL,1000B            ;parity bit generated
               OR    AL,10000B           ;even parity
               ADD   DX,3                ;point to line control register
               OUT   DX,AL               ;send the initialization value
```

```
;---INITIALIZE THE INTERRUPT ENABLE REGISTER:
                DEC   DX              ;point to interrupt enable register
                DEC   DX              ;
                MOV   AL,0            ;disable all interrupts
                OUT   DX,AL           ;send the byte
                 .                    ;continue
                 .
```

7.1.3 Set the current communications port

There are two ways by which a program can decide which of the COM channels is to be used. One means is by specifying the channel number in program statements. The second way is by writing the program for COM1, but changing which communications adaptor is accessed by COM1.

The BIOS data area contains space for four two-byte variables which hold the *base addresses* of the serial channels (PC-DOS supports only the first two). A base address is the lowest port address of the group of port addresses that access a particular serial channel. The base address of COM1 is at 0040:0000, and COM2 is at 0040:0002. To change serial ports, simply exchange the two values. Switching the addresses a second time restores the original port assignments.

High Level

In BASIC the OPEN"COM... statement may be set up in the form **OPEN C\$ + "1200,N,8" AS #2**, where C\$ may be either **"COM1:"** or **"COM2:"**. Alternatively, use PEEK and POKE to switch the base addresses:

```
100 DEF SEG=&H40                    'point to bottom of BIOS data area
110 X=PEEK(0):Y=PEEK(1)             'store the first 2 bytes
120 POKE 0,PEEK(2):POKE 1,PEEK(3)   'transfer the second 2 bytes
130 POKE 2,X:POKE 3,Y               'put 1st 2 bytes at higher position
```

Middle Level

If a program accesses the communication ports via BIOS INT 14H, then the COM port may be specified in DX as either 0 or 1 (for COM1 or 2). Rather than fill DX with an immediate value, fill it with a variable that can be set to either 0 or 1, as required. Programs that use communications functions 3 and 4 of DOS INT 21H always address COM1. In this case, switch the two base addresses:

```
;---EXCHANGE BASE ADDRESSES OF COM1 AND COM2:
            MOV   AX,40H        ;point ES to BIOS data area
            MOV   ES,AX         ;
            MOV   DX,ES:[0]      ;put 1st base address in DX
            MOV   AX,ES:[2]      ;put 2nd base address in AX
            MOV   ES:[0],AX      ;exchange the addresses
            MOV   ES:[2],DX      ;
```

7.1.4 Monitor the status of the serial port

The *line status* register of the 8250 UART sets up the communications protocol. This register is located at the port address that is 5 higher than the base address for the particular COM channel. Ordinarily it is constantly monitored during communications activity. During data transmission, the register tells when the prior character has been sent off, lest the program write the next character on top of it. In data reception, the register informs the program when a character arrives, so that the program can remove it before it is overlaid by the one that follows. The contents are as follows:

bit 0	1 = a byte of data has been received
1	1 = received data has been overrun (prior character was not removed in time)
2	1 = parity error (probably from line noise)
3	1 = framing error (transmission is out of sync)
4	1 = break detect (a long string of 1's has been received, indicating that the other station requests an end to transmission)
5	1 = transmitter holding register empty (this register is given output data)
6	1 = transmitter shift register empty (this register takes holding register data and converts it to serial form)
7	1 = time-out (off-line)

High Level

In BASIC, first find the base address for the COM channel in use, add 5 to it, and then use INP to get the byte at that port address. Appendix B explains how to perform bit operations in BASIC so that a program can interpret the byte. The following example checks the *break detect* bit:

```
100 DEF SEG=&H40            'point to start of BIOS data area
110 ADDRESS=PEEK(4)+PEEK(5)*256  'calculate COM2 base address
120 X=INP(ADDRESS+5)        'get status port value
130 IF X AND 16 THEN 500    'jump to subroutine if bit 4 is on
    .
    .
500 'begin BREAK routine
```

Middle Level

Function 3 of BIOS INT 14H returns the contents of the line status register in AH (AL receives the modem status register [7.1.5]). On entry DX holds the number of the communications port that is accessed, where COM1 = 0 and COM2 = 1. Like the one above, this example checks for the *break detect* condition:

```
MOV  AH,3             ;function number
MOV  DX,1             ;choose COM2
INT  14H             ;fetch the status byte
TEST AH,10000B       ;break detect?
JNZ  BREAK_DETECT    ;jump to break routine if so
```

Low Level

This example is much like the one given above for BASIC. Read the base address of the COM channel from the BIOS data area, add 5, and get the status byte from the resulting port address.

```
MOV   AX,40H            ;point ES to bottom of BIOS data area
MOV   ES,AX             ;
MOV   DX,ES:[2]         ;get COM2 base address
ADD   DX,5             ;add offset of 5 for status register
IN    AL,DX            ;get the status byte
TEST  AL,10000B         ;bit 5 set?
JNZ   BREAK_DETECT      ;if so, jump to break routine
```

7.1.5 Initialize and monitor the modem

There are six lines by which modems communicate with the computer (more advanced modems may have extra lines through the RS232 interface). Here are their names, abbreviations, and functions:

From computer to modem:

Data Terminal Ready (DTR)	informs modem that computer is powered up and ready for communications
Request To Send (RTS)	informs modem that computer wants to send data

From modem to computer:

Data Set Ready (DSR)	informs computer that modem is powered up and ready
Clear To Send (CTS)	informs computer that modem is ready to begin data transmission
Data Carrier Detect (DCD)	informs computer that modem has connected with another modem
Ring Indicator (RI)	informs computer that the phone line the modem is connected to is ringing

---

First the computer turns the *data terminal ready* signal on, and then it instructs the modem to dial the remote station. Once the modem has established a connection, it turns on the *data set ready* signal. This informs the computer that the modem is ready for communications, and at that point the computer can turn on the *request to send* signal. When the modem replies with *clear to send*, transmission can begin.

The two standard lines by which the computer controls the modem may be accessed through the *modem control register* on the 8250 UART chip. This register is located at an address that is 4 greater than the base address for the COM channel in use. Here is the bit pattern in the register:

Modem Control Register:

bits 7-5	(always 0
4	1 = UART output looped back as input
3	auxiliary user designated output #2
2	auxiliary user designated output #1
1	1 = "request to send" is active
0	1 = "data terminal ready" is active

Ordinarily bits 0 and 1 of the modem control register are set to 1, and the others are set to 0. Bit 2 is set to 0 unless a modem's manufacturer has given it a special use. Bit 3 is set to 1 only when interrupts are used [7.1.8]. Finally, bit 4 is a special feature that is useful for testing communications programs without actually going on line. The output signal from the UART is looped back so that the UART receives it as serial input. This feature may be used to test whether the chip is functioning properly. Loop-back is not available through the BIOS INT 14H communications routines.

The four lines by which the modem sends information to the computer are monitored through the *modem status register*. This register is located at the port address that is 6 higher than the base address of the communications adaptor in use. Here is the bit pattern:

Modem Status Register:

bit	7	1 = "data carrier detect"
	6	1 = "ring indicator"
	5	1 = "data set ready"
	4	1 = "clear to send"
	3	1 = change in "data carrier detect"
	2	1 = change in "ring indicator"
	1	1 = change in "data set ready"
	0	1 = change in "clear to send"

Programs constantly monitor these bits during communications operations. Note that the four low bits parallel the four high bits. These bits are set to 1 only when a change has occurred in the status of the corresponding high bit *since the last time the register was read*. All four low bits are automatically restored to 0 after the read operation. Programs of any level may read the register directly. Alternatively, function 3 of BIOS INT 14H returns the contents of the modem status register in AL (the line status register contents appear in AH). On entry to this function DX must hold the number of the COM channel (0 or 1).

Most modems have many more capabilities than the two modem-related registers reflect. Features like autodial and autoanswer are controlled by *control strings*. These strings are sent to the modem as if they were data being transmitted. The modem extracts the strings from the data by watching for a special character used only to signal the start of a control string. This character may be predefined (often it is ASCII 27, the ESCape character) or it may be user-selectable. The modem is able to determine how long each sequence must be, so that beyond the end of the string it again treats the transmission outflow as data. Every modem has its own set of commands. By way of example, here are those used by the internal modem of the PCjr:

Symbol	Meaning	Application
A	answer	enter answer mode
Bn	break	send a break signal n * 100 ms long
C	ncount	before answering count n rings
Dn...n	dial	dial the string of numbers n...n
Fn	format	set up communications protocol
H	hang-up	break the connection
I	initialize	initialize the modem
LR	long response	toggles code system used by modem
M	mode	make modem see characters as data
Nn	new	change command character to n
O	originate	enter originate mode
P	pick-up	enter voice mode
Q	query	request modem status
R	retry	retry dial command
Sn	speed	select baud rate
Tn...n	transparent	ignore ctrl sequences next n...n bytes
V	voice	force modem to voice mode
W	wait	do nothing until next command
X	xmit	transmit dial tones
Z	ztest	perform hardware diagnostics

In response to a *query* command, the modem returns status information, sending it to the 8250 like incoming data. Among other things, this information can report that the line is busy. All in all, a good deal of documentation is required to properly use a modem's command sequences and status information. For the PCjr's modem, see the PCjr Technical Reference Manual. The examples below give only the bare framework by which modem connections are established.

High Level

Because the telephone system works at less than blinding speed, establishing a modem link is perhaps the one point in communications programming where BASIC can work every bit as well as assembly language. Here is the framework:

```
100 OUT BASEADDRESS+4,1                    'turn on "data terminal ready"
110 '''now send control string to modem to dial number and establish
120 '''connection -- this code varies by the modem
  .
  .
200 X=INP(BASEADDRESS+6)                    'get modem status register value
210 IF X AND 2 <> 2 THEN 200                'keep looping until bit 1 is set
220 OUT BASEADDRESS+4,3                     'turn on "request to send" bit as well
230 X=INP(BASEADDRESS+6)                    'get modem status register value
240 IF X AND 1 <> 1 THEN 230                'keep looping until bit 0 is set
250 '''now being sending data...
```

Low Level

Here is the same general framework written in assembly language:

```
;---TURN ON THE "DATA TERMINAL READY" SIGNAL:
              MOV   DX,BASE_ADDRESS   ;start with base address
              ADD   DX,4              ;point to modem control register
              MOV   AL,1              ;turn on bit 1
              OUT   DX,AL             ;turn on DTR
;---SEND CONTROL STRING TO MODEM TO DIAL NUMBER...
                    .                 ;this code is modem-dependent
                    .

;---THEN WAIT UNTIL "DATA SET READY" SIGNAL IS ON"
              INC   DX                ;point to modem status register
              INC   DX                ;
   TRY_AGAIN: IN    AL,DX             ;get contents
              TEST  AL,10B            ;see if bit 2 is on
              JZ    TRY_AGAIN         ;don't continue until it is
;---TURN ON "REQUEST TO SEND":
              DEC   DX                ;return to modem control register
              DEC   DX                ;
              MOV   AL,3              ;turn on RTS, leaving DTR on
              OUT   DX,AL             ;send the new bit setting
;---WAIT FOR "CLEAR TO SEND"
              INC   DX                ;return to modem status register
              INC   DX                ;
   ONCE_MORE: IN    AL,DX             ;get the status byte
              TEST  AL,1              ;ready to send?
              JZ    ONCE_MORE         ;don't go on if not
;---NOW BEGIN SENDING DATA...
```

7.1.6 Transmit data

Transmitting data is simpler than receiving it, since a program has complete control over the composition of the data, and over the rate at which it is sent. Still, transmission routines can become elaborate if they process the data as they send it. And timing can be a problem when the XON/XOFF protocol is used. This protocol uses ASCII characters 17 (XON) and 19 (XOFF) to signal to the transmitting station that the receiver wants the transmission flow temporarily interrupted. To accommodate it, the program must constantly watch for incoming characters while it transmits (in the *full duplex* mode in which most modems operate, signals simultaneously flow both ways across the telephone line). Similarly, to detect that the remote station has sent a string of 0's and brought about a *break* condition, the transmitting status must intermittently monitor the status of the break bit (number 4) of the line status register [7.1.4]. Figure 7-2 (at [7.1.7]) shows how the data transmission routine interacts with the data reception code.

Because of these considerations, the presentation here of an isolated transmission routine is somewhat artificial. But it can be combined with the data reception routine shown at [7.1.7] to create a general framework. Obviously, a tremendous amount of elaboration is required to form a workable routine, particularly by way of error checking and recovery.

High Level

In BASIC, use PRINT#, PRINT#USING, and WRITE# to send characters out an opened communications port. The latter two statements have special formats that parallel those of the PRINT USING and WRITE statements used for video operations. Generally PRINT# is used. This example sends data taken directly from the keyboard. It assumes that COM1 has already been opened, as shown at [7.1.2]. The routine monitors the break bit of the line status register.

```
      .
      .
      .
500 C$=INKEY$:IF C$<>"" THEN PRINT#1,C$ 'if a keystroke, send it
510 X=BASEADDRESS+5              'read line status register
520 IF X AND 32=32 THEN 1000     'if bit 5 set then BREAK
530 IF EOF(1) THEN 500           'if input buffer empty, check for keystroke
540 ...                          'else, go receive data...
      .
      .
      .
        (data reception routine here)
      .
      .
      .
1000 '''BREAK routine begins here
      .
      .
      .
```

Middle Level

Function 1 of BIOS INT 14H sends the character in AL out the serial port. On entry, DX holds the COM port number (0-1). On return, AH holds a status byte in which bit 7 = 1 if the operation failed. In this case, the following bits are significant:

```
bit 4   Break detect (the receiving station signals "stop!")
    5   Transmission shift register empty
    6   Transmission holding register empty
```

DOS has an asynchronous communications function that transmits the character placed in DL. The function, number 4 of INT 21H, offers no advantage over the BIOS interrupt; indeed, it does not return status information, and it does not allow you to designate which COM port to use (it always addresses COM1).

To output strings of data, use function 40H of INT 21H. This is the common output function for all files and devices under the *file handle* method of access. COM1 has a predefined handle, number 0003. Place the handle in BX and the number of bytes to output in CX. Then point DS:DX to the output data buffer and call the function.

```
MOV   AH,40H           ;function number
MOV   BX,3             ;predefined COM handle
MOV   CX,50            ;output 50 bytes
LEA   DX,DATA_BUFFER   ;point DS:DX to the data buffer
INT   21H             ;send the data
JC    COM_ERROR        ;jump if there has been an error
```

Note that there is no need to "open" a predefined handle. If an error occurs, the carry flag is set, and AX returns 5 if the communications port was not ready and 6 if the handle number was wrong.

Low Level

When a character of data is placed in the 8250's *transmitter holding register*, it is automatically output to the serial line via the *transmitter shift register*, which serializes the data. There is no need to pulse a strobe bit to initiate the transfer, as is required on the parallel adaptor. Bit 5 of the *line status register* tells whether the transmitter holding register is free to receive data. The register is constantly monitored until bit 5 becomes 1. Then one byte of data is sent to the transmitter holding register, from where it is instantly output. Bit 5 changes to 0 while the byte is output, and only when it again becomes 1 may the next character be sent to the transmitter holding register. This process is repeated as long as required.

The following example gives the basic setup of such a routine. Of course, it can be made extremely complex (in particular, communications programming requires extensive error checking and recovery procedures). The example assumes that the serial port and modem have already been initialized, as shown at [7.1.2] and [7.1.5]. The first part is a loop that keeps checking for errors and received characters. [7.1.7] gives the code for the data reception routine.

```
;---WAIT UNTIL ALL RIGHT TO SEND A CHARACTER:
KEEP_TRYING:  MOV  DX,BASE_ADDRESS   ;base address from prior code
              ADD  DX,5              ;point to line status register
              IN   AL,DX            ;get status byte
              TEST AL,00011110B     ;test for error
              JNZ  ERROR ROUTINE    ;jump to error routine if a problem
```

```
                TEST  AL,00000001B        ;test whether data received
                JNZ   RECEIVE             ;go to receive routine [7.1.7]
                TEST  AL,00100000B        ;test if ready to transmit character
                JZ    KEEP_TRYING         ;if not, loop around

;---TRANSMIT A CHARACTER (GET IT FROM THE KEYBOARD):
                MOV   AH,1                ;BIOS function to check if keystroke
                INT   16H                 ;BIOS keyboard interrupt
                JZ    KEEP_TRYING         ;return to loop if no keystroke awaits
                MOV   AH,0                ;BIOS function to get a keystroke
                INT   16H                 ;keystroke now in AL
                SUB   DX,5                 ;point to transmitter holding register
                OUT   DX,AL               ;send the character
                JMP   SHORT KEEP_TRYING   ;return to loop
```

7.1.7 Receive data

A communications program is ready to receive data once a communications port has been initialized [7.1.2] and contact has been established with the remote station [7.1.5]. Data reception is never entirely separate from data transmission, since a program may need to send an XOFF signal (ASCII 19) to stop the data flow if data is received faster than it can be processed. XON (ASCII 17) tells the remote station to recommence transmission. Note that the PCjr cannot receive data while disk operations are taking place; XON and XOFF may be used to overcome this limitation.

Depending on the complexity of the data protocol, the incoming data may require only a little, or a good deal, of interpretation. Any of the various control codes listed at [7.1.9] might be received. Those that signal data boundaries are more often found in *synchronous* communications. When displaying the incoming data on the screen, consider the effect of line feed characters (ASCII 10), since some languages (BASIC included) automatically insert a line feed after a carriage return; in this case, eliminate the incoming line feed characters to avoid double-spacing on the screen. Figure 7-2 diagrams the basic communications routine, including the transmission code that is discussed at [7.1.6].

High Level

For communications routines written in interpreted BASIC, time is of the essence. Processing is slow, and if the input routine is improperly designed, the input buffer can fill (that is, *overflow*) while the program is still busy interpreting the prior data received. An obvious solution to this problem is to make the buffer extremely large. When BASIC is loaded the input buffer size is set by appending a /C: command. **BASICA/C:1024** creates a 1K buffer, and this is the minimum size for 1200 baud (4096 bytes may be required by complex routines). The default value is 256 bytes, and this buffer size has the advantage that when BASIC reads from the buffer it can fit the entire contents into a single string variable. Use it only at 300 baud or below.

BASIC reads from the buffer using the INPUT$ statement (INPUT# and LINE INPUT# also work, but INPUT$ is the most flexible). This statement is in the form **INPUT$(numberbytes,filenumber)**. For example, **INPUT$(10,#1)** reads ten bytes from the communications channel opened as #1. If the buffer size is under 256 bytes, it is most convenient to read the entire contents of the buffer at once. LOC tells how many bytes of data currently reside in the buffer. So write **S$ = INPUT$(LOC(1),#1)** and S$ is given all the data received since the buffer was last accessed. Of course, if **LOC(1) = 0** then the buffer is empty, and the routine must keep looping until data is received. Note that **EOF(1)** also reports on the buffer contents, returning -1 if empty, and 0 if there are any characters.

Once data is given to S$, the program seeks whatever control codes are of concern. The INSTR function performs this task most quickly. Recall that INSTR is followed by first the position in the string from which to begin searching, and then the name of the string, and finally the character (or string) that is sought. To find the XOFF character (ASCII 19) the statement would be **INSTR(1,S$,CHR$(17))**. To

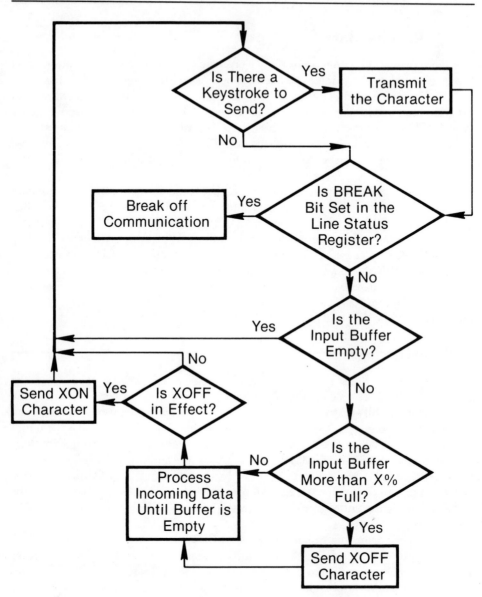

Figure 7-2. The basic communications routine.

find a second occurrence of a control code, search the string again, starting from the character following the position at which the first was located.

Ordinarily the input routine eliminates most control codes from the incoming data so that it appears properly on the display. Then the data is displayed, shunted around memory, and sometimes written to disk or dumped on to a printer. In the midst of all this, the program must constantly return to look for more data. If the buffer turns out to be filling too quickly, the program can send an XOFF character to the transmitting station, halting the data flow. Then the flow may be reenabled

to the transmitting station, halting the data flow. Then the flow may be reenabled after the received data has been decoded. Of course, XON and XOFF must be supported by the protocol in use. Programs written in interpreted BASIC usually can use XON/XOFF for "speed-matching" when they receive data; but often such programs cannot respond quickly enough when they *receive* an XOFF signal while they are transmitting.

```
.
.
500 '''transmission routine here (see [7.1.6])
.
.
.
600 IF LOC(1)>100 THEN XOFF=1:PRINT#1,CHR$(19) 'if buffer filling,
                              'turn XOFF status on by sending ASCII 19
610 C$=INPUT$(LOC(1),#1)         'read the contents of the buffer
620 '''filter the data for special characters:
630 IF INSTR(1,C$,CHR$(19))>0 THEN 800   'XOFF character received?
640 IF INSTR(1,C$,CHR$(17))>0 THEN 900   'XON character received?
  .
  .     (delete unwanted control codes)
  .
700 PRINT C$;                    'display the string
710 IF LOC(1)>THEN 600           'if more data arrived, go get it
720 IF XOFF=1 THEN XOFF=0:PRINT#1,CHR$(17)   'switch off XOFF
730 GOTO 500                     'goto start of transmission routine
  .
  .
800 'respond to XOFF
  .
900 'respond to XON
  .
  .
```

When applied to a communications port the LOF (length of file) function returns the amount of free space remaining in the input buffer. For example, if the COM port was opened as **#1**, then **LOF(1)** reports the amount of free space. This feature may be useful for telling when the buffer is nearly full. But note that the LOC statement returns the location of the buffer pointer, and this value can be used for the same purpose. For example, for a COM port opened as **#3**, in which the buffer size is 256 bytes, so long as LOC(3) does not return 256, the buffer is not full.

Middle Level

BIOS function 2 of INT 14H waits for a character from the serial port, places it in AL when received, and then returns. On entry, place the COM port number (0 or 1) in DX. On return AH holds 0 if no error has occurred. If AH is not 0, then a status byte has been returned in which only five bits are significant. These bits are:

```
bit 1   overrun error (new character before prior one removed)
    2   parity error (probably from a transmission line problem)
    3   framing error (start and stop bits not as they should be)
    4   break detect (received a long string of 0 bits)
    7   time out error ("data set ready" signal not received)
```

DOS also offers an asynchronous communications function that receives single characters, number 3 of INT 21H. The function waits for a character from COM1 and places it in AL. Note that there is no matching function to initialize the port, and so it must be done via the BIOS routine, or directly, as shown at [7.1.2]. The default initialization is 2400 baud, no parity, with one stop bit, and eight-bit characters. This interrupt offers no advantages over the BIOS routines (except to help with compatibility in other MS-DOS machines) and it returns no status information.

Low Level

When receiving data without the use of the communication interrupt [7.1.8], a program must constantly monitor the line status register, which is located at the port address that is 5 greater than the base address of the serial adaptor in use. Bit 0 of this register is set to 0 so long as no character has been received in the *receiver data register*. When bit 0 changes to 1, the character must immediately be removed from the register in order to avoid its being overrun by the next character to arrive. Once the character is removed, bit 0 immediately returns to 0, and it stays 0 until another character is received.

Although not shown here, be aware that communications routines usually set up a *circular buffer* to collect the incoming characters. Circular buffers are discussed at [3.1.1]. You also should know that if the incoming data is directed to the screen at 1200 baud, the BIOS scrolling routine [4.5.1] cannot act quickly enough, and an overrun will occur. An easy solution to this difficulty is to rely on communications interrupts, as explained at [7.1.8].

The following example duplicates part of that shown in the prior section, where characters are transmitted. What is shared is the infinite loop that begins the code. Combine the two routines along with the initializiation routines at [7.1.2] and [7.1.5] for a complete serial I/O routine.

```
KEEP_TRYING:    MOV   DX,BASE_ADDRESS      ;base address from prior code
                ADD   DX,5                 ;point to line status register
                IN    AL,DX                ;get status byte
                TEST  AL,00011110B         ;test for error
                JNZ   ERROR ROUTINE        ;jump to error routine if a problem
                TEST  AL,00000001B         ;test whether data received
                JNZ   RECEIVE              ;go to receive routine
                TEST  AL,00100000B         ;test if ready to transmit character
                JZ    KEEP_TRYING          ;if not, loop around
                .                          ;else, transmit a character...
                .
        ;---(transmission routine here--see [7.1.6])
                .
                .
        ;---RECEIVE DATA AND DISPLAY ON SCREEN:
        RECEIVE:        MOV   DX,BASEADDRESS       ;base address=receiver data register
                        IN    AL,DX               ;get the newly arrived character
                        CMP   AL,19               ;check for XOFF, etc
                        JE    XOFF_ROUTINE        ;
                        .                          ;etc...
                        .                          ;
                        MOV   DL,AL                ;prepare to display the character
                        MOV   AH,2                 ;DOS interrupt to display character
                        INT   21H                  ;display the character
                        JMP   SHORT KEEP_TRYING    ;return to loop
```

7.1.8 Send/receive data by communications interrupts

Elaborate communications programs have too much to do to devote full time to I/O operations. Incoming data must be analyzed, outgoing data must be gathered, and large blocks of data may need to be moved to and from disk. Communications interrupts let a program spend no more time in I/O operations than is required. For example, by setting up an interrupt, control is transferred to a data transmission routine only when the transmitter holding register is empty, and control reverts to the program once a byte of data is sent, allowing the program to continue until the transmitter holding register is ready again. Be sure to be familiar with the discussion of interrupts at [1.2.3] before reading on.

The IBM machines allot two hardware interrupt channels for communications, numbers 3 (COM1) and 4 (COM2). Note that on the PCjr the modem is on channel 3 and COM1 on channel 4. The 8250 UART for each channel allows four classes of interrupts, using the following binary code numbers:

```
00   change in modem status register
01   transmitter holding register empty
10   data received
11   reception error, or break condition received
```

These codes are contained in bits 2-1 in the *interrupt identification register*, which is located at the port address that is 2 greater than the base address of the serial port in use. Bit 0 of this register is set to 1 when an interrupt is pending; the other bits are not used, and are always set to 0.

To select one or more interrupts, program the *interrupt enable register*, which is located 1 higher than the base address. The bit pattern is:

```
bit 0   1=interrupt when data received
    1   1=interrupt when transmitter holding register empty
    2   1=interrupt when data reception error
    3   1=interrupt when change in modem status register
  4-7   unused, always 0
```

When one of these events occurs, a hardware interrupt is invoked, which takes place on channel 3 of the 8259 interrupt chip for COM1 and on channel 4 for COM2. The interrupt routine transfers control to whatever code is pointed to by the associated interrupt vectors. Because this is a hardware interrupt, it can be masked out [1.2.2]. Remember that the interrupt routines you provide must end with the standard exit code for hardware interrupts **MOV AL,20H/OUT 20H,AL**. Figure 7-3 illustrates the communications interrupt.

Any number of interrupt types may be enabled simultaneously. But if more than one is enabled, the routine must begin by checking the interrupt identification register to find out which it is. More than one interrupt can occur simultanously, and for this reason bit 0 of the identification register tells whether additional interrupts are pending. When two or more occur at the same instant, they are processed in the order shown in the table below. The additional interrupts must be processed before the interrupt routine returns. The prior interrupt condition is "undone" by taking the action shown in the righthand column of this table:

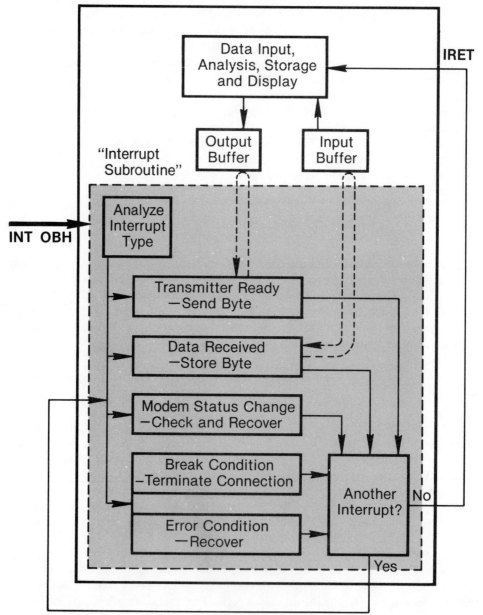

Figure 7-3. The communications interrupt.

Code	Type	Action for "reset"
11	error or break	read line status register
10	data received	read receiver data register
01	transmitter ready	output character to transmitter holding register
00	modem status change	read modem status register

Low Level

Here is the general form of a communications interrupt handler:

```
;---SET UP THE COMMUNICATION INTERRUPT VECTOR:
              PUSH  DS                  ;DS changed by function
              MOV   DX,OFFSET IO_INT    ;point DS:DX to COM routine
              MOV   AX,SEG IO_INT       ;
              MOV   DS,AX               ;
              MOV   AL,0BH              ;vector number for COM1
              MOV   AH,25H              ;function to change vector
              INT   21H                 ;change vector
;---INITIALIZE THE INTERRUPT-ENABLE REGISTER (COM1):
              MOV   AX,40H              ;point DS to BIOS data area
              MOV   DS,AX               ;
              MOV   DX,DS:[0]           ;get base address for COM1
              INC   DX                  ;point to interrupt enable register
              MOV   AL,3                ;enable both receive and transmit INTS
              OUT   DX,AL               ;send the byte
              POP   DS                  ;restore DS
                                        ;the program continues...


;---HERE IS THE INTERRUPT ROUTINE-FIRST FIND OUT TYPE OF INTERRUPT:
   IO_INT         PROC FAR
   NEXT_INT:      MOV   DX,BASEADDRESS    ;base address for COM1
                  INC   DX                ;
                  INC   DX                ;point to interrupt identification reg
                  IN    AL,DX             ;read the value
                  TEST  AL,10B            ;transmitter?
                  JNZ   TRANSMIT          ;go transmit a character
                                          ;else, must be receive interrupt:

   RECEIVE:       .                       ;begin character/line reception
                  .
                  .
                  JMP   SHORT ANOTHER     ;go see if another interrupt pending

   TRANSMIT:      .                       ;begin routine to transmit a character
                  .
                  .

;---BEFORE EXITING, CHECK THAT NO OTHER INTERRUPT REQUESTS PENDING:
   ANOTHER:       MOV   DX,BASEADDRESS    ;base address of COM1
                  INC   DX                ;point to interrupt identification reg
                  INC   DX                ;
                  IN    AL,DX             ;read the value
                  TEST  AL,1              ;request pending?
                  JNZ   NEXT_INT          ;if so, jump back to start of routine
```

```
                 MOV   AL,20H              ;else, send end-of-interrupt code
                 OUT   20H,AL              ;
                 IRET                      ;quit
IO_INT           ENDP                      ;end of interrupt procedure
```

7.1.9 Look up a communications control code

This table gives the 32 ASCII control codes that are used in communications or to operate printers or other devices. An extra code is added, ASCII 127 (DEL), because it is normally used as a control code, although there is no Ctrl key combination to produce it. The applications of some of these codes are invariant, such as the carriage return. But most are given a wide range of interpretations, much to the detriment of equipment compatibility.

ASCII Code Number			Ctrl		
decimal	hex	Symbol	Code	Mnemonic	Purpose
00	00	(null)	^@	NUL	Spacing character (meaningless, so also useful for delays).
01	01	☺	^A	SOH	Start Of Heading. Begins transmission of data block or new file.
02	0	☻	2^B	STX	Start Of Text. Marks beginning of text following header data.
03	03	♥	^C	ETX	End Of Text. May mark beginning of error checking data.
04	04	♦	^D	EOT	End Of Transmission. Sign-off code, but sometimes only marks end of file.
05	05	♣	^E	ENQ	Enquiry. Requests status information from remote station.
06	06	♠	^F	ACK	Acknowledge. Verifies the success of communications between stations.
07	07	•	^G	BEL	Bell. Beeps the speaker, signalling need of attention.
08	08	▫	^H	BS	Backspace.
09	09	○	^I	HT	Horizontal Tab.
10	0A	◎	^J	LF	Line Feed.
11	0B	♂	^K	VT	Vertical Tab.
12	0C	♀	^L	FF	Form Feed.
13	0D	♪	^M	CR	Carriage Return.
14	0E	♫	^N	SO	Shift Out. Changes character set.
15	0F	☼	^O	SI	Shift In. Changes character set.
16	10	►	^P	DLE	Data Link Escape. Modifies meaning of subsequent characters (like Esc).
17	11	◄	^Q	DC1	Device Control 1. Used as XON to signal remote station to transmit.
18	12	↕	^R	DC2	Device Control 2. General purpose toggle signal.
19	13	‼	^S	DC3	Device Control 3. Used as XOFF to signal remote station to not transmit.
20	14	¶	^T	DC4	Device Control 4. General purpose toggle signal.
21	15	§	^U	NAK	Negative Acknowledge. Signals transmission failure.

ASCII Code Number			Ctrl		
decimal	hex	Symbol	Code	Mnemonic	Purpose
22	16	▬	^V	SYN	Synchronous Idle. Used between data blocks in synchronous communications.
23	17	↕	^W	TB	End Of Transmission Block. Variant of ETX.
24	18	↑	^X	CAN	Cancel. Usually signals transmission error.
25	19	↓	^Y	EM	End Of Medium. Signals physical end of data-source.
26	1A	→	^Z	SUB	Substitute. Replaces characters that are invalid or impossible to display.
27	1B	←	^[	ESC	Escape. Marks following characters as a control sequence.
28	1C	∟	^/	FS	File Separator. Marks logical boundary between files.
29	1D	↔	^]	GS	Group Separator. Marks logical boundary between data groups.
30	1E	▲	^^	RS	Record Separator. Marks logical boundary between data records.
31	1F	▼	^__	US	Unit Separator. Marks logical boundary between data units.
127	7F	⌂	none	DEL	Delete. Eliminates other characters.

Section 2: Create a Device Driver

Device drivers are special programs that control input/output with a peripheral like a printer or hard disk. Since the specifications by which such peripherals operate vary by the manufacturer, a program intended for a wide range of users may need dozens of device drivers to accommodate the range of hardware it must work on. There are four ways of incorporating device drivers into programs:

1. Place the code for all devices right into the program. For example, to support a variety of printers, create a table of printer control sequences and look up the correct code each time it is used. This approach wastes memory, and it can be slow.

2. Create a number of device drivers, and have the program load the one that is needed as an overlay (that is, drop it into the program at an area that has been specially set aside for it [1.3.5]).

3. Set up the device driver as a separate program that is listed in the batch file that boots up the machine. The program is run, and it sets up the device routine that it contains as an interrupt. Then the program exits, but stays resident in memory, as explained at [1.3.4]. Thereafter, any program can use the device driver via the interrupt vector.

4. Set up a full-fledged *installable device driver*, in which the device is loaded at start-up by the CONFIG.SYS file. DOS makes provision for this kind of device driver, and once loaded it can make full use of DOS commands, including error checking. A special command, *IOCTL* ("I/O Control"), lets a program check a driver's status, and it can send control strings to the driver apart from the flow of data.

The first three strategies are easily accomplished using information given elsewhere in this book. Installable device drivers, on the other hand, are quite complex. But once they are in place, they are extremely powerful. DOS treats the device with as great a familiarity as the keyboard or a disk drive. The device may be given a name, such as SERIALPR for a serial printer, and the device may then be opened from any language for access. In BASIC, the statement **OPEN "SERIALPR" FOR OUTPUT AS #2** would ready the serial printer for output. In assembly language the printer could be accessed by both *file control block* and *file handle* commands, including the very powerful IOCTL function. And from the DOS user interface (that is, from the prompt A>, B>, etc.) the user could merely enter **COPY A:MYFILE SERIALPR:** and the contents of MYFILE would be dumped on to the serial printer.

Installable device drivers can only be written in assembly language. They serve two kinds of devices, *character* and *block* devices. These names describe the units by which the devices handle data. Generally, block device drivers serve disk drives and character device drivers serve just about everything else, from serial printers to robots. Block devices move large blocks of data, and so they are devoted to data *storage*. Character devices move data byte-by-byte, and so they are better suited for the *control* of devices and for data transfers where the lines cannot handle a high transfer rate. Block device drivers are quite complicated, and there is not adequate room here to explain their structure. It is the rare programmer that ever needs to write one. The DOS technical reference manuals give the necessary information and a complete example of a RAM-disk. You should be able to follow this information after you study the discussion of character device drivers found here.

Installable device drivers are unforgiving of programming mistakes. Because the drivers are automatically installed by DOS when COMMAND.COM is booted, it is essentially impossible to get at the programs with a debugger. So be meticulous about details.

Device driver programs break down into three parts, each of which is discussed separately in the sections that follow. These are (1) the *device header*, which names the device and keeps track of the other parts of the driver, (2) the *device strategy*, which keeps track of a data area set up by DOS called the *request header*, and (3) the *device interrupt handler* which actually contains the code that drives the device.

7.2.1 Set up the device header

Device drivers must be set up as a COM file [1.3.6]. They are not, however, true programs, since they must not have a program segment prefix (PSP). To achieve this, do not place an **ORG 100H** statement at the beginning of the program, as is required of ordinary COM programs. Either write **ORG 0**, or write nothing at all. Set the driver up as a *far* procedure, just as for any program. The example below begins with the initial code for a driver named DEVICE12. It replaces the default **AUX** device provided by DOS, so that it receives any data output by function 4 of DOS INT 21H. The entire device driver is comprised of the code in this subsection and the two that follow; place them end-to-end to arrive at the complete program.

A device driver begins with the *device header*. It is eighteen bytes long, divided into five fields. The first field (DD) is always given the value -1 (FFFFFFFFH), and when DOS loads the driver it places the starting address of the next driver at this position. In this way, when DOS seeks a particular driver it can search along the chain of addresses. The last driver loaded is left with -1 in the first field of the header.

The second field is the driver's *attribute byte*. Only seven bits are significant, as follows:

```
bit 15   1=character device/0=block device
    14   1=IOCTL supported/0=IOCTL not supported
    13   1=IBM block format/0=other block format
     3   1=clock device/0=not a clock device
     2   1=current NUL device/0=not NUL device
     1   1=standard output device/0=not standard output
     0   1=standard input device/0=not standard input
```

Ordinarily only bit 15 is set, or bits 15 and 14 are set if IOCTL is supported (as discussed at [7.2.4]). Bit 13 applies only to block devices. The others are used to replace DOS default devices (the "standard input and output devices" are the keyboard and video display; the clock device integrates the system's real-time clock with the BIOS time-of-day clock; and the NUL device is a dummy device designed for testing purposes).

The third and fourth fields hold the offsets of the strategy and interrupt routines, which are explained in the next two subsections. Finally, the last field contains the device name. The name may be up to eight characters long, and it must be left-justified in the eight-byte field, with trailing spaces. To replace an existing DOS device, such as LPT1 or COM2, use the same device name, as in the example here.

Low Level

This example sets up a driver for a serial device. "DEVICE12" is the name of the file that is placed in the DOS configuration file to load this device. The attribute byte has only bit 15 set to 1, showing that it is a character device and that it does not support IOCTL. DEV_STRATEGY and DEV_INTERRUPT are the names of the routines discussed in following subsections. The device is named *AUX* so that it replaces the ordinary DOS device by that name. This makes it especially easy to access the device, since DOS has a ready-made handle by which to access an AUXiliary (serial) device. Included in the example is the initial code for the driver, setting it up as a COM program. The ending counterparts of these lines occur in the third part of the program, two subsections ahead.

```
CSEG        SEGMENT PUBLIC 'CODE'               ;set up the code segment
            ORG 0                               ;this line is optional
            ASSUME CS:CSEG,DS:CSEG,ES:CSEG      ;all offsets from code segment
DEVICE12    PROC   FAR                          ;drivers are far procedures
            DD     0FFFFFFFFH                    ;address of next driver (-1)
            DW     8000H                        ;attribute byte
            DW     DEV_STRATEGY                 ;address of strategy routine
            DW     DEV_INTERRUPT                ;address of interrupt routine
            DB     'AUX     '                   ;device name (pad with spaces)
            .
            .
```

7.2.2 Set up the device strategy

The device strategy routine requires only five lines. When DOS loads the device, it sets up a data block called the *request header*. The request header has two functions. First, it acts as a data area for the internal operations of DOS. More important, the request header is the point through which information is passed between the driver and the program that calls it. For example, when a driver outputs data, it is given the address of that data by means of the request header. And when the driver is finished with its work, it sets a status byte in the request header which can then be made available to the calling program, alerting it to errors.

DOS creates the request header when the device driver is installed (when the system is booted). The device strategy routine is executed only once, at that time. ES:BX is found pointing to the newly formed request header, and the strategy routine needs merely to make a copy of ES:BX so that the request header can be found whenever the driver is accessed. The offset and segment addresses of the header are placed in two variables. You will find in the next section that, when the driver is called, one of the first things it does is to restore these values to ES:BX so that it can take information from the request header.

The request header varies in length, depending on the kind of request being made of the device driver (e.g., initialization, data output, or status return). The first thirteen bytes of the header are the same in all cases, however. The format is as follows:

1. Length of request header (DB)
2. Unit code (DB). Defines the device number for block devices.
3. Command Code (DB). The number of the most recent command sent to the device driver is kept here. These codes are listed at [7.2.3].
4. Status (DW). The status is set each time the driver is called. When bit 15 is on, then an error code is placed in the low eight bits. These are listed at [7.2.3].
5. Reserved Area (eight bytes). Used by DOS.
6. Data required for the driver's operation (variable length—see next section).

Low Level

Here are the five lines of the device strategy routine. Note how the two word-length variables that hold ES and BX *follow* the RET instruction, as required by the COM format.

```
               .
               .
               .
DEV_STRATEGY:MOV CS:KEEP_ES,ES   ;make copy of request header segment
             MOV CS:KEEP_BX,BX   ;make copy of request header offset
             RET                 ;that's all
KEEP_CS      DW ?                ;keep the 2 variables here
KEEP_BX      DW ?                ;
               .
               .
               .
```

7.2.3 Set up the device interrupt handler

A device driver begins with the two pieces of code shown in the prior two subsections. These are followed by the interrupt routine proper. It is actually a misnomer to call this routine an "interrupt," since the driver does not function like an interrupt, and the routine ends with an ordinary RET instruction.

There are thirteen kinds of functions that an installable device driver can perform. When the driver is called upon by a DOS function (say, by function 3FH of INT 21H, which reads data from a file or device) the function places a code number from 1 to 13 in the one-byte field at offset 2 in the request header (for input, code number 5). Control is then given to the driver interrupt routine by looking up its location in the device header [7.2.1]. The interrupt routine first restores ES:BX so that it points to the request header, and then it looks up this code number. Using the code, the interrupt routine calls the matching procedure that performs the requested function. The procedure is located by means of a thirteen-word table that contains the offsets for the thirteen kinds of functions. The functions are always listed in the following order:

```
1.      INITIALIZE
2.      CHECK_MEDIA
3.      MAKE_BPB
4.      IOCTL_IN
5.      INPUT_DATA
6.      NONDESTRUCT_IN
7.      INPUT_STATUS
8.      CLEAR_INPUT
9.      OUTPU_DATA
10.     OUTPUT_VERIFY
11.     OUTPUT_STATUS
12.     CLEAR_OUTPUT
13.     IOCTL_OUT
```

Once the procedure is completed, the interrupt routine terminates with a RET instruction, and control reverts to the calling program. The device driver may include code for only a few of the functions, or for many of them, depending on the device and the degree of control and error checking required. Function numbers for which no routine is supplied in the device driver are all directed to a line of code that simply exits the device driver, with nothing having been done. In this case, before exiting set bits 15, 8, 1, and 0 in the request header to inform the calling program that a non-existent function was called (bit 15 indicates an error, bit 8 that the driver functioned correctly, and bits 0 and 1 give the error code 3 for "command unknown").

One function *must* be present in all device drivers, and that is number 1, the initialization function. This function is automatically performed when the driver is loaded, and not again. One important task required of the procedure is that it set the address of the end of the driver in the four bytes beginning at offset 14 in the request header. The end of the program is marked in the example below by the label *eop:*. Beyond this task, the initialization routine should perform any initialization that the device itself requires. Figure 7-4 diagrams the device driver structure.

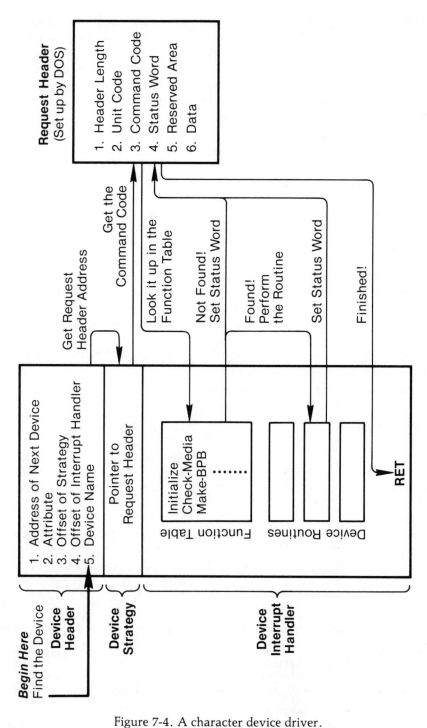

Figure 7-4. A character device driver.

Which of the other twelve possible functions are included in a device driver depends on what the driver has to do. Some, such as CHECK__MEDIA or MAKE__BPB, are relevant only to block devices (they set the type of disk, size of sectors, etc.). For character devices the two functions of primary importance are INPUT__DATA and OUTPUT__DATA (note that these names are arbitrary—it is the positions of the labels in the function table that are invariant). In either case, the request header has the following structure:

```
13 bytes    standard request header format
 1 byte     media descriptor byte (block devices only)
 4 bytes    offset/segment of data transfer buffer
 2 bytes    count of number of bytes to transfer
 2 bytes    starting sector number (block devices only)
```

The output function is used in the example below. The procedure that performs the output takes from the request header the address of the buffer in which the output data resides (offset 14). It also finds there the number of bytes that it should output (offset 18). When the procedure has finished sending out the data, it sets the status word in the request header (offset 3), and then it returns. If the operation is successful, set bit 8 of the status word to 1. The other possibilities are discussed below.

Low Level

This example gives the general form of the interrupt routine, without actually including the code that drives the device.

```
;---INITIALIZE THE DEVICE INTERRUPT HANDLER:
              .
              .
DEV_INTERRUPT: PUSH ES              ;save all registers
               PUSH DS              ;
               PUSH AX              ;
               PUSH BX              ;
               PUSH CX              ;
               PUSH DX              ;
               PUSH SI              ;
               PUSH DI              ;
               PUSH BP              ;
               MOV   AX,CS:KEEP_ES  ;set ES:BX to point to request header
               MOV   ES,AX          ;
               MOV   BX,CX:KEEP_BX  ;
               MOV   AL,ES:[BX]+2   ;get the command code from the header
               SHL   AL,1           ;multiply by 2 (since 2-byte entries)
               SUB   AH,AH          ;make AH 0
               LEA   DI,FUNCTIONS   ;point DI to offset of function table
               ADD   DI,AX          ;add offset into function table
               JMP   WORD PTR [DI]  ;jump to the address at that offset

FUNCTIONS      LABEL   WORD         ;here is the function table
               DW    INITIALIZE
               DW    CHECK_MEDIA
               DW    MAKE_BPB
               DW    IOCTL_IN
               DW    INPUT_DATA
               DW    NONDESTRUCT_IN
               DW    INPUT_STATUS
```

```
                     DW    CLEAR_INPUT
                     DW    OUTPUT_DATA
                     DW    OUTPUT_VERIFY
                     DW    OUTPUT_STATUS
                     DW    CLEAR_OUTPUT
                     DW    IOCTL_OUT

;---EXIT DRIVER IF UNUSED FUNCTION:
 CHECK_MEDIA:
 MAKE_BPB:
 IOCTL_IN:
 INPUT_DATA:
 NONDESTRUCT_IN:
 INPUT_STATUS:
 CLEAR_INPUT:
 OUTPUT_VERIFY:
 OUTPUT_STATUS:
 CLEAR_OUTPUT:
 IOCTL_OUT:
                     OR    ES:WORD PTR [BX]+3,8103H   ;modify status word to show error
                     JMP   QUIT                       ;jump to end of program

;---HERE ARE THE ROUTINES FOR THE 2 CODES PROVIDED FOR:
  INITIALIZE:   LEA   AX,E_O_P               ;offset of end-of-program in AX
                MOV   ES:WORD PTR[BX]+14,AX  ;place e_o_p offset in header
                MOV   ES:WORD PTR[BX]+16,CS  ;place e_o_p segment in header
                  .                          ;set up device initialization code
                  .
                  .
                JMP   QUIT


  OUTPUT_DATA:  MOV   CL,ES:[BX]+18          ;get character count from table
                CBW   CX                     ;use CX to count
                MOV   AX,ES:[BX]+16          ;get data buffer address
                MOV   DS,AX                  ;      (place in DS:DX)
                MOV   DX,ES:[BX]+14          ;
                  .                          ;now begin the output operations:
                  .
                  .
                JMP   QUIT

;---QUIT, MODIFYING THE STATUS BYTE IN THE REQUEST HEADER:
  QUIT:         OR    ES:WORD PTR [BX]+3,100H    ;set bit 8 to show that "done"
                POP   BP                         ;restore all registers
                POP   DI
                POP   SI
                POP   DX
                POP   CX
                POP   BX
                POP   AX
                POP   DS
                POP   ES
                RET
  E_O_P:                                         ;mark end of program
  DEVICE12      ENDP                             ;terminating code
  CSEG          ENDS
                END   DEVICE12
```

Before returning, the driver sets the status word in the request header. In the above example, this is done in two places, depending on whether or not the function called was one of those provided for. The lines read **OR ES:WORD PTR [BX] + 3,XXXXH**. The bit pattern for XXXX is set as follows:

bits	0-7	error code (if bit 15=1)
bit	8	set to 1 when function completed
bit	9	set to 1 while driver is "busy"
bits	10-14	reserved for DOS
bit	15	set to 1 when error occurs

The low byte of this word contains the following error codes when bit 15 is set to indicate an error:

0	tried to write to write-protected media
1	unknown unit
2	device not ready
3	unknown command
4	cyclic redundancy check error
5	bad drive request structure length
6	seek error
7	unknown media
8	sector not found
9	printer out of paper
A	write error
B	read error
C	general failure

7.2.4 Access the device driver

A device driver is installed by placing the name of the finished COM program in the DOS configuration file. To load the example program, place a line in CONFIG.SYS that reads **DEVICE = DEVICE12.COM.** Then reboot the system to install the driver. If the machine will not boot, there most likely is a bug in the driver's initialization code.

Once the driver is in place, use the regular DOS functions of INT 21H to access it. Which functions are used depends on whether the device replaces a standard DOS device (as in the example given here) or whether it is added as an entirely new device. To replace the standard DOS serial device, name the driver **AUX**, and then functions 3 [7.1.7] and 4 [7.1.6] of INT 21H respectively perform input and output. If the device is parallel, name it **PRN**, then use function 5 [6.3.1] of INT 21H to output printer data. Alternatively, use functions 3FH [5.4.4] for input and 40H [5.4.3] for output. In this case, use the file handle 0003H for a serial device and 0004H for a parallel one. Note that there is no need to "open" the device when these predefined handles are used.

If the device does not replace one of the DOS standard drivers (that is, if it is not named with one of the reserved words, PRN, AUX, etc.), open the device using the same functions that open files. You may use both the file control block and file handle methods of access, although the latter is preferred. To be sure that a disk file has not mistakenly been opened, place the file handle in BX, 0 in AL, and then execute function 44H of INT 21H. This is the IOCTL function, and if bit 7 of the value it returns in DL is 1, the driver is present.

IOCTL requires that the appropriate bit setting be made in the driver's attribute byte, and that at least the framework of an IOCTL routine be set up in the device interrupt handler. The IOCTL function has eight subfunctions, numbered from 0 to 7, and one of the following code numbers is placed in AL when the function is called:

```
0       Return device information in DX
1       Set device information, using DL (DH should be 0)
2       Read CX bytes from device driver via the control
        channel, and place them at DS:DX
3       Write CX bytes to the device driver via the control
        channel, taking them from DS:DX
4       Same as #2, but use the drive number in BL, where
        0=default drive, 1=A, etc.
5       Save as #3, but use the drive number in BL (as in #5)
6       Get input status
7       Get output status
```

Various information is returned, depending on which function was called. For subfunctions 0 and 1, DX is given the following bit pattern (providing bit 7 = 1, so that it is a device and not a file that is accessed):

```
0       1=device is console input
1       1=device is console output
2       1=device is null (test) device
3       1=device is clock device
4       reserved
```

5	1=no checks for `Ctrl-Z`, Ø=checks for `Ctrl-Z`
6	1=not yet end of `file`, Ø=end of `file`
7	1=is a `device`, Ø=is a `disk file`
8-13	reserved
14	1=if OK to use subfunctions 2 & 3, Ø=not OK
15	reserved

Subfunctions 2-5 allow arbitrary control strings to move between the program and the device. This allows control messages to operate outside of data flow through the device, simplifying matters considerably. On return, AX holds the number of bytes transferred. Subfunctions 6-7 allow a program to check if a device is ready for input or output. For devices, AL returns FF is the device is ready, and Ø if not. When used with an open file (bit $7 = \emptyset$), AL returns FF until the "end of file" condition occurs.

Note that BASIC 3.Ø adds IOCTL and IOCTL$ statements. These respectively allow a BASIC program to send and receive control strings through device drivers after they have been opened by an OPEN statement. The output string is enclosed in quotes, as in **IOCTL #3,"** . . . . ..**"**. Similarly, **A$ = IOCTL$(3)** receives status information via IOCTL.

7.2.5 Detect/analyze device errors

Devices malfunction for three kinds of reasons. The device may be physically damaged or out of condition. The software that controls the device may be faulty. Or the program may make a request of the device that is not allowed (for example, asking a disk drive to write on a write-protected diskette). DOS detects and analyzes most such errors, and it provides the possibility of recovery.

High Level

The BASIC interpreter detects a variety of errors, with device driver errors included among them. Error codes are returned when the error is encountered, and if no error recovery measures have been taken, a program simply stops in its tracks. However, it is possible to set up *error trapping*, so that when a "critical" (that is, *fatal*) error occurs, BASIC automatically shifts over to an error recovery subroutine that you have set up. The routine can analyze the code and find out on which line of the program it occurred. Once this is accomplished, the program can take steps to recover from the error, either by requesting help from the user or by executing some alternate code. Once finished, the program can be made to resume from any place in the program you like (with certain restrictions). All of the code required for extensive error checking can increase the size of a program considerably. Note that on the IBM BASIC compiler even a little error checking requires an overhead of more than four bytes for every line of the program.

To enable error trapping in BASIC, place at the beginning of the program the line **ON ERROR GOSUB** n, where n is the line number at which the error recovery subroutine begins. Whenever a critical error occurs, control is transferred to that line. At the beginning of the subroutine, set up a series of lines on the form **IF ERR = n THEN linenumber**, where n is an error number taken from the error message appendix in the BASIC Reference Manual. The line numbers mark the beginning of the section of the error recovery routine that is devoted to that particular error. These sections may in turn be divided according to a series of statements reading **IF ERL = n THEN linenumberr**. ERL returns the line number on which the error occurred, enabling the recovery routine to pinpoint the location of the error.

Once the recovery process is complete, use the statement **RESUME** to return to the line on which the error occurred. RESUME may be followed by a line number in order to return to some other line. Be cautioned, however, that you must not use RESUME to jump to a point in the program that is outside the subroutine in which the error occurred. If recovery is impossible but the program can continue anyway, then write **RESUME NEXT** so that the program resumes on the line following the one on which the error occurred. Here is the general setup for error recovery in BASIC:

```
100 ON ERROR GOTO 5000      'enable error trapping
  .
  .
  .
5000 IF ERR=61 THEN 5100     'disk full error
5010 IF ERR=71 THEN 5200     'disk not ready error
```

```
.
.
5100 IF ERL=2080 THEN 5120       'check where error occurred
5110 BEEP:PRINT"Disk in drive B is full":RESUME 'inform user, continue
5120 BEEP:PRINT"Disk in drive A is full":RESUME
.
.
5200 BEEP:PRINT"A disk drive is not ready"        'write error message
5210 PRINT"Strike any key when corrected"
5220 IF INKEY$="" THEN 5220                        'wait for a keystroke
5230 RESUME ERL-10                                  'retry the operation
```

BASIC 3.0 introduces the ERDEV and ERDEV$ instructions. Both fetch read-only variables from the INT 24H critical error handler. **Z% = ERDEV** returns a status word in Z%, where the high byte contains bits 13-15 of the attribute in the device header, and where the low byte contains the INT 24 error code. **Z$ = ERDEV$** places the eight-byte device name in Z$ for a character device, or the two-byte drive specifier for a block device.

Low Level

Sometimes device drivers incur errors that are so serious that a program simply cannot continue until they are corrected. When such an error occurs, DOS invokes the *critical error handler.* The critical error handler swings into action both for standard system devices and for installed device drivers. Users most often encounter it when a disk operation is tried on a drive that has an open door. The message appears: "Not ready error reading drive A—Abort, Retry, Ignore?"

The critical error handler may be rewritten to take advantage of your installed devices. Interrupt vector 24H points to the DOS routine, and you may redirect the vector to your own routine. When the routine is invoked, the high bit of AH equals 0 if the error was in a block device, and 1 if in a character device. BP:SI points to the device header of the faulty device, which can yield additional information. The eight bytes beginning at offset AH in the header give the device name, and the critical error handler places a word-length error code in DI. Here are the code *numbers* (they do not represent bit positions):

Code	Problem
0	attempted write on write-protected disk
1	unknown device
2	drive not ready
3	unknown command
4	data transfer error
5	bad request structure length
6	seek error
7	unknown media type
8	sector not found
9	printer out of paper
A	write fault
B	read fault
C	general failure

In the case of a disk error, AL contains the number of the drive that failed (0 = A, 1 = B, etc.), and bits 2-0 of AH indicate the kind of failure. Bit 0 is set to 1 if the error occurred during a write operation and 0 if during a read operation. Bits 2-1 hold information about where on the disk the error occurred, giving 00 for the initial DOS sectors, 01 for the FAT, 10 for the directory, 11 if elsewhere.

There are three ways in which a program can recover from a critical error:

1. The computer user can be instructed to remedy the problem (such as by closing the disk drive door) and DOS can be made to retry the device operation.
2. Control can be returned to the program at the instruction following the INT 21H function that attempted to use the driver.
3. The program can be terminated, with control transferred back to DOS.

Your error handling routine may recover from the error by issuing an IRET instruction after having placed 0 in AL to ignore the error, 1 to retry the operation, and 2 to terminate the program. If you want the routine to undertake the recovery itself, it must restore the application program's registers from the stack and then remove all but the last three words on the stack. An IRET instruction then returns control to the program, although DOS itself will thereafter be unstable until it has carried out a function call higher than number 12. Here is the stack configuration (from top to bottom) when the critical device handler is called:

```
Error handler return address:    IP,CS,FLAGS

User registers from when
          device was called:     AX,BX,CX,DX,SI,DI,BP,DS,ES
                                 IP,CS,FLAGS
```

DOS also processes many *non*-critical errors. These include the error codes that may show up in a result register when a DOS function is called. The codes are discussed in this book wherever the accompanying function is covered. Be aware, however, that beginning with version 3.0 DOS returns *extended error codes* for the functions that use FCBs or file handles. When the carry flag is set following one of these functions, the usual error codes are returned in AX. The additional *extended error* information is made available by executing INT 59H, with 0 placed in BX. This function also reports on critical errors, and it may be used from within an INT 24H critical error handler.

The function places in AX an error code taken from a list that contains all of the familiar error codes (like "insufficient memory") and some new ones (like "sharing violation" for multiuser systems). BH returns a code for the *error class*, telling what genre of error has occurred. For example, code 1 indicates "out of resources," telling that memory, file buffers, or *whatever* have run out. Other classes can point to software problems, media problems, formatting problems, etc. BL returns a code that suggests an action to take for recovery, such as "retry" or "abort" or "make a request of the user." Finally, CH gives a number reporting the *locus* of the problem: did it take place in a block device?..a serial device?..in RAM?

The data for these error codes is quite extensive. See the DOS 3.0 Technical Reference Manual for complete information. Since DOS 3.0 is not intended for use on the pre-AT machines, reliance on these codes limits the compatibility of your software. Still, a 3.0-only set of routines could be added on top of the traditional error checking procedures. [1.1.3] shows how a program can figure out what version of DOS it is running.

Finally, be aware that one process can pass an *exit code* to the process that calls it. The term *process* is applied to programs that interact. For example, when the EXEC function loads and runs one program from within another, the loaded program is the *child*, and the loading program is the *parent*. The parent may require information about how well the child performed. To make use of this feature, place the desired exit code in AL and execute function 4CH of INT 21H to terminate the program. When the parent process then regains control, it executes function 4DH of INT 21H (no input registers) and AL receives the code, which can then be analyzed and responded to. In addition, AH returns information about how the child process terminated: 0 for normal termination, 1 if by Ctrl-break, 2 if by a critical device error, and 3 if by function 31H, which leaves the process resident.

If a program terminates by means of this function (instead of 20H —see the discussion at [1.3.4]) DOS receives the exit code, and the code may be incorporated into the operation of batch files by using the IF subcommand. This subcommand allows for the conditional execution of other commands in the batch file. The exit code is treated as an ERRORLEVEL number, and the conditional operation is performed depending on whether the code is a certain number or higher. Using this feature, a batch file could be made to stop processing and display a message should an error occur in one of the programs it runs. For more information, see the *Batch Commands* section of the DOS operations manual.

Section 3: Use Special I/O devices

There are a vast variety of I/O devices available for the IBM microcomputers, including mice, bar code pens, graphics tablets, plotters, robot arms, and much more. This section discusses only those peripherals specifically supported by IBM hardware. These include cassette recorders, light pens, and the various devices that may be hooked up to a game port. The port addresses that control other devices in the system are discussed at their respective sections in this book. The mapping of the ports is much the same in all of the IBM machines:

Port Address	Function
00-0F	DMA chip (8237) (not on PCjr)
20-2F	Interrupt chip (8259) (AT controller #1: 20-3F)
40-4F	Timer chip (8253/8254)
60-6F	PPI chip (8255) (AT uses keyboard addresses only)
70-7F	Real-time clock (AT only)
80-83	DMA page registers (not on PCjr)
A0-BF	Interrupt chip #2 (AT only)
C0-C7	Sound chip (SN76496N) (PCjr only)
F0-FF	PCjr diskette controller, AT math coprocessor control
1F0-1F8	AT fixed disk
200-20F	Game adaptor
278-27F	AT serial port #2
2F8-2FF	Serial adaptor (COM2) (COM1 on the PCjr)
320-32F	XT Fixed disk
378-37F	Parallel printer adaptor cards for PC, XT, AT
3B0-3BF	Monochrome/parallel adaptors (not on PCjr)
3D0-3DF	Color graphics adaptor
3F0-3F7	Diskette controller
3F8-3FF	Serial adaptor (COM1) (PCjr modem, COM1 at 2F8)

7.3.1 Read from/write to a cassette recorder

Only very few IBM PCs or PCjrs have ever been used with a cassette recorder, and the XT and AT do not support cassette operations at all. Besides being notoriously unreliable, cassette I/O is inconvenient, and it allows only sequential, and not random, file operations. Still, there may be cause to program for cassette on the PCjr. Be cautioned that cassette operations use channel 2 of the 8253 timer chip [2.1.1], so do not attempt any simultaneous use of this channel. Note also that during cassette *read* operations the time of day interrupt is disabled, throwing off the BIOS time-of-day count.

High Level

Although cassette files are handled entirely differently than disk files, the commands that access them are similar. Only program files and sequential data files may be written to cassette. The latter may include memory-image files. Note that data may not be *appended* to sequential files. When created, the following one-byte extensions are given to the file names:

```
.B      BASIC program
.P      Protected BASIC program
.A      BASIC program in ASCII format
.M      Memory image file
.D      Sequential data file
```

To save a program on cassette, write **SAVE "CAS1:filename"**. To load a program, write **LOAD "CAS1:filename"**. In the latter case the tape is gone through until the file is found, and the name of each file encountered is shown on the screen (cassettes do not use a directory). By requesting a non-existent file a full listing of files on the cassette may be displayed.

Middle Level

BIOS operates on cassette tapes in units of 256-byte blocks rather than files. A series of blocks is prefaced by a "leader," which is comprised of 256 bytes of ASCII 1. The leader ends with a sync bit of 0. Then there follows a sync byte with the value 16H, followed by the 256 bytes of data. After that come two bytes of error checking, then the next data block, then another pair of error checking bytes, and so on. The entire sequence ends with a four-byte trailer, all of the ASCII 1.

To read data from cassette, use function 2 of INT 15H. There is no need to open a file as a program would for disk operations. ES:BX points to a buffer in memory to which the data is transferred, and CX holds the number of bytes to read. On return, DX reports how many bytes were actually read and ES:BX points to the last byte read plus one. The carry flag is set to 0 if the transfer was successful, otherwise AH contains 1 if error checking found a problem, 2 if data transfer failed, or 3 if the data was not found on the tape.

Function 3 of INT 15H writes data to cassette. ES:BX points to the first byte of data, and CX holds the number of bytes to write. Upon return ES:BX points to the byte following the last written. The motor is controlled by executing functions Ø (on) and 1 (off) of INT 15H. There are no input or return registers for either function.

7.3.2 Read the light pen position

Although few computers are equipped with a light pen, it is one of the few auxiliary peripheral devices supported by both hardware and the operating system. Light pens operate by a small optical detector in the tip of the pen. As the electron beam scans the screen, it initiates a pulse in the optical detector when the beam reaches the point of the screen at which the light pen is held. The timing of the pulse relative to the display's horizontal and vertical sync signals tells the light pen position.

High Level

BASIC can read the light pen by two methods. In the first, a program continuously monitors the pen status. In the second, whenever the light pen is used, control is instantly transferred to a subroutine provided by your program. To continuously monitor the pen, use the PEN statement as a function in the form $X = PEN(n)$, where n is a code number that determines what information X is given about the pen and its position. The values for n are:

```
0       returns -1 if pen switch down since last poll, 0 if not
1       returns last x coordinate (0-319 or 0-639) at which
            the pen was switched on (it may since have
            been moved while still switched on)
2       returns last y coordinate (0-199) at which the pen was
            switched on (as above)
3       returns -1 if pen currently switched on, 0 if not
4       returns the current (or most recent) x coordinate of
            the pen (0-319 or 0-639)
5       returns the current (or most recent) y coordinate of
            the pen (0-199)
6       returns last character-row position (1-24) at which
            the pen was last activated
7       returns the character-column position (1-40 or 1-80)
            at which the pen was last activated
8       returns the current (or most recent) character-row
            position (1-24)
9       returns the current (or most recent) character-
            column position (1-40 or 1-80)
```

This example finds out if the pen is switched on, and if so, it gets the current pixel position:

```
100 IF NOT PEN(3) THEN 130      'if pen not on, jump ahead
110 X=PEN(4)                    'get x-axis pixel position
120 Y=PEN(5)                    'get y-axis pixel position
130                             'continue
```

More flexible use of the light pen is offered by the **ON PEN GOSUB** statement. This statement gives the line number at which a subroutine begins that is activated when the light pen is switched on. BASIC accomplishes this by making a check on the pen status between every instruction that it executes. The subroutine may read the pen position and take whatever action is required. When the subroutine is finished, the program returns to wherever it was when the pen was switched on.

ON PEN GOSUB does not operate unless a **PEN ON** statement activates it. **PEN OFF** turns the feature back off. The point of this is that constantly checking the pen status between instructions slows down execution time, and so "trapping" should only operate when it is required. If a program enters a critical section of code that should not be interrupted by the ON PEN GOSUB routine, write **PEN STOP**. In this case, the pen status continues to be checked, and if the pen is switched on, that fact is remembered. But not until another PEN ON statement is encountered does ON PEN GOSUB send the program to the subroutine.

This example causes the program to be interrupted whenever the light pen switch is pressed. The pixel at the light pen position is turned on by the routine that the trapping brings into action.

```
100 ON PEN GOSUB 5000          'set light pen subroutine location
110 PEN ON                     'enable trapping
   .
   .
   .
5000 '''light pen routine
5010 X=PEN(4)                  'get the X coordinate
5020 Y=PEN(5)                  'get the Y coordinate
5030 PSET(X,Y)                 'turn on the pixel
5040 RETURN
```

Middle Level

Function 4 of BIOS INT 10H reports the current light pen position. There are no input registers. On return, AH contains 0 if the pen switch has not been triggered, and 1 if values for a *new* position have been received. Two sets of position coordinates are returned, both for the character position and the pixel position. The character position is given by DX, where DH contains the ROW (0-24) and DL contains the column (0-79). The pixel position is kept in CH and BX, where CH has the row (line) position (0-199), and BX has the column position (0-319 or 0-639, depending on the screen mode).

```
;---GET READING AND SAVE PIXEL ROW AND COLUMN POSITIONS:
        MOV   AH,4              ;function number
        INT   10H              ;BIOS video interrupt
        CMP   AH,1             ;new position?
        JE    NO_READING        ;jump ahead if not
        MOV   COL,BX           ;save pixel column position
        MOV   CL,CH            ;row position now in CL and CH
        MOV   CH,0             ;make CH,0
        MOV   ROW,CX           ;save pixel row position
```

Low Level

The light pen is essentially an extension of the video system and, as such, of the 6845 CRT controller chip. The light pen position is given by a single two-byte value contained in registers 10H (high) and 11H (low) of the chip. [4.1.1] explains how to read the chip registers. See the example there. Port address 3DCH sets the light pen latch, and 3DBH clears it.

```
;---TEST THE LIGHT PEN, AND READ ITS POSITION:
                MOV   DX,3DAH              ;point to status register
                IN    AL,DX               ;get the information
                TEST  AL,4                ;test switch
                JNZ   NOT_SET             ;quit routine
                TEST  AL,2                ;test trigger
                JZ    NOT_SET             ;quit routine
                SUB   DX,7                ;point to 6845 address register
                MOV   AL,10H              ;request low light pen reading
                OUT   DX,AL               ;send the request
                INC   DX                  ;point to 6845 data registers
                IN    AL,DX               ;get the value
                XCHG  AH,AL               ;store it in AH
                DEC   DX                  ;point back to address register
                MOV   AL,11H              ;point to low byte of data
                OUT   DX,AL               ;send the request
                INC   DX                  ;back to data registers
                IN    AL,DX               ;now AX holds reading, go calculate
                                          ;   position on basis of screen mode...
```

7.3.3 Take analog input from the game port

The game port can support two joysticks or four paddles. For a joystick it reports a pair of coordinates and the status of two buttons; for a paddle it reports one coordinate and the status of one button. A number of auxiliary devices—such as graphics tablets—may also be hooked up to the game port; their operation parallels that of a joystick. This section discusses how to read coordinates, and the next section discusses how to tell the status of the buttons.

High Level

The STICK function returns a position on the axis specified by the following code numbers:

0	X-axis of joystick A
1	Y-axis of joystick A
2	X-axis of joystick B
3	Y-axis of joystick B

You need only write $X = STICK(0)$, for example, and X will be given the X-axis value for joystick A. But this function has a quirk that you must not overlook. *Only* when code number 0 is used are the joystick coordinates actually read, and at that time it reads all four values. Code numbers 1 - 3 merely report the findings of code number 0. To use the latter three codes, write a $X = STICK(0)$ function immediately before, even if the program does not need to know the value returned by code 0.

Joysticks vary in their physical characteristics, and for this reason they must be aligned so that their extreme positions coincide with the edges of the video display. The following example shows how this is done. The example continuously draws pixels at the current joystick position, an action that requires that the range of values returned by the game port be converted to the range of screen positions.

```
100 '''get the extreme readings of the joystick
110 STRIG ON                            'enable button
120 V=STRIG(0)                          'clear any prior input
130 PRINT"briefly push button 1 when stick is farthest to left"
140 XLEFT=STICK(0)                      'get left-most stick reading
150 IF STRIG(0)=0 THEN 140              'loop until button pressed
160 STRIG OFF:FOR N=1 TO 1000:NEXT:STRIG ON  'make delay so user can let go
170 PRINT"briefly push button 1 when stick is farthest to right"
180 XRIGHT=STICK(0)                     'get right-most stick reading
190 IF STRIG(0)=0 THEN 180              'loop until button pressed
200 STRIG OFF:FOR N=1 TO 1000:NEXT:STRIG ON  'make delay so user can let go
210 PRINT"briefly push button 1 when stick is farthest to top"
220 V=STICK(0):YTOP=STICK(1)            'get top-most stick reading
230 IF STRIG(0)=0 THEN 220              'loop until button pressed
240 STRIG OFF:FOR N=1 TO 1000:NEXT:STRIG ON  'make delay so user can let go
250 PRINT"briefly push button 1 when stick is farthest to bottom"
260 V=STICK(0):YBOTTOM=STICK(1)         'get bottom-most stick reading
270 IF STRIG(0)=0 THEN 260              'loop until button pressed
280 STRIG OFF                           'finished
290 '''get multipliers to set screen coordinates, counting from 0
300 XRIGHT=XRIGHT-XLEFT                  'get horizontal difference
310 XMULTIPLIER=320/XRIGHT               'calculate pixels per unit
```

```
320 YBOTTOM=YBOTTOM-YTOP              'get vertical difference
330 YMULTIPLIER=200/B/YBOTTOM         'calculate pixels per unit
340 '''now figure coordinates in medium resolution graphics:
350 X=STICK(0)                        'get horizontal stick reading
360 Y=STICK(1)                        'get vertical strick reading
370 X=(X-XLEFT)*XMULTIPLIER           'figure horizontal pixel position
380 Y=(Y-YTOP)*YMULTIPLIER            'figure vertical pixel position
390 PSET(X,Y)                         'turn on the pixel
400 GOTO 350                          'repeat
```

Middle Level

Only the AT provides operating system support for joysticks. Function 84H of INT 15H returns coordinates, where:

$$
\begin{aligned}
AX &= \text{x-axis of joystick A} \\
BX &= \text{y-axis of joystick A} \\
CX &= \text{x-axis of joystick B} \\
DX &= \text{y-axis of joystick B}
\end{aligned}
$$

On entry, place 1 in DX. When 0 is in DX the function instead returns the joystick button settings [7.3.4]. On return, the carry flag is set if there is no game port in the machine.

Low Level

Information about coordinates is held for both joysticks or all four game paddles in just one byte that is found at port address 201H. Here are the respective bit patterns:

bit	Joystick	Paddle
3	Y-axis of stick B	Coordinate of paddle D
2	X-axis of stick B	Coordinate of paddle C
1	Y-axis of stick A	Coordinate of paddle B
0	X-axis of stick A	Coordinate of paddle A

A single bit describes a coordinate by means of *timing*. Begin by sending a byte of any value to the port. This causes the four low bits to be set to 0. Then continuously read the value of the port, timing how long it takes for the bit in question to become 1. The elapsed time is proportional to the joystick position on that axis. The longest times are taken for the down-position on the Y-axis and the right-position on the X-axis. No matter the position, the bits change from 0 to 1 very quickly relative to the speed at which the joystick or paddle is mechanically moved. A program can with fair accuracy test first the Y-axis position and then the X-axis position; there is no need to alternate between testing each. In this example a value is taken for the X-axis of joystick A.

```
;---GET X-AXIS POSITION OF JOYSTICK A
             MOV  DX,201H    ;game port address
```

```
               OUT   DX,AL          ;send an arbitrary value to the port
               MOV   AH,1           ;will test bit 1
               MOV   SI,0           ;initialize counter
NEXT:          IN    AL,DX          ;read the port
               TEST  AL,AH          ;test bit 1
               JE    FINISHED       ;jump ahead when bit turns to 1
               INC   SI             ;else increment the counter
               LOOP  NEXT           ;loop around
FINISHED:                           ;now SI has X-axis value for stick A
```

7.3.4 Take digital input from the game port

The game port supports four game paddles or two joysticks, as well as a variety of graphics devices. The status of up to a total of four buttons on the devices may be monitored. Monitoring the buttons can be a complex matter, since a program may not be free to check them at all times; yet a button could be pressed and then released while the program is busy elsewhere. Special *trapping* routines are created to deal with this problem. The status of the buttons is automatically read several times per second without the program specifically requesting that this be done; when it turns out that a button is down, control is transferred to a subroutine that figures out which button it is and then acts accordingly.

High Level

BASIC uses the STRIG statement to read the status of the buttons. STRIG is sophisticated in that it can *trap* the occurrence of the depression of a button even without the program immediately concerning itself with the button's status; that is, the program can ask "has the button been pressed since I last enquired?" This feature is extremely useful in video games, since a program can devote itself to manipulating the screen without constantly needing to check the button status. The feature slows down a program's operation, however, since BASIC is made to check the buttons after *every* instruction. For this reason, STRIG is operational only when it is purposely turned on, and it may be turned on and off as a program requires.

STRIG operates in two ways. First, it can act as a function that directly reads the current value of the buttons, in the form **X = STRIG(n)**. Here n is a code number:

```
0       Button A1 pressed since last call
1       Button A1 currently depressed
2       Button B1 pressed since last call
3       Button B1 currently depressed
4       Button A2 pressed since last call
5       Button A2 currently depressed
6       Button B2 pressed since last call
7       Button B2 currently depressed
```

In all cases, the function returns -1 if the description applies, and 0 if not.

The second way in which STRIG is used is in the form where it is set up to automatically switch the program over to a subroutine whenever a button is pressed. Write **ON STRIG(n) GOSUB line**. The line number refers to the starting line of the subroutine. The number n refers to the button, where 0 = A1, 2 = B1, 4 = A2, and 6 = B2. Each button may be interpreted by its own subroutine, or they may all be directed to the same subroutine.

To activate the STRIG function, include a program line reading **STRIG(n) ON**. Use the four code numbers above as values for n. To deactivate it (speeding up program execution) write **STRIG(N) OFF**. There is a third option. **STRIG(n) STOP** causes the button depressions to be trapped, but no action is taken until the next STRIG(n) ON statement. This feature keeps ON STRIG GOSUB from making undesirable interruptions. A program is still slowed during the STRIG(n) STOP condition.

The following example shows ON STRIG GOSUB in action. The example at [7.3.3] contains lines showing the X=STRIG form.

```
100 ON STRIG(0) GOSUB 5000        'set up transfer to 5000 if A1 pressed
  .
200 STRIG(0) ON                   'activate trapping
  .
300 STRIG(0) STOP                 'deactivate trapping, but monitor button
  .
400 STRIG(0) ON                   'goto 5000 if A1 has been pressed
  .
500 STRIG(0) OFF                  'stop checking button status
  .
5000 '''Subroutine to respond to button A1
  .
5500 RETURN                       'return to wherever left off
```

Middle Level

Only the AT offers operating system support for a joystick. Function 84H of INT 15H returns the button settings in bits 4-7 of AL, as discussed below. On entry, DX should contain 0; when DX contains 1 the joystick coordinates are returned instead [7.3.3]. On return, the carry flag is set if no game port is installed.

```
;---TEST BUTTON #2 OF STICK B (BIT 7):
            MOV   AH,84H             ;function number
            MOV   DX,0               ;request button settings
            INT   15H                ;call the function
            JC    NO_JOYSTICK        ;go to error routine if no joystick
            TEST  AL,10000000B       ;test bit 7
            JNZ   BUTTON_DOWN        ;jump if buttom down
                                     ;etc...
```

Low Level

Bits 7-4 of port address 201H contain the status of the buttons connnected to the game port. The bit assignments vary depending on whether joysticks or paddles are connected:

bit	Joystick	Paddle
7	Button #2 of stick B	Button of paddle D
6	Button #1 of stick B	Button of paddle C
5	Button #2 of stick A	Button of paddle B
4	Button #1 of stick A	Button of paddle A

A program need only read the value from the port and check the relevant bit settings:

```
MOV DX,201H        ;port address of game adaptor
IN AL,DX           ;get the value
TEST AL,0010B      ;is bit 1 on? (button A2 down?)
JNZ BUTTON_A2      ;if bit 1 on, jump to routine
```

Programs generally have better things to do than constantly watch the game port, but it is equally impractical to periodically check the port by interspersing a routine throughout the program. To achieve the trapping effect described above for BASIC, you will need to set up an addition to the time-of-day interrupt, as described at [2.1.7]. The interrupt is normally invoked 18.2 times per second, and each time a check of the game port can be made and appropriate action taken.

Appendices

APPENDIX A: Binary and hexadecimal numbers and memory addressing

The basic unit of computer data storage is the bit. In most microcomputers eight bits are combined to make a byte, and each bit of the byte may be set to be "on" (=1) or "off" (=0), allowing 256 combinations. Thus 256 different symbols may be expressed by one byte (the extended ASCII character set), or an integer from 0 to 255 may be held within one byte. While we are accustomed to writing these numbers in decimal form, they may as well be written in binary or hexadecimal form— their values are unchanged, and programming software can read them as easily in one form as in another. Instead of saying that a byte can hold a number from "0 to 255", one could say the value is from "00000000 to 11111111" in binary or from "00 to FF" in hexadecimal. Since the different forms can be confused, binary and hex numbers are specially marked. In assembly language, a binary number is followed by **B** and a hexadecimal number is followed by **H**, as in 11111111B or FFH. Microsoft BASIC prefixes hexadecimal numbers with **&H**, as in **&H**FF; unfortunately, it does not at all recognize numbers written in binary form.

Binary numbers:

When the contents of a byte are expressed in binary form, eight digits are required. Each digit corresponds to one of the bits, and the bits are numbered from 0 to 7. As with decimal numbers, the digits are laid out right to left from lowest to highest value. Unlike decimal numbers, where each successive digit counts to ten times higher than the digit to the right (10,100,1000), binary digits count to only *twice* as high as the digit to the right. Thus the rightmost digit counts to 1, the next counts to 2, the third counts to 4, and so on up to 128 for the eighth digit. This means that if the first digit is 1, then adding 1 to it causes it to go back to 0, with 1 *carrying over* to the second digit, just as $9 + 1 = 0$ plus a carry to the 10s place in decimal arithmetic. Here is what counting to 10 looks like in binary:

```
00000000    0
00000001    1
00000010    2
00000011    3
00000100    4
00000101    5
00000110    6
00000111    7
00001000    8
00001001    9
00001010   10
```

In this sequence, most of the zeros on the left are unnecessary; that is, the sequence could as well be written as 0, 1, 10, 11, 100, 101...etc. The zeros are included here only to remind you that each digit corresponds to a bit of a byte. While all the zeros and ones may be a little overwhelming, you will find binary numbers easy to deal with if you think of them this way:

bit:	7	6	5	4	3	2	1	0
value:	128	64	32	16	8	4	2	1

When you encounter the binary number 10000001, bits 7 and 0 are "on." Bit 7 is worth 128 and bit 1 is worth 1, so the decimal value of the byte is 129. If the byte represents a character, then it corresponds to ASCII 129, which is **u** with an umlaut. Conversely, to find the bit pattern for the letter **A**, which is ASCII 65, search the table above for the bit values it contains: 64 and 1, equalling 01000001B.

Why bother with binary numbers? One reason is that computers keep information in *status bytes* in memory or in *status registers* on support chips. Several pieces of information are crammed into one or two bytes. This is accomplished by allotting particular bits to particular data. For example, a status byte might, among other things, tell how many printers and disk drives are connected to the machine. Say that the two highest bits hold the printer number, and the two lowest bits hold the disk drive number. The status byte would be found at a particular memory location, and like any byte, it would have a value from 0 to 255. If the value of the byte is 66, then it would be 01000010 when converted to binary form (64 + 2). Now, the binary number held in the two high bits is 01, and in the two low bits it is 10. The first tells that there is one printer, and the second indicates two disk drives. A group of bits taken together in this way is referred to as a *field*. Often your programs will need to read status bytes or registers, and sometimes they will need to make changes in the bit settings. These operations are trivial in assembly language, but not in BASIC. Appendix B explains how they are performed.

Hexadecimal numbers:

Whereas in binary numbers each successive higher digit counts to twice as high as the digit to the right, in hexadecimal numbers each digit is 16 times higher. In decimal numbers there is first a 1's place, then a 10's place, and then a hundred's place. And in binary numbers the succession is from 1's place to 2's place to 4's place. But with hex numbers there is a 1's place, then a 16's place, then a 256's place, etc. This means that when the 1's place contains 9, adding 1 more to it does not result in a carry to the next highest digit, as would be the case with decimal numbers. But how do you write the decimal number 10 as a single digit? The answer is that hex numbers use the first six letters of the alphabet as additional numeric symbols:

hexadecimal symbol	decimal equivalent
A	10
B	11
C	12
D	13
E	14
F	15

Counting in hexadecimal numbers goes along like this: . . . 8, 9, A, B, C, D, E, F, 10, 11 . . . . . 19, 1A, 1B, etc.

The usefulness of hexadecimal numbers lies in the fact that one hex digit describes the contents of exactly 1/2 byte. For example, in the number F6, the F corresponds to the high four bits of a byte, and the 6 to the low four bits (four bits taken together are called a *nibble*). It is not too hard to calculate the binary equivalent of only four bits. FH = 1111B, and 6H = 0110B (remember the H and B suffixes: how else can you tell apart 11 binary, 11 decimal, and 11 hexadecimal?). So F6H has the bit pattern 11110110. A two-byte number (an integer) might equal 6FF6H. In this case, the bit pattern is 0110111111110110. If the number is only three digits, like F6FH, then the top half of the high-value byte of the number is 0: 0000111101101111.

Hexadecimal numbers are much easier to read than binary numbers. And, although they take some getting used to, they ultimately prove much more convenient to work with than decimal numbers.

Memory and port addresses:

Now that you understand hexadecimal numbers, the system by which the CPU addresses memory becomes comprehensible. First, it is important to note that there are two kinds of addresses: memory addresses and port addresses. The address numbers used for each are entirely separate; sending a value to memory address 2000 is completely different from sending a value to port address 2000. Port addresses are accessed via BASIC's INP and OUT instructions, or by IN and OUT in assembly language. Memory addresses are directly accessed by the PEEK and POKE instructions in BASIC, or by MOV in assembly. There are 65K possible port addresses and 1024K possible memory addresses.

Because the CPU uses 16-bit registers, it is fastest for it to calculate memory addresses if they are no more than 16 bits long. However, the largest number that 16 bits can hold is 65535. Think of this as the four-digit hexadecimal number FFFFH. It takes four more bits to hold a number as large as a million (FFFFFH), which is the size of a PC's address space (the PC AT can access more through *virtual* addressing, which is not covered here).

The CPU solves the problem of addressing more than 64K with a 16-bit pointer by breaking memory up into *segments*. A segment is any 64K stretch of memory; since it is only 64K, a 16-bit value can point to any byte within it. The CPU keeps track of just where in the one-megabyte address space a segment begins, and it counts the 16-bit address as an offset from that point. But how define the point? The answer is that a *second two-byte value is used to mark the beginning of a segment, and the value is multiplied by 16 (= 4 bits) before it is put to this use.* Thus, if this *segment value* is equal to 2, it is multiplied by 16 to make 32, and addresses are then calculated as an offset from the 32nd byte of memory. If an address in the segment is 7, then 32 + 7 means that the byte accessed is actually the 39th byte in memory, not the 7th. It's *relative* address (or offset) is 7, and its *absolute address* is 39.

In BASIC you can set the segment address using the DEF SEG statement. If you write **DEF SEG = 2**, then the beginning of the segment you wish to address is set to the 32nd byte, as in the example above. Then you may use PEEK or POKE to read or write to individual bytes of memory. PEEK(7), for example, would read the byte that is the 7th from the start of the segment, that is, the 39th byte in memory.

Now, in many places this book refers to absolute memory addresses. This is necessary since the operating system stores crucial information at particular places. An absolute address is given in the form 0000:0000, where the first four hexadecimal digits are the segment address and the second four digits are the memory address (offset). Using the example given above, the address of the 39th byte of memory could be written as 0002:0007. Note that the same address can be written differently if the segment register value is changed, as in 0001:0017. Alternatively, an address can be written as a single five-hex-digit number. For example, the video buffer begins at B000:0000, which can be written as B0000H. Note that the H suffix is omitted in the special address notation.

There is one last point to note about the use of memory. When a number is spread across two or more bytes, the lowest, least significant part of the number is placed at the lowest memory address. If the integer value A48BH begins at memory location 1000:0007, then :0007 holds 8B and :0008 holds A4. Similarly, in a single precision number like F58CA98DH, 8D would be found in the lowest of four memory addresses, and F5 would be in the highest.

APPENDIX B: Bit operations in BASIC

BASIC cannot use numbers in binary form. It sees the bit pattern **11000000** as equalling 11 million, not 192. But manipulating bit patterns is essential in sophisticated programming since the contents of status bytes and status registers are often read or changed.

Two *logical operators* are used for most operations on bit patterns. These are OR and AND, and both are available in BASIC. Used alone or in combination they enable a program to read or set individual bits of a byte. OR and AND operate on two values and give a third value as the result, just like the arithmetic operators: **Z = X OR Y**. When used with *byte*-length values, the operations are actually performed eight times, once for each bit. OR would examine bit 0 of the two bytes, and if the bit is on (= 1) in *either* byte, then bit 0 is turned on in the result byte that OR creates. The same process is performed on the other seven pairs of bits. The AND operation, on the other hand, would turn on a bit in the result byte only if *both* of the two corresponding bits are 1; otherwise the bit is 0. Examine the two operations in the diagrams below:

	operand 1		operand 2		result	operand 1		operand 2		result
bit 7	1		0		1	1		0		0
6	1		0		1	1		0		0
5	1		1		1	1		1		1
4	1	OR	1	=	1	1	AND	1	=	1
3	0		0		0	0		0		0
2	0		0		0	0		0		0
1	0		1		1	0		1		0
0	0		1		1	0		1		0

In programming, OR is used to turn on one or more bits in memory or in a status register. For example, there may be need to turn on the blink attribute at a particular character position on the display. This requires that bit 7 be turned on. Now, the program could simply write a whole attribute byte at this location, but the status of the other seven bits may not be known. Instead, the byte is first read from the video buffer and placed in an integer variable such as **X**. Then a second byte is made in which only bit 7 is turned on. As you know (or as you can learn from Appendix A), this byte equals 128. Simply write Y = X OR 128, and Y will become the same byte as X, but with bit 7 turned on. This diagram shows why:

bit	attribute		128		result
7	0		1		1
6	1		0		1
5	0		0		0
4	1	OR	0	=	1
3	0		0		0
2	0		0		0
1	0		0		0
0	1		0		1

In the number 128, *only* bit 7 is turned on. Whether bit 7 is on or off in the attribute byte, it will be turned on in the result byte. But in the case of the other 7 bits, they are turned on in the result byte only if they are already on in the attribute byte. The OR instruction can turn on more than one bit at once (but see the note of caution below). To turn on bits 2 and 3, use the combined value of these two bits: 4 + 8 = 12.

bit	attribute		12		result
7	0		0		0
6	1		0		1
5	0		0		0
4	1	OR	0	=	1
3	0		1		1
2	0		1		1
1	0		0		0
0	1		0		1

AND is used to *turn off* one or more bits. Here, calculate the value of the byte in which every bit is turned on except the one(s) you want turned off. Remember that both corresponding bits must be on to make the result bit also be on. To turn off bit 7, use 255 - 128 = 127:

bit	attribute		127		result
7	1		0		0
6	1		1		1
5	0		1		0
4	1	AND	1	=	1
3	0		1		0
2	0		1		0
1	0		1		0
0	1		1		1

Note how every bit set to 1 in the attribute byte (except bit 7) combines with a 1 in the byte value 127 so that the corresponding bit is set to 1 in the result byte. Bits that are set to 0 in the attribute byte remain 0.

Sometimes a program will need to set a group of bits (a *field*). For example, say that you want to change the three lowest bits of a video attribute byte, changing the foreground color of a character. Perhaps the new pattern should be, in descending order, 101. This value equals 5, but ORing the attribute byte with 5 will not necessarily do the job, since OR will turn on a bit in the result byte if *either* of the corresponding bits equals 1. If the middle bit is turned on in the attribute byte, it remains on in the result byte:

bit	attribute	12	result
2	0	1	1
1	1	0	1
0	0	1	1

In such a case a program must first turn off all three bits using AND, and then it can safely OR the bit pattern desired. In this case, $255-4-2-1 = 248$, so first calculate $Y = X \text{ AND } 248$ and then calculate $Z = Y \text{ OR } 5$.

It is not too difficult for a program to tell if one particular bit is on or off. In this case, AND the byte with the value for which all bits are off except the one tested (say, bit 5, which equals 32). If the result is non-zero the bit is shown to be on:

bit	attribute		32		result
7	1		0		0
6	0		0		0
5	1		1		1
4	1	AND	0	=	0
3	0		0		0
2	0		0		0
1	0		0		0
0	1		0		0

But what if a program needs to learn the settings of two or more bits? For example, bits 6 and 7 taken together may hold a number from 0 to 3, but if the two bits are isolated they result in one of four (decimal) values: 0, 64, 128, and 192. Since BASIC forces you to work in non-binary numbers, some fancy processing is required to figure out the bit patterns these numbers represent. Here are two subroutines that let you avoid these machinations. The first converts the decimal number retrieved from a byte into a string of eight 1's and 0's. Note that this is a character string, not a binary numeral. A second routine takes such a string (of any length) and converts it into decimal form. Using these routines, you can easily examine status bytes in memory. And with the help of the MID$ function you may snip out a bit field and convert the value it holds to decimal. Here is the decimal-to-binary routine:

```
100 STATUSBYTE=PEEK(13):GOSUB 1000        'get byte from memory, gosub binary
110 PRINT BITPATTERN$                      'on return BITPATTERN$ has string
  .
  .
1000 '''Convert decimal number to 8-character binary string
1010 BITPATTERN$=""                        'clear the variable
1020 FOR N=7 TO 0 STEP -1                   'work backwards from bit 7
1030 IF STATUSBYTE-2^N < 0 THEN 1060        'jump ahead if bit off
1040 BITPATTERN$="1"+BITPATTERN$           'else add a "1" to the string
1050 STATUSBYTE=STATUSBYTE-2^N:GOTO 1070   'and subtract bit value from total
1060 BITPATTERN$="0"+BITPATTERN$           'if off, add "0" to string
1070 NEXT                                   'repeat 7 times
1080 RETURN                                 'all done
```

It is important to note that the order of bits in these binary strings is reversed. Rather than moving left to right from bit 7 to bit 0, bit 0 resides at the left end of the string. The reason for this is so that MID$ can easily find the bits you want to isolate. Because MID$ counts from 1, and not from 0, think of the bits as numbered from 1 to 8. To isolate the fourth and fifth bits, write **BITFIELD$ = MID$(BITSTRING,4,2)**. Then to find the decimal value (0-3) held in the field, use this reconversion routine:

```
100 BITFIELD$=MID$(BITPATTERN$,4,2):GOSUB 2000   'cut out part of binary string
110 PRINT DECIMALVALUE                             'returns decimal value of field
  .
  .
2000 '''Convert variable length binary string to decimal number
2010 DECIMALVALUE=0                                'clear the variable
2020 FOR N=1 TO LEN(BITFIELD$)                     'repeat for length of field
2030 DECIMALVALUE=DECIMALVALUE+VAL(MID$(BITFIELD$,N,1))*2^(N-1) 'add values
2040 NEXT                                          'repeat
2050 RETURN                                        'all done
```

APPENDIX C: Some background on assembly language

A reader of this book who does not know assembly language quickly learns that many programming tricks can be accomplished through no other means. While learning assembly language requires a book in itself, this appendix provides basics that will help newcomers decode some of the assembly language examples. By keeping an inquiring eye on the middle- and low-level sections, you'll gradually develop a sensibility for how assembly language works, and this will make learning the specifics much easier. Not all assembly instructions used in this book are discussed here, but you will find those instructions that occur 95% of the time, and the function of the rest may be decipherable from the program notes.

The 8088 chip has thirteen 16-bit registers, each devoted to particular uses. While in a high-level language you might place two numbers into variables and then add the variables together, in assembly language the numbers are placed in two registers on the 8088 chip and then one register is added to the other. Everything in assembly language is a matter of moving numbers in and out of registers and then operating on the registers, changing individual bits, performing arithmetic operations, etc. Part of the reason assembly language operates so quickly is that data is kept on the chip registers; compilers tend to return everything to memory after each instruction, and accessing memory is very time consuming. Figure C-1 shows the thirteen registers on the 8088 or 80286 chips (the latter has extra facilities for multitasking that do not concern us here).

The AX, BX, CX, and DX registers are "general purpose registers." They are special in that operations may be made not only upon the whole register, but also upon only half of it. Each of the four registers is divided into a high part and a low part, where, for example AH stands for "AX high," and AL stands for "AX low." Similarly, an assembler program can access BH, BH, CH, CL, DH, and DL. This division is useful, since often programs work with one-byte values. The BP, SI, and DI registers are also fairly versatile, although they only take 16-bit values. In the *flag register* each bit indicates something about the CPU's status, such as whether an arithmetic operation results in a carry.

Generally speaking, values are placed in the registers by means of the MOV instruction. **MOV AX,BX** moves the contents of BX into AX, overlaying whatever value currently resides in AX. **MOV AH,BL** moves a byte between registers, but **MOV AX,BL** is not allowed—the values must be the same width. MOV also can fetch values from memory, as in **MOV AX,ACCT_NUMBER**. Here, ACCT_NUMBER is a variable name that the programmer makes up, just as in a high-level language. The variable is set up with a statement that would look like **ACCT_NUMBER DW 0**. This statement sets aside a "data word" (2 bytes), initializing it to zero. Other symbols include **DD** for double words, and **DB** for single bytes and strings. The assembler does the work of keeping track of where the variable is located, so that when the statement **MOV AX,ACCT_NUMBER** is assembled, an address is filled in for ACCT_NUMBER.

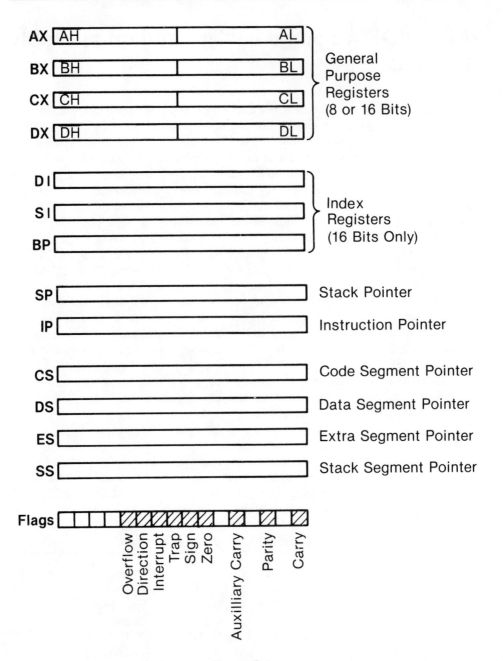

Figure C-1

Working with variable names is the easiest way of tracking down data in assembly language programs. But there are all sorts of fancy addressing techniques that enable a program to get at elaborate arrays or to use pointers. For example, **MOV AX,[BX][SI]** moves to AX whatever value is contained at the offset made up of the combined values found in the BX and SI registers. But an offset from where? The answer is that all data is sequestered into one part of the program, and all code is kept elsewhere. The data part is called the *data segment*, and the code part is called the *code segment*. Data variables are always defined as offsets from the start of the data segment.

The position in memory at which the data segment begins is set by the DS register, which is one of four segment registers. Like all registers on the chip, it is 16 bits wide, which means that it cannot hold a number larger than 65535. How then can the data segment point to locations high in the one-megabyte memory space that the CPU uses? The answer is that the contents of the segment register are automatically multiplied by 16, and the result points to the place in memory at which the segment starts. Thus segments always begin on 16-byte boundaries in memory. Once the segment is established, other registers can hold an offset to any point in the 65535 bytes that follows. The ES ("extra segment") register is also used to point to data in memory.

Among the assembler instructions you will often see in this book are those that load the segment and offset values for a variable. **MOV AX, SEG ACCT_NUMBER** places the segment in which ACCT_NUMBER resides into AX, and from there it is shifted to DS. **MOV BX,OFFSET ACCT_NUMBER** moves into BX the offset in the data segment of ACCT_NUMBER. Once accomplished, DS:BX points to ACCT_NUMBER. If ACCT_NUMBER is a one-dimensional array, then another offset could be used to get at a particular element in the array. You'll often also see the instruction **LEA**, which is another way of loading an offset.

The *code segment* holds the sequence of machine instructions that comprise the program. A MOV instruction, for example, exists as a few bytes of machine code where the values of the bytes indicate to which register the move is made, and from where. The IP (instruction pointer) register holds an offset value that tells at what point in the code segment instructions are currently being executed. After each instruction is carried out, IP is incremented to point to the next. In a trivial program IP would move from the first byte in the code segment to the last, and that would be the end of the program. But, like other programs, assembly language programs are broken up into procedures (subroutines), and so the instruction pointer is constantly jumping around from one place in the code segment to another.

When the instruction pointer jumps to another point in the code, its prior position must be remembered so that it can return to its starting point, just as a RETURN statement in a BASIC program brings control back to the place from which a subroutine is called. In assembly, the procedure is given a name, such as "COMBINE_DATA", and then the statement **CALL COMBINE_DATA** sends the program off to the procedure. The procedure ends with a RET ("return") instruction. At the time that the procedure is called, the CPU saves the current instruction pointer value by pushing it onto the *stack*.

The stack is just what it sounds like—a stack of data used for temporary storage. When the procedure is finished, the prior instruction pointer value is retrieved from the stack and the programs moves along. The stack is also kept in a separate memory segment called, naturally enough, the *stack segment*, which is set by the SS register. The SP register holds the *stack pointer*, and this number always points to the "top" of the stack, and it changes as items are added or taken away.

Now, a stack may seem like an awfully clumsy way of keeping information, but it has two advantages. First, access to its contents is much faster than to other variables kept in memory, and second, the stack can be used for many purposes. It can hold the return addresses for procedures within procedures within procedures. And the same memory space can later be used by the programmer to hold data that is in the midst of processing, but for which there is no available space on the chip. Programs PUSH the contents of a register on to the stack, and later they POP it off. You will find the assembly programs in this book studded with instructions like **PUSH BX** and **POP DX**. Getting the pushes and pops out of order is a favorite way of crashing assembly programs.

Once a programmer succeeds in setting up the three segments (CS, DS, and SS) and in getting the data on to the chip, there are a variety of built-in features provided by the CPU that help the assembly programmer. Here are some of the most prominent:

ADD AX,BX	adds BX to AX. There also is a SUB instruction, plus variants on each.
MUL BL	multiplies BL times AX. There also is a DIV instruction, plus variants on each.
INC BL	increments BL by 1. There also is a DECrement instruction.
LOOP XXX	loops the program back to the line labeled "XXX", repeating the process the number of times contained in CX (just like a FOR . . . TO . . . NEXT instruction in BASIC).
OR AL,BL	performs the logical OR instruction by BL on to AL, leaving the result in AL. There also are AND, XOR, and NOT instructions.
SHL AX,1	shifts left all bits in AX by one position. This effectively multiplies the contents of AX by 2. Other instructions shift the bits right, or roll them around from one end of register to the other. There instructions are invaluable for bit operations, such as setting pixels on the screen.
IN AL,DX	moves into AL the byte found at the port address given in DX. There also is an OUT instruction.
JMP	jmps program control to some other place in the program, like a GOTO instruction in BASIC. **JMP YYY** transfers control to the line of the program that is given the label "YYY:".
CMP AL,BL	compares the contents of AL and BL. A CMP instruction is followed by one of a host of jump instructions that operate conditionally. For example, if the CMP instruction is followed by JGE, then the jump is made only if BL is greater than, or

equal to, AL. CMP instructions achieve the same result as IF
. . . THEN instructions in BASIC (which is to say that IF . . .
THEN instructions are translated into CMP instructions by the
BASIC interpreter).

TEST AL,BL   tests if any of the bits that are on in BL are also on in AL. It is
followed by conditional jump instructions, just as CMP is.
TEST is useful for testing status bits (bit operations are very
easy to perform in assembly language).

MOVS   Movs a string of the length specified in CX from the place in
memory pointed to by SI to the place pointed to by DI. There
are several other instructions that facilitate string movement
and string searches.

Assembly language provides many variants of these instructions and quite a few
other special instructions besides. There is a whole class of instructions called
pseudo ops, which are instructions placed in the source code that tell the assembler
how to proceed. For example, one type of pseudo op can automatically insert fre-
quently used code throughout a program. These snips of code are called macros,
and it is this feature that earns the assembler its name "macro assembler."

Finally, assembly language has a capability that is (or should be) the envy of all
who program only in higher level languages. This is that assembly language can
make optimum use of the operating system *interrupts*. These are nothing more than
ready-made procedures. Rather than being accessed by CALL, however, they are
brought into action by an INT instruction. INT 21H calls up interrupt number hex
21. There are scores of these interrupts, both on the ROM BIOS and in DOS, and
some of the routines are extremely powerful. Some, in fact, are so thoroughly integrated with DOS that there is simply no way that you could write and integrate an
equivalent routine of your own. High-level languages make use of many of the
interrupts. They write on the screen using them, get keystrokes using them, and
access disk drives using them. But many really useful interrupts are commonly
ignored by high-level languages, such as the one that lets you run one program
from within another. Some compilers (such as Lattice C and Turbo Pascal) allow
access to the interrupts if you know how to set them up, and you may want to use
the middle-level sections of this book for that purpose.

Before an interrupt is called, certain information has to be placed in registers on
the CPU. The interrupt that scrolls the screen vertically, for example, needs to
know the dimensions of the window it is to scroll, the number of lines to shift, etc.
These are sometimes referred to as *input registers*. Again and again you'll see the
words "on entry, BH contains...", giving the input register specifications. Similarly, when the interrupt returns, certain registers will return a value, or give status
information. These are called *result registers*, and they are referred to by the words
"on return, AX contains...". Often a single interrupt contains many functions.
DOS, in particular, crams almost everything into INT 21H. And so often a function number is required on entry to an interrupt. Whether in BIOS or in DOS, the

function number always goes into AH (sometimes a sub-function number goes into AL).

   All of this is a lot of information to digest. But keep an eye on the simpler examples in this book, and gradually you'll see the underlying logic. Assembly language deserves its reputation for difficulty. What you've just read is the *simple stuff*. There are all sorts of intricacies that are encountered at more advanced levels. And bugs in assembly code can be terribly difficult to locate, if only because the source code is much longer than for equivalent code in a high-level language (the assembled code is much tighter, however). These days, many professionals write their programs in C, analyze the performance, and then rewrite critical, time-intensive routines in assembly language. The inability to write those assembly subroutines can sometimes condemn one's programming efforts to mediocrity. So find a good assembly primer and get going! Perhaps the greatest reward is finding one day that you really, truly understand how computers work.

APPENDIX D: Integrating assembly routines into BASIC programs

Assembly language subroutines consist of a string of bytes of machine code. When the routine is executed, BASIC jumps away from the sequence of instructions that comprise the BASIC program, and it begins to execute the sequence of instructions that are encoded in the assembly language string. When the assembly routine is finished, control jumps back to where the BASIC program left off.

This book provides assembly routines for BASIC programs in two ways. Both have the subroutine written into the program, rather than kept on a separate disk file. The first method requires that the program set aside memory to hold the routine, the second, less conventional, method does not.

In the first method, the routine is coded in DATA statements, and the program moves it to an unused part of memory and then accesses it with the CALL statement. Care must be taken that the routine is not inadvertently overwritten by data, or vice-versa. The usual solution to this problem is to place the routine at a memory location that BASIC can not reach. Since interpreted BASIC can not extend beyond 64K, systems that have, say, 256K of memory need only poke the routine into the highest 64K block. For 128K systems you should calculate how much memory will be required by DOS, BASICA, and any device drivers. Allow for at least 25K plus the 64K that BASIC will use. In 64K systems, at start-up use the CLEAR command to limit the amount of memory that BASIC can use. **CLEAR,n** limits BASIC to n bytes. Then poke the routine into the very top of memory.

Use DEF SEG to point to the first byte of the location at which the routine is to be deposited, and then use READ to fetch a byte of the routine and poke it into memory space, continuing until the whole routine is in place. For example:

```
100 DATA &Hxx,&Hxx,&Hxx,&Hxx,&Hxx          'a 10-byte routine
110 DATA &Hxx,&Hxx,&Hxx,&Hxx,&Hxx
   .
   .
300 '''poke the routine into memory:
310 DEF SEG=&H3000                         'point to memory location
320 FOR N=0 to 9                           'for each of 10 bytes
330 READ Q                                 'read the byte from DATA
340 POKE N,Q                               'poke it into memory
350 NEXT
```

Once the routine is loaded into memory and you wish to call it, be sure that the most recent use of DEF SEG points to the beginning of the routine. Then give the value of 0 to an integer variable, and CALL the name of that variable. If parameters are passed to the routine, they are placed in parentheses at the end of the CALL statement. For example:

```
500 DEF SEG=&H3000                 'point to start of routine
510 DOGS=12                        '3 parameters for the routine
520 CATS=44                        '
530 POSSUMS=1                      '
540 CASUALTIES=0                   'start executing from first byte
550 CALL CASUALTIES(DOGS,CATS,POSSUMS)   'execute the routine
```

There is a much easier and more economical way of setting up assembly language subroutines that avoids the problem of memory allocation. Simply set up the routine as a string variable in the program. Each byte may be coded using CHR$. Then use VARPTR to find the offset of the string in memory. The offset is held in the two bytes beginning from the byte after the one VARPTR points to (the first byte is the string length). Then use the address to call the routine. Note how DEF SEG is used to point to BASIC's data segment so that the string address will constitute an offset for the CALL statement. For example:

```
100 DEF SEG            'set segment to BASIC data area
110 X$="CHR$(B4)+.."   'the code for the subroutine
120 Y=VARPTR(X$)       'get the string descriptor (2nd and 3rd bytes are
                       '   the string's address
130 Z=PEEK(Y+1)+PEEK(Y+2)*256   'calculate the address
140 CALL Z             'call the subroutine
```

Many of the values expressed by CHR$( )can be more economically written as ASCII symbols. Rather than write **ROUTINE = CHR$(12) + CHR$(65) + CHR$(66)**, write **ROUTINE = CHR$(12) + "AB"**. In fact, most ASCII symbols can be entered by holding down the Alt key, typing in the ASCII number on the numeric keypad, and then releasing the Alt key. Codes 0-31, however, may not be entered in this way to serve this purpose.

APPENDIX E: Using the ANSI.SYS device driver

ANSI.SYS is a small program found on the DOS diskette that may optionally be loaded into memory to increase the capabilities of DOS. It was not made a part of COMMAND.COM so as to save memory when it is not in use. The facilities ANSI.SYS provides may be used as a matter of programming convenience; they also provide a way of achieving a certain degree of software compatibility with non-IBM MS-DOS machines. There is no feature that it adds to the machine that cannot be achieved in other ways; but ANSI.SYS makes certain kinds of control over the keyboard and video display much easier (and usually considerably slower). All of the ANSI.SYS features are described in this book under the relevant headings.

ANSI.SYS can be loaded only at the time that DOS is booted. Beginning with version 2.0, at start-up DOS automatically looks for a CONFIG.SYS file as well as for an AUTOEXEC.BAT file. The CONFIG.SYS file contains various parameters, such as the number of file buffers to set up. And it also contains the names of any device drivers that should be loaded and integrated into COMMAND.COM. ANSI.SYS is such a device driver. Simply place a line in the file that reads **DEVICE = ANSI.SYS**. It may be the only line in the file. To create this file, use the DOS COPY command. Simply type (from, say, A >):

```
COPY CON:CONFIG.SYS     <carriage return>
DEVICE=ANSI.SYS         <carriage return>
<F6>                    <carriage return>
```

Striking F6 after the final entry writes the Ctrl-Z character (ASCII 26) that marks the end of the file.

APPENDIX F: The 8088 instruction set

The number of clocks to add for the effective address (EA) is as follows:

	Components	Operands	Clocks
(a)	Base or index	[BX],[BP],[DI],[SI]	5
(b)	Displacement	label or disp	6
(c)	Base + index	[BX][SI],[BX][DI]	7
		[BP][SI],[BP][DI]	8
(d)	Displacement + base or index	[BX],[BP],[DI],[SI] + disp	9
(e)	Displace + base + index	[BX][SI],[BX][DI] + disp	11
		[BP][SI],[BP][DI] + disp	12

Add two clocks for segment overrides. Here are the instruction times:

instruction		clocks	bytes
AAA		4	1
AAD		60	2
AAM		83	1
AAS		4	1
ADC	register, register	3	2
ADC	register, memory	9(13) + EA	2-4
ADC	memory, register	16(24) + EA	2-4
ADC	register, immediate	4	3-4
ADC	memory, immediate	17(25) + EA	3-6
ADC	accumulator, immediate	4	2-3
ADD	register, register	3	2
ADD	register, memory	9(13) + EA	2-4
ADD	memory, register	16(24) + EA	2-4
ADD	register, immediate	4	3-4
ADD	memory, immediate	17(25) + EA	3-6
ADD	accumulator, immediate	4	2-3
AND	register, register	3	2
AND	register, memory	9(13) + EA	2-4
AND	memory, register	16(24) + EA	2-4
AND	register, immediate	4	3-4
AND	memory, immediate	17(15) + EA	3-6
AND	accumulator, immediate	4	2-3

instruction		clocks	bytes
CALL	near procedure	23	3
CALL	far procedure	36	5
CALL	word memory pointer	29 + EA	2-4
CALL	word register pointer	24	2
CALL	double word memory pointer	57 + EA	2-4
CBW		2	1
CLC		2	1
CLD		2	1
CLI		2	1
CMC		2	1
CMP	register, register	3	2
CMP	register, memory	9(13) + EA	2-4
CMP	memory, register	9(13) + EA	2-4
CMP	register, immediate	4	3-4
CMP	memory, immediate	10(14) + EA	3-6
CMP	accumulator, immediate	4	2-3
CMPS	destination, source	22(30)	1
CMPS	(REP) destination, source	9 + 22(30)/rep	1
CWD		5	1
DAA		4	1
DAS		4	1
DEC	word register	2	1
DEC	byte register	3	2
DEC	memory	15(23) + EA	2-4
DIV	byte register	80-90	2
DIV	word register	144-162	2
DIV	memory byte	(86-96) + EA	2-4
DIV	memory word	(154-172) + EA	2-4
ESC	immediate, memory	8(12) + EA	2-4
ESC	immediate, register	2	2
HLT		2	1
IDIV	byte register	101-112	2
IDIV	word register	165-185	2
IDIV	memory byte	(107-118) + EA	2-4
IDIV	memory word	(175-194) + EA	2-4
IMUL	byte register	80-98	2
IMUL	word register	128-154	2
IMUL	memory byte	(86-104) + EA	2-4

instruction		clocks	bytes
IMUL	memory word	(138-164) + EA	2-4
IN	accumulator, immediate byte	10(14)	2
IN	accumulator, DX	8(12)	1
INC	word register	2	1
INC	byte register	3	2
INC	memory	15(23) + EA	2-4
INT	3	52	1
INT	immediate byte other than 3	51	2
INTO		53 or 4	1
IRET		32	1
JCXZ	short-label	18 or 6	2
JMP	short-label	15	2
JMP	near-label	15	3
JMP	far-label	15	5
JMP	word memory-pointer	18 + EA	2-4
JMP	word register-pointer	11	2
JMP	dblword memory-pointer	24 + EA	2-4
Jxxx	short-label	16 or 4	2
LAHF		4	1
LDS	word register, memory dblword	24 + EA	2-4
LEA	word register, memory word	2 + EA	2-4
LES	word register, memory dblword	24 + EA	2-4
LOCK		2	1
LODS	source-string	12(16)	1
LODS	(REP) source	9 + 13(17)/rep	1
LOOP	short-label	17 or 5	2
LOOPE	short-label	18 or 6	2
LOOPNE	short-label	19 or 5	2
LOOPNZ	short-label	19 or 5	2
LOOPZ	short-label	18 or 6	2
MOV	memory, accumulator	10(14)	3
MOV	accumulator, memory	10(14)	3
MOV	register, register	2	2
MOV	register, memory	8(12) + EA	2-4
MOV	memory, register	9(13) + EA	2-4
MOV	register, immediate	4	2-3

instruction		clocks	bytes
MOV	immediate, register	10(14) + EA	3-6
MOV	segment register, word register	2	2
MOV	segment register, memory word	8(12) + EA	2-4
MOV	word register, segment register	2	2
MOV	memory, segment register	9(13) + EA	2-4
MOVS	destination, source	18(26)	1
MOVS	(REP) destination, source	9 + 17(25)/rep	1
MUL	byte register	70-77	2
MUL	word register	118-133	2
MUL	memory byte	(76-83) + EA	2-4
MUL	memory word	(128-143) + EA	2-4
NEG	register	3	2
NEG	memory	16(24) + EA	2-4
NOP		3	1
NOT	register	3	2
NOT	memory	16(24) + EA	2-4
OR	register, register	3	2
OR	register, memory	9(13) + EA	2-4
OR	memory, register	16(24) + EA	2-4
OR	register, immediate	4	3-4
OR	memory, immediate	17(15) + EA	3-6
OR	accumulator, immediate	4	2-3
OUT	immediate byte, accumulator	10(14)	2
OUT	DX, accumulator	8(12)	1
POP	register	12	1
POP	segment register	12	1
POP	memory	25 + EA	2-4
POPF		12	1
PUSH	register	15	1
PUSH	segment register	14	1
PUSH	memory	24 + EA	2-4
PUSHF		14	1
RCL	register,1	2	2
RCL	register,CL	8 + 4/bit	2
RCL	memory,1	15(23) + EA	2-4
RCL	memory,CL	20(28) + EA + 4/bit	2-4
RCR	register,1	2	2
RCR	register,CL	8 + 4/bit	2
RCR	memory,1	15(23) + EA	2-4
RCR	memory,CL	20(28) + EA + 4/bit	2-4

instruction		clocks	bytes
REP		2	1
REPE		2	1
REPNE		2	1
REPZ		2	1
REPNZ		2	1
RET	(intra-segment, no POP)	20	1
RET	(intra-segment, POP)	24	3
RET	(inter-segment, no POP)	32	1
RET	(inter-segment, POP)	31	3
ROL	register,1	2	2
ROL	register,CL	8 + 4/bit	2
ROL	memory,1	15(23) + EA	2-4
ROL	memory,CL	20(28) + EA + 4/bit	2-4
ROR	register,1	2	2
ROR	register,CL	8 + 4/bit	2
ROR	memory,1	15(23) + EA	2-4
ROR	memory,CL	20(28) + EA + 4/bit	2-4
SAHF		4	1
SAL	register,1	2	2
SAL	register,CL	8 + 4/bit	2
SAL	memory,1	15(23) + EA	2-4
SAL	memory,CL	20(28) + EA + 4/bit	2-4
SAR	register,1	2	2
SAR	register,CL	8 + 4/bit	2
SAR	memory,1	15(23) + EA	2-4
SAR	memory,CL	20(28) + EA + 4/bit	2-4
SBB	register,register	3	2
SBB	register,memory	9(13) + EA	2-4
SBB	memory,register	16(24) + EA	2-4
SBB	register,immediate	4	3-4
SBB	memory,immediate	17(25) + EA	3-6
SBB	accumulator,immediate	4	2-3
SCAS	destination	15(19)	1
SCAS	(REP) desination	9 + 15(19)/rep	1
SHL	register,1	2	2
SHL	register,CL	8 + 4/bit	2
SHL	memory,1	15(23) + EA	2-4
SHL	memory,CL	20(28) + EA + 4/bit	2-4
SHR	register,1	2	2
SHR	register,CL	8 + 4/bit	2

instruction		clocks	bytes
SHR	memory,1	15(23) + EA	2-4
SHR	memory,CL	20(28) + EA + 4/bit	2-4
STC		2	1
STD		2	1
STI		2	1
STOS	destination	11(15)	1
STOS	(REP) destination	9 + 10(14)/rep	1
SUB	register, register	3	2
SUB	register, memory	9(13) + EA	2-4
SUB	memory, register	16(24) + EA	2-4
SUB	register, immediate	4	3-4
SUB	memory, immediate	17(25) + EA	3-6
SUB	AL, immediate	4	
TEST	register, register	3	2
TEST	register, memory	9(13) + EA	2-4
TEST	register, immediate	5	3-4
TEST	memory, immediate	11 + EA	3-6
TEST	AL, immediate	4	2-3
WAIT		3 + 5n	1
XCHG	AL, 16-bit register	3	1
XCHG	memory, register	17(25) + EA	2-4
XCHG	register, register	4	2
XLAT	source-table	11	1
XOR	register, register	3	2
XOR	register, memory	9(13) + EA	2-4
XOR	memory, register	16(24) + EA	2-4
XOR	register, immediate	4	3-4
XOR	memory, immediate	17(15) + EA	3-6
XOR	AL, immediate	4	2-3

APPENDIX G: The 80286 instruction set

In keeping with the theme of the book, only instructions for the real address mode are listed here. The more powerful 80286 chip does not require effective address additions to the instruction times, nor are there differences in the number of clocks required for byte or word operands. An asterisk indicates that you should add one clock if three elements are summed in the offset calculation. The letter 'm' is the number of bytes in the next instruction, and 'n' stands for the number of repetitions.

		clocks	bytes
AAA		3	1
AAD		14	2
AAM		16	2
AAS		3	1
ADC	register/memory with register to either	2,7*	2
ADC	immediate to register/memory	3,7*	3-4
ADC	immediate to accumulator	3	2-3
ADD	register/memory with register to either	2,7*	2
ADD	immediate to register/memory	3,7*	3-4
ADD	immediate to accumulator	3	2-3
AND	register/memory and register to either	2,7*	2
AND	immediate to register/memory	3,7*	3-4
AND	immediate to accumulator	3	2-3
CALL	direct within segment	7 + m	3
CALL	register/memory indirect within segment	7 + m,11 + m*	2
CALL	direct intersegment	13 + m	5
CBW		2	1
CLC		2	1
CLD		2	1
CLI		3	1
CMC		2	1
CMP	register/memory with register	2,6*	2
CMP	register with register/memory	2,7*	2
CMP	immediate with register/memory	3,6*	3-4
CMP	immediate with accumulator	3	2-3

		clocks	bytes
CMPS	repeated cx times	5 + 9n	2
CMPS	byte or word	8	1
CWD		2	1
DAA		3	1
DAS		3	1
DEC	register/memory	2,7*	2
DEC	register	2	1
DIV	byte register	14	2
DIV	word register	22	2
DIV	byte memory	17*	2
DIV	word memory	25*	2
ESC		9-20*	2
HLT		2	1
IDIV	byte register	17	2
IDIV	word register	25	2
IDIV	byte memory	20*	2
IDIV	word memory	28*	2
IMUL	byte register	13	2
IMUL	word register	21	2
IMUL	byte memory	16*	2
IMUL	word memory	24*	2
IMUL	integer immediate multiply (signed)	21,24*	3-4
IN	fixed port	5	2
IN	variable port	5	1
INC	register/memory	2,7*	2
INC	register	2	1
INS	string	5 + 4m	2
INS	byte or word	5	1
INT	type specified	23 + m	2
INT	type 3	23 + m	1
INTO		24 + m or 3	1
IRET		17 + m	1
JCXZ		8 + m or 4	2
JMP	short/long	7 + m	2
JMP	direct within segment	7 + m	3
JMP	register/memory indirect within segment	7 + m,11 + m*	2
JMP	direct intersegment	11 + m	5

		clocks	bytes
Jxxx		7 + m or 3	2
LAHF		2	1
LDS		7*	2
LEA		3*	2
LES		7*	2
LOCK		∅	1
LODS		5	1
LODS	repeated cx times	5 + 4n	2
LOOP		8 + m or 4	2
LOOPZ/LOOPE		8 + m or 4	2
LOOPNZ/LOOPNE		8 + m or 4	2
MOV	register to register/memory	2,3*	2
MOV	register/memory to register	2,5*	2
MOV	immediate to register/memory	2,3*	3-4
MOV	immediate to register	2	2-3
MOV	memory to accumulator	5	3
MOV	accumulator to memory	3	3
MOV	register/memory to segment register	2,5*	2
MOV	segment register to register/memory	2,3*	2
MOVS	byte or word	5	1
MOVS	repeated cx times	5 + 4n	2
MUL	byte register	13	2
MUL	word register	21	2
MUL	byte memory	16*	2
MUL	word memory	24*	2
NEG		2	2
NOT	register/memory	2,7*	2
OR	register/memory and register to either	2,7*	2
OR	immediate to register/memory	3,7*	3-4
OR	immediate to accumulator	3	2-3
OUT	fixed port	3	2
OUT	variable port	3	1
OUTS	string	5 + 4m	2
OUTS	byte or word	5	1
POP	memory	5*	2
POP	register	5	1
POP	segment register	5	1
POPA		19	1

		clocks	bytes
POPF		5	1
PUSH	memory	5*	2
PUSH	register	3	1
PUSH	segment register	3	1
PUSH	immediate	3	2-3
PUSHA		17	1
PUSHF		3	1
RCA	register/memory by 1	2,7*	2
RCA	register/memory by CL	5 + n,8 + n*	2
RCA	register/memory by count	5 + n,8 + n*	3
RCR	register/memory by 1	2,7*	2
RCR	register/memory by CL	5 + n,8 + n*	2
RCR	register/memory by count	5 + n,8 + n*	3
RET	within segment	11 + m	1
RET	within segment adding immediate to SP	11 + m	3
RET	intersegment	15 + m	1
RET	intersegment adding immediate to SP	15 + m	3
ROL	register/memory by 1	2,7*	2
ROL	register/memory by CL	5 + n,8 + n*	2
ROL	register/memory by count	5 + n,8 + n*	3
ROR	register/memory by 1	2,7*	2
ROR	register/memory by CL	5 + n,8 + n*	2
ROR	register/memory by count	5 + n,8 + n*	3
SAHF		2	1
SAL	register/memory by 1	2,7*	2
SAL	register/memory by CL	5 + n,8 + n*	2
SAL	register/memory by count	5 + n,8 + n*	3
SAR	register/memory by 1	2,7*	2
SAR	register/memory by CL	5 + n,8 + n*	2
SAR	register/memory by count	5 + n,8 + n*	3
SBB	register/memory and register to either	2,7*	2
SBB	immediate from register/memory	3,7*	3-4
SBB	immediate from accumulator	3	2-3
SCAS	repeated cx times	5 + 8n	2
SCAS	byte or word	7	1
SEG	(segment override)	0	1
SHL	register/memory by 1	2,7*	2
SHL	register/memory by CL	5 + n,8 + n*	2
SHL	register/memory by count	5 + n,8 + n*	3

		clocks	bytes
STC		2	1
STD		2	1
STI		2	1
STOS	repeated cx times	5 + 3n	2
STOS		3	1
SRL	register/memory by 1	2,7*	2
SRL	register/memory by CL	5 + n,8 + n*	2
SRL	register/memory by count	5 + n,8 + n*	3
SUB	register/memory and register to either	2,7*	2
SUB	immediate from register/memory	3,7*	3-4
SUB	immediate from assumulator	3	2-3
TEST	register/memory and register	2,6*	2
TEST	immediate data and register/memory	3,6*	3-4
TEST	immediate data and accumulator	3	2-3
WAIT		3	1
XCHG	register/memory with register	3,5*	2
XCHG	register with accumulator	3	1
XLAT		5	1
XOR	register/memory and register to either	2,7*	2
XOR	immediate to register/memory	3,7*	3-4
XOR	immediate to accumulator	3	2-3

APPENDIX H: A glossary for IBM microcomputers*

146818:   The chip in the AT that holds the real-time clock and configuration information.

6845:   The video controller chip.

76496:   The PCjr's sound synthesizer chip.

765 (PD765):   The floppy disk controller chip.

8048:   The keyboard microprocessor.

8237:   The direct memory access (DMA) chip.

8250:   The serial communications adaptor chip.

8253:   The programmable timer chip.

8255:   The peripheral interface adaptor chip.

8259:   The interrupt controller chip.

8087:   The math coprocessor chip in the PC, XT, and PCjr.

8088:   The central processing unit (CPU) in the PC, XT, and PCjr.

80286:   The central processing unit (CPU) in the AT.

80287:   The math coprocessor chip in the AT.

Absolute address: A memory address given as an offset from the lowest address in memory (0000:0000), rather than from some offset within memory (a **relative address**).

Absolute coordinates: Coordinates specified in relation to a central axis, rather than by reference to the position of the prior coordinates used (**relative coordinates**).

Absolute disk sectors: To "access an absolute disk sector" means to read a sector at a particular, numbered position on the disk.

Access code: DOS Technical Reference Manual terminology for a **subfunction** number—that is, the code for one function of several performed by a particular interrupt.

Acknowledge: An I/O signal that indicates that a task has been performed, and that the hardware is ready to perform it again.

Address register: A register on some **support chips** that acts as a pointer to several data registers on the chip that are accessed through a single port address. A pro-

*****Note:** Boldfaced words in the definitions are themselves entries in the glossary.

gram first *indexes* the register it must access by sending a register number to the address register.

Addressing: The means of accessing particular locations in memory through a system of absolute positions and relative offsets.

AND: A logical operation in which the bit patterns of two values are compared and a third value is created in which all bits are turned on that are on in both of the two component values.

ANSI.SYS: A **device driver** supplied with DOS that performs many of the functions of BIOS. It is used to extend software compatibility to all machines that run MS-DOS, whether they are IBM microcomputers or not.

ASCII code: A code number from 0-127 that corresponds to one of the 128 ASCII characters. The IBM microcomputers use an *extended* ASCII set of 256 characters.

ASCII text file: A sequential text file in which all numbers are represented as ASCII characters, where data elements are separated by a carriage return/line feed pair, and where the end of the file is marked by a ^Z character (ASCII 26).

ASCIIZ string: Same as a **path string**.

Aspect ratio: The ratio of the number of vertical to horizontal dots along equal distances on the video display or in graphics printing.

Assembler: Software that converts assembly language **source code** into machine code.

Assembly language: The lowest level of programming language, in which the programmer writes instructions that directly control the actions of the CPU.

Asynchronous communications: Serial communications in which the time that passes between sending characters may vary.

Attribute: A characteristic imparted to a device or to data. Every character of a text screen has an attribute that sets its color, intensity, etc. Device drivers have attributes that tell how they handle data, control strings, etc. And files can have attributes that make them hidden, read-only, etc.

Attribute byte: In general, a byte containing a code that sets special characteristics for whatever medium it refers to. A file's attribute byte (in the disk directory) sets hidden status, read-only status, etc. In the **video buffer** there is for every character position on the screen an attribute byte that holds information about color, underlining, etc.

AUTOEXEC.BAT: The name of the batch file that is automatically executed when DOS is booted.

B: Suffix denoting a number expressed in binary form, as in 10111011B. See Appendix A.

Background color: The background color in use on the video display. It is the color to which the enter screen returns when the display is "cleared."

Background operation: A subsidiary process that occurs while a program runs. For example, a word processing program can send data to a printer while the program is used for editing. Background operations may work by the use of **interrupts**.

Base address: The lowest address of a group of contiguous **port addresses** through which a peripheral device is accessed.

Batch file: A file listing DOS commands and programs; these are automatically invoked either in the order in which they are listed or by conditional branching.

Baud rate: The number of bits-per-second at which data is transmitted.

BIOS: The "basic input/output system," which is the part of the operating system that is permanently kept in the machine on ROM chips.

BIOS data area: An area in memory starting at 0040:0000 where BIOS keeps status information and the **keyboard buffer.**

Bit field: When a byte or word is viewed as a bit pattern, several bits taken together may hold a particular item of information. For example, bits 0-3 of a text **attribute byte** form a bit field that holds a character's foreground color.

Bit operations: Program operations that read or change particular bits within data.

Bit Plane: On the EGA, the video buffer is divided into four sections, referred to as bit planes 0 - 3. In 16-color modes the four planes are in parallel, so that four bytes are located at a particular memory address (the **latch registers** intermediate movement of data between the CPU and video memory). In some cases the planes may be *chained*, that is, they are combined into one or two larger planes.

Block device: A device that sends or receives data in block units. Disk drives are the most common block device.

Boot record: A short program placed on a disk at the position at which the disk is first read when DOS is booted. The program provides the computer with the ability to load portions of DOS.

Boundary: A defined interval in memory, in a file, etc. For example, programs are placed in memory at 16-byte boundaries. This means that the absolute memory address of such a position is always evenly divisable by 16.

Break code: The kind of **scan code** that is generated when a key is released (the **make code** occurs when the key is first depressed).

Break detect: A capability of a serial communications adaptor to sense a long sequence of logical 0s. These signal that the remote station wants transmission broken off.

Buffer: An area of memory that is set aside as a holding area for information in transit from one part of the computer to another. The keyboard uses a buffer, as do the disk drives and video displays.

Carry flag: One of the bits in the CPU's **flag** register that is often used by DOS functions to indicate an error condition.

CD: "Carrier detect." See **DCD**.

Chaining: On the EGA, video memory is divided into four **bit planes**. When these are combined into one or two larger planes, they are said to be "chained."

Character device: A device that sends or receives data one character at a time, such as a printer. Compare this with **block devices**, which move data in block units.

Child process: A program that runs while another program (the **parent**) is in control.

Circular Queue: A kind of data buffer in which data is inserted at one end and taken from the other. The two ends of the buffer are constantly changing, and two **pointers** keep track of the current "front" and "rear."

Cluster: A group of disk sectors that form the basic unit in which disk space is allocated.

Code: The series of executable instructions that make up a program, as distinct from the *data* that they operate on. Generally, "code" refers to the sequence of machine instructions that a compiler or assembler produces from **source code**.

Code segment: The section of memory that holds the code used by a program (other segments hold the data and stack).

Color attribute: The bit pattern held in the video buffer that sets the color for a particular dot or character on the screen. On the monochrome and color cards, these attributes coincide with a system of **color code** numbers. In the PCjr and EGA, however, the color attributes refer to the number of a **palette register**, and that register contains the code for the color that the attribute is to be associated with.

Color code: A number from 0-15 that refers to one of the sixteen display colors. On an EGA attached to the IBM Enhanced Color Monitor there may be 64 color codes (0-63).

.COM: A type of file in which **relocation** has already been performed so that all addresses are already written into the file before it is loaded.

Command line: A line on the video display that receives command information, such as a line starting with the DOS prompt.

Communications interrupt: A hardware interrupt brought about by a serial adaptor. It can occur whenever a character arrives over the serial line, whenever it is time to send another, etc.

Compiler: A program that converts the **source code** instructions of a high-level language into a machine code file (or sometimes into *intermediate code* which is then executed by an **interpreter**).

CONFIG.SYS: The name of a special file that DOS searches for when booted. The file contains information about DOS parameters and **device drivers** that lets DOS configure the system.

Control block: See **parameter block**.

Control code: One of the first 32 characters of the ASCII character set. They are customarily used to control hardware rather than to encode data. The carriage return and line feed are among the most familiar.

Control string: A string of characters that controls hardware. Control strings are often embedded in data sent to printers and modems. They begin with a special character that signals their special status (usually the ESC character, ASCII 27).

CPU: The "central processing unit" which performs the instructions that make up a computer program. The Intel 8088 chip is the CPU for all IBM microcomputers except the PC AT, which uses the Intel 80206.

CRC: See **cyclic redundancy check**

Critical error: A device error that prevents a program from proceeding. It invokes the DOS **critical error handler**.

Critical error handler: A DOS interrupt that is invoked when a serious device error occurs. It can be replaced with an error-recovery routine.

CR/LF: "Carriage return/line feed." The pair of characters that is used to cause the cursor or print head to start a new line.

CRT: "Cathode ray tube." The video display.

CTS: "Clear to send." A signal from a modem to a communications port indicating that the modem is ready to begin data transmission. It is part of the **handshaking** procedure.

Current block: The 128-record block of file data that is currently referenced by the **file control block method** of file access. See **current record number**.

Current directory: The directory in a **tree-structured directory** to which all file operations are automatically directed unless a path string specifies otherwise.

Current record number: In the **file control block method** of file access, data is organized in blocks of 128 records. The **current record number** is the number of the record in the **current block**. For example, the current record number of **random record** 128 is 0, since it is the first record in block 1 (all counting starts from 0, so random record 128 is the 129th record in the file, block 1 is the second block, and the last record of block 0 is number 127).

Cyclic redundancy check: An error checking technique where a mathematically derived code follows the transmission of a block of data; the code is recalculated and compared to be sure that the data has not changed during transmission.

Cylinder: In disk drives, a cylinder is the group of **tracks** at a given distance from the center of the disk or disks mounted in the drive.

Data segment: An area in memory that contains a program's data. In assembly language this memory area is pointed to by the DS register.

Data transfer area: A buffer used by the **control block method** of disk access to hold data that is transferred to and from disk.

DB: An assembly language term indicating that a data object is one byte long, or that it is a string comprised of one-byte codes.

DCD: "Data carrier detect." A signal from a modem to a serial port indicating that connection has been made with another modem.

DD: An assembly language term indicating that a data object is four bytes long.

Default DTA: The 128-byte **data transfer area** every program is given, starting from offset 80H in the **program segment prefix**.

Delimiter: Special characters that separate data items.

Device: Generally speaking, a device is any peripheral that stores, displays, or processes information, such as a disk drive, video display, or printer.

Device driver: A software routine that controls and monitors a device, such as a printer or disk drive.

Device header: The beginning part of a DOS device driver routine; it identifies the device.

Device interrupt handler: The body of a DOS device driver routine; it holds the code that carries out the device driver functions.

Device strategy: A part of a DOS device driver routine that links the driver to the **request header**, which is the **parameter block** DOS creates to manage the driver.

Direct memory access: A way of making very rapid data transfers between peripherals and memory. It is especially useful for disk operations. DMA uses a special chip (not found on the PCjr).

Direct memory mapping: See **memory mapping**

DMA: See **direct memory access**

DOS prompt: The symbols at the start of a DOS command line: A>, B>, etc.

Drive specifier: A two-byte string naming a disk drive, in the form **A:, B:,** etc.

DSR: "Data set ready." A signal from a modem to a communications port indicating that the modem is ready.

DTA: "Disk transfer area." The buffer used when transferring data to and from disks by the **file control block** method of file access.

DTR: "Data terminal ready." A signal from a communications port to a modem indicating that the computer is ready.

DW: An assembly language term indicating that a data object is two bytes long.

Echo: Feedback for verification. For example, incoming keystrokes are usually echoed on the screen, and communications output also is usually echoed.

Entry: The words "on entry" refer to how the CPU registers are set up *before* an operating system function is executed.

Environment string: A string of one or more specifications that DOS follows when it executes a program. It contains configuration commands entered by the user, such as BUFFERS or BREAK.

EOF: Abbreviation for "end of file."

Error code: A code number produced by the operating system to indicate a particular error condition.

Error trapping: Coding that causes program control to be passed to a special error-recovery procedure whenever a **critical error** occurs.

Escape sequence: A **control string** that begins with the escape character (ASCII 27). Most printer control, for example, is performed using escape sequences.

.EXE: A program file that requires **relocation** when it is loaded. Not all addresses in the program can be set until the position of the program in memory is determined. EXE files have **headers** that hold the information for relocation. They take slightly longer to load, and are slightly larger on disk, than COM files.

EXEC: The DOS function that lets a program run another program. It also loads **overlays**.

Exit code: A code passed from a **child process** to the **parent process**. For example, when one program runs another, an exit code may be passed from child to parent when the child terminates. The programmer may define the codes.

Extended code: A key code used to identify those keystrokes (or keystroke combinations) for which there are no symbols in the ASCII character set, such as the function keys, or the Ctrl or Alt key combinations. Extended codes are two bytes long, where the first byte is always ASCII 0 to differentiate the code from an ordinary one-byte ASCII code.

Extended error code: Beginning with DOS 3.0, elaborate extended error codes are returned when an error occurs. These codes report not only the error, but also its type, its location in the hardware, and its probable means of recovery.

Extended file control block: A **file control block** that has an extra seven-byte **header** field that sets the **file attribute**.

Extra segment: The place in memory pointed to by the CPU's ES register. The settings in ES and DS (the **data segment** register) are often used in tandem to move data from one part of memory to another.

FAT: See file **allocation table**.

FCB: See file **control block**.

Field: A group of bits or bytes allocated to hold a particular data item.

File allocation table: A table found on every disk that keeps track of available disk space, and that records which **clusters** of disk space are allocated to which file.

File attribute: A setting in a file's directory entry that determines the status of the file, making it normal, hidden, read-only, etc.

File control block: A **parameter block** that a program sets up in memory to hold information required by DOS to operate on a file.

File control block method: A collection of DOS functions that access disk files by means of file control blocks. This method has been made obsolete by the **file handle method** of access.

File descriptor: In BASIC or other high level languages, a file descriptor is the buffer number under which the file was opened, e.g., as #1 or #3.

File handle: A code number returned by DOS when a file is opened using the **file handle method** of disk access. This code is used to identify the file in all subsequent disk operations. Certain *predefined* handles identify the video display, the printer, etc.

File handle method: The method of file access that makes use of **file handles**. This method largely replaces the earlier **file control block** method of access.

File pointer: A variable kept by DOS for every file it opens. The file pointer points to the position in the file from which read/write operations begin.

Flags: A flag is a variable that, by being either "on" or "off", tells whether or not a particular condition prevails. The CPU has a 16-bit *flag register* in which the bits act as indicators of various aspects of the CPU's operation.

Foreground color: The colors in which characters or graphics are drawn on the screen.

Framing error: An error in serial communications where the data flow gets out of sync, so that data bits, parity bits, start bits, and stop bits are misinterpreted.

Function: In high-level languages, a function generally refers to a procedure that converts data from one form to another. At operating system level, the word *function* can refer to any **interrupt** routine. More specifically, a particular interrupt may perform several services, and each of these is a function of that interrupt (the function number is always placed in the AH register when the interrupt is called). The functions themselves may contain a number of **subfunctions**.

Global character: Either of the characters ? or * as they are used in DOS for unspecified characters in file names.

H: A suffix denoting a number expressed in hexadecimal form, as in 0D3H. See Appendix A.

Handle: See **file handle**.

Handshaking: The exchange of predetermined signals between two devices to establish a connection between them.

Hardware interrupt: An interrupt brought about by the action of hardware, whether a peripheral device, **support chips,** or the CPU itself.

Hardware scrolling: A video vertical scrolling technique that works by changing the starting point in the **video buffer** from which data is displayed, rather than by shifting the contents of the buffer.

Header: A **parameter block** placed at the beginning of a program, a device driver, or some other body of code or data. The header contains information about the code or data that is essential for its use. The operating system, for example, places a 256-byte header before every program it loads—the **program segment prefix**— and uses the information it contains to manage the program.

Hidden file: A status that can be given to a file by setting its **attribute byte**. Hidden files are not shown in directory listings.

Installable device driver: A **device driver** that is fully integrated with DOS, so that it can make use of special error checking and control facilities.

Instruction pointer: A register on the CPU that points to the next machine instruction that is to be executed. It marks offsets within the **code segment**.

Interpreter: A program that translates source code one instruction at a time, executing it immediately. The programs BASIC.COM and BASICA.COM are interpreters.

Interrupt: Interrupts are software routines that are brought into action in two ways. *Hardware* interrupts are initiated by hardware, as when a key is pressed on the keyboard; they instantly take control of the CPU, do their job, and then return the CPU to its work. *Software interrupts* perform common program needs, such as sending a character to the screen or printer; they are supplied by the operating system, and they occur only when a program explicitly calls them.

Interrupt Handler: An interrupt routine. The term is used most often for **hardware interrupts.**

Interrupt vector: See **vector**.

IOCTL: "I/O Control." A mechanism provided by DOS allowing a program to interact with a **device driver**, sending and receiving control strings directly, rather than placing them in the flow of data that the device handles.

IRQ: Abbreviation for "interrupt request". Used in reference to the maskable **hardware interrupts**.

Keyboard buffer: A 15-character **circular queue** in which the keyboard interrupt deposits incoming characters.

Keyboard interrupt: A hardware interrupt that is invoked whenever a key is pressed down or let up. It converts **scan codes** received from the keyboard micro-processor into the codes used by programs, and it inserts these codes into the keyboard buffer.

Latch registers: On the EGA there are four one-byte latch registers that hold the four bytes of data at a particular memory address in the video buffer. When the CPU reads from the buffer, the latch registers are filled, and usually when the CPU writes to the buffer the latch contents are dumped into the corresponding memory location.

Linker: A program that links together program **object modules**, organizing their addresses so that the modules can communicate. Even single-module programs must be linked, since the linker also sets up the code for **relocation**.

Logical sector number: Rather than refer to disk sectors as "side x, track x, sector x," *logical* sector numbers reflect a sector's position by counting all sectors as a sequence, starting from the outside edge of the disk.

LSB: "Least significant bit" or "least significant byte."

Machine instruction: The numeric codes used by the CPU. For example, the INT instruction is encoded as *CD*, and the sequence *CD 21* causes the CPU to invoke interrupt 21H.

Machine language: The lowest level of programming, where the programmer writes his instructions directly in the binary codes used by the CPU. **Assembly language** programming more conveniently achieves the same results by creating the codes from mnemonics like MOV or TEST.

Machine language subroutine: A subroutine that is written in assembly language, assembled, and then integrated into a program written primarily in a high level language. Such subroutines are generally used for actions that are repeated many times and that must be performed very quickly. Depending on the **compiler** or **interpreter**, the machine code may be linked into the program, coded into the lines of the program, or separately loaded into memory from disk.

Make code: The kind of **scan code** that is generated when a key is depressed (the **break code** occurs when the key is subsequently released).

Marking: Said of a serial signal when it is "high," that is, equal to a logical 1. In particular, in **asynchronous communications** the signal is said to be "marking" during the time between the transmission of data units.

Mask: A bit pattern that determines what bits in a second pattern are active. For example, particular hardware interrupts are disabled by setting bits in the *mask* *register* on the interrupt controller chip; the fourth hardware interrupt is *masked out* by 00001000B.

Master boot record: A **boot record** on a hard disk. It contains the **partition table**, which points to the various disk partitions. Each partition begins with an ordinary boot record, which initiates loading of the associated operating system.

Memory allocation: The allocation by DOS of a block of memory for a program's use.

Memory control block: A 16-byte **parameter block** set up by DOS at the start of each block of memory it allocates to a program through its memory allocation functions.

Memory mapping: Placing video data directly into the **video buffer** (from which it is projected onto the screen) rather than using the functions provided by the operating system or a high level language.

Memory space: The range of memory addresses that the CPU can access. The address space of the 8088 chip is approximately one million bytes.

MSB: "Most significant bit" or "most significant byte."

Object module: A file of machine code in which the **relative addresses** are not yet fixed. The **linker** processes and combines object modules into finished EXE or COM program files.

OR: A logical operation in which the bit patterns of two value are compared and a third value is created in which all bits are turned on that are on in one or both of the two component values.

Overlay: A sub-program that is kept on disk until the main program requires it. It is loaded into memory on top of some part of the main program, overlaying it.

Overrun: An overrun occurs when data in a **buffer** or **register** is overlaid by incoming data before it has been processed.

Page: In video operations a *page* is a part of the video buffer that holds data for a single screen. The display can be switched to show the contents of one page, and then another. The term *page* also refers to a 256-byte section of memory.

Palette: The selection of colors available in a particular video mode.

Palette code: A number that corresponds to a particular color from the available **palette**.

Palette register: One of 16 registers in the EGA or PCjr that specifies the color that is displayed on the screen when its associated **color code** appears in video memory.

Paragraph: A 16-byte unit of memory that begins from a boundary that is evenly divisible by 16.

Paragraph number: A number that defines a position in memory by referring to memory in 16-byte units. Paragraph number 2, for example, refers to the second 16 bytes of memory, and when a pointer is directed at this paragraph, it points to the 17th byte of memory.

Parameter: A number that is supplied as a specification for the performance of a device, operating system function, or programming language statement.

Parameter block: A group of variables set up in memory to hold information used by a device or operating system function.

Parent Process: A program that makes use of other programs (the **child process**)

Parity Bit: An extra (9th) bit that is added to every byte of memory in order to check for transmission errors. Parity bits are also attached to data in serial communications.

Parse: To resolve a text string into its component parts. DOS can parse command line information and reformat it for use by the file access functions.

Partition: A section of a hard disk. A hard disk may be partitioned so that it can be used with more than one operating system.

Partition table: A table included in the **master boot record** of a fixed disk. It contains information about the size and location of each partition.

Path string: A string used to identify a file in the **file handle method** of disk access. The string is in the same form required by DOS at command level. It may begin with a drive specifier, it may contain subdirectory names separated by backslashes, and it must be followed by an ASCII Ø byte to mark its end. The maximum string length is 63 bytes.

Physical coordinates: The coordinates of a point on the video display as measured from the top left corner, which is regarded as Ø,Ø. See also **world coordinates**.

Pixel: A dot of video graphics. IBM documentation refers to a pixel as a "pel," for "picture element."

Pointer: A variable that holds the address of another variable.

Polling: Monitoring a peripheral device by continuously checking its status until a desired change comes about.

Port: A path through which data may be transferred between the CPU and its support chips.

Port A (Port B, Port C): One of the three registers that programs can access on the 8255 peripheral interface chip.

Port Address: A number from Ø to 65535 that addresses a **port**. Port addresses are separate from memory addresses. Ports are accessed by the IN and OUT instructions in assembly language, and by INP and OUT in BASIC.

Printer interrupt: A **hardware interrupt** that occurs when the printer adaptor sends a "not busy" signal. The interrupt routine ordinarily sends a character of output data to the printer and then returns control to the CPU; this procedure allows the printer to operate while the computer is used for other purposes.

Program segment prefix: The 256-byte **header** that DOS places before all EXE or COM programs when they are loaded into memory. It contains variables used by DOS to manage the program, plus space for a **file control block** and **data transfer area**.

Protocol: The system of **parameters** and data formats used by a **device**.

PSP: See **program segment prefix**

Random block: A block of records that are read or written by a single random file operation in the **file control block** method of file access.

Random record number: The number entered into the **random record field** of a file control block. Subsequent file operations convert the number into **current block** and **current record** values.

Real-time operations: Program operations that take place at a specified moment, rather than at whatever time the computer is able to accomplish them. Screen animation, alarms, and robots all use real-time operations.

Record: A block of data of specified size that is the unit in which information is output to/input from files.

Record number: A number giving the position of a record in a file, counting from 0. In a file that is organized into 10-byte records, record number 5 refers to bytes 50-59 of the file, even if lower numbered records have not been entered.

Register: A place on a chip where data is stored or manipulated. In the IBM microcomputers, most registers are either eight or sixteen bits long. Registers on the CPU receive values from memory and hold them while they are added, multiplied, etc. Registers on the video control chip are initialized with data that set the video characteristics.

Relative address: A memory address that is described as an offset from some point defined in memory. In **COM** files, for example, variables are positioned at addresses that are relative to the starting point of the program.

Relative coordinate: A coordinate that is fixed *relative* to the last coordinate used. In this case, **3,5** indicates "3 to the right and 5 upwards" and **-3,-5** indicates "3 to the left and 5 downwards."

Relocation: A process performed by DOS when an **EXE** program is loaded. DOS calculates the base addresses (segment addresses) from which all other addresses are offsets. These base addresses can not be set until the program is loaded because the position of the program in memory is not clear until that time. **COM** programs do not require relocation.

Request header: A parameter block set up by DOS to control a **device driver**.

Resident program: A program kept in memory after it terminates. DOS prevents it from being overlaid by subsequently loaded programs, which can access the routines it contains by means of interrupt vectors.

RTS: "Request to send." A signal from a communications port to a modem indicating that the computer wants to send data.

Return: The expression "on return..." refers to what information is found in the CPU registers *after* an operating system function has been executed.

RI: "Ring indicator." A signal from an auto-answer modem to a communications port that tells when the telephone the modem is connected to is ringing.

ROM BIOS: See **BIOS**

Root directory: The central directory on a disk. It is positioned at an invariable location on the disk. It may contain file listings, a **volume label**, and pointers to **subdirectories**.

Scan code: A code number sent from the 8048 keyboard microprocessor to the 8255 peripheral interface (or equivalent) telling which key has been struck or released. The **keyboard interrupt** converts scan codes into ASCII codes, extended codes, and settings in the status bytes that keep track of the toggle and shift keys.

Segment: A 64K area of memory set up to hold code, data, or the stack. Segments are always at 16-byte boundaries in memory, since they are derived by multiplying the value found in a **segment register** by 16.

Segment address: A misnomer for **segment value** or **paragraph number**.

Segment register: One of four registers on the CPU that point to the starting positions of memory **segments**. The value in the register is automatically multiplied by 16 so that it points to one of the 65535 16-byte boundaries within the 1-megabyte CPU address space. The names of the segment registers are CS (code segment), DS (data segment), SS (stack segment), and ES (extra segment).

Segment value: A number that defines a position in memory be referring to memory in 16-byte units. The same as a **paragraph number**.

SETBLOCK: A DOS function that can shrink or expand the amount of memory allocated to a program.

Software Interrupt: An **interrupt** brought about by a software INT instruction.

Source code: A program as it is originally written, before it is compiled, assembled, or interpreted.

Stack: An area in memory that a program sets up to temporarily hold data. The last element placed on the stack is the first retrieved. The stack can be accessed more quickly than variables.

Stack segment: An area of memory set aside by a program to hold the stack.

Start bit: In serial communications, a start bit precedes every word of data. It consists of a 0 bit, and it marks the end of the **marking** state (a series of 1's) that fills in the variable time that passes between words.

Starting cluster: The **cluster** starting from which a file is recorded on disk. The file's directory entry points to the starting cluster, and the **file allocation table** keeps track of any subsequent clusters used by the file.

Start line: The scan line at which the cursor image starts. For example, 14 horizontal scan lines make up a line of text on the monochrome display, and these are numbered from 0-13. The start line for a normal cursor is number 12, and the stop line is number 13.

Status byte: A memory location that holds a bit pattern describing the current status of a device.

Status register: An I/O register that holds a bit pattern describing the current status of a device.

Stop bit: In serial communications, stop bits follow every word of data. They place the communications line in a **marking** state and hold it there for the minimum time that must pass before the next word is sent.

Stop line: The scan line at which the cursor image stops. See **start line**.

Subdirectory: A directory that is structured exactly as a **root directory**, except that it is held on disk as a file, rather than at **absolute disk sectors**. The root directory may contain entries that point to subdirectories, and these may in turn hold entries for other subdirectories.

Subfunction: One routine of several performed by a **function** of an operating system interrupt. Whereas a function number is always placed in AH, subfunction numbers go in AL before the interrupt is executed.

Support Chip: Any of the major integrated circuits that connect the CPU to other parts of the computer or to external devices. This glossary begins with a list of the support chips discussed in this book.

Synchronous communications: Serial communications in which the sending and receiving stations transmit and receive data at a precisely synchronized rate.

System clock: The crystal that supplies the underlying pulse that drives all circuitry, including the 8253 timer chip.

System file: A special status that may be given to a file by way of its **attribute byte**. It marks the file as being part of the operating system.

Tiling: Filling in an area of a graphics display with a pattern, rather than in a single color.

Time-of-day count: A variable in the **BIOS data area** that is constantly incremented by the **timer interrupt**. Its value is used by the operating system to calculate the time of day.

Time Out: An expression used in input-output operations to indicate that a peripheral device is not operating.

Timer interrupt: An interrupt initiated by the 8253 timer chip 18.2 times per second. Each time it occurs the interrupt increments the BIOS **time-of-day count**.

Track: A ring of disk space. 360K diskettes are divided into 40 tracks, and each track is subdivided radially into nine sectors.

Tree-structured directory: A system of **subdirectories** organized like the branches of a tree, where the first level of subdirectories are referenced by the **root directory**, and where those subdirectories reference more distant subdirectories.

Typematic rate: The rate at which the keyboard keys repeatedly send a code when they are continuously held down.

Vector: The four-byte memory address of an **interrupt** routine. The high two bytes give the **segment**, and the low two bytes give the offset.

Vector Table: A table of pointers. Interrupt vectors are held in 256 four-byte fields that take up the lowest 1024 bytes of memory. Each field holds the address of an interrupt routine. INT 0 is pointed to by the first vector, INT 1 by the second, etc.

Video Buffer: An area in memory that is set aside to hold information displayed on the screen. The color graphics card, for example, uses a 16K buffer. Video circuitry continuously scans the buffer, decoding the buffer contents and projecting them on to the screen.

Video gate array: A chip in the PCjr's video system that holds a number of control and status registers, including the **palette registers**.

Volume label: A special directory entry used to provide an 11-character identifier for diskettes.

Word: Generally speaking, *word* refers to the size of the basic data unit used by a microprocessor. In this book the term almost always means a two-byte unit.

World coordinates: A screen coordinate system instituted by software that prescribes the range of x and y coordinates, which may or may not include negative numbers. For example, the left and right edges of the screen might be given the values -100 and 100. These coordinates are mapped on to the screen's **physical coordinate** system, in which the top left corner is always defined by $x = 0$ and $y = 0$, and in which only positive numbers are used.

XON/XOFF: A **handshaking** method in serial communications that uses ASCII characters 17 and 19, respectively, to signal to the transmitting station that it should resume or stop transmission. It is used when data is arriving too quickly to process.

XOR: A logical operation in which the bit patterns of two values are compared and a third value is created in which the only bits that are turned on are those in which only one bit is on out of the two compared.

INDEX

APPEND, 276

Cassette, 67, 412-413
CHDIR, 261
CIRCLE, 218-219
CLEAR, 145, 235
CLOSE, 271, 277, 305
CLS, 158
COLOR, 152-153, 156, 200
Color graphics adaptor, 137
    presence, 8-9
COM files, 26, 41
Command line, 287-288
Control codes, 129, 179, 182-183, 393-
        394
    modem, 379-380
    printer, 338-348
CSRLN, 171

Ctrl-Break, 23, 48, 126-127
CVI$/CVS$/CVD$, 320

Data transfer area, 269, 285-286
DATE$, 52
Device drivers,
    access, 405-406
    attributes, 397
    header, 397-398
    interrupt handler, 400-404
    IOCTL, 405-406
    request header, 399
    strategy, 399
Dip switches, 3, 43
Direct memory access chip, 46, 294-
        295
Disks,
    available space, 247, 250
    capacity, 241
    directories, 241-242, 252-261

Disks—cont.
    fixed, 241
    format, 10-11, 241-242
    sector operations, 300-302
    volume label, 265-267
Disk drives,
    number of, 4-5, 10-11, 12-13
    type, 10-11
DMA, see *direct memory access chip*
DRAW, 219-220, 224
DTA, see *data transfer area*

EGA, see *enhanced graphics adaptor*
Enhanced graphics adaptor, 138
    presence and configuration, 8-9
    special screen modes, 207-210, 215-
        217
Environment string, 31
EOF, 310-311, 385
ERDEV/ERDEV$, 408
ERL, 407
ERR, 407
Error trapping, 250, 324-326, 333-334,
        407-410
EXE files, 26, 41

FAT, see *file allocation table*
FIELD, 315, 320
FILES, 254, 259
File allocation table, 30, 241, 243-246,
        253
File control block, 268, 282-285
    extended, 255, 272, 285
File operations,
    append, 248, 306
    file pointer, 290, 318
    random, 289-290, 315-322
    random block, 317-318, 321-322
    sequential, 289, 304-314
    verification, 323

Floppy disk controller chip, 291-299
FRE, 15

Game port, 417-422
  presence, 12
GET#, 320

Handles, 183, 268

INKEY$, 93, 96-97, 98, 100, 107, 115
INPUT, 101, 167, 171
INPUT#, 310
INPUT$, 311, 385
INT 10H,
  function 0H, 145, 155, 158
  function 1H, 169-170
  function 2H, 163, 167
  function 3H, 171
  function 4H, 415
  function 5H, 180, 236
  function 6H, 158, 231
  function 7H, 158, 231
  function 8H, 185-186
  function 9H, 153, 158, 179
  function AH, 179
  function BH, 156, 201
  function CH, 204-205, 213
  function DH, 153, 216
  function EH, 179
  function FH, 145, 236
  function 10H, 156
  function 11H, 189-190
  function 13H, 183-184
INT 11H, 13
INT 12H, 15
INT 13H,
  function 1, 325
  function 2, 266, 301
  function 3, 266, 301
INT 14H,
  function 0, 371-372
  function 1, 375, 382-383

  function 2, 375, 387
  function 3, 376
INT 15H,
  function 0, 413
  function 1, 413
  function 2, 412
  function 3, 413
  function 84H, 120, 418, 421
  function 85H, 120
  function 86H, 57
  function 88H, 16
INT 16H,
  function 0, 97
  function 1, 95
  function 2, 105
  function 3, 122-123
  function 4, 122-123
INT 17H,
  function 0, 334, 351
  function 1, 329
  function 2, 332
INT 1AH, 54-55, 56-57, 58-59, 67
INT 1CH, 60-63
INT 1EH, 293
INT 1FH, 188, 227
INT 20H, 35
INT 21H,
  function 1H, 93, 98-99
  function 2H, 179
  function 3H, 375, 387, 405
  function 4H, 375, 383, 405
  function 5H, 351-352
  function 6H, 93, 100, 179
  function 7H, 93, 97
  function 8H, 93, 97
  function 9H, 179, 182-183
  function AH, 74, 93, 101-102
  function BH, 95
  function CH, 93
  function EH, 270
  function FH, 262, 277
  function 10H, 277-278
  function 11H, 255-256, 272
  function 12H, 255-256
  function 13H, 272
  function 14H, 311

INT 21H—cont.
  function 15H, 306-307
  function 16H, 271-272
  function 17H, 280-281
  function 19H, 270
  function 1AH, 286, 307
  function 1BH, 245-246
  function 1CH, 10, 22, 245-246
  function 21H, 321
  function 22H, 317
  function 23H, 126, 248
  function 24H, 321-322
  function 25H, 21-23
  function 27H, 321-322
  function 28H, 317-318
  function 29H, 287-288
  function 2AH, 52
  function 2BH, 52
  function 2CH, 50-51
  function 2DH, 50-51
  function 2EH, 323
  function 2FH, 286
  function 30H, 7
  function 31H, 37
  function 33H, 127
  function 35H, 21-23
  function 36H, 247
  function 39H, 257
  function 3AH, 258
  function 3BH, 261
  function 3CH, 272-273, 307
  function 3DH, 278, 285, 307, 312-
    314
  function 3EH, 278
  function 3FH, 102-103, 312-314,
    321-322, 405
  function 40H, 183, 307-308, 318,
    352, 383, 405
  function 41H, 273
  function 42H, 249, 308-309, 313,
    318-319
  function 43H, 263-264
  function 44H, 405
  function 45H, 279
  function 46H, 279
  function 47H, 261

  function 48H, 29-30
  function 49H, 29-30
  function 4AH, 29-30
  function 4BH,
    subfunction 0, 31-33, 34
    subfunction 3, 38-40
  function 4CH, 410
  function 4DH, 37, 410
  function 4EH, 256, 259-260, 273
  function 4FH, 256, 259-260
  function 54H, 323
  function 56H, 281
  function 57H, 262
  function 59H, 326
  function 5AH, 273-274
  function 5BH, 273
INT 23H, 126
INT 24H, 408
INT 25H, 301-302
INT 26H, 301-302
INT 27H, 35
INT 4AH, 55
Interrupts, 17
  additions to, 24-25
  communications, 19, 373, 389-392
  disk, 19, 294
  keyboard, 19, 109-113
  printer, 19, 349, 353
  timer, 19, 58-59, 60-63
Interrupt controller, 19
  mask register, 20

KEY, 124, 158
Keyboard,
  ASCII codes, 89, 132-134
  buffer, 89, 92-94, 95, 111
  click, 122-123
  extended codes, 89, 136
  function keys, 121
  interrupt, 46, 89
  shift keys, 104-105, 116, 129
  toggle keys, 104-105, 118, 129
  typematic rate, 122-123
KILL, 271

LEN, 277, 370
Light pen, 414-416
LINE, 218, 223
LINE INPUT#, 310
LOC, 316, 385
LOCATE, 163, 167, 169, 203
LOF, 248, 316, 387
LPRINT, 350-351
LSET, 315

Math coprocessor, 12-13, 19
Memory
    allocation, 28-30, 38
    availability, 12, 14-16
    extended, 16
    map, 2
MKDIR, 257
MKI$/MKS$/MKD$, 315-316, 320
Modems, 378-381
Monochrome adaptor, 137
    presence, 8-9

NAME, 280
NOISE, 85

ON ERROR GOSUB, 324-325, 407
ON PEN GOSUB, 415
ON STRIG GOSUB, 420
ON TIMER GOSUB, 60
OPEN, 271, 275-277, 304, 335, 350,
    370, 375, 395

Paging, 162, 234-237
PAINT, 223-224
Palette registers, 149-151, 198-202
PALETTE (USING), 200-201
Parallel port, 327-328
    number, 12
    switch between, 335-336
PEN, 414
Peripheral interface chip, 3, 67, 69-71,
    83, 87, 89, 109

PLAY, 72, 76-77, 80, 84
PCOPY, 235
PMAP, 204
POINT, 216
POS, 171
PRINT, 152, 176-178, 182
PRINT#, 305, 335, 350, 382
Printer,
    adaptors, 327-328
    errors, 331-332, 333-334
    initialization, 329-330
    interrupt, 353
Program segment prefix, 26-27, 35,
    41, 284, 287
PrtSc key, 128
PSET/PRESET, 203
PSP, see *program segment prefix*
PUT, 224-225
PUT#, 316

Random numbers, 64-65
RANDOMIZE, 64
Real-time,
    clock, 53-55
    operations, 60-63
Relocation, 38, 41
RESUME, 407
RMDIR, 257
RND, 64
RSET, 315-316

Scan codes, 89, 109-110, 119, 131
    phantom key, 131
Screen
    character attributes, 148-155
    border color, 156-157
    graphics attributes, 198-202
SCREEN, 143-144, 185, 200, 235
Scrolling, 229, 230-231, 232-233
    hardware scrolling, 238-239
Serial ports, 367-369
    initialization, 370-374
    interrupts, 389-392
    number, 12

SHELL, 31, 34
SOUND, 56, 72, 74, 83
Sound generator chip, 67-68
Speaker, 46, 66
STICK, 417
STRIG, 420
String descriptors, 101
Sys Req key, 119-120

TIME$, 50
Time-of-day clock, 45, 46, 56-57, 58-
59, 60-63
Timer chip, 45, 46-49, 67, 72-73, 77-
79, 80-82, 87

Vector table, 17, 23
Video,
    adaptor type and number, 8-9, 12
    blink bit, 146-7, 149, 153
    buffer, 138, 176, 180-181, 194-196,
        205-206
    controller chip, 140-142, 162-165,
        167-168, 170, 171-172, 181, 201
    enable bit, 146-7, 231
    gate array (PCjr), 141, 147, 156
    mode, 143-7, 195
    switching adaptors, 160-161

WIDTH, 143-144, 339, 350
WINDOW, 203-204
WRITE, 152, 176-178
WRITE#, 305, 382

Related Resources Shelf

Inside the IBM PC, revised & enlarged   Peter Norton

This best-seller has been thoroughly updated and expanded to include *every* model of the IBM microcomputer family! Detailed in content, yet brisk in style, INSIDE THE IBM PC provides the fascinating tour inside your machine that only the renowned Peter Norton can give. He'll lead you into a complete understanding of your IBM—knowing what it is, how it works, and what it can do. First review the fundamentals, then move on to discover new ways to master the important facets of using your micro to its fullest potential. Definitive in all aspects.

☐ 1986/400 pp/paper/0-89303-583-1/$21.95

Creating Utilities with Assembly Language: 10 Best for the IBM PC & XT
Stephen Holzner

With assembly language as its foundation, this book explores the most popular utility programs for the IBM PC and XT. For the more advanced user, this book unleashes the power of utilities on the PC. Utilities created and discussed include PCALC, ONE KEY, CLOCK, FONT, DBUG SCAN, DSKWATCH and UNDELETE. The author is a regular contributor to *PC Magazine.*

☐ 1986/352 pp/paper/0-89303-584-X/$19.95

Artificial Intelligence for Microcomputers: A Guide for Business Decision Makers   Mickey Williamson

This book discusses artificial intelligence from an introductory point of view and takes a detailed look at expert systems and how they can be used as a business decision-making tool. Includes step-by-step instructions to create your own expert system and covers applications to cost/benefit analysis, personnel evaluations and software benchtesting.

☐ 1986/216 pp/paper/0-89303-483-5/$17.95

Assembly Language Programming with the IBM PC AT   Leo J. Scanlon

Author of Brady's best-selling IBM PC & XT ASSEMBLY LANGUAGE: A GUIDE FOR PROGRAMMERS (recently revised and enlarged), Leo Scanlon is the assembly language authority. This new book on the AT is designed for beginning and experienced programmers, and includes step-by-step instructions for using the IBM Macro Assembler. Also included is a library of 30 useful macros, a full description of the 80286 microprocessor, and advanced topics like music and sound.

☐ 1986/464 pp/paper/0-89303-484-3/$21.95

To order, simply clip or photocopy this entire page, check your order selection, and complete the coupon below. Enclose a check or money order for the stated amount or include credit card information. Please add $2.00 per book for postage & handling, plus local sales tax.

Mail to: **Prentice Hall Press, c/o Prentice-Hall Mail Order Billing, Route 59 at Brook Hill Drive, West Nyack, New York 10994.** To order by phone, call 201-767-5937.

Name _____

Address _____

City/State/Zip _____

Charge my credit card instead: ☐ MasterCard   ☐ Visa

Credit Card Account # _____ Expiration Date _____ / _____

Signature _____

Dept. Y   D5831-BB

Prices subject to change without notice.

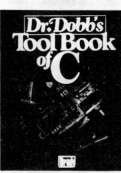

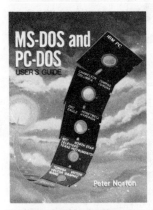

Fasten your seat belt!

For the serious computer user who wants to soup up his PC—make it faster, more powerful, more fun—the experts at PC WORLD have a fascinating new book and software program that can make your personal computer truly personal.

Called *The Fully Powered PC* with *PC World Utilities Disk*, it takes you under the hood of your PC. It shows you how to construct your own system, how to combine many single-purpose systems, and how to call up a dozen or more applications with little more than a keystroke.

It puts you on the fast track by showing you how to put applications programs into active memory so they run faster, design menus to

guide you through systems you've created, even customize your computer to find and dial telephone numbers. It even includes public-domain software that add still more powerful features to your PC.

In other words, *The Fully Powered PC* helps you create a system that performs exactly the way *you* want it to. And isn't that why you bought a PC in the first place?

For the IBM PC, XT, AT or compatible. $39.95 at all computer stores. To order direct, call TOLL FREE: 1-800-624-0023, (in N.J. 1-800-624-0024), or use the coupon below.

THE FULLY POWERED PC

PC World's experts explain how to customize your IBM Personal Computer to make it faster, more efficient and more productive.

//|||Brady